Microsoft® Windows® 98

Complete Course™

Dr. Donald Busché
Marly Bergerud
Saddleback College

JOIN US ON THE INTERNET
WWW: http://www.thomson.com
EMAIL: findit@kiosk.thomson.com   A service of I(T)P®

South-Western Educational Publishing
an International Thomson Publishing company I(T)P®

Cincinnati • Albany, NY • Belmont, CA • Bonn • Boston • Detroit • Johannesburg • London • Madrid
Melbourne • Mexico City • New York • Paris • Singapore • Tokyo • Toronto • Washington

Team Leader: Steve Holland
Managing Editor: Carol Volz
Project Manager: Dave Lafferty
Consulting Editor: Custom Editorial Productions, Inc.
Marketing Managers: Steve Wright & Larry Qualls
Design Coordinator: Mike Broussard
Production: Custom Editorial Productions, Inc.

ISBN: 0-538-72054-9 (spiral binding)
ISBN: 0-538-72119-7 (perfect binding)

Library of Congress Catalog Card Number: 97-48423

1 2 3 4 5 6 7 8 9 10 JH 03 02 01 00 99 98

Printed in the United States of America

I(T)P®
International Thomson Publishing

South-Western Educational Publishing is a division of International Thomson
Publishing, Inc. The ITP registered trademark is used under license.

Microsoft® and Windows® are registered trademarks of Microsoft Corporation.

Complete Course™ is a trademark of South-Western Educational Publishing.

The names of these and all commercially available software mentioned herein are used for
identification purposes only and may be trademarks or registered trademarks of their
respective owners. South-Western Educational Publishing disclaims any affiliation, association, connection with, sponsorship, or endorsement by such owners.

PREFACE

In the blink of an eye, we will cross over into the twenty-first century. What will your working, living, and playing be like in the year 2000? It is difficult to answer these questions, but one thing is certain: The information technologies are and will continue to play a critical role in your life. How we work, conduct business, and communicate with each other will, in many ways, change and be closely intermingled with the many kinds of information technologies.

This book, *Microsoft Windows 98: Complete Course*, is a text about one of the most popular software programs to be developed in the history of the personal computer. Windows 98, the operating system, will take you on one of the most exciting computer trips imaginable—it is the software designed to help you succeed in the next century.

Some of the new features you'll notice in Windows 98 include:

- Revised versions of the standard Windows desktop and an option to switch to an Active Desktop that gives you quick and easy access to Web sites.

- Upgraded support for multimedia called ActiveMovie that allows you to receive high-quality movies and audio directly on your desktop.

- A mechanism that selects and schedules downloads of information from the World Wide Web without you having to visit the site or even be connected to the Web.

- Easier, faster, and more powerful ways to work with applications, to access networks, and to safeguard your data.

As you use and learn Windows 98, you will cover a lot of rugged terrain (much of it will be new and strange to you!), and your travels will be frustrating if you do not have a guide and the right equipment. That's what *Microsoft Windows 98: Complete Course* provides you with—a guide. (You already have the equipment!)

Your guide (that is, this book) has broad, specific goals. One is to explain the Windows concepts you must understand. As you will see, Windows uses one consistent approach in all its applications, and because it is consistent, you have a head start even when you learn a new Windows application because you already know a lot about it! A second goal is to provide you with skills in using the new tools through ample practice in both normal, everyday tasks and more complex special projects. (After all, without practice, you cannot build skills.)

Right now, you're probably eager to dig in. The last thing you want to do is read a summary of "what's to come." But remember, this book is your guide. To get the most out of your trip, spend a few minutes looking at the following "road directions" so that you'll understand where you are going and how you are going to get there.

How this Book Is Organized

Microsoft Windows 98: Complete Course is organized into 11 units that address the major features of Windows 98. Each unit contains lessons that offer comprehensive hands-on exercises in a step-by-step format with carefully labeled screens to illustrate the application. Also provided is a detailed summary and end-of-lesson materials and applications designed to reinforce your learning. A description of the content of each unit follows on the next page.

Unit 1 Getting Started

This unit introduces you to the primary features of Windows 98, an operating system developed in a graphical environment (Windows' way of using pictures and menus), and describes Windows' consistent patterns. It introduces the Windows desktop, window screens, icons, the title bar, and the menu bar. It explains the Windows Help system and lets you use the mouse.

Unit 2 My Computer

This unit shows you how to find, view, and manage your files easily and efficiently using My Computer. From this point, you begin thinking of your disks as electronic filing cabinets that permit you to store your electronic files in folders and subfolders.

Unit 3 Windows Explorer

This unit focuses on tools for controlling and maintaining folders and files on your system. You see how Windows Explorer performs the same disk and folder maintenance operations as My Computer, but provides additional features.

Unit 4 Accessory Applications

This unit introduces the Windows Notepad, Calculator, and Phone Dialer accessories. These applications are designed to work like their actual desktop counterparts.

Unit 5 WordPad

This unit covers WordPad, an accessory program that provides you with the basic features common to all word processing programs, such as the ability to create, save, and retrieve document files; move, copy, enhance, and edit documents; set text margins and align text in various ways; and search for and replace words or phrases throughout the entire document. Although WordPad lacks a spell checker, a thesaurus, and other advanced features, WordPad does let you create basic documents such as letters, reports, and memos—complete with objects, such as sound recordings, if you wish.

Unit 6 Paint

This unit covers Paint, an accessory program designed specifically for creating graphics—for drawing images of all kinds, from simple to complex. Paint provides tools that make drawing images quite simple. It offers tools to create, save, edit, and print your drawings, and to import images from other sources.

Unit 7 Control Panel

This unit explains techniques for using the tools that control the way Windows looks, feels, and sounds. Here you will learn how to customize your desktop environment and your hardware and software settings. (Be sure to follow your instructor's directions so that you do not make system changes.)

Unit 8 Running DOS Applications

This unit provides techniques for running DOS programs and using them within the Windows 98 environment. These techniques include running DOS programs in a window and booting your computer to DOS rather than the Windows 98 interface.

Unit 9 Sharing Data

This unit covers the various methods for sharing data among Windows' applications and with other users. Using the Clipboard and OLE are explained, as is the Briefcase tool and Network Neighborhood.

Unit 10 Multimedia Accessories

This unit explains what multimedia is, ways it is used, and, if you have the proper hardware, how to use it. Multimedia is the combining of text, sound, video, animation, and images in a way that makes using computers easier, more fun, educational, and entertaining! If you want to use multimedia, you must have the appropriate multimedia hardware.

Unit 11 Internet Explorer

This unit introduces Microsoft's Internet Explorer, a Web browser that puts the resources of the World Wide Web at your fingertips. You learn how to search the Web for specified information, how to send and receive electronic mail messages, and how to save Web content to a computer disk.

Additional Learning Tools

This text contains a number of other aids that can help you learn and understand Windows 98's many features.

Windows Template Disk

A Windows Template disk stores the files you will need to complete the lesson exercises and unit applications. In addition to this Template disk, you will need several formatted, blank disks for storing data from your exercises.

Appendix—Computer Basics: Software and Hardware

This appendix discusses the basics of computer hardware and software. If you are familiar with computers, reviewing this discussion won't hurt; it will only expand your computer literacy. If you are not familiar with computers, this appendix will provide you with an essential foundation of computer terminology.

Glossary

A comprehensive Glossary serves as a handy reference for defining—or perhaps simply confirming—the meanings of the new terms you will read during your travels.

Conventions Used in this Text

Not surprisingly, describing any Windows 98 task requires special conventions and a host of special terms and instructions. These conventions make it easier for you to read the text and to complete the exercises and applications. To help you as you work through the exercises, terms and instructions are treated in a standard way throughout the text. Knowing this system will be even more helpful! Please note, then, the conventions used in this book.

Text Conventions

- To distinguish among the various meanings of the word *window*, the capitalized word Windows always refers to the software program Windows 98 (Microsoft Corporation). The capitalized word Window refers to a menu of that name, that is, the "Window menu." The lowercase word window means, broadly, "screen"; thus, you will read about window elements as well as specifically titled windows such as the "Explorer window" or the "Color window."

- When you must press and hold down two (or more) keys at the same time, the keys are shown with a plus sign and no space between the characters; for example: Alt+T.

- Boldface identifies characters that you must key; for example: Key **Word Processing** *in the Description text box.*

- The word *press* is used when you are to press function keys, or when you are to use a combination of function and alphanumeric keys, and the function key is listed first; for example, *Press* **Alt** or *Press* **Ctrl+S**.

- The names of menus, menu options, commands, dialog boxes, and specific windows are capitalized; for example, the *Help* menu, the *Print* option, the *Save As* command, the *Save As* dialog box, and the *WordPad* window.

- Glossary words are defined the first time they appear. The word is shown in italic type; for example: The *Clipboard* is a temporary storage place for data that is cut or copied.

Menu Conventions

One of the nice things about using Windows 98 is that the standard user interface menus look pretty much the same, regardless of the application being used. Of course, Windows has a few conventions of its own for using the menus.

- Windows commands that are selected from a menu are shown in exercises in bold followed by the name of the menu in bold type; for example: *Select* **Copy** *from the* **Edit** *menu.*

- Menu commands that are unavailable to you at the current time may appear dimmed, grayed out, or not visible. (You may need to select another item from the menu before you are allowed to use this command.)

- An ellipsis (...) following a command indicates that a dialog box will display after you choose the command. You will need to select items in the dialog box before the command can be carried out.

- A check mark (✓) next to a command indicates that the command is in effect. Selecting a checked command will remove the check mark; then the command will no longer be in effect.

- A triangle (▶) next to a command informs you that when this command is selected, a submenu will appear, listing additional commands.

- A keystroke combination next to a menu command tells you that you can use this combination of keys (instead of using the mouse) to select the command.

Acknowledgments

For the successes our Windows books have enjoyed we must thank, first, the outstanding editors and staff at South-Western Educational Publishing, most especially Dave Lafferty, for overseeing the day-to-day production responsibilities.

A major contributor to the success of a computer book is, of course, the technical editor, who has the challenging task of uncovering technical inaccuracies. In this case, we were doubly fortunate, because our technical editors also coordinated the print and software components, reviewed and tested the exercises, and contributed extensively to the organization of the text. Double thanks, then, to our technical editors Betsy Newberry and Catherine Skintik of Custom Editorial Productions, Inc.

One last group deserves special credit for their support and understanding—our families and close friends, the people who understood when we were late and why we were locked up with our PCs. They are especially delighted to see us, at last, without a keyboard or a mouse or a laptop before us!

Marly Bergerud
Don Busché

How to Use this Book

What makes a good computer software text? Sound pedagogy and the most current, complete materials. That is what you will find in the new *Microsoft Windows 98: Complete Course.* Not only will you find a colorful, inviting layout, but also many features to enhance learning.

SCANS (Secretary's Commission on Achieving Necessary Skills)–The U.S. Department of Labor has identified the school-to-careers competencies. The five workplace competencies (resources, interpersonal skills, information, systems, and technology) and foundation skills (basic skills, thinking skills, and personal qualities) are identified in the exercises throughout the text. More information on SCANS can be found on the *Electronic Instructor.*

Notes– These boxes provide necessary information to assist you in completing the exercises.

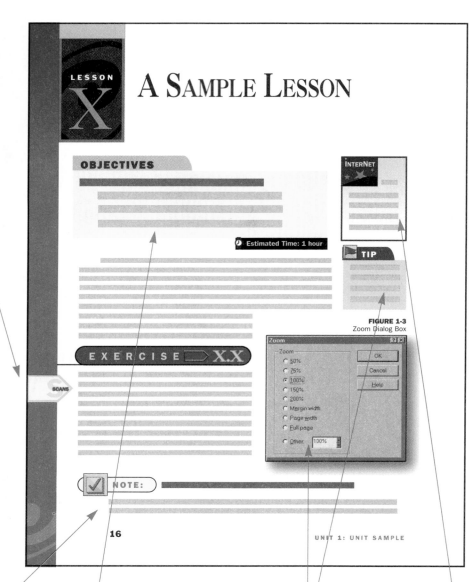

Objectives– Objectives are listed at the beginning of each lesson, along with a suggested time for completion of the lesson. This allows you to look ahead to what you will be learning and to pace your work.

Enhanced Screen Shots– Screen shots now come to life on each page with color and depth.

Tips– These boxes provide enrichment information about Windows features.

Internet– Internet terminology and useful Internet information is provided in these boxes located throughout the text.

How to Use this Book

Summary– At the end of each lesson you will find a summary to prepare you to complete the end-of-lesson activities.

Review Questions– Review material at the end of each lesson and each unit enables you to prepare for assessment of the content presented.

Lesson Projects– End-of-lesson hands-on application of what has been learned in the lesson allows you to actually apply the techniques covered.

End-of-Unit Applications– End-of-unit hands-on application of concepts learned in the unit provides opportunity for a comprehensive review.

Critical Thinking– A realistic simulation runs throughout the text at the end of each unit, reinforcing the material covered in the unit. Each activity gives you an opportunity to apply creative analysis to situations presented.

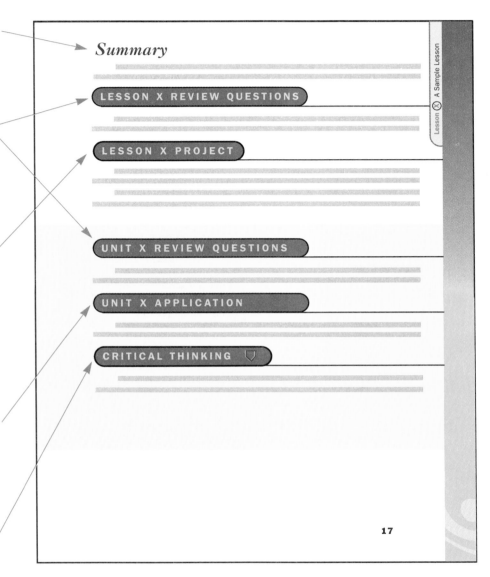

Summary

LESSON X REVIEW QUESTIONS

LESSON X PROJECT

UNIT X REVIEW QUESTIONS

UNIT X APPLICATION

CRITICAL THINKING

Lesson X   A Sample Lesson

17

NEW FEATURES

Windows 98 includes the following new features:

- Powerful Web integration capabilities that let you access and store Web resources quickly and easily.

- Easy access to Internet Explorer, Windows 98's Web browser. You can launch the browser from the Start menu. Or, simply click the Internet Explorer icon on the desktop or the Internet Explorer button on the Quick Launch toolbar, and you're ready to surf the Net.

- A Channel bar that enables you to receive information regularly from your favorite Web sites. By subscribing to a channel, information from a particular Web site is downloaded automatically to your computer at specified intervals. You don't even have to be connected to the Web!

- An Active Desktop option that displays the Channel bar and other "active" content from Web sites directly on your desktop.

- Navigation buttons and an Address bar in My Computer and Windows Explorer that help you move among your system's files, folders, and resources, as well as sites on the World Wide Web.

- A Links toolbar in My Computer and Windows Explorer that displays buttons for your favorite Web sites. Simply click a button to open the Web page.

- Outlook Express, Internet Explorer's e-mail program that you can access directly through Internet Explorer.

- A new Help system thatís structured like the World Wide Web. Help topics and key terms are underlined and in a different color, closely resembling links on a Web page that you can click to quickly access additional information.

- A Desktop Themes icon in the Control Panel that gives you complete control over the way your desktop looks, feels, and sounds.

- Powerful system tools and utilities designed to keep your computer running smoothly.

- ActiveMovie Control, a new accessory that enables you to play movies and other multimedia files from your computer, a network, or the Internet.

- Display options that let you connect several monitors to your computer, thus expanding your desktop area.

TABLE OF CONTENTS

UNIT 1   GETTING STARTED

UNIT 2   MY COMPUTER

Start-Up Checklist

HARDWARE

✓ An IBM or IBM-compatible PC.

✓ An 80486 DX2/66 processor (the standard) or higher (100 mHz 80486DX4s and Pentiums provide significantly improved performance, but Windows 98 runs like a champ on the minimum "standard").

✓ 8MB of RAM memory (12MB will be optimum for most users, but 16MB gives a noticeable performance boost to 32-bit applications).

✓ One hard disk (300MB or larger) with at least 110MB of free hard disk space. The amount of free hard disk space required by the Windows 95 to Windows 98 upgrade is determined by the cluster size of the target partition and the number of components already installed in Windows. Windows 98 requires at least 110MB of free hard disk space with the smallest cluster size and minimum installed components. This number can be as large as 243MB to install to a clean partition with the largest cluster size and all components selected. If Windows 98 stops the setup due to a lack of available free hard disk space, you can do the following to free additional hard disk space: Empty the Recycle Bin, empty the WWW Cache folder; delete **.tmp** and **.bak** files, or backup and move off the partition any MS/DOS programs.

✓ At least one 3½-inch disk drive.

✓ A display adapter.

✓ An enhanced keyboard.

✓ A mouse or pen pointer.

✓ A printer that is supported by Windows 98, if you want to print with Windows.

SOFTWARE

✓ Microsoft Windows 98.

JOIN US ON THE INTERNET

WWW: **http://www.thomson.com**
E-MAIL: **findit@kiosk.thomson.com**

South-Western Educational Publishing is a partner in *thomson.com,* an on-line portal for the products, services, and resources available from International Thomson Publishing (ITP). Through our site, users can search catalogs, examine subject-specific resource centers, and subscribe to electronic discussion lists.

South-Western Educational Publishing is also a reseller of commercial software products. See our printed catalog or view this page at:

http://www.swpco.com/swpco/comp_ed/com_sft.html

For information on our products visit our World Wide Web site at:

http://www.swpco.com/swpco/swpco.html

To join the South-Western Computer Education discussion list, send an e-mail message to: **majordomo@list.thomson.com.** Leave the subject field blank, and in the body of your message key: SUBSCRIBE SOUTH-WESTERN-COMPUTER-EDUCATION <your e-mail address>.

A service of I(T)P®

Progress Record

Name _____

UNIT 1 GETTING STARTED

		Score	Date Completed	Instructor
Lesson 3	Exercise 3.3	_____	_____	_____
	Project, step 3	_____	_____	_____
	Project, step 3	_____	_____	_____
	Project, step 5	_____	_____	_____
	Project, step 8	_____	_____	_____

UNIT 2 MY COMPUTER

		Score	Date Completed	Instructor
Lesson 8	Project 8 Report Form	_____	_____	_____

UNIT 3 WINDOWS EXPLORER

		Score	Date Completed	Instructor
Lesson 9	Project 9 Report Form	_____	_____	_____
Lesson 10	Project 10 Report Form	_____	_____	_____
Lesson 11	Project 11 Report Form	_____	_____	_____

UNIT 4 ACCESSORY APPLICATIONS

		Score	Date Completed	Instructor
Lesson 12	New Notes	_____	_____	_____
	Insurance	_____	_____	_____
Lesson 13	Billing	_____	_____	_____
	New Insurance	_____	_____	_____
Lesson 14	Billing Calculated	_____	_____	_____
	Project 14	_____	_____	_____
Unit 4 Review	Overtime	_____	_____	_____

UNIT 11 INTERNET EXPLORER

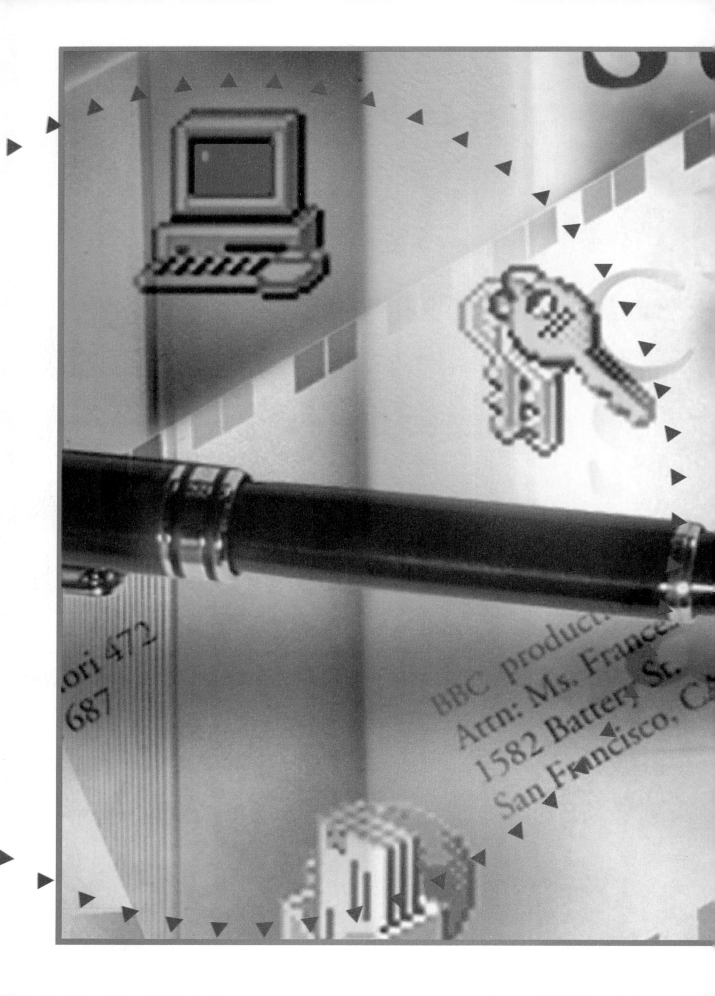

GETTING STARTED

INTRODUCTION TO WINDOWS 98

OBJECTIVES

Upon completion of this lesson, you will be able to:

■ Explain the most important features made possible by the taskbar.

■ Describe the difference between the standard Windows desktop and the Active Desktop.

■ Start Windows.

■ Examine the elements of the Windows opening screen.

■ Use a mouse to move around the desktop.

■ Shut down Windows.

🕐 **Estimated Time: 1.5 hours**

Windows . . . A simple, familiar word. Not a high-tech word. Yet Windows is, as you will see, an accurate name for a rich, powerful, high-tech software program. Reason: The word *windows* represents a visual or picture-oriented environment, the type of environment that Windows 98 uses. This environment provides an easy way for users to communicate or *interface* with the computer by way of pictures, often called a *graphical user interface* or GUI. Indeed, Windows' visual environment is the key to understanding and to using this impressive program.

But a graphical user interface does more than make Windows 98 easy to use. One key benefit of GUI is that it provides a *consistent* way to work within each program, a *consistent* way to work with other programs, and a simple, *consistent* way to switch between programs.

The Windows World

Imagine an electronic (not a physical) version of your desktop, complete with electronic tools and supplies, all accessible at your fingertips. That's the Windows 98 desktop! Its parallels with the physical desktop are not accidental; Windows is designed to be your workplace.

Here you will work with your mouse, by moving and clicking. Here you can place a clock before you, use your calculator, grab your files and folders, dial your phone, surf the Net, and open your briefcase. You can instantly see a complete listing of all your tools and supplies, a complete log of all your files and folders—a complete inventory of everything on your computer. And let's not forget that wastebasket (which Windows calls a Recycle Bin). You can even decorate your Windows desktop, as you will see later.

Windows Empowers You

Y*ou* can't appreciate the full potential of Windows 98 until you understand its powerful capabilities, such as linking files and automatic file updating. This powerful, yet friendly, software is an operating system, and that means it manages everything—both the hardware and the software that operates your entire computer system. With Windows 98, you shift to each new task and open and close applications as effortlessly and quickly as when you use your remote control to switch between TV channels. While one window remains open and active on the desktop, others remain open but inactive either on the desktop or as buttons on the taskbar. Just click on a taskbar button to reactivate it and place it in an open window.

This capability of running several tasks or applications at the same time is called *multitasking.* Multitasking allows you to process data in one application while you are working in another. For instance, while you are working on a spreadsheet in one window, you might be printing a word processing document in another window!

And, with Windows *linking* features, you can easily transfer data among applications and update the data automatically.

Windows 98—An Easy Transition

W*hether* you are new to Windows software or not, adapting to new software—even a new version of familiar software—can be taxing. Learning new tools and unfamiliar features can be time consuming and may require training. But Windows 98 simplifies the process considerably. Consequently, if you've used an older version of Windows, you'll make the "Win 98 transition" easily. As you make the transition, you'll see that Windows 98 provides:

- Easier, faster, and more powerful ways to work with application programs, special hardware settings, and increased speed for your network connections.

- Greater reliability and built-in support for hardware and software improvements, such as being able to use up to four monitors at a time.

- Revised versions of the standard Windows desktop and an option to switch to an Active Desktop which gives you quick and easy access to Web sites.

- Enhanced versions of desktop tools, the taskbar, and the Start menu.

- Upgraded support for multimedia that allows you to receive high-quality movies and audio—directly on your desktop.

- A single easy way to have automated access to and delivery of information—whether it is located on your machine, the local area network, or on the Internet.

- A mechanism that schedules delivery of information from the World Wide Web that you are interested in viewing regularly without having to physically visit the site or even connect to the Web.

- Advanced capabilities for Internet Explorer and support for all Internet standards.

Starting Windows

After you power up your computer, a box may appear on your screen that displays the message "Welcome to Windows." If this window displays, enter a user name and a password and then click OK. If several people are using the same system, you may be given a special user name and password. (You may need to ask your system administrator for assistance.) Then, after you click OK, Windows will open up to one of two desktops, the Windows *standard desktop* as displayed in Figure 1-1, or the *Active Desktop*, as shown in Figure 1-2.

FIGURE 1-1
Standard desktop

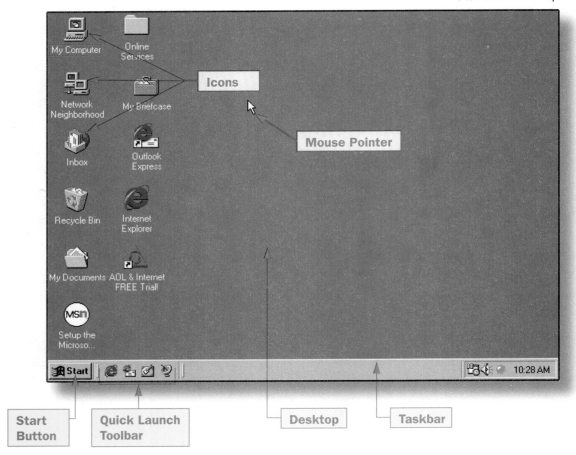

Your computer is probably set up to open with the Active Desktop. You will soon learn how easy it is to switch between the two desktop options. Through the Active Desktop you will be introduced to a whole new view of your computer—one in which it is part of the large world of networks, intranets, and the Internet. Take a minute to look over the differences in these two opening Windows screens before you get started with Windows!

FIGURE 1-2
Active Desktop

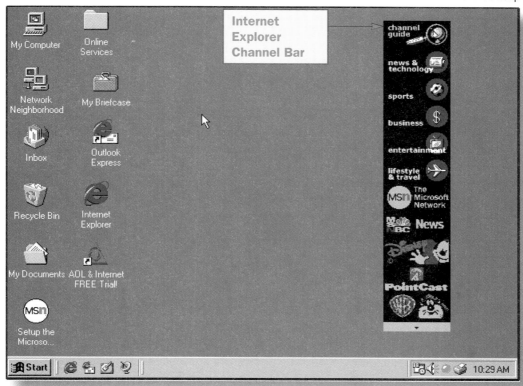

EXERCISE ⟶ 1.1

1. Power up your computer system. Windows should start automatically.

2. Compare your screen with the ones illustrated in Figure 1-1 and Figure 1-2. Your screen may differ slightly, but the basic elements should

be the same. Spend a few minutes looking at the layout of your screen and the position of the elements. If your screen does not display elements similar to those shown in Figure 1-1 or Figure 1-2, ask for assistance.

Examining the Windows Opening Screen

Now that you have started Windows 98, you are ready to explore its many features. As you explore Windows, remember what you have already learned about its graphical environment. As you work through each lesson in this course, you will be using the same consistent way of performing common tasks for different programs within Windows.

The Desktop

The *desktop* (see Figure 1-1) provides the overall work area on the screen and is the Windows equivalent of the top surface of your desk. Most Windows activity takes place on the desktop. You put things on your desk, take things off your desk, and move things around on your desk. In the same way, you can place items on, remove items from, and move items around on your Windows desktop.

Like any new desk, the Windows desktop is relatively neat when Windows is first installed on your computer. A new Windows desktop may have up to seven or more icons, depending on your system's configuration. As you work, placing elements on and removing elements from your desktop, these icons will generally stay on your desktop.

Look again at Figure 1-1, which identifies the main components of the opening Windows screen: the desktop, the taskbar, the Quick Launch toolbar, the Start button, the mouse pointer, and a number of small pictures, or *icons*, you can use to work with Windows 98 programs and features.

The opening Windows screen typically displays five or more icons, each of which represents a different feature or a different application you can use. In some cases, the icons represent specific parts of your computer system or shortcuts to applications.

While many icons can be placed on the desktop and removed from the desktop, several icons will generally appear on all Windows desktops: *My Computer, Network Neighborhood, Recycle Bin, My Briefcase,* and *Internet Explorer.* These icons are discussed in detail below.

- **My Computer** displays the contents of your computer. You can see the hardware devices, resources, programs, and files that are stored on your computer. My Computer also provides information about different system resources, such as the size of the hard disk and how much space is available on it. You can also use My Computer to format disks and to run applications.

- **Network Neighborhood** lists all of the computers on your network, if you are connected to one. Network Neighborhood permits you to browse through files on a networked computer.

- **Recycle Bin** contains files you delete from your hard disk. You can retrieve files from the Recycle Bin if you deleted them by mistake. A lifesaver!

- **My Briefcase** permits you to store and synchronize different versions of files and folders between two or more computers.

- With **Internet Explorer**, you get a fast, personalized Web browser. It provides you with far-reaching communication capabilities, including sending and receiving e-mail, surfing the Net, designing your own Web site, or building a video conference.

The Taskbar

Locate the *taskbar* in Figure 1-1 or Figure 1-2. There you will see the taskbar in its usual location, at the bottom of the screen, but you can move it to the top, left, or right side of the desktop to suit your needs. Wherever you choose to position it, you will find the taskbar to be a very convenient helper!

You use the taskbar for two important tasks: to display the Start menu and to switch among currently running applications that you wish to keep open. Every application that you keep open is represented by a button on the taskbar that offers easy access to all your running applications—just click the button. For example, if you open Excel, the taskbar displays a button for that application. If you then decide to run CorelDRAW, the taskbar adds a button for that application. One glance at the icons on the taskbar buttons tells you which applications are running (active). Want to switch to another active application? Just click the appropriate button on the taskbar!

If you right-click on a blank area of the taskbar, the taskbar shortcut menu appears, as illustrated in Figure 1-3. Select Toolbars from the menu to display a submenu that contains options for displaying various toolbars. In Figure 1-3, notice that a check mark appears beside Quick Launch. This means that the Quick Launch toolbar is currently displayed on the desktop.

FIGURE 1-3
Taskbar shortcut menu showing its Toolbars submenu

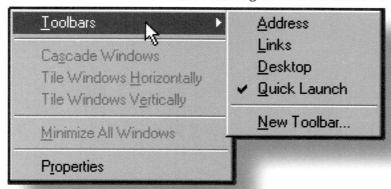

The Start Menu

You click the *Start button* on the taskbar to display the Start menu, as shown in Figure 1-4. The Start menu contains a list of options you will use throughout this book that enable you to complete frequently performed tasks quickly and easily. For example, you can launch programs from the Start menu, open recently used files, change your system's settings, find files or folders, access Help topics, and close and shut down Windows.

The options that appear on your Start menu will vary, depending on the setup of your system. Following is an explanation of the options commonly found on the Start menu:

- **Programs** allows you to launch programs quickly from the desktop.

- **Favorites** lists the Web sites, folders, or files you access regularly. Figure 1-5 shows the Favorites menu and the Links submenu.

FIGURE 1-4
Windows Start button and menu

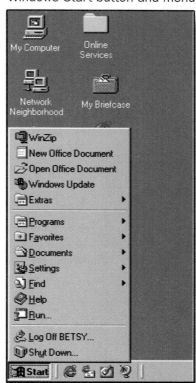

FIGURE 1-5
Favorites menu and Links submenu

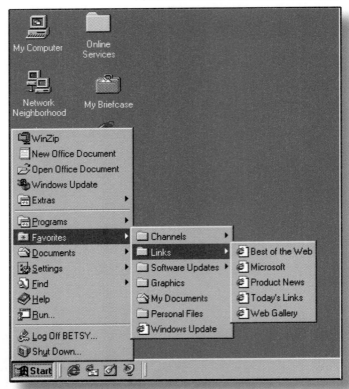

- **Documents** contains a list of the last 15 documents you opened and worked on most recently on your computer. It gives you quick access to these documents and the applications in which they were created.

- **Settings** displays options for customizing the look and "feel" of your desktop. For instance, the Control Panel option lets you change settings such as the computer's date/time, desktop background, display colors, keyboard language, and mouse controls. The Taskbar and Start Menu option lets you make changes to what appears on your taskbar and Start menu.

- The **Find** option is one of the most important capabilities in the Windows program: it helps you find files and folders. This option also lets you search for Web sites you visit frequently, plus it provides a quick way to find people whose names are stored in a variety of your electronic address books.

- The **Help** option opens the Windows Help facility, an easy-to-use Windows facility that provides you information about Windows and its applications.

- The **Run...** command allows you to begin a program quickly from the Start menu. You can also use this command to find a file or program.

- The **Log Off...** command identifies the name of the user who is logged on to the computer.

- The **Shut Down...** option provides options for safely shutting down and/or restarting Windows and your computer.

The Mouse Pointer

The arrow you see on the desktop (see Figure 1-1 or Figure 1-2) is the *mouse pointer*, a graphical element you move around the screen to select items (such as icons and menu options), issue commands, and move and manipulate screen elements (such as text or windows). The arrow is one of several shapes the pointer may assume. Other shapes and their meanings will be explained later in this lesson.

The Channel Bar

Windows' Active Desktop looks similar to the standard desktop with one exception: the Internet Explorer Channel bar (see Figure 1-2). The Channel bar is designed to provide you quick and easy access to particular Web sites, or *channels*. By subscribing to a channel, information from that site is delivered to your computer at scheduled times. You simply click the channel on the Channel bar to review that site's content.

To switch from the standard desktop to the Active Desktop, right-click on any blank area on the desktop. A shortcut menu displays, like that shown in Figure 1-6. Point to Active Desktop, and then click View As Web Page on the submenu. To switch back to the standard desktop, you simply click the View As Web Page option again to deselect it.

FIGURE 1-6
Switching to Active Desktop

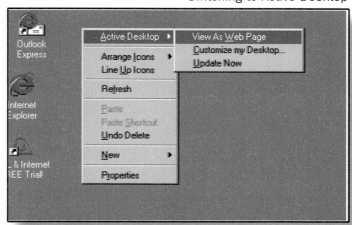

EXERCISE ⟹ 1.2

1. If the standard desktop appears when you start Windows, change it to the Active Desktop: Position the mouse pointer on any blank space on the standard desktop and click the right mouse button.

2. On the menu that opens, point to **Active Desktop**. On the submenu, point to **View As**

Web Page and click the left mouse button once. The special features of the Active Desktop allow you to bring your favorite Internet Web pages to your desktop, click on Web links, view animation, listen to sound, and much more! You will learn about Internet Explorer in Unit 11.

Moving Around the Desktop

Question: "How do I move around the Windows desktop?" Answer: "With a mouse!" The mouse lets you race all over the screen—and, if you want, carry materials with you as you move!

Introducing the Mouse

The *mouse* is an input device that allows you to find files, access tools, and grab folders you need to move or place on the Windows desktop. Of course, you can also use the mouse to put those tools, files, or folders away. But that's not all: The mouse serves a number of other convenient uses. Your desktop is a visual work area, and the mouse is the key to that work area.

Some laptop and notebook computers use a *trackball*. Consider a trackball an upside-down mouse. Use your thumb to rotate the ball and move the pointer.

MOUSE BASICS

Next to the keyboard on your computer desk, clear an area (at least 1 square foot) for moving the mouse. This area must be clean and smooth because the mouse uses a rotating ball to sense movement: Any grease or dust on the desk surface can clog the ball and cause difficulty in operating the mouse. For best performance, try a *mouse pad*. It's specially designed to sit under your mouse and facilitate its movement.

Hold the mouse so that the cable extends outward (away from your hand) and the body of the mouse rests under the palm of your hand. Rest your index finger lightly on one of the buttons.

THE MOUSE POINTER

The mouse controls the on-screen mouse pointer. To move the pointer up or down, to the left or right, just slide the mouse in that direction. When you get "cornered," that is, when you run out of room on your real desk or mouse pad, just lift the mouse off your desk (or mouse pad), move the mouse, then set it back down—all without moving the on-screen pointer.

The on-screen pointer changes its appearance depending on the task Windows is engaged in. Most of the time, the pointer looks like an arrow, but it may assume a number of other shapes. For example:

- When you are working with text, the pointer changes to an I-beam.

- When Windows is working on an instruction and isn't ready to accept any further input from you, the pointer changes to an hourglass. The hourglass means "Wait! Windows is busy finishing a task!"

- When an arrow is attached to the hourglass, this indicates that Windows is working on a task but you can still select and move objects.

- When the pointer turns into a circle with a slash through it—the international "no" symbol—the message is "This action is not allowed!" For example, if you try to drag an icon onto the taskbar, you'll see this pointer shape.

When you move the pointer over parts of a window, the different pointer shapes give you visual clues about how you can move the mouse.

MOUSE BUTTONS

So, the mouse lets you move around the screen quickly, but what do you do when you "get there"? Besides moving the pointer around the screen, the mouse allows you to move windows and to choose various applications. How? By using *mouse buttons*.

Every mouse has one, two, or three buttons, depending on the manufacturer. By default, the button on the left is the *primary button* (the one you will use most often). It is also referred to as the select/drag button because it is the one you use to select and move elements around the screen.

The secondary button, usually the button on the right, is called the *shortcut menu button* (shortcut menus are discussed later in this lesson), and using it is called *right-clicking*. You'll learn when to right-click as you practice using Windows.

Are you left-handed? Windows allows you to reverse the primary and secondary mouse buttons so you can use your left hand. You'll learn how in a later lesson.

Operating the Mouse

In addition to moving the pointer, the mouse is used to select objects and to move objects or icons around the screen. You *select* or *highlight* an item by pointing to it and pressing and then releasing the left mouse button. Pressing and then releasing the left mouse button is referred to as *clicking*; some commands require you to *double-click* (that is, click twice quickly). If you don't double-click the button fast enough, Windows interprets your action as two single clicks rather than one double-click. (With a little experience, you'll double-click expertly.)

Moving objects with the mouse is known as *dragging*. You drag an object by placing the mouse pointer on the item to be moved, then pressing and holding down the mouse button while moving the object. When the pointer is at the right location, release the mouse button.

Table 1-1 lists and explains five common techniques for using a standard two-button mouse device.

Using the mouse proficiently requires a little practice—and a little patience. In a very short time, you'll use the mouse comfortably and smoothly.

TABLE 1-1
Operating the mouse to accomplish common procedures

Mouse Techniques

To	Do this . . .
Drag	Press the mouse button and move the mouse in the desired direction.
Click	Press and release the left mouse button.
Double-click	Click the left mouse button twice in rapid succession.
Right-click	Press and release the right mouse button.
Select	Point to an item and click the mouse button.

EXERCISE 1.3

1. Move the mouse on your desk (or mouse pad). As you move the mouse, watch the screen to see how the pointer moves:
   a. Move the pointer to the far left of your screen by sliding the mouse to the left on the desk or mouse pad. Do not lift the mouse.
   b. Move the pointer to the far right of your screen by sliding the mouse to the right.
   c. Move the pointer to the top of your screen by moving the mouse toward the top of your desk or mouse pad.
   d. Move the pointer to the bottom of your screen by moving the mouse toward the bottom of your desk or mouse pad.

2. Display and then close the Start menu:
   a. Point to the **Start** button on the lower left corner of the taskbar.
   b. Click the left mouse button.
   c. Point to a clear area of the desk and click the mouse button. The Start menu closes.

3. Select and rearrange the icons on the desktop:

   a. Point to the **My Computer** icon and click the mouse button. Notice that when you click an icon, it changes color. The change in color means the icon is selected.
   Point to the **Network Neighborhood** icon (or any other icon if you don't have this one on your desktop). Now click to select it. As you do so, notice that My Computer is deselected (that is, it returns to its original color).
   b. Again point to the **My Computer** icon.
   c. While holding down the mouse button, drag the icon about 1 inch to the right and release the mouse button. As you drag the icon, note how a "ghost image" of the icon follows the mouse pointer to indicate where the icon will be placed when you release the mouse button.
   d. Drag the My Computer icon back to its original position.

4. Double-click the **My Computer** icon. The My Computer window opens as shown in Figure 1-7. Remain in this screen for the next exercise.

FIGURE 1-7
Double-clicking an icon

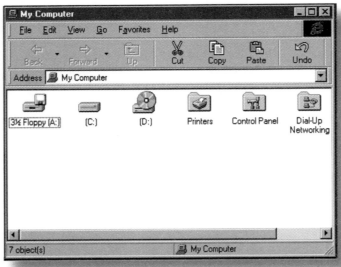

Shutting Down Windows

Shutting down Windows is a two-step process. First, you should close any programs you have been running. (As with any application software package, closing an application before you turn off the computer will guard against losing current work.) Second, once you have closed all applications that have been active, you are ready to shut down Windows.

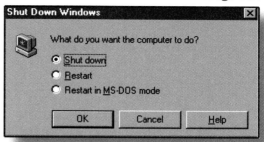

FIGURE 1-8
Shut Down Windows message box

To shut down Windows, select the Shut Down option from the Start menu. Each time you shut down Windows, a message box will be displayed, giving you choices similar to those shown in Figure 1-8. These choices are discussed below.

- **Shut down**. Selecting this option quits Windows and prepares your computer to be shut down. A message displays telling you when it is safe to turn your computer off.

- **Restart**. This option quits Windows and restarts your computer.

- **Restart in MS-DOS mode**. This option closes Windows and places your system in the Windows DOS environment. In the Windows DOS environment, you will be unable to use some of the commands that are available in other DOS versions. When you have finished your DOS session, you can shut down your system or launch Windows by keying *exit* or *win* and pressing Enter.

E X E R C I S E ⟩ 1.4

1. Click the **Start** button and select the **Shut Down** option from the **Start** menu.

2. Select the **Restart in MS-DOS mode** option by clicking the option button preceding the words, then clicking the **Yes** button. Windows closes, and the DOS prompt is displayed.

3. Launch Windows by keying **win** at the DOS prompt and pressing **Enter**.

4. If instructed, shut down Windows again and turn off your computer.

Summary

This lesson introduced you to Windows 98 and summarized some of its key features. You learned that:

- Windows 98 allows multitasking; that is, processing information in more than one application at the same time.

- Windows 98 permits data transfer; that is, moving information or graphics from one application window to another, as well as automatically linking transferred data when the original data file is revised.

- Windows 98 provides a choice of two desktops for you to work with: the standard desktop and the Active Desktop.

- The opening screen on the standard desktop provides five or more icons, small images or pictures, each of which represents a different feature or a different application you can choose.

- Most Windows activity takes place on the desktop. While many elements can be placed on the desktop and removed from the desktop, several icons will generally appear on all Windows desktops: My Computer, Network Neighborhood, Recycle Bin, My Briefcase, and Internet Explorer.

- The Windows opening screen has the following basic components: the desktop, the taskbar, the Quick Launch toolbar, the Start button, the mouse pointer, and a number of desktop icons.

- Through the Internet Explorer Channel bar, the Active Desktop lets you bring your favorite Internet Web pages to your desktop, click on Web links, view animation, listen to sound, and much more.

- You use the taskbar to open programs and documents and to switch back and forth between running applications. The taskbar is generally displayed at the bottom of the screen, but you can move it to the top, left, or right side of the desktop to suit your needs. Two key features of the taskbar are the Start button and task switching.

- The Start menu options let you launch programs, open recently used files, change your system's settings, find files or folders, access Help topics, list your favorite Web sites, folders, or files, and close and shut down Windows.

- The mouse controls an on-screen pointer. The shape of the pointer will change depending on where you are on-screen and what you are doing.

- Mouse buttons let you make selections by clicking (pressing and releasing once), right-clicking (clicking the right mouse button), and double-clicking. The left button is the most used. The right button is used for shortcuts.

- The mouse also lets you move ("drag") objects. Place the pointer on the object to be moved, press and hold down the mouse button while moving the object, and release the button when the object is in position.

- Close all programs you have been running before you shut down Windows.

- Select the Shut Down option from the Start menu when you want to shut down Windows. You can then shut down the computer, restart the computer, or restart the computer in MS-DOS mode.

LESSON 1 REVIEW QUESTIONS

MATCHING

Write the letter of the term in the right column that matches the definition in the left column.

_____ 1. It appears when you right-click on the desktop.

_____ 2. The icon on the desktop that represents a network.

_____ 3. A graphical element you move around the screen to select, move, and manipulate screen elements.

_____ 4. The action of moving an object with the mouse.

_____ 5. Icon on the desktop that contains deleted files.

A. dragging

B. Network Neighborhood

C. Recycle Bin

D. the Active Desktop

E. mouse pointer

TRUE/FALSE

Each of the following statements is either true or false. Indicate your answer on the left by circling T if the statement is true and F if the statement is false.

T F 1. The standard desktop is the name of the Windows operating system.

T F 2. The Recycle Bin stores newly created documents.

T F 3. A trackball is similar to an upside-down mouse.

T F 4. The taskbar is usually located at the bottom of the screen.

T F 5. Multitasking means running one or more applications simultaneously.

LESSON 2

MANIPULATING WINDOWS

OBJECTIVES

Upon completion of this lesson, you will be able to:

- Identify parts of the window.

- Open, move, resize, minimize, maximize, and restore windows.

- Work with menus and menu elements.

- Work with dialog boxes.

- Manipulate multiple windows.

⏱ Estimated Time: 1.5 hours

You are now familiar with the Windows 98 desktop. In this lesson, the various parts of a window are identified. You will learn how to work with a window and how to manage multiple windows. Using menus and dialog boxes to issue commands is also discussed.

Identifying the Parts of a Window

A *window* is an on-screen area in which you view program folders, files, or icons. At first sight, a window like the one in Figure 2-1 may look rather complicated because you aren't familiar with its symbols and labels. Let's examine the features of the window shown in Figure 2-1. The elements labeled in Figure 2-1 are common to most windows you'll work with in Windows 98.

- In Figure 2-1, find the *title bar* at the top of the window. The title bar displays the name of the application running in a window—in this case, "My Computer."

- Directly below the title bar is a *menu bar*, which lists available menus (the specific choices depend on the application you are running). The Figure 2-1 menu bar lists six choices: File, Edit, View, Go, Favorites, and Help.

- The *Standard toolbar* contains buttons that permit you to access various functions and issue commands. The toolbar in the My Computer window has buttons for navigating your computer's resources and for changing the display of the objects in the window.

 **NOTE:**

The buttons on the Standard toolbar vary from window to window, depending on the window or application program, but the position of the toolbar is consistent.

16

- The *Address Bar* displays the name of the open folder or object. It also permits you to quickly key the address of a Web page without opening your browser.

- In the rectangular window are icons, which you learned about in Lesson 1. In this window, the icons represent the parts of your computer system and applications to control the system.

- The *Minimize, Maximize/Restore*, and *Close buttons* appear at the upper right corner of the window, on the same line as the title bar. The Minimize button reduces the window to a button on the taskbar, and the Maximize button enlarges the window to fill the screen. Once the window is full-screen size, the Maximize button changes to a Restore button, which enables you to restore the window to its previous (smaller) size. The Close button quickly closes the window.

- The *Launch Internet Explorer Browser button* lets you start Internet Explorer at the click of a button.

- The *borders* are the four lines that define the limits of the window.

- The *status bar* provides information on the currently selected object or the task you are performing. As you choose menu items, select window objects, or issue commands, the action is described on the status bar.

- The *resize tab* provides a large spot to grab when you want to resize a window.

- When the window is not large enough to display everything in one window, *scroll bars* are displayed (not shown in Figure 2-1). Clicking on the scroll bar moves (scrolls) the contents of a window so that you can view objects that are hidden.

FIGURE 2-1
Parts of the window

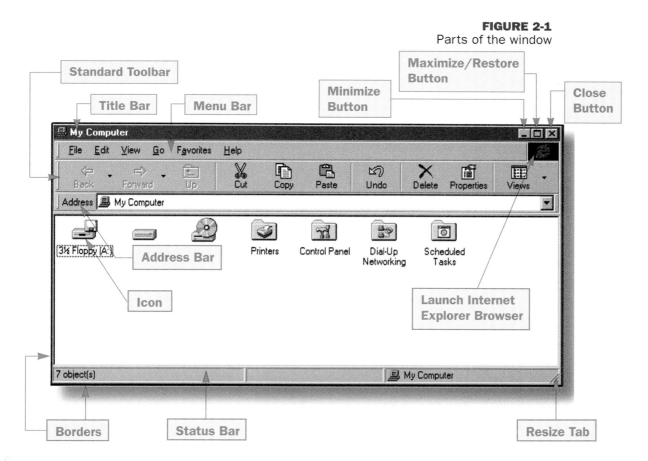

Manipulating Windows

When you open a window, the software determines the window size and location on the desktop. A predetermined software choice or setting is called the *default*. If you wish, you can change many defaults; for example, you can control the position and size of your windows by changing the default settings.

Moving a Window

At times, you may need to move a window to uncover another window or an object on the desktop. The quickest way is to drag the window by its title bar. If the window is maximized, you must first restore it to its previous size before you move it.

Resizing a Window

If the window has a resize tab, as shown in Figure 2-1, you can resize the window without moving the upper left corner. You resize by dragging the resize tab in any direction.

If you want greater control over the position of the resized window, resize the window by dragging one of the three types of window borders (horizontal, vertical, or corner), as shown in Figure 2-1.

- If you drag on a horizontal border, you make the window taller or shorter. The pointer changes to a vertical double-headed arrow, indicating that you can drag the border up or down.

- If you drag on a vertical border, you make the window wider or narrower. The pointer changes to a horizontal double-headed arrow, indicating that you can drag the border right or left.

- If you drag from one of the corners, you can change two window dimensions with one movement. The pointer changes to a diagonal double-headed arrow, indicating that you can drag in either a vertical or a horizontal direction.

Minimizing, Maximizing, and Restoring a Window

Although it is easy to resize a window by dragging its borders, Windows 98 also gives you three additional ways to resize a window. The Maximize, Restore, and Minimize buttons allow you to change the window's size with one click of the mouse.

Study the resizing buttons shown in Figure 2-2. To use one of these buttons, click on it.

- The Minimize button reduces the active window to a button that appears on the taskbar. The window is still available but it is hidden, allowing more room on your desktop.

- The Maximize button enlarges the active window to its maximum size so that it fills the entire window—helpful if you need a larger view of one window. Once you select the Maximize button, it is replaced by the Restore button.

- When a window has been maximized, clicking the Restore button returns the window to its former size.

FIGURE 2-2
Minimize, Maximize, and Restore buttons

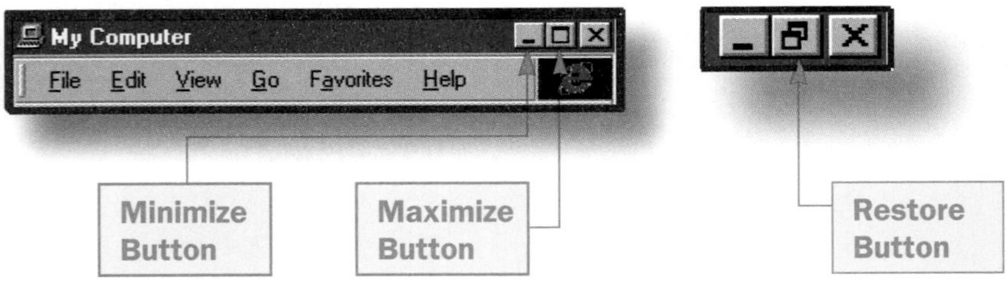

Minimize Button

Maximize Button

Restore Button

E X E R C I S E ⟹ 2.1

1. If necessary, start your computer. Double-click the **My Computer** icon on your desktop.

2. Move the My Computer window until its upper left corner is 1 inch from the top and 1 inch from the left side of the desktop:
   a. Position the pointer over the title bar and press and hold down the mouse button.
   b. Drag the window to the desired position.

3. Resize the window by using the resize tab:
   a. Position the pointer over the resize tab (see Figure 2-1). The pointer should change to a diagonal double-headed arrow.
   b. Drag the tab down and to the right to enlarge the window.

4. Click the **Minimize** button. The window minimizes to a button on the taskbar. Did you notice the visual effect of the window minimizing to a button on the taskbar?

5. Click the **My Computer** button on the taskbar to restore the window to its former position on the desktop.

6. Click the **Maximize** button. The window expands to fill the display and the Maximize button changes to a Restore button.

7. Click the **Restore** button to restore the My Computer window to its former size.

8. Resize the My Computer window by dragging a vertical border:
   a. Position the pointer over the left border of the My Computer window. When the pointer is in the correct position, it will change to a horizontal double-headed arrow.
   b. Drag the border to the left until it is at the left edge of the desktop.

9. Leave the My Computer window on-screen for the next exercise.

Working with Menus

A *menu* is a list of options or choices. Every window you open in Windows 98 contains a menu bar offering menus. The My Computer window currently on your screen has a menu bar with six menus: File, Edit, View, Go, Favorites, and Help. Each of these menus in turn offers a number of *commands* you can issue to perform a task or function.

If all these menu choices appeared on the desktop at the same time, your work area would be too cluttered to be useful. Windows' menus organize the choices so that they are out of sight but within reach.

To find out what choices are available on a particular menu, you display the menu by clicking on it. When you click on the menu name, the menu drops down, as shown in Figure 2-3.

Besides the menus on the menu bar that are specific to each window you open, Windows 98 also has a menu you can access at any time: The *Start menu*, which you open by clicking the Start button, offers a number of choices you can select among (see Figure 2-4).

Before you learn how to choose an item from a menu, read the following section to understand more about menus.

FIGURE 2-3
Menu in the My Computer window

FIGURE 2-4
Start menu

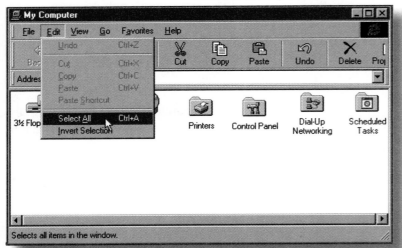

Identifying Menu Elements

Look again at Figures 2-3 and 2-4 and notice the differences among the listed options. One is highlighted, some are in black print, some are in a light color, and some are followed by three periods. All menu choices have one letter underlined. Each visual element has a special meaning, as explained below.

HIGHLIGHTING

In Figure 2-3, the Select All menu option is highlighted; that is, the words appear in white letters within a dark box. Highlighting indicates that an option is currently selected.

COLORS

Not all menu options are available to you all the time. The dark or black print indicates options that are currently available. Light or grayed print indicates options that are not available. Look closely at the Edit menu in Figure 2-3. Which two options are currently available?

ELLIPSES

An ellipsis is the series of three periods (...) following some commands. See the Run... and Shut Down... commands in Figure 2-4, for example. An ellipsis tells you that if you choose this option, a second window or dialog box will be displayed, requesting more information from you. (You'll learn more about dialog boxes later.)

SELECTION LETTERS

Each menu option has one underscored letter or number, indicating a keyboard command you can use as an alternative to the mouse. On the keyboard, press the underscored letter or number to choose that command. You can press the selection letters only while the menu is displayed.

SHORTCUT KEYS

Some menu options list *shortcut keys* to the right, as shown in Figure 2-3. Unlike selection letters, shortcut keys can be used even when the menu is not displayed.

RIGHT-POINTING ARROW

The right-pointing arrows shown in Figure 2-4 indicate that if you point on an option that has one of these arrows, another menu will appear with more options. This second menu is a *submenu*. Windows automatically opens submenus after the pointer has been resting on an option for a short period of time. You can click on the option to display the submenu immediately.

Selecting an Option from a Menu

To select an option from a menu, first open the menu. You'll find that as you move the pointer down the menu, the highlight also moves. Stop the pointer on the option you want to choose, then click. The command you have chosen will execute.

You can also execute a command using the command's shortcut keys, if available. After you have become familiar with commands, you may find it easier to use shortcut keys for the commands you use most often.

Shortcut keys enable you to select commands without using menus. Shortcut keys generally combine the Alt, Ctrl, or Shift key with a letter key; in this text, such combinations are expressed as follows: Alt+X or Ctrl+O. Look again at Figure 2-3. The shortcut keys for the Select All command are Ctrl+A. To execute this command using the shortcut keys, press the Ctrl key and hold it down while pressing the *a* key. Then release both keys at the same time.

NOTE: You can use either capital or lowercase letters for shortcut keys.

E X E R C I S E ▷ 2.2

1. Display a topic from the Help menu in the My Computer window:
   a. Click the **Help** menu name in the menu bar.
   b. Select **About Windows 98** by pressing the letter **a.**
   c. Close the window by clicking the **Close** button.

2. Select all the icons in the My Computer window:
   a. Click the title bar on the My Computer window to verify that it is selected.
   b. Key the shortcut **Ctrl+A**. All the icons are now selected.
   c. Click somewhere in the blank (white) space in the My Computer window to deselect the icons.

3. Close the My Computer window by clicking its **Close** button.

4. Open the Start menu by clicking the **Start** button.

5. Point to **Settings**. Notice how another menu opens to the right of the Start menu.

6. Move the pointer to the **Run...** command on the start menu and click. The Run dialog box appears, as shown in Figure 2-5.

7. Leave the Run dialog box on screen for the next exercise.

FIGURE 2-5
Run dialog box

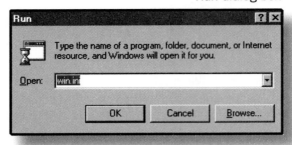

Working with Dialog Boxes

Some menu options, such as the Run... command you selected in the last exercise, need more information before they can be executed. For example, before Windows can run (start) a program, it needs to know the program name. The ellipsis (...) that follows such a command signals that need for additional information. You provide the needed information by responding to a *dialog box*, such as the one shown in Figure 2-5.

A dialog box is itself a window and has some of the same features as a window, such as an identifying title bar and a Close button. But dialog boxes contain a number of other elements that help you give information to your computer.

Let's take a look at the elements you will find most often in dialog boxes.

Buttons

There are two types of buttons: *command buttons* and *option buttons*.

■ Command buttons carry out your instructions using the information selected in the dialog box. Command buttons are always rectangles. When you press a command button, the program accepts your instructions. If there is an ellipsis on the button (for example, Browse...), choosing it will open another dialog box. Typical command buttons are Open, Help, Cancel, and OK. The Run dialog box currently on your screen contains three command buttons: OK, Cancel, and Browse....

■ Option buttons (sometimes called radio buttons) allow you to choose one option from a group of options. (See Figure 2-6.) To change a selection, simply choose a different button.

FIGURE 2-6
Option buttons and text boxes

Option Button

| Orientation |
| Portrait |
| Landscape |

| Margins (inches) |
| Left: 1.25" | Right: 1.25" |
| Top: 1" | Bottom: 1" |

Text Box

Boxes

There are four types of boxes: *text boxes, check boxes, list boxes,* and *drop-down list boxes.* A *combo box* combines two types of boxes.

■ Text boxes allow you to key information in the dialog box. A text box may contain a blinking insertion point to show you where to begin keying, or it may already contain text that you can change as necessary. To change existing text, highlight it by double-clicking on it and then key the new text. Figure 2-6 shows several text boxes.

■ Check boxes also allow you to make choices from a group. However, unlike option buttons, you can check several boxes; that is, you can select a variety of options. Clicking with the mouse selects (✔) or deselects (no ✔) a check box. Figure 2-7 shows two check boxes.

■ List boxes present a set of options in list format. List boxes are found in both windows and dialog boxes. When the list of options is too lengthy to fit in the box, *scroll bars* are available to allow you to *scroll* through the items. Drag the scroll box to move up or down the list. Figure 2-7 shows scroll bars on the Font and Size list boxes.

FIGURE 2-7
A dialog box containing several kinds of boxes

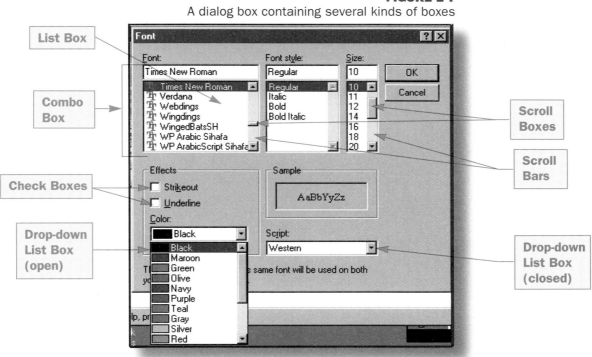

■ A drop-down list box displays only one option and a special arrow symbol. Click on the arrow symbol to reveal the entire list box. Figure 2-7 shows two drop-down list boxes, with one of the lists displayed.

■ A combo box is a combination of a text box and a list box. You can select from the list or enter your own choice by keying it in the text part of the combo box. Figure 2-7 shows a combo box.

2 3

1. If the Run dialog box on your screen contains text, make sure the text is highlighted.

2. Key your first name in the text box—do not press Enter.

3. Click the **OK** command button. You now see a message box (another form of dialog box) similar to the one illustrated in Figure 2-8.

Windows is telling you that it cannot locate the file you asked to run.

4. Click the **OK** command button to cancel the message display.

5. Click the **Cancel** command button to cancel the Run... command.

FIGURE 2-8
Message box

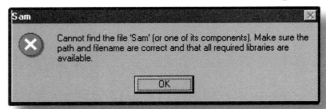

Managing Multiple Windows

Windows' multitasking ability allows you to perform more than one task at a time. As a result, you may have a lot of windows open on the desktop at one time, and this can be confusing. How can you manage those windows and switch between them? By rearranging the windows on your desktop!

Arranging Windows on the Desktop

Earlier you learned to drag a window to a different location on the desktop. Dragging can be very time-consuming when you have a number of open windows. A *shortcut menu* hidden on the taskbar makes it easy to arrange open windows. The shortcut menu contains the options that are most commonly performed from the current window display. While the shortcut menu is handy, not all options are included on a shortcut menu. To access this shortcut menu, point on any portion of the taskbar that does not contain a button and right-click. The shortcut menu shown in Figure 2-9 displays, allowing you to instruct Windows to organize the open windows on your desktop. You can choose one of three different arrangements: Cascade, Tile Horizontally, or Tile Vertically.

FIGURE 2-9
Shortcut menu

■ The Cascade Windows option *cascades* the open windows into a stack with title bars showing; the active window is always in front of the stack, on the top layer.

■ The Tile Windows Horizontally option *tiles* the open windows across the desktop from top to bottom, without overlapping any portion of any window.

■ The Tile Windows Vertically option divides the desktop evenly among the open windows and aligns the windows across the screen, left to right, without overlapping any window.

The shortcut menu also contains a Minimize All Windows command, which reduces all windows to buttons on the taskbar. And you can cancel whichever option you select by using the Undo command. For example, the shortcut menu shown in Figure 2-9 lists an Undo Cascade option. Selecting this option restores the display to its previous arrangement.

Switching Between Windows

When multiple windows are open on your desktop, the one you are working with is called the *active window*. The active window is easy to recognize because its title bar is a different color or intensity. You can make any open window the active window in one of two ways:

■ If any portion of the window you want to work with is visible, click on it. It will come to the front and become the active window.

■ At any time, press and hold down the Alt key, then press Tab. A small window appears in the center of the display. The window contains icons for all items currently open. This display includes those items open on the desktop as well as those items minimized on the taskbar. If you hold down the Alt key and then press and release Tab, you can cycle through all the icons. A box surrounds the item's icon and a description appears at the bottom of the window as each item is selected. When the one you want is selected, release the Alt key and that item comes to the front and becomes the active window. This is called the *fast Alt+Tab* method for switching to a different window.

E X E R C I S E ⇨ 2.4

1. Open the My Computer window by double-clicking its icon on the desktop.

2. Open the Recycle Bin window by double-clicking its icon on the desktop.

3. Open the Find: All Files window:
   a. Display the Start menu by clicking the **Start** button.
   b. Move the pointer to the **Find** option.
   c. Click **Files or Folders** to open its window.

4. Tile the open windows using the shortcut menu:
   a. Point on a blank area in the taskbar and right-click to display the shortcut menu.

   b. Select the **Tile Windows Vertically** option. The windows are now arranged differently; they are arranged in a tiled format.

5. Select the **Tile Windows Horizontally** option from the shortcut menu. The windows are rearranged into this tiled format.

6. Select the **Cascade Windows** option from the shortcut menu. The windows are rearranged into a cascade format.

7. Change the active window:
   a. Click the My Computer window. If it wasn't in front, it comes to the foreground and becomes the active window.

(continued on next page)

b. Click the **Recycle Bin** window and make it the active window. The Recycle Bin comes to the front as the active window.

c. Click the **Find: All Files** window and make it the active window. This window comes to the front as the active window.

8. Undo the cascade format and return the windows to the Tile Windows Horizontally format:

a. Point on the taskbar and right-click to display the shortcut menu.

b. Select the **Undo Cascade** option. The windows are again arranged in a horizontal tiled format.

9. Minimize all windows to buttons on the taskbar by selecting the **Minimize All Windows** option on the shortcut menu.

10. Open the Recycle Bin window using the Alt+Tab feature:

a. Press and hold down the **Alt** key.

b. Press and release the **Tab** key until the Recycle Bin icon is outlined, then release the Alt key.

11. Notice that this window is still in tile format. Display the Recycle Bin window in the cascade format by selecting the **Cascade Windows** option on the shortcut menu.

12. Open the My Computer window and the Find: All Files window using the Alt+Tab feature. Display all the open windows in cascade format.

13. Close all open windows by clicking their **Close** buttons. If instructed, shut down Windows and your computer.

Summary

This lesson discussed how to manage and manipulate windows, and how to issue commands through menus and dialog boxes. You learned that:

■ Any window with Minimize and Maximize/Restore buttons can be resized. A window can also be resized by dragging one of its borders or corners. The resize tab provides a large spot to grab when you want to resize a window.

■ A menu is a list of options or choices. You make selections from a menu by pointing at and clicking on an option or using the up or down arrow keys.

■ On a menu, a highlighted option (white letters within a dark box) indicates that this option is currently selected, and light or grayish letters (as opposed to black) means that an option is not available.

■ A series of three periods (...), called an ellipsis, following a command tells you that if you choose this option, a dialog box will open to request more information.

■ A dialog box is a window. In it, you will find command buttons and option buttons. Command buttons are rectangular and, as their name clearly tells, clicking a command button executes a command. Option buttons (also known as radio buttons) let you choose one option from a group of options.

■ A dialog box may also have check boxes, list boxes, text boxes, and drop-down list boxes, each of which allows you to make selections or key information.

■ Windows is able to multitask (do more than one task at a time). This means more than one window can be open at a time. The windows can be arranged on the desktop in a cascade, horizontally tiled, or vertically tiled format. Click on any window or use Alt+Tab to bring a desired window to the front and make it the active window.

LESSON 2 REVIEW QUESTIONS

MATCHING

Write the letter of the term in the right column that matches the definition in the left column.

_____ 1. A list of options or choices.

_____ 2. A predetermined choice made by the software.

_____ 3. The window in which you are presently working.

_____ 4. In a dialog box, the buttons that carry out your instructions using the information selected.

_____ 5. In a dialog box, the buttons that represent a group of choices from which you can select one.

A. option buttons

B. default

C. menu

D. command buttons

E. active window

MULTIPLE CHOICE

Complete the following questions by circling the correct multiple choice letter.

1. The list of choices on a Windows menu bar
   A. is the same for all applications
   B. will vary according to the application
   C. displays as icons
   D. none of the above

2. Shortcut keys
   A. can be used even when the menu is not displayed
   B. are keystrokes that must be used rather than the mouse
   C. always use the Alt key
   D. cannot be used unless the menu is displayed

3. When a window is not large enough to display everything,
   A. you can click the Restore button to enlarge it
   B. the status bar will indicate there is more to be displayed
   C. you should drag its title bar to resize it
   D. you can click the Maximize button to enlarge it

4. The visual element that indicates whether a menu option is available is
   A. an ellipsis
   B. the color of the option
   C. an underscored letter
   D. highlighting

5. If additional information is needed before a command can be executed, Windows displays a
   A. message box
   B. dialog box
   C. control-menu box
   D. prompt box

GETTING HELP

OBJECTIVES

Upon completion of this lesson, you will be able to:

- Start the Windows Help system.

- Use the Help system's Contents, Index, and Search tabs.

- Print a Help topic.

- Use the "What's This?" feature.

> ⏱ **Estimated Time: 1.5 hours**

If you need assistance while working in Windows, use Windows Help, a built-in help facility designed to provide you with information about Windows and its applications. In this lesson, you learn how to use the Windows Help system.

Starting the Help System

The Windows Help facility looks and acts the same in each application, but the information is specific to that application.

You can access Help in three ways:

1. Select the Help option from the Start menu.

2. Press F1.

3. Select Help whenever you see a Help command button or Help as an item on a menu (almost every menu bar has this item).

Selecting the Help option from any menu displays a Help window like the one shown in Figure 3-1. The title bar of the Help window reads "Windows Help" because this window provides general information about the Windows program. The title bar of each Windows application Help screen is specific to the application. For example, the Help window title bar for the WordPad accessory is "Wordpad Help."

FIGURE 3-1
Help window

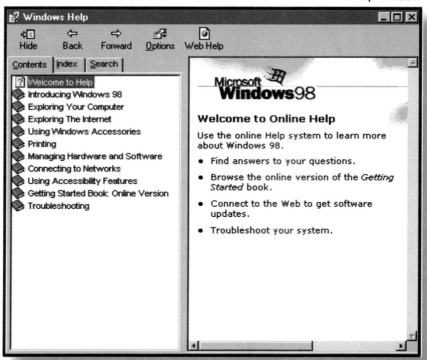

Think of the Help system as an electronic reference book complete with a table of contents and an index. Notice the three tabs at the top of the left frame of the window: Contents, Index, and Search. Each tab offers a different way to use the Help system.

Using the Contents Tab

The Contents tab shown in Figure 3-1 offers a number of general topics, represented by book icons. To view the topics listed under each of these general topics, click the book icon. You will notice that when you point to a topic, it changes to a different color and is underlined, similar to a link you might see on a Web page. The topics icon changes to an open book icon and a list of subtopics displays. The subtopics are also represented by book icons that can be opened, as shown in Figure 3-2. Help entries for a subtopic are represented by a question mark icon.

To view a particular Help entry, click the entry. The entry displays in the right frame of the Help window. Figure 3-3 shows the Help entry that displays if you select *Find a topic* from the Contents tab.

INTERNET The Web is a graphical system of linking and pointing to documents and sites on the Internet, a worldwide network of computers. A link is underlined text or a graphic that you can click to jump to another document or site on the Internet.

FIGURE 3-2

Contents tab with a list of topics and subtopics

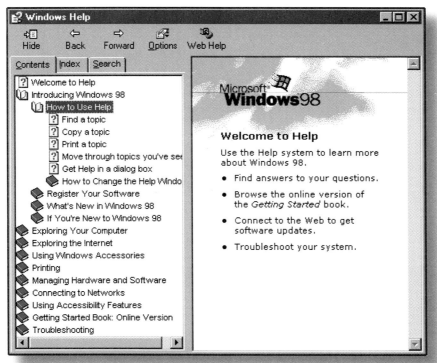

FIGURE 3-3

Displaying a Help entry

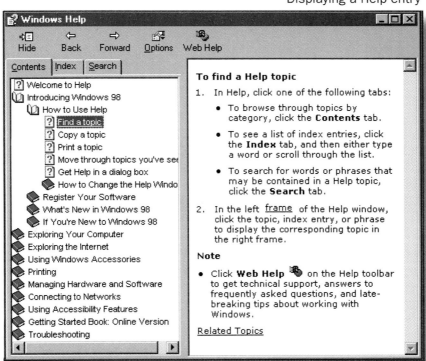

EXERCISE 3.1

1. Select the **Help** option from the **Start** menu. The Windows Help window displays.

2. Verify that the Contents tab is displayed on top. If it is not, click the **Contents** tab.

3. Display the How to Use Help entry:
   a. Click the **Introducing Windows 98** listing in the Contents list box. The subtopics for this option display.

   b. Click the **How to Use Help** listing to display the available Help entries.

   c. Click the **Move through topics you've seen** listing. The Help entry displays in the right frame of the window, as shown in Figure 3-4.

4. Read the information in the window and leave it on-screen for the next exercise.

FIGURE 3-4
Move through topics you've seen Help entry

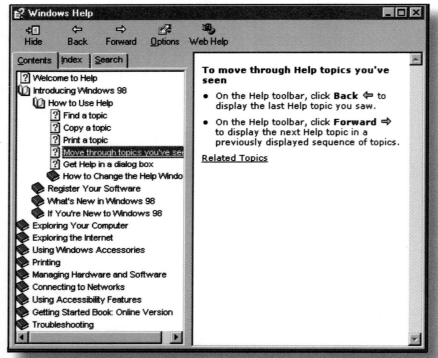

> **TIP**
>
> To widen the Contents tab so you can see the entire Help topic listed, position the pointer between the two frames. When it turns into a horizontal double-headed arrow, drag to the right.

Using the Help Toolbar

Let's look closer at the Help entry shown in Figure 3-4. Notice the toolbar at the top of the window. The Help toolbar includes various buttons. These buttons help you navigate and customize the Help system. You will see this toolbar on all Help entry windows.

- The Hide button removes the left frame of the Help window from view. It changes to a Show button that you can click to redisplay the frame.

- The Back button returns you to previous Help entries. Clicking this button once takes you to the most recent entry; clicking again takes you to the next most recent entry.

- The Forward button takes you to the next Help topic in the previously displayed sequence of topics.

- The Options button displays a menu with options for moving through the Help files, for refreshing Help topic content from the Web, for customizing the look of Help entries, and for printing Help entries.

- The Web Help button lets you connect to a Windows 98 Web page that contains information on Windows 98.

EXERCISE ▷ 3.2

1. Click the **Back** button to return to the Help opening window.

2. Click the **Forward** button.

3. Click the **Hide** button to remove the left frame of the window from view.

4. Click the **Show** button to redisplay the entire window.

5. Click the **How to Use Help** topic in the Contents list. Click it again to close the book.

6. Click the **Introducing Windows 98** listing. Click it again to close the book.

7. Remain in this screen for the next exercise.

Printing a Help Topic

When you are working with a new Windows program or feature, you may find it handy to have a hard copy (printout) of selected Help topics so you don't have to keep Help open while you are learning.

You can print a chosen topic by clicking the Options button and selecting Print. The Print dialog box shown in Figure 3-5 appears. If you select the *Print the current page* option, you print the topic displayed in the right frame of the window. If you select the *Print everything contained in the current heading* option, you print all the topics listed under the selected heading on the Contents tab. If you select the *Print everything contained in the contents* option, you print all the Help topics listed on the Contents tab. Click the OK button after you have selected a print option.

FIGURE 3-5
Print Help dialog box

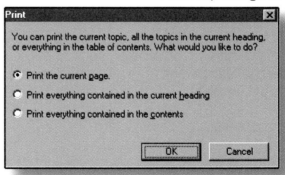

Another Print dialog box opens, like the one shown in Figure 3-6. You will learn more about the options in the Print dialog box when you print documents later in this course. For now, you only need to know how to verify that your computer is connected to the appropriate printer (as indicated in the Name text box). Click OK to print the Help entry.

FIGURE 3-6
Print dialog box

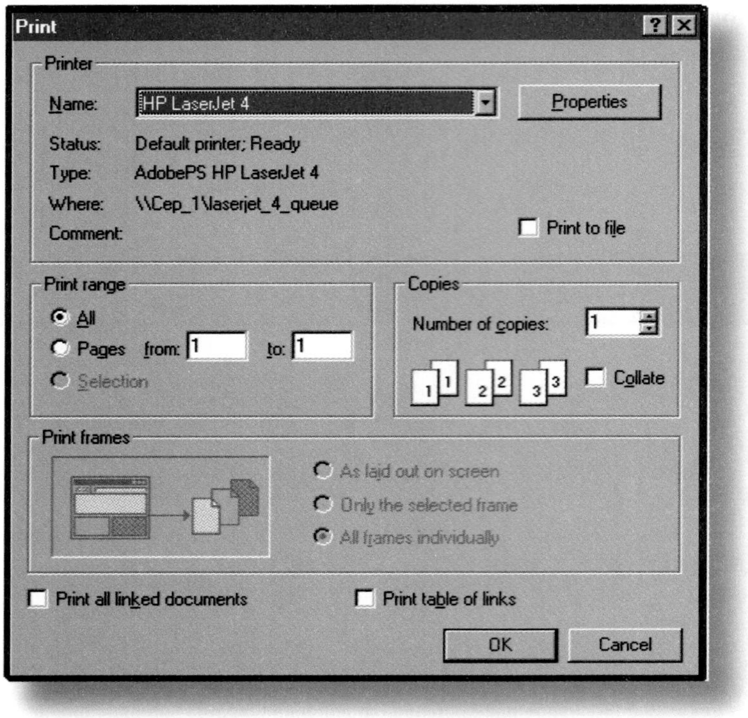

E X E R C I S E ▷ 3.3

In order to complete this exercise, you must have a printer connected to your computer system. If you are sharing a printer, be sure you have access to the printer and it is online. If you do not know how to access your printer, ask for assistance before you begin this exercise.

1. Click **Introducing Windows 98** in the Contents list.

2. Click **How to Use Help** and then click **Print a topic**.

3. Click the **Options** button and then click **Print**.

4. In the first Print dialog box, verify that the first option to print only the current page is selected. Click **OK**.

5. In the second Print dialog box, make sure you are connected to the appropriate printer and click **OK**.

6. Remove the page from the printer when printing is finished.

7. Close the How to Use Help and Introducing Windows 98 books on the Contents tab.

8. Remain in this screen for the next exercise.

Help Entry Objects

Look carefully at the Help entry in Figure 3-7. Notice the three items listed in the middle of the window. You can click on one of the items to display more information about that topic. In the figure, the Disk Defragmenter item has been clicked to display more information below it.

Notice the formats of the Tune-Up Wizard and the FAT32 items. They look very similar to hyperlinks you might click on a Web page. The Tune-Up Wizard is underlined and grayed, indicating that it has been "jumped to" in the past. The FAT32 item is underlined and in a different color, indicating it has not yet been opened. At the end of the Disk Defragmenter information, you see another link, *click here*. Clicking it opens a Help entry, like that shown in Figure 3-8.

Do you see the small button with an arrow pointing upward and left? This is a *shortcut button*. In addition to text, many Help entries contain one or more such buttons, each a shortcut for performing an action associated with the topic you are viewing. For example, clicking on the shortcut button displayed in Figure 3-8 would start the Disk Defragmenter.

FIGURE 3-7
Clicking links in a Help entry

FIGURE 3-8
Help entry with a shortcut button

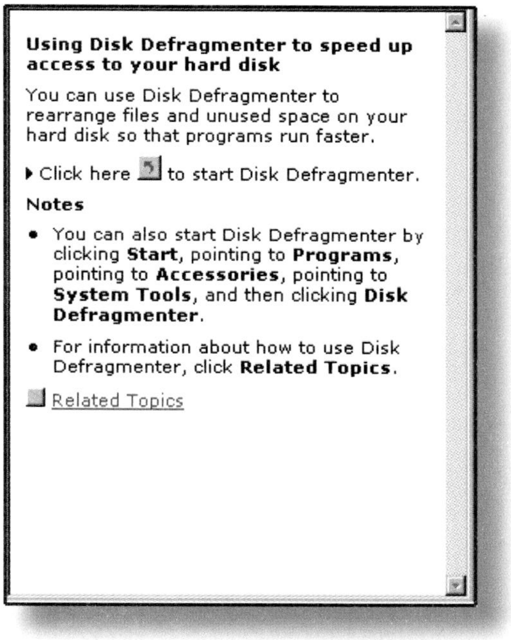

Some Help entries have a button in the lower left corner labeled *Related Topics* (see Figure 3-8). Click the button to display a list like that shown in Figure 3-9. You can move quickly to any of the topics listed by clicking the topic.

A Help entry might also contain a word or term that is underlined, like that shown in Figure 3-10. This is known as a *pop-up*. Clicking on the pop-up *program log* in Figure 3-10 displays a box that defines the term. When you are finished reviewing the information in the box, click the mouse button.

When the window is too small to show all the text of an entry, scroll bars will be displayed so you can scroll the text into view. Scroll bars are especially important for dialog boxes and other windows that cannot be resized by dragging on the borders or clicking on the Maximize button.

FIGURE 3-9

List of related topics

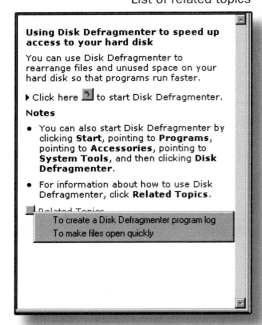

FIGURE 3-10

Clicking a pop-up displays a definition of the term

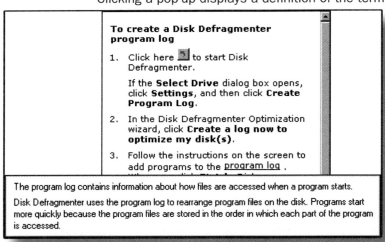

To scroll text, click the up or the down scroll arrow. Clicking the up arrow moves the text *downward*; the down arrow moves text *upward*. Each time you click, the text will scroll one line in the direction you've chosen. If you hold down the mouse button instead of clicking, the text will continue to scroll.

The scroll bar also has a scroll box. You can move through the text quickly by dragging the scroll box to a position that corresponds approximately to the location you want to view. For example, to view the middle of the text, move the scroll box to the middle of the scroll bar.

EXERCISE ⟹ 3.4

1. On the Contents tab, click the **Managing Hardware and Software** listing to display its subtopics.

2. Click the **Tuning Up Your Computer** listing to display its topic files.

3. Click the **Make files open quickly** listing to display its Help entry in the right frame.

4. Click the pop-up *defragment* to display a definition for the term.

5. Read the definition and then click anywhere to close the box.

6. Click the **Related Topics** link in the lower left corner of the topic page. You may have to scroll in the right frame to see the link.

7. Click the **To check your disk surface, files and folders for errors** related topic.

8. Read through the entry.

9. Close all open books on the Contents tab and remain in this screen for the next exercise.

Using the Help Index

If you don't find the information you want on the Contents page, or if you don't like browsing the book titles in search of the desired information, use the Help Index. Like a book index, the Help Index provides an alphabetical listing of topics covered in the Help system. Simply click on the Index tab in the Windows Help window to bring an alphabetical listing of topics into view (Figure 3-11).

To find a topic using the Index, key a word or a phrase in the text box (or select one from the list), then click the Display button at the bottom of the window. The topic displays in the right frame.

Instead of keying a word or phrase in the Help Topics text box, you can scroll the topic list and double-click to select a topic.

FIGURE 3-11
Help's Index tab

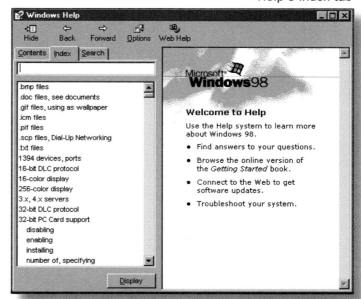

1. In the Windows Help window, click the **Index** tab. The Index tab should move to the foreground with a blinking cursor in the text box.

2. Key the word **creating** in the text box, but do not press Enter. This enters the topic for which you want help. The highlight moves to the first entry that matches the word you keyed.

3. Click the **Display** button. The Help entry for that topic displays in the right frame. Read through the entry.

4. On the Index tab, double-click on the **creating documents** listing. A Topics Found box listing related topics is displayed.

5. Double-click **Using WordPad**.

6. Read through the entry and then remain in this screen for the next exercise.

Using the Search Tab

Have you ever tried to locate a specific topic in an index when you weren't quite sure of the precise wording? If so, you probably tried a number of different words or phrases until you guessed the correct one. In the Windows Help system, you have to know the topic title before you can locate it in the Contents or Index listings. But the Search tab now comes to your rescue! The Search tab enables you to search for specific words and phrases within a Help topic, select among listings, and display the topic.

The Search tab looks similar to that shown in Figure 3-12. In the text box at the top of the left frame, you key the word or phrase for which you want to find more information. The Search feature is case sensitive. Click the List Topics button and all the Help entries that contain the word or phrase are listed in the Topic list box. Double-click a topic in the list box to display it in the right frame.

FIGURE 3-12
Search tab

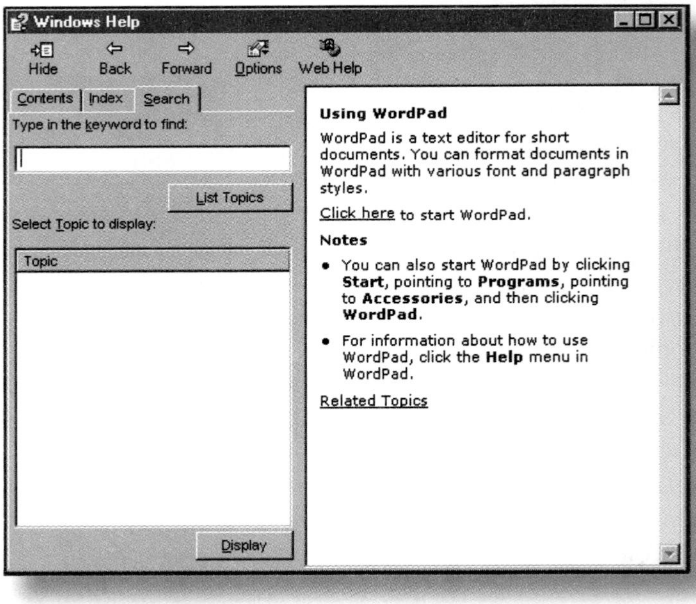

If the Help system cannot find the word or phrase in any entries, it displays a message box telling you that no topics were found.

EXERCISE ⟹ 3.6

1. In the Help window, click the **Search** tab. The Search tab should move to the foreground with a blinking cursor in the text box.

2. Key **calendar** in the text box. Click the **List Topics** button.

3. The Help system finds only one entry that contains the word *calendar*. Double-click the topic to display it in the right frame.

4. Read through the entry.

5. Click the **Close** button for the Windows Help window to close the Help system.

Getting Help on a Specific Item

All dialog boxes and some windows have their own special Help feature called *What's This?* This feature employs a special pointer with which you select any option in a dialog box. Thus "What's This?" means "What's this option?"

Here's how it works: Look at Figure 3-13. See the ? icon in the upper right corner of the dialog box? When you select the ? icon, a large question mark attaches to the mouse pointer, and with this question mark pointer you can click on any option in the dialog box or window. When you click an option, a box displays with a short description of the item you selected. The mouse pointer returns to its normal arrow shape after displaying a description.

You can also right-click on any option in a dialog box to display a small box labeled "What's This?" Click on this box to display a description of the option you right-clicked.

FIGURE 3-13
Using the "What's This?" feature

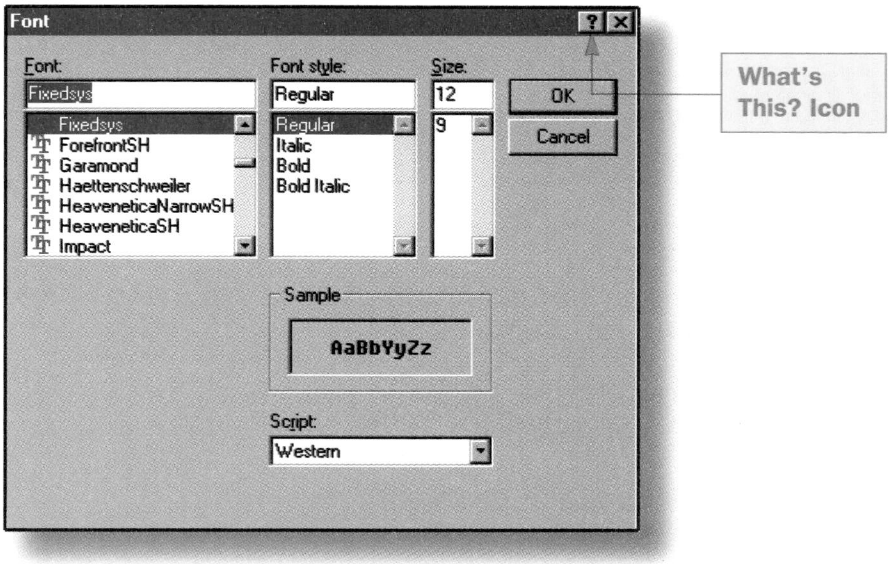

3 9

1. Click the **Start** button and then click **Run** on the Start menu. The Run dialog box opens.

2. Click the **?** icon in the upper right corner of the dialog box. The mouse pointer becomes an arrow with a large question mark beside it.

3. Click the **Browse** button. A description of this button displays.

4. Click anywhere to close the description box. Click **Cancel** to close the Run dialog box.

5. If instructed, shut down Windows and your computer.

Summary

This lesson discussed how to use the Windows Help system. You learned that:

■ To access Windows Help, press F1 whenever you see Help on the menu bar, select the Help option from the Start menu, or select Help whenever you see a Help command button. Different applications give different kinds of help.

■ Windows' Help system is like an electronic reference book with a table of contents and an index. Files can be searched by word or phrase. The information on a Help entry can be printed for easy reference.

■ The Help Options menu provides options for moving through the Help files, for refreshing Help topic content from the Web, for customizing the look of Help entries, and for printing Help entries.

■ Help entries may contain different objects. Click the shortcut button to perform an action associated with the selected topic. Select a pop-up to display a definition or short description of the pop-up word or term. Click the Related Topic button to see a listing of topics related to the selected topic.

LESSON 3 REVIEW QUESTIONS

TRUE/FALSE

Each of the following statements is either true or false. Indicate your answer on the left by circling T if the statement is true and F if the statement is false.

T F 1. When using the Help Search feature, keying in the text box with uppercase or lowercase letters will produce the same results.

T F 2. Most dialog boxes contain the "What's This?" icon.

T F 3. You can access the Help system by pressing the F11 key.

T F   4.   You cannot print Help topics.

T F   5.   If the Contents tab is currently displayed in the Windows Help window, clicking the Forward button takes you to the Index tab.

MULTIPLE CHOICE

Complete the following questions by circling the correct multiple choice letter.

1.   Terms in a Help entry that are underlined are called
   A.   pop-ups
   B.   annotations
   C.   shortcuts
   D.   none of the above

2.   An alphabetical listing of topics covered in the Help system is found in the
   A.   Contents tab of the Help Topics list box
   B.   Index tab of the Help Topics list box
   C.   Search tab of the Help Topics list box
   D.   Options button on the Help toolbar

3.   Windows Help
   A.   can be accessed only from the Help menu
   B.   is a menu option on all menu bars
   C.   is an optional feature that must be purchased separately
   D.   cannot be active when you are running an application program

4.   To display a previously selected topic quickly in a Help entry window, use the
   A.   Back button
   B.   Show button
   C.   Help Topics button
   D.   Options button

5.   When you want to find Help entries that contain a certain word or phrase, you key the words or phrase you want to find in the
   A.   Contents tab
   B.   Index tab
   C.   Search tab
   D.   All of the above

LESSON 3 PROJECT

This project gives you the opportunity to review the concepts in this lesson and practice the techniques in the exercises. Be sure you have access to a printer before beginning the activity.

1. Launch Windows if it is not already active.

2. Access Windows Help and select the **Contents** tab.

3. Locate and display the entry for the following topics, then print each topic.

    Exploring Your Computer
       The Windows Desktop
       Tips and Tricks
       Start a program from the taskbar
    Exploring the Internet
       Publish Your Own Web Page
       Use Microsoft Personal Web Server (PWS)

4. Search the Help system to locate the topics containing the word *piracy*, then go to *What is software piracy?*

5. Print the Help entry.

6. Using the Help Index tab, locate the topics for *printers*.

7. Double-click the **settings** listing under *printers*. Then, display the *To change printer settings* topic.

8. Print a copy of the entry.

9. Quit the Help system.

10. Assemble your printout pages for submission to your instructor as follows:
    a. Arrange the printouts in the order in which they were produced.
    b. Write your name and class information in the upper right corner of each printout.

11. If instructed, shut down Windows and your computer.

TIP

Remember to obtain access to the printer if you are sharing a printer, and be sure the printer is ready before you issue the Print command.

UNIT 1 REVIEW QUESTIONS ▽

WRITTEN QUESTIONS

Answer the questions below on a separate piece of paper.

1. Describe the taskbar and explain how and why you use it.

2. Briefly explain multitasking.

3. Identify the basic shapes the mouse pointer may assume, and when it assumes each.

4. Explain the five common mouse operations.

5. Identify four visual elements that are used in Windows menus and explain their meaning.

6. Explain the use of keyboard shortcuts and give two examples.

7. Identify the four types of boxes that may appear in a dialog box and explain the purpose of each.

8. Distinguish between the functions of the Help system's Contents, Index, and Search tabs.

9. Distinguish between the three different Windows shut-down methods.

10. Describe two ways that a window can be resized.

UNIT 1 APPLICATION ▽

SCANS

Aleta Lopez is the owner of a corporate newsletter publishing business, named Corporate Communique. The office has recently made the transition from Windows 95 to Windows 98. Needless to say, many employees are a little nervous about working with a new operating system.

To help ease their anxiety, Aleta wants to organize a training session that shows employees how to use the Windows 98 Help system. She knows that if employees understand how to look up information and find answers to their questions, then working in a new computing environment will not be nearly as intimidating to them!

Create an outline for Aleta to use in the training session. Make sure the outline covers the following:

- Starting the Windows Help system.

- Using the toolbar buttons.

- Using the Help system's Contents, Index, and Search tabs.

- Understanding the objects in a Help window.

- Using the "What's This?" feature.

- Printing a Help topic.

Then, make up a list of topics that employees should search for in the Help system that will help them understand the Windows 98 environment. You can create your outline and list by writing it on paper or by composing it in a word-processing program on your computer.

CRITICAL THINKING

On Monday morning, you arrive at your office and find that Windows 98 has been loaded on your computer. You notice that your computer desktop looks a little different than it used to.

Using the Windows Help system, look up information on the items that now appear on your desktop and print copies of the Help entries. Write a brief report on why you selected these topics to print. Then, assemble the topics in a fashion that would make it easy for a new user of Windows 98 to quickly get acquainted with the desktop.

MY COMPUTER

UNIT 2

🕐 **Estimated Time for Unit 2: 8.5 hours**

USING MY COMPUTER

Files, folders, and disks—these are your key system resources. Windows offers two tools for browsing, accessing, and managing these resources: My Computer and Explorer. Both are easy to access. You see the My Computer icon on the desktop every time you start Windows. You access Explorer from the Programs option on the Start menu. This lesson will introduce you to My Computer.

Understanding File Management Concepts

Before you can appreciate and use either of Windows 98's file management tools, you must understand the foundation on which they are built: files, folders, and disks.

Files

Imagine large file drawers for paper files. If papers were simply stacked in the drawer, not separated or grouped in any way, finding what you wanted would be a nightmare! But if one folder contained, say, all reports together, another all letters, another all memos—well, then you'd find what you want much faster, with less searching. The same applies to storing computer data.

In terms of paper documents, a "file" may describe a wide range of documents—short or long, formal or informal, handwritten or typed, and so on. In computer terms, too, file describes a wide range of objects: A *file* may be the instructions the computer needs to operate (called program files or executable files). Or a file may contain a text document that you can read (often referred to as a document file).

Folders

Files are stored on a disk. Disks are discussed in greater detail below, but for now, note that some very common disks can store the equivalent of many thousands of pages of information. But as with paper files, finding what you want may be time consuming. In both cases, folders are helpful!

For example, a disk can be organized to have a *folder* that contains only files relating to application programs, another folder only for correspondence files, another only for reports, another only for forms, and so on. Like paper folders, disk folders organize files into manageable groups, and *subfolders* further separate groups of files within a folder. As you start working with disks later in this lesson, you will see more clearly how files are grouped into subfolders and how subfolders are grouped within folders.

Disks

Files, folders, and subfolders are stored on disks. Think of a computer disk as an "electronic file cabinet." Instead of storing paper files, however, computers store electronic files—program instructions or data documents.

Now let's distinguish between the terms *disk* and *drive*. A *disk* is the magnetic medium on which data are stored. A *disk drive* is the hardware that finds, reads, and writes information to and from a disk. To clarify the distinction, just pick up a portable floppy disk (or diskette) and insert it into a built-in disk drive.

While a *floppy disk* is small and portable, a second kind of disk, a *hard disk*, is not. A hard disk and a hard drive are one integrated unit; further, the unit cannot easily be removed from the computer. In fact, because it is permanently installed, a hard disk is also called a *fixed* disk. Because a hard disk drive is one unit, people sometimes use the terms *disk* and *drive* interchangeably.

The Computer Window

As you learned earlier, you start My Computer by double-clicking its icon on the desktop. The My Computer window that displays contains the familiar title bar, menu bar, display area, and several other parts, as shown in Figure 4-1. The objects displayed in the window reflect your computer's setup and will differ from computer to computer.

FIGURE 4-1
My Computer window

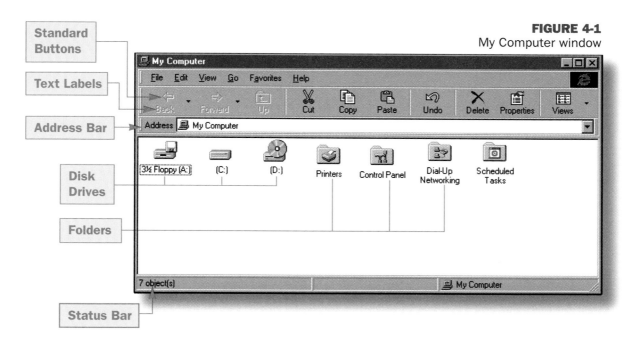

1. Double-click the **My Computer** icon on the desktop. The My Computer window opens.

2. In its display window, examine the icons that represent your system's computer resources.

3. Leave the My Computer window on screen for the next exercise.

Identifying the Icons in the Display Window

As indicated on Figure 4-1, the My Computer window contains two types of icons: disk drive icons and folder icons.

Disk drive icons identify (by letter and type) the disk drives that you can access on your system. Thus the icons will vary, depending on the computer system. The appearance of each disk drive icon varies according to the type of drive—hard disk drive, floppy disk drive, or CD-ROM drive.

A disk drive is named by letter. For most computers:

- Drives A: and B: are floppy disk drives.

- Drive C: designates the hard disk. Some computers have more than one hard disk, and some computers have partitioned hard disks—disks divided into separate sections or "logical drives." Additional hard drives and partitions are usually labeled D:, E:, F:, and so on.

Figure 4-1 shows a computer system with one floppy drive, called 3½ Floppy (A:); one hard drive, called (C:); and one CD-ROM, called (D:).

The My Computer window shown in Figure 4-1 also contains folder icons for the Control Panel, Printers, Dial-Up Networking, and Scheduled Tasks. You will learn more about these folders in later lessons.

Setting My Computer Options

The View menu (Figure 4-2) lets you control the way the My Computer window looks and functions. The key options on the View menu are discussed in the following sections.

Toolbars

When you select the Toolbars command, the Toolbars submenu displays, like that shown in Figure 4-3. Notice that the Standard Buttons, Address Bar, and Text Labels options have a check mark beside them. This means that they are currently selected or displayed.

The Standard Buttons are those buttons that appear on the standard toolbar directly below the menu bar (see Figure 4-1). You can choose to hide the labels that identify the buttons by deselecting Text Labels on the Toolbars submenu.

The Address Bar (see Figure 4-1) identifies the name of the system resource that's currently selected. You can click the drop-down list arrow at the end of the Address Bar text box to display a list of the objects contained in the

FIGURE 4-2
My Computer's
View menu

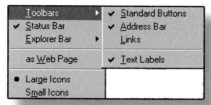

FIGURE 4-3
Toolbars submenu

selected resource. From this list you can select an object for viewing. The bar also lets you type a Web page address without first opening your browser.

The Links option on the Toolbars submenu displays to the right of the Address Bar when it is selected. You can add shortcuts to important Web sites to this toolbar to make accessing them a snap.

Before we continue our discussion of the options on the View menu, let's take a closer look at the buttons on the standard toolbar.

Back and Forward Buttons. Clicking the Back button returns you to the resource previously displayed in the Address Bar. Clicking the Forward button takes you to the next resource in the previously displayed set of resources. You can click the drop-down list arrows on the Back and Forward buttons to display a list of the resources you can move to.

Up Button. The Up button takes you up one level in your system's resource hierarchy.

Editing Buttons—Cut, Copy, and Paste. To the right of the Up button are three editing buttons, which are used to edit objects in the My Computer display window. The icon on the face of each button provides a visual clue as to its function.

Scissors identify the **Cut button**. Select (highlight) an object, and then click the Cut button to remove *(cut)* that object from the display window. The object that you cut is held in a special temporary storage area called the *Clipboard*.

Two identical sheets of paper identify the **Copy button**. Select an object and then click the Copy button to *copy* it, which will temporarily store a duplicate of that object on the Clipboard. When you're ready to insert the object, you use the Paste button.

A sheet of paper in front of a miniature clipboard identifies the **Paste button**. The clipboard represents the temporary storage area where cut and copied objects "go," and the paper represents the object itself. When you click on Paste, you insert, or *paste*, an object from the Clipboard to your current display window.

Undo Button. To "undo" means to cancel your last action. For example, if you cut an object and then realize you should *not* have cut it, click immediately on Undo to restore the object to the display window.

Delete Button. Use the Delete button to remove selected objects from the display window. Delete is different from Cut. When an object is deleted, it is *not* placed on the Clipboard for temporary storage. Therefore, use Delete only when you do not intend to paste that object elsewhere.

IMPORTANT:

While Undo provides a safety net, that net disappears if you take *any* action after clicking Delete! You must use Undo immediately.

Properties Button. Click the Properties button to display the Properties dialog box for the selected object. The Property sheets will be discussed shortly.

Views Button. Click the Views button drop-down list arrow to display options for displaying the contents of the My Computer window. These same options (as Web Page, Large Icons, Small Icons, List, and Details) also appear on the View menu. These options are discussed below.

Status Bar

The second option on the View menu is Status Bar, which also toggles on and off and displays a check mark when selected. When selected, the status bar appears at the bottom of the My Computer window (see Figure 4-1). The status bar indicates how many objects appear in the window. When an object is selected, as in Figure 4-4, the status bar indicates how many objects are selected and gives available information about the object(s).

FIGURE 4-4
Status bar when an object is selected

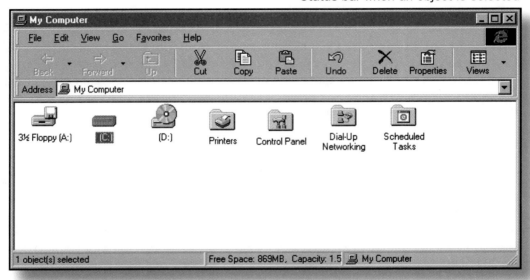

Explorer Bar

When you select Explorer Bar on the View menu, a submenu like that shown in Figure 4-5 displays.

Selecting an option from the Explorer Bar submenu starts your Web browser and lets you access the Web directly from the My Computer window. A frame opens on the left side of the My Computer window. In Figure 4-6, the Search option was selected, allowing you to search the Web from the My Computer window.

FIGURE 4-5
Explorer Bar submenu

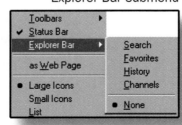

INTERNET A Web browser is a type of software that lets you access sites and information on the World Wide Web. You will learn about Window 98's Internet Explorer in Unit 11.

FIGURE 4-6
Web Search option selected in My Computer window

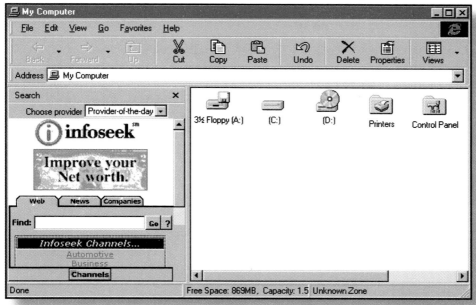

As Web Page

Selecting the as Web Page option on the View menu changes the My Computer window to resemble a site you might visit on the Web (see Figure 4-7).

FIGURE 4-7
Viewing My Computer as a Web page

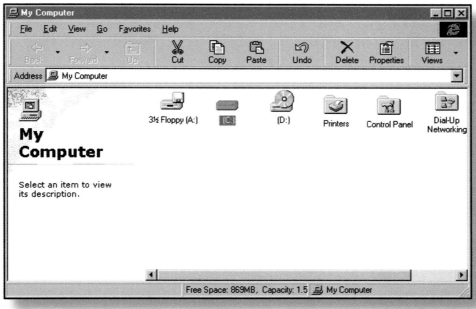

Display Options

The four display options—Large Icons, Small Icons, List, and Details—are also accessible from the Views drop-down list. As shown in Figure 4-2, a bullet (dark circle) appears to the left of the selected option.

The Small Icons option shows icons in a "normal" size; Large Icons, in an extra-large size. In both cases, the items in the My Computer window are arranged from left to right, in rows.

The List option arranges the contents of the My Computer window in a straight list, from top to bottom, starting a second column when the first is complete, column by column.

Clicking the Details button on the toolbar arranges the items in the My Computer window in a single column from top to bottom, but it also provides additional columns of information (such as the type of file, size of resource, date that the file was last modified, etc.) for each item in the list.

Arrange Icons

As you resize or change the contents of the My Computer window, some of its objects may become hidden or scattered around the white space. The two options in the fourth section of View menu options, Arrange Icons and Line Up Icons, allow you to control the order and placement of objects in the My Computer window.

Arrange Icons. The Arrange Icons option offers a submenu that allows you to organize the contents of a drive or folder by name, type, size, or date. Depending on how Windows 98 has been installed on your computer, you may also have the options to organize by total size and free space.

Line Up Icons. When you are working in the Large Icons or Small Icons view and the icons become disarrayed, you can arrange them in neat rows and columns by selecting the Line Up Icons option. This option is convenient when you wish to align the icons without changing the order in which they appear in the window.

Refresh

The Refresh command updates what is displayed in the My Computer window. The Refresh option can be used if the contents of the window have been changed by a command or by another user on a network system, and the changes are not updated automatically.

Folder Options

Selecting the last item on the View menu, Folder Options, displays the Folder Options dialog box. As you see in Figure 4-8, the Folder Options dialog box offers three tabs: General, View, and File Types.

The General tab contains options for the style of your desktop. Click an option to display a sample in the window. Click the Settings button to further customize your desktop. The Custom Settings dialog box opens, as shown in Figure 4-9.

FIGURE 4-8
Folder Options dialog box

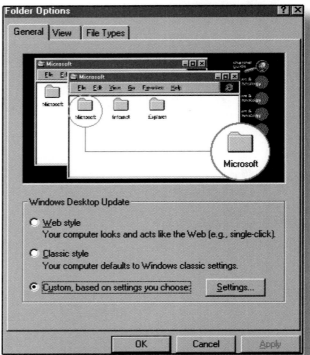

FIGURE 4-9
Custom Settings dialog box

The Custom Settings dialog box provides you with various options for customizing the way you organize and manage the objects and files on your computer. You can use the What's This? icon to learn more about the various options in the dialog box. We'll discuss the browse options, though, in a little more detail below:

■ **Open each folder in the same window.** Select this option to display the contents of each folder you open in the same window. In other words, only one window is open on screen at a time—a handy feature when you have to open several folders before you get to the one you really want! Use the Back and Forward buttons on the toolbar to move to and from folders.

■ **Open each folder in its own window.** This option opens a new window every time you open a folder or resource in My Computer. The previous folder will still be displayed in a window, so you can switch between them.

Accessing Disk Drives

Most disk operations require you first to identify the drive you want to use. The first floppy drive is generally drive A:; if a system has a second drive, that drive is generally drive B:. A hard drive is designated drive C:; additional drives are labeled D:, E:, and so on.

When My Computer is displayed in the Address Bar, each disk drive available is represented by an icon in the display window. To select a drive, click the appropriate drive icon and the drive is highlighted, as shown in Figure 4-10. You access a drive by selecting its name in the Address Bar drop-down list or by double-clicking its icon in the window.

FIGURE 4-10
Selected disk drive is highlighted

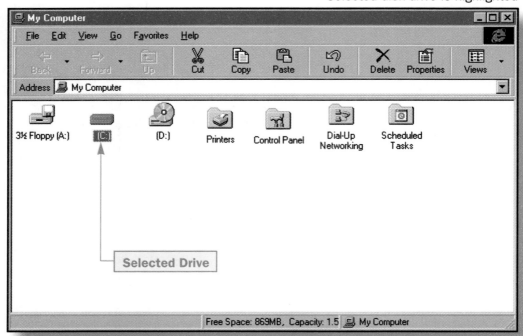

If there is no disk in the drive you select, or if you forget to close the door (if there is one), the error message box shown in Figure 4-11 will display. Insert the disk or close the drive door (if necessary), and then click the Retry button—or simply click the Cancel command button.

FIGURE 4-11
Warning message tells you the disk drive is not ready

TIP

If you insert an unformatted disk into the drive, a message box will display informing you that the disk isn't formatted and giving you the opportunity to format the disk.

Viewing the Contents of a Drive or Folder

You can display the contents of a selected drive or folder in the My Computer display window by double-clicking the object. Once displayed, the objects can be viewed as large icons, small icons, a simple list, or a detailed list, as you learned earlier.

E X E R C I S E ▷ 4.2

1. Select **Folder Options** from the **View** menu and click the **Settings** button. Select the **Open each folder in the same window** browse option and then click the **OK** button. Click **Close** to close the Folder Options dialog box.

2. Click the drop-down list arrow on the **Views** toolbar button and select **Large Icons,** if necessary.

3. Click the **Address Bar** drop-down list arrow; then select **Desktop.** You may have to scroll up to see the top of the list. Notice that the objects listed are the same objects that appear on your desktop, although they may differ somewhat from those shown in Figure 4-12.

4. Double-click the **My Computer** icon to once again show your system's resources in the display window.

5. Click the **Back** button to redisplay the Desktop in the window.

6. Choose **Details** on the **View** menu. Then, change to the **Large Icons** view.

7. Click the **Forward** button to return to My Computer. Make sure the view is **Large Icons**.

8. Double-click the **3 1/2 Floppy (A:)** icon to access the drive. Click **Cancel** in the message box that tells you the drive is not ready.

9. Select the Windows folder from your hard drive:
   a. Double-click the drive containing the Windows folder (usually drive C:).
   b. Locate the Windows folder on your hard drive; then double-click the **Windows** folder. Notice that the window's title bar now consists of an open file folder icon and the word *Windows*, indicating that you have selected the Windows folder. Notice also that the Windows folder is displayed in the Address Bar. Look at the status bar. How many objects are within the Windows folder? How much disk space do these objects use?

10. Make sure the **Large Icons** view is selected. Scroll in this window until your screen resembles Figure 4-13. Leave the window on screen for the next exercise.

5 5

FIGURE 4-12

Selecting Desktop shows all objects on the desktop

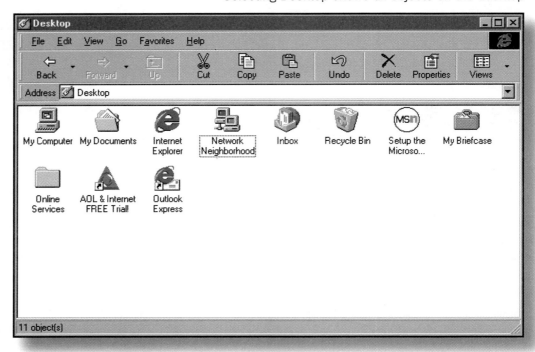

FIGURE 4-13

Contents of the Windows folder

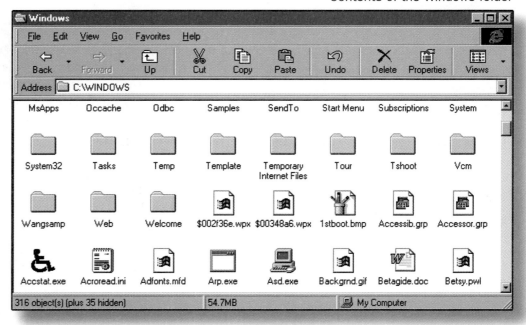

Identifying Object Icons and Using the Details View

Study Figure 4-13 carefully and notice the following:

■ The display window shows subfolders.

■ The display window shows several additional icons, each a different type of object (thus *object icons*). For example, the calculator application program is represented by a calculator, and files that are created with the Windows Paint program have an icon that looks like a piece of paper with an abstract painting and a paintbrush resting on it.

With practice, you'll easily identify many icons. But what about those icons you don't know? Simple solution: Display the window in the Details view (Figure 4-14). To do so, select the Details option from the View menu.

FIGURE 4-14

The Type column identifies the file type for each object in the Details view

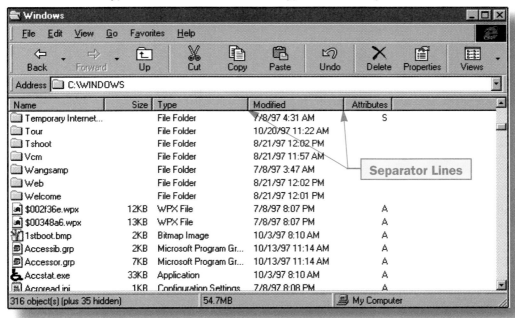

When you choose Details, the screen displays four new columns of information: Size, Type, Modified, and Attributes. As you can see in Figure 4-14, listings under Type may be truncated (that is, cut off) because the Type column is rather narrow. You can easily change the width of a column by dragging one of the vertical separator lines (labeled in Figure 4-14) that mark the column's boundaries. To drag a separator line, place the mouse pointer on the line. It becomes a double-headed arrow. Hold down the mouse button and drag in the desired direction, then release the button.

1. Click the **Views** button drop-down list arrow and select **Details** to expand the display.

2. Expand the Type column to see all entries:
   a. Place the mouse pointer over the separator line between the Type and Modified columns. The pointer becomes a double-headed arrow.
   b. Drag the separator line to the right until you can read all the entries in the column.

3. Click the **Up** button on the toolbar to close the Windows folder.

4. Click the **Up** button again to return to My Computer and display your system's resources.

5. Select **Folder Options** on the **View** menu and click the **Settings** button.

6. Change the browsing method back to **Open each folder in its own window**. Click **OK**, and then click **Close** to close the Folder Options dialog box.

7. Click the **Close** button of the My Computer window to close My Computer.

8. If instructed, shut down Windows and your computer.

Summary

This lesson discussed how to use My Computer. You learned that:

■ Computer disks store electronic files, which they organize in folders and subfolders. A disk is like a file cabinet. A folder is like a file drawer in the cabinet, a subfolder is like a hanging file within a drawer, and a file is like a document of one or more pages within a subfolder or a folder. Using My Computer to create folders and subfolders lets you group and organize electronic files the way that cabinets and folders allow you to organize paper documents—systematically!

■ When you start My Computer, you see a window with the familiar title bar, menu bar, display window, and status bar.

■ The My Computer window contains two types of icons: disk drive icons, which identify the disk drives you can access on your system; and folder icons, which represent the folders containing files on your system.

■ Floppy disk drives are generally labeled A: and B:; hard drives are labeled C:, D:, E:, and so on. To access a drive, double-click the drive icon in the My Computer display window.

■ Buttons on the My Computer toolbar let you navigate among your system's resources and control the display of objects. The toolbar also contains editing buttons that let you cut, copy, and paste objects.

- You can display the contents of a selected drive or folder by double-clicking the icon in the display window.

- You can display the contents of a selected drive or folder in four views: Large Icons, Small Icons, List, and Details. The specific details shown and the icon arrangement will vary depending on the view you choose.

- Objects within folders are represented by various types of icons.

LESSON 4 REVIEW QUESTIONS

MULTIPLE CHOICE

Complete the following questions by circling the correct multiple choice letter.

1. The object selected in the My Computer window is identified in the
   - **A.** menu bar
   - **B.** standard toolbar
   - **C.** Address Bar
   - **D.** status bar

2. A hard disk is different from a floppy disk; specifically, a hard disk
   - **A.** is portable and easy to remove
   - **B.** is normally inserted into a built-in disk drive
   - **C.** cannot be easily removed from the computer
   - **D.** is sometimes called a diskette

3. The major difference between copying a file and moving a file is that
   - **A.** when you copy a file, it is removed from its original location
   - **B.** when you move a file, it appears in more than one place
   - **C.** when you copy a file, you do not have to specify a destination
   - **D.** when you move a file, it is removed from its original location

4. If you select a drive without a disk in it,
   - **A.** a message box will display saying the drive is not accessible and the device is not ready
   - **B.** you will lock up the system and have to reboot the computer
   - **C.** the system will default to the hard disk
   - **D.** a message box will display saying "Please insert disk"

5. In My Computer the Details display *does not* include a file's
   - **A.** size
   - **B.** type
   - **C.** file name
   - **D.** author

MATCHING

Write the letter of the term in the right column that matches the definition in the left column.

_____ 1. Magnetic medium on which data are stored.

_____ 2. Hardware that finds, reads, and writes information to and from a disk.

_____ 3. Small, portable storage device.

_____ 4. Fixed unit within the computer.

_____ 5. Used to organize files and subfolders on a disk.

A. floppy disk

B. disk

C. folder

D. hard disk

E. disk drive

LESSON 4 PROJECT

This project gives you the opportunity to review the concepts in this lesson and practice the techniques in the exercises.

1. Start Windows if it is not already running.

2. Open **My Computer** and do the following:
   a. Change the view to **Details**.
   b. Change the view to **List**.
   c. Change the view to **Small Icons**.
   d. Select **Folder Options** from the **View** menu and click the **Settings** button. Select the browse option to **Open each folder in the same window** and then click the **OK** button. Click **Close** again to close the Folder Options dialog box.

3. Click the **Address Bar** drop-down list arrow and select **Recycle Bin**.

4. Click the **Back** button to return to My Computer.

5. Double-click the icon that represents your computer's hard disk.

6. Double-click a folder on your computer's hard disk to view its contents.

7. Change the view to **Large Icons**.

8. Click the **Up** button until My Computer appears in the Address Bar.

9. Change the folder browsing option back to **Open each folder in its own window**.

10. If necessary, change the view to **Large Icons**.

11. Click the **Close** button to close My Computer. If instructed, shut down Windows and your computer.

WORKING WITH DISKS

Upon completion of this lesson, you will be able to:

■ Format a floppy disk.

■ Magnetically label a floppy disk.

■ Use ScanDisk to locate and fix disk errors.

■ Run the Disk Defragmenter on a hard disk.

🕐 **Estimated Time: 1.5 hours**

My Computer makes disk handling easy. In this lesson, you'll learn how to use My Computer to manage and format floppy disks.

Formatting and Labeling Disks

Floppy disks are commonly used to save and transfer files from one computer to another. It's important that you know how to properly prepare a disk to safely store your files. Formatting and labeling are the two procedures you should be familiar with when working with floppy disks.

Formatting a Floppy Disk

Formatting prepares a disk for use on a specific type of drive—that is, it imprints a disk with the information it needs to work in that particular kind of drive. *But beware: The formatting process removes all the information from a disk!* Of course, Windows provides a safety net, in the form of the dialog box shown in Figure 5-1.

Some manufacturers of floppy disks sell their products "preformatted," so there is no need to format these disks. Just use them straight from the box.

FIGURE 5-1
Format dialog box

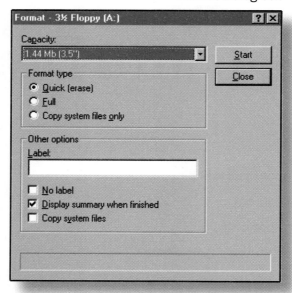

The Format dialog box offers you a number of options for formatting a disk. These options are discussed below.

CAPACITY

First, the dialog box asks you to identify the disk by its *capacity* (360KB or 1.2MB for $5^{1}/4$-inch disks; 720KB or 1.44MB for $3^{1}/2$-inch disks). The lower settings (360KB and 720KB) are for *double-density* disks. The higher settings (1.2MB and 1.44MB) are for *high-density* disks.

FORMAT TYPE

Next, you must select from among the following format types:

■ **Quick (erase)** or **Full**. The **Full** format option checks a disk for problem areas (bad sectors); the **Quick (erase)** option does not. You must select Full for new disks; for used disks, you may save time by using Quick (erase). Limit Quick (erase) to disks that you are confident are in good condition.

■ **Copy system files only**. Selecting this option transfers the system files to an already-formatted disk.

OTHER OPTIONS

Finally, choose from among these additional options:

■ **Label** or **No label**. "Electronic" labels are not essential, but they can be very helpful. For example, you may label one disk *Invoices* and another *Reports*. Unlike paper labels, electronic labels are visible only when you access the drive. If you want to add an electronic label, enter the label text in the Label text box. If you prefer not labeling the disk, check the No label check box.

■ **Display summary when finished**. If you check this box, Windows formats the disk and then displays a report telling you the number of bytes available on the disk, the number of bad sectors (if any), and other related information.

■ **Copy system files.** Checking this option transfers the appropriate system files to the floppy disk. Result: A bootable disk, one you can then use to boot the system. But remember, system files take up disk space, so don't check this option unless you need to make a bootable disk.

THE FORMATTING PROCESS

To format a disk, insert it into the appropriate disk drive, select the drive, and choose Format from the File menu. Select the desired options from the Format dialog box and click Start. A formatting scale displays a "progress report" at the bottom of the dialog box as the task is completed. When the format is completed, a Format Results box displays, like that shown in Figure 5-2.

FIGURE 5-2
Format Results dialog box

Format - 3½ Floppy (A:)

Capacity:
1.44 M

Format Results - 3½ Floppy (A:)

1,457,664 bytes total disk space

0 bytes used by system files

0 bytes in bad sectors

1,457,664 bytes available on disk

512 bytes in each allocation unit

2,847 total allocation units on disk

10DB-1773 serial number

Close

Progress Report

Click the Close button to close the Format Results dialog box. You are returned to the Format dialog box so that you may format additional disks. If you do, make the appropriate selections for each disk, and when you are ready, click the Start button to format. If you don't want to format additional disks, click the Close button to close the Format dialog box.

EXERCISE ⇨ 5.1

In this exercise you will format a disk (preferably a high-density or a high-capacity disk) in drive A: (unless your instructor gives you alternate instructions).

1. Using a felt pen, write *Windows Practice* on a disk label. Then place the label on your disk.

2. Insert the Windows Practice disk in the correct drive.

3. Start **My Computer** by double-clicking its icon

TIP

Develop the habit of writing on the label before you place it on the disk.

(continued on next page)

on the desktop. Click the **Views** button drop-down list arrow and select the **List** view.

4. Click the icon of the drive where you inserted the disk to select it.

5. Select **Format** from the **File** menu. The Format dialog box appears.

6. Verify that the appropriate capacity is indicated:

   High-density: 1.44MB for 3½-inch disk; 1.2MB for 5¼-inch disk.

   Double-density: 720KB for 3½-inch disk; 360KB for 5¼-inch disk.

7. Click the **Full** check box to select this format option.

8. Check the **No label** check box; then verify that all of the check boxes under Other options are unchecked.

9. Click the **Start** command button. The formatting scale at the bottom of the dialog box shows the progress of the format.

10. When the format is complete, click the **Close** button to close the Format Results dialog box. Then click the **Close** button to quit the Format dialog box.

Labeling Disks

Just as a paper label identifies a disk on the outside, a *disk label* identifies a disk on the inside—that is, electronically—with a magnetic label. You can label a disk when you format the disk, or you can add the label after the disk is formatted. You can also change the label whenever you wish. To label a disk, click the Properties button on the toolbar. The Properties dialog box for your floppy disk drive opens, as shown in Figure 5-3. On the General tab, key the name of the disk in the Label text box. A label can have up to 11 characters.

The disk label will not display in the My Computer window. The label can be viewed only by displaying the Properties dialog box.

NOTE:

Because you can view but not change the General properties of a remote network drive, you can't change its label.

FIGURE 5-3

Label a disk in the disk's Properties dialog box

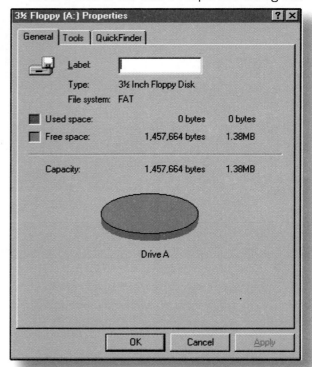

EXERCISE ▭▷ 5.2

1. Verify that your Windows Practice disk is in one of the floppy drives. Then select that drive.

2. Click the **Properties** button on the toolbar.

3. Verify that the **General** tab is selected (Figure 5-3).

4. An insertion point is blinking in the Label text box. Key your last name (or a shortened version of it if it is longer than 11 characters). If the disk already has a label, the Label text box will display it. Keying a new label replaces the former name.

5. Click the **OK** button to record the label or **Cancel** if you do not want to record the label. The Properties dialog box closes.

Managing Disks

A trouble-free hard disk is extremely important to the Windows program. Windows uses your hard disk for temporary storage, and many Windows application programs create temporary files on the hard disk as you use the application. If your hard disk is not in good working order, you may find your system slow in responding, or you may have problems running programs and opening documents.

Windows 98 comes with a number of tools to keep your system in good working order. You can review all of these by looking up *system tools* in the Windows Help facility. For the remainder of this lesson, we'll discuss two important disk maintenance tools: ScanDisk and Disk Defragmenter.

ScanDisk is a diagnostic tool—a program that reads a disk's "vital signs" and either warns you about problems or fixes them. *Disk Defragmenter* rearranges the files on your disk, repositioning the files so the disk performs optimally.

Locating and Fixing Disk Errors

You can use ScanDisk with hard disks or floppy disks (but not with CD-ROM disks). The ScanDisk program finds and fixes a variety of problems associated with the data structure of a disk, as well as physical problems (such as bad portions of the disk). ScanDisk doesn't actually repair a disk; it avoids storing data in any problem area.

Defragmenting a Disk

Disks—both hard and floppy—store data in clusters. A cluster is a group of 128 bytes. When you store files on a newly formatted disk, Windows writes each file's data in adjacent clusters. For example, the data for the first file saved might be stored in clusters 3 through 15, the next file's data might use clusters 16 through 30, and a third file's data might use clusters 31 and 32. In this way, Windows stores data in contiguous clusters; that is, in clusters that are adjacent on the disk.

What happens when you delete files? Each time you delete a file, you empty clusters and make them available for new data. To optimize your disk space, Windows uses these now-empty clusters as you save new files. First Windows saves as much data as possible in the first available cluster, then the next available cluster, and the next, and so on, until it has stored all the remaining file data. In this way, Windows splits file data among clusters that are not contiguous. In other words, in its efforts to optimize disk space, Windows creates *fragmented files*, files that are not stored in contiguous clusters. In the normal process of saving new files and deleting old files, your disk becomes quite fragmented.

Fragmentation does not harm a disk, but heavy fragmentation can slow down the disk's read and write times, thus reducing hard-disk efficiency. To enhance disk performance, use Windows' Disk Defragmenter, or a similar program. Disk Defragmenter rearranges disk files, storing each file in contiguous blocks.

NOTE:

Disk Defragmenter cannot be used with network drives or read-only drives.

First Defragmenter looks at your disk and tells you what percentage of the disk is fragmented. If the disk is not heavily fragmented, you may not want to proceed, so the Defragmenter gives you an option: continue or quit. If you continue, Disk Defragmenter begins to reposition the files. While Defragmenter is working, you can click on the Show Details button to see a graphic display of the program's progress.

IMPORTANT:

Do not run the Disk Defragmenter on your hard disk unless your instructor asks you to do so.

EXERCISE ⟹ 5.3

You must have your Windows Practice disk in one of the floppy drives before you begin this exercise. Since this disk was recently formatted, it won't be fragmented, but you will be able to see how the Disk Defragmenter works.

1. Open the **Start** menu.

2. Select the **Programs** option, select the **Accessories** option, choose the **System Tools** option, and then select the **Disk Defragmenter** option. The Select Drive dialog box displays (see Figure 5-4).

3. Click the drop-down list arrow at the end of the text box. Select the drive that contains your Windows Practice disk, and then click the **OK** button. Be patient: It may take Windows a few seconds to access the drive.

4. A message box displays, indicating that the fragmentation process is complete (see Figure 5-5). Click the **Yes** button.

5. Remove your Windows Practice disk from the floppy disk drive. If instructed, shut down Windows and your computer.

FIGURE 5-4
Select Drive dialog box

FIGURE 5-4
Select Drive dialog box

FIGURE 5-5
A message box tells you Disk
Defragmenter is done

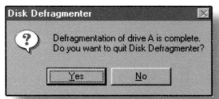

Summary

This lesson covered how to format, label, and manage your computer disks. You learned that:

- Formatting prepares a disk for use on a specific type of drive. In this context, formatting means imprinting a disk with the information it needs to work in that kind of drive. At the same time, formatting erases any information previously stored on the disk.

- You can give a disk an "electronic label." You can relabel a disk by keying a new name in the Label text box in the disk's Properties dialog box.

- You can use ScanDisk to find and fix a variety of problems associated with the data structure of a hard disk or floppy disk.

- Disk Defragmenter rearranges the files on a disk so that the disk performs optimally.

LESSON 5 REVIEW QUESTIONS

TRUE/FALSE

Each of the following statements is either true or false. Indicate your answer on the left by circling T if the statement is true and F if the statement is false.

T   F   1. Double-density disks will store approximately twice as much data as high-density disks.

T   F   2. If you format a previously used floppy disk, you can retain all the information on the disk.

T   F   3. The Quick (erase) format process deletes all information previously stored on a disk.

T   F   4. Disk labels can only be added when you format a disk.

T   F   5. A fragmented disk will operate more efficiently than a defragmented disk.

FILL IN THE BLANKS

Complete the following sentences by writing the correct word or words in the blanks provided.

1. A(n) _____ disk has a capacity of 360KB or 720KB.

2. The _____ format option checks a floppy disk for problem areas.

3. _____ prepares a floppy disk for use on a specific type of disk drive.

4. The Windows program that reads a disk's vital signs is called _____.

5. _____ files are not stored in contiguous clusters.

LESSON 5 PROJECT

This project gives you the opportunity to review the concepts in this lesson and practice the techniques in the exercises.

1. Insert a blank floppy disk in the appropriate drive.

2. Start **My Computer** and click the icon of the drive where you inserted the disk to select it.

3. Format the disk:
   a. Select **Format** from the **File** menu.
   b. Verify that the appropriate capacity for the floppy disk is indicated.
   c. Select the **Full** format option and check the **No label** check box; then verify that all of the check boxes under Other options are unchecked.
   d. Click the **Start** command button.
   e. When the format is complete, click the **Close** button to close the Format Results dialog box. Then click the **Close** button to quit the Format dialog box.

4. Apply a label to the disk:
   a. Click the **Properties** button on the toolbar.
   b. Verify that the General tab is selected.
   c. Key your last name (or a shortened version of it if it is longer than 11 characters) in the Label text box.
   d. Click the **OK** button to record the label.

5. Run the Disk Defragmenter on the disk:

   a. Open the Start menu. Select **Programs**, **Accessories**, **System Tools**, and then **Disk Defragmenter**.

   b. In the Select Drive dialog box, select the drive that contains your floppy disk and then click the **OK** button.

   c. When the message box displays, indicating that Disk Defragmenter is done, click the **Yes** button.

6. Remove the disk from the floppy disk drive. If instructed, shut down Windows and your computer.

WORKING WITH FOLDERS AND SUBFOLDERS

OBJECTIVES

Upon completion of this lesson, you will be able to:

- Create folders and subfolders.
- Name and rename folders.
- Delete and undelete folders.
- Restore a deleted folder from the Recycle Bin.

⏱ Estimated Time: 1.5 hours

My Computer gives you a number of options for working with folders. In this lesson, you will learn how to create new folders on a disk, and then create subfolders within them. You will also learn how to name, rename, and delete folders.

Creating a Folder

As you have learned, folders are used to organize files on a disk. When you want to create a folder to store files, your first decision is, "On which disk will I place the new folder?" To create a subfolder, your decision is, "Under which *parent folder* will I place the new subfolder?" Remember, this is a creation process, a building process. You decide where to create or where to build!

With My Computer, you create folders and subfolders using a similar process. To create a folder, first select the disk where you want the new folder to appear, then select New from the File menu. From the submenu, select Folder. A New Folder icon (Figure 6-1) appears in the display window. To create a subfolder, first double-click the folder where you want the subfolder to appear, then follow the instructions for creating a folder.

FIGURE 6-1
New Folder icon

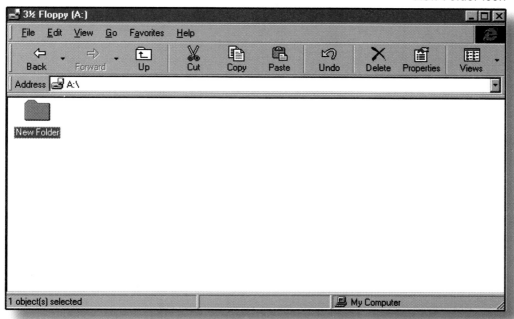

Naming Folders and Files

Are you familiar with DOS or older versions of Windows? If so, perhaps you know that both use a file-naming convention called 8.3 (pronounced "eight dot three"). The "eight" part means that a file's name may be up to eight characters long. The "three" part is an extension (no longer than three characters) to the name. And the "dot" is the period that separates the 8 from the 3. Neither spaces nor special characters can be used in the DOS naming system.

For example, in the *file name* **letter.doc**, the name is *letter*, the separator is the standard period, and the *extension* is *doc*. There you have it: *8.3*.

Windows 98 allows long names (up to 255 characters) for folders and files, and it allows spaces, punctuation marks, and most characters in the names. It allows you to name a folder **J. L. Smith & Company Contract**, instead of a code name such as **jlscocon.doc**.

But only application programs designed specifically for Windows 98 (and its predecessor Windows 95) will permit long file names. To compensate, Windows 98 (and Windows 98 application programs) assigns a short file name, called an *8.3 alias*. Programs that don't support long file names see this 8.3 alias as the file's name.

Be extra careful working with programs that don't recognize long file names:

■ If you copy a folder or file with a long file name to a system that doesn't support long file names, the system will use an 8.3 alias.

■ When you open a file that has a long file name in a program that doesn't recognize long file names, the long file name could get lost.

■ Backup and restore programs that don't support long file names will destroy the long file names.

To name a new folder, simply key the folder name. As you key, your folder name replaces the words *New Folder*. Press Enter to display the new folder name.

1. Start **My Computer** by double-clicking its icon on the desktop.

2. Change the view in the My Computer window to Large Icons.

3. Verify that your Windows Practice disk is in the appropriate floppy drive; then double-click the disk's icon in the display window. Notice that the drive is now displayed in the Address Bar. Notice also that there are no icons in the display window. Why? Because your Windows Practice disk is a newly formatted disk—a "clean" disk.

4. Turn on the Auto Arrange feature so the folder icons will be arranged neatly in the display window as you create them: From the **View** menu, select **Arrange Icons**, then choose **Auto Arrange** from the submenu.

5. Create a new folder called **Reports**:
   a. Select **New** from the **File** menu, then select **Folder** from the submenu.
   b. The New Folder icon—with the name **New Folder** highlighted—appears in the display window. Because Auto Arrange is turned on, this new folder is automatically placed in the upper left corner of the window.

   c. Key the folder name **Reports**. Be sure to key upper- and lowercase as shown.
   d. Press **Enter**. Do you see the new Reports folder in the display window?

6. Create three subfolders in the Reports folder:
   a. Double-click the **Reports** folder icon to open it. The Reports folder icon and name are now displayed in the Address Bar.
   b. Choose **New** from the **File** menu, and then select **Folder** from the submenu. The new folder appears.
   c. Key the folder name **Monthly**; then press **Enter**.
   d. Click anywhere in the display window except on the newly created folder to deselect it.

> **TIP**
>
> Make sure that the parent folder in which you want to create a subfolder is displayed in the Address Bar before you select New from the file menu.

7. Following the instructions in steps 6b–6d, create two additional subfolders in the Reports folder and name them **Quarterly** and **Final**. Your screen should resemble Figure 6-2 on the next page. Remain in this screen for the next exercise.

Renaming a Folder

It often happens that after you have used a folder for a time, you find you need to rename it. This is a simple process in My Computer:

- Click the folder to be renamed to select it.

- Choose Rename from the File menu.

- A box appears around the folder name, along with a blinking cursor.

- Key the new name within the box, and then press Enter.

FIGURE 6-2
Three subfolders in the Reports folder

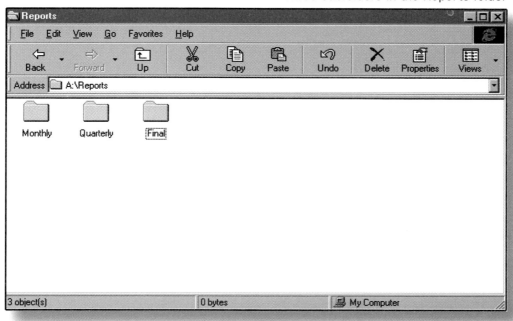

6.2

1. Click the **Up** button to close the Reports folder and return to the floppy disk display window.

2. Click the **Reports** folder icon in the display window to select it.

3. Choose **Rename** from the **File** menu.

4. Key the new name **Status Reports**; then press **Enter**.

IMPORTANT:

Rename folders with care. Application programs will not work if they cannot locate the folder names they search for.

Deleting a Folder

You can delete a folder in three ways:

1. Click the folder to select it; then click the Delete button on the toolbar.

2. Click the folder to select it; then select Delete from the File menu.

3. Click the folder to select it; then press the Delete key.

When you delete a folder or subfolder, you also delete all the files in it! Use extreme caution, therefore, before you attempt to delete a folder. To make sure that's what you really want to do, Windows displays a Confirm Folder Delete message box (Figure 6-3). Windows provides one additional safety net when you are deleting a folder from a hard disk. Folders deleted from a hard disk are transferred by default to the Recycle Bin, from which they can be recovered. But a folder or a file deleted from a floppy disk is gone—period. No Recycle Bin!

FIGURE 6-3
Confirm Folder Delete message box

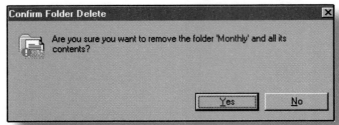

 **NOTE:**

My Computer allows you to turn off this Confirm Folder Delete message by checking the appropriate box in the Recycle Bin Properties dialog box. To prevent accidents, keep this option checked!

EXERCISE ▷ 6.3

1. Double-click the **Status Reports** folder to open the folder and display its subfolders.

2. Delete the Monthly subfolder:
   a. Click the **Monthly** subfolder to select it.
   b. Click the **Delete** button on the toolbar. The Confirm Folder Delete message box appears (Figure 6-3).
   c. Verify that the correct folder name (Monthly) is shown before you click the **Yes** button. Watch as Windows graphically illus-

trates the folder being deleted from the Status Reports folder.

3. Click **Up** until you return to My Computer.

4. Click the **Close** button to close My Computer.

5. Remove your Windows Practice disk from the floppy disk drive. If instructed, shut down Windows and your computer.

Undeleting a Folder

Recycle Bin

As discussed above, a folder deleted from a hard disk goes to the Recycle Bin. The Recycle Bin keeps track of where deleted files and folders were originally. Then, if you need to recover a deleted folder, you can use the Recycle Bin to restore the folder to its original location on the hard disk.

To restore a deleted folder from the Recycle Bin, double-click the Recycle Bin icon on the desktop to open the Recycle Bin window (Figure 6-4), which displays files deleted from the hard disk. Choose the file or files to be restored, and then select Restore from the File menu. The selected file will be returned to its original location.

FIGURE 6-4
Recycle Bin window

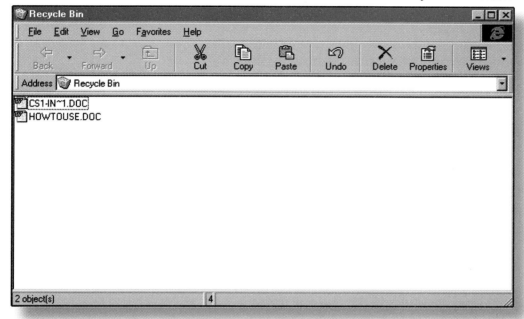

NOTE:

The Recycle Bin stores only hard disk deletions, not floppy disk deletions.

Summary

This lesson covered how to manage folders and subfolders on your computer system. You learned that:

■ You can assign folders and files descriptive names up to 255 characters long; however, only Windows 98 and Windows 98 applications (as well as Windows 95 and Windows 95 applications) can accommodate long names. Windows will assign a short file name, called an "alias," to each of these files so they can be used with programs that don't support long file names.

- You can easily rename a folder by selecting it, choosing Rename from the File menu, and then keying the new name.

- Deleting a folder or subfolder deletes all the files in it as well. Folders deleted from a hard disk are transferred to the Recycle Bin. Folders deleted from a floppy disk are deleted permanently.

- You can restore a deleted folder from the Recycle Bin by double-clicking the Recycle Bin icon on the desktop, selecting the folder to be restored, and then selecting Restore from the File menu.

LESSON 6 REVIEW QUESTIONS

TRUE/FALSE

Each of the following statements is either true or false. Indicate your answer on the left by circling T if the statement is true and F if the statement is false.

T   F   1. The parent folder is the folder in which the subfolder is located.

T   F   2. A parent folder can contain only one subfolder.

T   F   3. A long file name cannot exceed 25 characters.

T   F   4. All application programs can recognize long file names.

T   F   5. Folders deleted from the hard disk can be retrieved from the Recycle Bin.

WRITTEN QUESTIONS

Answer the following questions in the space provided.

1. What are the rules for the 8.3 method of assigning file names, and how do they differ from those for assigning long names?

   _____

   _____

2. How do you create a folder?

   _____

   _____

3. How would you rename an existing folder?

   _____

   _____

4. Why is it important to keep the Confirm Folder Delete message option turned on?

_____

_____

5. What happens to folders once you delete them from a hard disk?

_____

_____

LESSON 6 PROJECT

This project gives you the opportunity to review the concepts in this lesson and practice the techniques in the exercises. In order to complete this application you will need your Windows Practice disk.

1. Start Windows if it is not already running.

2. Open **My Computer** and do the following:
   a. Select the **Details** view.
   b. Maximize the My Computer window.
   c. If necessary, change the browsing option to browse folders by opening a separate window for each folder.

TIP

To change the Browsing option, use the **Folder Options** command on the **View** menu.

3. Insert your Windows Practice disk in the appropriate floppy drive; then select that drive.

4. Create a folder named **Project 6**.

5. Open the **Project 6** folder.

6. Create the following subfolders in the Project 6 folder: **Marketing**, **Sales**, and **Accounting**.

7. Create the following subfolders in the Sales subfolder you created in step 6: **Reports**, **Correspondence**, and **Miscellaneous**.

8. Rename the Miscellaneous subfolder **Budget**.

9. Change the browsing option to browse folders by opening a single window.

10. Close all open folder and subfolder windows, then close My Computer. If instructed, shut down Windows and your computer.

WORKING WITH FILES

OBJECTIVES

Upon completion of this lesson, you will be able to:

■ Manage the display and organization of files.

■ Copy and move files from one folder to another.

■ Recognize and distinguish between different file icons.

■ Run applications from My Computer.

⏱ Estimated Time: 1.5 hours

As you learned earlier, a file may be the instructions the computer needs to operate, or it may be the data you enter and save. In this lesson, you will learn how to identify, manage, and open files.

Selecting Files

My Computer permits you to control how your files are organized on a disk by assisting you to move and copy files between disks and folders and to delete files. The first step in performing any of these functions is to select the files.

To select a single file, click it. To select two or more files that are adjacent to one another, click the first in the series, press and hold down the Shift key, and then click the last (see Figure 7-1). To select files that are not adjacent, press and hold down the Ctrl key, then click each of the files. In Figure 7-2, for example, four nonadjacent objects are selected (note the status bar).

You can use the scroll bars to move around the display window when selecting files. Don't worry if the selected object moves out of view. An object will remain selected until you select another object or cancel the selection. When you want to cancel all the selections in the window, click a blank area in the window.

In the first exercise of this lesson (which begins on page 80), you will need to access the Windows folder on your system. If the folder is not called Windows, your instructor will give you alternate instructions.

FIGURE 7-1

Selecting adjacent files

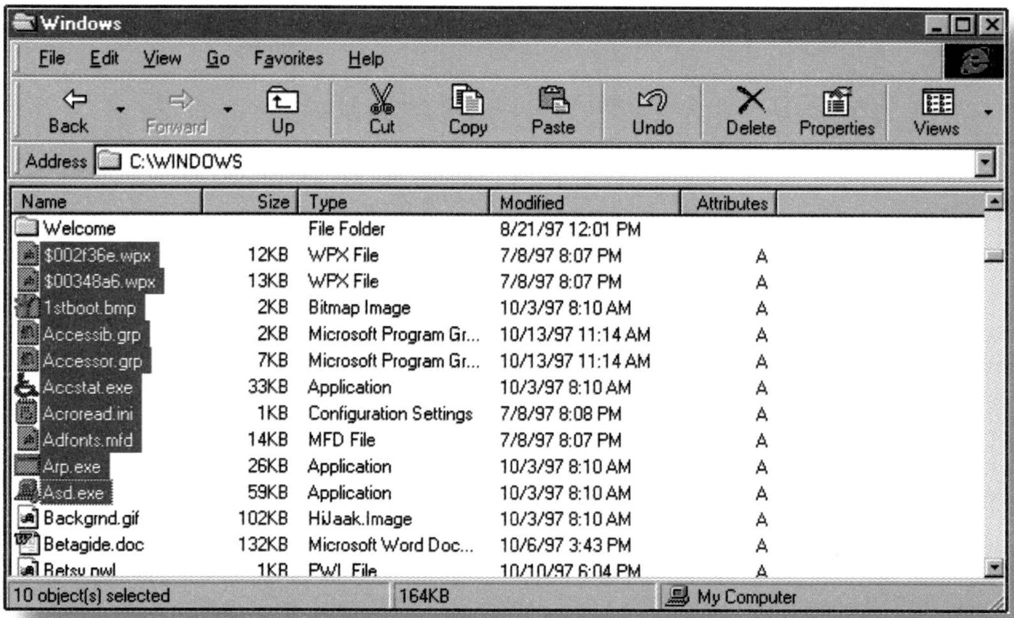

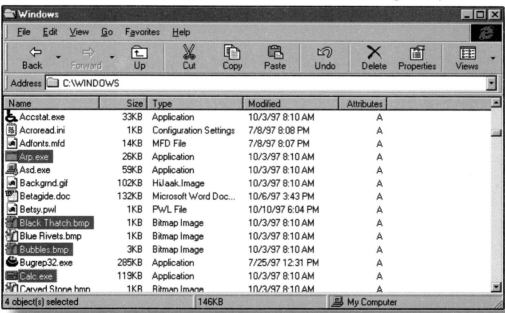

FIGURE 7-2

Selecting nonadjacent files

1. Start **My Computer**.

2. In the display window, double-click the drive that contains the Windows folder (usually your hard drive—drive C:).

3. Scroll the window until the Windows folder is in view; then double-click the **Windows** folder to open it.

4. Select the **Details** view, if necessary.

5. Select the first file (not folder) in the display window by clicking it once. (Be careful not to double-click or you may open the file.)

6. Select nonadjacent files:
   a. Press and hold down **Ctrl**.
   b. Click on every other file name you currently see in the window.

7. Deselect the first selected file by pressing **Ctrl** and clicking the file's icon in the display window.

8. Deselect all the selected files by clicking once on a clear area in the display window.

9. Select adjacent files:
   a. Scroll to the first file in the list.
   b. Click the first file.
   c. Press and hold down **Shift**. Then click the tenth file in the listing. All the intervening files will be selected, as illustrated in Figure 7-1 (your displayed list may not be exactly the same, but it should look similar).

10. Deselect all the selected files by clicking once on a clear area in the display window.

11. Keep the window open for the next exercise.

Changing the Order of Files Listed in the Display Window

So far, you have used My Computer's defaults to display the order of folders and files in the display window. But at times you may want to change the display order—for example, you may want to see all files of one type grouped together. The Arrange Icons options on the View menu (Figure 7-3) allow you to control the order in which objects are arranged in the display window.

The Arrange Icons submenu gives you the following options:

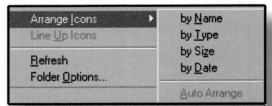

FIGURE 7-3
Arrange Icons options on My Computer's View menu

■ **by Name**. This option sorts and displays folders and files in normal alphabetic order by folder or file name (with symbols first, then numbers, and finally letters). Names are case sensitive: **Windows** is not the same as **windows** or **WINDOWS**. Folders are always placed before files when using this option.

■ **by Type**. This option displays folders and files grouped according to type (application, bitmapped image, folder, and so on). By default, folders are shown first.

■ **by Size**. This option lists folders and files in order by size. By default, folders are listed first. Files are listed in ascending order.

■ **by Date**. The By Date option lists folders and files in order by date, from most recent to oldest.

You can use the above options in combination. For example, you can arrange the folders and files first by size and second by name. The result: A list of files arranged by size, with objects of the same size arranged in alphabetical order by name.

E X E R C I S E ⟹ 7.2

1. Verify that the My Computer window is displayed on your screen.

2. If necessary, open the **Windows** folder and change the view to **Details**.

3. List the files by name in the display window:
   a. Select **Arrange Icons** from the **View** menu.
   b. Click **by Name**.

4. List the files by size in the display window:
   a. Select **Arrange Icons** from the **View** menu.
   b. Click **by Size**. Notice the files are now arranged by size.

5. List the files by date in the display window:
   a. Select **Arrange Icons** from the **View** menu.
   b. Click **by Date**.

6. Scroll the list and notice the files are now arranged by date.

7. Change the listing back to **by Name**.

8. Click the **Up** button until My Computer is displayed in the Address Bar.

Copying and Moving Files

One of the key advantages of using Windows is the ease with which you can copy or move files from one location to another. Once you become proficient on a computer, you will probably need to use these techniques frequently. For example, you will often want to copy a file as a backup, move a file to another folder, or reorganize the files on a disk.

You move or copy files from a "source" to a "destination." The *source* is the file to be copied and the *destination* is the location (folder or disk) where the copied file will then reside. Whenever you need to move or copy files, make both the source and destination visible. In this way, you can see what you are moving or copying and where it is going. In My Computer, you make the source and destination windows visible at the same time by changing the Browsing option in the Folder Options dialog box to *Open each folder in its own window*. Using this option, you can open both the source and the destination windows and see them at the same time on your screen.

When you *copy* a file, you place a duplicate of the file in a different location, and the original file remains in place. To copy a file to a new location on a different disk, first select it. You can select more than one file to copy using the techniques you learned earlier. You can also select a folder to copy. Then, drag the object from its current location and drop it onto its destination; that is, to where you want to copy it. A dialog box titled Copying... appears with a graphic that shows the object "flying" from source to destination, and the copied file appears immediately in the destination window.

IMPORTANT:

To copy an object to a new location on the same disk, you must hold down the Ctrl key as you drag the object. Otherwise, Windows moves the file rather than copies it.

The moving process is similar to the copying process. When you *move* a file, however, you remove it from its original location and place it in the destination window. To move an object to a new location on a different disk, select it, hold down the Shift key, and drag it to the destination window. A Moving... dialog box appears to show the progress of the move.

If you attempt to copy or move a file to a destination where an identically named file exists, Windows displays the Confirm File Replace message box shown in Figure 7-4. Click the Yes button to replace the existing file; click No to cancel the copy or move.

IMPORTANT:

To move an object to a new location on the same disk, simply drag it to the new location.

FIGURE 7-4
Confirm File Replace message box

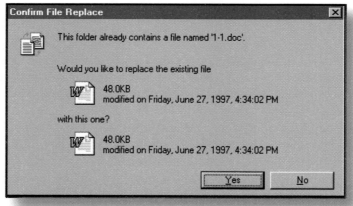

EXERCISE ▭⟩ 7.3

1. Place your Windows Practice disk in the appropriate floppy drive.

2. Change the browsing option so that each folder is opened in its own window:
   a. Select **Folder Options** from the **View** menu.
   b. Click the **Settings** button and then click **Open each folder in its own window**. Click the **OK** button and then click **Close**.

3. Double-click the icon representing your hard disk. Notice that both the My Computer window and your hard disk drive window appear as buttons on the taskbar.

4. In the hard disk drive window, double-click the **Windows** folder to open it in a new window.

5. Switch to the My Computer window (click the **My Computer** button on the taskbar) and double-click the drive in which you have placed your Windows Practice disk. You should see the Status Reports folder in the window.

6. Double-click the **Status Reports** folder icon. A fifth window opens.

7. Double-click the **Final** folder. A sixth window opens.

8. Close all open windows except for the Final folder window and the Windows folder window (see Figure 7-5).

9. Right-click on a blank area of the taskbar; then select the **Tile Windows Vertically** option from the shortcut menu.

10. Scroll the Windows window to bring the *Readme* file into view.

11. Point to the **Readme** file. Then drag the icon from the Windows folder window to the Final folder window. Notice that as you move the icon onto the Final folder window, there is a small plus sign (+) next to the pointer. This plus sign is a visual clue that you are copying the file.

12. After the Copying... dialog box closes, you will see the copied file in the Final folder window.

13. Select the **Calc** file from the Windows window. Hold down the **Shift** key and drag the file to the **Final** folder window.

14. Notice the Moving... dialog box that shows the process of the move. The Calc file now appears only in your Final folder window.

15. Move the **Calc** file back to the Windows folder window. Hold down the **Shift** key and drag the file from the Final folder to the Windows folder. It will reappear at the end of the Windows file list.

16. Change the browsing option back to display each folder in the same window.

17. Close both open windows and remain in this screen for the next exercise.

FIGURE 7-5
Open both the source and the destination windows when copying or moving files

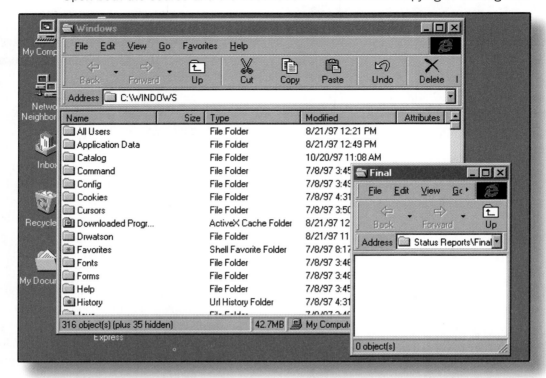

Running Applications from My Computer

There are several ways to run an application, and one is by using My Computer. To start an application program with My Computer, you can double-click an icon or select the icon and then choose the Open option on the File menu. However, you cannot click just any icon to start an application. Only certain icons will start applications. Windows typically contains several types of icons, so you need to learn how to recognize the different types.

Recognizing File Icons

Running applications from My Computer is easier when you can distinguish among the different types of icons. My Computer's display window shows two basic file icons—application file icons and document file icons. Each has distinguishable characteristics.

APPLICATION FILE ICONS

An *application file icon* starts an application. The icon may look like a miniature version of the program icon, or it may look like a miniature window (see Figure 7-6). In both cases, double-clicking an application file icon will start the application program.

FIGURE 7-6
Application file icons

DOCUMENT FILE ICONS

Document file icons share the same distinctive feature: a piece of paper with a superimposed graphic (Figure 7-7). When you create a document file, you can associate that file with an application. For Windows, this means you can create a link between a document and an application. In practical terms, this means you can open a document file *directly*—you do not need to open the application first.

FIGURE 7-7
Document file icons

Starting an Application Using the Open Command

One of the easiest ways to start an application from My Computer is to use the Open command on the File menu. As you will see in the next exercise, this is a simple process: Click the application icon, then choose Open from the File menu.

EXERCISE ⟹ 7.4

1. If necessary, open **My Computer**.

2. Double-click the disk drive containing the Windows folder, usually drive C:.

3. Double-click the **Windows** folder. If necessary, change the view to **Large Icons**.

4. Scroll the Contents pane until you locate the Calculator application icon (a small hand-held calculator with the caption *Calc*).

5. Click the Calculator application icon.

6. Select **Open** from the **File** menu. The Calculator application program opens in a window on top of the My Computer window, as shown in Figure 7-8.

7. Click the **Close** button on the Calculator window to close the Calculator application program.

FIGURE 7-8
Starting an application using the Open command on the File menu

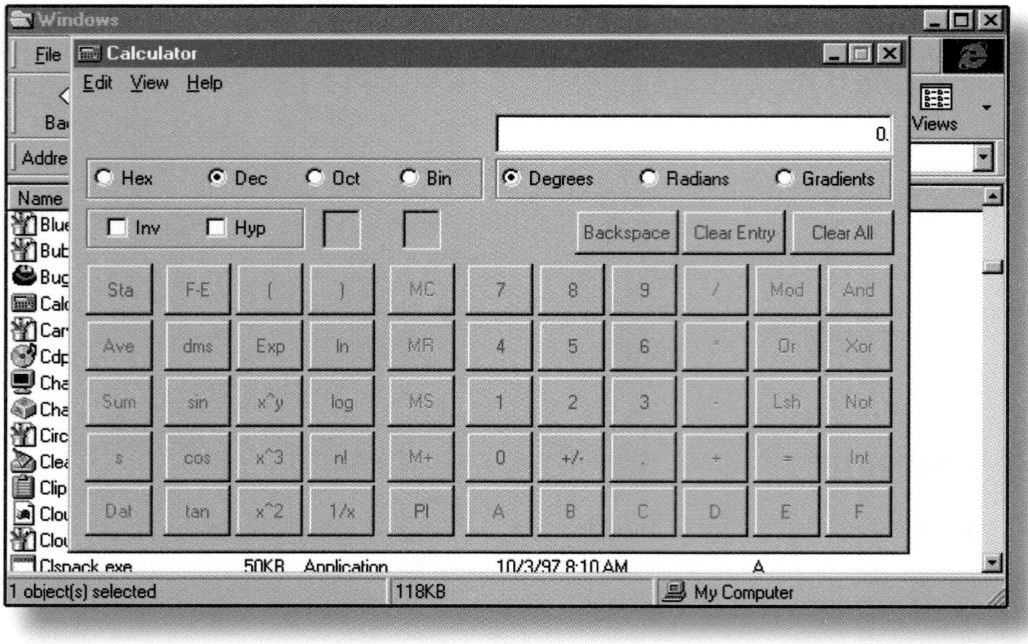

Starting an Application Using an Application File Icon

Rather than using the Open option, you can double-click an application file icon in My Computer's display window to start the application.

EXERCISE ⟹ 7.5

1. The Windows folder should still be displayed in the My Computer window.

2. Scroll the display window until you locate the Notepad application icon (a small spiral-bound tablet with the caption *Notepad*).

3. Double-click the **Notepad** application icon. The Notepad application program opens in a window on top of My Computer's window. It displays a blank window with a blinking cursor in the upper left corner, signaling that the application is ready for you to use.

4. Click the **Close** button on the Notepad application window to close the application.

Starting an Application Using a Document File Icon

To open an application from a document file icon, double-click any document that is associated with an application. A document file icon is easy to spot because it shows the application icon on top of a sheet of paper (often with the upper right corner of the paper turned down).

EXERCISE 7.6

1. The Windows folder should still be displayed in the My Computer window.

2. Drag the vertical scroll bar close to the end.

3. Locate the *Tips* document file icon. Look closely at the icon. Does it look familiar? This icon resembles the Notepad application because the document file is associated with the Notepad application program.

4. Double-click the **Tips** icon. The Notepad application opens, with the title bar "Tips.txt - Notepad" displayed.

5. Click the **Close** button on the Notepad application window to close the document and the application.

6. Close My Computer.

Using the Run... Command

You have learned how to open and run applications and their associated documents using several methods. Windows offers you another way to start applications and open files and folders: the Run... command on the Start menu.

When you select the Run... command, the Run dialog box shown in Figure 7-9 displays. The Open line in the dialog box contains the highlighted last document or program opened using the command.

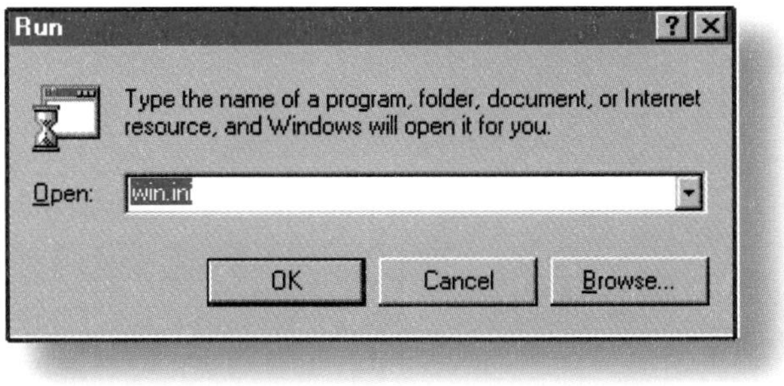

If you know the name of the document or program you want to open, you key it in the

FIGURE 7-9
Run dialog box

Open text box and then click the OK button to carry out the command. Your typing automatically replaces the highlighted text. If you're not sure of the name or location of the file or program, you can *browse* for it by clicking the Browse button. Windows then displays a Browse dialog box that closely resembles the My Computer window. In this dialog box you can open folders and scroll among files until you find the one you want. Double-clicking the found object returns you to the Run dialog box, where you'll find that Windows has filled in the name and path of the object. You then click the OK button to run the file or program.

1. Select **Run...** from the **Start** menu.

2. If the Open line contains text, make sure it is highlighted.

3. Key **Notepad** and click the **OK** button. The Notepad application displays in a window.

4. Close the Notepad window.

5. Select **Run...** again from the **Start** menu. This time, use the Browse button to find the Notepad file named **Tips:**
   a. Make sure any entry in the Open line is highlighted.
   b. Click the **Browse** button. In the Browse window, double-click **My Computer** and then select the drive where your Windows folder is located.
   c. Open the **Windows** folder. Click the down arrow on the **Files of type** drop-down list and select **All Files (*.*)**.
   d. Scroll to locate the **Tips** document file, then double-click it.

6. Notice that the file name and its path now appear in the Open text box. Click the **OK** button. The **Tips** document displays in a Notepad window.

7. Close the **Tips** document.

Reopening a Document

The commands you key on the Open line in the Run dialog box are stored on the drop-down list, as shown in Figure 7-10. Clicking the drop-down list arrow on the Open line displays a list of up to 20 of your most recently used Run commands. If you use this command often to run or open programs and documents, you can select them quickly from this drop-down list. Simply click any "stored" Run command on the Open drop-down list, click the OK button, and Windows does the rest!

FIGURE 7-10
Open drop-down list in the Run dialog box

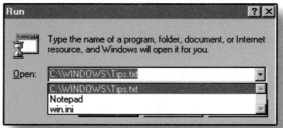

Opening a Folder Using the Run... Command

You can also use the Run command to open folder windows without actually running any program. To open a window for the folder C:/Windows, for example, simply key that string of characters in the Open text box and click the OK button.

EXERCISE ▷ 7.8

1. Select **Run...** from the **Start** menu.

2. Click the **Open** drop-down list arrow to display the list of previously used commands.

3. Click **notepad** and click the **OK** button. The Notepad window displays, just as it did in Exercise 7.7.

4. Close the Notepad window.

5. Select **Run...** again from the **Start** menu.

6. In the Open line, key **c:\Windows** and click the **OK** button. The Windows folder displays in a window similar to the one shown in Figure 7-11.

7. Close the folder window. If instructed, shut down Windows and your computer.

FIGURE 7-11
Using the Run... command to open a folder window

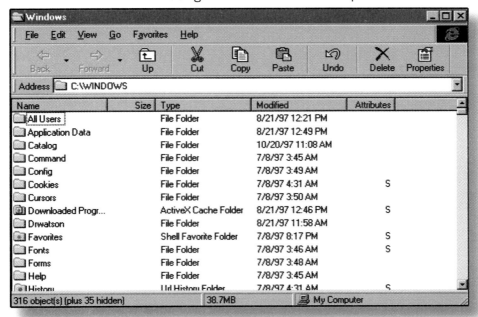

Summary

This lesson covered how to identify, manage, and open files. You learned that:

■ Files are moved or copied from a "source" to a "destination." The source is the file to be copied, and the destination is the location (folder or disk) where the moved or copied file will be placed.

■ When you copy a file, you duplicate the original. When you move a file, it is removed from its original location and placed in a new location.

- An application file icon looks like a miniature version of the program icon, or it may look like a miniature window.

- A document file icon looks like a piece of paper with a graphic on it. You can open an associated document file without having to open the application first.

- To run an application, select the application's icon and use the Open command in the File menu. If you prefer, double-click the application's icon in the My Computer display window. Yet another option: If a document is associated with an application program, double-click the document's icon.

- Use the Run… command to open a file or window. You can key the path of the file or window, choose it from the Open drop-down list, or use the Browse… button to locate it.

LESSON 7 REVIEW QUESTIONS

TRUE/FALSE

Each of the following statements is either true or false. Indicate your answer on the left by circling T if the statement is true and F if the statement is false.

T F 1. When copying files to a different disk, the source is the file to be copied.

T F 2. A destination file is the file you are copying.

T F 3. When you move a file, a copy of it is retained in the original location.

T F 4. When you arrange files by date, the most recently created or modified files are listed first.

T F 5. Double-clicking an application file icon starts the application.

MATCHING

Write the letter of the term in the right column that matches the definition in the left column.

_____ 1. To place a duplicate of a file in a different location, while maintaining the file in its original location.

_____ 2. To remove a file from its original location and place it in a new one.

_____ 3. The location (folder or disk) where a copied or moved file will reside.

_____ 4. The file to be copied.

_____ 5. Icon that looks like a piece of paper with a superimposed graphic representing an application.

A. move

B. document file

C. copy

D. source

E. destination

LESSON 7 PROJECT

This project gives you the opportunity to review the concepts in this lesson and practice the techniques in the exercises. You will need your Windows Template disk and your Windows Practice disk in order to complete this project.

1. Start Windows if it is not already running, and open **My Computer.**

2. Change the browsing option to **Open each folder in a separate window**.

3. Place your Windows Template disk in the appropriate floppy drive.

4. Copy the Project 7 folder from the Windows Template disk to the desktop:
    a. Double-click the disk drive containing the Windows Template disk.
    b. Switch to the My Computer window, and click the **Up** button to display **desktop** in the Address Bar.
    c. Drag the **Project 7** folder from the floppy disk drive window to the desktop window.

5. Move the Project 7 folder to your Windows Practice disk:
    a. Remove your Windows Template disk from the floppy drive and insert your Windows Practice disk.
    b. Hold down the **Shift** key and drag the **Project 7** folder from the Desktop window to the floppy disk drive window.

6. Open the Project 7 folder on your Windows Practice disk and do the following:
    a. Add a new subfolder called **Special Report #1** to the Project 7 folder.
    b. Copy all the files with the words *Sales Manual* in their file names to the Special Report #1 subfolder.
    c. In the Special Report #1 subfolder, rename the files that contain the word *Chapter* in their file names by changing the word *Chapter* to **Part**.
    d. Add a new subfolder to the Project 7 folder called **Quarterly Reports**.
    e. Move the Progress Reports (Q 1, Q 2, Q 3, and Q 4) files from the Progress Reports subfolder to the Quarterly Reports subfolder.
    f. Delete the **Progress Reports** subfolder.

7. Change the browsing option to **Open each folder in the same window**.

8. Close all folder and subfolder windows, then close **My Computer**. If instructed, shut down Windows and your computer.

LESSON 8

USING SHORTCUTS

If you use particular programs or documents frequently, you might want to create shortcuts for them so you can access them quickly and easily. In this lesson, you will learn how to create and use shortcuts.

What Is a Shortcut?

A *shortcut* functions as a pointer to an application or document file, wherever the file is located. When you double-click the shortcut icon, you're opening the actual item to which the shortcut is pointing.

The shortcut is represented by an icon on your desktop. A shortcut icon is identified by a small arrow in its lower left corner (see Figure 8-1). Here's how a shortcut works. Suppose you create a shortcut to the Tips document you opened in the last lesson. When you double-click the Tips shortcut icon to open it, you are actually opening the Windows folder, running the Notepad application program, and opening the Tips document. Now you see why it is called a shortcut! Shortcuts save time because you don't have to open and browse through several folders to find the file you need.

FIGURE 8-1
Shortcut icon

Creating Shortcuts

You can create a shortcut in one of two ways: by dragging a file to the desktop or by using the Create Shortcut command on the File menu.

Creating a Shortcut Using Drag and Drop

If you can display an item in the My Computer window, you can create a shortcut for it by *dragging and dropping*:

■ *Right-drag* the item from its current location to wherever you want the shortcut to appear.

■ *Drop* it by releasing the mouse button.

■ A shortcut menu appears, giving you several options. Click *Create Shortcut(s) Here*.

■ The icon appears with the shortcut arrow showing and a default name.

You may want to change the shortcut's default name to something different. To rename the shortcut, right-click the shortcut icon to display the Shortcut menu shown in Figure 8-2. Choose Rename and key the new name in the shortcut icon's text box. You can use this shortcut menu for a number of tasks, such as deleting a shortcut or changing its properties.

FIGURE 8-2
This shortcut menu gives you options for changing a shortcut

EXERCISE ▷ **8.1**

1. Open **My Computer** and locate the **Winnews** document file icon in the Windows folder.

2. Using the right mouse button, drag the Winnews document file icon to the desktop. Release the mouse button.

3. Select **Create Shortcut(s) Here** from the shortcut menu.

4. Close the My Computer window. The Winnews document shortcut appears on your desktop.

5. Rename the shortcut:
   a. Right-click the **Shortcut to Winnews** icon.
   b. Select **Rename** from the shortcut menu. Notice that the icon's name is now highlighted and has a blinking insertion point.
   c. Key **My Shortcut** and press **Enter** to rename the icon.

6. Leave the shortcut on screen.

 **IMPORTANT:**

If you use the left mouse button, you will *move* the **Winnews** document file icon.

Creating a Shortcut Using the File Menu

You can also create a shortcut by selecting the item you want to create the shortcut for in My Computer. Then, select Create Shortcut from the File menu. A shortcut icon for the item appears as the last item in the My Computer window (see Figure 8-3). Drag the icon to the desktop. Then, you can rename it as you have already learned.

FIGURE 8-3
Using the Create Shortcut command on the File menu

E X E R C I S E ⟹ **8.2**

1. Display the **Windows** folder in the My Computer Window.

2. Locate and select the **Defrag** program icon.

3. Select **Create Shortcut** from the **File** menu.

4. Drag the shortcut from the My Computer Window to the desktop.

5. Leave the shortcut on screen.

FIGURE 8-4
Defrag shortcut

Assigning a Shortcut Key to a Shortcut

A *shortcut key* is a keystroke combination that runs a program or opens the dialog box to which it is linked. For example, if you assign the shortcut key Ctrl+Alt+M to your My Shortcut, your new shortcut key will then open the Winnews document. You assign a shortcut key in the shortcut's Properties dialog box.

E X E R C I S E ⟹ 8.3

1. Right-click the **My Shortcut** icon. Select **Properties** from the shortcut menu. The My Shortcut Properties dialog box displays.

2. Make sure the **Shortcut** tab is displayed (see Figure 8-5).

3. Click an insertion point in the Shortcut key text box; then press and hold down **Ctrl**. Notice that the keystroke combination Ctrl+Alt+ displays. It ends with "+" because it is waiting for you to complete the shortcut. While holding down Ctrl, press **m**, then release **Ctrl.** The shortcut key Ctrl+Alt+M is displayed in the Shortcut key text box.

4. Click the **OK** button to save the shortcut key and close the My Shortcut Properties dialog box.

FIGURE 8-5
Shortcut tab

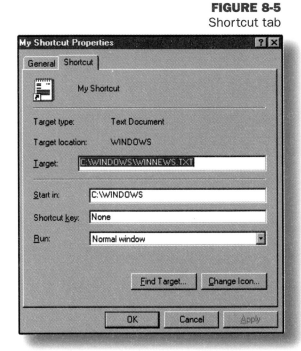

Using a Shortcut

You can activate a shortcut in two ways:

1. Double-click the shortcut icon.

2. Issue the shortcut key.

In the next exercise you will practice each of these methods.

NOTE:

If Windows is already using your selected keystroke combination for another shortcut, Windows runs the other shortcut. In this case, just open the shortcut's Properties dialog box and select a different keystroke combination.

EXERCISE 8.4

1. Double-click the **My Shortcut** icon. Did the Winnews document open?

2. Close the Winnews window.

3. Issue the shortcut key Ctrl+Alt+M:
   a. Press and hold down **Ctrl**.

   b. Press and hold down **Alt**.
   c. Press **m** and release all keys.

4. The Winnews document once again opens. Click its **Close** button to close it.

Which method do you prefer—double-clicking the icon or issuing the shortcut key? You probably found the first method simpler, but as you become more familiar with creating shortcuts, you will see that shortcut keys are very useful when the shortcut is not in view.

Deleting a Shortcut

Like most functions, shortcuts can be deleted. To delete a shortcut:

■ Select the shortcut, then press the Delete key.

   or

■ Right-click the shortcut and then select Delete from the shortcut menu.

In either case, Windows displays the message box shown in Figure 8-6, asking you to confirm the deletion. Deleting a shortcut deletes only the shortcut, not the file that the shortcut points to.

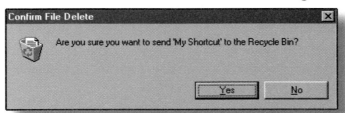

FIGURE 8-6
Confirm File Delete message box

E X E R C I S E ⇨ **8.5**

1. Right-click the **My Shortcut** icon on the desktop, and then select **Delete** from the shortcut menu.

2. Confirm that you do intend to delete the shortcut by clicking the **Yes** button on the message box.

3. Click the **Defrag** shortcut icon on the desktop, and then press the **Delete** key.

4. Click **Yes** in the message box to confirm the deletion.

5. If instructed, shut down Windows and your computer.

Summary

This lesson covered how to create, use, and delete shortcuts. You learned that:

■ A shortcut functions as a pointer to a file—wherever it is located. Double-click the shortcut icon to open the actual item to which the shortcut is pointing.

■ You create a shortcut by dragging and dropping or by using the Create Shortcut option on the File menu.

■ You can add a shortcut key to a Windows shortcut. A shortcut key is a keystroke combination that runs a program—or in this case, runs the Windows shortcut to which it is linked. Shortcut keys to Windows shortcuts always use Ctrl+Alt+ and one additional character.

TRUE/FALSE

Each of the following statements is either true or false. Indicate your answer on the left by circling T if the statement is true and F if the statement is false.

T F   1.   When you double-click a shortcut icon, you're opening a copy of the item to which the shortcut is pointing.

T F   2.   A shortcut icon is identified by an exclamation point in its lower left corner.

T F   3.   You can only create shortcuts to application programs, not specific folders or files.

T F   4.   Right-clicking a shortcut icon displays the shortcut menu.

T F   5.   You cannot delete a shortcut icon.

FILL IN THE BLANKS

Complete the following sentences by writing the correct word or words in the blanks provided.

1.   A(n) _____ functions as a pointer to an application or document file.

2.   You can create a shortcut by using the Create Shortcut command on the _____ menu.

3.   _____-clicking on a blank area on the desktop displays a shortcut menu.

4.   A(n) _____ is a keystroke combination that runs a program or opens the dialog box to which it is linked.

5.   A(n) _____ icon is represented by a small arrow in its lower left corner.

LESSON 8 PROJECT

This project gives you the opportunity to review the concepts in this lesson and practice the techniques in the exercises. You will need your Windows Template disk in order to complete this project.

1.   Start Windows if it is not already running.

2.   Place the Windows Template disk in the appropriate disk drive.

3. Open **My Computer**.

4. Create a shortcut to the Project 8 folder on your Windows Template disk:
   a. Display the Windows Template disk in the My Computer window.
   b. Right-drag the **Project 8** folder to the desktop.
   c. Choose **Create Shortcut(s) Here** from the shortcut menu.
   d. Rename the shortcut **Project 8 Folder**.

5. Using the Project 8 Folder shortcut, access and print a copy of the **Project 8 Report Form** in the Project Reports folder:
   a. Double-click the shortcut to open the Project 8 folder.
   b. Double-click the **Project Reports** subfolder.
   c. Verify that your printer is accessible and ready.
   d. Select the **Project 8 Report Form** file, then select **Print** from the **File** menu.

6. Using the Project 8 Report Form you printed in step 5, do the following:
   a. Fill in the heading with the appropriate information.
   b. Answer all questions on the Report Form using My Computer to display the subfolders and files in the Project 8 folder.

7. Close all windows, then close **My Computer**.

8. Delete the **Project 8 Folder** shortcut from the desktop.

9. If instructed, shut down Windows and your computer.

UNIT 2 REVIEW QUESTIONS

WRITTEN QUESTIONS

Answer the questions below on a separate piece of paper.

1. List and briefly explain the purposes of My Computer.

2. Identify the buttons on My Computer's toolbar and explain the purpose of each button.

3. Distinguish between folders and files.

4. Describe each of the following types of icons: folder icon, disk icon, document file icon, and application file icon.

5. Contrast double-density disks with high-density disks.

6. Explain the rules for the 8.3 method of assigning file names, and contrast these rules with those for assigning long names.

7. Distinguish between copying a file and moving a file.

8. Explain the purpose of formatting a disk and give an example of when you might wish to reformat a disk.

9. Explain the purpose of a shortcut key and briefly describe how it works.

10. Identify the two Windows disk management tools and explain how they help manage your disks.

UNIT 2 APPLICATION

SCANS

Aleta Lopez wants to organize Corporate Communique's client information in folders on her hard drive. Currently, all client files, including invoices, memos and letters to clients, and actual newsletter projects, are stored in a single folder named CorpComm. Help Aleta reorganize the files using My Computer.

Insert your Windows Template disk in the appropriate disk drive. Start My Computer and copy the **CorpComm** folder on the Template disk to the desktop. Remove the Windows Template disk and insert your Windows Practice disk. Create a folder on your Windows Practice disk that's named **CorpComm Clients**. Copy the contents of the **CorpComm** folder on the desktop to the **CorpComm Clients** folder.

Create folders in the CorpComm Clients folder for each of the following clients, using the client name as the folder name: **Townsend & Co.**, **Bartles Shipping**, **Leon Supply Co.**, and **Perdix & Stolley**.

Move the client files in the CorpComm Clients folder into the appropriate client folder. File names begin with the initials of the client's name, e.g., *TC* for Townsend & Co., *BS* for Bartles Shipping, *LS* for Leon Supply Co., and *PS* for Perdix & Stolley.

Create another folder in the CorpComm Clients folder and name it **Invoices**. Move all the invoice files in the individual client folders to the Invoices folder.

Delete the **CorpComm** folder from the desktop. If instructed, shut down Windows and your computer.

CRITICAL THINKING

Before you begin this exercise, determine whether your instructor wants to look at your screen before you delete anything.

On Monday morning, when you arrive at your office, the new microcomputer you have been waiting for is sitting on your desk. When you power up the system, you discover that it boots to Windows 98.

What a day! You feel as though you spent more time getting your folders and files set up on your new computer than you did at your assigned tasks. It's almost 5 o'clock, and your best friend, Dan Estrada, asks for your help. He, too, has a new computer with Windows 98, and he asks you to help him get organized. You stay after work to help Dan.

After some time, you and Dan have found and categorized all of his computer files as shown below:

Category	File Name	Explanation
Most often used:	budgetcy.xls	Current year's budget
	jones.doc	Proposal currently being developed
	taxrptq1.xls	Quarter 1 tax report spreadsheet
	taxrptq2.xls	Quarter 2 tax report spreadsheet
	acmebus.doc	Business plan being developed for a client
	taxrptq3.xls	Quarter 3 tax report spreadsheet
	customer.dbf	Customer database
	expense.dot	An expense reimbursement template
	status.dot	A status report template
	address.dbf	Customer mailing list
Occasionally used:	budgetny.xls	Next year's budget planning worksheet
	planny.xlt	Planning worksheet template
	shipping.dbf	Vendor database
	prodrpt.dot	Weekly production report tax template
	prodtpt.xlt	Weekly production report spreadsheet template

Category	File Name	Explanation
Seldom used:	budgetly.xls	Previous year's budget worksheet
	manual1.doc	Part 1 of department manual currently being written
	manual2.doc	Part 2 of department manual currently being written
	manual3.doc	Part 3 of department manual currently being written
Backup copies:	budgetcy.xlb	Backup copy of current year's budget
	taxrpt.xls	Blank tax report worksheet
	customer.bak	Backup copy of customer database
	shipping.bak	Backup copy of vendor database

Using the information above, create a folder system for Dan. Format a blank disk and create the folder structure on the disk by creating appropriate folders and subfolders. If your instructor asks to see your completed folder structure, display it in the My Computer window. Save the disk for use in the Unit 3 review activities.

When you are finished, write a short paper discussing your directory structure. Include the following in your report:

1. A sketch showing the folder structure.

2. The purpose of each of the subfolders.

3. The long file names that you would use in place of the 8.3 names Dan uses. Indicate the location of each file and the reason for placing it in the folder.

4. A sample of the written instructions you would give Dan on how to use the new folder and file system.

WINDOWS EXPLORER

UNIT 3

Estimated Time for Unit 3: 6 hours

103

LESSON 9

USING EXPLORER

OBJECTIVES

Upon completion of this lesson, you will be able to:

- Define uses for Windows Explorer.
- Start Explorer.
- Identify the parts of the Explorer window.
- Identify the icons in the display window.
- Expand and collapse the folder list.
- Set Explorer display options.

⏱ **Estimated Time: 1.5 hours**

Like My Computer, *Windows Explorer* is designed to help you find, view, and manage files—and to use files easily and efficiently. In this lesson, you'll learn how to start Explorer and set options to control the display of files and folders.

Introducing Windows Explorer

Explorer is a handy Windows program that gives you even more control over the organization and management of your files and folders. Like My Computer, Explorer makes it easy to view the contents of selected disks and folders. Explorer also gives you the capability to search for certain files and folders. That's why the Explorer icon is a magnifying glass superimposed over a file folder (Figure 9-1).

FIGURE 9-1
Explorer
icon

All of the disk and folder maintenance operations you use with My Computer are available in Windows Explorer as well. Explorer simply provides additional features to make the tasks easier and faster. For example, the Explorer window has two *panes*, or portions: a left pane and a right pane. The right pane looks just like the My Computer window and functions the same way. The left pane displays the contents of your hard disk, floppy disk, CD-ROM drive, or any resource attached to your computer or that is available on your desktop. Explorer's left pane makes it easy to move quickly between folders, lets you see the structure of your folders at a glance, and allows you to move and copy files by dragging them from the right pane to the left.

You access Explorer from the Programs option on the Start menu (see Figure 9-2). As you have already learned, you click the Start button to display the Start menu. To start Explorer, open the Programs menu from the Start menu, move the highlight to Windows Explorer, and click. Explorer's opening window is shown in Figure 9-3.

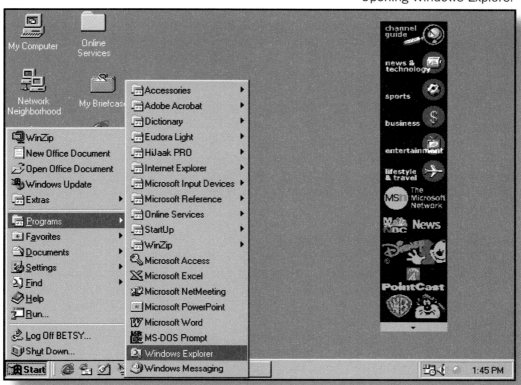

FIGURE 9-2
Opening Windows Explorer

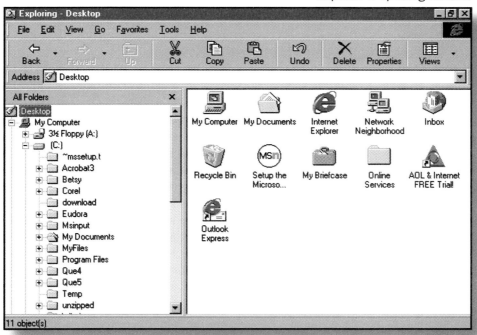

FIGURE 9-3
Explorer's opening window

EXERCISE ▭⟹ 9.1

1. Click the **Start** menu. Move the highlight to the **Programs** option.

2. Select **Windows Explorer** from the **Programs** menu. The Explorer window displays. Your screen may differ somewhat from the one shown in Figure 9-3.

Identifying the Parts of the Explorer Window

By now you should recognize the window features common to many Windows screens. If you are new to Windows, however, you may not know the functions of the two panes in the display window. The left pane is called the *All Folders pane*. The right pane is called the *Contents pane*. These panes are discussed below.

ALL FOLDERS (TREE) PANE

The All Folders pane is also called the Tree pane, because its hierarchical display of all of the objects on the desktop is like a tree's trunk and branch system. But in this case, the tree is upside down: Its main *root* (Desktop) is at the top, and its major branches (folders) and lesser branches (subfolders) follow downward toward the bottom.

CONTENTS PANE

What the right pane, the Contents pane, displays depends on which folder, disk, or other object is selected in the left pane. In other words, the two panes—Tree and Contents—work together. For example, note in Figure 9-3 that Desktop is selected. Now note that the Address Bar says *Desktop*, thus matching the object selected in the left pane. If the Windows folder were selected in the Tree pane, the listing in the Contents pane would change to show what's in the Windows folder, and the Address Bar would then read *C:\Windows*. Explorer's title bar also displays the name of the disk or folder that you're currently "exploring" in the Contents pane.

Identifying the Icons in the Display Window

Each time you open Explorer, the objects on the desktop appear in the Tree pane. The icons representing these objects should look familiar to you from the My Computer window, but they are displayed in a different fashion in Explorer.

At the top of the Tree pane is the Desktop icon. You may have to scroll to bring it into view. This icon represents the Windows desktop, and since all the objects in your system are placed on the desktop, all icons are shown in the Tree pane as stemming from the Desktop icon. Look again at Figure 9-3 and note how the My Computer icon appears below and to the right of the Desktop icon. The dotted line marking this connection makes it clear that My Computer is subordinate to—or down one level from—the Desktop.

The My Computer icon in turn has icons below and to the right of it: at least one floppy drive and the hard drive. The hard drive icon has a number of folders displayed below and to the right of its icon. These are the applications and other folders stored on the drive.

Finally, Explorer offers you a way of determining whether each of these folders has subfolders within it. Notice in Figure 9-3 the small boxes to the left of some icons. Boxes containing a plus sign (+) indicate folders that have subfolders not currently displayed. If a box contains a minus sign (–), the subfolders are displayed below the folder. In Figure 9-3, for example, the minus sign next to the drive C: icon indicates that all the folders on that drive are displayed below. The plus signs next to the MyFiles and Program Files folders indicate that these folders contain subfolders which are not displayed.

As you can see from a careful look at the Tree pane, Explorer shows in one view the same information that would require several views in My Computer. You'll find that this view makes it very easy to handle file management tasks.

The Contents pane also shows several types of icons, depending on what object is selected in the Tree pane. Look at Figure 9-4. This figure shows that the Windows folder has been selected—the label *Windows* is highlighted and the folder appears to be open. The Contents pane shows the contents of this folder, which include both subfolders (Tshoot, Vcm, Web, and so on) and files (*Black Thatch*, *Acroread*, and so on). You'll recognize application file icons (the Accstat icon, for instance) and document file icons from the discussion in Lesson 7.

FIGURE 9-4
Contents pane displays contents of selected object or folder

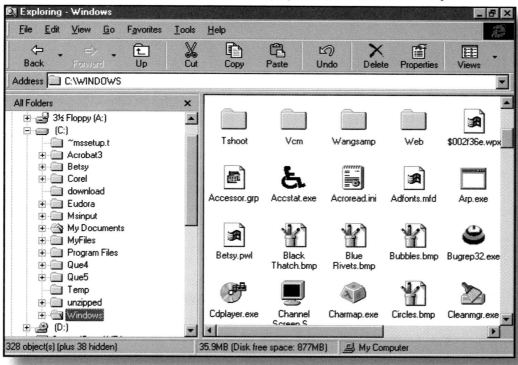

You can see the subfolders in the Contents pane even when they are not displayed in the Tree pane. Being able to control each pane independently of the other gives you great flexibility when you are copying, moving, viewing, or otherwise manipulating files.

Expanding and Collapsing the Tree

When you open Explorer, it does not display subfolders, except for those that appear on your hard drive. If you want to display subfolders for any other folder, you must *expand* the folder list (increase the subfolder display level). Expanding the folder list is easy: Just click the plus sign in the box to the left of the folder. As the subfolders display below the folder, the plus sign changes to a minus sign. If you then click the minus sign, you *collapse* the folder list (decrease the subfolder display level).

Collapsing a folder makes it possible to view more objects in the tree. This is useful if you are trying to copy or move files between different folders. Collapsing folders also makes the folder list less cluttered and makes it easier to locate files and folders.

1. Find the drive on which the Windows folder is stored (generally drive **C:**).

2. Locate the Windows folder, and note whether there is a plus or a minus sign in the box to the left of the icon.

3. Click the box to the left of the **Windows** folder icon. If the box has a plus sign, the tree will expand showing the subfolders below Windows; if the file icon displays a minus sign, the tree will collapse.

4. If necessary, click again on the box to the left of the **Windows** folder icon to display the Windows subfolders in the Tree pane.

5. Notice that at least two of the Windows sub-folders have additional subfolders, as indicated by a plus sign in the box to the left of the subfolder.

6. Expand the Start Menu folder (you may have to use the Tree pane's scroll bar to find it) and display all of its subfolders and their subfolders:
   a. Click the plus sign in front of the **Start Menu** folder. Note that its subfolder, Programs, is displayed with a plus sign.
   b. Click the plus sign in front of the **Programs** folder. Note that one of its subfolders, Accessories, is displayed with a plus sign.
   c. Click the plus sign in front of the **Accessories** folder. Note that none of these subfolders has a subfolder (no plus or minus signs).

7. Click the minus sign in front of the **Start Menu** folder. Notice that the Start Menu folder list collapses.

8. Click the plus sign in front of the **Start Menu** folder. Notice that the Start Menu folder list is still fully expanded (Figure 9-5). Collapsing a folder does not collapse any expanded sub-folders.

FIGURE 9-5
Start Menu folder with fully expanded folder list

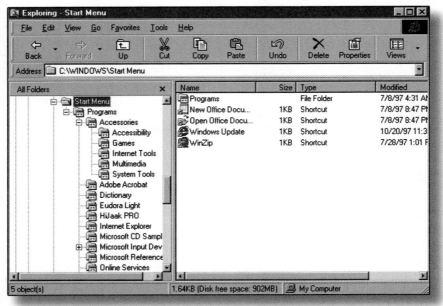

Setting Explorer Options

Explorer's View menu is identical to My Computer's View menu. You can choose to display the toolbar and the status bar, for example, and the Folder Options choice allows you to choose from among a number of options that control the way files are displayed.

Explorer's toolbar is also the same as My Computer's. You will see the familiar navigation buttons and Up button, which help you to navigate in the Tree pane. The Views button at the far right of the toolbar lets you change the way objects are displayed in the Contents pane only. These displays are the same as those you learned about in Lesson 4.

EXERCISE 9.3

1. Click the **Views** button drop-down list arrow on the toolbar and select **Details**, if this view is not already selected. Note that the display is the same as the Details view in My Computer.

2. Select the other views on the **Views** drop-down list to see how the display in the Contents pane changes.

3. Select **List** to display the Contents pane in List view.

Viewing the Contents of a Drive or Folder

Most folder and file operations require you first to identify the drive you want to use. In Explorer, the available disk drives are represented by icons in the Tree pane. To select a drive, click the appropriate drive icon. The drive is highlighted in the Tree pane and its contents appear in the Contents pane, as shown in Figure 9-6.

You can also select a drive or other desktop object (such as the Recycle Bin) by clicking the object in the Address Bar drop-down list. This action moves you directly to the object in the Tree pane. If you have a very large tree displayed, it is easier to select an object this way than to scroll in search of it.

To view the contents of a folder, click the folder in the Tree pane. The folder "opens" and its contents appear in the Contents pane. If the folder has subfolders, you can double-click the subfolder in the Contents pane. When you do so, the subfolder's contents are displayed in the Contents pane and the Tree pane also expands to show the subfolders.

FIGURE 9-6

In the Tree pane, highlighting shows which disk drive is selected

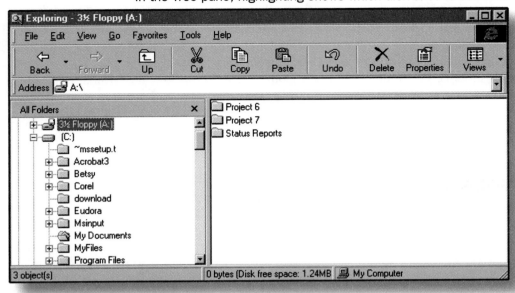

E X E R C I S E ⟹ 9.4

1. Insert your Windows Practice disk in the appropriate disk drive.

2. Click the icon of the drive where your Windows Practice disk is located. The Contents pane shows the contents of the disk.

3. Double-click the **Status Reports** folder in the Contents pane. Notice how the folder's contents now appear in the Contents pane and the Tree pane shows the open folder under the drive icon.

4. Display the contents of the Windows folder on your hard drive: Click the **Windows** folder in the Tree pane.

5. In the Contents pane, double-click the **System** folder. Your display should resemble Figure 9-7.

6. Click the **Up** button on the toolbar to select the Windows folder again.

7. From the Address Bar drop-down list, select the drive that contains your Windows Practice disk.

8. Click the **Close** button to close Windows Explorer. Then, if instructed, shut down Windows and your computer.

FIGURE 9-7
Contents of the System folder

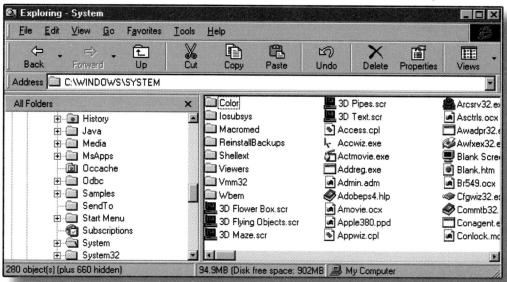

Summary

This lesson covered how to start Windows Explorer and view the contents of a drive and folder. You learned that:

■ When you start Explorer, you see a window with the familiar title bar, menu bar, display window, and status bar. The display window is divided vertically into two panes—a Tree, or All Folders, pane on the left and a Contents pane on the right.

■ The Tree pane displays all the objects on the desktop in a hierarchical structure, and it displays the folder structure for the currently selected disk. The Contents pane displays the contents of the folder selected in the Tree pane.

■ In the Tree pane, the open folder is the active folder. In the Contents pane, a folder icon represents a subfolder of the open folder.

■ Each time you access Explorer, the Tree pane displays the structure of your desktop. You can select a disk and display the structure of its contents. You can collapse (decrease the levels shown in) the tree, so that the folders and subfolders do not appear. You can also expand (increase the levels shown in) the tree, so that it shows folders of all levels.

■ Explorer's View menu options and Views button allow you to control how files are displayed in the Contents pane. You can select Large Icons; Small Icons; List, which shows small icons in list format; or Details, which shows small icons organized under the columns Name, Size, Type, and Modified (that is, date created or modified).

TRUE/FALSE

Each of the following statements is either true or false. Indicate your answer on the left by circling T if the statement is true and F if the statement is false.

T F 1. To start Windows Explorer, you select Documents on the Start menu and then select Windows Explorer.

T F 2. In Windows Explorer, the All Folders pane is also called the Contents pane.

T F 3. You can collapse the folders list on all drives so that subfolders do not display.

T F 4. The contents of the folder selected in the Contents pane will display in the Tree pane.

T F 5. A plus sign next to a folder in Explorer's Tree pane indicates folders that have subfolders not currently displayed.

MULTIPLE CHOICE

Complete the following questions by circling the correct multiple choice letter.

1. Explorer is designed to help you
    a. find, view, and manage files
    b. use files easily and efficiently
    c. create and delete folders and subfolders
    d. all of the above

2. Collapsing the folder list
    a. makes the folder list more cluttered
    b. makes it more difficult to copy or move files between different folders
    c. makes it possible to view more objects in the tree
    d. makes it more difficult to display objects in the Contents pane

3. In the Tree pane, a folder icon with a plus (+) sign indicates that the folder
    a. has recently been added
    b. does not contain any files
    c. has subfolders
    d. has been expanded

4. Which icon is at the very top of the tree in the Tree pane?
    a. Folder
    b. My Computer
    c. Desktop
    d. Drive C:

5. Which is not a display option for objects in Explorer's Contents pane?
   a. Details
   b. Filed
   c. Large Icons
   d. Small Icons

LESSON 9 PROJECT

This project gives you the opportunity to review the concepts in this lesson and practice the techniques in the exercises. You will need your Windows Template disk in order to complete this project.

1. Start Windows if it is not already running.

2. Open **Explorer** and select the **Details** view. Maximize the Explorer window.

3. Insert your Windows Template disk in one of the floppy drives; then select that drive in the Tree pane.

4. In the Tree pane, expand the **Project 9** folder.

5. Double-click the **Project Reports** folder in the Contents pane.

6. In the Contents pane, select the **Project 9 Report Form** and then select **Print** from the **File** menu.

7. Using the **Project 9 Report Form**, do the following:
   a. Fill in the heading with the appropriate information.
   b. Answer all questions on the Report Form using Explorer to display the subfolders and files in the Project 9 folder.

8. Collapse all open folders in the Tree pane.

9. Close **Explorer**. Then, if instructed, shut down Windows and your computer.

USING EXPLORER TO MANIPULATE FILES AND FOLDERS

OBJECTIVES

Upon completion of this lesson, you will be able to:

- Create and name folders and subfolders in Windows Explorer.
- Select folders and files.
- Change the order of files in the Contents pane.
- Copy, move, and delete folders and files.
- Rename folders and files.
- Set and delete file attributes.

Estimated Time: 1.5 hours

Many of the techniques for working with folders and files that you learned for My Computer work the same way in Explorer. Because of the different way that objects are displayed in Explorer, however, you'll want to practice them again in this lesson. Explorer also offers some additional ways to manipulate folders and files, as you'll see later.

Creating and Naming Folders and Subfolders

You create a folder in Explorer just as you do in My Computer. First, in the Tree pane you select the drive or parent folder where you will place the new folder. Then choose New from the File menu and Folder from the submenu. A New Folder icon appears at the bottom of the files list in the Contents pane, as shown in Figure 10-1. Key the new folder name in the text box that appears to the right of or below the New Folder icon. Press Enter, and the new folder name appears in the Contents pane and in the folder list in the Tree pane.

FIGURE 10-1
New Folder icon in the Contents pane

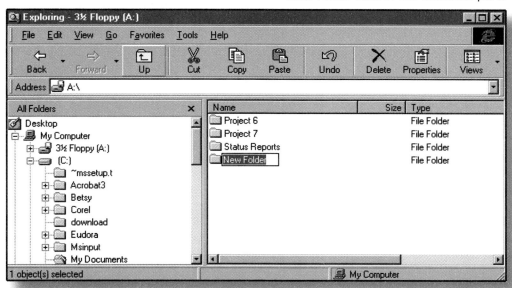

EXERCISE ⟹ 10.1

1. Start **Explorer** by clicking the **Start** button, selecting **Programs**, and then selecting **Window's Explorer**.

2. Change the view to **Large Icons**, if necessary.

3. Verify that your Windows Practice disk is in the appropriate floppy drive; then click the disk's icon in the Tree pane.

4. Create a new folder called Desktop Publishing Files:
   a. Select **New** from the **File** menu, and then **Folder** from the submenu.
   b. Key the folder name **Desktop Publishing Files** in the New Folder text box. Be sure to key upper- and lowercase as shown.
   c. Press **Enter**.

5. If necessary, expand the drive's file level in the Tree pane to show the new Desktop Publishing Files folder.

6. Create three subfolders in the Desktop Publishing Files folder:
   a. Select the **Desktop Publishing Files** folder icon in the Tree pane. The folder opens, indicating that it is the selected folder.
   b. Select **New** from the **File** menu; then select **Folder** from the submenu.
   c. Key the name **Stories** in the New Folder text box; then press **Enter**.
   d. Click the plus sign in front of the Desktop Publishing Files folder in the Tree pane to expand the tree. Notice that Stories is shown as a subfolder under the Desktop Publishing Files folder.
   e. Following steps 6a–6d above, create the new subfolders named **Documents** and **Graphics**. Notice that the subfolders display in alphabetical order in the Tree pane below the Desktop Publishing Files folder.

Selecting Folders and Files

Before you can take advantage of Explorer's power to manipulate files, you need to know how to select objects in the two panes. In the Tree pane, you can select only one object at a time. But in the Contents pane, you can select single or multiple folders and files.

You should already know these techniques for selecting multiple folders and files:

■ To select a single folder or file, click it.

■ To select files or folders randomly scattered through the Contents pane, press and hold down Ctrl while you click each of the desired objects. As shown in Figure 10-2, the selected objects will be highlighted.

FIGURE 10-2

Five objects selected in the Contents pane

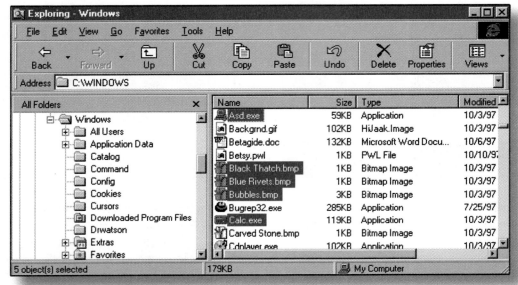

■ To select consecutive folders or files, as shown in Figure 10-3, click the first object of the group, press and hold down the Shift key, and click the last object of the group.

■ Explorer gives you an additional way to select consecutive files: Place the mouse pointer to the right and slightly above the first object of the group. Press and hold down the mouse button and drag a rectangle to the left and downward until all of the files in the group are highlighted. Release the mouse button. Be sure not to point on an icon or a name when you begin this operation, or you'll select and drag that object.

You can use the scroll bars to move around the Contents pane when you are selecting objects. Don't worry if the selected object moves out of view. An object will remain selected until you select another object or cancel the selection. When you want to cancel all the selections in the Contents pane, click a blank area in the Tree pane.

FIGURE 10-3

Selected group of consecutive folders and files

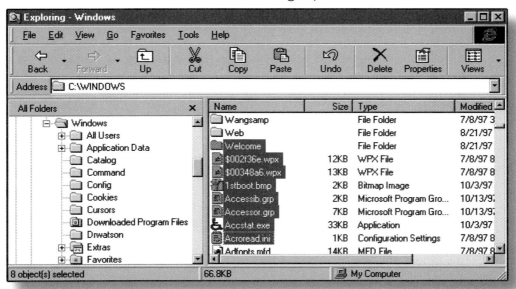

EXERCISE 10.2

1. Maximize the **Explorer** window.

2. Scroll the Tree pane until the **Windows** folder is in view and click the folder to display its contents in the Contents pane.

3. Select the **Blue Rivets** file in the Contents pane. Hold down the **Ctrl** key and select **Black Thatch** and **Bubbles**.

4. Click a blank area in the Tree pane to cancel the selection.

5. Select the first five subfolders in the Windows folder by dragging an outline around them.

6. Cancel the selection.

Changing the Order of Files in the Contents Window

It is often easier to select files if the Contents pane is sorted according to one criterion, such as file type or file size. There are two ways to sort and arrange the objects in the Contents pane:

■ Use one of the Arrange Icons options from Explorer's View menu. These options allow you to re-order the files according to name, type, size, or date.

■ Another method of arranging the objects in the Contents pane is available only when the Details view is selected. The column headings Name, Size, Type, and Modified act as command buttons. Clicking any one of these headings sorts the Contents pane objects in that order. For example, if you click the column heading Type, the objects in the pane are arranged according to their type (by default, in ascending order, from *a* to *z*, from *1* to *10*, and so on). If you click the same column heading a second time, the objects are arranged in descending order (from *z* to *a*, from *10* to *1*, and so on).

1. Select the **Details** view.

2. Click once on the **Type** column head in the Contents pane. When you arrange objects by type, folders are always shown first; then files are shown, in alphabetic order by type. If file folders are not listed first, click once again on the column head Type.

3. Select all files that are 200KB or larger:
   a. Click twice on the **Size** column head in the Contents pane to arrange the objects in descending order by size.

   b. Click the first file in the listing.
   c. Press and hold down **Shift**; then click on the last file in the listing that is 200KB or larger. Your display should look similar to Figure 10-4.

4. Click once on a clear area in the Tree pane. All the selected folders will be deselected.

5. Leave the window open for the next exercise.

FIGURE 10-4
Sorting and then selecting displayed objects

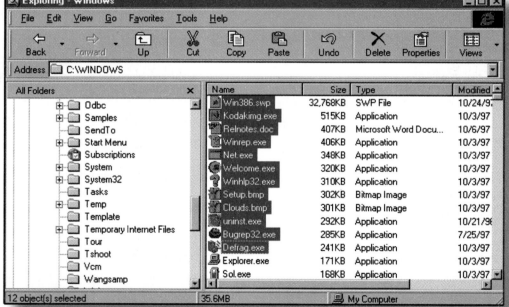

Copying Folders and Files

Folders and files are moved or copied by dragging the object from the Contents pane to the destination drive or folder in the Tree pane. This is easily done if you "set up" the Tree pane and Contents pane before you begin. To set up the Contents pane, select the appropriate drive or folder in the folder list so that the source folder or file is displayed in the Contents pane. To set up the destination drive or folder, expand the folder list in the Tree pane until the destination drive or folder is in view (do not select the object or you will deselect the source object). To copy a folder or file to a new location on a different disk, drag it from the Contents pane to the Tree pane. To move a folder or file to a new location on a different disk, hold down the Shift key and drag the object to the destination drive or folder in the Tree pane.

NOTE:

Hold down the Ctrl key when copying to a location on the same disk. To move a file or folder to a new location on the same disk, simply drag it to the destination drive or folder.

EXERCISE ▷ 10.4

1. Scroll the Tree pane to bring into view the drive where your Windows Practice disk is located.

2. If necessary, expand the tree: Click the plus sign in front of the drive in which you have placed your Windows Practice disk. *Careful:* If you click the drive, you will select the drive and deselect the Windows folder.

3. If necessary expand the **Desktop Publishing Files** folder by clicking the plus sign in front of the drive icon.

4. Click the **Type** column head to rearrange the files in the Contents pane by type.

5. Scroll to bring the Bitmap Image files into view, then select the first five Bitmap Image files. Your screen should resemble Figure 10-5.

6. Point to one of the selected files in the Contents pane, hold down the mouse button, and drag toward the **Graphics** subfolder in the Tree pane. Note how the entire group of selected files moves.

7. Move the group over the **Graphics** subfolder until the Graphics label is highlighted. Release the mouse button.

8. The animated illustration shows files being copied from one folder to another. The scale at the bottom of the window illustrates the progress of the task being performed.

9. When the animation window clears, notice that the five files are still displayed in the Contents pane.

10. Click the **Graphics** subfolder in the Tree pane. Notice that the five Bitmap Image files are displayed in the Contents pane. The files are located in both folders because they were copied.

11. Click the **Black Thatch** file in the Graphics subfolder, hold down the **Shift** key, and drag the file to the **Stories** subfolder in the Tree pane.

12. When the animation window clears, notice that the **Black Thatch** file is no longer displayed in the Contents pane; it has been moved.

13. Click the **Stories** subfolder in the Tree pane. Notice that the **Black Thatch** file is displayed in the Contents pane. The **Black Thatch** file is now located only in the Stories subfolder because it was moved, not copied. Remain in this screen for the next exercise.

119

FIGURE 10-5
Selecting objects to copy

Renaming Folders and Files

You rename folders and files in Explorer as you did in My Computer:

1. Select the folder or file to be renamed.

2. Select the Rename command from the File menu.

3. Key the new name in the text box.

4. Finally, press Enter.

E X E R C I S E ⟶ 10.5

1. Select the **Desktop Publishing Files** folder in the Tree pane.

2. Select **Rename** from the **File** menu.

3. Key the new name **Electronic Publishing**; then press **Enter**.

4. Select the **Graphics** subfolder in the Tree pane. The Bitmap Image files will display in the Contents window.

5. Select the **Blue Rivets** file in the Contents pane.

6. Select **Rename** from the **File** menu.

7. Key the new name **Color Dot**; then press **Enter**. Remain in this screen for the next exercise.

IMPORTANT:

Rename folders and files with care. Application programs will not work if they cannot locate the file names or folder names they search for.

Deleting Folders and Files

Using Explorer, you can delete folders and files in a single action. But when you delete a folder or subfolder, you also delete *all* the files in it! Before you attempt to delete a folder, make sure you really don't need it anymore.

Note this distinction between deleting files and folders from a hard disk and from a floppy disk:

■ When you delete a folder or a file from a hard disk, by default it is sent to the Recycle Bin, and the Confirm Folder Delete message (Figure 10-6) or the Confirm File Delete message (Figure 10-7) displays. You can recover a folder or a file from the Recycle Bin if you decide later you need it.

FIGURE 10-6
Confirm Folder Delete message box

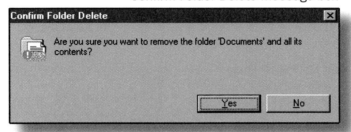

FIGURE 10-7
Confirm File Delete message box

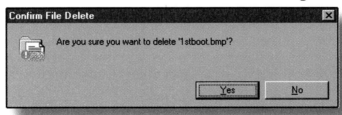

■ When you delete a folder or a file from a floppy disk, it is deleted—period. No Recycle Bin! First, however, the Confirm Delete message displays to warn you, because you cannot recover an object deleted from a floppy disk.

NOTE:

For information on how to restore a folder or file from the Recycle Bin, see *Undeleting a Folder* in Lesson 6.

121

You delete files in Explorer the same way you do in My Computer:

- Select the folder or file you wish to delete; then press the Delete key.

or

- Select the folder or file you wish to delete; then press the Delete button on the toolbar.

or

- Select the folder or file you wish to delete; then select Delete from the File menu.

In each case, a Confirm Delete message window will display. Click the Yes button if you want to delete the file or the folder (and the folder's contents), or the No button if you want to cancel the action.

EXERCISE ▷ 10.6

1. Select the **Stories** subfolder in the Tree pane.

2. Select **Delete** from the **File** menu; then click the **Yes** button in the Confirm Folder Delete message box.

3. Select the **Graphics** subfolder in the Tree pane. The Bitmap Image files will display in the Contents pane.

4. Select the first file name in the Contents pane; then press **Shift** and click the third file name.

5. Press **Delete**; then click the **Yes** button in the Confirm Multiple File Delete message box.

Changing File Attributes

If you've ever accidentally deleted or changed files, you know how annoying and upsetting it can be. And if you haven't, you surely do not want to experience this! With Windows, you can take every precaution to avoid such time-wasting, irritating, frustrating accidents.

Windows permits you to place controls on file operations by assigning one or more attributes to a file. An *attribute* is a hidden code or "flag" placed in a file. Windows uses such flags both to identify the type of file and to determine the operations that are permissible.

For example, you want to avoid the possibility of accidentally deleting system files. Your computer simply will not operate without certain system files! To protect them from the possibility of being deleted, you can flag system files with the *hidden attribute*. *Hidden files* will not be displayed when you use conventional commands to show or list files. Of course, the files are stored on your disk, but the Hidden attribute protects them, hides them away, gives them anonymity. The idea is, if they're hard to find, they're hard to delete!

You can assign up to four attributes to a single file. The four attributes, their flag codes, and brief explanations of each are shown in Table 10-1.

TABLE 10-1
File attributes

Attribute	Flag Code	Explanation
Read-only	R	Prevents a file from being changed. Flags the file and limits its contents to being read into memory or copied, but not written to.
Archive	A	Automatically assigned to any file you create or modify. Some backup and copy utility programs turn off the Archive attribute.
Hidden	H	Conceals the file name from routine folder listings. (Especially useful if others use your computer or if you work on sensitive or confidential information.)
System	S	Identifies a file that is critical to system operation. A system attribute can be assigned only by the operating system (that's why this option is unavailable—grayed out—in Figure 10-8).

FIGURE 10-8
General tab in a file's Properties dialog box

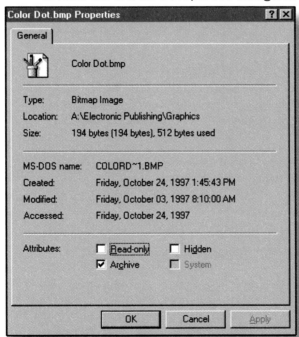

The *read-only attribute* is the most frequently used attribute. Let's say you have created a long report and saved it as a file. You want coworkers to have access to and to read the file data, but how can you make sure they do not change the text? Answer: By assigning the read-only attribute, you limit other users to only reading the file; they cannot *change* the file. The read-only attribute also helps protect your files from many destructive viruses.

How do you assign a file attribute? By selecting the file and then clicking the Properties button on the toolbar. At the bottom of the General properties tab (Figure 10-8) the four attributes are listed, and three are available to you. (The system attribute is assigned only by Windows.) Just click a check box to assign that attribute.

Above the check boxes in Figure 10-8, you see information about the selected file, mostly the same information you see when you select the Details view in Explorer's Contents window.

You remove a file attribute using the same process: Display the Properties dialog box and click the check box of the attribute you want to remove.

EXERCISE ⇨ 10.7

1. Select the **Graphics** subfolder in the Tree pane.

2. Select the **Color Dot** file in the Contents pane. Click the **Properties** button on the toolbar. The Properties dialog box for the **Color Dot** file displays on your screen.

3. Click the **Read-only** check box to assign the read-only attribute, click the **Apply** button, and then click the **Close** button. Now let's rename **Color Dot** to **Blue Dots**.

4. Select the **Color Dot** file in the Contents pane; then select **Rename** from the **File** menu.

5. Key the new name **Blue Dots**, and press **Enter**. The message shown in Figure 10-9 displays asking you whether you want to change this read-only file.

6. Click **No** to close the message box.

7. Click the **Color Dot** file in the Contents pane; then select the **Properties** button on the toolbar.

8. Click the **Read-only** check box to remove the check mark.

9. Click the **Apply** button, and then click the **Close** button.

10. Click the **Close** button to close Windows Explorer. If instructed, shut down Windows and your computer.

FIGURE 10-9
Confirm File Rename dialog box

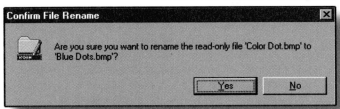

FIGURE 10-9
Confirm File Rename dialog box

Summary

This lesson covered how to work with files and folders in Windows Explorer. You learned that:

■ View menu options in Explorer allow you to sort the Contents pane by name, type, size, or date.

■ Before you can copy, delete, rename, or use an object, you must select it.

■ In the Tree pane, you can select only one folder at a time. In the Contents pane, you can select any number of objects displayed. You can drag a rectangle around adjacent files you want to select.

■ Objects are copied and moved from a source to a destination. Explorer simplifies both processes by allowing you to use the mouse to drag the selected file or folder to its destination.

■ You can delete folders and files in a single action. When you delete a folder or subfolder, you also delete all the files in it. Folders and files deleted from the hard disk are placed in the Recycle Bin and can be recovered (undeleted); objects deleted from a floppy disk are not placed in the Recycle Bin and cannot be recovered!

■ File attributes are hidden codes or flags that allow you to place controls on files. The four file attributes are read-only, archive, hidden, and system.

MATCHING

Write the letter of the term in the right column that matches the definition in the left column.

_____ 1. A file that can only be read into memory or copied from one location to another.

_____ 2. A code or "flag" placed in a file to identify the type of file and to control the type of operations that can be performed on that file.

_____ 3. A file that does not appear on a regular folder listing.

_____ 4. Key you press to select consecutive files or folders.

_____ 5. Key you press to select nonconsecutive files or folders.

A. Shift

B. Ctrl

C. attribute

D. read-only

E. hidden

FILL IN THE BLANKS

Complete the following sentences by writing the correct word or words in the blanks provided.

1. To copy a file or folder to a location on the same disk, you hold down the _____ key while dragging.

2. To move a file or folder from the Contents pane to a different disk in the Tree pane, you hold down the _____ key while dragging.

3. The _____ attribute is assigned automatically to any file you create or modify.

4. The _____ attribute is useful if your files are confidential or sensitive.

5. The _____ attribute can be assigned only by the operating system.

LESSON 10 PROJECT

This project gives you the opportunity to review the concepts in this lesson and practice the techniques in the exercises. You will need your Windows Template disk and Windows Practice disk in order to complete this project.

1. Start **Explorer**. Insert the Windows Template disk in the floppy disk drive. Copy the **Project 10** folder to the desktop.

2. Insert your Windows Practice disk and move the **Project 10** folder from the desktop to your Windows Practice disk.

3. Select the drive containing your Windows Practice disk in the Tree pane, expand the **Project 10** folder in the Tree pane, and then display the contents of the **Project Reports** folder in the Contents pane. Select the **Project 10 Report Form** file and then choose **Print** from the **File** menu.

4. With the Project 10 folder selected in the Tree pane, do the following:
   a. Add a new subfolder called **Special Report** to the Project 10 folder.
   b. Copy all Microsoft Word files from the Project 10 folder to the Special Report subfolder.
   c. Rename each of the Chapter files in the Special Report subfolder by changing the word *Chapter* to **Part**. (You will have to rename the four files one file at a time.)
   d. Move all of the Progress Report files from the Progress Reports subfolder to the Special Report subfolder.
   e. Delete the **Progress Reports** subfolder.

5. Assign the read-only attribute to all of the files with *Budget* in their name in the Project 10 folder.

6. Using the **Project 10 Report Form** you printed in step 1, do the following:
   a. Fill in the heading with the appropriate information.
   b. Answer all questions on the Report Form using Explorer to display the appropriate folder and subfolder contents.

7. Close **Explorer**. If instructed, shut down Windows and your computer.

Using Explorer's Find Feature

OBJECTIVES

Upon completion of this lesson, you will be able to:

■ Search a folder for a specific file.

■ Search files and folders using wildcards.

■ Search by date.

■ Search by type of file, by text, and by size.

■ Use the Find command to select specified files.

■ Run applications from Explorer. ⏱ **Estimated Time: 1.5 hours**

Being able to quickly find files or folders is a feature of Windows Explorer that will help you work more efficiently. In this lesson, you will learn how to use the Find option to locate files and folders that meet specified criteria.

The Find Option

Explorer's Find feature allows you to locate:

■ One file among many within a folder.

■ One folder among many on a disk.

■ All folders and files with similar names.

■ All files that share a common characteristic (file type, file size, or text).

To find a file or folder, select Explorer's Find option from the Tools menu; then from the submenu, select the Files or Folders option. The Find: All Files dialog box displays, as shown in Figure 11-1. If you are searching for a specific file or folder, key the name in the Named text box on the Name & Location tab. If you do not know the exact name or you want to search for a group of files, you can use the asterisk (*) as a wildcard character (explained in the next section). You can even key a list of file names in the text box (leave a space after each file name). The text box will accommodate long lists, and it will keep scrolling the file names as you add to the list.

FIGURE 11-1

FIGURE 11-1
Find: All Files dialog box

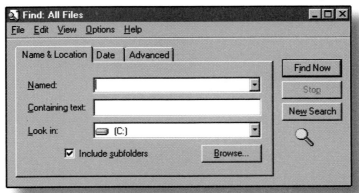

If the Include subfolders option is checked, when you click the Find Now button Explorer searches the selected folder and all its subfolders (if any) for the search text. If Include subfolders is not selected, the search is limited to the currently selected folder.

EXERCISE 11.1

1. Launch Windows Explorer.

2. Select drive **C:** (or the drive that contains the Windows folder).

3. Select the **Windows** folder in the Tree pane.

4. Verify that the **Details** view is selected.

5. Select **Find** from the **Tools** menu; then select **Files or Folders** from the submenu. Verify that the **Name & Location** tab is displayed and that the appropriate drive and folder are displayed

in the Look in text box (**C:\Windows** if the Windows folder is stored on drive C:).

6. Key the file name **Ansi.sys** in the **Named** text box.

7. Verify that the **Include subfolders** check box is selected (checked).

8. Click the **Find Now** button to start the search. The Search Results window displays in the Find: All Files dialog box, as shown in Figure 11-2.

FIGURE 11-2
Search Results window

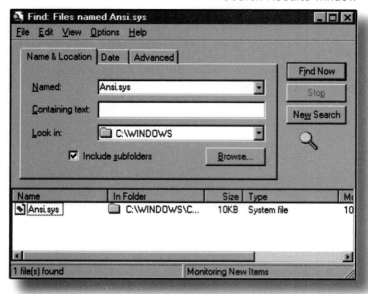

Like the Explorer window, the Search Results window can be displayed in four views: Large Icons, Small Icons, List, and Details. When the Details view is selected, the Search Results window displays the match data in five columns, one for each criterion in the match: Name, location (In Folder), Size, Type, and date last modified (Modified).

In Figure 11-2, the location listing—that is, the In Folder column—offers very useful information, namely, the *path* to the file you were searching for: C:\WINDOWS\COMMAND. The path is always written in a standard direction from general to specific. Thus the complete path for the file **Ansi.sys** is:

C:\WINDOWS\COMMAND\ANSI.SYS

In other words: "The **Ansi.sys** file is located in the Command subfolder in the Windows folder on drive C:."

The above search was not case sensitive (usually used only for long file name and text searches). To activate this option, select Case Sensitive on the Options menu.

You can save the results of a search for later use by selecting the Save Search option on the File menu. Explorer will create an icon on the desktop that, when opened, will display the Find: All Files dialog box with the specified search criteria already filled in. To complete the search, simply click the Find Now button.

You do not have to close and reopen the Find: All Files dialog box between searches. Clicking the New Search button (see Figure 11-2) in the dialog box displays a message box informing you that you are clearing the current search. Click the OK button to begin a new search. When you begin a new search in this way, you must once again specify the appropriate drive and folder in the Look in box. The simplest way to do this is by using the Browse button. When you click this button, Windows displays a Browse for Folder dialog box that closely resembles Explorer's Tree pane. In this dialog box you can expand levels as necessary to find the drive or folder where you want your search to begin. Click the desired drive or folder and then the OK button to return to the Find: All Files dialog box. The Look in box then shows the drive or folder you selected.

Searching with Wildcards

People who create lots of files may at times forget an exact file name. To simplify the search for files when you are not sure of the exact and complete name, Explorer lets you use the asterisk (*) as a *wildcard character* for help. In a path, an asterisk (*) means "I'm not positive of the exact characters up to this point (or from this point on)—in fact, there may be no additional characters up to this point or from this point on!"

Previous versions of DOS and Windows had a one-asterisk limit, but Windows 98 lets you use multiple asterisks within a file name specification for a file search. And to simplify searches even further, by default Windows ignores case in the Named text box.

Here are some examples to show how you might use wildcards effectively in the Named text box on the Name & Location tab:

- If you know the file name is *Readme* (for example) and you know it has an extension, but you do not remember the extension, use * for the extension. In the Named text box, enter: **Readme.***. The search finds **Readme.doc**, *readme*.txt, *readme* (a file with no extension), and so on.

- If you know the extension is *.txt* (for example) but you do not know the file name, use * for the file name. In the Named text box, enter: ***.txt**. The search finds all files with the extension *.txt* (**Chapter1**.*txt*, **Readme**.*txt*, **report**.*txt*, and so on).

- If you know the file begins with the name *Read* (for example) but you do not know the entire name or extension, use * to represent what you do not know. In the Named text box, enter: **Read***. The search finds all file names that begin with the letters *Read*: **Read**me.doc, *read*er.txt, **Read**y, **Read**e (a person's name), and so on.

- If you know that the file name includes the letters *up* (for example) somewhere in its name but you are not sure whether the name *begins* with *up* or *ends* with *up*, use * twice—before and after *up*. In the Named text box, enter: ***up***. The search finds the file names **Start**U*p*, **Back**up.cnt, S*up*port.doc, *up*s, invoice.*up*s, and so on.

EXERCISE ⟹ 11.2

1. The Find: All Files dialog box should still be open on your screen.

2. Maximize the **Find: All Files** dialog box window.

3. Click the **New Search** button, then click the **OK** button to clear the last search.

4. Key ***.cnt** in the Named text box.

5. Reset the C:\Windows path in the Look in text box by using the Browse button:
   a. Click the **Browse** button.
   b. In the Browse for Folder dialog box, navigate the tree to locate the Windows folder.

   c. Highlight the **Windows** folder and click the **OK** button to return to the Find: All Files dialog box.

6. Check the **Include subfolders** check box if it is not already checked.

7. Click the **Find Now** button to start the search.

8. The number of files located will display in the status bar at the bottom of the dialog box. If the listing is very long, scroll bars will be provided.

Searching by Date

Even occasional computer users fill their disks easily! When you do, you will appreciate the benefits from using the Find: All Files dialog box's Date tab (see Figure 11-3). Rather than search through all the files on a disk or in a folder, the Date tab lets you narrow your search according to the file's creation date or modification date.

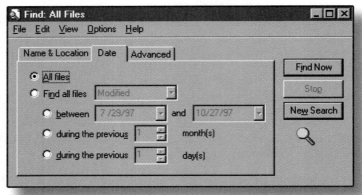

FIGURE 11-3
Date tab in the Find: All Files dialog box

To use this feature to find files, click the Find all files button; then select one of the three available options to search by date:

- **Between x and x.** Select this option to specify a range of dates—that is, the month, day, and year of both the starting and the ending dates (for example, you might enter "January 1, 1997," and "December 31, 1997"). Explorer will then find any file or folder that was created or modified within the range specified.

- **During the previous x month(s).** Select this option to search for files or folders that were created or modified within the last x months—you specify how many months by keying the number or clicking the up and down arrows to set the number. For example, you may key "2" to locate all the files that were created or modified within the last two months.

- **During the previous x day(s).** Select this option to search for files or folders that were created or modified within the last few days. For example, you may use this option to find a file you created a few days ago when you don't know where you saved it.

EXERCISE ⟹ 11.3

1. The **Find: All Files** dialog box should be displayed and maximized.

2. Click the **New Search** button; then click the **OK** button in the message box to indicate you wish to begin a new search.

3. Key the search characters *win* plus the wildcard * in the Named text box: **win***.

4. Verify that the c: is the path and that the **Include subfolders** check box is checked.

5. Click the **Find Now** button to start the search. Do not close the Find: All Files dialog box when the search is completed.

6. Note how many files Explorer found (the number is displayed in the status bar at the bottom of the search results window).

7. Now narrow the search to files that were created or modified between June 1, 1997, and July 31, 1997: Click on the **Date** tab in the **Find: All Files** dialog box.

8. Click the **Find all files** button; then click on the **between** button.

9. Double-click in the text box immediately after the word *between* to select the default date; then key the beginning date, **6/1/97**. Did you notice that when you began to key the date, the former date was deleted from the text box?

10. Double-click in the ending date text box; then key the ending date, **7/31/97**.

11. Click the **Find Now** button. Explorer locates all of the files and folders on drive C: (a) that have names beginning with the letters *win* and (b) that were created or modified between June 1, 1997 and July 31, 1997.

12. Note how many files Explorer found. Are there more, fewer, or the same number of files as in the previous search?

13. Select **Save Search** from the **File** menu. You won't see anything happen.

14. Click the **Close** button to close the **Find: All Files** dialog box; then minimize **Explorer** (and any other application you may have open). The search results you saved will be displayed on your desktop as an icon of a folder and computer similar to the one shown in Figure 11-4. Remain in this screen for the next exercise.

FIGURE 11-4
Search results saved on desktop

Performing Advanced Searches

You can use the third tab in the Find: All Files dialog box, Advanced (Figure 11-5), in combination with the other two tabs (Name & Location and Date) to further narrow your search criteria.

FIGURE 11-5
Advanced tab in the Find: All Files dialog box

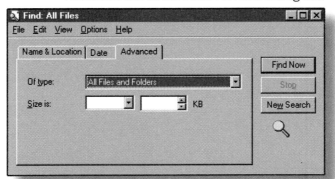

The Advanced tab has two search criteria:

- **Of type**. Use this option to select exactly which type of folder or file you want to include in the search. The drop-down list contains all the file types that Windows recognizes by their application. For example, if you want a list of only Microsoft Word documents that match your search criteria, select Microsoft Word Document from the Of type drop-down list.

- **Size is**. Use this option to search for files or folders by size. You have the option of selecting files that are "at least" as large as a specified size or "at most" the specified size. For example, if you want a list of only those files no larger than 350KB, you would select the At most option from the drop-down list box and then key "350" in the size box. The size can also be set by clicking the up or down arrow to the right of the size box.

Now let's further narrow our search of all files and folders that begin with the letters *win*. Let's limit our search to only application files of 50KB or larger.

E X E R C I S E ⟹ 11.4

1. Double-click the saved search results icon on the desktop to open the **Find: All Files** dialog box.

2. Maximize the **Find: All Files** dialog box; then click the **Find Now** button to display the search results.

3. Click the **Advanced** tab.

4. Click the **Of type** drop-down list arrow; then select **Application**.

5. Click the **Size is** drop-down list arrow; then select **At least**.

6. Press **Tab** to move to the next text box; then key **50**.

7. Click the **Find Now** button to begin the search. Note the number of files that are listed in the Search Results window. Do they meet your criteria? (Do they begin with the letters *win*? Are they larger than 50KB? Are they application programs? Were they created or modified between June 1, 1997, and July 31, 1997?)

8. Click the **Close** button to close the **Find: All Files** dialog box.

9. On the desktop, delete the saved search results icon: Click to select the icon, then press the **Delete** key.

Explorer can also search computers on your network (if you are connected to a network). Select the Computer option on the Find submenu. To search for a site on the Internet, select On the Internet on the Find submenu. A dialog box, similar to the one shown in Figure 11-6, opens. Fill in the address of the Web page you want to find.

FIGURE 11-6
Finding a site on the Internet

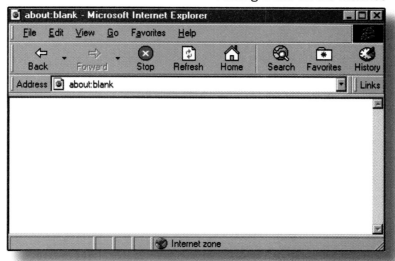

   NOTE:

The Explorer's QuickFinder tool lets you find files by name or content. You open QuickFinder by selecting using QuickFinder on the Find submenu.

Using the Find Command to Select Files

You can also use the Find command as a way to select nonadjacent files that have some common feature. Once Find shows the files in the search results box, you can select them just as you would select files in the Explorer Contents pane.

E X E R C I S E ⟹ 11.5

1. Select **Find** from the **Tools** menu; then select **Files or Folders**.

2. Maximize the **Find: All Files** dialog box.

3. If necessary, click the **Name & Location** tab.

4. Key the wildcard and extension ***.ini** in the **Named** text box, press **Tab**, and then select the drive where the Windows folder is located (usually drive **C:**).

5. Click the **Advanced** tab in the **Find: All Files** dialog box; then click the **Size is** drop-down list arrow and select **At least** from the drop-down list.

6. Press **Tab** and key **4** or click the up arrow until the number 4 appears in the box; then click the

(continued on next page)

Find Now button. Your screen should resemble Figure 11-7.

7. Select all the files using one of the methods you learned earlier.

8. Close the **Find: All Files** dialog box. Remain in this screen for the next exercise.

FIGURE 11-7
Search results

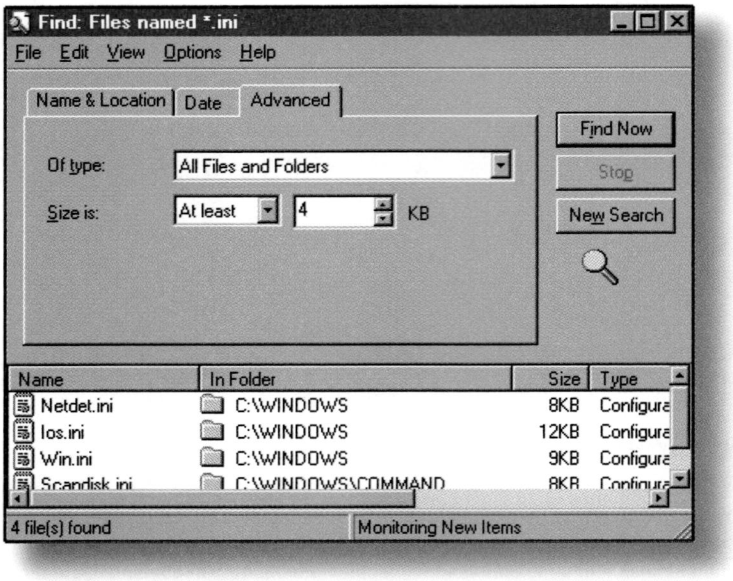

Running Applications from Explorer

In Lesson 7, you learned that you can start an application or open a document and its associated application at the same time by clicking the appropriate icons in the My Computer display window. You can use the same techniques to start applications and open documents in Explorer.

Remember that an application file icon looks like a miniature version of a program icon or like a miniature window. To start an application in Explorer using an application file icon:

■ Double-click the icon in the Contents pane.

or

■ Click the icon to select it, then choose Open from the File menu.

Remember that a document file icon resembles a piece of paper with a superimposed graphic that represents the associated application. To open a document and start its associated application at the same time in Explorer, double-click the document file icon in the Contents pane.

EXERCISE 11.6

1. In the Explorer Tree pane, select the **Windows** folder.

2. Scroll the Contents pane until you locate the Pbrush application icon, which looks like a small paint palette.

3. Double-click the **Pbrush** application icon. The Paint accessory application starts and displays a blank Paint screen, as shown in Figure 11-8.

4. Click the Paint window's **Close** button to close the application.

5. Scroll the Contents pane until you find a file called **Setup.bmp** identified by an icon showing

an abstract image and paintbrush on a piece of paper. The art image suggests the association of this file with the Paint program.

6. Double-click the **Setup** file. The Paint application starts and displays the Paint file Windows uses when setting up Windows 98 on a hard drive, as shown in Figure 11-9.

7. Click the **Close** button on the Paint document to close the application.

8. Close **Explorer**. If instructed, shut down Windows and your computer.

FIGURE 11-8
The application file icon opens the Paint program

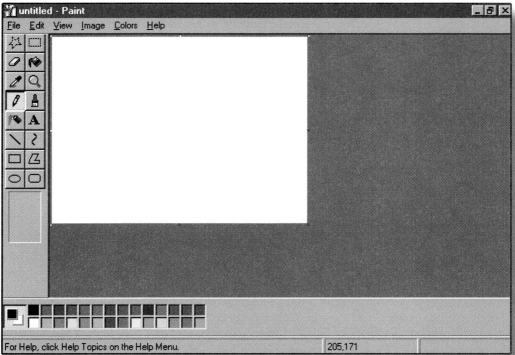

FIGURE 11-9

Clicking a document file icon opens both the application and the document

Summary

This lesson covered how to search for files and folders in Windows Explorer. You learned that:

■ Explorer's Find option lets you search for a specific file or for a specific group of files. You can use the wildcard character * (which means "any character") to substitute for a name or extension that you do not know.

■ The Find: All Files dialog box's Date tab lets you narrow a search according to the file's creation date. You can search for a file created or modified within a range of dates, during a specified number of months, or within a few days.

■ Using Explorer's advanced search features, you can narrow your search criteria by type of file or folder, files containing a specified string of characters, or a specified size or range of sizes.

■ Explorer can search computers on your network (if you are connected to a network) and on the Internet.

■ To run an application, select the application's icon and use the Open command in the File menu or double-click the application's icon in the Contents pane. Yet another option: If a document is associated with an application program, double-click on the document's icon in the Contents pane.

LESSON 11 REVIEW QUESTIONS

TRUE/FALSE

Each of the following statements is either true or false. Indicate your answer on the left by circling T if the statement is true and F if the statement is false.

T   F   1. You can key several names in the Named text box of the Find: All Files dialog box if you leave a space after each file name.

T   F   2. A search for files or folders can contain only one criterion for each search.

T   F   3. The search results window can be displayed in Details view only.

T   F   4. The asterisk (*) is a commonly used wildcard character.

T   F   5. When you save a search, the results are automatically saved in the My Documents folder on your computer's hard disk.

MULTIPLE CHOICE

Complete the following questions by circling the correct multiple choice letter.

1. The Find option on the Tools menu allows you to locate
   - **A.** one file among many within a folder
   - **B.** one folder among many on a disk
   - **C.** all the folders and files with similar names
   - **D.** all of the above

2. Which of the following would you key in the Named text box in the Find: All Files dialog box to locate all files containing the words *service* and *reservation*?
   - **A.** serv*
   - **B.** *serv
   - **C.** *serv*
   - **D.** none of the above

3. The Of type search criteria on the Advanced tab of the Find: All Files dialog box lets you search for
   - **A.** all files and folders that share a common name
   - **B.** all files saved in a specified file format
   - **C.** all files that share a common character
   - **D.** all files of a specified size

4. If you wanted to find a file that was created yesterday, which option on the Date tab would you choose:
   A. Between x and x
   B. During the previous x month(s)
   C. During the previous x day(s)
   D. None of the above

5. When you save a search, the results are saved as:
   A. an icon on the taskbar
   B. an icon on the desktop
   C. a file in the My Documents folder
   D. a file in an unnamed folder on the desktop

LESSON 11 PROJECT

This project gives you the opportunity to review the concepts in this lesson and practice the techniques in the exercises. You will need your Windows Template disk in order to complete this project.

1. Start **Explorer**. Insert your Windows Template disk in the appropriate disk drive. Expand the contents of the disk in the Tree pane and then select the **Project 11** folder to display its contents in the Contents pane.

2. Use the **Find** feature to find and print the **Project 11 Report Form** file.

3. Using the Project 11 Report Form you printed in step 2, fill in the heading with the appropriate information.

4. Using Explorer's **Find** option, search your Project 11 folder to find the answers to the questions on the Project 11 Report Form.

5. Close **Explorer**. If instructed, shut down Windows and your computer.

UNIT 3 REVIEW QUESTIONS 🔽

WRITTEN QUESTIONS

Answer the questions below on a separate piece of paper.

1. List and briefly explain the purposes of Explorer.

2. Identify the parts of the Explorer window and explain the purpose of each part.

3. Explain how the wildcard character can be used to search for files.

4. Discuss the different techniques available to select multiple folders or files.

5. Explain the purpose of a file attribute, and give at least two examples of how different attributes may be used.

6. Discuss the two options available when using the Advanced tab in the Find: All Files dialog box and give an example of when each might be used.

7. Discuss what happens to a file that is deleted from the hard disk, whether the file can be restored, and what you must do to restore it.

8. List three reasons for collapsing the All Folders tree and discuss each reason.

9. Identify each of the options available on Explorer's Date tab and give an example of when each option would be used.

10. Explain how to save search results, and then how to delete the saved search results.

UNIT 3 APPLICATION 🔽

SCANS

    Shawna Walker, the office manager for Corporate Communique, wants to organize the files and folders on her computer using Windows Explorer. Shawna maintains all types of files, including payroll spreadsheets, vendor lists, client information, form letters, and the like.

Start Windows Explorer. Insert your Windows Template disk in the appropriate drive and copy the **CorpComm Operations** folder to the desktop. Remove the Windows Template disk and insert your Windows Practice disk. Move the CorpComm Operations folder to your Windows Practice disk. Rename the folder **CC Operations**.

Create folders in the CC Operations folder named **Employees**, **Vendors**, **Clients**, and **Miscellaneous**.

Move the **Client List** text file, the **Clients** database file, and the **Invoice** spreadsheet file to the Clients folder. Move the **Vendors** text file to the Vendors folder. Move the **Payroll**, **Expense Report**, and **Timecards** spreadsheet files to the Employees folder. Move the **IRS Letter**, **Moving Announcement**, and **Open House** text files to the Miscellaneous folder.

Close all open folders. Then, search your Windows Practice disk for the **Timecards** file.

Close Windows Explorer. If instructed, shut down Windows and your computer.

CRITICAL THINKING

In the Unit 2 Critical Thinking activity, you were instructed to create a folder system on a blank disk using My Computer. Insert the disk and display its contents using Windows Exporer. Display the disk's folders and subfolders in the Tree pane. Display subfolders of the various parent folders in the Contents pane.

Create a sketch of the expanded folder structure as it appears in the Explorer's Tree pane. Make sure you include the plus and minus icons to the left of each folder. Write a short explanation of why a folder has a plus or minus icon beside it. When you are done, collapse the folders and close Explorer.

ACCESSORY APPLICATIONS

UNIT 4

Estimated Time for Unit 4: 7.5 hours

LESSON 12

USING NOTEPAD

OBJECTIVES

Upon completion of this lesson, you will be able to:

- Identify an accessory application.
- Start Notepad.
- Key text in a Notepad document.
- Move around in a Notepad document.
- Save and close a Notepad document.
- Print a Notepad document.

⏱ **Estimated Time: 1.5 hours**

A major feature of Windows is that it can run several programs simultaneously. In fact, Windows comes with a number of helpful accessory applications, often called *applets* or just *accessories*, that are designed to be used while you are working in a program application—that's why they are called "accessory applications." In this lesson, you will learn how to use *Notepad*—a simple word processing program.

Introducing the Accessory Applications

The names of some Windows accessories broadly hint at the features you can expect from them: Notepad, Calculator, WordPad, Character Map, Phone Dialer, and Paint. You can use the accessories to perform the functions for which you'd use "real" desk accessories. Just as you keep a real notepad and a real calculator within reach on your desk, on screen you can keep the Notepad icon and the Calculator icon handy.

Notepad, Calculator, and Phone Dialer are often called *Personal Information Managers*, or *PIMs*. These are the accessories that most closely resemble the physical objects you might keep on your real desk to help you manage your work, your files, and your notes. That's why these particular desktop accessories deserve the special title Personal Information Managers.

PIMs are loaded into memory while you are working with them, and they remain loaded in memory when you move to other applications. As a result, you can access PIMs and other applications easily by pressing Alt+Tab or by clicking the application on the taskbar.

The Notepad Application

Notepad is a simplistic word processing program. It uses only one *font* (a set of letters, numbers, and symbols of the same size and shape), and it reads and writes ASCII *text files* only (files that contain words and numbers but no formatting codes or control characters). Thus you won't want to use Notepad to create long, complex documents. But Notepad's limitations enable it to work more quickly on-screen than more sophisticated programs with full font and text displays.

Notepad is generally used to:

■ Create files that can be sent to a computer bulletin board or through an electronic mail system.

■ Create and modify DOS files such as those with .BAT file extensions or Windows system files with .INI file extensions.

■ Key simple notes, quick reminders, records of phone calls, and daily "to do" lists.

You may want to leave Notepad open on the taskbar to make it easy to quickly jot down reminder notes—for example, notes from phone calls.

Starting Notepad

You start Notepad (and other Accessories applications) by clicking the Start menu, moving the mouse to Programs, and then to Accessories. The accessories icons display on a submenu, as shown in Figure 12-1. (Your Accessories menu may differ as a result of your system's configuration.) Figure 12-2 shows a closer view of the Accessories menu. Note that Windows supplies an icon representing each accessory's function, plus its name.

FIGURE 12-1
Starting an accessory application

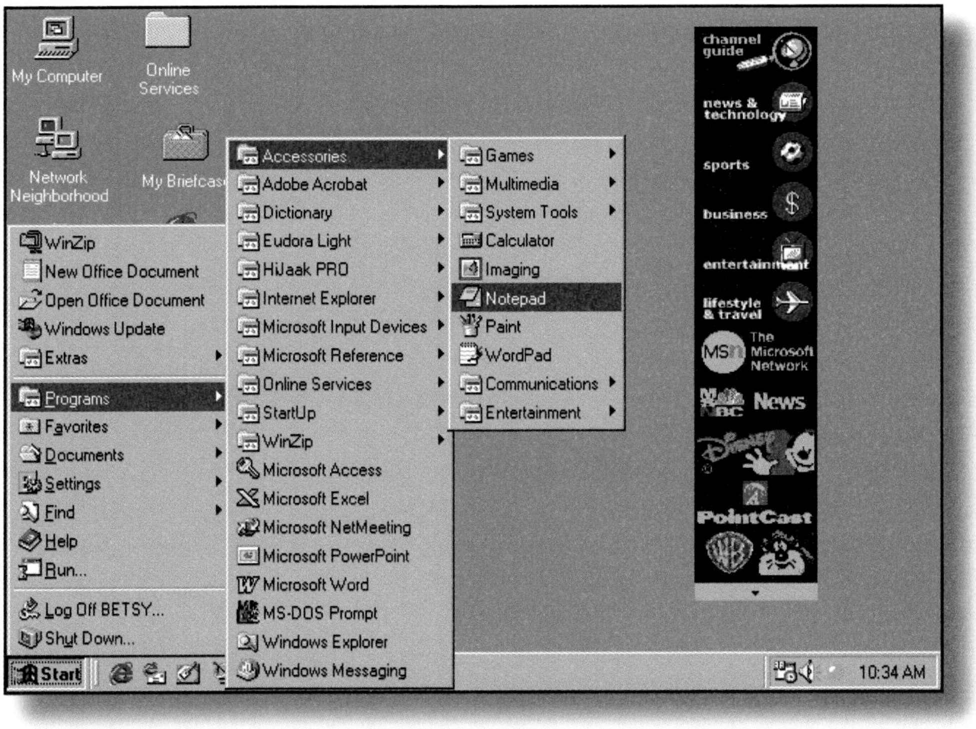

You can start Notepad by clicking Start, moving the pointer to Programs and then to Accessories, and finally clicking the Notepad icon on the Accessories submenu. The Notepad window displays, as shown in Figure 12-3.

As you see in Figure 12-3, the Notepad title bar reads "Untitled - Notepad." Below the title bar is a menu bar with four menu options: File, Edit, Search, and Help. Below the menu bar is the work area, where you will key text. The cursor, a thin blinking vertical line that indicates the insertion point, appears at the top of the work area. The cursor marks the place where text will be entered when you begin keying. When you key text, each character you key appears to the left of the cursor. You will notice that the mouse pointer changes shape to look like a letter *I*. This is called an *I-beam pointer*.

Keying Text

Although the word *notepad* may bring an image to your mind of a program that is very small, a Notepad document can hold nearly 50,000 characters (eight to ten pages). If you create a larger file, an error message will display saying you have insufficient memory (the message displays regardless of how much memory your system has).

FIGURE 12-3
Opening Notepad window

In Notepad you may choose *Word Wrap*, an option on the Edit menu, to let the computer determine end-of-line breaks for you. Notice that in Notepad, Word Wrap is not the default, which means you have to click Word Wrap if you want your text to wrap around to the next line. Figure 12-4 shows Notepad text with and without the Word Wrap option activated.

FIGURE 12-4
Notepad text without (top) and with (bottom) the Word Wrap
option selected

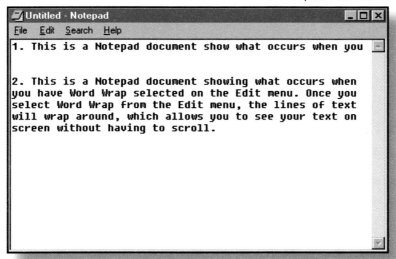

Once Word Wrap is selected, you simply start keying text at the blinking cursor. Of course, making mistakes while keying text is to be expected, and there are a couple of ways to correct mistakes as you are going along in the document:

1. Press the Backspace key if your cursor is to the right of the error you wish to correct.

2. Press the Delete key if your cursor is to the left of the error you wish to correct.

As you key text, use the Shift key to capitalize letters and to use most common symbols on the keyboard. Also, be sure to use Enter only when you finish keying text at the end of a paragraph, not at the end of each line.

EXERCISE 12.1

1. Start Windows, if it is not already running.

2. Open Notepad by clicking the **Start** button, moving the highlight to **Programs** and then **Accessories**; then select **Notepad** from the **Accessories** menu.

3. Select **Word Wrap** from the **Edit** menu.

4. Now key the following text:

   Windows 98 is software that
   provides a simpler way to manage
   your computer, your
   applications, your documents,
   and your printer. It provides
   you with state-of-the-art
   Internet access capabilities,
   and gives you the power to
   transform your PC into an
   interactive multimedia center.

5. Use Backspace and Delete to correct any keying errors.

6. Leave the text on screen for the next exercise.

Moving Around in a Notepad Document

You can move around the Notepad window using either the mouse or the keyboard.

MOVING WITH THE MOUSE

■ If your document has more text than can be displayed in the current window, Notepad offers a vertical scroll bar. If text is not wrapped, Notepad displays a horizontal scroll bar. Click on these scroll bars as necessary to bring other parts of the document into view.

■ To move the cursor anywhere in the document, position the I-beam and then click.

MOVING WITH THE KEYBOARD

■ To scroll a page, press Page Up or Page Down.

■ To move to the beginning of a line, press Home.

■ To move to the end of a line, press End.

■ To move to the beginning or end of a document, press Ctrl+Home or Ctrl+End, respectively.

■ To move the cursor anywhere in the document, press the arrow keys.

EXERCISE ⟹ 12.2

1. Move the cursor anywhere in the text: Position the I-beam and then click.

2. Press the up arrow or the down arrow to scroll one line at a time.

3. Press the **Home** key to move to the beginning of the line. Press the **End** key to move to the end of the line.

4. Press **Ctrl+End** to move to the end of the document.

5. Use arrow keys to return to the beginning of the document.

6. Leave the text on screen for the next exercise.

Saving a Notepad Document

You can save Notepad documents on disk by using either the Save or the Save As option on the File menu. Use Save As the first time you save a file, because Save As requires you to name your file. After you have saved a file the first time, you can select Save to store revisions to the file.

Choosing Save As opens the Save As dialog box shown in Figure 12-5. This dialog box should remind you of the My Computer window. In this dialog box, you can choose where to save the file by clicking appropriate drives or folders. The File name text box (which currently reads Untitled) lets you supply a name for the file. Using the Save as type drop-down list, you can choose a file type for the document. If you decide you don't want to save the file after all, click the Cancel button to return to your document.

FIGURE 12-5
Save As dialog box

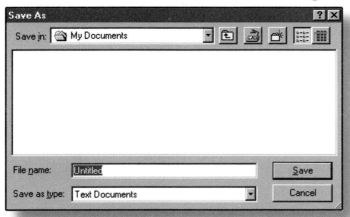

FIGURE 12-5
Save As dialog box

The Save As option also provides a way to copy files. You can use Save As to copy a file on the same disk using a new file name, or to copy a file on a different disk using the same file name.

EXERCISE ▷ 12.3

1. Insert your Windows Practice disk in the appropriate floppy disk drive.

2. Select **Save As** from the **File** menu. The Save As dialog box displays.

3. Select the drive that contains your Windows Practice disk from the Save in drop-down list. The contents of the Windows Practice disk display in the window.

4. The Save as type list box should display Text Documents. If it doesn't, click the down arrow

to display the drop-down list, then click **Text Documents**.

5. Highlight the *Untitled* name in the **File name** text box. Key a new file name: **New Notes**.

6. Click the **Save** button.

7. The file is saved and you are returned to the Notepad window. Note that the new file name now appears in the title bar.

Printing a Notepad Document

Notepad offers only a few printing options—namely, margins, headers, and footers. To see the default settings for these options, select Page Setup on the File menu. The Page Setup dialog box (see Figure 12-6) displays these default settings:

■ Paper size: Letter

■ Left and right margins: 0.75 inch

■ Top and bottom margins: 1 inch

- Orientation (which direction the text prints on the paper): Portrait (text prints across, not lengthwise).

- Header: &f (indicates that the name of your file will print as the header text).

- Footer: Page &p (indicates that the word Page followed by the page number will print as the footer text).

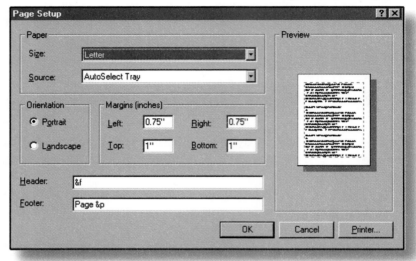

FIGURE 12-6
Page Setup dialog box

The Preview area at the right of the dialog box shows you how your printed page will look with the current settings. As you change the settings, the preview also changes.

You can change these defaults by entering new data in the text boxes. You can also change these defaults by entering any of the special header and footer codes listed in Table 12-1.

TABLE 12-1
Special Notepad codes used to format headers and footers

KEY	TO GET
&d	Current date
&t	Current time
&f	Name of your file
&p	Page number
&l	Flush left alignment
&r	Flush right alignment
&c	Center alignment

When you are satisfied with your page setup, click the OK button to return to the document. Then choose Print from the File menu to print the document.

EXERCISE ▭⟶ 12.4

1. Select **Page Setup** from the **File** menu.

2. Key these header codes: **&r&d**. These codes will position the header flush with the right margin (&r) and print the current date (&d).

3. Key these footer codes: **&cPage &p**. This command produces a footer with the word Page followed by the page number (&p) centered between the right and left margins (&c).

4. Click the **OK** button to accept the changes and to close the Page Setup dialog box.

5. Select **Print** from the **File** menu to print the document. Inspect your printed document.

6. Save the file and leave it on screen.

Closing a Notepad Document

Notepad does not have a "close document" command, but there are actually four ways you can close a Notepad document:

■ Select New from the File menu, which closes the file and opens a new Notepad file.

■ Select Open from the File menu, which closes the file and opens an existing Notepad file.

■ Select Exit from the File menu, which closes both the document and Notepad.

■ Click the Close button, which closes both the document and Notepad.

EXERCISE ▭⟶ 12.5

1. Close your Notepad document by clicking the **Close** button.

2. If a message box appears, asking if you want to save the document, click **Yes**.

3. If instructed, shut down Windows and your computer.

Summary

This lesson covered how to start, save, print, and close a Notepad document. You learned that:

■ Windows provides a number of personal information managers (PIMs)—desktop accessory applications (applets) designed to help you manage time efficiently, coordinate schedules, keep track of phone numbers, and so on. These accessories are designed to be used while you are working in a program application.

151

- Notepad lets you create simple notes, quick reminders, records of phone calls, and daily "to do" lists.

- You must choose Notepad's Word Wrap option to automatically wrap text to the next line.

- You can use the keyboard to quickly move to certain locations in the Notepad document.

- You use the Save As command to save a Notepad document for the first time or to save it with a new name or to a different location. You use the Save command to periodically save the document.

- You can control the way a Notepad document prints by changing the default settings in the Page Setup dialog box.

LESSON 12 REVIEW QUESTIONS

TRUE/FALSE

Each of the following statements is either true or false. Indicate your answer on the left by circling T if the statement is true and F if the statement is false.

T F 1. No more than one accessory program can be running in Windows at a time.

T F 2. Windows Notepad is a powerful word processing program that contains advanced features such as spell checking.

T F 3. Notepad does not automatically word wrap.

T F 4. The Save As option in Notepad can be used to copy a file.

T F 5. Selecting New from the File menu closes an open Notepad file.

MULTIPLE CHOICE

Complete the following questions by circling the correct multiple choice letter.

1. An example of a Personal Information Manager (PIM) is
    A. Notepad
    B. Phone Dialer
    C. Calculator
    D. all of the above

2. When you open Notepad, the insertion point
    A. will appear in the middle of the screen
    B. appears as a thick box-like symbol
    C. indicates the place where text will be entered when keyed
    D. none of the above

3. When you enter text in Notepad, each character you key
    A. will appear to the right of the cursor
    B. will appear to the left of the cursor
    C. will appear just above the cursor
    D. none of the above

4. Notepad will permit you to
    A. record nearly 50,000 characters in a document
    B. add pictures to the file
    C. search and replace according to the information keyed in the Find dialog box
    D. none of the above

5. Which of the following is not a method for closing a Notepad file?
    A. Click the Close button
    B. Select New from the File menu
    C. Select Close from the File menu
    D. Select Exit from the File menu

LESSON 12 PROJECT

This project gives you the opportunity to review the concepts in this lesson and practice the techniques in the exercises. You will need your Windows Practice disk in order to complete the project.

1. Start a new Notepad document.

2. Make sure that the Word Wrap option is selected. Then key the following text:

    ```
    Research the following for presentation to the Health and Safety
    Committee:

    a. Value of property owned and replacement cost.

    b. Risk potential.

    c. Medical and hospitalization insurance fringe benefit package.
    ```

3. Save the document on your Windows Practice disk; use the file name **Insurance.**

4. Proofread your document and correct any errors. Save the file.

5. Print a copy of your corrected document.

6. Close the document and Notepad.

LESSON 13

USING ADVANCED NOTEPAD FEATURES

OBJECTIVES

Upon completion of this lesson, you will be able to:

- Insert, delete, and replace text in a Notepad document.
- Copy and cut text using the Clipboard.
- Search a document.
- Use Notepad's time and date stamp feature.

⏱ **Estimated Time: 1.5 hours**

Notepad offers a number of features to help you change or *edit* the text in your documents. In this lesson, you will learn how to apply these features to create more professional-looking documents.

Editing a Notepad Document

Before you can edit text, you must select the text you wish to change. To select means to *highlight* or *block* text. Then, you can delete it, replace it, or insert new text.

Selecting Text

Select text when editing your document using any of these methods:

- Click at the beginning of the text you want to select, hold down the mouse button, and drag to the last character of the text.
- Double-click a single word.
- Choose Select All from the Edit menu to select an entire document.

    To remove the highlight from a selection, click on any blank area in the document.

Inserting, Deleting, and Replacing Text

It is simple to insert, delete, or replace text in a Notepad document.

- Add characters by moving the cursor to the desired location and then keying the text.
- Delete characters by pressing the Delete or the Backspace key, depending on the position of the cursor, or by selecting the text and then pressing Delete.

■ Replace characters by keying new text over old text: First select the text to be replaced. Next replace the highlighted text (the "old text") with the "new text"—just key the new text, and watch as it replaces the old highlighted text.

Undo changes you have just made by selecting the Undo option on the Edit menu. The Undo command gives you an opportunity to change your mind. Undo will reverse only your most recent edit.

E X E R C I S E ⟹ 13.1

1. Start **Notepad**.

2. Insert your Windows Template disk in the appropriate floppy drive.

3. Select **Open** from the **File** menu. Select the drive where your template disk is located from the Look in drop-down list.

4. Double-click the **Sample** document.

5. If necessary, select **Word Wrap** from the **Edit** menu. Resize the window if desired.

6. Click an insertion point immediately after the letter *g* in the word *working* in the second sentence.

7. Press **Spacebar** once; then use **Delete** to delete the words *on a*. Now key **with**, plus a space.

8. Click an insertion point immediately following the letter *r* in the word *computer* and insert an **s**.

9. Click an insertion point at the beginning of the first sentence of the second paragraph, click and hold down the mouse button, drag to the end of the word *though* in the next sentence, and release the mouse button.

10. Key **Although** and watch as the keyed text replaces the original highlighted text. If nec-essary, adjust space between the words *Although* and *Notepad*.

11. Click an insertion point immediately after the comma following *capabilities* in the last sentence of the second paragraph.

12. Drag to highlight the text up to the period at the end of the sentence (do not include the period), and then release the mouse button.

13. Press **Delete** to delete the text. *Do not do anything else* until you have read the next instruction.

14. Select **Undo** from the **Edit** menu. Notice that the text you just deleted is replaced in its former position. Click in a blank space to remove the highlight.

15. Remove your Windows Template disk from your floppy drive and insert your Windows Practice disk.

16. Select **Save As** on the **File** menu to save your revisions to the **Sample** document on the Windows Practice disk: Select the drive where your practice disk is located from the Look-in drop-down list. Use the existing file name, and then click **Save**.

155

Copying and Cutting Text Using the Clipboard

Notepad's Edit menu (see Figure 13-1) offers a number of additional options for editing text. The most often used editing features are Copy, Paste, and Cut.

Copy and Paste let you duplicate text (Copy) and then position it (Paste) where you wish:

- Highlight the text you want to duplicate.

- Select Copy from the Edit menu.

- Position the cursor where you want to insert the duplicated copy.

- Select Paste from the Edit menu. The duplicated text is now in its new position.

    It's that simple!
    Cut moves or removes text using a similar procedure:

- Highlight the text you want to move or remove.

- Select Cut from the Edit menu to remove text from the document.

- Select Paste from the Edit menu if you want to insert the cut text in a new position.

The Copy, Paste, and Cut features use the Windows Clipboard as a temporary storage area for a block of text. When you use the Copy or the Cut commands, you are placing text on the Clipboard; when you use the Paste command, you are emptying the contents of the Clipboard where you have positioned the insertion point.

FIGURE 13-1
Notepad's Edit menu

TIP

Right-click the mouse for quick access to Edit menu options, including Cut, Copy, and Paste.

EXERCISE 13.2

1. Open the **New Notes** file from your Windows Practice disk. If a message box appears asking if you want to save the **Sample** document, click **Yes**.

2. Select the text to copy and move: Choose **Select All** from the **Edit** menu to highlight the entire document, including the period.

3. Select **Copy** from the **Edit** menu. Selecting Copy places the text on the Clipboard. Notice that the text still appears in the document; you see no visible change. Click in any blank area to remove the highlight.

4. Open a second Notepad window: Click the **Start** button on the taskbar; move to **Pro-**

grams; then to **Accessories**; and finally, click **Notepad**.

5. In the new window, open the **Sample** file from your Windows Practice disk.

6. Choose **Word Wrap** from the **Edit** menu, if necessary.

7. Click an insertion point immediately before the first word in the first paragraph (*Windows*).

8. Press **Enter** twice to create a blank line before the first line of this document; then move your insertion point back up to the beginning line.

9. Select the **Paste** option from the **Edit** menu. Watch as the text selected in **New Notes** is copied from the Clipboard and pasted to your document at the insertion point position.

10. Click **Save As** on the **File** menu and save the document on your Windows Practice disk as **Windows Information**.

11. Click the **New Notes** document window to make it active. Close this document window by choosing **Exit** from the **File** menu.

12. Leave the **Windows Information** document on screen.

Searching a Notepad Document

The Search menu (Figure 13-2) lets you quickly locate words and phrases in a Notepad document. Starting from the insertion point, Notepad searches the document in either a forward or a backward direction.

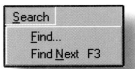

FIGURE 13-2
Notepad's
Search menu

The Search menu has two options—Find and Find Next. When you select Find, the Find dialog box (Figure 13-3) displays. To begin the search, key the text you are searching for (called the *text string*) in the Find what text box. In the Direction box choose Up (if you want to search to the beginning of the document) or Down (if you want to search to the end of the document). Remember: The starting point is the cursor's present location. Click the Find Next button to begin the search. Find then locates all occurrences of the text string.

If you want, you can limit the text search to a specific capitalization ("case") pattern. If you click the Match case check box, Find will locate only those occurrences of the text string that match the specific uppercase/lowercase pattern you've indicated. For example, if you key *File* in the Find what text box and check Match case, Find will report only instances of *File*—not *FILE*, not *file*, not *files*. In other words, Match case tells Find to report only exact string matches.

FIGURE 13-3
Find dialog box

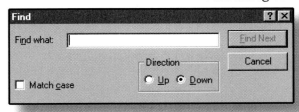

When you key a word in the Find box, Find locates not only whole words that match the text string but also parts of words that match. For instance, if you key *file* in the Find what text box, Find locates *file*, *files*, and *filename*. To find only whole words, key a space before and after the word you want to find.

E X E R C I S E ▭⟩ **13.3**

1. Move the insertion point immediately before the first word in the document.

2. Select **Find** from the **Search** menu. The Find dialog box opens.

(continued on next page)

3. In the Find what text box, key **task**.

4. Verify that the **Down** button is selected under Direction; then click the **Find Next** button. When Notepad finds the first occurrence of *task*, it highlights the word. The Find dialog box remains displayed in front of the Notepad document. (You may need to move the Find dialog box to see the highlighted word.)

5. Click **Find Next** to find further instances of *task*. Note that Find locates *taskbar* and *tasks*, which contain the text string.

6. When Notepad finds no more occurrences of the text string, it displays the Cannot find message box shown in Figure 13-4. Click the **OK** button. Move the cursor back to the beginning of the document.

7. In the **Find** dialog box, highlight **task** and key [**space**]**task**[**space**]. Click the **Find Next** button to perform the new search. Note that Find locates only the whole word *task*.

8. Close the Find dialog box and leave the **Windows Information** document on the screen.

FIGURE 13-4
The Cannot find
message box

Using Notepad's Time and Date Stamp Feature

Notepad lets you automatically place a current time and date stamp in a document each time you open the document. You can use this feature to keep a record of your activities and to log how much time you spend on each task or project—a very handy feature for the office!

To use this feature, on the first line in a Notepad document key .LOG exactly as shown (period first, followed by capital letters). Then each time you open the file, Notepad will add the current time and date to the end of the file, using your computer's clock.

1. Notepad should still be open on your screen. Select **New** from the **File** menu. Select **Yes** if you are asked if you want to save the **Windows Information** document.

2. At the cursor, key **.LOG**.

3. Select **Save As** from the **File** menu. Save the document on your Windows Practice disk as **Billing**.

4. Even though the document is still open, select **Open** from the **File** menu and double-

click **Billing**. The document displays with the current time and date. Each time you reopen the document, the time and date will display automatically.

5. Key the following text below the time and date stamp:

   ```
   Harry and Sally scheduled a
   luncheon meeting today at The
   Plaza Hotel.[Enter]
   ```

6. Select the **Save** option from the **File** menu.

7. Now wait for about two minutes (otherwise the new time and date will be exactly the same as before).

8. Select **Open** again (click **Yes** if the message box appears asking if you want to save the

Billing document) and double-click the **Billing** file name. The document displays the current time and date below the line you keyed in step 5.

9. Key the following text below the new time and date stamp:

   ```
   The Johnston contract has been
   signed. Go ahead with the lease
   purchase agreement.[Enter]
   ```

10. Select **Save** from the **File** menu.

11. Print the document.

12. Close Notepad: Select **Exit** from the **File** menu, or click the **Close** button, and click **Yes** if you are asked if you want to save changes.

Summary

This lesson covered how to edit and modify a Notepad document. You learned that:

■ You must first select text before you can edit it. You can select text by clicking at the beginning of the text you want to highlight, holding down the mouse button, and dragging to the last character of the text; by double-clicking a single word; or by choosing Select All from the Edit menu to select an entire document.

■ You can delete characters by using the Delete or Backspace keys, or by selecting the text and pressing the Delete key.

■ You can replace characters by selecting the text to be replaced and then keying the new text.

■ The Undo command on the Edit menu lets you reverse your most recent edit.

■ Notepad's Edit menu allows you several options for editing text, including copying and moving text using the Clipboard.

■ The Search menu contains commands that let you quickly locate words and phrases in a Notepad document.

■ You can place the current time and date in a document using the current time and date stamp feature.

FILL IN THE BLANKS

Complete the following sentences by writing the correct word or words in the blanks provided.

1. To select an entire Notepad document, you can choose the Select All command from the _____ menu.

2. You can _____-click a word to select it.

3. The _____ command will reverse your most recent edit in a document.

4. Cut or copied text is temporarily stored on the _____.

5. To insert the current time and date in a Notepad document, you key _____ on the first line in the document.

MATCHING

Write the letter of the term in the right column that matches the definition in the left column.

_____ 1. A Notepad feature that lets you duplicate text and place it in another location in the document.

_____ 2. A feature that allows you to find a specific text string.

_____ 3. A feature that lets you reverse your most recent change.

_____ 4. A feature that lets you remove text from a document and store it on the Clipboard.

_____ 5. A feature that lets you permanently remove text from a document.

A. Undo

B. Delete

C. Copy and Paste

D. Find

E. Cut

LESSON 13 PROJECT

This project gives you the opportunity to review the concepts in this lesson and practice the techniques in the exercises. You will need your Windows Practice disk in order to complete this project.

1. Start **Notepad** and open the **Insurance** file from your Windows Practice disk. Make sure that the **Word Wrap** option is selected.

2. Choose the **Select All** option from the **Edit** menu.

3. Select **Copy** from the **Edit** menu.

4. Open a second Notepad window. Select the **Word Wrap** option.

5. Select **Paste** from the **Edit** menu.

6. Insert two blank lines at the beginning of the document.

7. On the first line, key the following:

   `.LOG[`**`Enter`**`]`

8. Select **Time/Date** from the **Edit** menu to insert the current date and time.

9. Make the following changes to your document:
   a. Move item (c) so that it follows item (a) and realphabetize the items.
   b. Insert the word **all** before the word *property* in item (a).
   c. Insert the word **its** before the word *replacement* in item (a).
   d. Delete the words **and hospitalization** in the new item (b).

10. Proofread your document and correct any errors. Save the file to your Windows Practice disk as **New Insurance**.

11. Print a copy of your corrected document.

12. Exit Notepad. If instructed, shut down Windows and your computer.

USING CALCULATOR

Upon completion of this lesson, you will be able to:

- Open and close Calculator.

- Use the standard calculator.

- Use memory functions.

- Use Calculator's scientific mode.

- Use Calculator with other programs.

⏱ Estimated Time: 1.5 hours

As you have learned, *Calculator* is another one of Windows' handy personal information managers. In this lesson, you will learn how to start and close Calculator, and how to work in its two operating modes.

The Calculator Application

The Calculator accessory application has two operating modes—*standard* and *scientific*. On screen, Calculator appears in its own window, and its title bar reads *Calculator*. As you see in Figure 14-1, both the standard calculator and the scientific calculator offer the same three menu options: Edit, View, and Help.

You can minimize Calculator to a button on the taskbar, but the Calculator has no Maximize button. The Calculator window cannot be resized.

In either calculator mode, you can use the mouse or the keyboard to enter the numbers and arithmetic operators for your calculations. If you want to use the keyboard, you must enter numbers and arithmetic operators on the numeric keypad (located to the right of your alphabetic keyboard). Just turn on Num Lock to activate the numeric keypad.

The standard calculator can compute addition, subtraction, multiplication, and division, as well as square roots, percentages, and reciprocals. The scientific calculator is capable of very complex computations. The scientific calculator works the same as the standard calculator but contains 30 or more advanced mathematical features. Both calculators can store data in memory.

FIGURE 14-1
The standard (top) and scientific (bottom) calculators

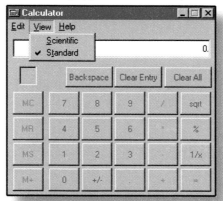

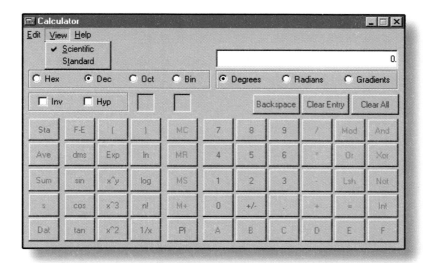

Opening and Closing Calculator

To open Calculator, click its icon on the Accessories menu. Whether the Calculator opens in the standard or in the scientific mode depends on its last setting. When you wish to change the mode, select the Standard or the Scientific option on the View menu, as shown in Figure 14-1. To close Calculator, simply click its Close button.

EXERCISE 14.1

1. Click **Calculator** on the **Accessories** menu to open the Calculator window.

2. Select **Scientific** from the **View** menu. Notice that the scientific calculator has more buttons than a standard handheld calculator.

3. Select **Standard** from the **View** menu.

Using the Standard Calculator

To operate Calculator, press the appropriate buttons, using either the mouse or the numeric keypad. This is one Windows application where you may find that using the mouse is *not* easier, at least not until you get used to it! Using the mouse, you select number and function keys by clicking the keys displayed on the calculator on your screen. Numbers appear in the display window as you select them or as Calculator computes them.

Using the numeric keypad, press the appropriate numbers and arithmetic operators on the 10-key pad. Be sure Num Lock is on before you begin to use the numeric keypad. (A light should display under Num Lock on your keyboard.) Notice all the basic arithmetic operators (/, *, −, +) appear on the keypad. See Table 14-1 for a list of the functions you can use to edit the display or to perform calculations using the keyboard or a mouse on both the standard and the scientific calculators.

TABLE 14-1

Keyboard and mouse calculator functions in both standard and scientific modes

Calculator Functions

Press	Click	To
+	+	Add
−	−	Subtract
*	*	Multiply
/	/	Divide
= or Enter	=	Execute an operation
Delete	CE	Clear last function or displayed number
Backspace or left arrow	Back	Delete the last number in the displayed value
Esc	C	Clear the current calculation
Ctrl+L	MC	Clear (erase) the value in memory
Ctrl+R	MR	Recall value from memory and retain the value in memory
Ctrl+M	MS	Store displayed value in memory

continued on next page

Calculator Functions (cont.)

Press	Click	To
Ctrl+P	M+	Add displayed value to current value in memory and place result in memory
@	sqrt	Compute square root of displayed number
%	%	Calculate the current value as a percentage
F9	+/−	Change the sign of the displayed number
.	.	Insert a decimal point in the displayed number
R	1/x	Calculate the reciprocal of the displayed number

Note that for division, you press the / key or click the slash (/) button; for multiplication, you press the * key or click the asterisk (*) button. If you make a mistake, you can erase the last digit or arithmetic operator from the display by pressing the Backspace key or clicking on the Back button. Continue erasing one character at a time.

To clear the last entry in a series of entries, press Delete or click the CE (Clear Entry) button. For example, if you are adding a series of numbers and make a mistake on the third entry, simply click the CE button immediately after entering the incorrect number; then reenter the last number. You need not start over. To clear the calculator entirely and return the display to 0, press Esc or click the C button.

The simplest way to learn to use Calculator is to practice! In the exercises below, you will use both the mouse and the keyboard.

EXERCISE 14.2

1. Compute the sum of 4 + 2:
   a. Click **4** and then **+**. The number 4 appears in the display.
   b. Click **2** and then click **=**. The answer 6 appears in the display.

2. Compute the remainder of 100 − 60:
   a. Click **100** and then **−**. The number 100 appears in the display.
   b. Click **60** and then click **=**. The answer 40 appears in the display.

3. Compute the product of 50 × 3:
   a. Click **50** and then *****. The number 50 appears in the display.
   b. Click **3** and then click **=**. The answer 150 appears in the display.

4. Compute the quotient of 100/25 (100 divided by 25):
   a. Click **100** and then **/**. The number 100 appears in the display.
   b. Click **25** and then click **=**. The answer 4 appears in the display.

After you click =, you can repeat the last instruction by pressing Enter or clicking = again. For example, in problem 4 above, the first time you click = you are instructing Calculator to divide by 25. You get the answer 4. If you repeat this instruction, Calculator will divide 4 by 25 (to give the answer 0.16). Each time you click =, you will divide by 25 again.

EXERCISE 14.3

1. Find 28% of 75:
   a. Key **75** and then *****. The number 75 appears in the display.
   b. Key **.28** and then press **Enter**. The answer 21 appears in the display.

2. Find the square root of 144:
   a. Key **144**.
   b. Press **@**. The answer 12 appears in the display.
   c. Press **Esc** to clear all numbers and functions.

Using Memory Functions

Calculator's memory buttons (MC, MR, MS, and M+) on both the standard calculator and the scientific calculator let you save or store numbers in memory for later use or to accumulate totals. New values placed in memory either add to or replace the old values. To store the number in the display in memory, click the M+ button. To save the result of a calculated number, click the MS (memory store) button once the result is calculated. To recall a stored number from memory, click the MR (memory recall) button.

The memory function is especially useful when you want to multiply or divide a number of values by the same amount. Storing that amount in memory allows you to easily use it again and again.

EXERCISE 14.4

1. Compute the sum of $(15 \times 23) + (224 \div 16)$:
   a. Key **15** and then *****; key **23** and then press **Enter**. The answer 345 appears in the display.
   b. Key **Ctrl+P**. The letter *M* appears in the display above the memory function buttons.
   c. Key **224** and then **/**; key **16** and then press **Enter**. The answer 14 appears in the display.
   d. Key **Ctrl+P**. The 14 remains in the display.
   e. Key **Ctrl+R**. The number 359 appears in the display.
   f. Key **Ctrl+L** to clear the memory.
   g. Press **Esc** to clear the display.

2. Compute the earnings at $5.50 an hour for 32.5, 43, and 27 hours:
   a. Key **5.5** and then **Ctrl+P**. The letter *M* appears in the display window above the memory function buttons.
   b. Key **32.5** and then *****. The value 32.5 appears in the display window.
   c. Key **Ctrl+R**. The memory value 5.5 appears in the display window.
   d. Press **Enter**. The result, 178.75, appears in the display window. The answer is $178.75.
   e. Key **43** and then *****. The value 43 appears in the display window.
   f. Key **Ctrl+R**. The memory value 5.5 appears in the display window.

g. Press **Enter**. The result 236.5 appears in the display window. The answer is $236.50.

h. Key **27** and then *. The value 27 appears in the display window.

i. Key **Ctrl+R**. The memory value 5.5 appears in the display window.

j. Press **Enter**. The result 148.5 appears in the display window. The answer is $148.50.

3. Clear the memory and display.

Using the Scientific Mode

The scientific calculator performs all the arithmetic functions of the standard calculator plus these advanced functions:

- Exponential and logarithmic operations.

- Trigonometric calculations.

- Arithmetic calculations in the binary, octal, and hexadecimal number systems

- Statistical calculations such as average and standard deviation.

If you need such specialized features, you should explore them in detail on your own.

USING THE STATISTICS BOX

The scientific calculator's statistics feature makes working with a long series of numbers much easier. When you click the statistics button, *Sta*, a separate window opens that displays a running tally, similar to an adding machine's paper tape, as shown in Figure 14-2. Thus the *Statistics Box* can be used for many functions unrelated to statistics.

FIGURE 14-2
The scientific calculator's
Statistics Box window

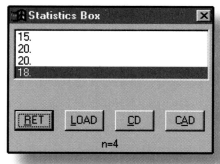

To use the Statistics Box, display the scientific calculator, and then click the Sta button. The Statistics Box window always opens on top of the scientific calculator window. You will have to drag the Statistics Box off the calculator in order to use the calculator.

To transfer a number to the Statistics Box from the scientific calculator's display, press the Insert key on the keyboard, or click the Dat key on the Calculator display.

To obtain statistical information about the sum of a list of numbers, click one of the three statistical functions that appear below the Sta button on the scientific calculator (Figure 14-1, bottom):

- *Ave* calculates and displays the average of the numbers in the list.

- *Sum* adds the numbers in the list and displays the sum.

- *s* calculates the standard deviation, using a population parameter of $n-1$. To use a population parameter of n, select Inv before pressing *s*.

At the bottom center of the Statistics Box, you always see the total number of items ($n=$) in the list. When the list is blank, you see $n=0$; as numbers are entered, n increases.

USING COMMAND BUTTONS IN THE STATISTICS BOX

The four command buttons in the Statistics Box (Figure 14-2) help you to insert and delete entries and to control interaction with the Calculator:

- *RET* switches the active window to the Calculator without closing the Statistics Box. To return to the Statistics Box, click the Sta button, or click the Statistics Box to make it the active window.

- *LOAD* makes the Calculator window display the number that is currently selected in the Statistics Box window.

- *CD* deletes the selected number from the Statistics Box window.

- *CAD* deletes all numbers from the Statistics Box window.

EXERCISE 14.5

1. Select **Scientific** from the **View** menu to display the scientific calculator.

2. Click the **Sta** button to open the **Statistics Box** window.

3. Drag the Statistics Box window to make both it and the main Calculator window visible.

4. Click the Calculator window to make it active.

5. Key **80** and then press **Insert**. (Be sure to press the key labeled *Insert* and not the one labeled *Ins*.) The value 80 is displayed in the Calculator window and in the Statistics Box window.

6. Key **85** and then press **Insert**. The value 85 is displayed in the Calculator window and below the value 80 in the Statistics Box window.

7. Key **70** and then press **Insert**. The value 70 is displayed in the Statistics Box window.

8. Now that you have entered all the numbers for your problem, you can calculate the mean of the values. Click the **Ave** button on the main calculator. The arithmetic mean, 78.333, displays in the Calculator window.

9. Click the **CAD** button in the Statistics Box window to clear all numbers.

10. Click the Statistics Box window's **Close** button to close the window.

11. Clear the value in the Calculator's display window.

Using Calculator with Other Programs

Calculator's value is not limited to its uses as a computation tool. You can use Calculator to paste Calculator results into other programs, and you can paste figures from other programs into Calculator.

If, for example, you need to total numbers in Notepad as you compose your document, key the numbers as a formula followed by an equal sign. Then copy the formula and the equal sign to the Calculator via the Clipboard, get the result, and paste the result back in the Notepad document. Exercise 14.5 will give you hands-on practice.

E X E R C I S E 14.6

1. Open **Notepad**.

2. Open the **Billing** document from your Windows Practice disk. Notice the current time and date stamp.

3. Verify that the **Word Wrap** option is selected on the **Edit** menu.

4. Below the most recent time and date stamp, key the following text (do not press Enter):

   The amount of vacation pay is computed by adding your regular pay and your minimum commission amount. For example, your vacation pay for next week will be 320 + 120 =

5. Click an insertion point immediately before the number 3 in the value 320 and drag across the formula up to and including the = sign.

6. Select **Copy** from the **Edit** menu. The calculation is copied to the Clipboard.

7. Make the **Calculator** active.

8. Select **Paste** from the **Edit** menu. The numbers in the calculation are inserted into the Calculator and the sum, 440, appears in the Calculator display.

9. Select **Copy** from the Calculator **Edit** menu.

10. Switch back to the **Billing** document and click an insertion point after the equal sign.

11. Select **Paste** from the **Edit** menu. The sum, 440, is pasted in the document, as shown in Figure 14-3.

12. Select **Save** from the **File** menu and then close the Notepad.

13. Click the Calculator's **Close** button to close Calculator.

14. In Notepad, save the Billing document as **Billing Calculated**. Then, print a copy of it.

15. Exit Notepad. If instructed, shut down Windows and your computer.

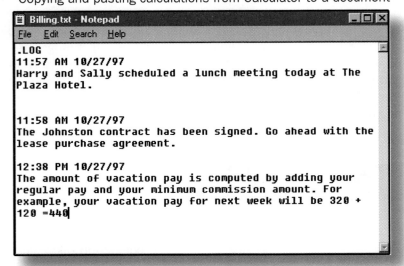

```
Billing.txt - Notepad
File  Edit  Search  Help
.LOG
11:57 AM 10/27/97
Harry and Sally scheduled a lunch meeting today at The
Plaza Hotel.


11:58 AM 10/27/97
The Johnston contract has been signed. Go ahead with the
lease purchase agreement.

12:38 PM 10/27/97
The amount of vacation pay is computed by adding your
regular pay and your minimum commission amount. For
example, your vacation pay for next week will be 320 +
120 =440
```

Summary

This lesson covered how to use the Calculator accessory application. You learned that:

- Calculator has two operating modes: standard and scientific. The standard calculator can compute addition, subtraction, multiplication, division, square roots, percentages, and reciprocals. The scientific calculator is capable of more complex computations.

- You can use the numeric keypad or the mouse to enter computations in either Calculator mode.

- The scientific calculator has a Statistics Box that displays a running tally of numbers. You can then sum, average, or calculate a standard deviation of the numbers.

- You can paste Calculator results into other programs and paste figures from other programs into Calculator.

LESSON 14 REVIEW QUESTIONS

TRUE/FALSE

Each of the following statements is either true or false. Indicate your answer on the left by circling T if the statement is true and F if the statement is false.

T F 1. You can minimize Calculator, but you cannot maximize it.

T F 2. The numeric keypad on your computer lets you enter numbers into Calculator if the Num Lock key is on.

T F 3. The scientific calculator permits you to work with number systems other than the decimal number system.

T F 4. The Statistics Box can be used only for statistical calculations.

T F 5. You resize the Calculator window by dragging its resize tab.

MULTIPLE CHOICE

Complete the following questions by circling the correct multiple choice letter.

1. The multiplication symbol in Calculator is
   A. /
   B. *
   C. x
   D. Esc

2. To open the Statistics Box window on the scientific calculator, click
   A. Sta
   B. Ave
   C. Insert
   D. Dat

3. When using the keyboard to key numbers on the Calculator, you must
   A. simply press the assigned letter or number
   B. press Num Lock on and the assigned letter or number
   C. press Ctrl, Alt, and the assigned letter or number
   D. none of the above

4. To clear the current calculation, you press
   A. F1
   B. Enter
   C. Esc
   D. Backspace

5. To store a number in memory that's currently displayed, you click the
   A. MC button
   B. MR button
   C. MS button
   D. M+ button

This project gives you the opportunity to review the concepts in this lesson and practice the techniques in the exercises. You will need your Windows Practice disk in order to complete this project.

1. Open a new Notepad document; then key the following text:

   ```
   Sales for 9/16:

   Department A =

   Department B =

   Department C =

   Department D =
   ```

2. Open the standard calculator.

3. Compute the sum for each of the departments listed below and copy them to the Notepad document using the following steps:
   a. Compute the sum for Department A.
   b. Copy the sum to the Clipboard.
   c. Make Notepad active and paste the sum for Department A after the equal sign on the appropriate line in the document.
   d. Return to Calculator.
   e. Clear the Calculator window.
   f. Repeat the procedure above until you have pasted the sum of each department's sales in the appropriate place in the Notepad document.

Dept. A	Dept. B	Dept. C	Dept. D
42.50	167.76	32.60	1713.50
157.75	234.10	342.90	154.40
235.11	17.34	275.10	923.50
17.34	164.98	324.16	
34.67	134.20	23.46	
10.76	237.56		

4. Insert a comma in the proper location in the total for Department D.

5. Save the Notepad document as **Project 14** to your Windows Practice disk.

6. Print the **Project 14** document.

7. Exit Notepad and Calculator. If instructed, shut down Windows and your computer.

USING PHONE DIALER

Upon completion of this lesson, you will be able to:

■ Enter and call a number.

■ Store and edit speed dial entries.

■ Set Phone Dialer properties.

🕐 **Estimated Time: 1 hour**

*P*hone Dialer is an accessory program that dials your voice telephone calls for you. In this lesson, you will learn how to place calls using Phone Dialer, and how to set properties to make storing and sending calls quicker and easier.

Understanding Phone Dialer

Phone Dialer allows you to place up to eight phone numbers into its speed-dial memory; then, with just a click of a button, you can dial any of the stored numbers. When Phone Dialer has finished dialing the number, you simply pick up the receiver of the phone to take your call.

Using your system's modem, Phone Dialer acts as an interface between your computer and your telephone. Its sole purpose is to quickly access often-used phone numbers; thus it facilitates voice communications. (In a later lesson you will see how HyperTerminal facilitates computer-to-computer communications.)

To begin using Phone Dialer, select the Communications option on the Accessories menu, and then click Phone Dialer. The Phone Dialer opening window looks like that shown in Figure 15-1. A Call Log dialog box may open as well. You will learn more about this later in the lesson. Once Phone Dialer is open, you have several options: You can enter and then call a number, you can store numbers for future use, you can edit stored numbers, and more. These options are discussed below.

Entering and Calling a Number

You may place a call with Phone Dialer in several ways.

■ To place a new call with Phone Dialer, enter the number in the Number to dial text box and then click the Dial command button (or simply press Enter). You may enter the number in one of three ways:

1. Key a number using the number keys on the top row of the keyboard.

2. Key a number using the numeric keypad. Be sure that Num Lock is on.

3. Use the mouse to click the appropriate number-pad buttons in the Phone Dialer dialog box.

FIGURE 15-1
Phone Dialer's opening window

- To call a recently dialed number, click the drop-down list arrow in the Number to dial text box. For your convenience, Phone Dialer stores over a dozen of the last numbers you've dialed. Click the number you want to call, and then click the Dial button to place that call.

- To call a number stored on a Speed dial button, just click the appropriate button. Phone Dialer immediately places the call; you do not even need to click the Dial button!

All these options are easy to use, and all are helpful. Clearly, however, the speed dial options are the most useful and most helpful. Let's see how you can store numbers in speed dial.

Storing Speed Dial Entries

To store a new Speed dial entry, click a free (that is, a blank) speed dial button. When the Program Speed Dial dialog box opens (Figure 15-2), fill in the two text boxes (Name and Number to dial). Proofread the information just to make sure, and then click Save. The name and number are now stored and will be displayed on a speed dial button whenever you access Phone Dialer.

FIGURE 15-2
Program Speed Dial dialog box

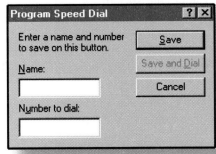

EXERCISE 15.1

1. Open Phone Dialer by clicking Communications on the **Accessories** menu and then **Phone Dialer**.

2. Click the first speed dial button (number 1). The Program Speed Dial dialog box opens.

3. Key a name in the Name text box.

4. Tab to the Number to dial field (or click in the text box). Key a telephone number with no spaces or dashes.

5. Click the **Save** button. The dialog box closes, and Speed dial button 1 now shows the name you entered.

6. Repeat steps 2–5 using speed dial buttons 2 and 3.

7. Place a call to button 1: Just click the button! Because this is a practice exercise, you may click **Hang Up** immediately after you hear the phone dialing.

NOTE:

If your computer is not connected to a modem, Windows displays a warning box. Click the OK button to cancel it.

8. Now make a call without using speed dial:
   a. Enter a number in the **Number to dial** text box using any of the methods discussed above. Note that as soon as you enter the first digit, the Dial button becomes active.
   b. Click the **Dial** button. You now see the Dialing screen and hear the phone dialing. Click **Hang Up**.

9. Click the **Minimize** button to keep Phone Dialer on the taskbar.

Editing Stored Speed Dial Entries

The Edit option on the menu bar provides the usual Cut, Copy, Paste, and Delete functions. It also offers another option: Speed Dial.

When you select the Speed Dial option, the Edit Speed Dial dialog box appears (Figure 15-3), allowing you to edit or replace entries. Click the button that you want to revise or update, and then enter the new data in the appropriate text boxes.

You can also delete Speed Dial entries. Select Speed Dial on the Edit menu. Click the Speed dial button you want to delete. Highlight the name in the Name text box and press Delete. Then, do the same to the number in the Number to dial text box.

FIGURE 15-3
Edit Speed Dial dialog box

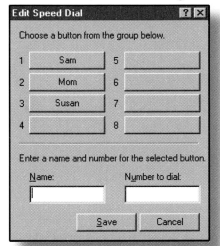

1. Maximize **Phone Dialer**.

2. Select **Speed Dial** from the **Edit** menu. The Edit Speed Dial dialog box opens.

3. Click button **1**.

4. Edit the name information in the **Name** text box: Replace the name with the name of a friend or colleague not already stored on the speed dial buttons.

5. Edit the phone number in the **Number to dial** text box.

6. Repeat steps 3–5 for each of the other buttons you want to edit.

7. Now, delete the speed dial numbers: In the **Phone Dialer** dialog box, select **Speed Dial** on the **Edit** menu.

8. Click a button with a speed dial entry. Highlight the name in the **Name** text box and press **Delete**. Highlight the number in the **Number to dial** text box and press **Delete**. Do the same for each speed dial button.

9. Click the **Save** button. Leave Phone Dialer maximized on screen.

Using the Tools Menu Options

As you see in Figure 15-4, clicking Tools on the Phone Dialer menu bar displays three options: Connect Using, Dialing Properties, and Hide/Show Log.

FIGURE 15-4
Tools menu

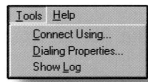

CONNECT USING

When you select this option, the Connect Using dialog box displays (Figure 15-5), allowing you to change the modem settings for the program by using Line, Address, and Line Properties.

FIGURE 15-5
Connect Using dialog box

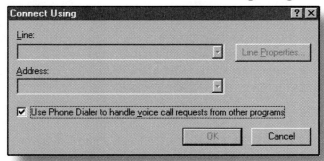

DIALING PROPERTIES

Selecting this option opens the Dialing Properties dialog box (Figure 15-6), which permits you to change key Phone Dialer properties, such as:

- **I am dialing from** and **I am in this country/region:** If you move your computer to another location or if you use a portable computer, you may need to change the location, area code, and country settings.

- **When dialing from here:** If your company telephone system requires you to dial 9 to make an outside call, then enter "9" in the box following "For local calls, dial." Likewise, enter the appropriate numbers if dialing outside the company for long distance calls. Doing so "informs" Phone Dialer how to make calls outside the company. Similarly, you can change the settings in the Dialing Properties dialog box to enter the information needed to make calling card calls, to disable call waiting, and to indicate whether your system uses tone or pulse dialing.

FIGURE 15-6
Dialing Properties dialog box

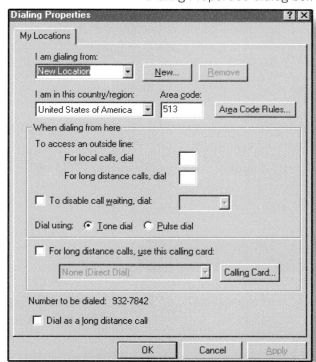

SHOW LOG/HIDE LOG

Phone Dialer keeps a detailed record of your calls, a *Call Log*. Figure 15-7 shows the log before any calls have been dialed. The log provides a detailed record of your calls by name, number, date, time, and length of call. If you want the Call Log on screen at all times behind your Phone Dialer, select the Show Log option. If you do not, select Hide Log. (Show Log and Hide Log "toggle"; that is, when you check one on the menu, that option disappears and the other then becomes "available.")

FIGURE 15-7
Call Log window

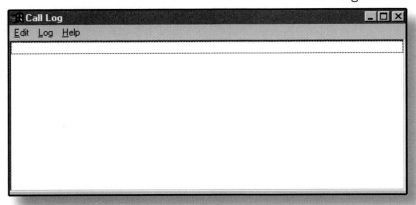

You can use Call Log in interesting ways; for example, you may find it helpful to:

- Cut or copy calls and paste them into a report or documentation for accounting or phone-tracking purposes. To place the information in another document, highlight the calls, select Cut or Copy from the Edit menu, and use the Paste command.

- Redial a number listed on the log. To redial, click the call listing and choose Dial from the Log menu.

- Edit your Call Log by cutting entries. To delete one or more entries, highlight the calls in the log and then choose Delete from the Edit menu.

- List only incoming calls, only outgoing calls, or both in your Call Log. In the Call Log window, click the Log option and then click a check box to show your choices.

E X E R C I S E ▷ 15.3

1. Maximize **Phone Dialer** if it is not already maximized on your screen.

2. Select **Show Log** from the **Tools** menu.

3. In the Call Log, select each entry and then select **Delete** from the **Edit** menu.

4. Select **Hide Log** on the **Tools** menu.

5. Select **Dialing Properties** from the **Tools** menu. The Dialing Properties dialog box opens.

6. Click the **What's This?** button in the dialog box and click the pointer on the various options.

7. When you have reviewed the various options in the Dialing Properties dialog box, close it and then close Phone Dialer by clicking its **Close** button. If instructed, shut down Windows and your computer.

Summary

This lesson covered Window's Phone Dialer accessory application. You learned that:

- Phone Dialer stores up to eight phone numbers and dials stored numbers quickly—just click a button.

- You can edit speed dial numbers by simply keying new numbers in the Edit Speed Dial dialog box.

- Phone Dialer offers options for storing your calling card number, displaying a Call Log on screen, and other useful assistance that facilitates phone dialing.

LESSON 15 REVIEW QUESTIONS

TRUE/FALSE

Each of the following statements is either true or false. Indicate your answer on the left by circling T if the statement is true and F if the statement is false.

T   F   1. Phone Dialer acts as an interface between your computer and your telephone.

T   F   2. You can enter phone numbers to dial using the numeric keypad only.

T   F   3. The Number to dial drop-down list in the Phone Dialer dialog box contains recently dialed numbers.

T   F   4. You can place up to eight phone numbers in speed-dial memory.

T   F   5. You cannot remove the Call Log from your screen.

MATCHING

Write the letter of the term in the right column that matches the definition in the left column.

_____ 1. A record of calls by name, number, date, time, and length of call.

_____ 2. A feature that lets you place phone calls by clicking on a button.

_____ 3. Option that allows you to change modem settings.

_____ 4. Option that allows you to change settings such as your area code.

_____ 5. Option that lets you keep track of all your calls.

A. Dialing Properties

B. Show Log/Hide Log

C. Call Log

D. Connect Using

E. Speed Dial

This project gives you the opportunity to review the concepts in this lesson and practice the techniques in the exercises.

1. Open **Phone Dialer**.

2. Enter four speed dial numbers.

3. Click the **Save** button.

4. If your computer is set up so that it can place calls, try placing a call to one of the numbers stored in Speed Dial.

5. Select **Speed Dial** from the **Edit** menu.

6. Delete one of the numbers stored in Speed Dial. Add a new name and number.

7. Click the **Save** button.

8. Place a call to the number you just added.

9. Delete all the entries from Speed Dial.

10. Close Phone Dialer by clicking the **Close** button. If instructed, shut down Windows and your computer.

UNIT 4 REVIEW QUESTIONS

WRITTEN QUESTIONS

Answer the questions below on a separate piece of paper.

1. List the Personal Information Managers (PIMs) discussed in this unit, and give an example of how you may use each to increase your productivity.

2. Distinguish between Cut and Paste and Copy and Paste, and describe an instance where each may be used.

3. Discuss the results of keying *do*, *do*[space], *Do*[space], and [space]*do*[space] when searching text in Notepad.

4. Briefly explain how the Notepad time and date stamp feature works, and give at least two practical uses for this feature.

5. Identify the code for creating a Notepad document header that prints the word *Page* and the page number in the center of each page. Explain the purpose of each of the symbols used in your code.

6. Give the steps you would follow to calculate the average of the following numbers using the Statistics Box feature of the scientific calculator: 45, 40, 60, 65, and 43.

7. Indicate the steps you would follow to store eight phone numbers in Phone Dialer.

8. Describe Call Log and explain its uses.

9. Explain how the Dialing Properties dialog box can be used to customize your dialing needs.

10. Briefly describe a couple of applications for which you would use the scientific calculator.

UNIT 4 APPLICATION

SCANS

Jim Monnin, a project manager for Corporate Communique, has requested some budget information concerning a client's newsletter project from Shawna Walker. Jim wants to know how much overtime was charged to the project's account.

Using the scientific calculator, help Shawna calculate the figures. Display the scientific calculator. Then, open the Notepad document **Overtime** from your Windows Template disk. Complete the document by using Calculator to compute the needed figures. Copy and paste the results from Calculator into the document. (Use the memory feature to store the overtime rate, and compute the average overtime wage by adding the overtime earnings to the Statistics Box and pressing the **Ave** key.)

Save the Notepad document to your Windows Practice disk. Print a copy of the document. Then, close all open applications. If instructed, shut down Windows and your computer.

CRITICAL THINKING

Two weeks ago you were promoted to the position of Information Technology Trainer for all 325 employees at the Radon Inc. facility. For the past three days you have been attending the national Telecon Conference; you returned to work this morning.

Your new boss, the vice president for Information Technology, sent you several e-mail messages while you were away. One requires your immediate attention: He has requested your first-draft announcement telling employees of the five Microsoft Office training sessions, which are to begin in four weeks. He expects the announcement to list the session dates and titles, and he wants the announcement out by the end of this week!

Because you anticipated this request, you began drafting this announcement on your laptop while you were away at your conference. Since you started the announcement in Notepad, continue in Notepad—at least for now. Continue to use your Windows programs to create an appropriate announcement or flyer that includes a schedule of seminar sessions, and place the trainers' phone numbers on Phone Dialer. Keep a Call Log of your long distance phone calls to seminar trainers and establish a budget for each seminar using Calculator to finalize your calculations.

1. Start **Notepad** and insert your Windows Template disk into one of the floppy drives. Open the file **Seminars**. Make sure that the **Word Wrap** option is selected.

2. Insert the following text as a new, third paragraph:

    What you will get from this session:

    The Windows basics you will need.

    Master the basic functions of each application: Word, Excel, PowerPoint, and Access.

3. Revise the text as follows:
    a. List the dates, times, and locations of the five available seminars.
    b. Print an update of the draft copy of the announcement.
    c. Write a short cover letter to accompany the announcement to the departments within your company.

4. Use this list of selected workshop trainers and place their phone numbers in the Phone Dialer for easy access when you or your manager needs to contact them.

Seminar Topic	Software Trainers	Phone Numbers
Windows Basics	Jan Anderson (Rochester, GA)	(555) 555-3255
Word	Schorree Fisher (Berkeley, SC)	(500) 555-1313
Excel	JoAnn Weatherwax (New Earl, NY)	(600) 555-4333
Access	Carolyn Voet (Princetown, WA)	(009) 555-9945
PowerPoint	Maureen Smith (Sunnydale, FL)	(100) 555-9984
Mail	Pat Grignon (Dana Pointe, MA)	(700) 555-1189
Train-the-Trainer	Robert D. Stewart (San Cuesta, CA)	(400) 555-8903

5. Use the Calculator and Notepad programs to develop and print out a preliminary budget for your manager next week, including the following items:

a. Speaker fees (vary by hourly rate and number of days retained):

Jan Anderson	3 days @ $500/day (18 hours)
Schorree Fisher	5 days, 15 hours total @ $50/hour
JoAnn Weatherwax	4 days, 12.5 hours total @ $50/hour
Carolyn Voet	2 days @ $750/day, plus 1 day @ $1,000
Maureen Smith	3 days @ $700/day (24 hours)

b. Hotel conference room and audiovisual costs:

5 days @ $350 for 4 breakout rooms

1 day @ $500 for 1 auditorium

5 days of audiovisual costs is $350/day for each of 4 breakout rooms for 5 days.

c. Banquet/luncheon costs based on cost per person, 210 persons attending:

Day 1	Buffet $7.50 ea.	Lunch $12.00 ea.	Dinner $15.75 ea.
Day 2	Buffet $7.50 ea.	Lunch $10.00 ea.	Dinner $16.05 ea.
Day 3	Buffet $7.50 ea.	Lunch $12.00 ea.	Dinner—On Your Own
Day 4	Buffet $7.50 ea.	Lunch $9.50 ea.	Dinner $17.75 ea.
Day 5	Buffet $9.00 ea.	Lunch $13.00 ea.	Dinner $15.50 ea.

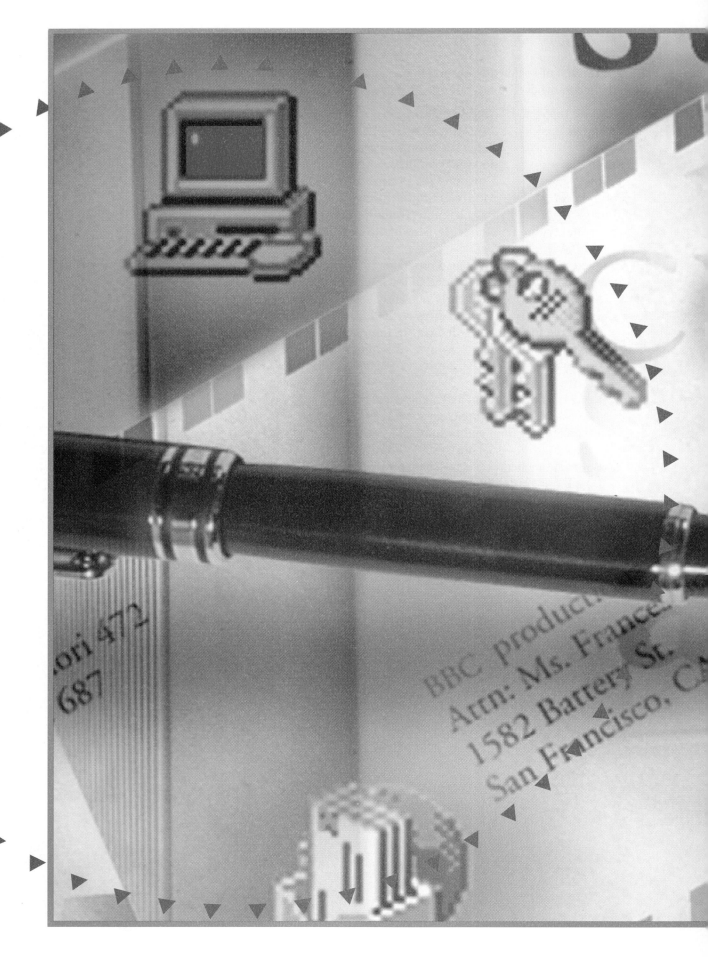

WORDPAD

CREATING DOCUMENTS WITH WORDPAD

OBJECTIVES

Upon completion of this lesson, you will be able to:

- Start WordPad.

- Key text in a WordPad document.

- Save a document.

- Close a document.

- Open an existing document.

- Print a document.

⏱ Estimated Time: 1.5 hours

Windows *WordPad* is an easy-to-use word processing program. It contains basic features common to all word processing programs, such as the ability to create, save, and retrieve document files; move, copy, enhance, and edit text; set text margins and align text in various ways; and search for and replace words or phrases throughout the entire document.

In the next four lessons, you will learn how to use WordPad to create simple documents such as letters, reports, and memos—complete with objects, if you wish. The object may be a sound recorded in an earlier meeting that you want to be heard by the person reading the report you are creating in WordPad. Or the object may be a picture or spreadsheet created in another software program.

Starting WordPad

Windows WordPad is an application found on the Accessories menu. To start WordPad, click the Start button, move the highlight to Programs, and then to Accessories. Finally, click the WordPad icon.

When you launch WordPad, you will see the opening window shown in Figure 16-1. Note the menu bar, toolbar, ruler, and status bar. The blank area is the *workspace* for inputting your document. Your window may also show a format bar, an optional tool that we'll discuss a bit later.

Look at the six options on WordPad's familiar menu bar. Do you see that one letter of each word is underlined? Now look at the underlined letters in the File menu options shown in Figure 16-2. Underlining is a code for *keyboard commands*: As an alternative to using the mouse, you can use this letter in combination with the Alt key to select a menu. Thus you can press Alt+F *instead of* clicking on File. When a menu is displayed, you can issue commands by simply pressing the underlined letter. Thus you can press *o* to issue the Open command. Chances are you prefer using your mouse, but remember the

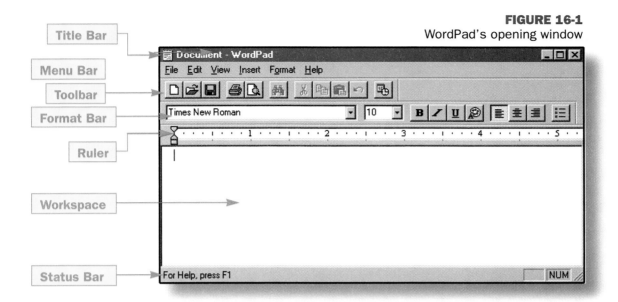

FIGURE 16-1
WordPad's opening window

Title Bar

Menu Bar

Toolbar

Format Bar

Ruler

Workspace

Status Bar

meaning of the underlined letters just in case your mouse is ever disabled or you are working on a laptop computer that doesn't have a mouse.

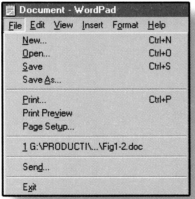

FIGURE 16-2
WordPad's File menu

Keying Text

Wordpad's opening window offers you a blank workspace, clear and ready for your text. The *cursor*, a thin vertical blinking line, indicates the start position, just as in Notepad. As you key text, the cursor moves; you might say you *push* the cursor along as you key. Remember that the cursor's location is called the *insertion point*, the point where the next character you key will be inserted.

Keying text in WordPad is exactly like keying text in Notepad, except for one feature: WordPad automatically wraps text to the next line. You do not have to choose this option, as you did in Notepad. Once you have keyed text in a new document, you can move around in the document using the same mouse and keyboard techniques as in Notepad.

Now, let's begin using WordPad!

EXERCISE ▭ 16.1

1. Start Windows if it is not already active.

2. Click the **Start** button, move the highlight to **Programs**, and then **Accessories**, and finally click **WordPad**.

3. Click the **Maximize** button to maximize the WordPad window.

4. In the workspace, key the following two paragraphs of text at the cursor position. Press **Enter** twice at the end of each paragraph, as indicated.

   Computer technology has genuinely revolutionized the world of business. For most of us, the first image of this revolution is the office. In the 1990s administrative assistants, managers, top executives--all have personal computers (PCs) on their desktops. Armed with PC power, office workers at all levels (and in all industries) rely on their computers to draft and revise their letters, memos, reports, and proposals; to develop spreadsheets and databases; to create object images; and to communicate with one another via e-mail.[**Enter**][**Enter**]

   But offices aren't the only businesses benefiting from the computer revolution. Repair shops use PCs for billing. Auto parts dealers use PCs for inventory. Video rental stores rely on PCs to track customer returns. And take-out restaurants network two computers--one at the front counter, the other in the kitchen--to show cooks the orders as they are entered! In addition, many, many home businesses thrive only because a PC allows a sole entrepreneur to handle correspondence, invoicing, inventory, and more, all by herself or himself.[**Enter**][**Enter**]

5. Look over the document and correct any errors you made, using the **Backspace** or **Delete** key.

6. Keep this document open on your screen for the next exercise.

Saving a WordPad Document

It is a good idea to save your work frequently—every 10 minutes or so—to avoid accidental loss. Like Notepad, WordPad offers two File menu options for saving:

- Use Save for documents that are already named as you want them named.

- Use Save As for documents that are not yet named (or for documents that you wish to rename).

The Save As command can save you a lot of time by allowing you to use existing files and then give them new names. Imagine, for example, a short letter to Mary Linton already saved under the file name *Linton Letter*. A week later you want to send the same letter to Greg Chin—with a revised inside address and the current date, of course. Once you make the copy changes, select Save As from the file menu and save your new file as *Chin Letter*. Perhaps nothing is more critical than saving your files for the future, so learn to master the Save As command!

The Save As dialog box gives you an important option for saving files. The Save as type drop-down list (Figure 16-3) displays five options you can choose from when saving your file. These file types are discussed below.

FIGURE 16-3
Save As dialog box

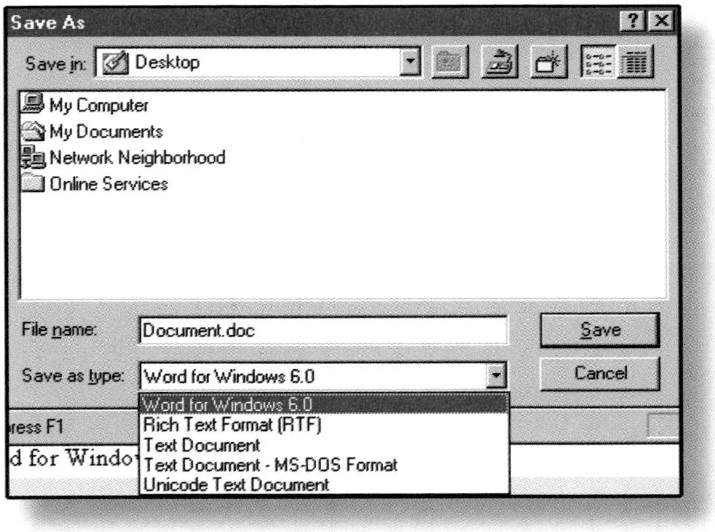

- **Word for Windows 6.0**. Choosing this option lets you save a WordPad document as a Word for Windows document. In WordPad, you can open documents created in any version of Word for Windows.

- **Rich Text Format (RTF)**. RTF text files instruct the word processing software how the docu-ment's text should look on screen or appear when printed—that is, it shows text as bold, justified, centered, and so on. Thus WordPad allows you to exchange RTF files between operating systems or word processors easily, without wasting time to convert the documents.

- **Text Document**. Here, text does not mean "words" or "copy." A text docu-ment is a file with no formatting, not even paragraph breaks—text only!

- **Text Document – MS-DOS Format**. This option saves a file in ASCII format (ASCII, pronounced "ASKee," refers to an international standard for exchanging text files). Files saved in this format can be recognized by all PC word processing programs and most other applications as well.

- **Unicode Text Document**. This is another text-only format in which all the formatting is removed.

You will usually want to accept the default, Word for Windows 6.0.

TIP

Notice that the WordPad toolbar has a Save button. To save your document using this button, simply click it.

You will need your Windows Practice disk to complete this assignment.

1. Insert your Windows Practice disk in the appropriate disk drive.

2. Select **Save As** from the **File** menu. The Save As dialog box appears.

3. Select the drive in which you have placed your Windows Practice disk.

4. Key the file name **Practice** in the text box. From the Save as type drop-down list, select **Word for Windows 6.0**, if necessary, and click the **Save** button.

5. Leave the document on screen for the next exercise.

Closing a WordPad Document

Like Notepad, WordPad does not have a "close document" command that allows you to close a document while leaving WordPad open. You close a document the same ways as in Notepad:

- Select New from the File menu to replace the current document with a new blank screen.

- Select Open from the File menu to replace the current document with another WordPad document.

- Select Exit from the File menu or click the Close button to quit the document and WordPad simultaneously.

If you select New before saving the current document, WordPad displays the warning message shown in Figure 16-4, reminding you that your document hasn't been saved. Select Yes to save the document.

FIGURE 16-4
Message window reminds you to save the current document

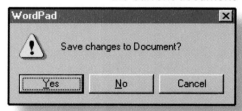

Opening a New WordPad Document

When you choose New from the File menu to begin a new document, WordPad displays the New dialog box shown in Figure 16-5. From this dialog box you can select a type for the new document. These choices should look familiar to you—they are the same document types that appear in the Save as type drop-down list in the Save As dialog box. Usually, you will want to select the default choice, Word 6 Document. When you click the OK button in this dialog box, WordPad displays a blank screen for your new document.

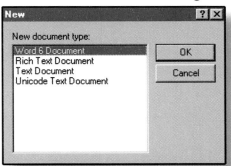

FIGURE 16-5
New dialog box

E X E R C I S E ▭ 16.3

1. Choose **New** from the **File** menu. The New dialog box appears.

2. Accept the default document type of Word 6 Document by clicking the **OK** button.

3. The current document is replaced by a new, blank screen.

4. Leave this new document on screen.

Opening an Existing WordPad Document

WordPad offers several ways to open existing documents:

■ Select Open from the File menu to display the Open dialog box.

■ Display the File menu. Toward the bottom of the menu is a section showing the four most recently opened files. Click a file name from this list to open the file.

■ Click the Open button on the toolbar to display the Open dialog box.

The Open dialog box gives you further options for opening a file: You can key the file name in the File name text box. You can specify the type of files to display in the Files of type drop-down list. Use the Look in drop-down list to display the contents of the desired drive or folder, then double-click the file you want to open.

E X E R C I S E ▭ 16.4

1. If necessary, insert your Windows Practice disk in the appropriate disk drive.

2. Select **Open** from the **File** menu. The Open dialog box displays.

3. In the Open dialog box, select the drive containing your Windows Practice disk.

4. Double-click the **Practice** file. The document opens.

(continued on next page)

5. Move the insertion point to the end of the **Practice** document, if it is not already there; the insertion point should be positioned to begin paragraph 3.

6. Key the following copy:

   The power of computers is one obvious reason for their widespread use today. But would they be as popular if they were still as large and as cumbersome as the roomsize monsters of years ago? Would they be available to small businesses and homes if they cost as much today as they did years ago? Hardly! Over the years computer engineers have made computer chips smaller and smaller--and at the same time more and more powerful AND less expensive! One wit noted that if what happened to computers would happen to automobiles, then a Rolls Royce would soon cost about two dollars![Enter][Enter]

7. Save the revised document by clicking the **Save** button on the toolbar.

8. Key the following copy as the fourth and final paragraph:

   Computers . . . What would your world be without them?

9. Select **Save As** from the **File** menu.

10. If necessary, select the drive in which you have placed your Windows Practice disk.

11. Key **New Stuff** in the File name text box, and then click the **Save** button.

Printing a WordPad Document

WordPad lets you print documents by using the Print option on the File menu. Before you print, however, you should always select the *Print Preview* option (also on the File menu). These options are discussed in detail below.

Print Preview

To see the way your document will look when printed, select the Print Preview option from the File menu, or click the Print Preview button on the toolbar. The "preview" is a miniature version of the document, an outline of the text area framed against the full page, as shown in Figure 16-6. The mouse pointer becomes a magnifying glass that you can click on any area of the document to see a closer view.

At the top of the Preview window, the buttons offer you the opportunity to Print the document, to advance to the Next Page or return to the Previous (Prev.) Page, to get a Two-Page view, to Zoom In (magnify the page view) or Zoom Out (reduce the page view), and, finally, to Close the Print Preview window. As usual, unavailable button options are grayed out; for example, when you preview a one-page document, Next Page is unavailable.

Print

To print an open document in WordPad, select Print from the File menu. The Print dialog box appears, as shown in Figure 16-7. You have a number of options to choose from in this dialog box. A discussion of the most important of these begins on page 194.

FIGURE 16-6
Print Preview window

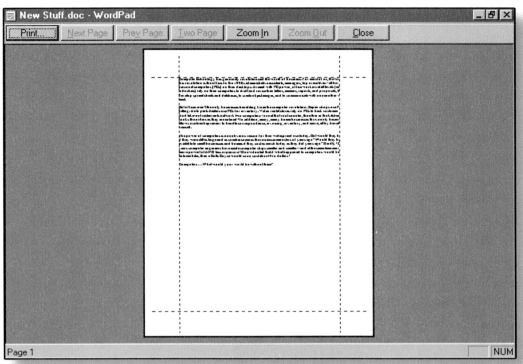

FIGURE 16-7
Print dialog box

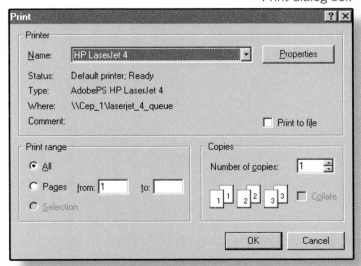

- **Printer**. The top half of the Print dialog box is devoted to the properties of your printer—information that you can change when you install a new printer or wish to send the print job to a different printer. To send the print job to a different printer, select the new printer from the Name drop-down list.

- **Print range**. Select All (the default) when you want to print all pages in the current file. Otherwise, select Pages and key the page numbers in the two boxes (*from* and *to*). The selection option lets you print selected text only.

- **Copies**. The default is 1 copy. To print additional copies of each page, key a number in the Number of copies box. Below the Number of copies you can choose how you want the printed pages to be collated.

You can also print a document by clicking the Print button on the toolbar. Clicking this button, however, causes your document to begin printing immediately. You will not see the Print dialog box.

NOTE:

Windows 98 has multitasking capability. While your document is printing, you can work on some other task. And if your printer is located at a distance from your computer, you can keep track of the printing process by checking the printer icon that appears next to the clock on the taskbar. When this icon disappears, your printing is completed.

E X E R C I S E ▷ 16.5

1. Check the **New Stuff** document in Page Preview:
   a. Select **Print Preview** from the **File** menu.
   b. Use **Zoom In** to check the general format.

2. Print one copy of the document.

3. Close **WordPad**. If you are asked, save the document.

4. If instructed, shut down Windows and your computer.

Summary

This lesson introduced you to Windows' WordPad word processing application. You learned that:

- Windows WordPad is located on the Accessories menu. WordPad allows you to create, save, and retrieve document files; move, copy, enhance, and edit documents; set text margins and align text in various ways; and search for and replace words or phrases throughout a document.

- The WordPad opening screen shows "Document – WordPad" in its title bar. After you have saved your document, your new file name replaces the word *Document* in the title bar.

- The cursor, a thin vertical line that blinks on and off, appears at the top left of the workspace when you open WordPad. As you key text, the cursor (also called the insertion point) moves ahead, always indicating the position where the next character you key will be inserted.

- You must name a new document in order to save it. To save a new document, use the Save As command on the File menu. Use the same procedure when you want to save a revised document with a new file name.

- To save an already-named document (for example, after you revise the text), use the Save command on the File menu. (If you want to give that revised document a new name, then you must use the Save As command.) Or you can click the Save button on the toolbar.

- To open a file, use the Open option on the File menu, or click the Open button (appropriately, an opened folder) on the toolbar.

- To see the layout of a page and to check page breaks on screen before printing, use the Print Preview option on the File menu.

- Selecting the Print option on the File menu displays the Print dialog box, where you can specify whether you want to print the entire document (All), a selected range of pages (enter page numbers after the words *from* and *to* in the Print range section), or only highlighted text (Selection). You can also enter (after Copies) the number of copies you want to print.

LESSON 16 REVIEW QUESTIONS

TRUE/FALSE

Each of the following statements is either true or false. Indicate your answer on the left by circling T if the statement is true and F if the statement is false.

T   F   1.   WordPad lets you create basic documents, such as letters, reports, and memos.

T   F   2.   As you key text in a WordPad document, you push the cursor forward.

T   F   3.   If you select the New option from the File menu before you save the current document, you immediately lose your current document.

T   F   4.   You cannot print a document from the Print Preview window.

T   F   5.   You use the Save As command to save a document for the first time.

MULTIPLE CHOICE

Complete the following questions by circling the correct multiple choice letter.

1.   The cursor in the WordPad program is a
    A.   short horizontal bar
    B.   small blinking square
    C.   thin vertical blinking line
    D.   starlike symbol

2.   To save a new, unnamed WordPad document, select
    A.   Save As on the File menu
    B.   Save on the File menu
    C.   either of the above
    D.   neither of the above

3. To check a document on screen before printing,
   A. open the View menu and select Page Breaks
   B. open the File menu and select Print Preview
   C. open the Window menu and select Preview Page
   D. none of the above

4. Whenever you call up a file and update it, you can
   A. save the new, updated file under the same file name
   B. keep the old file and save the new file under a new file name
   C. either of the above
   D. neither of the above

5. To print a WordPad document, select
   A. Print Preview on the File menu
   B. Print on the File menu
   C. Page Preview on the File menu
   D. any of the above will work

LESSON 16 PROJECT

This project gives you the opportunity to review the concepts in this lesson and practice the techniques in the exercises. You will need your Windows Template disk and Windows Practice disk in order to complete this project.

1. Start the **WordPad** program.

2. Open the file named **Literacy** from the Windows Template disk.

3. Go to the end of the document and press **Enter** three times. Then key the following paragraph:

   ```
   . . . Can You?
   ```
   [**Enter**] [**Enter**]
   ```
   If you or someone you know would benefit from literacy training, ask
   your employer, your local librarian, or your nearest school or community
   college district for information. And if you can help as an instructor,
   consider becoming a Literacy Volunteer!
   ```

4. Save the revised document on your Windows Practice disk under the new file name **Literacy Revisions**.

5. Check your document using **Print Preview**.

6. Print a copy of your document.

7. Proofread your printed copy and correct any errors.

8. Save your revised copy and print a fresh copy, if necessary.

9. Close the file and exit **WordPad**. If instructed, shut down Windows and your computer.

EDITING AND FORMATTING WORDPAD DOCUMENTS

OBJECTIVES

Upon completion of this lesson, you will be able to:

- Use Page Setup to format a document.
- Display editing and formatting tools.
- Select text.
- Use the Edit menu to edit text.
- Use the Format menu and toolbar buttons to format text.
- Find and replace text.

🕑 **Estimated Time: 1.5 hours**

W ordPad makes it easy for you to edit or revise text as necessary, and to modify the appearance of text in a document. In this lesson, you'll learn how to use WordPad's editing tools and how to apply various formatting techniques.

Using Editing and Formatting Tools

E diting means revising or changing the words in text. Using WordPad's Edit menu, you can easily update a report, correct sales figures, delete sentences or paragraphs, or otherwise change documents.

Formatting means changing the look or the arrangement of text, whether that text is of individual characters, words, sentences, or the entire document.

WordPad offers a host of editing and formatting tools that give you great power in developing documents. Further, WordPad gives you options in displaying the tools at your command.

Using Page Setup to Format a Document

What will your printed document look like? WordPad has preset choices (called defaults) for paper size, left and right margins, top and bottom margins, and so on. To see—or change—WordPad's defaults, select Page Setup on the File menu. The Page Setup dialog box, shown in Figure 17-1, will display.

FIGURE 17-1
Page Setup dialog box

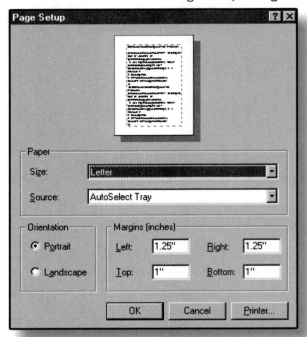

The top of the Page Setup dialog box displays a sample of what a printed page would look like with the current specifications for paper size, margins, and the like. In the areas beneath, you can change any of the specifications, and as you do so, you will simultaneously see the sample page change.

PAPER

Change Size if you are not going to print on standard 8½-by-11-inch paper (WordPad's default, which it calls Letter). Click the arrow to the right of the text box and select one of the nine options listed.

Change Source if, for example, you are feeding special letterhead into the printer. Again, click the arrow to the right of the text box to see a list of Source options.

ORIENTATION

Portrait is the standard term used to identify 8½-by-11-inch paper positioned with the 8½-inch dimension from left to right. *Landscape* is when the 11-inch dimension is positioned from left to right.

MARGINS

WordPad's default settings are 1.25-inch left and right margins, and 1-inch top and bottom margins. To change any or all, click in the appropriate box and enter your desired margin. (WordPad's default is to measure in inches.)

Remember "What's This?"? If you have questions, use the ? icon at the top right corner. In the Page Setup dialog box, for example, if you click ?, a question mark attaches to your mouse pointer. If you then drag the pointer to, say, the word *Portrait* (under Orientation) and click, you're essentially saying "What's Portrait?" WordPad answers: "Specifies how the document is positioned on the printed page."

Displaying Editing and Formatting Tools

Do you want to see the various bars, buttons, and rulers on your screen at all times? Or do you prefer not having them on screen? Your choice! WordPad equips these tools with toggle switches that you can turn on or off, as you please.

To change display options, click the View menu (Figure 17-2). You have the following choices:

FIGURE 17-2
WordPad's View menu

- The first four items on the View menu (Toolbar, Format Bar, Ruler, and Status Bar) have toggle switches: select one and a check mark appears, showing that it's on; select a checked item and the check mark disappears, showing that it's off. In this way you turn the toolbar, format bar, ruler, or status bar on or off.

- The last choice on the View menu is Options. When you select Options, the Options dialog box (Figure 17-3) appears, with the Word tab selected. This tab provides you with three choices under Word wrap and four choices under Toolbars. The Options dialog box also offers an Options tab that, when selected, allows you to select the unit of measurement of your choice (inches, centimeters, etc.).

FIGURE 17-3
Options dialog box

Selecting Text

As you have learned, before you can cut (delete) a block of text, move a few words, copy a sentence, italicize a phrase, underline a key statement, or otherwise change your copy, you need to select the text.

You select text in WordPad in the same ways as in Notepad:

- Hold down the mouse button and drag across the text you want to select.

- Double-click any word to select it.

- Choose Select All from the Edit menu to select the entire document.

In addition, WordPad lets you quickly select various quantities of text using the mouse. First position the mouse pointer in the margin to the left of the first line in the paragraph. The mouse pointer changes from an I-beam to a right-pointing arrow. Then, to select:

- The current line, click once.

- The current paragraph, double-click.

- Multiple paragraphs, double-click to select the first paragraph, hold down Shift, point on the second paragraph, and then click once. Both paragraphs are now selected. (After you select the first paragraph, you can also drag the mouse to the end of the text you wish to highlight.)

- The entire document, hold down Ctrl and click once.

Using the Edit Menu to Edit Text

Once you have highlighted or selected text, you may delete it, move it, or copy it using commands on the Edit menu (Figure 17-4). You'll be familiar with many of these commands from Notepad:

- To delete highlighted text, press Delete or Backspace.

- To move text, first highlight the text, then select Cut. Position the cursor at the new destination for the moved copy, then select the Paste command. The highlighted copy now appears in its new position.

- To copy text, first highlight the text, then choose Copy. Position the cursor at the new destination for the copied text, then select the Paste command. The new copy is now inserted (and the original text is untouched).

- The Undo command is a safety feature; use it to cancel your last editing command.

WordPad's toolbar includes buttons for these editing commands. They are not active, however, until text is selected.

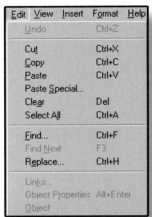

FIGURE 17-4
WordPad's Edit menu

E X E R C I S E 17.1

1. Insert your Windows Template disk in the appropriate disk drive.

2. Open the file **XTI Ad**.

3. Change the side heading *Consulting Manager* to *Consulting Project Manager*:
   a. Click an insertion point immediately before the letter *M* in the word *Manager*.
   b. Key **Project** and space once.

4. Cut item 7 from the first paragraph under *Requirements* and renumber the remaining items:
   a. Click immediately before the word *management* in item 7. Press the mouse button and drag through the number *8*, including

the space following the second parenthesis. Release the mouse button when you are in the desired position.
   b. Select **Cut** from the **Edit** menu.
   c. Click an insertion point between the number 9 and the parenthesis that follows it.
   d. Press **Backspace** once to delete the number 9.
   e. Key **8**.

5. In the last paragraph, reverse the order of two sentences:
   a. Highlight the sentence beginning *Applicants...*, including the space following the period.

b. Select the **Cut** button from the toolbar.

c. Click an insertion point immediately after the period in *Employer*. Space once.

d. Select the **Paste** button from the toolbar.

6. Save the document to your Windows Practice disk and leave it on screen for the next exercise.

Using the Format Menu to Format Text

The Format menu (Figure 17-5) offers four options for formatting your document. Three of these options (Font, Paragraph, and Tabs) offer additional options, as you can tell by the ellipses following their names.

Let's look in detail at each of the four choices listed under Format.

FONT

What's the easiest way to change more than one characteristic or "the look of" alphabetic or numeric characters on your keyboard? Choose Font from the Format menu. The Font dialog box displays, as shown in Figure 17-6, allowing you to change text in a number of ways:

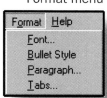

FIGURE 17-5
WordPad's Format menu

FIGURE 17-6
Font dialog box

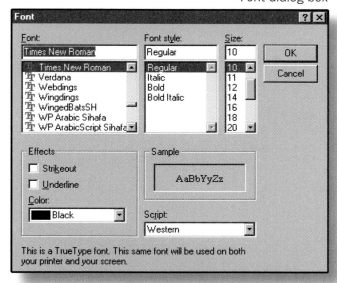

- To change the font, select a new font from the Font list box. A sample of each new font selection displays in the Sample box.

- To change the font style, select a new style from the Font style list box. Again, the Sample box displays your new selection.

- To change the font size, select the desired size from the Size list box, or key a size in the text box. The Sample box changes once again.

- To choose strikeout or underline, click the options under Effects.

- To choose colors, click the arrow at the right of the Color list box to display color choices.

- To choose language scripts, click the scroll arrow to the right of the Script list box.

BULLET STYLE

Another way to format text is to use *bullets*. Bullets are symbols such as dots or diamonds that appear at the beginning of a line of text, making the text stand out (see Figure 17-7). To use Bullet Style, position the insertion point where the bullet list starts, then choose Bullet Style from the Format menu. Now as you enter your text, each time you press Enter, a bullet displays on the next line. To end automatic bullet insertion, choose Bullet Style again.

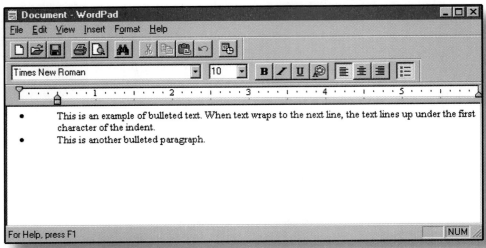

FIGURE 17-7
Bullet style applied to WordPad text

You can also change an existing paragraph to Bullet Style: Click anywhere in the paragraph, then select Bullet Style from the Format menu.

PARAGRAPH

The Paragraph dialog box on the Format menu (see Figure 17-8) lets you apply indentation and alignment formats.

FIGURE 17-8
Paragraph dialog box

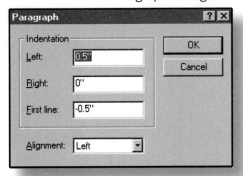

- **Indentation** offers three options. In the Left and Right boxes, you can specify (in inches) the left and the right margin indent you prefer, if any. The default is zero—no indentation. For example, entering 0.5 for Left indents all paragraphs a half-inch from the left margin; entering 0.5 in both boxes indents paragraphs from both sides. The third option, First line, indents only the first line of each paragraph.

- The **Alignment** option, at the bottom of the Paragraph dialog box, displays three choices in a drop-down list that you access by clicking the arrow to the right of the list box: Left, Right, and Center. The default is Left. Selecting Right justifies text at the right margin; Center, of course, centers each line across the full width.

TABS

A *tab stop* marks the place where the cursor will stop when you press the Tab key. WordPad has default tab stops every half-inch, but you can add a tab stop wherever you need one by selecting Tabs from the Format menu. The Tabs dialog box (see Figure 17-9) opens, with a blinking insertion point in a box labeled Tab stop position. You enter tab stops one at a time by keying the location and clicking the Set button. For example, to set a tab stop at 2 inches, key 2 in the Tab stop position text box and then click the Set button. Each tab stop you set is displayed in the large window below the Tab stop position box.

FIGURE 17-9
Tabs dialog box

You can also set tabs using the ruler bar, a full-length, numbered, horizontal ruler that displays directly under the format bar. To set a tab stop, position the mouse pointer at any position on the ruler where you want a tab stop and click the ruler. A small L-shaped symbol marks each tab stop. To delete a tab stop, just click the tab symbol and drag it off the ruler.

Using the Format Bar to Format and Enhance Text

Chances are you'll be editing and formatting constantly as you create or revise documents. To simplify both processes, WordPad provides a handy format bar (see Figure 17-10) at the top of your WordPad window, immediately below the menu bar. The buttons on the format bar are shortcuts for formatting text. All you do is highlight text, then use the appropriate format bar buttons as needed.

FIGURE 17-10
Format bar

The format bar contains two groups of items:

- A Font text box (with the name of a font displayed) and a Font Size box (with the type size displayed).

- Eight buttons that control various types of formatting.

TIP

If the formatting toolbar is not displayed, select Format Bar from the View menu.

Now, let's take a closer look at these format bar features.

THE FORMAT BAR BOXES

The Font box identifies the typeface you are currently using. To change to another face, click the drop-down list arrow at the right of the Font box. A drop-down list shows other available fonts. To choose another font, move the pointer to the desired font name and click it.

The next box, Font Size, works the same way. To change the type size, click the drop-down list arrow and a numerical listing of sizes (from 8 to 72 points) displays. Use your mouse pointer to find and then click your choice. You can also double-click in the Font Size box to highlight the current size, then key a new size.

THE FORMAT BAR BUTTONS

Following the two boxes is a row of eight buttons that allow you to easily toggle on and off a number of features. Let's identify these eight buttons (refer again to Figure 17-10):

- The first three buttons are labeled **B** (for bold), *I* (for italic), and <u>U</u> (for underline). Easy enough!

- The fourth button shows a color palette—the Color button. Clicking the Color button opens a drop-down list of more than a dozen colors you can choose for the text color.

- The next three buttons are Left, Center, and Right alignment buttons. Look closely and you will see that the horizontal lines, though small, sufficiently identify each.

- Last is the Bullets button, which activates the Bullet Style format.

Except for Colors, all buttons are toggle switches. To activate and deactivate the toggle buttons, highlight the text that you want to format and then just click the appropriate button. If you are keying text, click the appropriate button where you want the new formatting to begin. Click the button again to deactivate the feature.

EXERCISE ▷ 17.2

1. The **XTI Ad** document should be on your screen.

2. Center the first heading, *XYTRON INSTITUTE INC.*:
   a. Move the I-beam to the left margin. When the I-beam becomes a right-pointing arrow, move the arrow to point at the heading *XYTRON INSTITUTE INC.*
   b. Click the left mouse button once. The entire line is highlighted.
   c. Click the **Center** button on the format bar.

3. In the first paragraph, italicize the words *among the world's 10 largest*:

   a. Highlight the phrase by dragging from *among* to the end of the word *largest*.
   b. Click the **I** (Italic) button on the format bar.

4. Change all three headings to 14-point Helvetica bold. As you proceed, note that you highlight copy only once to perform several different actions to the same block!
   a. Highlight the heading **XYTRON INSTITUTE INC.**
   b. Click the **Font** box arrow to display the drop-down list. Highlight **Helvetica** and click it.
   c. Click the **Font Size** box arrow. Highlight and select **14**.

d. Click the **B** (Bold) button on the format bar. Click anywhere on the text screen to de-select the highlighted copy and see the re-sults of your changes.

e. Repeat steps 4a–4d for each of the two subheadings.

5. Indent the text paragraphs a half-inch:

a. Move the insertion point anywhere in the first paragraph.

b. Select **Paragraph** from the **Format** menu to open the Paragraph dialog box.

c. In the First line text box, key **.5**.

d. Click the **OK** button.

e. Repeat steps 5a–5d for each of the other text paragraphs (not for headings!).

6. Center the name and address information in the next-to-last para-graph. First separate the address into one block of six individual lines, as follows:

TIP

You can apply an indent or other for-matting to several ad-jacent para-graphs by highlighting them and then choosing the formatting option.

a. Click an insertion point immediately before the letter *S* in *Sandra*.

b. Backspace once, key a colon, and press **Enter** twice.

c. Click an insertion point immediately before the *H* in *Human*, backspace twice, and press **Enter**.

d. Click an insertion point immediately before the *X* in *Xytron*, backspace twice, and press **Enter**.

e. Click an insertion point immediately before the *I* in *Industry*, backspace twice, and press **Enter**.

f. Click an insertion point immediately before *[your city, state, and ZIP]*, backspace twice, and press **Enter**.

g. Click an insertion point immediately before the *F* in *Fax*, backspace twice, and press **Enter**. Delete the period following the Fax number.

h. Highlight the entire six-line address block and center it using the **Center** button on the format bar.

7. Save the updated file and leave it on screen for the next exercise.

Finding and Replacing Text

Flipping through pages of even a short document in an effort to find a word or phrase can be time consuming and frustrating. WordPad simplifies such searches. With WordPad, you can easily find the copy you are looking for and, if you wish, replace that copy with revised copy.

Look again at WordPad's Edit menu in Figure 17-4. There you will see Find, Find Next, and Re-place, three time-saving search options. Note that unlike the other two, Find Next is grayed out, an indi-cation that it is unavailable to you now. Each of these options is discussed below.

Find

The first option, Find, helps you locate a word or phrase. Select Find and the Find dialog box (Figure 17-11) displays, prompting you to enter the search word or phrase in the text box la-beled Find what. As soon as you key text, the Find Next button darkens, showing that it is now available to you. You can also access the Find dialog box by clicking the Find button on the toolbar.

FIGURE 17-11
Find dialog box

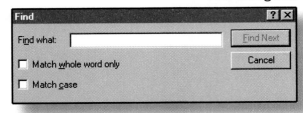

Below the text box are two options:

- **Match whole word only**. This option limits the search to whole words. If you do not check the Match whole word only option, Find will locate all words containing the text string entered in the Find what text box. For example, if you enter *the* in the Find what text box, all words containing those letter, such as *theory* and *apotheosis*, will be found.

- **Match case**. This option makes the search case sensitive: It matches upper- and lowercase letters exactly. For example, if you want to find only instances of the word *The*, not *the*, key *The* in the text box and click this option.

Find Next

Obviously, this choice is available only after Find has been used. That's why, as explained earlier, it first appears grayed out (unavailable) on the Edit menu. Clicking on the Edit menu and then clicking on Find Next quickly repeats the last search—no dialog box!

But there is an even faster way to use Find Next! Look at the Edit menu and note the shortcut key next to the Find Next option: F3. This is one time when using a shortcut key is faster than mousing around: one quick keystroke.

Replace

Selecting the Replace option displays the Replace dialog box (see Figure 17-12), which prompts you to enter two key pieces of information: Find what and Replace with. Key the search target in the Find what box, and then key your desired replacement in the Replace with box.

FIGURE 17-12
Replace dialog box

Begin a Replace operation by clicking either Find Next or Replace All. Find Next shows you the first occurrence of the text in the Find what box. You can then click the Replace button to change the highlighted search string to the text you keyed in the Replace with text box, or click Find Next to find the next occurrence. Clicking Replace All at any point changes all occurrences of the search string without showing you each one. Click Cancel to stop the Replace operation at any time.

E X E R C I S E ⇒ 17.3

1. The **XTI Ad** document should be on your screen.

2. Find all occurrences of the word *customer* and replace each use with *client:*
   a. Click an insertion point at the top of the document.
   b. Select **Replace** from the **Edit** menu.
   c. Key **customer** in the **Find what** text box, then press **Tab** to move to the Replace with text box (or click an insertion point in the text box).
   d. Key **client** in the **Replace with** text box.
   e. Click the **Find Next** button. WordPad searches the text and highlights the first occurrence of the search word. (To better see the highlighted word in the text window, move the Replace dialog box as necessary.)
   f. Click the **Replace** button. WordPad replaces the word and automatically moves to the next occurrence of customer.
   g. Continue replacing all occurrences of *customer* with *client*. Click the **OK** button when the message box tells you WordPad has finished searching the document.
   h. Click the **Close** button to close the Replace dialog box.

3. Find the word *reports* and change it to read *status reports*:
   a. Select **Find** from the **Edit** menu.
   b. Key **reports** in the **Find what** text box.
   c. Click the **Find Next** button. The search word is now highlighted on the text screen.
   d. Click **Cancel** to close the **Find** dialog box.
   e. In the text window, click an insertion point immediately before the *r* in the word *reports*.
   f. Key **status** followed by one space.

4. Check the **XTI Ad** document in Page Preview:
   a. Select **Print Preview** from the **File** menu.
   b. Use **Zoom In** to check the general format.

   c. Note that the name and address lines you centered in Exercise 17.2 are a little too far to the right because each line maintains the first-line indent of the paragraph they were originally part of.
   d. Close **Print Preview**. Highlight the six-line block of name and address information and remove the first-line indent in the **Paragraph** dialog box.
   e. Return to Print Preview and note the change in the centered copy.
   f. Make any other necessary changes to the document.

5. Save the document.

6. News Update: Xytron announced today that Sandra Kotes has been promoted to Executive Vice President of Corporate Development and that Tyrone Millrose has been named Human Resources Manager. You need to correct the file and print a corrected copy of the classified ad.

7. Correct the document:
   a. Select **Replace** from the **Edit** menu.
   b. Key **Sandra D. Kotes** in the **Find what** text box, then press **Tab**.
   c. Key **Tyrone Millrose** in the **Replace with** text box.
   d. Find and replace all occurrences of the search string.

8. Save the document.

9. Print one copy of the revised document.

10. Close **WordPad**. If instructed, shut down Windows and your computer.

Summary

This lesson covered WordPad's editing and formatting features. You learned that:

■ WordPad offers four helpful bars—the ruler bar, the toolbar, the format bar, and the status bar—all of which are optional. To display one or all of the bars on screen, pull down the View menu and click the option for the desired bar. A check mark next to the option name tells you that the option is selected (on). To deselect (turn off) an option, click once again on that option in the View menu.

■ Editing means changing the words in text (correcting spelling errors, updating figures, cutting superfluous words and phrases, adding or deleting punctuation—any kind of "content change"). Formatting means changing the look or the arrangement of text (that is, changing margins or indents; using italics, boldface, or underline; changing type sizes; changing fonts—visual changes, as compared to content changes).

■ The first step in making an editing or a formatting change is to select text; that is, highlight or identify the block of copy. You may select one character, or you may select an entire document.

■ To delete highlighted text, use the Cut option on the Edit menu. To move highlighted text, first cut the block, then paste it into its new position. To copy highlighted text, use Copy and Paste the same way you use Cut and Paste to move text. To retract a command just initiated, click the Undo option on the Editing menu, or click the Undo button (a curved arrow) on the toolbar.

■ Use WordPad's format bar to change character attributes—that is, to enhance text copy by using bold, italic, or underline.

■ Use the Font option on the Format menu to change more than one attribute at a time. When the Font dialog box displays, select the Font, Font Style, and Size of your choice. As you make each selection, the Sample box shows you what your choice looks like.

■ Select the Paragraph option on the Format menu to change the left, right, or first-line indent. The Paragraph dialog box also allows you to align paragraphs at the left margin or the right margin, as well as to center paragraphs.

■ Select the Find option on the Edit menu to search for a word or phrase in text. The Find dialog box then prompts you to enter copy in the Find what box. Select the Replace option on the Edit menu to find and then replace a word or a phrase with another word or phrase. The Replace dialog box prompts you to enter copy in both the Find what box and the Replace with box.

MULTIPLE CHOICE

Complete the following questions by circling the correct multiple choice letter.

1. In the Page Setup dialog box, you can change
   A. paper size
   B. orientation
   C. margins
   D. all of the above

2. In WordPad documents, you can select text by
   A. dragging across the text
   B. clicking once in the left margin to select the current line
   C. double-clicking on a word to select that word
   D. all of the above

3. To change the look of characters or numbers in a WordPad document, use the
   A. format bar
   B. Edit menu
   C. toolbar
   D. View menu

4. You set a tab stop by
   A. keying the location in the Tab stop position box and clicking Set
   B. clicking on the ruler to display a small L at the tab stop position
   C. either of the above
   D. neither of the above

5. You can use the WordPad toolbar to
   A. begin a new document
   B. open an existing document
   C. save the current document
   D. all of the above

MATCHING

Write the letter of the term in the right column that matches the definition in the left column.

_____ 1. Changing the words in text.

_____ 2. Changing the look or the arrangement of text.

_____ 3. The WordPad menu that contains commands to cut, copy, and paste text.

_____ 4. The WordPad menu used to change the look of text.

_____ 5. The screen element that contains buttons to bold, italicize, and underline text.

A. format bar

B. editing

C. formatting

D. Format menu

E. Edit menu

This project gives you the opportunity to review the concepts in this lesson and practice the techniques in the exercises. You will need your Windows Practice disk in order to complete this project.

1. Start WordPad.

2. Make the following document format settings:
   a. Font: Times New Roman, Regular, 12
   b. Ruler On
   c. Page Setup: Left and Right margins, 1.5 inches; Top and Bottom margins, 1 inch

3. Create a memo heading:
   a. Key **M E M O R A N D U M**, in bold capital letters with one space between letters, as shown.
   b. Center the heading.
   c. Click an insertion point after the word *MEMORANDUM*, and then press **Enter** three times.

NOTE:

If you press Enter while MEMORANDUM is highlighted, the highlighted copy will disappear.

   d. Click the **Left** align button on the format bar.

4. Click the ruler at the 0.75-inch mark to set a tab stop.

5. Key the following heading block, pressing **Tab** and **Enter** as indicated.

```
Date:[Tab]          October 12, 199-[Enter]

To:[Tab]            Ray T. Kleinst[Enter]

From:[Tab]          Shelley Wintergreen[Enter]

Subject:[Tab]       Training Seminars[Enter][Enter][Enter]
```

6. Key the body of the message shown below. Follow the line spacing shown. Before you key the tabular matter, use the Tabs dialog box to set tab stops at 2.25, 3.25, and 4.5 inches.

```
Employees have shown an especially strong interest in two seminars
listed in the Training Seminars Bulletin we distributed last week. To
meet employees' needs, therefore, we are adding three additional
sections of two seminars that were closed on the first day of
registration.

The additional sections are listed below:

Seminar                         Date        Time          Room
"Writing Reports"               July 12   8 am to 4 pm    T201
                                Aug. 4    8 am to 4 pm    T204
                                Sept. 6   8 am to 4 pm    T212

"Proofread with Confidence!"    July 19   8 am to 4 pm    T209
                                Aug. 21   8 am to 4 pm    T209
                                Sept. 13  8 am to 4 pm    T209

To register for any of these seminars, please call Training (Ext. 4321).
```

7. Proofread your document and correct any errors.

8. Save your memorandum on your Windows Practice disk with the file name **Seminars**.

9. Print one copy of your memorandum.

10. Close WordPad. If instructed, shut down Windows and your computer.

INSERTING OBJECTS IN A WORDPAD DOCUMENT

OBJECTIVES

Upon completion of this lesson, you will be able to:

■ Create an object.

■ Edit an object.

■ Revise and change objects.

■ Use Character Map in a WordPad Document.

🕐 **Estimated Time: 1.5 hours**

WordPad lets you combine text with illustrations, giving you plenty of opportunities to be creative and innovative. In this lesson, you will learn how to insert various objects in a WordPad document.

Creating Objects

You can insert a wide range of objects into your WordPad document: object images, pictures, media clips, worksheets, charts, and so on. You can create your own object; for example, you can draw or paint an object using a software application, or you can create a worksheet or a chart using Excel. Or you can pick up existing objects from "stock" sources; for example, if your system has the Microsoft ClipArt Gallery, you can browse the gallery for ideas and then insert a ClipArt image into your document with little more than a mouse click.

To insert an object into your WordPad document, select Object from the Insert menu. The Insert Object dialog box opens, as shown in Figure 18-1. This dialog box is your key to a host of object possibilities, so let's look at its features in detail.

Create New

Create New (the default; note that its button is selected) allows you to choose from any of the options listed in the Object Type list box; how many object types are available to you depends on your particular system. If Microsoft Office is installed on your system, you will have a substantial selection of applications, including Excel and PowerPoint. Of course, WordPad Document is always on the list (usually near the bottom, because the order is alphabetical). As you change selections, the Result box at the bottom of the window tells you what that option will do if selected. To select an object type, either double-click it or select it and click the OK button.

FIGURE 18-1
Insert Object dialog box

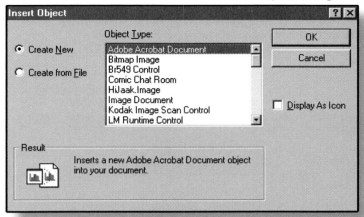

An application window opens, allowing you to create an object using that application. For example, if you choose Bitmap Image, a window (see Figure 18-2) opens with a small framed canvas next to a complete palette, inviting you to draw, paint, or airbrush an object (which will then be saved as a bitmap image). If you choose PowerPoint Presentation or PowerPoint Slide, the application opens, allowing you to create an object using PowerPoint. Likewise, you may choose Excel Chart, Excel Worksheet, or Excel Graph to create objects. There, in each application window, you create the object; then, with a simple double-click, you insert your new object into your "target" WordPad document and return to the document at the same time!

FIGURE 18-2
When you select Bitmap Image in the Insert Object
dialog box, this window opens

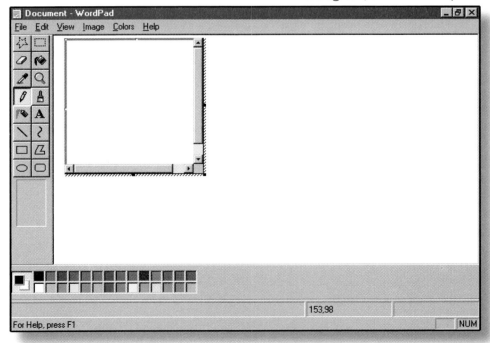

Create from File

Use this option when you have already created and saved an object and now want to insert that object into a WordPad document. When you click this button, the Object Type window disappears and in its place the smaller File text box displays, as shown in Figure 18-3.

FIGURE 18-3
Selecting the Create from File option to
insert an existing object

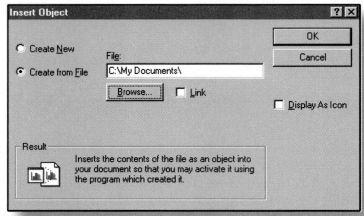

To locate your object file, you may key the path (complete file name, including disk drive letter and folder) in the File text box. To do so, highlight the name that now appears in the text box and key the correct path. The highlighted name disappears as you key. Or you may click an insertion point in the text box and then replace the path information. Or, you can click Browse to display the Browse dialog box (Figure 18-4). Select the object you want to insert and then click the Insert button.

FIGURE 18-4
Browse dialog box

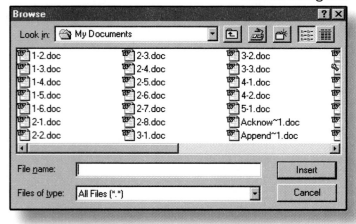

Before you insert an object, determine where you want the object to be positioned in the destination document. An object will be inserted immediately before the insertion point in a WordPad document.

Once the object is inserted in the document, the image can be sized (enlarged or reduced) and moved.

EXERCISE ⟹ 18.1

1. Open the **WordPad** program.

2. Place your Windows Template disk in the appropriate disk drive.

3. In a new WordPad document, key the following sentence:

   ```
   The object illustrated below was
   inserted from my Windows
   Template disk into my WordPad
   document.
   ```

4. Press **Enter** to move the cursor to a new line.

5. Select **Object** from the **Insert** menu. The Insert Object dialog box displays.

6. Click the **Create from File** button. The Object Type window closes, and the File text box opens.

7. Click the **Browse** button to display the Browse dialog box. In the **Look in** list box, click the drive that contains your template disk.

8. Look for the **Pencils** file in the display window and click to highlight it.

9. Click the **Insert** button in the lower right corner. The Browse dialog box closes, and the Insert Object dialog box reopens.

10. In the Insert Object dialog box, the File text box now reads *A:\Pencils.rtf* (or *B:\Pencils.rtf*).

11. Click the **OK** button. The object is inserted into your WordPad document, nearly filling the window. Scroll the window to note the placement of the object: It is precisely where your insertion point was positioned.

12. Save the document to your Windows Practice disk as **My Object**.

Editing Objects

Once an object is inserted into your document, you can edit the object in the following ways:

■ You can size the object (make it larger or smaller).

■ You can move (reposition) the object.

■ You can revise or change certain objects (not all).

Sizing Objects

To enlarge or reduce an object inserted into a WordPad document, you must first select the object. Click anywhere on the object, and it appears in a frame or a box, indicating that it is selected and that you are working with the object as a whole. Figure 18-5 shows a selected object. To deselect an object, move the pointer anywhere off the object and click the mouse button.

FIGURE 18-5
Selected object

Look carefully along the perimeter of the box that encloses the graphic in Figure 18-5 and find the eight small boxes, or *handles*, that appear at the four corners and at the four midpoints. Why "handles"? Because these eight handles are your key to sizing objects. With your mouse pointer, you grab these handles to resize the object! When you move the mouse pointer over a handle, the pointer becomes a double-headed arrow. The orientation of the double-headed arrow—vertical, horizontal, or diagonal—depends on whether the mouse pointer is on a top/bottom, side, or corner handle.

To reduce the size of an object, click on a handle and push inward, toward the object. To enlarge the size of an object, click on a handle and pull outward, away from the object. When you push or pull a corner, you reduce or enlarge the graphic in two directions, in two dimensions. But when you push or pull a center point, you reduce or enlarge in one direction only, thereby changing only one dimension. Think of it as compressing or stretching a box.

Moving or Positioning Objects

You can relocate an object in two ways:

- With the object selected, click on it and hold down the mouse button until a small gray box appears below the mouse pointer. Move the pointer to the place you want to move the object. A gray vertical line marks the point where the object will appear. Release the mouse button and the object moves to the new location.

NOTE:

This technique, called drag and drop, can be used with any selected object, including text.

- Select the object and then click any alignment button on the toolbar. The object moves to its new position.

Revising or Changing Objects

Once inserted into WordPad, the objects you created are not unchangeable, preserved in stone forever and ever. You can change them if you wish.

Not surprisingly, when you want to change or revise an inserted object, WordPad returns you to the original application in which the object was created. Let's say, for example, that you selected Bitmap Image, sketched a picture, and inserted that graphic as an object into a WordPad document. Now you open that document, see that graphic, and decide that you want to change its colors or redraw some lines. How do you proceed?

Select the Edit menu and look at the last option on the menu. These options change, depending on where the object was originally created. Figure 18-6 shows the submenu available for a document object. Choosing either Edit or Open from the Document Object submenu will reopen the application in which the graphic object was created. Once you are "there," you can change the object as you wish. Then double-click to insert the new, revised object into your WordPad document.

Note that not all inserted objects can be revised.

FIGURE 18-6
Document Object submenu

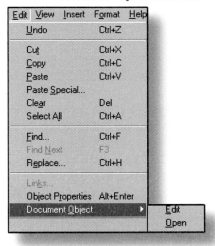

1. If necessary, select the object on your screen by clicking it.

2. Practice finding the double-headed arrows:
   a. Move the mouse pointer on the midpoint handle on the left side of the frame. It should become a horizontal double-headed arrow.
   b. Now move the pointer to the midpoint handle at the top of the frame. It should become a vertical double-headed arrow.
   c. Move the pointer to the top left corner handle. The pointer becomes a diagonal double-headed arrow.

3. Reduce the size of the object:
   a. With the pointer on the right middle handle, hold down the mouse button and drag to the left until you "crop out" the extra white space around the object.
   b. Release the mouse button. The object should appear smaller.

4. Use the other side handles to remove the white space from the other sides of the object. Try not to distort the image by making it either too narrow or too wide.

5. With the object still selected, click the **Center** alignment button on the format bar.

6. Save the file and print it.

7. Close **WordPad**.

Using Character Map in a WordPad Document

Like WordPad, *Character Map* is a Windows accessory application. Use Character Map to find a special character or symbol and copy it into your WordPad document—or copy a string of characters or symbols, if you wish.

To start Character Map, select the System Tools option on the Accessories menu, and then click Character Map. The Character Map window shown in Figure 18-7 opens, displaying the character set for the currently selected font, which is identified in the Font box. To change fonts, click the arrow to the right of the Font box; the Font drop-down list box opens, allowing you to select another font. Each time you select a new font, its character set is displayed in the window.

Admittedly, the box display is small, and you can't change the size of the window. But you can slightly enlarge the view of a character by pointing on it and holding down the mouse button (see Figure 18-8). When you find what you want, click the character to highlight it, and then click the Select button. Your choice will be displayed in the Characters to copy box. To make a *second copy* of that symbol, click Select again. To copy another symbol, click that symbol and then Select. With Character Map, you can create a string of characters, but you can choose only one character or symbol at a time.

When you have finished, click the Copy button. Your selection is now stored on the Clipboard. Minimize the Character Map window if you plan to return to it; close the window if you do not. When you return to your WordPad document, position the cursor where you want to insert the character (or the

FIGURE 18-7
Character Map window

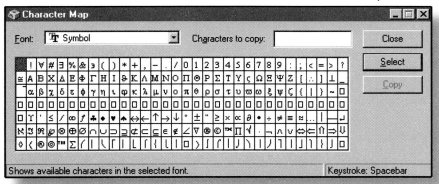

FIGURE 18-8
Enlarging the view of a character

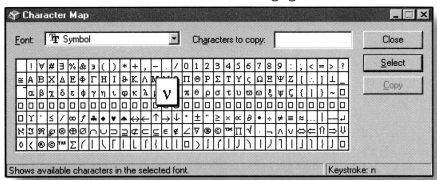

TIP

Notice that in the lower right corner of the Character Map window (see Figure 18-7), the Keystroke box tells you how to form the selected character directly from your keyboard without opening Character Map. Useful information!

character string), and then click the Paste button or select Paste on the Edit menu. Your symbol or your string is now inserted in your WordPad document. To insert it again, click Paste again (the character or string of characters remains stored until you clear the Clipboard).

E X E R C I S E ⟩ 18.3

1. Open **WordPad** and **Character Map**.

2. In WordPad, select font and size: Choose **Times New Roman** and **24** from the Font and Font Size boxes.

3. Click the **Center** button on the toolbar.

4. Key your full name on one line. When you finish keying, position the insertion point immediately before the first letter in your first name.

5. Click **Character Map** on the taskbar.

(continued on next page)

6. When Character Map opens, confirm that the Font box shows Times New Roman. If it does not, click the scroll arrow and select this font.

7. In the character set, find the copyright symbol (©). It should be on the fifth row, 10 boxes in from the left. Click the **Select** button, then click the **Copy** button.

8. Minimize the **Character Map** window so that you can access it again later.

9. In your WordPad document, confirm that the insertion point is positioned immediately before the first letter in your first name (see step 4).

10. Click the **Paste** button on the toolbar—the copyright symbol appears! Then space once.

11. Move the insertion point to the end of the line, after your name. Press **Enter** three times. Confirm that the Center command is still active.

12. Key the following copy, substituting your last name where indicated:

```
[your last name] Software
Applications
```

13. Click **Character Map** on the taskbar. The Character Map window opens.

14. Highlight the copyright symbol in the **Characters to copy** box and press **Delete**.

15. Find the trademark (™) symbol. It should be on the fourth row, seven boxes from the right. Click the **Select** button, and then click the **Copy** button.

16. Close **Character Map**.

17. With the insertion point positioned after the *s* in *Applications*, click the **Paste** button on the toolbar.

18. Save your document on the Windows Practice disk using your last name as the file name.

19. Select **Print Preview** from the **File** menu to view your work, click the **Print** button, and then click the **OK** button to print the document.

20. Close **WordPad**. If instructed, shut down Windows and your computer.

Summary

This lesson explained how to insert objects in a WordPad document. You learned that:

- You can insert a range of objects, including graphic images, pictures, media clips, spreadsheets, and charts, in a WordPad document.

- To insert an object in a WordPad document, click Object on the Insert menu. The Insert Object dialog box offers an array of choices for creating new objects and for using existing objects.

- Objects inserted into a WordPad document can be sized and moved on the page.

- Character Map is an application that lets you find and copy special symbols and characters and then insert the characters selected into your WordPad document. Character Map also tells you the keystroke combinations you can use to access a special character or symbol directly while keying a document, without even opening Character Map.

LESSON 18 REVIEW QUESTIONS

TRUE/FALSE

Each of the following statements is either true or false. Indicate your answer on the left by circling T if the statement is true and F if the statement is false.

T F 1. WordPad allows you to insert only short worksheets and charts.

T F 2. To insert an object, you select Object from the Edit menu.

T F 3. Selecting the Create New option in the Insert Object dialog box lets you create an object in a selected application that you can then insert in WordPad.

T F 4. You can resize and reposition most inserted objects.

T F 5. You can resize a selected object by dragging one of its handles.

FILL IN THE BLANKS

Complete the following sentences by writing the correct word or words in the blanks provided.

1. An object is inserted immediately _____ the insertion point in your WordPad document.

2. _____ are the small boxes that appear on the perimeter of a selected object.

3. The technique of moving an object with the mouse is known as _____.

4. Microsoft _____ contains many predesigned graphic images that you can insert in a WordPad document.

5. To insert an object in a WordPad document, click Object on the _____ menu.

LESSON 18 PROJECT

This project gives you the opportunity to review the concepts in this lesson and practice the techniques in the exercises. You will need your Windows Practice disk in order to complete this project.

1. Start **WordPad**.

2. Open the **Seminars** file from your Windows Practice disk.

3. Use the information in this document to create a one-page flier:
    a. Create a large centered title at the top of the page:

    `Improve Your Communications Skills!`

    b. Adapt the memo copy, revising it to make it "grab" employees and interest them in the seminars offered. Use your imagination in both the writing and the formatting, and have fun!

4. Save your flier copy on your Windows Practice disk as **New Flier**.

5. Insert a graphic object into your new document:
    a. Determine where you want to locate the object on your flier.
    b. Locate the **Books** file on your Windows Template disk.
    c. Insert the object in your flier.
    d. Resize the object if necessary.

6. Save your document.

7. Print a copy of the flier.

8. Proofread your flier. Revise the copy and the object as necessary and reprint the flier.

9. Close **WordPad**. If instructed, shut down Windows and your computer.

UNIT 5 REVIEW QUESTIONS ▽

WRITTEN QUESTIONS

Answer the questions below on a separate piece of paper.

1. How are the Save and the Save As commands different?

2. What is the difference between editing a document and formatting a document? Give an example of each.

3. What is the procedure for cutting several sentences of text?

4. What is a first-line indent? Describe its appearance and give an example of when you would use one.

5. What is the specific procedure you would follow to replace every occurrence of the word *normal* with the word *regular* in a WordPad document?

6. What is the general procedure for inserting an object into a WordPad document?

7. Why might you want to use Print Preview before printing a document?

8. Explain how you would locate and build a string of special characters to be inserted in a WordPad document.

9. What is portrait orientation and what is landscape orientation?

10. Distinguish between the New and the Open command on the WordPad File menu.

UNIT 5 APPLICATION ▽

SCANS

    A Corporate Communique project team is preparing the next issue of the Townsend & Co. newsletter. The cover story for the newsletter is an announcement about the company's new Web site. The story still needs to be edited and formatted so that it can be sent to the client for approval.

    Using WordPad, open the **TC Cover Story** document from your Windows Template disk. Read through the document and correct any misspelled words. Note that the client's name has been misspelled throughout. Use the Find and Replace options to correct the misspelled name. Add a title, or "headline," to the story.

Then, format the document. Change the type size, style, and alignment of text, as you feel is necessary. Break up the story into shorter paragraphs. Add indents and insert bullets if you think it will make the text easier to read. Boldface the names of buttons to make them stand out.

When you are satisfied with the appearance of the document, save it to your Windows Practice disk, and then print a copy.

Close all open applications. If instructed, shut down Windows and your computer.

CRITICAL THINKING

SCANS

Since you started working for R&P Industrial Products Inc., you realize that R&P is really two companies. One "half" is the manufacturer. The company operates plants across the country, each with state-of-the-art equipment, thanks to intelligent planning, purchasing, and management over the past ten years.

The other "half" is its headquarters office, home to a staff of hundreds—engineers, marketing experts, administrative assistants, data entry clerks, corporate trainers, accountants and bookkeepers, advertising copy writers, legal staff, sales representatives, and so on. Since you were first hired at R&P, you've witnessed how the entire staff does indeed work collaboratively on projects.

One report, one proposal, one set of specifications may have input from more than a dozen staff members! The flow of paper and floppy disks is dizzying! Which draft is the "latest"? Which is the "updated and revised" disk? Has the Executive Committee seen and approved the latest corrections to this proposal? And on and on . . .

A year ago R&P's president said that she wanted the office to function as smoothly as the plants now function. She created the Project Workgroup Task Force to research these questions: How can R&P use software to support collaborative writing, facilitate the workflow of documents, and manage document-creation and storage needs? She realized that if R&P is to remain competitive, its employees must have and use state-of-the-art software.

That software is here! The task force has researched, purchased, and installed DocPath and DocStore, two powerful software packages. Now your employees must be trained to use each sophisticated software package.

As a member of the Project Workgroup Task Force, you're now working with the Training Department to develop courses for all office employees. The Task Force chair, Myra Menendez, has asked you to develop an in-company flier to explain why the company needs the new software and to invite employees to a general meeting where they will receive complete details about the long-range training program. As a result, you drafted the information called **R&P Draft Flier** found on your Windows Template disk.

Revise that draft: Edit the text as necessary, add bold or italics for emphasis, change the font and the type size, use bulleted lists, and so on. Your flier will be distributed to all employees and posted on all bulletin boards.

PAINT

WORKING WITH THE PAINT TOOLS

OBJECTIVES

Upon completion of this lesson, you will be able to:

■ Open the Paint program.

■ Use the tool box.

■ Use the color box.

■ Use the drawing tools.

■ Use the paint tools.

■ Print a Paint document.

⏱ Estimated Time: 1.5 hours

Windows *Paint* is an accessory designed specifically for graphics—drawings and images of all kinds, from simple to complex. Paint provides tools that make the process of drawing images quite simple, and it offers many features that make revising and modifying artwork more fun than work (even for people who tremble at the thought of sketching on paper). The finished art can be used as a stand-alone image or placed in a newsletter, poster, letterhead, advertisement, notice, flier, or other document.

In the next four lessons, you will use Paint tools to create, save, edit, and print your drawings. You will also learn how to "import" images (that is, transfer to Paint an image created in another graphics program and then save the image as a Paint file). Paint may be puzzling at first, but stick with it. After a while, the results will be rewarding.

Introducing the Paint Tools

Windows Paint is accessible from the Accessories menu. The Paint icon resembles a bucket of paintbrushes. When Paint opens, you see an opening screen (Figure 19-1) with these familiar features: a title bar; Minimize, Maximize, and Close buttons; a work area (but this time, for drawing); a status bar; and, of course, a menu bar. In addition, the Paint window has two unique tool areas: a *tool box* and a *color box*.

🖌 Paint

FIGURE 19-1
Opening Paint window

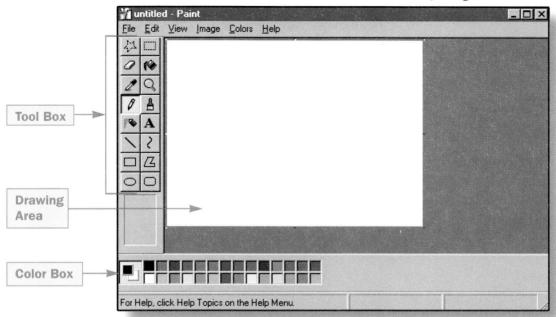

Tool Box

Drawing Area

Color Box

EXERCISE 19.1

1. Start Paint: Click the **Start** button, select **Programs**, then **Accessories**, and then choose **Paint**. The Paint screen appears.

2. Maximize the screen.

3. Display the **View** menu and make sure that the first three menu options are checked.

4. Leave the Paint screen open for the next exercise.

Using the Tool Box

The drawing area of the Paint window is where all the action takes place. The tools you need are to the left of the drawing area in the tool box, and the color box is beneath it. Take a look at Figure 19-2, an enlarged picture of the tool box. Notice that each tool is represented by an icon that illustrates the tool's function.

The 16 tools in the Paint tool box can be classified in four groups: *drawing tools*, *painting tools*, *modifying tools*, and a *text tool*:

■ Eight drawing tools are provided. The four line tools are used to draw lines, boxes, and circles. These tools are Pencil, Brush, Curve, and Line. Four shape tools (or geometric tools) are used to form shaped objects. The shape tools are Rectangle, Rounded Rectangle, Ellipse, and Polygon. Each shape tool is available in outline, filled/bordered, and filled (no border) styles.

■ Two painting tools are used to paint or "color" objects: Airbrush and Fill With Color.

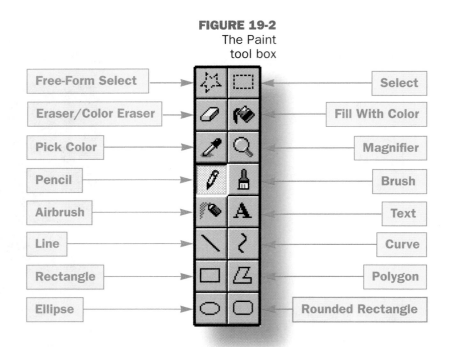

FIGURE 19-2
The Paint
tool box

Free-Form Select → Select

Eraser/Color Eraser → Fill With Color

Pick Color → Magnifier

Pencil → Brush

Airbrush → Text

Line → Curve

Rectangle → Polygon

Ellipse → Rounded Rectangle

■ Five modifying tools allow you to edit drawings and paintings: Select, Free-Form Select, Eraser/Color Eraser, Pick Color, and Magnifier.

■ One text tool lets you add text to your graphic.

To draw or paint, click the desired tool in the tool box. Then when you move the pointer to the drawing area, the pointer changes to the tool you selected or to a crosshair that allows you to draw a shape or line. When you select a tool, the bottom portion of the tool box may provide further options for the tool, such as line style or weight. Figure 19-3, for example, shows the different shapes available for the Brush tool and the kinds of lines that can be created with them. Simply click one of the options in the selection area to change the shape of the line.

FIGURE 19-3
Lines created using the Brush tool

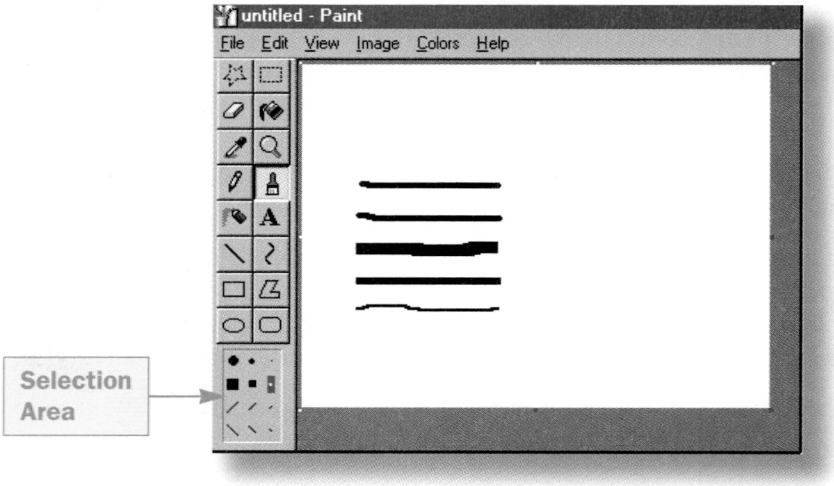

Selection
Area

Using the Color Box

The color box offers a palette of colors that you can use to select foreground and background colors. The two small overlapping squares at the far left of the color box indicate the current selections for foreground (top square) and background (bottom square) colors. By default, Paint selects black as the foreground color and white as the background color.

Generally, foreground color is controlled by the left mouse button and background color by the right button. When you are creating a filled shape, the foreground color is the outline and the background the fill. When you create a filled shape with no border, the foreground color is the fill. If you create the shape using the right mouse button, however, foreground and background colors reverse. Figure 19-4 shows how foreground and background colors are applied to various shapes drawn with the left and right mouse buttons.

FIGURE 19-4
The foreground color is red and the background color is black

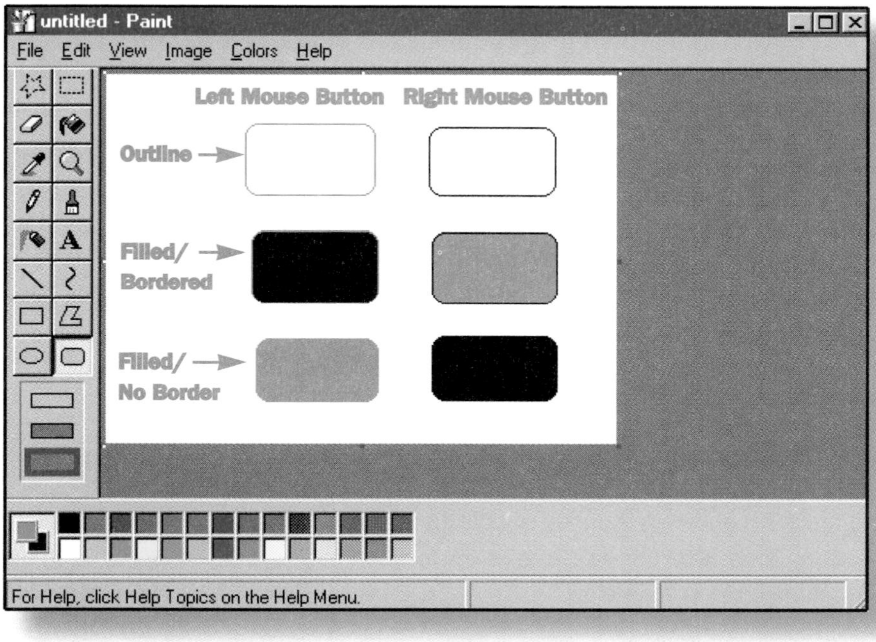

Color box colors and patterns can be changed easily. To change the foreground color or pattern, point to the desired color or pattern and click the left mouse button. To change the background color or pattern, point to the desired color or pattern and click the right mouse button.

Using the Drawing Tools

Now let's prepare to use Paint's drawing tools. First a few general guidelines:

■ To use a drawing tool, select it from the tool box. Position the tool's icon or crosshair where you want to begin the object, click and hold down the mouse button, drag until the object is the desired size, then release the mouse button.

■ To delete everything you've created with the current tool, select Undo from the Edit menu.

■ To clear your screen at any time, choose Clear Image from the Image menu.

The four line tools are used for drawing lines:

■ Use the Pencil tool to draw thin, free-form lines.

■ Use the Curve and the Line tools to draw curved and straight lines. To draw a perfectly straight line, hold down the Shift key as you draw.

■ Use the Brush tool to draw free-form lines using any of 12 brush shapes and sizes.

Before you use any line tools (except the Pencil), determine the size and/or the shape of the line by selecting from the palette of brush shapes or line sizes below the tool box.

The four shape tools (or geometric tools) are used for drawing objects:

■ Use the Rectangle and Rounded Rectangle tools to draw rectangles with square or rounded corners. If you want a perfect square, hold down the Shift key as you draw.

■ Use the Ellipse tool to draw circles and ovals. For a perfect circle, hold down the Shift key as you draw.

■ The Polygon tool is used to draw multisided closed objects with straight sides. Draw the first line of the object using the crosshair. Position the crosshair where you want the next side of the object *to end*, then click the mouse button. Double-click when you want to finish the object.

To change the weight of the line for these shapes, first select the Line tool and choose a line weight. To change outline and fill options, select foreground and background colors from the color box.

You're ready to use the drawing tools to create simple drawings. Don't worry about "artistic ability"! Your graphic may differ slightly from the illustrations in the Paint exercises. Just do your best and have fun!

E X E R C I S E 19.2

1. Figure 19-5 shows a number of objects in the drawing area. Use this figure as a guide when completing the steps below.

2. Draw a thick vertical line down the center of the screen:
   a. Select the **Line** tool from the tool box.
   b. Select the thickest (the last) line from the selection area.
   c. Position the crosshair at the top center of the drawing area—not on the menu bar.
   d. Press and hold down the **Shift** key, press

   > **TIP**
   >
   > If you make an error or you click or release the mouse button too soon, select the Undo option on the Edit menu.

   and hold down the mouse button, and then drag to the bottom of the drawing area. Release the mouse button, and then release the **Shift** key.

3. In the upper half of the left side of the page, draw a perfect square box with a thin border:
   a. With the Line tool still selected, choose the thinnest line from the selection area.
   b. Select the **Rectangle** tool.
   c. Select the first option (outline) from the selection area.
   d. Position the crosshair in the upper portion of the drawing area.
   e. Press and hold down the **Shift** key, press and hold down the left mouse button, and then drag down and to the right until you

have a box similar to the one in Figure 19-5. Release the mouse; then release the **Shift** key.

4. Draw a perfect filled circle in the lower half of the left side of the page:
   a. Select the **Ellipse** tool and choose the second option from the selection area.
   b. Select a foreground color or pattern by clicking in the color box with the left mouse button.
   c. Position the crosshair in the lower portion of the drawing area.

d. Press and hold down the **Shift** key, press and hold down the right mouse button, and then drag up and to the right until you have a circle similar to the one in Figure 19-5. Release the mouse; then release the **Shift** key.

5. Use the drawing tools to draw lines and objects similar to those in Figure 19-5. Do not draw anything on the right side of the screen.

6. Leave your practice drawing on screen for the next exercise.

FIGURE 19-5
Drawing objects in Paint

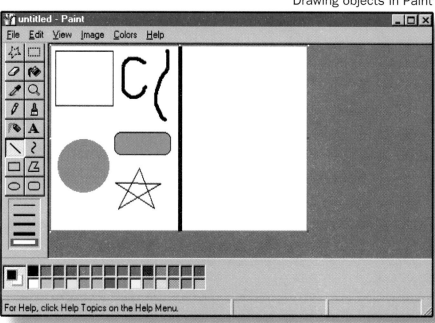

Using the Painting Tools

You can use the two painting tools to draw free-form objects and to fill graphic objects:

■ Like a can of spray paint, the Airbrush tool sprays a light circular pattern of colored dots, not a solid color. Click once on the mouse button to get one "spurt" of color; hold down the mouse button and drag to get a "trail" of spray color.

■ The Fill With Color tool fills a shape with color or shading. The shape must be completely enclosed (such as a box or a circle); any opening will cause the paint to spill out of the shape. The Fill With Color icon looks like a paint jar pouring paint.

1. Figure 19-6 shows several new objects added to the practice drawing. Use this figure as a guide as you complete the following steps.

2. Draw a thin horizontal line across the center of the right half of the screen using the Line tool.

3. Using the Brush tool, write your first name in the upper portion of the right side of the drawing area:
   a. Select the **Brush** tool.
   b. Select the last brush shape in the third row of the selection area.
   c. Select a foreground color (or pattern) of your choice by clicking on your selection on the color box with the left mouse button.
   d. Position the brush-shape mouse pointer where you want to start, press the mouse button, and "write" your name.

4. Using the Brush tool, draw three different closed shapes in the lower portion of the right side of the drawing area:
   a. Select the **Brush** tool, if it is not already selected.
   b. Select a foreground color (or pattern) of your choice.
   c. Draw the shape. Be sure you make a closed shape.
   d. Repeat steps 4a–4c to create two additional objects.

5. Use the Fill With Color tool to fill the interior of two of the objects you created in step 4 with a different color or pattern:
   a. Select the **Fill With Color** tool from the tool box.
   b. Select a foreground color or pattern from the color box.
   c. Position the tip of the pouring paint from the Fill With Color mouse pointer inside the object you want to fill.
   d. Click the left mouse button.
   e. Repeat steps 5b–5d to fill one more object.

6. Use the Airbrush to fill the interior of the last of your three objects with a different color or pattern:
   a. Select the **Airbrush** tool from the tool box.
   b. Select a foreground color or pattern from the color box.
   c. Position the Airbrush tool mouse pointer inside the object where you want the airbrush stroke, press and hold the mouse button, and "spray" the interior of the object.

7. Leave the Paint document on screen for the next exercise.

FIGURE 19-6
Using the painting tools

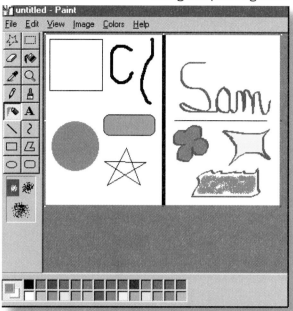

Saving and Printing a Drawing

Saving and printing a drawing is the same process as saving and printing a Notepad or WordPad document.

You select Save As on the File menu to save the drawing for the first time. Select Save to periodically save your work. To print a drawing, select Print from the File menu to display the Print dialog box. Here you can choose what pages to print and how many copies to print.

To change page settings before you print, choose Page Setup from the File menu. The Page Setup dialog box lets you change paper size, orientation, and margins.

To see how your drawing will appear on the page before you print it, choose Print Preview from the File menu. The Print Preview window allows you to zoom in on your drawing and to print it if you are satisfied with it.

EXERCISE ⇨ 19.4

1. Insert your Windows Practice disk.

2. Select **Save As** from the **File** menu and save your drawing to the Windows Practice disk as **My Drawing**.

3. Choose **Print Preview** from the **File** menu to view your drawing as it will look when printed.

4. Click the **Print** button in the **Print Preview** window.

5. Choose **Exit** from the **File** menu to quit the drawing and close **Paint**.

Summary

This lesson introduced you to Windows' Paint accessory application. You learned that:

■ Paint is a powerful tool for producing stand-alone artwork or developing graphics to be incorporated into documents such as newsletters, reports, letters, and memos.

■ Paint can perform electronically an assortment of graphic-arts tasks, such as coloring and shading lines; creating geometric shapes; moving and copying partial images; and inserting, cutting, copying, and moving text.

■ Paint provides a variety of easy-to-use drawing and painting tools that allow you to create graphics from simple to complex.

■ Paint is located on the Accessories menu. To open Paint, click its icon (a bucket of paintbrushes).

■ In addition to familiar window features, the Paint window displays two unique tool areas: a tool box and a color box. But the drawing area of the Paint window is where all the action takes place.

■ The tool box provides many tools to support your drawing activities and enhance your graphics—drawing tools, painting tools, modifying tools, and a text tool.

■ The color box lets you place color in the foreground or in the background of your drawing.

LESSON 19 REVIEW QUESTIONS

MULTIPLE CHOICE

Complete the following questions by circling the correct multiple choice letter.

1. All of the following are drawing tools except the
   A. Curve tool
   B. Rounded Rectangle tool
   C. Free-Form Select tool
   D. Ellipse tool

2. When painting an object,
   A. position the tool's icon inside the area you wish to paint
   B. be sure the area is a closed area
   C. select the fill color before clicking inside the object
   D. all of the above

3. When drawing, if you release the mouse button before you intend to, you can
   A. select the Clear Image option from the Image menu
   B. select the Undo option from the Edit menu
   C. select a different drawing tool and start over
   D. none of the above

4. The Ellipse tool is used to draw
   A. perfect circles
   B. filled circles
   C. ovals
   D. all of the above

5. The left mouse button controls the
   A. foreground color or pattern
   B. background color or pattern
   C. width of the drawing line
   D. density of the Airbrush tool's spray

MATCHING

Write the letter of the term in the right column that matches the definition in the left column.

_____ 1. The portion of the Paint window where you create and modify your graphic.

_____ 2. A tool used to draw a circle.

_____ 3. A painting tool that sprays a light circular pattern of colored dots.

_____ 4. The color controlled by the left mouse button.

_____ 5. The color controlled by the right mouse button.

A. Ellipse

B. Airbrush

C. foreground

D. background

E. drawing area

LESSON 19 PROJECT

This project gives you the opportunity to review the concepts in this lesson and practice the techniques in the exercises. You will need your Windows Practice disk in order to complete this project.

1. Figure 19-7 shows a drawing that was created using the Paint tools you learned about in this lesson. Use this figure as a guide to create a similar drawing.

2. When you are done, save the drawing as **Project 19** to your Windows Practice disk.

3. Exit **Paint.** If instructed, shut down Windows and your computer.

FIGURE 19-7

WORKING WITH THE MODIFYING TOOLS

OBJECTIVES

Upon completion of this lesson, you will be able to:

- Use the selection tools.

- Work with selected objects.

- Use the Eraser/Color Eraser tool.

- Save a drawing using a different file type.

⏱ **Estimated Time: 1.5 hours**

E ven if you have steady hands and a good imagination, you may want to modify your work. Paint offers several tools that can help you modify a drawing. In this lesson, you will learn how to use Paint's modifying tools.

Modifying a Drawing

A s you have already learned in previous lessons, before you can edit an object, you must select it. Paint has two selection tools: Select and Free-Form Select. The Select and Free-Form Select tools perform essentially the same function: They select a part of a drawing so that you can modify it. The Free-Form Select tool is used to select irregularly shaped portions of a drawing; its icon shows an irregular shape. The Select tool is used to select rectangular areas; its icon shows a rectangular shape.

To select a shape with the Select tool, first click on the tool. Then position the crosshair just above and to the left of the object to be selected. At this position, press the left mouse button and drag the crosshair down and to the right until the dotted line completely encloses the desired selection. Be sure that the entire object is within the displayed dotted rectangle. Only the area within the dotted rectangle can be modified.

To select a shape with the Free-Form Select tool, first click on the tool. Then position the crosshair near the object to be selected, press the left mouse button, and drag a line around the shape to be selected. Since you control the form the line takes, you can enclose as much or as little within the selected area as needed. Once you release the mouse button, a rectangular dotted line appears around your selection.

Working with Selected Objects

When an area is selected with either the Select tool or the Free-Form Select tool, the selection—called a *cutout*—can be resized, moved, cut, copied, or further modified.

RESIZING AN OBJECT

Paint allows you to easily resize a selected object. The selected object has handles that can be used to change the width or height of the object. This process is exactly the same as the one you learned in Lesson 18 to resize objects in WordPad.

You should keep in mind these points, however, about resizing:

■ Paint will allow you to resize a filled object, but the resizing process leaves behind a rectangle of the fill color. You can erase this rectangle by using the Eraser (you'll learn more about the Eraser shortly), but if you think you may have to adjust sizes of objects, you should create them as out-lines and then use the Fill With Color tool to add the fill once you are satisfied with the object sizes.

■ Because Paint creates objects one dot at a time, resizing an object can sometimes make the lines of the object very jagged. You are encouraged to create your objects as near to their final size as possible to avoid the "jaggies" that may appear when you resize.

MOVING, CUTTING, OR COPYING AN OBJECT

To move a cutout, place the pointer inside the selection rectangle. The mouse pointer becomes a four-headed arrow. Hold down the mouse button and drag the cutout to its new location. To copy a cutout, hold down Ctrl while dragging the cutout to its new location.

You can move or copy a cutout in one of two ways: *transparently* or *opaquely* (the default):

■ When you move or copy a cutout transparently, any part of the cutout that is in the background color assumes the underlying color of the location to which it is moved or copied. To move or copy transparently, click the Draw Transparent icon in the selection area.

■ When you move or copy a cutout opaquely, all parts of the cutout retain their original colors at the new location. To move or copy opaquely, click the Draw Opaque icon in the selection area.

If you want to use a cutout in a new drawing or an existing drawing, you can use the Cut, Copy, and Paste commands on the Edit menu. First select the object to be cut or copied, then choose the appropriate command. The cutout is stored on the Clipboard and is available to be pasted into another drawing. You can also use this process to paste a number of identical objects in the current drawing, as a way of ensuring consistency.

USING COPY TO AND PASTE FROM

Paint offers two more ways to work with cutouts: the Copy To and Paste From commands.

The Copy To command on the Edit menu allows you to save only a portion of a drawing. To use the Copy To command, select the object or portion of the drawing you want to save, then choose Copy To from the Edit menu. In the Copy To dialog box, indicate where you want to save the object, give it a name, and choose a file type. The next time you open the file, Paint displays only the selected object.

The Paste From command allows you to specify where a pasted object will be located. When you paste an object from the Clipboard using the Paste command, the pasted object always appears in the top left corner of the screen. To use Paste From, draw a selection rectangle where you want to insert an object and then choose Paste From from the Edit menu. In the Paste From dialog box, choose the name of the object you want to insert. Paint pastes the object in the selection rectangle you drew, enlarging the rectangle if necessary to accommodate the object.

Using the Eraser/Color Eraser Tool

The Eraser/Color Eraser tool has two functions. Eraser erases by changing all colors in its path to the current background color. To use the Eraser, first click it, choose one of the four eraser sizes shown in the selection area, and then drag using the *left* mouse button over the area to erase.

The Color Eraser erases only the selected foreground color by changing it to the selected background color. To use the Color Eraser, first click the Eraser/Color Eraser tool, check that the appropriate foreground and background colors are chosen, and then drag using the right mouse button over the color to be changed.

E X E R C I S E ⟹ 20.1

1. Start **Paint**, and open the **Star** file from your Windows Template disk.

2. Delete the yellow square behind the blue star. Use the Color Eraser tool for this task:
   a. Select white as the background color if necessary: click white with the *right* mouse button.
   b. Select yellow as the foreground color: click yellow with the *left* mouse button.
   c. Click the **Eraser/Color Eraser** tool. Choose the largest eraser from the selection area. Press and hold the right mouse button as you drag the eraser across the picture. All yellow color should be erased.

 **NOTE:**

If you hold down the left mouse button by mistake and erase some of the drawing, stop immediately and choose Undo from the Edit menu. Then begin again holding down the right mouse button.

3. Select the star and resize it:
   a. Choose the **Select** tool.
   b. Place the crosshair above and to the left of the star.

c. Press the mouse button and drag the dotted rectangle around the star. If the rectangle does not enclose the entire star when you release the mouse button, click on any blank area to remove the selection rectangle and then start over.

d. Place the mouse pointer on the lower right corner handle and drag upward and inward to reduce the size of the star by about one-quarter. Your screen should resemble Figure 20-1.

4. Create and position a copy of the object:
   a. With the object still selected, place the mouse pointer anywhere inside the selection rectangle. The pointer becomes a four-headed arrow.
   b. Hold down the **Ctrl** key and drag downward and to the right until the copy of the object is no longer overlapping the original object. Release the **Ctrl** key and the mouse button. You now have two stars in the work area.

5. Leave the drawing on-screen for the next exercise.

FIGURE 20-1
Selecting and resizing an object

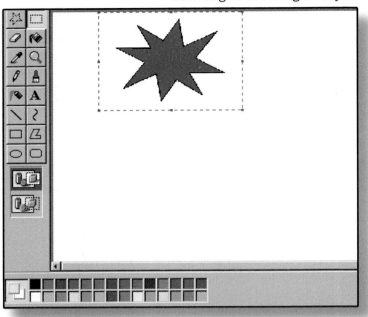

Saving a Drawing

Y ou learned in the last lesson that you save a drawing in Paint in the same way you saved documents in Notepad and WordPad. Choose Save As to save the drawing the first time or with a new name or location; choose Save to store changes to an existing drawing.

You have an important decision to make, however, the first time you save a drawing, and that is what file format to use. Paint's Save As dialog box contains the Save as type drop-down list shown in Figure 20-2. You can see that Paint offers you a number of options for saving your file, from monochrome bitmap to 24-bit bitmap. The default, 24-bit bitmap, gives you the most options for color and provides the best resolution, but files saved in this format can be very large. If you are working on a floppy disk, you may not be able to store many 24-bit Paint files to the disk. For the purposes of this course, the 256 Color Bitmap option provides adequate color range and resolution and results in files of manageable size.

FIGURE 20-2
Save as type drop-down list

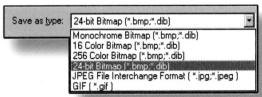

EXERCISE 20.2

1. The **Star** file should be on your screen. Save it to your Windows Practice disk:
   a. Remove your Windows Template disk and insert your Windows Practice disk.
   b. Choose **Save As** from the **File** menu.
   c. In the **Save As** dialog box, click the **Save as type** down arrow to display the drop-down list. Select **256 Color Bitmap**.
   d. In the **File** name box, key **Gala Flier**.
   e. Click the **Save** button.

NOTE:

Be patient! It takes longer to save a drawing than to save a text file.

2. Print a copy of the document.

3. Exit **Paint**. If instructed, shut down Windows and your computer.

Summary

This lesson covered Paint's modifying tools. You learned that:

■ Paint has two selection tools. The Select tool is used to select rectangular areas. The Free-Form Select tool is used to select irregularly shaped portions of a drawing.

■ A selected area is called a cutout, and the cutout can be resized, moved, cut, copied, and modified.

■ You can resize a selected object by dragging a handle. When you resize a filled object, you must use the Eraser tool to remove fill color that is left behind.

■ You can move or copy a cutout in one of two ways: transparently, where any part of the cutout that is in the background color assumes the underlying color of the location to which it is moved or copied; and opaquely, where all parts of the cutout retain their original colors at the new location.

■ The Eraser tool erases by changing all colors in its path to the current background color. The Color Eraser tool erases only the selected foreground color by changing it to the selected background color.

LESSON 20 REVIEW QUESTIONS

TRUE/FALSE

Each of the following statements is either true or false. Indicate your answer on the left by circling T if the statement is true and F if the statement is false.

T   F   1.   You press the right mouse button when using the Free-Form Select tool and the left mouse button when using the Select tool.

T   F   2.   You would use the Select tool to select a rectangular area.

T   F   3.   You cannot resize filled objects.

T   F   4.   A transparent cutout assumes the underlying color of the location to which it is moved or copied.

T   F   5.   The default file type for Paint drawings is 24-bit bitmap.

MATCHING

Write the letter of the term in the right column that matches the definition in the left column.

_____ 1. That portion of a drawing that is cut or copied.

_____ 2. A modifying tool that lets you select irregular shapes.

_____ 3. A modifying tool that lets you select rectangular shapes.

_____ 4. A modifying tool that erases by changing all colors in its path to the current background color.

_____ 5. A modifying tool that erases only the selected foreground color by changing it to the selected background color.

A. Eraser

B. Color Eraser

C. Select

D. Free-Form Select

E. Cutout

LESSON 20 PROJECT

This project gives you the opportunity to review the concepts in this lesson and practice the techniques in the exercises. You will need your Windows Template disk and Windows Practice disk in order to complete this project.

1. Start **Paint** and open the **Picture** file from your Windows Template disk.

2. Copy the turquoise chess piece (the one in the upper right of the window) to the Clipboard using the **Free-Form Select** tool.

3. Select **New** from the **File** menu to close the **Picture** file and start a new drawing.

4. Paste the chess piece into the new document.

5. Remove the black color from the object using the Color Eraser tool. (*Remember*: Use the *right* mouse button to erase with the Color Eraser.)

6. Place a copy of the object to the right of it and below it.

7. Add an unfilled black rectangle around the two objects using the third line thickness.

8. Save the drawing to your Windows Practice disk as **Chess**. Use the **256 Color Bitmap** file type.

9. Print the drawing and exit **Paint**. If instructed, shut down Windows and your computer.

EXPLORING OTHER PAINT OPTIONS

OBJECTIVES

Upon completion of this lesson, you will be able to:

■ Flip and rotate objects in a drawing.

■ Stretch, shrink, and skew objects in a drawing.

■ Create text blocks using the Text tool.

■ Format text in a drawing.

🕐 **Estimated Time: 1 hour**

In addition to the modifying tools you learned about in the last lesson, Paint provides you with even more options for changing and enhancing the appearance of your drawings. In this lesson, you will learn how to apply special effects to drawings, and how to add text.

Using Special-Effects Options

Paint's Image menu, shown in Figure 21-1, offers three special-effects options:

■ **Flip/Rotate**. Use this option to flip the selected object horizontally or vertically or rotate it 90, 180, or 270 degrees.

■ **Stretch/Skew**. This option allows you to stretch and shrink your selection horizontally and vertically (you specify the percentage). You can also skew (distort) your selection horizontally and vertically (you specify the number of degrees).

■ **Invert Colors**. This option changes the color of the selected object to the color opposite its position on the RGB color wheel. For example, black becomes white, and white becomes black.

To use these special effects, first select an object with either the Select tool or the Free-Form Select tool. Then choose the desired option from the Image menu. If you choose Flip/Rotate or Stretch/Skew, Paint opens a dialog box to allow you to choose among further options. Remember, if you want to reverse the special effect you applied, just use the Undo command.

FIGURE 21-1
Image menu

Image	
Flip/Rotate...	Ctrl+R
Stretch/Skew...	Ctrl+W
Invert Colors	Ctrl+I
Attributes...	Ctrl+E
Clear Image	Ctrl+Shft+N
✔ Draw Opaque	

EXERCISE  21.1

1. Start **Paint** and open the **Gala Flier** Paint file from your Windows Practice disk.

2. Rearrange the star arrangement currently on your screen:
   a. Use the **Select** tool to draw a selection rectangle around the star on the right.
   b. Drag the cutout so that it is just below and to the right of the star on the left, as shown in Figure 21-2.

3. Resize and create a copy of the star arrangement currently on your screen:
   a. Use the **Select** tool to draw a selection rectangle around both stars.
   b. Drag the cutout to the top left of the screen.
   c. With the cutout still selected, reduce the size of the object by about one-quarter.
   d. With the cutout still selected, hold down the **Ctrl** key and drag a copy of the object near the top right of the screen.

4. Flip the object horizontally:
   a. With the object still selected, choose **Flip/Rotate** from the **Image** menu. The Flip and Rotate dialog box appears as shown in Figure 21-3.
   b. Make sure **Flip horizontal** is selected, and then click the **OK** button.
   c. The object "changes direction" from left to right.

5. Move the object into the top right corner of the screen if necessary.

6. Your screen should resemble Figure 21-4.

7. Save the file as **Gala Flier Enhanced** to your Windows Practice disk.

8. Leave the file on screen for the next exercise.

FIGURE 21-2
Rearranging objects

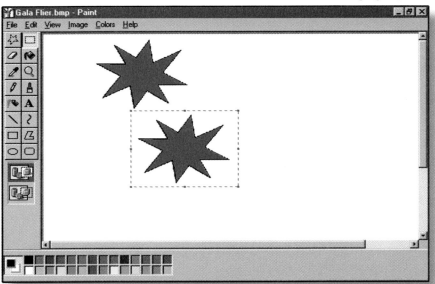

FIGURE 21-3
Flip and Rotate dialog box

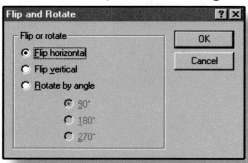

FIGURE 21-4
Stars have been copied and flipped

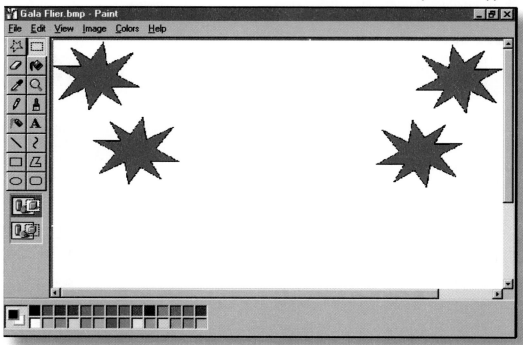

Changing Image Attributes

While you will usually want to use Paint's default settings for color, measurement, and screen size, particular projects may require you to change these settings. You can do so by choosing Attributes from the Image menu. Paint displays the Attributes dialog box shown in Figure 21-5. Here you can change screen size, unit of measurement, and whether Paint uses colors or a black and white palette. To restore the original settings, click the Default button.

FIGURE 21-5
Attributes dialog box

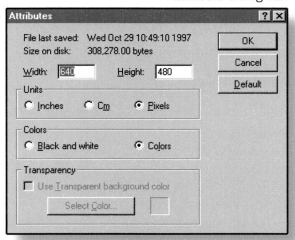

Working with the Text Tool

The Text tool allows you to add text to any drawing. Paint considers text to be an object just like a line or shape, so once you have completed your text, you can select it and move it just as you would any other object. When creating a text block for a drawing, you might find it easier to create the text block elsewhere on the screen and then move it into place as you would move any other object.

To use the Text tool:

■ Select the Text tool in the tool box.

■ Position the crosshair where you want your text to begin; then drag diagonally down and to the right to create a text frame. The insertion point will blink in the upper left corner of the frame and the Fonts dialog box shown in Figure 21-6 appears. If the Fonts dialog box does not open, select Text Toolbar from the View menu.

■ Key the text. Click outside the text frame to complete the entry.

You may change the appearance or specifications of the text type, but you must do so before you complete the text entry. You change the font, style, or size of the text by using options on the Text toolbar. Select font and size from the drop-down lists and click the appropriate buttons to change the style. As you make selections from the Text toolbar, the text immediately changes to reflect your choices. Once you click outside the text frame or choose another tool, you can no longer edit your text.

FIGURE 21-6
Text toolbar

A text block can have only one font, size, and style. If you want text to show different fonts, styles, or sizes, create a series of text blocks and then drag them into place.

E X E R C I S E ▷ 21.2

1. Add text to your flier:
   a. Select the **Text** tool from the tool box.
   b. Draw a text frame at the top center of the screen, between the two sets of stars, about 1 inch high.
   c. Choose **Text Toolbar** from the **View** menu, if the Text toolbar does not automatically appear.
   d. Select **Times New Roman**, **24**, and **B** on the Text toolbar. If desired, select a foreground color other than black from the color box.
   e. Click in the text frame. Key **Children's Hospital** and then click elsewhere on the drawing to close the text frame.
   f. Select the text block using the **Select** tool and reposition it if necessary to center it between the stars.

2. Using the instructions above, create three more text blocks containing the following information. Create each block below the stars and move it into place at the top of the flier between the two sets of stars.

   New Year's Benefit Gala
   [Set in **Times New Roman, 18, Bold Italic**]

Special Guest
Appearance by:
   [Set in **Times New Roman, 14, Bold**]

The Starlight
Quartet
   [Set in **Book Antiqua, 24**]

TIP
If these fonts are not available on your system, select a comparable font.

3. Create a final text block to be positioned below the stars, using the font, size, and style of your choice:

   December 31   8:00 pm   Addiston
   Ballroom   R.S.V.P.

4. If desired, change the colors of the stars by using the **Fill With Color** tool.

5. Your drawing should resemble Figure 21-7.

6. Save the drawing and print a copy.

7. Exit **Paint**. If instructed, shut down Windows and your computer.

FIGURE 21-7
Adding text to a drawing

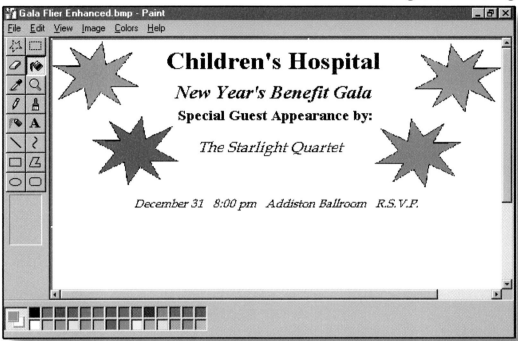

Summary

This lesson covered Paint's special effects options and the Text tool. You learned that:

- The Image menu options allow you to create a variety of special effects.

- You can flip a selected object horizontally or vertically or rotate it 90, 180, or 270 degrees.

- You can stretch and shrink your selection horizontally and vertically. You can also skew (distort) your selection horizontally and vertically.

- You can change the color of the selected object to the color opposite its position on the RGB color wheel. For example, black becomes white, and white becomes black.

- The Text tool allows you to add text to any drawing.

- Paint treats a text block like any other object.

TRUE/FALSE

Each of the following statements is either true or false. Indicate your answer on the left by circling T if the statement is true and F if the statement is false.

T F 1. You use the Flip/Rotate option to switch the color of a selected object to the color opposite its position on the RGB color wheel.

T F 2. You find the special effects options on the Image menu.

T F 3. The Undo command cannot be applied to special effects applied to an object.

T F 4. You can rotate an object either vertically or horizontally.

T F 5. When you select the Text tool, the mouse pointer changes to a crosshair.

FILL IN THE BLANKS

Complete the following sentences by writing the correct word or words in the blanks provided.

1. The _____ special-effects option lets you turn a shape 90, 180, or 270 degrees.

2. The _____ tool is used to add blocks of words to a drawing.

3. The _____ toolbar contains buttons that let you change the look of text you add to a drawing.

4. To display the Text toolbar, you select Text Toolbar from the _____ menu.

5. The _____ special-effects option lets you quickly change the color of a selected object.

LESSON 21 PROJECT

This project gives you the opportunity to review the concepts in this lesson and practice the techniques in the exercises. You will need your Winodws Template disk and Windows Practice disk in order to complete this project.

1. Start **Paint**. You will create the card shown in Figure 21-8.

2. Use the **Select** tool to draw a rectangle in the middle of the drawing area.

3. Use **Paste From** on the **Edit** menu to paste the **Face** file from your Windows Template disk in the drawing area. Enlarge the bitmap to accommodate the image if necessary.

4. Create the image of the boy's face in the center of the drawing area:
   a. Use the **Select** tool to select the parts of the image.
   b. Drag each part into place using the left mouse button.

5. Add the balloon:
   a. Flip the balloon vertically before moving it into place.
   b. Enlarge the balloon a bit.

6. Insert the text in the balloon shown in Figure 21-8 using **Arial**, **12** point, **bold**, and **italic**.

7. Add the double-line box around the image. First draw the thin inside box, then select the **Line** tool, choose a thicker line style, and reselect the **Rectangle** tool to draw the heavier box.

8. Insert the text in the box as shown in Figure 21-8, creating each line separately and using **Arial**, **18** point, **bold**.

9. Save the graphic on your Windows Practice disk with the file name **My Face** in the **256 Color Bitmap** file type.

10. Print a copy of your drawing and then exit **Paint**. If instructed, shut down Windows and your computer.

FIGURE 21-8

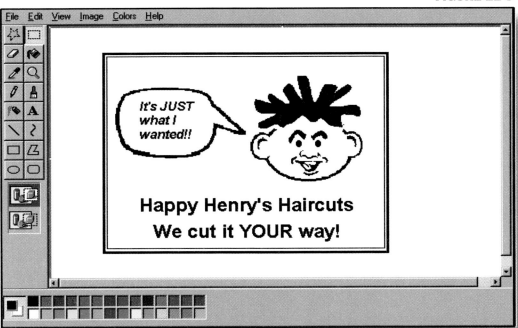

LESSON

22

USING ADVANCED PAINT FEATURES

OBJECTIVES

Upon completion of this lesson, you will be able to:

- Import graphic files into a Paint drawing.

- Use the View Bitmap command to control the display of an imported graphic.

- Use the Zoom option to work with different areas of a Paint drawing.

- Define pixel and use pixel coordinates to manage objects on the screen.

🕐 **Estimated Time: 1 hour**

By now you probably have a good idea how to use the basic features of the Paint program. Paint includes a number of other features and capabilities that allow you to create more sophisticated drawings and edit them more exactly. These features are covered in the lesson.

Using Other Sources for Drawing Material

Until now, you have created simple objects yourself and worked with an object supplied on your Windows Template disk. But there are a number of other sources for material that you can use in your drawings.

Importing Graphic Files into Paint

Import means to bring into Paint a graphic file that was created outside of Paint. You can import graphic files that were created with another painting or drawing program. You can also convert a paper drawing or photograph to an electronic file format. How? With a device called a *scanner*. Then, once converted to a graphic file, that drawing or photograph too can be imported into Paint.

You must follow these guidelines when importing graphic files:

- You can import only graphic files that have BMP, MSP, or PCX formats. BMP is the original format for *Bitmap* (thus the extension **.bmp**). *MSP* is the format for **M**icrosoft **P**aint files (from earlier versions of Windows). *PCX* is the graphic-file format used in PC Paint (an application by ZSoft Corporation). PCX is a well-known standard for graphic files.

- You need both a monitor and a video adapter capable of displaying all of Paint's 256 colors. If your equipment is capable of displaying only 16 colors, when you import a 256-color image Paint will adjust the colors to the 16-color limitation (obviously, the imported graphic will lose some of the original's color). If you have a monochrome monitor, your images will display only in shades and patterns of black and white.

To import a file into Paint, use the Open command on the File menu. Save the imported file using any of Paint's file types.

CAPTURING SCREENS

Another source of material for Paint is your computer screen itself. You can capture any image that appears on the screen by using the Print Screen key. (Your key may read Prt Scrn or Print Scrn.)

To capture a screen:

- Press the Print Screen key to capture the entire screen.

- Press Alt+Print Screen to capture only the active window.

NOTE:

Some keyboards require that you press Shift+Print Screen to capture and copy the entire display to the Clipboard.

Nothing noticeable happens when you capture the screen, but the captured screen is stored on the Clipboard just like a cut or copied object. To use the capture, use the Paste command to place it in your drawing.

Viewing a Bitmap Larger Than the Screen

When you use the Open command to import a graphic file or when you paste an image from the Clipboard into Paint, Paint adjusts to accommodate the imported image. If the image is larger than the drawing area, the entire graphic will be placed in memory, *but only part of it will be visible*. You can use the scroll bars to view those areas outside the drawing area.

If the image is only *slightly* larger than the drawing area, you can create more space by closing the tool box, color box, and status bar (click each on the View menu). Of course, you can select them again whenever you're ready.

If you still need more space, click View Bitmap on the View menu to hide everything except your picture. To reverse the View Bitmap command, press any key; the hidden screen components will reappear.

EXERCISE 22.1

1. Start **Paint** and maximize the Paint window, if necessary.

2. Screen-capture a copy of the Solitaire window:
   a. Click the **Start** button on the taskbar. Point to **Programs**, then **Accessories**, then **Games**, and then click **Solitaire**. Maximize the **Solitaire** window.

   b. Press the **Print Screen** key. A copy of the Solitaire window is copied to the Clipboard.
   c. Close the **Solitaire** program.
   d. Return to **Paint** using the taskbar.

3. Select **Paste** from the **Edit** menu. If the message box appears asking if you'd like the bitmap enlarged, click **Yes**.

(continued on next page)

4. Scroll the image with both the horizontal and the vertical scroll bars. Notice that the entire Solitaire window has been reproduced on your drawing area.

5. Leave the image on screen for the next exercise.

Using the Zoom Option

The Zoom option magnifies the drawing on your screen and is therefore useful for editing. You can use the Zoom option to repair a drawing, change color in very small areas, or even redraw a portion of a graphic.

When you select Zoom from the View menu, a submenu allows you to choose Large Size or Custom. Large Size enlarges your drawing by 400%. If you choose Custom, the Custom Zoom dialog box appears as shown in Figure 22-1, letting you select from among five zoom sizes. Paint's Zoom mode is also called a *fat-bit editor* because it enlarges each bit (makes it "fat") so that you can edit it.

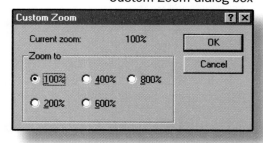

FIGURE 22-1
Custom Zoom dialog box

While you are zoomed in on the drawing, you can add a thumbnail that shows the area in its 100% size. To add the *thumbnail* to the screen, choose Zoom again and then choose Show Thumbnail from the submenu. In the upper left corner of the drawing area, a small window appears with a normal-size view of the magnified area. Any changes you make to the image will be reflected in the thumbnail.

Paint also offers a grid option to help you in the editing process. To display the grid, choose Zoom and then Show Grid from the submenu.

Each square in the magnified area represents one *pixel* of the image. You can change any pixel to either the foreground or the background color by clicking the mouse on that pixel with one of the tool box tools. To put the current foreground color in a pixel, click the left button; to put the current background color in, click the right button. You can paint a group of pixels at once in either the foreground color or the background color by holding down the appropriate mouse button and dragging the mouse.

1. Your screen should show the image of the **Solitaire** window.

2. Select **Zoom** from the **View** menu, and then choose **Custom** from the submenu.

3. In the **Custom Zoom** dialog box, click the **800%** option, and then click the **OK** button.

4. Select **Zoom** again and choose **Show Grid** from the submenu. Your screen should resemble Figure 22-2.

5. Choose **Zoom** once again and select **Show Thumbnail** to show a portion of the Solitaire screen in normal size. Point to the title bar of the Thumbnail window and drag it to the right side of the screen.

6. Choose the **Pencil** tool, if necessary.

7. Select dark red for the foreground color and yellow for the background color.

8. Paint all the blue pixels inside the box of cards (the Solitaire icon) red:
   a. Point to one of the blue pixels on the box front.
   b. Press and hold down the left mouse button and slowly drag across all the blue pixels.

9. Paint all the white pixels on the card sticking out of the box yellow by holding down the right mouse button and slowly dragging across the white pixels. Your screen should resemble Figure 22-3.

10. Fill the Solitaire title bar with dark red (if you have a color monitor) or a pattern (if you have a monochrome monitor):
    a. Choose the **Fill With Color** tool.
    b. Position the tip of the icon anywhere in the blue area of the Solitaire title bar.
    c. Click the left mouse button.

11. Fill with dark red the interior of any letters that still contain blue. (Move the Thumbnail window out of the way, if necessary.)

12. Close the **Thumbnail** by clicking its **Close** button.

13. Choose **Zoom** and **Normal Size** to return to normal size.

14. Leave the image on screen for the next exercise.

FIGURE 22-2
Zooming in on a graphic

FIGURE 22-3
Changing the color of individual pixels

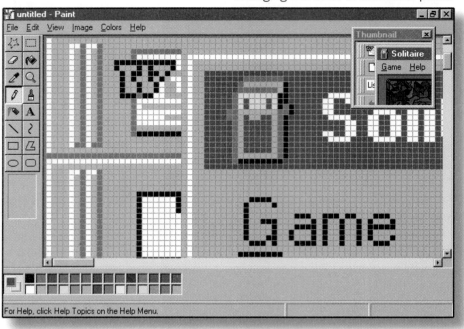

Using Pixel Coordinates

Paint provides two ways for you to control exactly where an object is located and how big it is. The two measurement boxes at the far right of the status bar show you as you draw where the object is located on the screen and the size of your object. Paint measures objects in *pels* (for **p**icture **el**ement), the individual dot that makes up an image. The rectangle shown in Figure 22-4, for example, was started at pixel location 126,82 and measures 259 by 183 pels. The first pixel location number reflects your position from left to right; the second number indicates the position from top to bottom.

EXERCISE 22.3

1. Choose **New** from the **File** menu to display a new screen. Do not save changes to the current drawing.

NOTE:

If the new screen is yellow, make sure that white is selected as the background color in the color box and choose New again.

2. Create the logo shown in Figure 22-5 on page 258 by following the steps below.

3. Draw the parts of the logo:
   a. Choose the **Line** tool and select the thinnest line from the selection area.
   b. Choose the **Rectangle** tool. Start at 45,50 and create a box that measures 321 × 117 pels.

256

FIGURE 22-4
Pixel measurement boxes

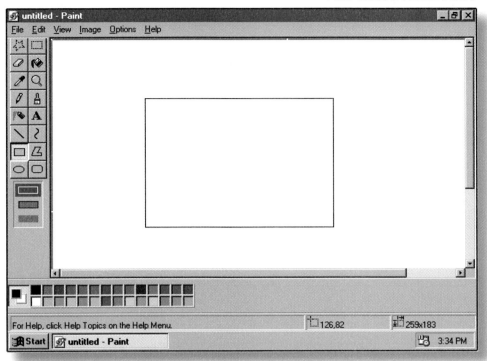

c. Create another box that starts at 66,84 and measures 18 × 67 pels.

d. Choose the **Ellipse** tool. Start at 65,64 and create an ellipse that measures 21 × 14 pels.

e. Choose the **Rounded Rectangle** tool. Start at 106,64 and create a rectangle that measures 249 × 87 pels.

4. Paint the background area blue (color monitor) or black (monochrome monitor).

5. Add the text:

a. Change the foreground color back to black.

b. Use **Arial**, **14** point, **bold italic** and key the text shown in Figure 22-5.

6. Select the graphic. Select **Copy To** from the **Edit** menu to save it on your Windows Practice disk. Use the file name **Logo** and the **256 Color Bitmap** file type.

7. Print a copy of the logo and close **Paint**. If instructed, shut down Windows and your computer.

TIP

Remember that it is easier if you create the text elsewhere on the drawing area and then drag the text into place.

2 5 7

FIGURE 22-5

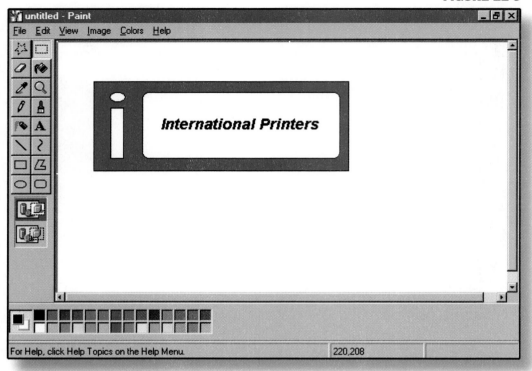

Summary

This lesson covered Paint's advanced features. You learned that:

- Paint permits you to import images (that is, to bring into Paint images that were created in other sources).

- The View menu offers the Zoom option (also called a fat-bit editor), which lets you magnify graphics so that you can see each bit in the drawing.

- You can use pixel coordinates to control exactly where an object is located and how big it is.

LESSON 22 REVIEW QUESTIONS

TRUE/FALSE

Each of the following statements is either true or false. Indicate your answer on the left by circling T if the statement is true and F if the statement is false.

T F   1. You can import only files that have the .MSP extension into Paint.

T F   2. You import a screen capture into a Paint file by using the Print Screen key and then pasting the image from the Clipboard.

T F   3.   Paint's Zoom mode is also called a fat-bit editor.

T F   4.   You can magnify an object up to 800% using the Custom Zoom options.

T F   5.   The first pixel location number reflects your position from top to bottom.

FILL IN THE BLANKS

Complete the following sentences by writing the correct word or words in the blanks provided.

1.   A(n) _____ is a unit of measurement that represents an individual dot that makes up an image.

2.   In a magnified area of an object, each square represents a(n) _____.

3.   The Zoom mode is also called the _____.

4.   The _____ option magnifies a drawing on the screen to make it easier to edit.

5.   A(n) _____ is a small window within the drawing area that contains a normal-size view of a magnified area.

LESSON 22 PROJECT

This project gives you the opportunity to review the concepts in this lesson and practice the techniques in the exercises. You will need your Windows Template disk and Windows Practice disk in order to complete this project.

NOTE:

You may need to have a second Practice disk ready to save the file you create in this application.

1.   Open **Paint**, or clear the image area if Paint is already running. You will create the announcement shown in Figure 22-6.

2.   Open the **Map** file from your Windows Template disk.

3.   Modify the graphic to include only the seven states shown in Figure 22-6:
    a.   Use the **Free-Form Select** tool to outline those states you do not want.
    b.   Use **Cut** to delete those states from the drawing area.
    c.   Use the fat-bit editor to clean up any ragged edges on the remaining image.

4.   Position the image in the center of the image area.

5. Paint each state with a contrasting color or pattern.

6. Add the text shown in Figure 22-6. Use **Times New Roman**, **16** point and **12** point. Use bold as desired.

7. Add the "pointing" lines.

8. Add the Rounded Rectangular border lines in a color of your choice.

9. Save the graphic to your Windows Practice disk as **Western** using the **256 Color Bitmap** file type.

10. Print a copy of your announcement.

11. Close Paint. If instructed, shut down Windows and your computer.

TIP

To make sure each of the seven lines begins in the same place, note the starting pixel coordinates when you begin to draw the first line.

FIGURE 22-6

UNIT 6 REVIEW QUESTIONS ▽

WRITTEN QUESTIONS

Answer the questions below on a separate piece of paper.

1. Distinguish between drawing and painting in the Paint program.

2. Name five tools in the tool box and explain the function of each.

3. Explain why the Fill With Color tool can be used only within a closed area.

4. Discuss the purpose and function of the color box.

5. Explain the roles of your monitor and your video adapter card in the Paint program.

6. Contrast the Select and Free-Form Select tools. Describe a situation in which each tool would be the best choice.

7. Explain how the fat-bit editor works, and why you might need to use it.

8. Distinguish between copying a cutout opaquely and transparently.

9. Explain the purpose of the Copy To command on Paint's Edit menu.

10. Explain how to determine the height and the width of an image.

UNIT 6 APPLICATION ▽

SCANS

The Corporate Communique project team assigned to the Townsend & Co. account wants to come up with a new masthead for the client's newsletter. Using Paint, create a masthead for the newsletter. A basic sample masthead is shown in Figure U6-1. The masthead must fit across the top of an 8½-by-11-inch page. Be as creative and imaginative as you want, and try to use as many of Paint's drawing and painting tools as you can.

Save the graphic as **TC Masthead** to your Windows Practice disk. Print a copy of the masthead. Then, close all open applications. If instructed, shut down Windows and your computer.

Volume I, Issue 1

TOWNSEND & CO.
REAL ESTATE REPORT

CRITICAL THINKING ▽

Like many other concerned companies, your firm participates in the Annual Giving Campaign, a fund-raiser that helps a number of worthwhile causes through United Assistance. This year's campaign is just beginning, and you have been named Campaign Chair. Congratulations!

You've edited a copy of last year's letter (Figure U6-2). You will mail the final letter to your coworkers to solicit their support and persuade them to donate generously. With the mailing, you plan to include a chart to inform your colleagues how the donations will be distributed. In addition, you need a payroll deduction form for employees (1) to indicate how much they wish to donate from each paycheck, (2) to indicate to which category of assistance they wish their contributions to be pledged, and (3) to authorize the Payroll Department to make payroll deductions.

Develop your letter and payroll deduction form in WordPad. Include these three categories on the payroll deduction form as three areas for which money will be designated to care for your community: (1) Community Care (helping the greatest number of people through one donation), (2) Targeted Care (Family Violence Prevention, Youth Development, Child Care and Development, Homeless and Families in Crisis, and Health Services), and (3) Specific Care (specific agencies such as Red Cross, United Way, and other nonprofit organizations).

Use Paint to create a chart which has the following two parts:

SPECIFIC THINGS PROVIDED BY YOUR GENEROSITY

$5	50 pounds of food
$10	2 hours of reading services for a blind student
$20	1 hour of individualized counseling
$35	a car seat for a baby in foster care
$45	a hot lunch, a day of exercise, and activities for 2 seniors
$60	enables a homeless woman to find housing and receive counseling
$80	provides immunizations against measles virus for 16 children
$100	provides a hot meal for 285 homeless individuals

NATIONWIDE CORPORATE CONTRIBUTIONS TO UNITED ASSISTANCE

CC	Community Care (one donation)		$30,000
TC	Targeted Care		
	FV	Family Violence Prevention	$8,000
	CD	Child Care and Development	$12,000
	YD	Youth Development	$48,000
	HF	Homeless and Families in Crisis	$38,000
	HS	Health Services	$19,000
	SC	Specific Care (specific nonprofit organizations)	$21,000

Print the letter, the payroll deduction form, and the chart. You may wish to create two separate charts and place them within the text of your letter or provide them as a separate page to your letter.

FIGURE U6-2

(Current Date)

Dear Colleague

People helping people has been part of the American tradition since our nation began. You now have the opportunity to become a part of this fine tradition--by participating in your company's annual campaign for United Assistance, a nonprofit organization that helps people and solves community problems.

Our company has a proud tradition of supporting United Assistance; we are contributing to the five categories for caring for your community shown in the chart below that make our community a better place to live and work. #

Our annual campaign for United Assistance takes place from October 15 through November 15. We urge you to give generously through a convenient payroll deduction-- a small monthly deduction is painless and adds up in a big way. To participate, complete the attached contribution form and return to your United Assistance coordinator. If you currently contribute, fill out the form only if you wish to change your donation. In filling out the attached form, please note specifically if you wish to indicate for which category you would like your dollars to be earmarked. *payroll deduction*

No one is obligated to give, but every dollar you give may help you or someone you know. This year's United Assistance campaign sponsors more causes than ever before, including child care and substance abuse programs, to name a few. *Women's shelters*

Helping others through contributing to United Assistance can make a difference. Thank you for caring.

Your donations are also tax deductible.

(Your name)
Corporate Giving Campaign Chair

Enclosure: Payroll Donation Form

kss

263

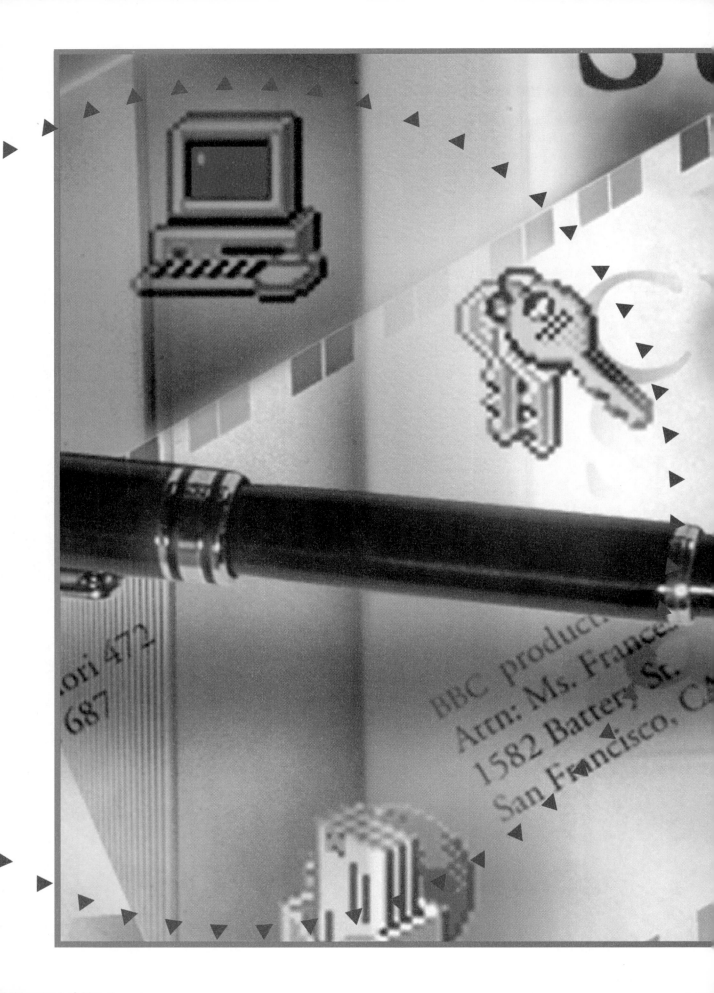

CONTROL PANEL

SETTING ACCESSIBILITY OPTIONS

OBJECTIVES

Upon completion of this lesson, you will be able to:

■ Explain how to use the Windows Control Panel.

■ Set keyboard accessibility options.

■ Set display accessibility options.

■ Set mouse accessibility options.

⏱ Estimated Time: 1 hour

The more you use Windows, the more you realize how its graphical user interface provides a desktop environment complete with icons, color, sound, and a mouse. But this environment isn't static. You can change it to suit your taste or your needs! How? By using the *Control Panel*. In the next six lessons, you will learn how to customize and personalize your computer desktop by adjusting Control Panel settings.

Starting the Control Panel

The Control Panel contains built-in tools to give you control of the way Windows looks, feels, and sounds. These tools permit you to customize both the desktop environment and several of your system's original hardware and software settings. (And Windows implements most of the Control Panel changes immediately, without requiring you to reboot, unlike most other software programs.)

The Control Panel is located on the Settings menu. You open the Control Panel by clicking Start, selecting Settings, then selecting the Control Panel option. The Control Panel window opens, as shown in Figure 23-1, displaying a variety of icons. The number and the types of icons displayed will vary from one system to another, depending on several factors.

■ If your system is using the Power Management option, you will see the Power Management icon.

■ If your system has any multimedia devices, you will see additional icons.

■ If you have installed any applications that display their own icons on the Control Panel, you will see those icons.

FIGURE 23-1
Control Panel

EXERCISE ▭ 23.1

1. Start Windows if it is not running.

2. Select **Settings** on the **Start** menu; then select **Control Panel** from the submenu.

3. Verify that the **Status Bar** option is selected on the View menu, and that the **Standard Buttons**, **Address Bar**, and **Text Labels** options are checked on the Toolbars submenu.

4. If necessary, change the view to Large Icons by clicking the **Views** button's drop-down list arrow and selecting **Large Icons**.

5. Leave the Control Panel on screen for the next exercise.

Looking at the Control Panel

A quick glance at Figure 23-1 tells you that the Control Panel window is similar to other windows: It has a title bar, menu bar (with the familiar File, Edit, View, Go, Favorites, and Help options), and Address bar that identifies the name of the selected folder or system resource. And as you saw in the previous exercise, you have four choices (views) for arranging the icons: Large Icons, Small Icons, List, and Details.

Each icon in the Control Panel enables you to customize one particular aspect of Windows. Double-click an icon to open a dialog box containing options that you can modify. Many of the commonly used Control Panel icons are covered in this unit. In this lesson, we'll explore the *Accessibility Options*.

Setting Accessibility Options

If you have vision, hearing, or dexterity impairments, you can use the Accessibility Options icon to choose from a variety of options that will make the system easier for you to use. For example, if you have hearing impairments, you can arrange to have visual warnings and to see display captions whenever your system makes a sound. If you need to increase screen readability, you can choose contrasting colors and different fonts.

Clicking the Accessibility Options icon opens the Accessibility Properties dialog box (see Figure 23-2), which displays five tabs: Keyboard, Sound, Display, Mouse, and General. The options on each tab are explained below.

FIGURE 23-2
Accessibility Properties dialog box

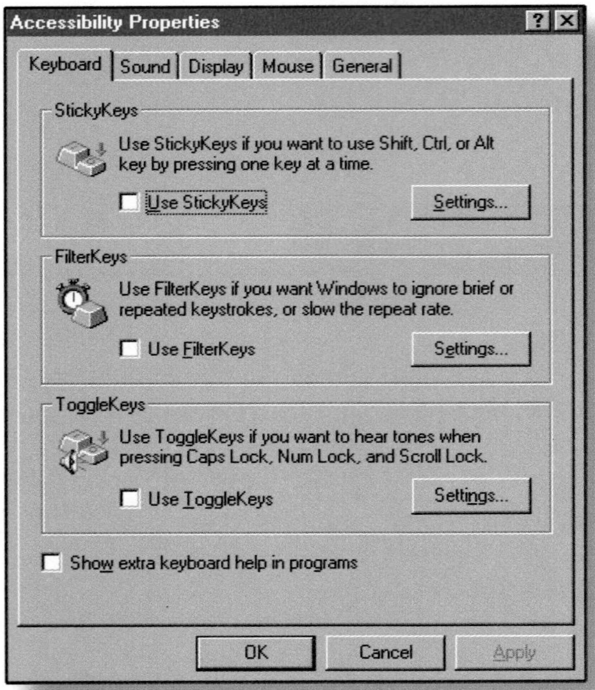

Keyboard Accessibility Options

The Keyboard tab in the Accessibility Properties dialog box helps individuals who have dexterity impairments that make using some standard keyboard functions difficult. The keyboard accessibility options are explained below.

- **StickyKeys.** It sounds funny, but StickyKeys is an accurate name. Typically you must press and hold down two keys simultaneously to issue a keyboard command. One of the two keys is generally Ctrl, Alt, or Shift. Checking the Use StickyKeys feature makes the next key you press remain active (makes it "sticky") until you press another key. Because one key is "sticky," you do not have to hold down two keys at once to issue a keyboard command.

  Take, for example, the keyboard command for Copy: Ctrl+C. Ordinarily, you must press and hold down both keys to issue the command. But when you turn on StickyKeys, you can press and release Ctrl and then press C. You can see how helpful this feature is to individuals who have difficulty pressing two keys simultaneously.

  Look again at the Keyboard tab in Figure 23-2. Notice the three Settings buttons, one to the right of each option. Pressing any of these buttons opens another dialog box offering further options. The Settings for the StickyKeys dialog box permits you to turn the StickyKeys feature on or off from the keyboard, make one of the StickyKeys active until you press the key again, or have your computer play unique tones to indicate when Ctrl, Alt, or Shift is pressed, locked, or released.

- **FilterKeys.** This feature instructs the keyboard to ignore (filter) accidental or repeated keystrokes. FilterKeys adjusts the number of seconds your computer waits between keystrokes. So if you have difficulty releasing a key quickly, or if you press a key too many times, you can filter out these unwanted keystrokes.

- **ToggleKeys.** A key toggles when it can be turned on and off, like an electric light switch. On the standard keyboard, the Caps Lock, Scroll Lock, and Num Lock keys all toggle. Press Caps Lock and it is active (on); press it again and it is inactive (off). How do you know? A tiny light informs you—that is, it informs you only if you can see that light.

  If you have difficulty seeing these tiny toggle lights, select ToggleKeys and your computer will play a high-pitched sound to let you know that a toggle key is on, and a low-pitched sound when a toggle key is off.

- **Extra Keyboard Help.** Some programs can display extra help about using the keyboard. Check the box at the bottom of the Keyboard tab if you would like to see when extra help is available.

Sound Accessibility Options

Sound has become an important Windows feature, providing audio clues to a variety of Windows activities. Later in this unit you will learn how to assign sounds to activities such as minimizing or maximizing a window, opening a program, or displaying an error message. Obviously, audio clues are of little value if you have difficulty hearing. If that is the case, you can use two Sound options, SoundSentry and ShowSounds (see Figure 23-3), to convert audio cues to visual cues.

FIGURE 23-3
Sound properties

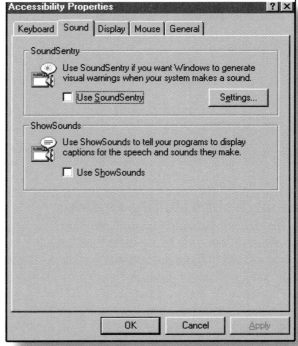

269

- **SoundSentry.** This feature instructs your computer to flash a selected screen element every time the system's built-in speaker plays a sound. You can specify which part of the screen flashes by clicking the Settings button.

- **ShowSounds.** Some programs convey information by sound. The ShowSounds feature instructs such programs to also provide the information visually; for example, by displaying text captions or informative icons.

Display Accessibility Options

If you have difficulty distinguishing screen colors, you can change a program's default color scheme. On the Display tab (see Figure 23-4), click the Settings button to open the Settings for High Contrast dialog box (Figure 23-5). There you will find options for changing the default colors and for creating a custom color scheme. You will learn more about Windows color schemes later in this unit.

Note that when the Use High Contrast accessibility option is on, Windows will increase the legibility of the display whenever possible.

FIGURE 23-4
Display properties

FIGURE 23-5
Settings for High Contrast dialog box

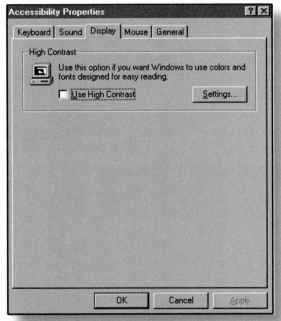

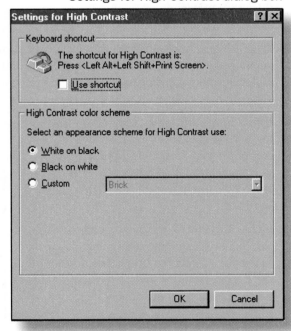

Mouse Accessibility Options

If you have difficulty manipulating the mouse, the Mouse tab offers the MouseKeys feature (Figure 23-6), which allows you to use the numeric keypad to move the mouse pointer and to click, double-click, and drag to select. Table 23-1 shows how to use the numeric keypad for basic mouse functions.

FIGURE 23-6
Mouse tab

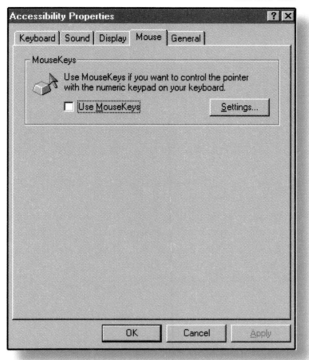

TABLE 23-1
Manipulating the mouse with the numeric keyboard

Using MouseKeys	
If you want to	**Then**
Move the mouse pointer	Press the directional keys (left arrow, right arrow, up arrow, down arrow) on your numeric keypad
Click the mouse	Press 5 on the numeric keypad
Double-click the mouse	Press + (the plus key) on the numeric keypad
Drag to select	Press the Ins key on the numeric keypad to begin highlighting; press the Del key on the numeric keypad to end highlighting

The Settings for MouseKeys dialog box (Figure 23-7) gives you several additional options. For example, you can adjust the pointer's top speed and how quickly it accelerates. You can also opt to use Num Lock as a MouseKeys toggle when MouseKeys is selected. Further, you can display a status indicator for MouseKeys on the taskbar, if you wish.

General Accessibility Options

The General tab (see Figure 23-8) in the Accessibility Properties dialog box controls how the other accessibility options operate. For example, the Automatic reset option turns StickyKeys, SoundSentry, MouseKeys, FilterKeys, ToggleKeys, and Use High Contrast features off after your computer has been idle for a specified period of time. This option is handy for computers used by more than one person. The SerialKey feature is not turned off by default because this feature is useful if more than one person uses the same computer.

You may have noticed that there is a shortcut key to turn on and off each of the accessibility features. Checking the Notification options on the General tab will give you a confirmation message every time you use a shortcut key to turn an accessibility feature on or off—a useful alert against turning on a feature accidentally.

Alternative input devices are available for individuals who are unable to use the standard keyboard and mouse. Use the SerialKey feature to attach such alternative input devices to your computer's serial port. Simply put a check in the box labeled Support SerialKey devices.

FIGURE 23-7
Settings for MouseKeys dialog box

FIGURE 23-8
General tab

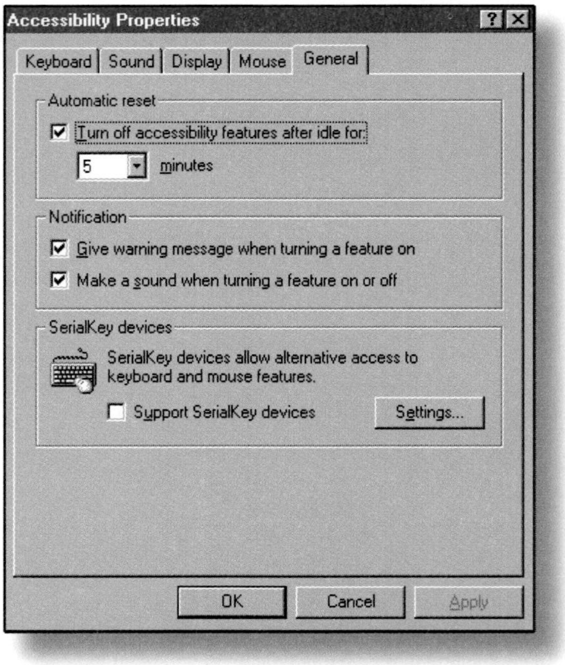

EXERCISE ⟹ 23.2

1. Double-click the **Accessibility Options** icon in the **Control Panel** to display the Accessibility Properties dialog box.

2. Set the Keyboard, Sound, and Mouse options:
  a. Select the **Keyboard** tab, click the **Use StickyKeys** check box, and then click the **Settings** button.
  b. Uncheck the **Turn StickyKeys off if two keys are pressed at once** option, verify that all of the remaining Options and Notification check boxes are checked, and then click the **OK** button.
  c. Select the **Sound** tab, click the **Use Sound-Sentry** check box, and then click the **Settings** button. The Settings for SoundSentry dialog box opens (Figure 23-9).
  d. In the **Settings for SoundSentry** dialog box, verify that the visual warnings are set as shown in Figure 23-9; then click the **OK** button. If you must change a setting, select the appropriate option from the drop-down list before clicking the OK button.
  e. Select the **Mouse** tab, and then check the **Use MouseKeys** check box.
  f. Select the **General** tab and set the **Turn off accessibility features after idle for 10 minutes** by keying **10** in the text box.
  g. Click the **Apply** button, and then click the **OK** button.

3. Open **Notepad** and minimize all windows except the Notepad window. Do not maximize the Notepad window. Select **Word Wrap** from the **Edit** menu if it is not already selected.

4. Practice using the Keyboard, Sound, and Mouse accessibility options:
  a. Press and release the **Shift** key. Did you hear the sound and/or see the screen flash when you pressed the Shift key? This is a verification that you have set the Shift key on so the next letter key you press will be a capital letter.
  b. Key the following sentence without holding down the Shift key:

```
The screen will flash and the
speaker will beep as I work on
this Exercise.
```

5. Edit the sentence using the numeric keypad:
  a. Using the keypad directional arrow keys, move the I-beam mouse pointer to the position immediately before the *s* in the word *screen*.

 **NOTE:**

Your I-beam may move very slowly. Be patient!

  b. Press and release the **Ins** key on the numeric keypad. The cursor moves to the location of the I-beam.
  c. Click before the word *screen*. Using the right arrow key on the numeric keypad, drag the highlight across the word *screen* (but not the space following it) to select the word.
  d. Press the **Del** key on the numeric keypad to stop highlighting. Press **Ctrl** and then press **x** to cut the selected word. Did you notice that you issued a keyboard shortcut without having to hold down the two keys simultaneously?
  e. Key the word *monitor* at the cursor position.
  f. Using the arrow keys on the numeric keypad, move the I-beam mouse pointer immediately after the word *work* near the end of the sentence.

(continued on next page)

g. Using the **Ins** key and the right arrow key, highlight the words *on this Exercise* (do not include the period). Press the **Del** key to stop highlighting.

h. Press **Ctrl+x**.

6. Turn off the accessibility options:

a. Open the **Control Panel** and double-click the **Accessibility Options** icon.

b. Uncheck the **Use StickyKeys**, **Use Sound-Sentry**, and **Use MouseKeys** options. Click

on the General tab, change the Automatic reset back to **5** minutes. Click the **Apply** button, and then click the **OK** button.

c. Close the **Control Panel**.

7. Close **Notepad**. Do not save changes. If instructed, shut down Windows and your computer.

FIGURE 23-9
Settings for SoundSentry dialog box

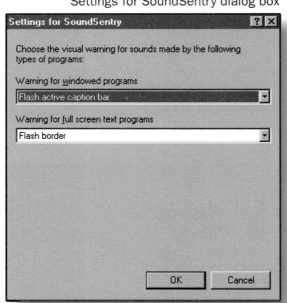

Summary

This lesson covered the accessibility options in the Control Panel. You learned that:

- The Control Panel provides capabilities different from most of the other Windows applications. Control Panel is the tool that allows you to control the Windows environment by customizing Windows and changing its default settings.

- When you start Windows, you will find the Control Panel option on the Settings menu. The Control Panel window opens with a number of icons that enable you to customize many aspects of Windows.

- Control Panel allows you to customize Windows to accommodate physical disabilities.

- For people who have trouble pressing and holding down two keys at once, the Keyboard accessibility options offer StickyKeys, FilterKeys, and ToggleKeys.

- The Sound accessibility options enable people with hearing difficulties to convert sound messages to visual messages.

- The Display accessibility option permits you to select a color scheme with a higher contrast—helpful to anyone who has difficulty distinguishing the default colors.

- The MouseKeys accessibility option provides an alternative for people who have difficulty manipulating the mouse.

- The General accessibility options control how the other accessibility options operate.

LESSON 23 REVIEW QUESTIONS

TRUE/FALSE

Each of the following statements is either true or false. Indicate your answer on the left by circling T if the statement is true and F if the statement is false.

T F 1. The Control Panel lets you change only hardware settings.

T F 2. To open Control Panel, you select it from the Start menu.

T F 3. The FilterKeys feature lets you adjust the number of seconds your computer waits between keystrokes.

T F 4. The SoundSentry feature instructs a program that conveys information by sound to provide the same information visually.

T F 5. With the MouseKeys feature, you can use the numeric keypad to control movement of the mouse pointer.

MATCHING

Write the letter of the term in the right column that matches the definition in the left column.

_____ 1. Option that lets you use the Shift, Ctrl, or Alt key by pressing one key at a time.

A. MouseKeys

B. ToggleKeys

_____ 2. Option that lets you hear tones when pressing Caps Lock, Num Lock, and Scroll Lock.

C. StickyKeys

_____ 3. Option that instructs your computer to flash a screen element every time the computer plays a sound.

D. ShowSounds

E. SoundSentry

_____ 4. Option that tells your programs to display captions for the speech and sounds they make.

_____ 5. Option that lets you use the numeric keypad to control the mouse pointer.

LESSON 23 PROJECT

This project gives you the opportunity to review the concepts in this lesson and practice the techniques in the exercises.

1. Open the **Control Panel** and double-click the **Accessibility Options** icon.

2. On the **Display** tab, click the **Use High Contrast** option. Click the **Settings** button and select the **White on black** option. Click **OK**. Then click **Apply** on the Display tab.

3. On the **Mouse** tab, click the **Use MouseKeys** option. Click **Apply** and then click **OK**.

4. Use the directional keys on the numeric keypad to move the pointer around the Control Panel window. Move the pointer to the **Accessibility Options** icon. Press + on the numeric keypad to open the Accessibility Options dialog box.

5. Change the accessibility options back to their default settings:
   a. On the **Display** tab, deselect the **Use High Contrast** option. Click **Apply** and then click **OK**. You may have to resize the taskbar. Position the pointer on its top border. When the pointer turns into a double-headed arrow, drag the border down to return the taskbar to its original size.
   b. On the **Mouse** tab, deselect the **Use MouseKeys** option. Click **Apply** and then click **OK**.

6. Close the **Control Panel**. If instructed, shut down Windows and your computer.

CUSTOMIZING THE DESKTOP

LESSON

24

OBJECTIVES

Upon completion of this lesson, you will be able to:

- Apply a predefined background pattern to the desktop.

- Create and add a new background pattern.

- Remove a background pattern.

- Hang desktop wallpaper.

- Use a bitmap file as desktop wallpaper.

⏱ **Estimated Time: 1 hour**

Windows applications run on the desktop, and objects are placed on the desktop. When you install Windows, the original desktop you see is rather plain, but you can customize it to suit your personal tastes! In this lesson, you will learn how to change the look of your desktop's background.

Changing Display Properties

You customize the desktop using the Control Panel. Specifically, you select the Control Panel's Display icon, and the Display Properties dialog box appears (Figure 24-1).

As you see in Figure 24-1, the Display Properties dialog box has several tabs you can use to change the appearance and the behavior of your desktop.

- The **Background** tab offers you a wide selection of wallpaper graphics and enables you to place a background and pattern on your desktop. You can use one of the wallpaper graphics or patterns that comes with Windows or create one of your own.

- The **Screen Saver** tab helps you to prevent screen burn-in. When your system is on but idle, Screen Saver displays a moving graphic or a blank screen.

- The **Appearance** tab permits you to control the color, fonts, and size of various screen elements. You can change the appearance of these elements by selecting from a set of predefined schemes or by creating your own scheme.

FIGURE 24-1
Display Properties dialog box

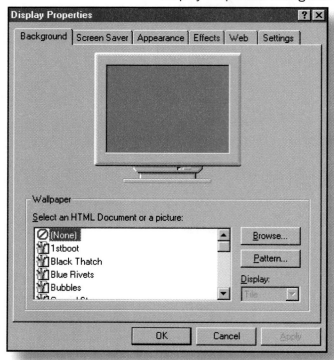

- The **Web** tab gives you options for changing the display of the Active Desktop.

- The **Settings** tab permits you to change the resolution and the number of colors used by the display, change the display type, and change other display characteristics.

Customizing the Background

When Windows is first installed, your desktop is a solid color. However, using the Background tab you can change the desktop to a predefined wallpaper or background pattern, create your own background pattern, or use a graphic file prepared in a paint program to create a background pattern.

Setting the Background Pattern

You can apply a pattern to your desktop by clicking the Pattern button on the Background tab (see Figure 24-1). The Pattern dialog box opens, as shown in Figure 24-2.

The list box provides predefined background patterns. Scroll through the list; as you click any of the patterns listed, that pattern is displayed in the Preview window. Click OK and you are returned to the Background tab where the pattern appears in the

FIGURE 24-2
Pattern dialog box

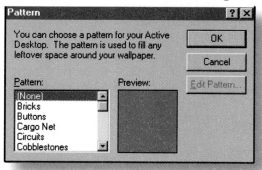

large monitor. Click the Apply button, and your selection will take effect immediately. When you make your final selection, click the OK button to make your selections the default.

EXERCISE ▭▷ 24.1

Since a background pattern lies behind all open windows, in order to see the results of this exercise you must minimize all windows except the Display Properties dialog box.

1. Open the **Control Panel**; then double-click the **Display** icon.

2. Minimize all windows except the Display Properties dialog box.

3. Select the Daisies background pattern:
   a. Click the **Pattern** button.

b. In the Pattern dialog box, use the scroll bar to the right of the Pattern list box to locate and then select **Daisies**. Click **OK**.

c. Notice that the Daisies pattern displays on the screen in the center of the Background tab. Click the **Apply** button and then click **OK**. The selected pattern displays on the desktop behind the Display Properties dialog box.

4. Repeat steps 3a–3c to select the **Triangles** background pattern. Remain in this screen for the next exercise.

Creating and Adding a New Background Pattern

If you wish to edit the pattern you have selected or wish to create a new pattern, you can do so by clicking the Edit Pattern button in the Pattern dialog box. The Pattern Editor dialog box opens, as shown in Figure 24-3.

The Pattern Editor dialog box has two main areas:

■ A Pattern box on the left shows you one "unit" that makes up the selected background pattern.

■ A Sample box on the right shows you what the pattern looks like in its normal size.

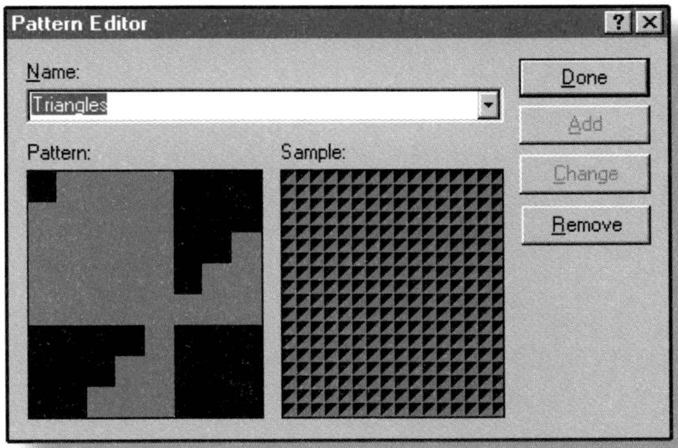

It's important to understand that every image you see on your computer screen is "drawn" by dots—light dots and dark dots. If you were to magnify a newspaper picture,

FIGURE 24-3
Pattern Editor dialog box

you would see that dots similarly make up newspaper pictures. Likewise, the dots on your computer screen are too small to see, but together they form a pattern, a picture, an image. The "unit" gives you a magnified view of the larger sample in the Sample box. In other words, it gives you a glimpse of all the small dots that make up the larger sample.

By now, you may have figured out that by changing the small dot pattern you can change the larger sample. To simplify the process, the Pattern Editor shows you the "unit" in a grid of squares. Each square represents a dot on screen. A dot can be either light or dark. To edit the image, you change the dots in the Pattern box by changing light to dark or by changing dark to light. The result will be a new pattern, and of course a new sample.

How do you change dots from light to dark and vice versa? Simply click on the dot; that is, on the square in the Pattern box. With each change, you will see the effect in the Sample box.

Once you've finished, you can add your newly created pattern to the others available. Key a new name for the pattern in the Name text box and click the Add button. Your new pattern will be listed in alphabetic order with the others. You can then add the new pattern to your desktop.

EXERCISE 24.2

1. In the **Control Panel**, double-click the **Display** icon.

2. Click the **Pattern** button. Then select the **Bricks** background pattern by clicking its name in the Pattern list box.

3. Click the **Edit Pattern** button to open the Pattern Editor.

4. In the Name text box, key **My Pattern**, the name of the pattern you will create.

5. To create your new pattern, use the pattern illustrated in Figure 24-4 as your guide. Click on the squares to re-create the pattern of light and dark illustrated in Figure 24-4. As you click, note

> **TIP**
>
> The dots toggle with each click. If you click on the wrong square, just click again to "erase"!

that you can see your pattern take shape in the Sample box.

6. Click the **Add** button and then click **Done** to add the pattern name (**My Pattern**) to the list in the Pattern dialog box and close the Pattern Editor.

7. Click **OK** to close the Pattern dialog box. The Display Properties dialog box reappears.

8. Click the **OK** button to apply **My Pattern** to the desktop and to close the Display Properties dialog box.

FIGURE 24-4
My Pattern dot pattern

Removing a Background Pattern

To remove a desktop background pattern, use the Remove command button in the Pattern Editor dialog box.

EXERCISE 24.3

1. In the **Control Panel**, double-click the **Display** icon.

2. Click the **Pattern** button. In the Pattern dialog box, select **My Pattern** from the Pattern list box.

3. Click the **Edit Pattern** button.

4. Make sure **My Pattern** appears in the **Name** text box. Click the **Remove** button. A message box appears asking you to confirm your request.

5. Click the **Yes** button in the message box.

6. Click the **Done** button in the Pattern Editor dialog box.

7. In the Pattern dialog box, select the **(None)** option from the Pattern list box and then click **OK**.

8. Click **OK** to close the Display Properties dialog box. The pattern disappears from the desktop.

Hanging Desktop Wallpaper

In addition to a background pattern, you can add wallpaper, or a graphic file, to the desktop's background. You can select from Windows' preexisting wallpaper files that are listed on the Background tab (see Figure 24-1). Or you can create your own wallpaper. You can center wallpaper on the desktop, or you can tile it to fill the entire desktop, or you can stretch it so that a section of it is expanded to stretch across the screen. These options are shown in Figure 24-5. You select the option from the Display drop-down list box on the Background tab.

FIGURE 24-5
Wallpaper that's tiled (left), centered (center), and stretched

  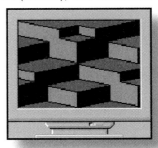

EXERCISE 24.4

1. In the **Control Panel**, double-click the **Display** icon.

2. Select the **Triangles** wallpaper:
   a. Click the down scroll arrow in the **Wallpaper** list box until the **Triangles** option displays, then select it.
   b. Click the **Display** drop-down list arrow and select **Center** to center the wallpaper on the screen.

3. Click the **Apply** button to "hang" the wallpaper. Do *not* click the OK button.

4. Notice that the wallpaper is centered on the desktop. If you have selected a background pattern, the background pattern fills the area of the desktop not covered by the wallpaper.

5. Click the **Tile** option from the Display drop-down list in the Display Properties dialog box.

6. Click the **Apply** button to "rehang" the wallpaper.

7. Click the **OK** button to close the Display Properties dialog box.

TIP

You will need to minimize all the windows on your screen and move the Display Properties dialog box in order to see the actual wallpaper on your desktop.

The Triangles wallpaper now covers the entire desktop. If you look closely at the desktop, you will see that the graphic has been duplicated enough times to fill the area.

Any bitmapped graphic file (usually files with the .BMP extension) can be used as wallpaper. You can create your own graphic in Paint and save it as a bitmapped file, or you can bring a favorite graphic file into Windows' Paint program and save it as a bitmapped file.

INTERNET You can download a graphic file or image from the Web, save it in the bitmapped file type, and hang it as wallpaper on your desktop.

EXERCISE 24.5

1. In **Control Panel**, double-click the **Display** icon.

2. Use the **Starburst** file from your Windows Template disk to create a wallpaper:
   a. Click the **Browse** button on the **Background** tab to open the Browse dialog box.
   b. Select the drive that contains your Windows Template disk.
   c. Double-click the **Starburst.bmp** file. The Browse dialog box closes, and the Display Properties dialog box reappears.
   d. Verify that the **Tile** option is selected from the Display drop-down list in the Display Properties dialog box.
   e. Click the **OK** button to hang the wallpaper. The Display Properties dialog box closes, and the wallpaper fills the desktop.

3. Reset the wallpaper to (None):
   a. Reopen the Display Properties dialog box.
   b. Scroll the wallpaper list box, locate the **(None)** option, and click it.
   c. Click the **Apply** button.

4. Click the **OK** button to close the Display Properties dialog box.

5. Close the **Control Panel**. If instructed, shut down Windows and your computer.

IMPORTANT:

Wallpaper is pretty, but it's also costly—in terms of computer memory. If you want to use your computer's memory to its fullest, reconsider using a wallpapered desktop.

Summary

This lesson covered the desktop background display options in the Control Panel. You learned that:

- Double-clicking the Display icon opens the Display dialog box, where you can adjust the desktop's background pattern and hang wallpaper.

- You can select from Windows' existing background patterns. You can also edit these patterns in the Pattern Editor dialog box. New patterns can be saved with their own names.

- Windows comes with a number of preexisting wallpaper styles that you can hang on your desktop. A wallpaper can be tiled to fill the whole screen, centered on the screen, or stretched across the screen.

- You can use any bitmapped graphic file as a wallpaper. For example, you might create a graphic in Paint or download a graphic from the Web, and use it as wallpaper on the desktop.

LESSON 24 REVIEW QUESTIONS

TRUE/FALSE

Each of the following statements is either true or false. Indicate your answer on the left by circling T if the statement is true and F if the statement is false.

T F 1. The Background tab in the Display Properties dialog box lets you change the color, fonts, and size of various screen elements.

T F 2. By default, your desktop's background is a solid color.

T F 3. You edit a pattern by clicking dots in the Sample box in the Pattern Editor dialog box.

T F 4. You can save an edited pattern with a new name.

T F 5. Once you add a new pattern to the Patterns list, you cannot remove it.

MATCHING

Write the letter of the term in the right column that matches the definition in the left column.

_____ 1. Tab in the Display Properties dialog box that lets you create a moving graphic that helps protect your monitor's screen.

_____ 2. Tab in the Display Properties dialog box that provides you with background patterns you can apply to the desktop.

_____ 3. Tab in the Display Properties dialog box that lets you modify the appearance of the Active Desktop.

_____ 4. Tab in the Display Properties dialog box that lets you change the color of various screen elements.

_____ 5. Tab in the Display Properties dialog box that lets you change the number of colors used by the display.

A. Settings

B. Web

C. Appearance

D. Background

E. Screen Saver

LESSON 24 PROJECT

This project gives you the opportunity to review the concepts in this lesson and practice the techniques in the exercises. Before you begin, ask if your instructor wants to see the custom desktop pattern you will create in this project.

1. Open the **Control Panel**, open the Display Properties dialog box, and click the **Background** tab if necessary:
   a. Select any background pattern except (None).
   b. Use the Pattern Editor to create one of the patterns shown in Figure 24-6 or create a pattern of your own design.

2. Display the pattern on your desktop. If you have been instructed to do so, notify your instructor.

3. Remove the pattern from the desktop.

4. Close the Display Properties dialog box and the **Control Panel**. If instructed, shut down Windows and your computer.

FIGURE 24-6

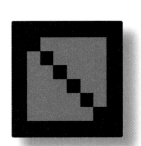 

CHANGING OTHER DISPLAY PROPERTIES

OBJECTIVES

Upon completion of this lesson, you will be able to:

■ Select and apply a screen saver.

■ Modify a screen saver.

■ Change the desktop color scheme.

■ Create and save a desktop color scheme.

■ Change desktop fonts.

🕐 **Estimated Time: 1.5 hours**

You can use the Display Properties dialog box to customize much more than just the desktop's background. In this lesson, you will learn how to use options on the Screen Saver and Appearance tabs to alter the look of your desktop.

Using Screen Saver

Screen saver programs were originally developed to protect monitors from "burning" an image on the screen permanently! Today, most monitors are not susceptible to burn-in, so screen savers have outlived their original use. But screen savers are still popular because they serve another useful function: They block others from seeing your display when you step away from your computer. (You can even equip a screen saver with a password.) Besides, they provide a fun way to personalize your computer!

In a word, the screen saver works when you don't. When you do not touch the keyboard or the mouse for a specified period of time, the screen saver takes over the display, showing a blank screen or a moving image (moving images will not burn into the screen—and they're fun!). You specify the period of idle time after which the screen saver takes over. The screen saver disappears as soon as you touch a key or move the mouse; the original screen returns (that is, the original screen returns unless you specify a password that must be entered first).

Windows provides several different screen savers. To review the screen savers available, click the Screen Saver tab in the Display Properties dialog box. It looks like that shown in Figure 25-1. Click the Screen Saver drop-down list box and select the screen saver of your choice. The monitor graphic on the tab shows what the screen saver looks like.

FIGURE 25-1
Screen Saver tab

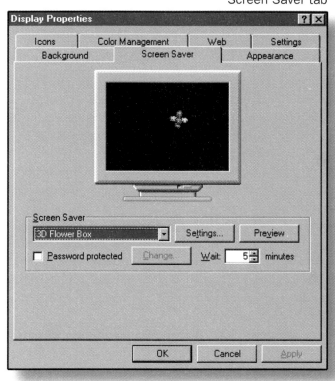

In the Wait box, click the up ("increase") or the down ("decrease") arrow to specify the amount of "idle time" that must elapse before the screen saver is activated, or simply key the desired number (in minutes) from 0 to 99.

Each screen saver option (except Blank Screen) can be customized by clicking the Settings button. A dialog box with options related to that screen saver opens. Figure 25-2 shows the Options for Scrolling Marquee dialog box.

FIGURE 25-2
Options for Scrolling Marquee dialog box

EXERCISE 25.1

1. Open the **Control Panel**; then double-click the **Display** icon.

2. Click the **Screen Saver** tab, and then write down the name of the screen saver currently selected. (You will be asked to return the screen saver to this setting when you complete this exercise.)

3. Click the **Screen Saver** drop-down list arrow and select the **Scrolling Marquee** screen saver.

4. Click the **Settings** button to display the **Options for Scrolling Marquee** dialog box (Figure 25-2). As you make the following selections, look at the Text sample box to see the results. (Again, write down the options that currently are selected.)

5. Click the **Centered** button in the Position section (to position the text to scroll across the middle of the screen; clicking Random will scroll text randomly).

6. Move the marker on the **Speed** bar to the middle.

7. Click the **Background color** drop-drown list arrow and select black, if necessary.

8. In the Text box, key the text **Windows is fun . . . and easy too!** The Text sample box will display your text as you key.

9. Click the **Format Text** button and choose the following settings in the Format Text dialog box (write down the current settings before you make changes to them):
   Font: **Times New Roman**
   Font Style: **Italic**
   Size: **48**
   Color: **Fuchsia**

10. Click the **OK** button.

11. Click the **OK** button again to return to the Display Properties dialog box. The screen in the center of the dialog box displays your screen saver.

12. Note the time setting in the Wait text box. Double-click the **Wait** text box, key **1**, and then click the **OK** button.

13. Sit back and don't touch the keyboard or mouse for at least 1 minute (the time you set in the Wait text box). After 1 minute, your marquee will display on the screen.

14. Interrupt the screen saver by moving the mouse or pressing a key.

15. In the **Screen Saver** list box, select the screen saver you wrote down in step 2. Change the **Wait** time back to its original setting. Click the **Settings** button and change the settings in the Options for Scrolling Marquee dialog box back to the settings you wrote down in step 4.

16. Click the **Format Text** button and change those options back to the settings you wrote down in step 9. Click **OK**. Click **OK** again to close the Options for Scrolling Marquee dialog box.

17. Click the **OK** button to close the Display Properties dialog box.

Controlling Desktop Colors and Fonts

The colorful Windows desktop was designed for a VGA (or better) monitor. (With a monochrome monitor, you will see shades of gray.) So far you have seen the default desktop, Windows' stock appearance scheme; however, you have complete control over your monitor's color scheme.

The Appearance tab in the Display Properties dialog box (Figure 25-3) offers options for setting a new color scheme. You can select from a set of predefined schemes, or you can create your own scheme.

FIGURE 25-3
Appearance tab

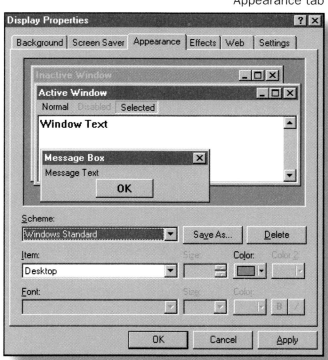

The top portion of the Appearance tab displays a sample window with most of the window elements shown in their selected color, size, and font. Together, the various colors, sizes, and fonts in this sample box make up a *color scheme*. Each color scheme has its own name, and the name of the currently displayed scheme is highlighted in the Scheme text box (Windows Standard is shown in Figure 25-3).

Using a Predefined Color Scheme

To select one of the predefined color schemes, click the drop-down list arrow to the right of the Scheme list box. Then click any name on the list; as you do so, that scheme is displayed in the sample window. In this way, you can review the selections available. To choose one of the schemes, click the Apply button and then the OK button. Your selection will become the new color scheme.

1. In the **Control Panel**, double-click the **Display** icon.

2. Click the **Appearance** tab.

3. Click the **Scheme** drop-down list arrow and scroll, if necessary, to bring the Brick color scheme into view.

4. Click the **Brick** color scheme (Figure 25-4). Take a few minutes to study the new scheme.

What do you notice about the color and the fonts?

5. Select a different color scheme from the **Scheme** list box (use the up and down arrows to scroll through the list).

6. Click the **Cancel** button to close the Display Properties dialog box.

FIGURE 25-4
Brick color scheme

Creating a New Color Scheme

If you prefer a customized scheme over a predefined scheme, you can change the colors, fonts, and element sizes in an existing scheme and create your own. You also can use the Bold and Italic buttons to apply formatting to font options. As you change the various elements, the changes are displayed in the sample screen. (If you wish, you can click an element in the sample window to select that element and display its current settings.)

Changing a color scheme is a two-step process:

1. Select a screen item you want to change.

2. Select a size and color for the elements—and if the item has text, a font name, size, color, and attribute—from the appropriate boxes.

The simplest way to select a screen element is to click that element in the sample window. However, if you know the element's name, you can select the element from the Item drop-down list box on the Appearance tab. The change is immediate; you can see it in the sample window.

E X E R C I S E ▭⟹ 25.3

This exercise assumes that you have a color monitor. If you have a monochrome monitor, select a shade or pattern in place of a color.

1. In the **Control Panel**, double-click the **Display** icon.

2. Click the **Appearance** tab.

3. Scroll and select the **Red, White, and Blue (VGA)** scheme from the Scheme drop-down list.

4. Click the **Item** drop-down list arrow; then scroll upward to select the **Active Title Bar** item.

5. Click the drop-down arrow on the **Color** list box to the right of the Item text box. Note that a color palette is displayed (Figure 25-5). This color palette controls the background color of the element selected in the Item list box.

6. Click a color other than the current color. The selected color becomes the active color, and the selected Item displays with this background color in the sample window.

7. Click the **Font** drop-down list arrow; then select **Courier**.

8. Click the Font **Size** box; then key **15**. Did you see the font size change in the sample window?

9. Click the **Italic** (**I**) attribute button.

10. Click the drop-down list arrow on the Font **Color** box to display the color palette; then click a color other than the current color. Check your color scheme in the sample window. Is the text legible? Continue selecting colors until you have a good contrast between the item background color and the font color.

11. Continue selecting screen items and changing the items until you have a pleasing color scheme.

12. Click the **Cancel** button to return to the Control Panel window, which will revert to the original color scheme.

FIGURE 25-5
Displaying the color palette

Saving or Removing a Color Scheme

To save a new color scheme, you must click either the OK button to use the scheme on a temporary basis or the Save As button to save the color scheme. You can save a color scheme with or without a name.

To save the color scheme with a name, select the Save As button; when the Save Scheme dialog box appears, key a name in the text box. A prompt appears asking which name (up to 32 characters long) you want to assign to the new color scheme. If you click the Cancel button, the color scheme will be saved, but the previous color scheme will remain displayed. If you click the OK button after saving your color scheme, the color scheme takes effect and the settings are stored on the hard disk as the new default. The next time you start Windows, the new color scheme displays.

Removing a color scheme is easy: Simply select that color scheme from the Scheme list box and click the Delete button. If you are currently using the color scheme, it will remain active until you select another scheme or close Windows.

EXERCISE ▷ 25.4

1. In the **Control Panel**, double-click the **Display** icon.

2. Click the **Appearance** tab.

3. Save the current color scheme using the name **Current Colors**:
   a. Click the **Save As** button. The Save Scheme dialog box opens.
   b. Key **Current Colors** in the text box.
   c. Click the **OK** button.

4. From the **Scheme** list box, select **Marine (high color)**.

5. Make the following changes to the **Marine (high color)** color scheme:
   a. Change the **Active Window Border** to size **15**, **red**.
   b. Change the **Desktop** to **blue** (select a shade of blue other than the one used by the Active Title Bar).
   c. Change the **Inactive Title Bar** to **white**; change the font to **Arial**, **10**, **blue**, **italic**.
   d. Change the **Inactive Window Border** to size **5**, blue (select a shade of blue not currently used by another element).

6. The color scheme sample should now have only red, white, and blue elements while the text remains black.

7. Click the **Save As** button. The Save Scheme dialog box displays with the current scheme name, **Marine (high color)**, highlighted.

8. Key **My Color Scheme** in the **Save Scheme** text box; then click the **OK** button.

9. Click the **OK** button. Your screen elements now display as **My Color Scheme**.

10. Delete **My Color Scheme** from the Scheme list box:
    a. Redisplay the **Appearance** tab in the **Display Properties** dialog box.
    b. Verify that **My Color Scheme** is selected in the Scheme list box.
    c. Click the **Delete** button.

11. Select **Current Colors** from the **Scheme** list box; then click the **OK** button.

TIP

The Desktop Themes icon in the Control Panel gives you access to a number of pre-existing display settings and themes. For example, you might choose the Nature theme to transform your desktop into a scene complete with the sights and sounds of nature.

Creating Custom Colors

Instead of using Windows' predefined colors, you can create your own set of custom colors using the Color dialog box (Figure 25-6), which has the following features:

- A large color matrix box, which occupies most of the right half of the Color window.

- A luminosity bar (the long vertical bar to the right of the color matrix box).

- A Color/Solid box, which displays your custom color selection as you make it.

- Two sets of measuring scales: Hue/Sat/Lum on one side, which measure hue, saturation, and luminosity; and Red/Green/Blue (RGB) for the primary colors.

FIGURE 25-6
Color dialog box

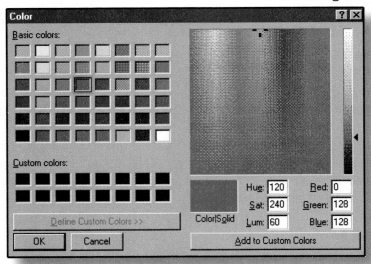

Using the color matrix box or these scales, you can customize your own colors, as explained below.

USING THE COLOR MATRIX BOX

Click anywhere in the color matrix box and a dark crosshair will display. When it does, look down at the Color/Solid box and the two sets of scales: Your selection is displayed in the Color/Solid box and its settings are displayed in the scales. Click elsewhere in the color matrix box and the crosshair reappears in that new box position; when it does, the Color/Solid box displays your new selection and the scales display its new settings. Instead of clicking here and there, you can click and hold down the mouse pointer and move the crosshair around the color matrix box. As you move, watch the Color/Solid box and the scales!

Stop when you are satisfied with the color. Then move to the luminosity bar to the right of the color matrix box. Do you see the small left-pointing arrow just outside the box? Click that arrow and hold down the mouse pointer while you drag the arrow up and down to adjust brightness.

When you are satisfied with your selection, click the Add to Custom Colors button. Your custom color will be placed in the first available blank box in the Custom colors palette. Repeat the process to make other selections. Click the OK button to close the box.

USING THE RGB SCALE

In Windows, all colors are made by combining the three primary colors—red, green, and blue (RGB). For example, when you combine red, green, and blue in full strength, you create white. When you combine all three colors in half strength, you produce a medium gray. And when you combine only red and blue in full strength with no green, you get purple.

The RGB scale values range from 0 to 255 (full strength). Thus red 255, blue 255, and green 255 will produce white; red 127, blue 127, and green 127 will produce medium gray. One way to create a custom color, therefore, is simply to change the numbers in the RGB boxes.

USING THE HUE/SAT/LUM SCALE

Just as you can change the values in the RGB scale, you can change the *hue* (the specific color), the *saturation* (the purity of color), and the *luminosity* (the brightness of the color) by using the Hue/Sat/Lum scale (see Figure 25-6).

In Windows, a color can have:

- A hue value from 0 to 239.

- A saturation value from 0 (gray) to 240 (pure color).

- A luminosity value from 0 (black) to 240 (white).

Remember that as you create your custom color, you see the results in the Color/Solid box.

USING THE COLOR/SOLID BOX

Computer monitors vary in how many colors they can display. Therefore, Windows uses a process called dithering to approximate the colors that your monitor can't display. The dithered color displays in the Color sample box. The Solid sample box displays a closely related color, one your system can display without dithering. If you are using a super VGA or better monitor, the custom color displays in both the Color and Solid sample boxes.

E X E R C I S E ⟶ 25.5

1. If necessary, open the Display Properties dialog box and click the **Appearance** tab.

2. Delete the Current Colors scheme: If necessary, select **Current Colors** from the Scheme list box and click the **Delete** button. Then select **Windows Standard** from the Scheme drop-down list box.

3. Create a custom color in the orange family:
   a. Click the **Item Color** box (*not* the drop-down list arrow) to display the Color palette.
   b. Click the **Other** button at the bottom of the palette to display the Color dialog box.
   c. Key the following numbers in the scales:
      Hue: **16**; Sat: **188**; Lum: **116**
      Red: **220**; Green: **104**; Blue: **27**
   d. If your screen shows different colors in the Color and Solid boxes, double-click the right side of the Color/Solid box to use the solid color most closely resembling the one you have created.

TIP

You can also create this color by dragging the crosshair in the color matrix box and adjusting the luminosity bar arrow.

   e. Click the **Add to Custom Colors** button to add the solid orange color to the Custom colors palette.
   f. Click the **OK** button to close the Color dialog box. Since the Desktop was selected in the Item drop-down list box, it was changed to the new color.
   g. Click the Color drop-down list arrow, and select the color your Desktop was previously.

4. Apply your custom color:
   a. Select **Active Title Bar** in the Item drop-down list box.
   b. Click the **Color** box drop-down list arrow, click the **Other** button, select the custom color on the Custom colors palette, and then click the **OK** button. The Active Title Bar changes to the new color in the sample window.

5. Click the **Cancel** button on the **Appearance** tab to close the Display Properties dialog box and cancel the color change.

6. Close the **Control Panel**. If instructed, shut down Windows and your computer.

Summary

This lesson covered techniques for changing screen savers and for adjusting the color, size, and font of items on the screen. You learned that:

- A screen saver is used to protect your monitor from screen burn-in and to block others from seeing what is on your display.

- You can select from Windows' existing screen savers. You can also customize these screen savers to suit your tastes.

- You can modify the desktop color scheme by selecting one of Windows' predefined schemes or by creating your own. You can save a scheme with a new name and you can delete a scheme.

- You can change the typeface, size, attributes, and color of text that appears in a window.

- You can create new colors to include in a color scheme by using the scales in the Color dialog box.

LESSON 25 REVIEW QUESTIONS

TRUE/FALSE

Each of the following statements is either true or false. Indicate your answer on the left by circling T if the statement is true and F if the statement is false.

T F 1. You must create a custom color scheme in order to change the currently displayed color scheme.

T F 2. The three primary colors used by Windows to create all colors are red, green, and black.

T F 3. The amount of "idle time" that must elapse before a screen saver is activated can be up to 99 seconds.

T F 4. You can save a customized color scheme with a new name.

T F 5. Windows does not let you delete color schemes.

FILL IN THE BLANKS

Complete the following sentences by writing the correct word or words in the blanks provided.

1. To select a different screen saver, you select the _____ tab in the Display Properties dialog box.

2. To change the color scheme of your desktop, you select the _____ tab in the Display Properties dialog box.

3. In the Hue/Sat/Lum scale in the Color dialog box, the _____ indicates the specific color.

4. In the Hue/Sat/Lum scale in the Color dialog box, the _____ indicates the purity of color.

5. In the Hue/Sat/Lum scale in the Color dialog box, the _____ indicates the brightness of color.

LESSON 25 PROJECT

This project gives you the opportunity to review the concepts in this lesson and practice the techniques in the exercises. Before you begin, ask if your instructor wants to see the screen saver you will create in this project. Also, make sure you write down the original settings for the screen saver so you can reapply them once you've completed the project.

1. Open the **Control Panel**; then double-click the **Display** icon.

2. Select the **Scrolling Marquee** screen saver and make the following settings in the Options for Scrolling Marquee dialog box:

   Position: **Random**
   Speed control: **moderate setting**
   Background color: [your choice]
   Message: **This project is completed!**
   Text format: **MS Serif, italic, 24**-point, [your choice of color]
   Delay: **1 minute**

3. Run your screen saver. If you have been instructed to do so, notify your instructor when your screen saver is running.

4. Change the screen saver settings back to their original settings. Then close the Display Properties dialog box and the **Control Panel**.

5. If instructed, shut down Windows and your computer.

CUSTOMIZING ADDITIONAL WINDOWS FEATURES

OBJECTIVES

Upon completion of this lesson, you will be able to:

- Control the keyboard response rate.

- Change regional settings.

- Change the date and time settings.

- Customize mouse operations.

- Assign a sound to an event.

⏱ **Estimated Time: 1.5 hours**

Now that you have reviewed how to customize your desktop display, you will learn how to customize your Windows software using the Keyboard icon, the Regional Settings icon, the Date/Time icon, the Mouse icon, and the Sounds icon in the Control Panel.

Controlling the Keyboard Response Rate

In Lesson 23 you learned that keyboard response is controlled by two factors:

1. How long the computer waits from the time you press a key to the time it repeats the character.

2. How quickly a key repeats characters once the key is held down.

In Windows, you control keyboard response through the Keyboard icon in the Control Panel. Double-clicking the Keyboard icon opens the Keyboard Properties dialog box (Figure 26-1), which offers two tabs for adjusting keyboard settings: Speed and Language.

The Speed tab displays three sliders that allow you to control the keyboard response rate: The first slider at the top of the Speed tab (under Character repeat) adjusts Repeat delay; the second, Repeat rate. The Speed tab offers a text box below the second slider so that you may test the rate. Just click the text box and hold down any alphabetic key. The third slider controls the Cursor blink rate box. When you're satisfied with the keyboard response, click the OK button to record your new settings.

FIGURE 26-1
Keyboard Properties dialog box

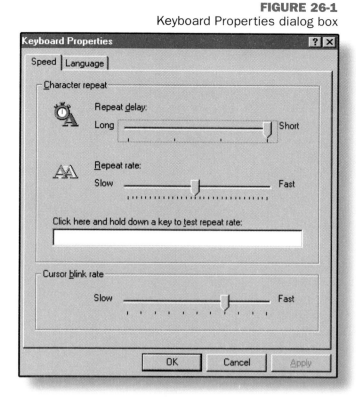

EXERCISE ▭▷ 26.1

1. Open the **Control Panel** and then double-click the **Keyboard** icon.

2. Adjust the Repeat delay rate:
   a. Click the slider and drag it to the far left (**Long** setting).
   b. Click in the text box and hold down the **h** key on your keyboard. Notice how long it takes before the letter *h* begins to repeat. (The actual time will vary, depending on your computer speed.)
   c. Click the slider and drag it to the far right (**Short** setting).
   d. Click in the text box and hold down the **h** key on your keyboard. Notice that it now takes less time for the letter *h* to repeat.
   e. Move the slider to a position that best suits you. You may have to test several settings.

3. Adjust the Repeat rate:
   a. Click the slider and drag it to the far left (**Slow** setting).
   b. Click in the text box and hold down the **h** key on your keyboard. Notice how fast the letter repeats in the text box.
   c. Click the slider and drag it to the far right (**Fast** setting).
   d. Click in the text box and hold down the **h** key on your keyboard. Notice how fast the letter repeats in the text box.
   e. Move the slider to a position that best suits you. You may have to test several settings.

4. Click the **Cancel** button to reapply the original settings.

Changing Regional Settings

The Regional Settings icon allows you to control most of the settings that vary by country. Since your system is already set up with the settings specific to your country, you may never need to change them—but you should know how to, just in case.

When you double-click the Regional Settings icon, the Regional Settings Properties dialog box opens (Figure 26-2). It contains five tabs:

FIGURE 26-2
Regional Settings Properties dialog box

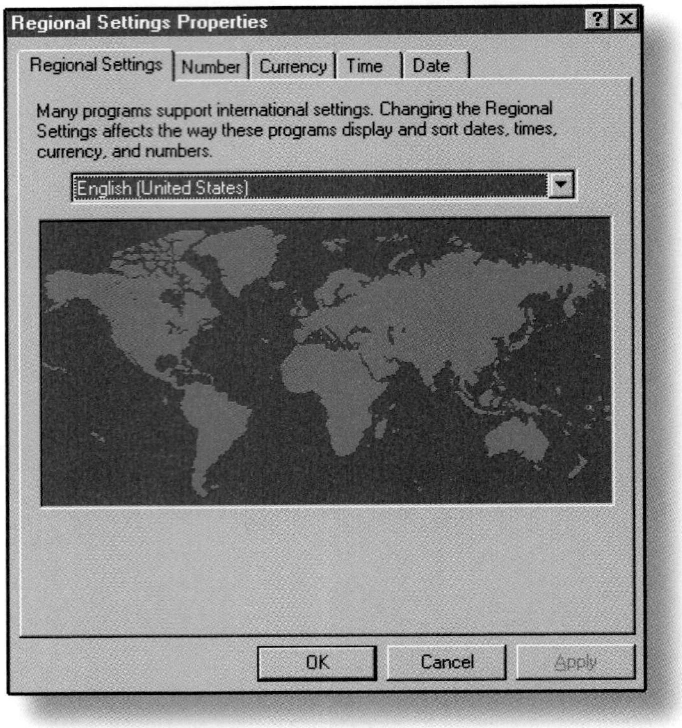

- **Regional Settings**. Sets Windows' defaults to match the region selected. When you choose a region from the drop-down list, Windows changes the settings on the other four tabs (Number, Currency, Time, Date) to reflect your regional choice.

- **Number**. Controls the way numbers are displayed, including the number of decimal places, the decimal separator, format of positive and negative numbers, and leading zeros; the character to be used to separate items in a list; and the measurement system (English or metric).

- **Currency**. Controls the display of the currency symbol (for example, $), the placement of the symbol, the number of decimal places, and the format of negative numbers.

- **Time**. Adjusts how hours and minutes are displayed and which symbol specifies A.M. and P.M.

- **Date**. Controls month-day-year order in date displays and the punctuation used to separate month-day-year; also allows you to choose whether the date display is short (1/06/98) or long (January 6, 1998).

Changing Date/Time Settings

By now you've surely noticed the time display on the right side of the taskbar. Obviously, you want to be sure that your system displays the correct time and date. One good reason: Many application programs allow you to insert the date and time automatically into your documents.

Double-clicking the Date/Time icon opens the Date/Time Properties dialog box (Figure 26-3), which contains two tabs: Date & Time and Time Zone. On the Date & Time tab, use the mouse to click the text box and then click the arrows to adjust the value. If you prefer, you may use the Tab key to move around.

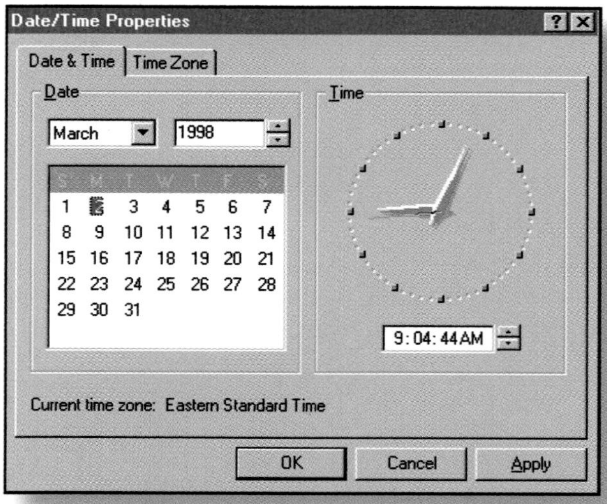

FIGURE 26-3
Date/Time Properties dialog box

Customizing the Mouse

If you want to customize mouse functions, double-click the Mouse icon in the Control Panel and use the Mouse Properties dialog box to make the needed adjustments. As you see in Figure 26-4, there are several tabs providing you with options for changing mouse settings. The options available on each are explained below.

- **StepSavers**. This tab provides shortcuts for selecting items with the mouse.

- **Pointers**. This tab lets you change the shape the mouse pointer assumes during certain activities.

- **Basics**. This tab lets you adjust the speed of the mouse pointer, the double-click speed, and it also lets you swap the functions of the mouse buttons.

- **Visibility**. This tab lets you control the location and visibility of the mouse pointer.

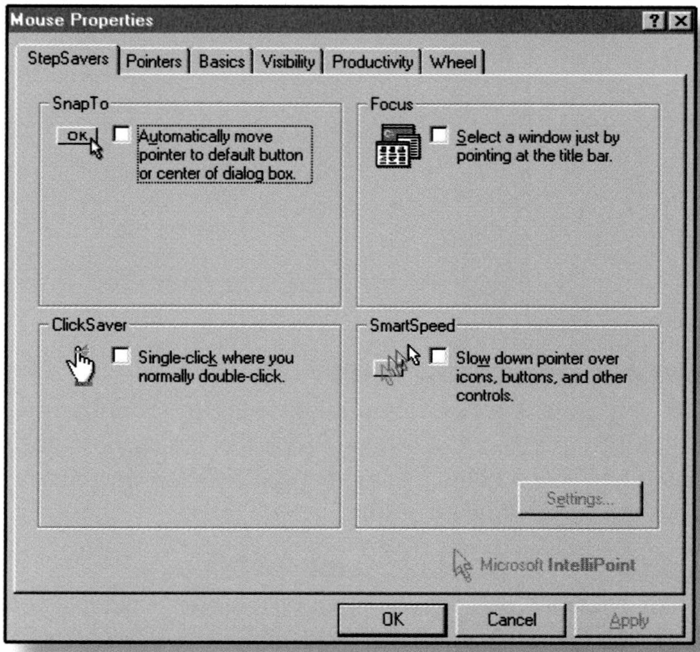

FIGURE 26-4
Mouse Properties dialog box

- **Productivity**. This tab lets you track the distance you move your mouse and it also lets you adjust the relationship between how you hold the mouse and the direction the mouse pointer moves on screen.

- **Wheel**. This tab lets you control the movement of the wheel button (if your mouse is equipped with one).

The Basics Tab

Let's take a closer look at the options on the Basics tab in the Mouse Properties dialog box.

SETTING POINTER SPEED

The Pointer speed option (see Figure 26-5) enables you to control the speed and acceleration of the mouse pointer. To adjust how fast the pointer moves on the screen, drag the marker on the speed bar in the desired direction.

FIGURE 26-5
Basics tab

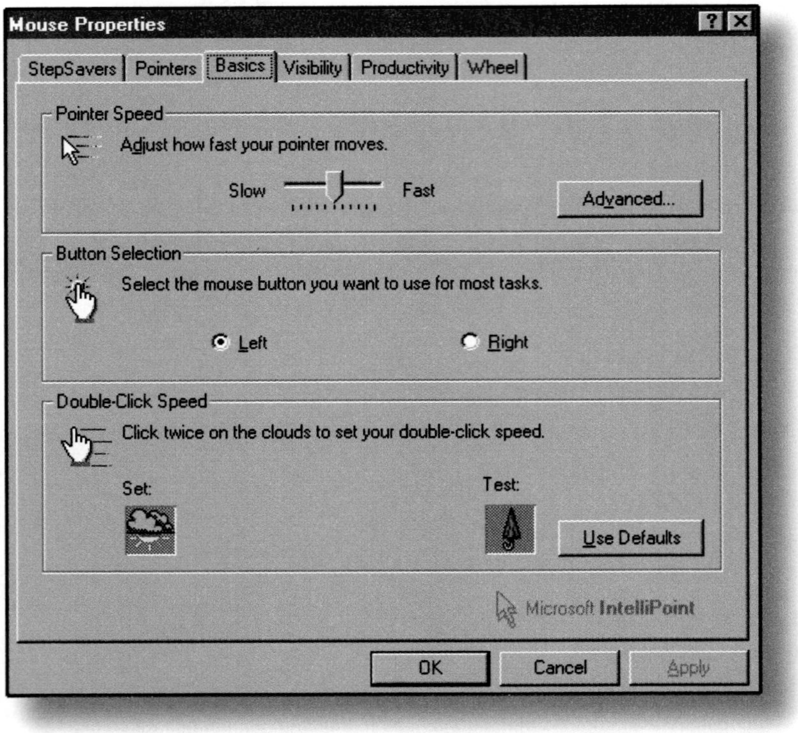

SWAPPING MOUSE BUTTONS

If you are left-handed, you might want to swap the functions of the mouse buttons. To do this, select the Basics tab in the Mouse Properties dialog box (see Figure 26-5). From the Button Selection options, click Right. This means that the right mouse button is now the primary button, and the left button is the shortcut menu button.

ADJUSTING THE DOUBLE-CLICK SPEED

The Double-Click Speed option on the Basics tab lets you set the amount of time allowed between the first and second clicks of a double-click. If you have trouble double-clicking the mouse fast enough, you can slow down the double-click speed. Double-click the clouds icon to set the double-click speed you desire. Then, double-click the Test icon to test the speed. If Windows recognizes the action as a double-click, the umbrella will open or close.

EXERCISE ⇨ 26.2

1. In the **Control Panel**, double-click the **Mouse** icon.

2. Adjust the double-click rate:
   a. Select the **Basics** tab.
   b. Double-click quickly on the **clouds** icon to set your double-click speed.
   c. Double-click slowly on the **umbrella** icon. Does it open or close? If it does not open, double-click on the icon until it opens or closes in recognition of your double-click action.

3. Click the **Use Defaults** button to reset the double-click speed at its original setting.

4. Adjust the pointer speed:
   a. Move the **Pointer Speed** slider to its slowest speed.
   b. Move the mouse to the left and right on the desktop. Notice the speed at which the mouse pointer moves on the screen.
   c. Move the **Pointer** speed slider to its fastest setting.
   d. Move the mouse to the left and right on the desktop. Notice the speed at which the mouse pointer moves on the screen. Did you notice that the mouse moves quickly across the screen?

5. Click the **Cancel** button to reset the **Pointer Speed** at its default setting.

The Pointers Tab

As you have seen in past exercises, the mouse pointer shape changes depending on what Windows is doing. Each shape is a visual clue to one particular Windows task. Windows comes with a number of pointer schemes. To see what the pointers look like in a scheme, select the Pointers tab in the Mouse Properties dialog box (see Figure 26-6). Select one of the schemes from the Scheme drop-down list box. The pointers for the selected scheme will display in the large window below.

You can create your own pointer scheme. Simply select one of the pointers in the display window, click the Browse button, and then double-click the file name of a different pointer. The new pointer will appear in the list in place of the former one. If

FIGURE 26-6
Pointers tab

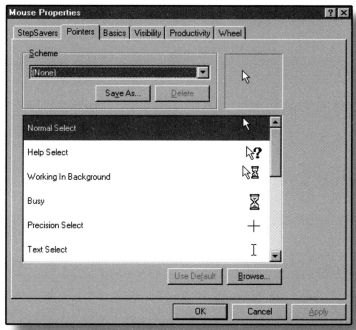

your display supports animated pointers, you can preview the animation in the preview box in the upper right corner of the tab.

After creating your new scheme, you must save it by clicking the Save As button and naming the file. You can always return to Windows' default settings: Just select the (None) option from the Scheme drop-down list.

The Visibility Tab

The options on the Visibility tab in the Mouse Properties dialog box are shown in Figure 26-7. The Sonar option lets you quickly locate the pointer on screen. Selecting the Vanish option hides the pointer as you type. If you are using a laptop computer with a liquid crystal display (LCD), you may find it helpful to add a trail to the mouse pointer to make it easier to follow the mouse as it moves around the screen. To change the length of the pointer trail, click the Settings button and drag the slider toward Short or Long. The PointerWrap option "wraps" the pointer to the opposite edge of the screen when you move it off the screen.

FIGURE 26-7
Visibility tab

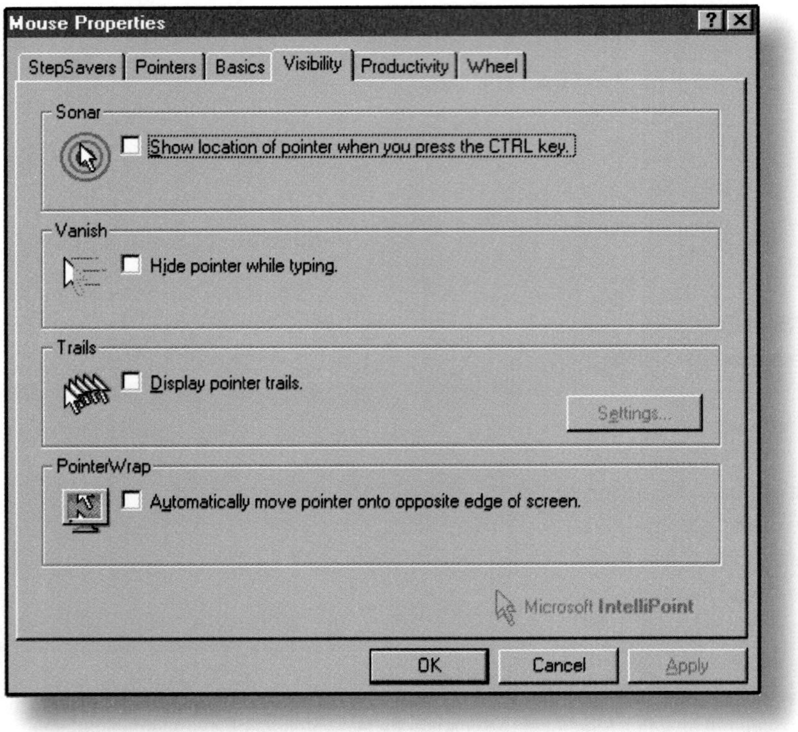

E X E R C I S E ⟹ 26.3

1. In the **Control Panel** double-click the **Mouse** icon.

2. Change the pointer scheme:
   a. Click the **Pointers** tab.
   b. From the **Scheme** drop-down list, select **Reptiles**.
   c. Click the **Cancel** button to return to the default pointer scheme.

3. Test the pointer trail feature:
   a. Redisplay the **Mouse Properties** dialog box and click the **Visibility** tab.

   b. Click a check in the **Display pointer trails** check box. Notice that this feature activates immediately.
   c. Move the mouse pointer to observe the pointer trails.
   d. Turn off the pointer trails feature by clicking in the **Display pointer trails** check box.

4. Click the **Cancel** button to close the Mouse properties dialog box.

Assigning Sounds

If your system has a sound card, Windows lets you assign sounds to standard events. For example, you can hear a bell each time you maximize a window or a beep each time you shut down Windows. To begin, double-click the Sounds icon in the Control Panel to open the Sounds Properties dialog box (Figure 26-8).

FIGURE 26-8
Sounds Properties dialog box

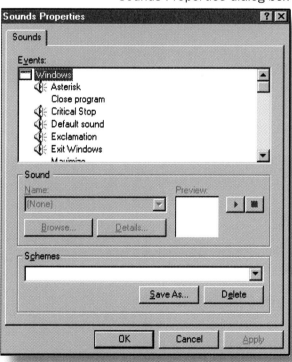

By default, Windows does not display sounds; therefore, you must first select the Windows Default scheme from the Schemes list box (Figure 26-8). To assign a sound from the scheme to an event, select the event from the Events list box (use the scroll bar to bring the event into view if it is not displayed), click the Browse button to display a listing of sound files (those files with the .WAV extension), and select one of the listed sounds. To test the sound, click the Preview play (➤) button in the Sound area of the dialog box. To stop playing a sound before it is finished, click the Stop (■) button.

When you have assigned all the sounds you want, click the OK or the Apply button to put the changes into effect. To save the sound scheme, click the Save As button; then key a scheme name in the Save this sound scheme as text box (Figure 26-9). In addition to the Windows default sound files, you can use sound files from other sources. Sound files can be downloaded from the Internet, purchased from a software dealer, or taken from recordings—that is, if your computer has a sound card and you have the appropriate equipment.

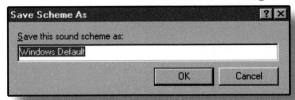

FIGURE 26-9
Save Scheme As dialog box

E X E R C I S E ▭▷ 26.4

If your computer does not have a sound card, skip this exercise.

1. In the **Control Panel** double-click the **Sounds** icon.

2. Assign The Microsoft Sound to the Close program event:
   a. Select the **Windows Default** scheme from the **Schemes** drop-down list if it is not already selected. If a message box displays asking if you want to save the current scheme, click **No**.
   b. Scroll the **Events** list to locate the **Close program** event; then click the event to select it.
   c. Click the down arrow in the **Name** drop-down list box; then click **The Microsoft Sound**. Did you notice the speaker icon that now appears in front of the event name in the list? This icon is a visual clue that a sound has been associated with the event.

3. Test the sound:
   a. Click the **Preview** play button. Did your system play the sound? If not, verify that

your computer has a sound card; then repeat step 2.
   b. Click the **Apply** button.

4. Click the **OK** button to close the Sounds Properties dialog box. Your sound should play as the dialog box closes.

5. Delete the sound you just added:
   a. Double-click the **Sounds** icon to open the Sounds Properties dialog box.
   b. Select the **Close program** event.
   c. Click the down arrow in the **Name** drop-down list box; then click **(None)** to remove the associated sound. Notice the speaker icon is no longer in front of the event name.
   d. Click the **Apply** button; then click **OK** to close the Sounds Properties dialog box. Notice that you hear no sound when you close the window.

6. Close the **Control Panel**. If instructed, shut down Windows and your computer.

Summary

This lesson covered the Control Panel's icons for adjusting the keyboard, mouse, sound, date and time, and regional settings. You learned that:

- You control keyboard response through the Keyboard icon in the Control Panel.

- The Regional Settings Properties dialog box options let you change country-specific settings for measurement (English or metric), number format, time, and currency.

- The Date/Time icon lets you change the date and time that displays in the right corner of the taskbar.

- You can change all activities and operations associated with the mouse in the Mouse Properties dialog box.

- In the Sounds Properties dialog box you can assign sounds to various system events.

LESSON 26 REVIEW QUESTIONS

TRUE/FALSE

Each of the following statements is either true or false. Indicate your answer on the left by circling T if the statement is true and F if the statement is false.

T   F   1.   Your computer system must have a sound card in order for you to assign sounds to Windows events.

T   F   2.   The Pointer trail option helps make the pointer more visible on screen.

T   F   3.   The Mouse icon is used to adjust the keyboard repeat delay and repeat rate.

T   F   4.   You cannot modify the pointer schemes that come with Windows 98.

T   F   5.   You can use sound files from a variety of sources to assign to Windows' events.

MATCHING

Write the letter of the term in the right column that matches the definition in the left column.

_____ 1. Tab in the Mouse Properties dialog box that lets you change the pointer scheme.

_____ 2. Tab in the Mouse Properties dialog box that lets you slow down the pointer's movement over icons, buttons, and other controls.

_____ 3. Tab in the Mouse Properties dialog box that lets you hide the pointer while typing.

_____ 4. Tab in the Mouse Properties dialog box that lets you adjust the pointer speed.

_____ 5. Tab in the Mouse Properties dialog box that lets you track the distance that your mouse moves.

A. StepSavers

B. Pointers

C. Basics

D. Visibility

E. Productivity

LESSON 26 PROJECT

This project gives you the opportunity to review the concepts in this lesson and practice the techniques in the exercises.

1. Open the **Control Panel**; then double-click the **Mouse** icon.

2. Change the pointer scheme to one of your choice.

3. Select one of the pointers in the list and click the **Browse** button. Change the pointer shape to one of your choice.

4. Click the **Cancel** button to return to the default pointer scheme.

5. Turn on the pointer trail feature.

6. In the **Date/Time Properties** dialog box, adjust the date and time, if necessary.

7. Turn off the pointer trail feature.

8. Switch the functions of the mouse buttons: Select the **Basics** tab in the Mouse Properties dialog box, and then click **Right** in the Button Selection area. Click the **OK** button with the *right* mouse button.

9. Switch the functions of the mouse buttons: Double-click the **Mouse** icon with the *right* mouse button. Click the **Basics** tab with the *right* mouse button, and then click the **Left** button with the *right* mouse button.

10. Close the Mouse Properties dialog box and the **Control Panel**.

11. If instructed, shut down Windows and your computer.

WORKING WITH PRINTER SETTINGS

OBJECTIVES

Upon completion of this lesson, you will be able to:

- Add and configure printers.
- Connect a printer to a port.
- Set the default printer.
- Remove a printer.

Estimated Time: 1 hour

One key area in which Control Panel lets you customize Windows is the Printers settings. In this lesson you will learn how to add and configure printers to work with your Windows system. You will also learn how to remove a printer.

Adding and Configuring Printers

You can use Windows with most printers, but first you must *configure* the *printer*—that is, install the printer and supply some printer settings. Configuring a printer may be as simple as selecting a name from a list of available printers. On the other hand, the installation may be more complex for an additional printer.

Windows provides a Printers icon for adding a printer, changing the settings on an already-installed printer, and identifying the default printer. Double-clicking the Printers icon in the Control Panel displays the Printers window (Figure 27-1) where you define these settings.

There are many, many different kinds of printers. To work with your printer, Windows needs basic information about the printer's paper sources, page sizes, control characters, fonts supported, and so on. This information is available in software called a *printer driver*, which must be installed on your hard drive. With the printer driver on your hard disk, you can configure your printer for use in Windows.

Windows software supplies hundreds of printer drivers on its installation CD, and Microsoft provides updates as new printer models are introduced. Printer drivers are also provided by dealers and by printer manufacturers.

Windows makes it easy to add and configure a new printer by supplying the Add Printer Wizard. This wizard guides you through the process in a series of dialog boxes, as you'll see in the following exercise.

TIP

The Printers window can also be opened by selecting Settings on the Start menu and then clicking Printers on the submenu.

FIGURE 27-1
Printers window

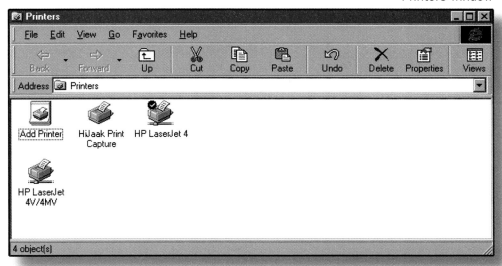

E X E R C I S E ⬜⟩ 27.1

To give you experience in adding and configuring a new printer, in this exercise you will add a duplicate of the printer currently on your system.

1. Open the **Control Panel** and double-click the **Printers** icon.

2. Write down the name of one of the printers shown in the Printers window.

3. Double-click the **Add Printer** icon to display the Add Printer Wizard dialog box.

4. Click the **Next** button to display the next set of instructions. Here you may be asked whether the printer is a Local printer or a Network printer.

5. If asked, choose **Local printer**; then click the **Next** button. The wizard displays a list of man-

ufacturers in the Manufacturers list box and printer models in the Printers list box.

6. Select the manufacturer's name of the printer you wrote down in step 2 from the Manufacturers list box (for example, HP); then select the printer model from the Printers list box (for example, HP LaserJet 4M Plus).

7. Click the **Next** button. If the wizard informs you that a driver is already installed for the printer you selected and recommends that you keep the existing driver, click the **Next** button. If the wizard jumps to the dialog box in which it wants to connect the printer to a port, do *not* click the **Next** button at this pointer. The wizard now wants to connect the printer to a port. Leave this dialog box on screen for the next exercise.

Connecting a Printer to a Port

In the process of adding a printer, you must identify the port to which the printer is attached. A *port* is a physical connection at the rear of the computer. The ports on a computer are generally not labeled or numbered, so you have to know something about computer hardware to properly identify them. Windows offers a *Plug and Play* feature that allows the wizard to select the port (for example, LPT1, LPT2, COM1, or COM2) to which it believes your printer is connected. A *COM port* is a *serial port*, or a connection in which information is sent serially, or bit by bit. A port with an LPT name is a *parallel port*, a connection in which information is sent in segments, not bit by bit. Generally printers are connected to parallel ports. If you wish to change the connection, click the desired port in the Available ports list box.

EXERCISE 27.2

1. Click the **Next** button to accept the wizard's selected port. The wizard permits you to accept the default name or give the printer a different name.

2. Verify that the **Printer** name box is highlighted; then key **My Printer**. Notice that the default printer name is replaced with the name you keyed.

3. Verify that the **Yes** button is selected at the bottom of the dialog box; then click the **Next** button. The wizard will now give you an opportunity to print a sample from the new printer.

4. Skip this printing step by clicking the **No** option button; then click the **Finish** button. A new printer icon now displays in the Printers window, with the name *My Printer*.

IMPORTANT:

When adding a printer, a message box may appear when you click the Finish button that instructs you to insert the Windows 98 CD. See your instructor for more information, or if you have the Windows 98 CD, insert it and follow the instructions that appear on screen.

Setting the Default Printer

Windows will automatically use one printer it calls the *default printer*. Each time you launch Windows, the default printer is the active printer. Whenever you need to change the default printer, just click the icon of the printer you want to become the default printer. Choose Set As Default from the File menu. That's all there is to it!

It's easy to identify the default printer. A small circle with a check mark inside it appears on the default printer's icon, as shown in Figure 27-2.

FIGURE 27-2
Default printer

HP LaserJet 4

E X E R C I S E ⟶ 27.3

1. Open the **Printers** window, if necessary.

2. Click any printer that appears in the window, except the one that's currently set as the default printer.

3. Select **Set As Default** from the **File** menu. Notice that a small circle with a check mark inside appears on the default printer's icon.

4. Change the default printer back to the original printer: Select the printer originally set as the default printer, and then select **Set As Default** from the **File** menu. Remain in the Printers window for the next exercise.

Removing a Printer

Removing a printer is a three-step process:

1. Click the printer icon for the printer you wish to delete.
2. Select Delete from the File menu.
3. Verify that the proper printer name is displayed in the Delete message box before you click the Yes button.

> **TIP**
>
> You can also delete a printer by selecting it in the Printers window and then clicking the Delete button on the toolbar.

E X E R C I S E ⟶ 27.4

1. In the **Printers** window click the **My Printer** icon.

2. Select **Delete** from the **File** menu.

3. Verify that the printer name, *My Printer*, is displayed in the message box (see Figure 27-3); then click the **Yes** button. Click the **No** button if any other printer name is displayed in the message box. The My Printer icon disappears from the Printers window.

4. Click the **Close** button to close the **Printers** window. Then close the **Control Panel**. If instructed, shut down Windows and your computer.

FIGURE 27-3
Message box asks you to confirm printer deletion

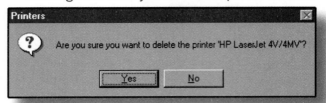

Summary

This lesson covered the techniques for adding and removing printers using the Control Panel's Printers icon. You learned that:

- You can open the Printers window by double-clicking the Printers icon in the Control Panel, or by selecting Settings on the Start menu and then Printers from the submenu.

- Printer drivers are a type of software that gives Windows the basic information it needs about a printer. Windows comes with hundreds of printer drivers on its installation CD, and updates are available when new printers are introduced on the market.

- The Add Printer Wizard guides you through the process of adding a printer. The wizard starts when you double-click the Add Printer icon in the Printers window.

- You can determine which printer you use is the default printer, or the one that document files are automatically sent to when you issue the command to print.

- You can remove a printer by simply selecting it in the Printers window, and then selecting Delete from the File menu, or clicking the Delete button on the toolbar.

LESSON 27 REVIEW QUESTIONS

TRUE/FALSE

Each of the following statements is either true or false. Indicate your answer on the left by circling T if the statement is true and F if the statement is false.

T   F   1.   You open the Printers window by selecting Printers on the Start menu.

T   F   2.   When you double-click the Add Printer icon in the Printers window, the Add Printer Wizard automatically starts.

T   F   3.   A printer must be named according to its manufacturer.

T   F   4. You cannot change the default printer.

T   F   5. You can remove a printer from the Printers window by selecting it and then clicking the Delete button on the toolbar.

FILL IN THE BLANKS

Complete the following sentences by writing the correct word or words in the blanks provided.

1. A(n) _____ is a software program that provides Windows with basic information about a printer.

2. A(n) _____ is a physical connection on the back of the computer that connects the unit to a printer.

3. You can open the Printers window by selecting _____ on the Start menu and then selecting Printers.

4. A small circle containing a check mark identifies the _____ printer in the Printers window.

5. LPT1, LPT2, and COM1 are examples of _____.

LESSON 27 PROJECT

This project gives you the opportunity to review the concepts in this lesson and practice the techniques in the exercises.

1. Open the **Printers** window.

2. Write down the name of one of the printers shown in the Printers window.

3. Double-click the **Add Printer** icon to display the Add Printer Wizard dialog box.

4. Click the **Next** button. If you are asked whether the printer is a Local printer or a Network printer, choose **Local printer**; then click the **Next** button.

5. Select the manufacturer's name of the printer you wrote down in step 2 from the Manufacturers list box; then select the printer model from the Printers list box.

6. Click the **Next** button. If the wizard informs you that a driver is already installed for the printer you selected and recommends that you keep the existing driver, click the **Next** button. If the wizard jumps to the dialog box in which it wants to connect the printer to a port, click the **Next** button to accept the wizard's selected port.

7. Verify that the Printer name box is highlighted; then key **Project Printer** as the printer's new name.

8. Verify that the **Yes** button is selected at the bottom of the dialog box; then click the **Next** button.

9. Skip the wizard's printing step by clicking the **No** option button; then click the **Finish** button.

10. Select the **Project Printer** in the **Printers** window and set it as the default printer.

11. Change the default printer back to the original printer.

12. Delete the **Project Printer** from the Printers window.

13. Click the **Close** button to close the Printers window. Then close the **Control Panel**. If instructed, shut down Windows and your computer.

WORKING WITH FONTS

Upon completion of this lesson, you will be able to:

■ View available fonts.

■ Print a font sample.

■ Arrange fonts by similarity.

■ Add and remove fonts.

⏱ Estimated Time: 1.5 hours

Windows lets you display text as it will look when printed! In other words, What You See Is What You Get, or WYSIWYG for short. This is possible because Windows supports a number of standard fonts as part of its graphical interface, and these same fonts are available in nearly every Windows application. You have already had some experience with choosing fonts for WordPad documents and Paint drawings. In this lesson, you'll learn more about fonts.

An Introduction to Fonts

F*ont* and *typeface* are printing terms that have been adopted for use with computers. Times New Roman and Arial identify two popular typefaces. But the name of a typeface by itself does little more than identify a general family of characters. In actual practice, you always need more specific information. What size Times New Roman? In regular type, **bold** type, *italic* type, or ***bold italic*** type? In ALL CAPITAL LETTERS or SMALL CAPITAL LETTERS?

Figure 28-1 shows samples of two different type sizes for two different typefaces. Each set shows a sample of regular, italic, bold, and bold italic. Each sample describes itself.

Look closely and you will see that each typeface is distinctive—Arial regular looks nothing like Times New Roman regular. Note the increase in size from the left column (10-point type) to the right column (12-point type). And note, too, the distinctive look of italic, bold, and bold italic in each typeface. Add to all this the ability to select all-capital letters or small-capital letters and you can see the endless possibilities you have for type design.

Let's summarize the key terms:

■ **Typeface** identifies one specific design or style of type, with no reference to size. Among the many popular typefaces are Arial, Helvetica, Century Schoolbook, and Times New Roman.

■ **Font** refers to the complete set of characters (all the letters, numbers, and symbols) in one size and one style in a given typeface (see Figure 28-2).

FIGURE 28-1

Samples of typefaces

10-point Arial regular	12-point Arial regular
10-point Arial italic	*12-point Arial italic*
10-point Arial bold	**12-point Arial bold**
10-point Arial bold italic	***12-point Arial bold italic***
10-point Times New Roman regular	12-point Times New Roman regular
10-point Times New Roman italic	*12-point Times New Roman italic*
10-point Times New Roman bold	**12-point Times New Roman bold**
10-point Times New Roman bold italic	***12-point Times New Roman bold italic***

FIGURE 28-2

Times New Roman fonts

- **Size** refers to type height, measured in points. In the type-measurement system, *points* and *picas* are the key terms. Fortunately, both are easily related to inches:

  12 points = 1 pica
  6 picas = 1 inch
  72 points = 1 inch
  1 point = 1/72 inch

Most Windows applications provide fonts in sizes ranging from 6 points to 72 points; some programs offer an even wider range of font sizes.

Now that you know the distinction between a font and a typeface, beware: Many computer users and desktop publishers use these terms interchangeably! But knowing the distinctions may be helpful.

Computer Fonts

Your computer needs two sets of fonts to do its work—one set to display characters on screen and another set to print characters on paper. The fonts designed to display type on the screen are called, appropriately, *screen fonts*. The fonts designed to produce printed copy are called *printer fonts*. The resolution of a screen font depends on the monitor. The resolution of a printer font depends on the printer. Because of the great variety of monitors and printers available, there is no "standard" for resolution.

SCREEN FONTS

Windows uses three different methods to display fonts on screen. Each method requires a separate font information file on the hard disk. In the discussion below, these methods are classified according to how the fonts are generated.

Bitmapped Fonts. Bitmapped fonts create characters dot by dot (much like the graphic desktop patterns and wallpapers you learned about earlier in this course), and they are displayed on screen pixel by pixel. Since they are formed by a pattern of dots, screen fonts are called *bitmapped fonts* (see Figure 28-3).

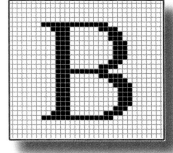

FIGURE 28-3
Bitmapped font

Bitmapped fonts are not scaleable (that is, you cannot change their size). As a result, the computer must store each size of each font separately, and that requires a lot of storage space. To conserve disk space, Windows screen fonts are available only in predefined point sizes (8, 10, 12, 14, 18, and 24 points) and in limited typefaces (Courier, MS Serif, MS Sans Serif, Small Fonts, and Symbol, depending on your monitor type).

Outline (Vector) Fonts. *Outline fonts* are created by drawing lines called *vectors* between points. Since these fonts are created by calculation and not from dots in a bitmapped matrix, vector fonts can be easily scaled to almost any size, and they can be rotated.

As you just learned, bitmapped fonts must be stored individually. Not so with outline fonts. For outline fonts, unlike bitmapped fonts, the computer stores only one outline of each letter, number, and symbol (including punctuation marks). Then the computer scales (that is, sizes) each outline as needed to produce larger or smaller or bolder letters and numbers.

Windows has only one outline font: Modern. For Modern, the computer stores only one outline for a lowercase *a*, one outline for a lowercase *b*, and so on. Then the computer adapts each outline character as needed to produce an *a* in 10-point type, an *a* in 12-point type, and so on—all sizes of that particular lowercase letter are generated from that one outline. Do you see how economical it is (in terms of computer memory and hard drive storage) to store one complete set of outline characters rather than one complete set for each size? This is one benefit of a *scaleable typeface*.

TrueType Fonts. Windows has its own version of outline fonts, called TrueType fonts. Whereas outline fonts build each character from lines and curves, *TrueType fonts* store a description of each character's shape and store and use the same information both for displaying on screen and for printing. As a result, TrueType fonts look the same on screen as they do when printed—thus true type!

Windows includes five TrueType fonts: Arial, Courier New, Times New Roman, Symbol, and WingDings. (The Symbol font is available in both a bitmapped and a TrueType version.) The first three are available in italic, bold, bold italic, and roman.

PRINTER FONTS

Printer fonts provide directions to the printer for printing. Windows supports printer fonts typically through the printer driver, which contains the definitions that support the printer fonts. The printer driver downloads the font information to the printer's memory. In any case, when you use printer fonts, you merely select typeface, style, and size. (Refer to the section on printer drivers earlier in this unit.)

There are three types of printer fonts: *built-in* (hardware) *fonts*, *soft fonts*, and *cartridge fonts*. Your limitations in using fonts are determined by your printer.

Built-In Fonts. Because built-in fonts are those that come with the printer, they are also called *resident fonts*. Some printers are limited to two or three fonts only; others have 35 or more resident fonts.

When you are printing using a printer's resident font, Windows will match that font as closely as possible on screen with one of its bitmapped screen fonts. When the match is not exact, your printed pages will not match your screen image precisely.

Soft Fonts. You can buy soft fonts, also called *downloadable fonts*, on floppy disks from commercial sources. You copy the font information from the floppy disks to your hard disk; then the files can be sent (that is, downloaded) to the printer as needed. The printer must have enough memory to hold the fonts, so printer memory capacity is important when using soft fonts. Time is also a consideration because downloading fonts is time consuming. (Printing is faster with built-in fonts.)

When used as printer fonts, TrueType fonts are downloaded just as soft fonts are downloaded, with this difference: TrueType fonts are downloaded to the printer at the time of printing, not before. Therefore, printing with TrueType is often faster than with soft fonts.

Cartridge Fonts. Fonts are also available in cartridges that physically plug into your printer. Just insert the cartridge into the cartridge slot on your printer. As with soft fonts, your printer must have enough memory to use cartridge fonts.

Viewing Available Fonts

The Fonts icon in the Control Panel lets you view samples of the fonts installed in your Windows system, but not printer fonts. However, printer fonts do appear in the Fonts list of Windows-based programs such as WordPad, Microsoft Word, and Microsoft Excel.

When you double-click the Fonts icon, the Fonts window opens (Figure 28-4) with the usual title bar, menu bar, toolbar, Address Bar, and display area.

FIGURE 28-4
Fonts window

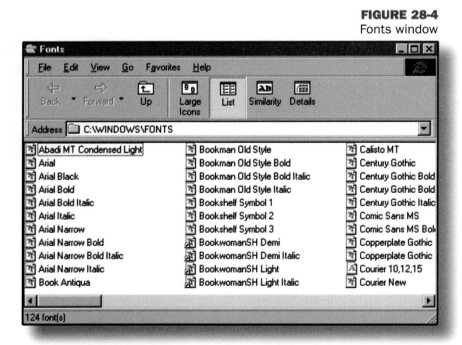

The display window shows the fonts installed on your computer system. The arrangement and the appearance of the listing are controlled by the view buttons on the toolbar. (These same options are available on the View menu.) The four display options are: Large Icons, List (the option selected in Figure 28-4), Similarity, and Details. The Similarity view is unique to the Fonts window and will be explained later in this lesson.

If you look closely at the display window in Figure 28-4, you will notice that two different icons are used: One is a sheet of paper with the letter A (used to identify bitmapped and outline fonts); the other is a sheet of paper with the letters TT (used to identify TrueType fonts). To get more information about any installed font, double-click the font's name. A dialog box opens to display samples of the font and information about it.

TIP

If the Standard toolbar is not displayed, select the View menu, Toolbars, and then Standard Buttons.

E X E R C I S E 28.1

1. Open the **Control Panel** and double-click the **Fonts** icon.

2. Click the **List** button on the toolbar.

3. Double-click **Arial** to open the Arial font's sample window, as shown in Figure 28-5.

FIGURE 28-5
Font sample window

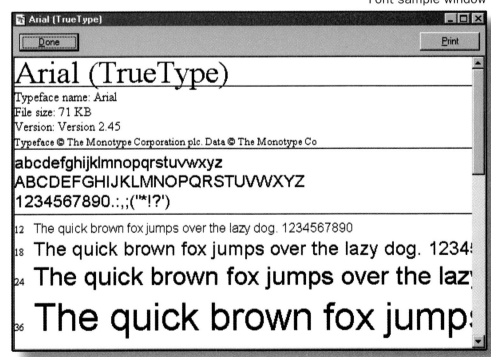

The Font Sample Window

As you can see in Figure 28-5, the font sample window is divided by horizontal lines into four sections (from top to bottom):

■ The font name is shown in the first section.

■ Technical information such as file size and version is shown next.

■ A full character set follows. This information is useful since some fonts do not contain all the characters and symbols that are available on the keyboard.

■ Samples of the typeface are displayed in several sizes. Which sizes are shown depends on the font. Scaleable TrueType fonts are shown in 12, 18, 24, 36, 48, 60, and 72 points. Nonscaleable bitmapped and outline fonts are displayed in the installed sizes only.

You will also notice the Print button in the upper right corner of the font sample window. This button allows you to print the information shown in the window. When you've finished using the font sample window, click the Done button to return to the Fonts window.

E X E R C I S E ▷ 28.2

1. Print a copy of the font sample:
   a. Verify that your printer is on and that you have access to it.
   b. Click the **Print** button, and then click the **OK** button in the **Print** dialog box.

2. Click the **Done** button when the font sample window is redisplayed.

3. Display and print a copy of the **Times New Roman** font.

4. Leave the Fonts window on screen for the next exercise.

Distinguishing Typefaces

Earlier in this lesson you learned that each typeface has certain distinguishing characteristics. Compare your two printouts from the last exercise. Which distinctive characteristics do you see? Look at the letters T and q. Note, for example, how the T in Arial is made of two very straight lines in the form of a cross. Now compare this with the T in Times New Roman, which is a very different "cross." In Times New Roman, the T has small "stems" called serifs that stick out from the two main cross pieces. Look for the serifs that drop down from the top cross piece and stick out from the bottom of the upright line. Times New Roman is a *serif* face; Arial is a *sans serif* face (*sans* means "without").

Arranging Fonts by Similarity

When you install Windows or a new font, an information file called a *Panose information file* is stored with each font. When this information is available, Windows is capable of comparing the Panose information for two or more files and listing the fonts in the sample window according to their similarities.

Buy why would you want to know if fonts are similar? The answer is that you may want to choose a font that has similar characteristics, but is not identical, to a specified font. If you don't have the "eye" for selecting similar fonts, ask Windows to compare the fonts for you: Just select the Similarity viewing option.

Arranging fonts by similarity is a two-step process. First you click the Similarity button (or select the List Fonts By Similarity option from the View menu); then you specify the base font in the drop-down list. For example, the fonts shown in Figure 28-6 are arranged according to their similarity to Arial. The base font, Arial, is shown in the drop-down list box. Notice that all the fonts listed are very similar or fairly similar. Further down the list, a number of fonts are listed that are "not similar." If no Panose information is available for a font, the font appears at the bottom of the list, with this comment in the Similarity to column: "No PANOSE information available."

If the listing is too long or you do not want the variations—that is, the bold and italic versions of the font—displayed, you can narrow your listing by selecting the Hide Variations (Bold, Italic, etc.) option from the View menu.

FIGURE 28-6
Similarity viewing option in Fonts window

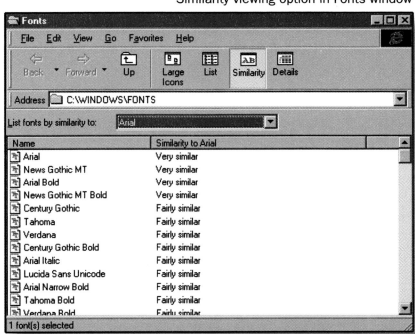

EXERCISE ⟹ 28.3

1. Display the fonts according to their similarity to Times New Roman:
   a. Click the **Similarity** button on the toolbar.
   b. Click the drop-down list box and select **Times New Roman**.

2. Select **Hide Variations (Bold, Italic, etc.)** on the **View** menu. Only the "regular" (no bold, italic, or bold italic) style of each installed font should be displayed.

3. Select **Hide Variations (Bold, Italic, etc.)** on the **View** menu again to deselect the option and display all the fonts.

4. Click the **Close** button to close the **Fonts** window.

Adding Fonts

Although Windows offers a variety of fonts, you may want to install additional fonts. Fonts are available from shareware, freeware, computer stores, mail order catalogs, and manufacturers. When purchasing and installing additional fonts, be sure to specify the printer you use. The screen fonts that match the printer fonts are installed automatically.

Any fonts purchased after Windows is installed on your system must be added to the Windows environment. Soft fonts and cartridge fonts come with a font-installation program that generates the screen fonts to match the new printer fonts. Some font programs, however, can generate screen fonts as they are needed, eliminating the need to store screen fonts on the hard disk (remember, you need one screen font for each size and type of font being used). If you are adding a large number of fonts, this feature can save a lot of disk space.

Font programs vary widely in the way they are installed and the way they make new fonts available. One purpose of the Fonts icon in the Control Panel is to allow you to install and remove fonts.

To install a new font, choose Install New Font from the File menu. The Add Fonts dialog box appears. The Add Fonts dialog box includes a list box for selecting a font from a disk drive or a network drive (Figure 28-7).

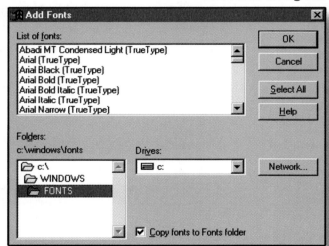

FIGURE 28-7
Add Fonts dialog box

EXERCISE ⇒ 28.4

1. In the **Control Panel** double-click the **Fonts** icon. If necessary, change the view to **Details**.

2. Insert your Windows Template disk in the appropriate drive.

3. Select **Install New Font** from the **File** menu; the Add Fonts dialog box displays.

4. Click the **Drives** drop-down arrow; then select the drive that contains your Windows Template disk. When you select the drive, Windows will search your Windows Template disk, will find *Small Fonts (EGA res)*, and will display its name in the List of fonts list box.

5. Verify that there is *no* check in the box labeled *Copy fonts to Fonts folder.* If this box is checked, the font will be copied to the Fonts folder on your computer's hard disk. Copying is not necessary here because you can use the font directly from the Windows Template disk.

6. Click the **Small Fonts (EGA res)** name in the List of fonts list box to select it.

7. Click the **OK** button. Since you are adding a font to the TrueType font management system but not storing it on your hard disk, Windows

displays a message to remind you that the disk containing the font must be in the disk drive when you wish to use that font in a document (see Figure 28-8).

8. Click the **Yes** button after reading the message. The font will be added to your installed fonts list. Then the Add Fonts dialog box will close and the added font will be displayed in the fonts list (see Figure 28-9).

9. Click the **Close** button to close the **Fonts** dialog box.

FIGURE 28-8
Message appears when you opt not to store a font
on the hard disk

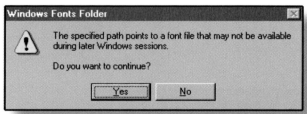

FIGURE 28-9
New font appears in the fonts list

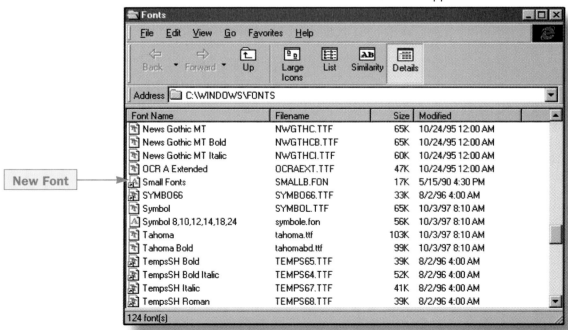

Removing Fonts

Storing fonts is costly in terms of memory. To free up space on your hard disk, you may decide to remove fonts that you rarely use.

 **IMPORTANT:**

Be extremely careful not to delete any font *you* did not add. Windows may need the font(s) to display non-Windows applications!

To remove a font, you can delete its file from the hard disk, or you can use the Fonts icon on the Control Panel. In the Fonts window, select the font name, then select Delete from the File menu. A message box will appear asking you to confirm that you want to delete the font (Figure 28-10). Click the Yes button to delete or No to cancel your decision.

FIGURE 28-10
Message asks you to confirm font deletion

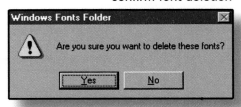

EXERCISE 28.5

1. In the **Control Panel** double-click the **Fonts** icon.

2. Click the **Small Fonts (EGA res)** font (the icon with the arrow in the lower left corner) in the fonts listing.

3. Select **Delete** from the **File** menu. The message box shown in Figure 28-10 will appear asking you to confirm that you want to delete the font. Be sure that only **Small Fonts (EGA res)** is selected or you may remove a font that your system needs.

4. Click the **Yes** button to delete the font.

5. Scroll the fonts list to verify that the font has been removed.

6. Click the **Close** button to close the Fonts dialog box. Close the **Control Panel**. If instructed, shut down Windows and your computer.

Summary

This lesson introduced you to the world of fonts and typefaces. You learned that:

■ Typeface identifies one specific design or style of type, with no reference to size. Among the many popular typefaces are Arial, Helvetica, Century Schoolbook, and Times New Roman. Font refers to the complete set of characters (all the letters, numbers, and symbols) in one size and one style in a given typeface. Size refers to type height, measured in points. One point equals 1/72 of an inch.

■ Your computer needs two sets of fonts to do its work—one set to display characters on screen, which are called screen fonts, and another set to print characters on paper, which are called printer fonts.

■ Windows uses three different methods to display fonts on screen: bitmapped, where a font is formed by a pattern of dots; outline or vector, which are created by drawing lines called vectors between points; and TrueType, which store a description of each character's shape and store and use the same information both for displaying on screen and for printing.

■ There are three types of printer fonts: built-in (or resident) fonts are those that come with the printer; soft (or downloadable) fonts are available on floppy disks or on the Internet from commercial sources and can be sent (that is, downloaded) to the printer as needed; and cartridge fonts, which are fonts that come on cartridges that physically plug into your printer.

■ You open the Fonts window by double-clicking the Fonts icon in the Control Panel. You can change the view of the Fonts window by clicking a view button on the toolbar or selecting a view option on the View menu.

■ You can use the Similarity view option to identify the similarities between a selected font and others on your hard disk.

■ You can double-click a font in the Fonts window to view information about it and see what it looks like displayed in various sizes. You can print a copy of the font information that appears in the sample window.

■ You can add fonts to and remove fonts from your hard disk. To add a font, you select the Install New Font option from the File menu. To delete a font, select it in the Fonts window and then select Delete from the File menu.

LESSON 28 REVIEW QUESTIONS

MULTIPLE CHOICE

Complete the following questions by circling the correct multiple choice letter.

1. An example of a font is
   A. Times New Roman
   B. Times New Roman in 10 point
   C. Times New Roman regular, bold, and italic in 10 point size
   D. Times New Roman in 10 point, 12 point, and 14 point

2. Scaleable fonts
   A. are created more quickly by your system than bitmapped fonts
   B. take up more disk space than bitmapped fonts
   C. are seldom used as screen fonts
   D. are generally sans serif fonts

3. What are the two basic types of computer fonts?
   A. bitmapped and outline
   B. screen and printer
   C. Panose and Windows
   D. TrueType and Soft

4. When measuring type size, 12-point type would equal:
   A. 12 picas
   B. 6 picas
   C. 1 inch
   D. 1/6 inch

5. The information file that is associated with each font installed on a hard disk is called a
   A. Panose file
   B. TrueType file
   C. Bitmapped file
   D. Typeface file

MATCHING

Write the letter of the term in the right column that matches the definition in the left column.

_____ 1. A type of font in which the characters are created dot by dot.

_____ 2. A type of font that you can get on a floppy disk from commercial sources.

_____ 3. A type of font in which a description of each character's shape is stored on the computer and is used for both on-screen display and printing.

_____ 4. A type of font in which the characters are created by drawing lines between points.

_____ 5. A type of font that comes already loaded on the printer.

A. TrueType

B. Soft

C. Outline

D. Bitmapped

E. Built-in

LESSON 28 PROJECT

This project gives you the opportunity to review the concepts in this lesson and practice the techniques in the exercises.

1. Open the **Control Panel** and double-click the **Fonts** icon.

2. Click the **List** button on the toolbar.

3. Double-click **Courier 10, 12, 15** to open the Courier font's sample window.

4. Print a copy of the font sample.

5. Click the **Done** button when the font sample window is redisplayed.

6. Find the fonts that are similar to Courier.

7. Close the **Fonts** window and then close the **Control Panel**. If instructed, shut down Windows and your computer.

UNIT 7 REVIEW QUESTIONS

WRITTEN QUESTIONS

Answer the questions below on a separate piece of paper.

1. Explain two ways you can set a Windows color scheme.

2. Describe how to create a custom color with the color palette.

3. Distinguish between a desktop pattern and a wallpaper.

4. Give two ways you can adjust the mouse pointer and explain the benefit of each.

5. Explain the original purpose of screen savers, name their major current use, and describe how a screen saver functions.

6. Discuss the purpose of a printer driver.

7. Distinguish between a screen font and a printer font.

8. Distinguish between a font and a typeface.

9. List the Windows accessibility options and briefly explain how they are used.

10. Discuss the purpose of mouse pointer trails and name an example when this feature might be helpful.

UNIT 7 APPLICATION

SCANS

Shawna Walker, Corporate Communique's office manager, has become very proficient with Windows 98. She now feels comfortable enough with the new operating system to start adjusting her desktop and display settings using the Control Panel. Help Shawna customize her computer desktop.

Open Paint and create a graphic that Shawna can hang as wallpaper on her desktop. Create a screen saver for Shawna. Change Shawna's desktop color scheme and fonts. Assign sounds to various events of your choosing.

When you are done adjusting the settings, write a short report in WordPad that explains what you changed. Include in the report an explanation of how to return the desktop to its default settings. Save the report as **Unit 7 Application** to your Windows Practice disk. Print a copy of the document.

Close all open applications. If instructed, shut down Windows and your computer.

CRITICAL THINKING

You have some free time before lunch—a perfect opportunity to customize your Windows desktop! Do the following:

- Create a custom color scheme with your favorite colors.

- Create a desktop pattern of your own design.

- Create a Scrolling Marquee screen saver that displays "I'm ready when you are!"

Just as you finish, several of your colleagues stop by to see if you want to go to lunch. You proudly show them your customized Windows desktop. Not surprisingly, they ask you to help them customize their Windows desktops.

You agree to do the following for them:

- Evelyn Lee, who works in the Accounting Department, wants a "business-like" wallpaper and screen saver.

- Tim Harris, who works in the Customer Service Department, wants a "fun" screen saver. Tim's system has a sound board, and he'd like to add sounds to some Windows events.

- Michael Moore, who is an account executive, will travel to Spain next week on business, and of course he'll take his new color laptop with him. Michael wants to know how he can use the Spanish keyboard while he is away and how to change the regional settings for Spain.

With this information, use the Control Panel to create these environments for your colleagues. Your instructor may wish to see each desktop and screen saver. When you are finished, write a short paper describing what you did for each colleague. Be sure to include the reasons for your choices.

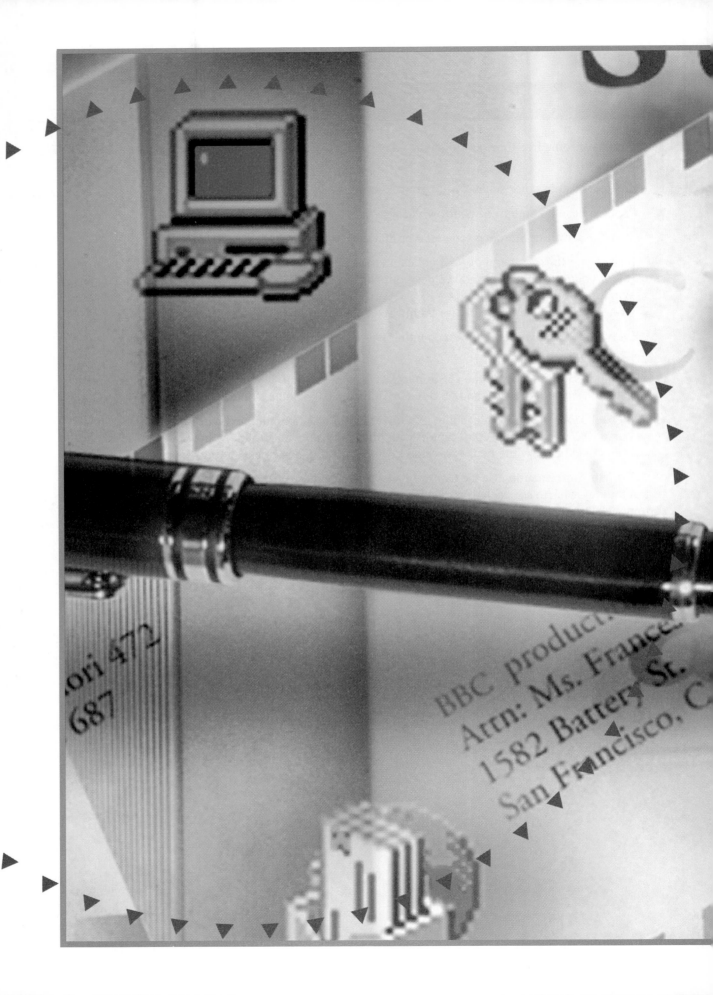

RUNNING DOS APPLICATIONS

UNIT 8

RUNNING A DOS SESSION

Before Windows 95 and now Windows 98, all IBM-compatible personal computers used a version of an operating system called *DOS* (short for Disk Operating System). When IBM developed the original IBM PC, they contracted the development of the operating system to the Microsoft Corporation, and Microsoft developed an operating system called *MS-DOS* (Microsoft Disk Operating System). IBM named its PC version of this program PC-DOS. Essentially, MS-DOS and PC-DOS are identical. In this unit, we will simply refer to DOS.

Basics of Running a DOS Session

Although DOS is not the operating system for Windows 98, DOS is still important for a number of reasons. First, over 80 million computer users today still use one or more application programs written for DOS. Second, a large number of computers operate an earlier version of Windows, which is itself a DOS-based program. And third, many software developers have adapted their DOS-based programs to run with Windows 98. For all these reasons, therefore, DOS-based programs will continue to be used for some time. Now you can see why Windows 98 can run DOS-based programs and why knowing some DOS basics can be very helpful.

Windows 98 runs DOS in a very special way. Windows 98 replaces DOS as the computer's operating system and assumes primary responsibility for managing its resources. That's why Windows 98 is classified as a fully integrated operating system. Windows handles DOS-based programs using *virtual machines* (VMs for short). Simply stated, a virtual machine is a block of memory configured to perform DOS operations just as if the block were an older DOS-based computer. This is like having an 8086 IBM-compatible personal computer in RAM.

The Windows 98 operating system is a true multitasking system. You'll remember from Lesson 1 that multitasking means you can run several applications—including DOS-based programs—at the same time. In Windows 98, you can run as many DOS-based programs simultaneously as your computer's memory will permit. You have the option of running DOS-based programs in two different ways: in a window (it will look and act like any Windows 98 program) or full screen (it will look and act as it would in the DOS environment).

Accessing DOS from Windows

You access DOS by using the MS-DOS Prompt command on the Programs menu. Clicking this option opens the MS-DOS Prompt window (Figure 29-1) in which you can run your DOS-based program or issue DOS commands.

FIGURE 29-1
MS-DOS Prompt opening window

Look closely at Figure 29-1 and notice the parts of the MS-DOS Prompt window. You see the familiar title bar, sizing buttons, and Close button. Notice that an optional toolbar is displayed beneath the title bar. When visible, this toolbar provides a convenient way to manage your DOS session.

Unlike most windows, the MS-DOS Prompt window does not have a menu bar. It does, however, have a *Control menu* (Figure 29-2) that gives you menu options corresponding to the toolbar buttons and window-sizing buttons. You access the Control menu by clicking the MS-DOS Prompt icon in the far left corner of the title bar.

FIGURE 29-2
Control menu

MS-DOS Prompt
Restore
Move
Size
Minimize
Maximize
Close
Edit
Toolbar
Properties
soft Corp 1981-1998.

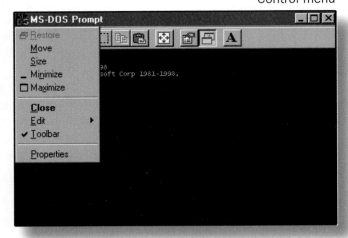

EXERCISE 29.1

1. Launch Windows if it is not already running.
2. Click the **Start** button, select **Programs**, then select **MS-DOS Prompt**. An MS-DOS Prompt window similar to the one shown in Figure 29-1 opens on your desktop, and the MS-DOS Prompt button appears on the taskbar.

The MS-DOS Prompt Window Toolbar

The toolbar is toggled on or off by selecting the Toolbar command from the Control menu. When displayed, the DOS toolbar has eight items. Each of these items is identified in Figure 29-3 and its function is described below.

FIGURE 29-3
DOS window toolbar

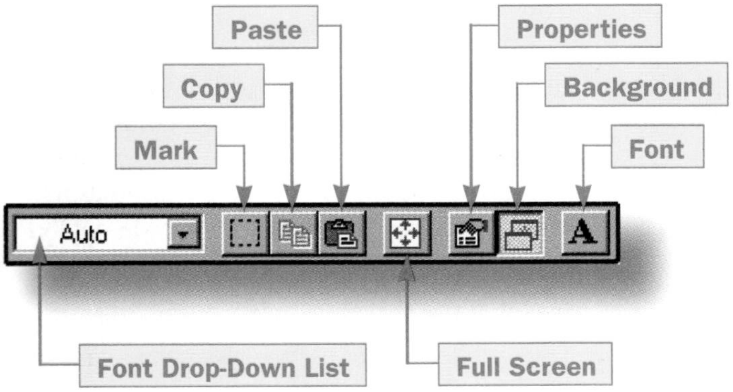

Paste
Copy
Mark
Properties
Background
Font
Auto
Font Drop-Down List
Full Screen

- **Font Drop-Down List**. Click the down arrow to display the font list, which permits you to select from a number of font options. These options are not font names, as in other Windows programs, but number combinations that describe the font's height and width. If you select the Auto font setting, Windows automatically scales the size of the display font so that the entire DOS screen fits within the current window. You'll see how this works later in this unit.

- **Mark**. Use this icon to select an item to be copied.

- **Copy**. Click this icon to copy a selected item to the Clipboard.

- **Paste**. Click this icon to paste a copied item from the Clipboard.

- **Full Screen**. Click this icon to toggle between a windowed display and a full-screen display.

- **Properties**. Click this icon to display the DOS-based program's Properties dialog box, which provides you with many options relating to the DOS window's display.

- **Background**. Click this icon to permit a DOS-based program to continue to run when you switch to other applications.

- **Font**. This icon displays the Font tab that appears in the program's Properties dialog box.

Switching Between a Windowed Display and a Full-Screen Display

As you will see later, at times you will want to work with the DOS window displayed full screen. You can toggle between a full-screen display and a windowed display in one of two ways:

1. Press Alt+Enter.

2. Click the Full screen icon on the toolbar.

The toolbar disappears in the full-screen mode. Press Alt+Enter to switch from a full-screen display to a windowed display.

EXERCISE ▷ 29.2

1. If the toolbar is not displayed on your screen, access the Control menu by clicking the **MS-DOS Prompt** icon and select **Toolbar**.

2. Click the **Font** drop-down list arrow and select the **7 × 14** option (or the option closest to 7 × 14). Notice how the window resizes to accommodate the new font.

3. Click the **Full screen** icon on the MS-DOS Prompt window toolbar. Notice that the MS-

DOS Prompt window is now displayed full screen (see Figure 29-4). Do you see any differences in the display? (*Answer:* The display shows none of the familiar Windows features—no title bar, toolbar, scroll bars, and so on.)

4. Press and hold down **Alt**, press **Enter**, and then release both keys. The MS-DOS Prompt is now toggled back to a windowed display.

FIGURE 29-4
DOS full-screen display

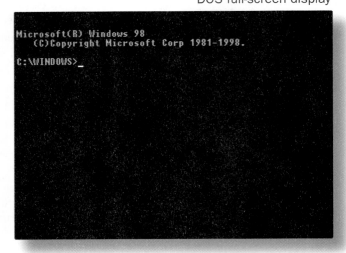

```
Microsoft(R) Windows 98
    (C)Copyright Microsoft Corp 1981-1998.

C:\WINDOWS>_
```

Creating Program Information Files (PIFs)

When you start a DOS-based program, Windows uses various settings to control the way the program runs and the way the program uses the computer's resources. These settings are stored in *PIFs* (*Program Information Files*). When you start a DOS-based program by double-clicking its icon, Windows searches for a PIF with the same name as the application's startup file. If it finds a matching PIF, Windows uses the settings stored in the PIF to run the program. If a DOS application has no PIF, Windows uses default settings to control the DOS application. You can make a PIF file by changing the application program's properties. Windows will save your choices in a newly created PIF for the application. Then the next time you run the DOS-based program, Windows will run it using the newly created PIF.

FIGURE 29-5
Properties dialog box

Adjusting DOS-Based Program Properties

You adjust a DOS-based program's properties by changing the information in the program's Properties dialog box. In a DOS program's Properties dialog box, five tabs allow you to change options: Program, Font, Memory, Screen, and Misc (for Miscellaneous), as shown in Figure 29-5. These five tabs are discussed below.

Setting Program Properties

The settings on the Program tab (see Figure 29-5) control various general properties for the application.

■ **Title**. The application's title is shown in the top text box. Changing this setting does not affect the application's file name.

■ **Cmd Line**. Normally, the name of the application's startup file is shown in this text box. A *startup file* is an executable file that runs the program. The command line can include optional command line parameters (switches) that control the way the program starts. You can also specify the name of a document on the command line rather than an application name if the application is properly associated.

■ **Working**. This entry specifies the directory that Windows makes "current" when it starts the DOS application.

■ **Batch File**. In this text box, you key the name of any batch file that must be run each time you start this program.

■ **Shortcut Key**. Use this entry to specify a key sequence that, when pressed, switches quickly to the DOS application. Issuing the shortcut key brings the DOS-based program to the foreground.

■ **Run**. The Run drop-down list specifies how the window is displayed when you start the DOS-based program. You can display it as a normal window; reduced to a button on the taskbar; or, if the DOS-based program permits, enlarged to take up the whole screen.

Setting Font Properties

You have already seen that you can change the font size of a windowed display by selecting one of the options on the toolbar's Font drop-down list. However, you have more font display choices on the Font tab (see Figure 29-6). As you study Figure 29-6, notice that the Font tab is divided into four sections. You make choices in the two upper sections; you see the results of your choices in the two lower sections. All four sections are discussed below.

FIGURE 29-6
Font tab

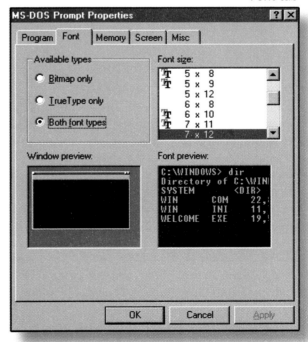

■ The Available types section (in the upper left corner of the tab) controls the type of fonts shown in the Font size list (in the upper right corner). You may use two types of fonts in windowed DOS-based programs—bitmapped and TrueType. Click the appropriate button to display Bitmap fonts, TrueType fonts, or Both font types (your choice is then displayed in the Font size section).

■ The Font size list box (in the upper right corner) displays the same list of font sizes as displayed in the Font drop-down list on a DOS-based program window. The font sizes are not measured in points (the traditional system used in word processing) but instead in picture elements. For example, in the 7 × 12 font size illustrated in Figure 29-6, each character occupies part of an area measuring 7 pixels wide by 12 pixels high. If you select any of the size options other than Auto, Windows adjusts the dimensions of the window to fit the selected font.

- The relative position of the window on the desktop is illustrated in the lower left corner of the Font tab, in the section titled Window preview.

- A sample of the selected font size is displayed in the Font preview window (lower right corner).

E X E R C I S E ▭⟩ 29.3

1. Click the **Font** button on the toolbar to display the **Font** tab in the MS-DOS Prompt Properties dialog box.

2. Click the **TrueType only** button in the Available types section of the Font tab. Notice that all the font sizes in the Font size listing are preceded with the symbol TT, which indicates that only TrueType fonts are listed.

3. Click the **Bitmap only** button in the Available types section of the Font tab. Now only Bitmap fonts are listed—no TT symbol!

4. Click the **Both font types** button to display both types of fonts.

5. If necessary, click the **Auto** selection in the Font size listing. (You may have to scroll to the top of the listing to locate the Auto selection.)

6. In the Font size list, click the **7 × 12** option; then click the **OK** button.

Setting Memory Properties

The settings on the Memory tab (see Figure 29-7) control the way the DOS-based application uses the computer's memory. Settings are provided to control conventional, expanded, and extended memory, as well as the amount of DOS protected-mode (DPMI) memory to allocate to this program. If you are unsure as to which settings to use, select the Auto option. Auto means "as much as possible"; it allows Windows to determine appropriate memory settings.

Because each DOS application operates in its own virtual machine (VM), the settings made on this tab affect only the memory that is allocated for the DOS-based application's VM. The settings do not affect the general Windows environment.

Setting Screen Properties

The settings on the Screen tab (see Figure 29-8) contain options for controlling the window display when the DOS-based program first starts. The options are in three sections: Usage, Window, and Performance.

FIGURE 29-7
Memory tab

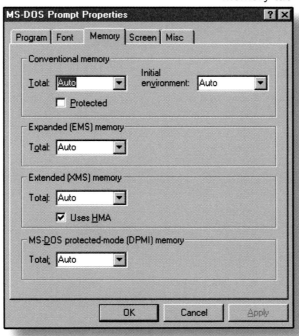

FIGURE 29-8
Screen tab

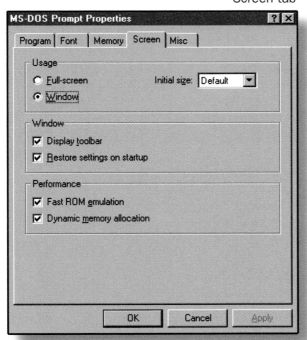

USAGE

Usage specifies how the application uses the screen:

■ Select the Window option for text-based DOS programs. The Initial size setting specifies the number of screen lines the application uses. Most DOS-based programs display 25 lines of text per screen. Some allow you to set a 43-line or a 50-line display. Select the Default option if you want the program to make its own decision.

■ Select the Full-screen option if you want the program to run in full screen or if you are running a graphics program.

WINDOW

These two options are available only if you select the Window option in the Usage section. Check the Display toolbar option to display the DOS toolbar in the DOS window. If you want Windows to save your settings, check the option labeled *Restore settings on startup*. The next time you start the MS-DOS Prompt, the saved settings are restored.

PERFORMANCE

The Performance options control miscellaneous video functions and are used in running DOS-based graphics applications.

E X E R C I S E ▭▷ 29.4

1. Click the **Properties** toolbar button; then select the **Screen** tab (see Figure 29-8).

2. Click the **Full-screen** option button; then click the **OK** button. The MS-DOS Prompt window now displays full screen.

3. Press **Alt+Enter** to switch to a windowed MS-DOS Prompt window.

4. Click the **Properties** toolbar button; again select the **Screen** tab. Notice the Window option button is checked. This option was selected when you issued the keyboard command, Alt+Enter.

5. Click the down arrow to the right of the Initial size drop-down list box, select **43** lines, and then click the **OK** button.

6. Click the down arrow to the right of the Font drop-down list; select **Auto**.

7. Close the **MS-DOS Prompt** window.

8. Open the **MS-DOS Prompt** window.

9. Notice that the MS-DOS Prompt window opens at the size specified by the options you selected on the Screen tab; that is, the window opens with space to display 43 lines of text (see Figure 29-9).

10. Click the **Properties** button on the toolbar; then select the **Screen** tab.

11. Select **25** lines, and then click the **OK** button.

12. Close the **MS-DOS Prompt** window.

13. Open the **MS-DOS Prompt** window. Notice that the MS-DOS Prompt window is resized to display the 25 lines you set on the Screen tab.

14. Click the Font drop-down list arrow; then select the **7 × 12** font option. Notice that the window is resized to accommodate your new setting.

15. Close the MS-DOS Prompt window.

FIGURE 29-9
Adjusting the Screen properties

Setting Miscellaneous Properties

The Misc(ellaneous) tab controls mouse behavior and several other items (see Figure 29-10).

FOREGROUND

You must clear the Allow screen saver check box if for any reason you do not want Windows' screen saver to start while you are running a DOS-based program.

MOUSE

Windows has no control over the mouse if you are running a DOS-based program full screen. If you are running a DOS-based program in a window, you must specify whether Windows or the DOS-based program controls the mouse. When the DOS-based program controls the mouse, the mouse pointer can be used to select menu options and items within the program window only. When the mouse pointer is moved outside the DOS program window, the mouse is controlled by Windows. When Windows controls the mouse, the pointer can be used only for Windows functions; the mouse cannot be used by the DOS-based program. In other words, the function of who controls the mouse is applicable only when the mouse pointer lies within the program window.

FIGURE 29-10
Misc tab

Note the two mouse options:

- Check the QuickEdit check box in the Mouse section of the tab if you want to be able to use your mouse to mark text in the DOS-based program window for cutting and copying. Clear the QuickEdit check box if you want the DOS-based program to have full control over your mouse.

- Select the Exclusive mode option if you want the DOS-based program to have exclusive (total) control over the mouse. When this is the case, the mouse pointer appears as a block pointer rather than as the standard arrow pointer. The block pointer follows the mouse, moving from one position to another as the mouse moves.

When the Exclusive mode is turned on, you can return mouse control to Windows by pressing Alt+Spacebar to display the Control menu. Then click the Properties button on the toolbar or select the Properties option from the menu. You can then select the Misc tab and deselect the Exclusive mode check box.

BACKGROUND

You must clear the Always suspend check box if you want a DOS-based program to be able to continue processing information while you work with another program. If you want to suspend background processing, check this box.

TERMINATION

Check the Warn if still active check box if you want a warning message to display whenever you try to quit a windowed DOS-based program by using a Windows procedure (clicking the Close button) or by closing Windows.

WINDOWS SHORTCUT KEYS

Windows reserves the keystroke combinations listed in this section for its own use. So, to make any of these shortcuts available to your DOS-based program, you must clear the appropriate check box. The actions of each of the Windows shortcut keys are explained in Table 29-1.

TABLE 29-1
Seven keystroke combinations reserved by Windows

Windows Shortcut Keys

Key This	To Do This
Alt+Tab	Switch to a different program
Ctrl+Esc	Display the Start menu
Alt+Print Scrn	Copy the current window as a bitmap graphic to the Clipboard
Alt+Spacebar	Display the program's Control menu
Alt+Esc	Switch directly to another program
Print Scrn	Copy the desktop as a bitmap graphic to the Clipboard
Alt+Enter	Toggle between full-screen and windowed display

EXERCISE 29.5

1. Open the **MS-DOS Prompt** window.

2. Move the mouse pointer on the desktop around the MS-DOS Prompt window. Notice that you can move the pointer anywhere on the screen.

3. Point inside the MS-DOS Prompt window and click the mouse button two or three times in different locations inside the window. Notice that nothing happens.

4. Select the QuickEdit option:
   a. Click the **Properties** button on the toolbar; then select the **Misc** tab.
   b. Click the **QuickEdit** check box; then click the **OK** button.

5. Point to the letter *M* in the word *Microsoft*, click, and drag across the line. Notice that the line is highlighted.

6. Press **Esc** to deselect the line.

7. Select the Exclusive mode option:
   a. Click the **Properties** button on the toolbar; then select the **Misc** tab.
   b. Uncheck the **QuickEdit** check box.
   c. Click in the **Exclusive mode** check box; then click the **OK** button.

8. Move the mouse on the desktop or mouse pad. Notice that the mouse pointer does not display on the screen. When the Exclusive mode is checked, the mouse is inactive.

9. Deselect the Exclusive mode and return mouse control to Windows:
   a. Press and hold down **Alt**, press **Spacebar**, and then release both keys. The Control menu displays.
   b. Use the down arrow to move the highlight to the **Properties** option on the **Control** menu, and then press **Enter**. Notice also that the mouse pointer reappears.
   c. Select the **Misc** tab and deselect the **Exclusive mode** check box.
   d. Click the **OK** button.

10. Move the mouse on the desktop or mouse pad. When the Exclusive mode is unchecked, the mouse is also active in the MS-DOS Prompt window.

11. Close the **MS-DOS Prompt** window.

Issuing DOS Commands

Windows has eliminated the need to learn DOS commands. Question: "Why, then, does Windows allow you to run applications by keying commands at the DOS prompt?" Answer: "Because so many computer users are very familiar with DOS commands and rely on them often." In this section, therefore, we will discuss how Windows 98 lets you issue DOS commands.

When you access the MS-DOS Prompt, the *command prompt* appears on the screen. The command prompt tells you that your system is in the DOS environment and identifies the default drive (usually drive C:). If the drive is drive C:, then the command prompt may appear as follows: C:\>.

At the command prompt, you can issue DOS commands that will perform many of the tasks Windows Explorer performs. For example, you might issue a command at the DOS prompt to display a list of files; copy, move, or delete files and folders; change folders; and so on.

Two DOS commands will be used in the following exercise: **dir,** the directory command, and **cd,** the change directory command

■ Keying the Directory command **dir** displays a listing of the folders and the files on the default disk. (In DOS, files are placed in "directories" rather than "folders"; hence "dir," short for directory.) Key the command at the DOS prompt as follows: **C:\>dir[Enter].**

■ Keying the Change Directory command **cd** followed by the name of a directory (folder) at the DOS prompt moves you into that new directory (folder). To change into the Windows directory, for example, you key: **C:\>cd Windows[Enter].**

In the same way you can issue other DOS commands at the prompt whenever it is convenient for you to take advantage of your DOS know-how.

E X E R C I S E ▭▷ 29.6

The following exercise assumes that Windows is the default directory (folder). If this is not the case for your system, your instructor will give you alternate instructions.

1. Open the **MS-DOS Prompt** window if it is not already open.

2. At the DOS prompt, key **dir** and press **Enter**. The directories and files on the default drive will display (Figure 29-11). Because the listing is long, it will scroll off the screen. In Figure 29-11, notice that the listing contains many of the same details that Explorer shows. The listing gives the traditional directory or file name (eight characters and an optional three-character extension), file size, date and time created or modified, and, on the far right side, the long file name, if one is used.

Notice that the DOS prompt is displayed a few lines below the last line of the directory listing ready for you to issue a new command.

3. At the DOS prompt, key **cd command** and press **Enter**. You now have moved to the Command subdirectory.

4. At the DOS prompt, key **dir** and press **Enter**. Because you are now "in" the Command subdirectory, the listing shows the contents of the Command subdirectory; that is, its directories and files.

5. Now run DOS full screen so you can see more of the directory listing: Press **Alt+Enter**. The MS-DOS Prompt window expands to full-screen size.

6. At the DOS prompt, key **dir** and press **Enter**. Note that you see more of the directory listing when you are running DOS full screen.

7. Toggle the DOS display back to a windowed display by pressing **Alt+Enter**.

FIGURE 29-11

Displaying directories in a DOS window

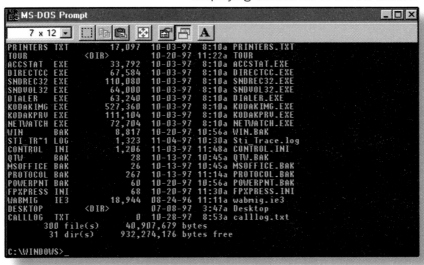

Booting to DOS

Occasionally you might need to boot your computer to the DOS environment, rather than starting Windows and then starting DOS, and having both systems running. Imagine, for example, that you experience a problem booting Windows; if so, you might be able to correct the problem working in the DOS environment. Or you might need to run a DOS application that doesn't work well under Windows. Knowing how to boot to DOS will prove helpful in both cases.

If you are booting to DOS because you want to run a DOS-based program that does not run well under Windows, you should use Windows' single DOS application mode instead. Then after you exit the DOS application, you can restart Windows by keying *exit*. This is similar to exiting Windows, running the DOS application, and then starting Windows again. The advantage is that you do not have to reboot your system in order to run the application or reboot to start Windows (which is necessary if you boot to a pre-Windows 98 version of DOS). Instead, you simply drop out of Windows temporarily!

EXERCISE 29.7

1. Close all open applications and shut down your system:
   a. Select **Shut Down** from the **Start** menu.
   b. Click the option **Restart in MS-DOS mode**.
   c. Click the **Yes** button.

   Notice that the DOS prompt (C:\Windows> or a similar prompt) indicates your system is in Windows' single DOS application mode.

2. Key **exit** and press **Enter** to restart Windows.

3. If instructed, shut down Windows and your computer.

Summary

This lesson introduced you to the MS-DOS operating system and how it works with Windows 98. You learned that:

- Before Windows 95 and now Windows 98, all IBM-compatible PCs used an operating system called DOS (Disk Operating System). The IBM PC version of this program is called PC-DOS; the Microsoft Corporation's version is called MS-DOS.

- Windows 98 is classified as a fully integrated operating system. Windows handles DOS-based programs using virtual machines (VMs), blocks of memory configured to perform DOS operations. A VM is the equivalent of having an 8086 personal computer in RAM.

- Windows 98 is a true multitasking system; it permits you to run several applications simultaneously—both Windows-based and DOS-based programs.

- A DOS-based program can be run in a window that looks and acts like any Windows 98 program window, or it can be run full screen. When a DOS-based program is run full screen, it looks just as if it were running in the DOS operating environment.

- An MS-DOS Prompt window is opened when the MS-DOS Prompt command is selected on the Programs menu. This window has the familiar title bar, resizing buttons, Close button, and an optional toolbar—but no menu bar.

- Eight items on the MS-DOS Prompt window toolbar permit access to the most common commands, enabling you to work with the DOS application as if it were a Windows application.

- To toggle between a windowed and a full-screen display, press Alt+Enter or click the Full screen icon on the toolbar. Because there is no toolbar in the Full screen mode, you must press Alt+Enter to toggle from a full screen display to a windowed display.

- DOS-based applications have properties, just like Windows-based applications do. A DOS-based application can be configured by changing its properties. Five tabs in a Properties dialog box allow you to change options: Program, Font, Memory, Screen, and Misc(ellaneous).

- DOS-based programs use Program Information Files (PIFs) to control the way the program runs and the way the program uses the computer's memory. A PIF file can be created by changing the application program's properties.

- Bitmapped and TrueType fonts may be used in a windowed DOS-based program. Font sizes are measured in pixels. Windows adjusts the dimensions of the window to fit the selected font type and size.

- Settings on the Memory tab control the way DOS-based applications use computer memory. Memory settings affect only the memory that is allocated for the DOS-based application's virtual machine (VM) and do not affect the general Windows environment.

- The Screen tab options control how a DOS-based application window is displayed when it opens. Options include Full-screen or Window mode, the number of text lines that will display in Window mode, and miscellaneous video functions for DOS-based graphics applications.

■ Windows has no control over the mouse when a DOS-based program is running full screen. Several mouse options are available when a DOS-based program is windowed. These options are selected on the Misc tab. Check the QuickEdit option to give Windows control over the mouse in the DOS-based program window. Uncheck the QuickEdit option to give MS-DOS control over the mouse when the mouse pointer is within the DOS-based program window (Windows then controls the mouse when the mouse pointer is outside the DOS-based program window). Click the Exclusive option to give MS-DOS full control of the mouse.

■ Seven Windows shortcut keys are listed on the Misc tab. A shortcut key can be unchecked to give the DOS-based program use of this keystroke combination if it is needed for a program function.

■ At the DOS prompt, commands can be issued that perform most of the tasks that Windows Explorer performs.

■ You can drop out of Windows temporarily and work in the DOS environment by selecting the option to Restart in MS-DOS mode in the Shut Down Windows dialog box.

LESSON 29 REVIEW QUESTIONS

MULTIPLE CHOICE

Complete the following questions by circling the correct multiple choice letter.

1. The Windows 98 operating system
   A. does not permit you to run several DOS-based applications at the same time
   B. uses a technical concept called visual machines
   C. is itself a DOS-based program
   D. permits you to run a DOS-based program just as it would if it were running on a DOS-based machine

2. You toggle between a full-screen display and a windowed display by
   A. pressing Alt+Enter
   B. clicking the Full screen icon on the toolbar
   C. setting the Full-screen option on an application's Screen tab in the MS-DOS Prompt Properties dialog box
   D. any of the above

3. A windowed DOS-based program display font
   A. must be a TrueType font
   B. must be a scaleable font
   C. can be either a bitmap or TrueType font
   D. must be a bitmap font

4. The Screen tab in the MS-DOS Prompt Properties dialog box contains an option for
   A. controlling the screen font used
   B. specifying how the application uses memory
   C. controlling whether the program is a text or graphic program
   D. specifying the number of screen lines the application uses

5. While running a DOS-based application,
   A. DOS always controls the mouse if you run the application full screen
   B. Windows always controls the mouse when running a DOS-based program in a window
   C. the mouse can never be moved outside a windowed DOS-based application
   D. the QuickEdit check box should be unchecked if you want the DOS-based program to have full control over the mouse

MATCHING

Write the letter of the term in the right column that matches the definition in the left column.

_____ 1. A block of memory configured to perform DOS operations just as if they were performed by a DOS-based computer.

_____ 2. The tab in the MS-DOS Prompt Properties dialog box that lets you switch from a full-screen view to a window view of DOS.

_____ 3. An icon on the MS-DOS Prompt window toolbar that displays the Font tab in the MS-DOS Prompt Properties dialog box.

_____ 4. A file containing various settings used to control the way a DOS-based program runs and the way a program uses the computer's resources.

_____ 5. Tab in the MS-DOS Prompt Properties dialog box that controls various general properties for a DOS-based program.

A. PIF

B. Font

C. Screen

D. Virtual machine

E. Misc

LESSON 29 PROJECT

This project gives you the opportunity to review the concepts in this lesson and practice the techniques in the exercises. You will need your Windows Template disk in order to complete this project.

1. Start Windows if it is not already running.

2. Open and print a copy of the **Project 29 Report Form** document stored on your Windows Template disk.

3. Complete the heading of the Project 29 Report Form by writing your name, class, and the date in the spaces provided.

4. Open the **MS-DOS Prompt** window.

5. Now you will issue a series of DOS commands. After each command, fill in the appropriate blank in the Project 29 Report Form. Proceed as follows:
   a. Key **dir** and press **Enter**. Then answer question 1 on the report form.
   b. Key **dir /o** and press **Enter**. Then answer question 2 on the report form.
   c. Key **dir /o-s** and press **Enter**. Then answer question 3 on the report form.
   d. Key **dir /ad** and press **Enter**. Then answer question 4 on the report form.
   e. Key **dir /o-n** and press **Enter**. Then answer question 5 on the report form.

6. Close the **MS-DOS Prompt** window. If instructed, shut down Windows and your computer.

WORKING IN DOS-BASED PROGRAMS

Upon completion of this lesson, you will be able to:

- Start a DOS-based program from the DOS prompt.
- Close a DOS-based program.
- Start a DOS-based program using the Start command.
- Start a DOS-based program using the Run command.
- Copy text from MS-DOS to a Windows program.

⏱ Estimated Time: 1.5 hours

Now that you are familiar with the MS-DOS environment, you will learn how to start DOS-based programs. This lesson covers several methods for launching a DOS-based application. You will also learn how to share data between DOS-based and Windows-based programs.

Starting DOS-Based Programs

You start a DOS-based program in one of three ways:

1. Double-click an application or a shortcut icon.

2. Key a program startup file name at the DOS prompt.

3. Use the Run command on the Start menu.

Double-clicking an icon is the easiest and most direct way to start a program, but DOS-based applications often don't have icons. Therefore, you must know how to use the other two methods of running DOS-based programs.

In the next few exercises you will run the DOS-based text editing program called Edit that comes with Windows 98. Most likely, you use a Windows-based word processing program, not the Edit program, but Edit can come in handy when you need to make changes in a DOS-based program.

Starting a DOS-Based Program from the DOS Prompt

Every DOS-based program has a startup file that runs the program. The startup file name generally is the same name as the application program and is followed by the extension **.exe** or **.com**. For example, the startup program name for the Edit program is **edit.com**. The extension **.exe** identifies the file as an executable file; the extension **.com**, as a command file. Thus, in Windows, you do not need to key the extension, just the startup name.

E X E R C I S E 30.1

1. Open the **MS-DOS Prompt** window by clicking the **Start** button, pointing to **Programs**, and then selecting **MS-DOS Prompt**.

2. At the DOS prompt, key **edit** and press **Enter**. The Edit program displays in the MS-DOS Prompt window, as shown in Figure 30-1.

3. Leave the Edit program on screen for the next exercise.

FIGURE 30-1
Edit program in the MS-DOS Prompt window

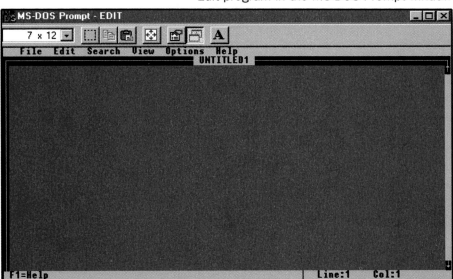

Closing a DOS-Based Program

When you are running a DOS-based program, be sure to use the program's normal quit or exit command to ensure that the program closes properly and that you will have an opportunity to save any open file. If you are running the program full screen, you will be returned to Windows after the program closes.

When you are running the program in a window, you can close the program in three additional ways:

1. Click the Close button.

2. Select the Close option from the Control menu.

3. Double-click the program icon on the title bar.

If you use any of these ways to close a DOS-based program that you start from the DOS prompt, Windows displays a warning message similar to the one shown in Figure 30-2. You can choose to ignore the warning and close the program, or you can go back to your DOS-based program and use its closing procedure.

FIGURE 30-2
Warning message

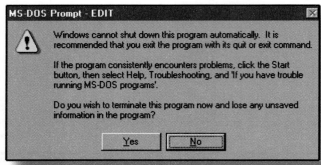

Depending on the option chosen in the DOS-based program's Properties dialog box, the program may remain visible in a window after you close the application. If it does, the title bar for the closed program will include the word *finished*, giving you a visual clue that the program is closed and it's safe to close the window. The program window remains visible because it may contain the program's final output or error messages that displayed when the program shut down.

EXERCISE 30.2

1. Click the **Close** button to close the DOS-based program and the MS-DOS Prompt window. A message box similar to the one shown in Figure 30-2 displays.

2. Read the message in the message box; then click the **Yes** button.

Starting a DOS-Based Program Using the Start Command

Another way to run DOS-based programs from the DOS prompt is to use the Start command. Key Start and then the startup file name. For example, to use the Start command to run the Edit program, you key **C:\>start edit[Enter].**

The advantage of using the Start command is that it runs the DOS-based program in its own virtual machine, thus giving as much memory to the program as possible. Also, the program opens in its own window.

The Start command also allows you to specify whether the program will be maximized, restored, or minimized when it starts. Table 30-1 lists the available Start command options; using the Edit program's Start command as an example.

TABLE 30-1
Specifying window size with the Start command

Start Command Options

Key	To Do This
Start/min edit	Start the Edit program in a minimized window
Start/max edit	Start the Edit program in a maximized window
Start/r edit	Start the Edit program in a restored window

E X E R C I S E 30.3

1. Open the **MS-DOS Prompt** window.

2. At the DOS prompt, key **start edit** and press **Enter**. Notice that the Edit program opens in its own window.

3. Close the MS-DOS Editor window by clicking its **Close** button. Do not close the MS-DOS Prompt window.

4. At the DOS prompt, key **start/max edit** and press **Enter**. Notice that the Edit program opens in a maximized window.

5. Close the **MS-DOS Edito**r window.

6. At the DOS prompt, key **start/min edit** and press **Enter**. Notice that the Edit program opens as a button on the taskbar.

7. Click the **MS-DOS Editor** button on the taskbar, and then close the window.

8. Close the **MS-DOS Prompt** window.

Starting a DOS-Based Program Using the Run Command

The *command processor* is the program that permits you to issue DOS commands. Whenever you access the DOS prompt, the command processor is loaded into memory. If your DOS-based program requires a lot of memory, you should avoid loading the command processor by using the Run command on the Start menu instead. When you use the Run command to start a DOS-based program, you free memory to run the DOS-based program.

Starting a program using the Run command is a three-step process:

1. Select the Run command from the Start menu.

2. Key the startup file name in the Open text box.

3. Click the OK button.

E X E R C I S E ▭ 30.4

1. Select **Run** from the **Start** menu.

2. Key the startup program name **edit** in the Open text box and click the **OK** button (see Figure 30-3). The Editor program window displays.

3. Click the **Close** button to close the program. Notice that the warning message does not display. The message appears only when you start a DOS-based program from the DOS prompt.

FIGURE 30-3
Run dialog box

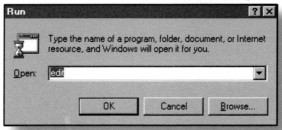

Sharing Data Between DOS-Based and Windows-Based Programs

Transferring data between DOS-based and Windows-based programs is like transferring data between Windows applications. If you copy or cut the desired data from one application, you can then paste it into another application.

Copying Text from an MS-DOS Program

In transferring information from a DOS-based application to a Windows-based application, you will need to keep track of the QuickEdit option on the application's Misc tab in its Properties dialog box.

■ If the QuickEdit option is unchecked, you must click the Mark button on the toolbar before you can use the mouse to select text.

■ If the QuickEdit option is checked, you do not have to click the Mark button before using the mouse to select the desired information.

How do you know if the QuickEdit option is checked without accessing the Misc tab? Drag the mouse pointer across the desired text. If QuickEdit is checked, the word *Select* appears in the program's title bar as soon as you start dragging (Figure 30-4). If it does not, the QuickEdit option is unchecked; you need to click the Mark button in order to select text. This process of selecting text is called *marking*.

In Exercise 30.5, you will transfer text from a DOS-based spreadsheet to Notepad. A simulated DOS-based spreadsheet, the **Report** file, is provided on your Windows Template disk. (Because the spreadsheet is simulated, you cannot use any spreadsheet functions.)

FIGURE 30-4
The word *select* appears in the title bar when QuickEdit is on

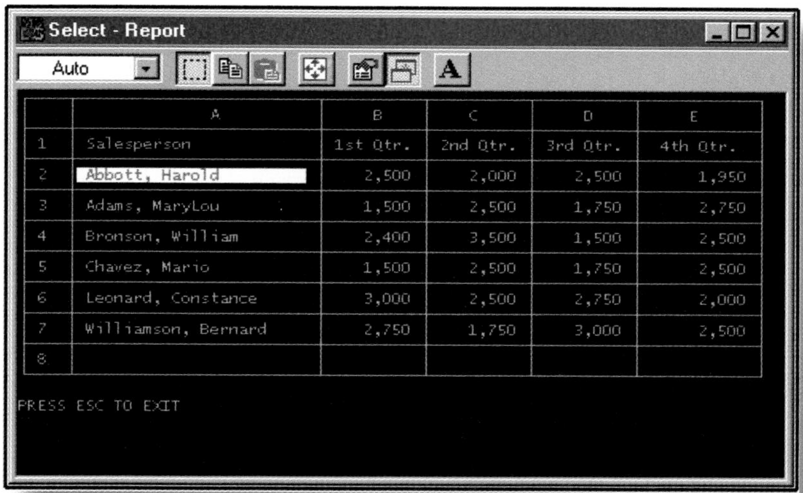

EXERCISE ▷ 30.5

1. Start the DOS-based application:
   a. Select **Run** from the **Start** menu.
   b. Click the **Browse** button.
   c. Select the disk drive your Windows Template disk is in.
   d. Select the **Report** file in the directory window, and then click the **Open** button.

   The Run dialog box displays with the file name **Report.com** in the text box.
   e. Click the **OK** button to run the simulated DOS-based spreadsheet.

(continued on next page)

2. If the DOS-based application runs full screen, toggle to a windowed display by pressing **Alt+Enter**.

3. Open a new Notepad document. Maximize the Notepad window, and then key the following text in the Notepad document:

The following information was copied from a DOS-based spreadsheet.**[Enter][Enter]**

4. Copy the data to be transferred:
- **a.** Click the **Report** button on the taskbar to display the Report window.
- **b.** Click the **Font** drop-down list box and select the **6 × 10** option, if it is not already selected.
- **c.** Click the **Mark** button on the toolbar. A blinking block cursor appears in the top left corner of the window. This block represents the starting point of the data to be marked and copied.
- **d.** Click the letter **S** in the word **Salesperson** (cell A1) and drag down and to the right below the

rule under the last number in the table, **2,500** (cell E7). The data you have selected will be highlighted, as shown in Figure 30-5.

5. Copy the data by clicking the **Copy** button on the toolbar.

6. Paste the data to the Notepad document:
- **a.** Click the **Untitled - Notepad** document to make the Notepad window active.
- **b.** Verify that the cursor is two lines below the text you keyed.
- **c.** Select the **Paste** option from the **Edit** menu. The spreadsheet information copied from the DOS-based spreadsheet will be pasted in your Notepad document.

7. Print and close the file without saving, and then exit **Notepad**.

8. Exit the DOS-based application:
- **a.** Press **Esc** to close the DOS-based application. The title bar reads "Finished - Report."
- **b.** Close the **MS-DOS** Prompt window.

FIGURE 30-5
Highlighting text with the Mark button

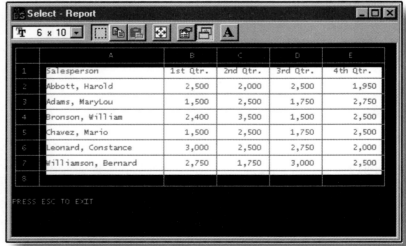

Summary

This lesson covered the various methods for opening a DOS-based application and sharing data between DOS-based and Windows-based programs. You learned that:

- A DOS-based program may be started by double-clicking an application icon or a shortcut icon; however, most DOS-based programs are not represented by an icon.

- Two additional methods for starting a DOS-based program are to key a program startup file name at the DOS prompt, or to use the Run command on the Start menu.

- To ensure that a DOS-based program is closed properly, use the program's normal quit or exit command.

- There are three options for closing the MS-DOS Prompt window: click the Close button; select the Close option from the Control menu; or double-click the program icon on the title bar.

- To transfer data between a DOS-based program and Windows-based program, you copy or cut the desired data from one application, and then paste it into another application. To select data with the mouse, make sure the QuickEdit option on the Misc tab is checked. If the option is unchecked, you must click the Mark button on the toolbar before you can use the mouse to select text.

LESSON 30 REVIEW QUESTIONS

TRUE/FALSE

Each of the following statements is either true or false. Indicate your answer on the left by circling T if the statement is true and F if the statement is false.

T F 1. You can start a DOS-based program in Windows the same way you start a Windows program.

T F 2. Every DOS-based program has a startup file that runs the program.

T F 3. The program extension **.exe** identifies a program as an extension of a DOS-based program.

T F 4. When you are running a DOS-based program, you should use the program's normal quit or exit command to close the program.

T F 5. You will be returned to Windows after closing a DOS-based program that was running full screen.

FILL IN THE BLANKS

Complete the following sentences by writing the correct word or words in the blanks provided.

1. The **.exe** extension on a startup file that runs a DOS-based program identifies the file as _____.

2. You would key _____ to start a DOS-based program in a minimized window.

3. You would key _____ to start a DOS-based program in a maximized window.

4. You would key _____ to start a DOS-based program in a restored window.

5. The _____ method for starting a DOS-based program at the DOS prompt runs the program in its own virtual machine.

LESSON 30 PROJECT

This project gives you the opportunity to review the concepts in this lesson and practice the techniques in the exercises.

1. Start Windows if it is not already running.

2. Open the **MS-DOS Prompt** window.

3. Maximize the **MS-DOS Prompt** window.

4. Run the DOS-based program **Greeting** (on your Windows Template disk) using the Start command:
    a. Key **Start** and space once.
    b. Key the letter of the drive in which you have placed your Windows Template disk and a colon (example: **A:**). Do not space.
    c. Key the file name **Greeting** and press **Enter**.

5. Close the **Greeting** program window.

6. Close the MS-DOS Prompt window by keying **exit** at the DOS prompt and then pressing **Enter**.

UNIT 8 REVIEW QUESTIONS

WRITTEN QUESTIONS

Answer the questions below on a separate piece of paper.

1. Why are none of the familiar Windows screen elements present when a DOS-based program is displayed full screen?

2. What is a PIF? Why are PIFs used?

3. What is the difference between starting a DOS-based program using the Start command and the Run command?

4. Explain the measurement system used by the fonts in the MS-DOS Prompt window.

5. Discuss the options you have for controlling the mouse in a windowed DOS-based program.

6. How can you return mouse control to Windows when the Exclusive mode is turned on?

7. Name the seven reserved Windows keystroke combinations. Explain the purpose of each.

8. What are the different ways a DOS-based program can be started? Give at least one example of when each method is appropriate.

9. Why does running a DOS-based program from the DOS prompt consume more memory than running it in other ways?

10. Explain the use of the QuickEdit option on the Misc tab when selecting text in a DOS-based program.

When you checked your e-mail this morning, you found the following message from Evelyn Lee of the Accounting Department:

```
                    I N T E R O F F I C E   M E M O R A N D U M

Date:        27-Sep 08:00am
From:        Evelyn Lee
Dept:        Accounting
Tel No:      555-6784
To:          [Your name]
Subject:     HELP WITH DOS-BASED PROGRAM

I have another problem I hope you can help me solve. As you know, I
recently began using a new computer system with Windows 98. I love the
system, but I have an old DOS-based database program that contains the
company telephone directory. I must update the directory and distribute
copies by next Monday, but of course I don't want to re-enter all the
data into a new Windows database program.

How can I pick up the copy from my old program and use it in Windows 98?
I have attached a file called DATABASE.COM that runs the program and
produces a sample phone listing for the sales department.

Thanks!
```

You write to Evelyn to say that you'll see what you can do, and then you download the file *Database.com* from her e-mail. When you run the program, you see that the program produces text that can be copied and pasted into a WordPad document.

Using the **Database.com** file stored on your Windows Template disk and the WordPad program, produce a sample telephone listing for the Sales Department. Make note of the procedures you used to produce the report, and then prepare a WordPad document that explains how Evelyn can use the DOS-based database reports and the WordPad program to produce her directory. Be sure to include the directory listing you prepared for the Sales Department as a sample.

SHARING DATA

SHARING DATA USING CUT AND PASTE

OBJECTIVES

Upon completion of this lesson, you will be able to:

- Understand how the Clipboard stores data.
- Display Clipboard Viewer text formats.
- View Clipboard format options.
- Share data in spreadsheet format.
- Share data in graphic format.
- Save Clipboard files.
- Create a scrap.

⏱ Estimated Time: 2 hours

A key benefit of Windows is that it eliminates repetitive tasks. Suppose that every month you develop an income report, a spreadsheet of cumulative financial information several pages long. Each month, you take the latest financial information from the spreadsheet and insert it into your sales analysis, a much longer text report. Do you rekey the financial information every time you need it for the sales analysis report? Of course not. You use the software's ability to share data. In the next five lessons, you will learn how to share data using a variety of methods.

Data Sharing

Sharing data allows you to create *compound documents*. A compound document is a document that consists of different types of data from different sources. In other words, a compound document is created by sharing data between and among documents. As you might expect, there are two documents involved in data sharing, a *source document* and a *destination document*.

- The document from which the data is copied is called the source document.
- The document to which the data is pasted is called the destination document.

The data is called the *object*. An object may be any type of data—for example, text, a sound clip, or a video clip.

Windows offers three options for sharing data. One is the Clipboard, which you have used in previous lessons. The others are *embedding* and *linking*, which are forms of object linking and embedding (abbreviated OLE and pronounced "o-LAY").

Sharing Data Using the Clipboard

You have used the Clipboard in previous lessons to copy and move data within and among documents of various types. You learned that the Clipboard is a temporary holding place in the computer's memory that stores text or a cutout until you place a new object on the Clipboard or exit Windows.

But the Clipboard has a number of features that you have not yet explored. In this section, you'll learn more about how the Clipboard stores objects, how to share data among different types of programs using the Clipboard, and how to view the contents of the Clipboard.

CLIPBOARD FORMATS

When a Windows application places an object on the Clipboard, it often uses multiple formats. The *format* is the code a program uses to display characteristics and/or attributes of text or graphics. WordPad, for example, places text on the Clipboard using three different formats (see Figure 31-1): Text, Picture, and OEM Text. The multiple-format arrangement provides more choices for pasting the object into other applications and, as you will learn later, for embedding and linking data. Many standard Clipboard formats exist. Table 31-1 describes some of the more common formats.

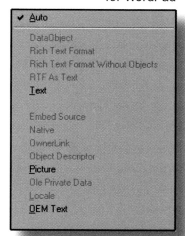

FIGURE 31-1
Clipboard formats
for WordPad

TABLE 31-1
Types of file formats available for objects placed on the Clipboard

Common Clipboard Formats	
TEXT FORMAT	**DESCRIPTION**
Text	Unformatted text in the current Windows system font.
OEM Text	Unformatted text in the character set created by the **O**riginal **E**quipment **M**anufacturer.
Rich Text Format (RTF)	**R**ich **T**ext **F**ormat is a standard format that is understood by most popular word processing application programs. RTF text retains formats such as italic, bold, centering, and so on.
Unicode Text	A 16-bit text-encoding format that allows for both Latin and non-Latin characters, as well as for commercial, mathematical, and scientific symbols.
Picture	Graphic image of text font created by drawing lines, rectangles, circles, and so on.

(continued on next page)

GRAPHIC FORMAT	DESCRIPTION
Bitmap	A device-dependent graphic format composed of an array of dots of various colors (or black and white).
DIB Bitmap	**D**evice-**I**ndependent **B**itmap format.
Picture	Graphic image created by drawn lines, rectangles, circles, and so on.

SPREADSHEET FORMAT	DESCRIPTION
SYLK	Microsoft **SY**mbolic **Lin**K format used to transfer spreadsheet data.
BIFF	**B**inary **I**nterchange **F**ile **F**ormat that is the standard data format used by Microsoft Excel.
Link, Object, Owner Link	Formats used to establish OLE links between documents.

The text formats are used for displaying text, the graphics formats are used for displaying images, and the spreadsheet formats are used for data that contain formulas. The most common formats for information are the text formats.

Most applications have standard options available, but not all formats are available for each application. The formats available depend on which application was used to create the object. By using the Clipboard Viewer, you can see which formats are available.

The Clipboard Viewer

Clipboard Viewer is a simple utility program that lets you view the contents of the Clipboard and also clear the Clipboard. Clipboard Viewer appears in the System Tools folder on the Accessories menu, and you open it the same way as any other accessory. The Clipboard Viewer window (Figure 31-2) has a standard menu bar (with File, Edit, Display, and Help menus), sizing buttons, and a Close button.

The Display menu is the key to transferring data using Clipboard Viewer. The Display menu indicates the present data format and permits you to select other formats for viewing Clipboard data. Which "other" formats appear active on the menu depends on the source application from which the object was copied.

FIGURE 31-2
Clipboard Viewer window

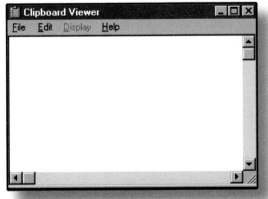

EXERCISE 31.1

1. Create a new WordPad document and key the following text:

   ```
   This text has been keyed
   directly in the WordPad program
   and copied to the Clipboard.
   ```

2. Copy the text to the Clipboard using the **Copy** button on the toolbar.

3. Display the contents of the Clipboard Viewer: Click the **Start** button, then **Programs**, **Accessories**, **System Tools**, and finally **Clipboard Viewer**.

4. Click the **Display** menu to view the default format of the data on the Clipboard.

   The check mark indicates that the default

setting for the data on the Clipboard is Auto, which means that the Clipboard Viewer has selected one of the three available formats (those shown in black) listed on the menu. "Auto" doesn't represent a format—it simply indicates that the Clipboard Viewer has selected the format it considers best for displaying the data. In this example, the Clipboard Viewer selected the Text format because the object is text created in WordPad.

Let's see how the other format options display the text.

EXERCISE 31.2

1. Select **OEM Text** on the Display menu. Notice that the display changes—a different font is used, so the text takes on a different appearance.

2. Select **Picture** on the Display menu. The display changes again because the Picture format is a graphic format and not a text format. Click the scroll bars to see if you can display more of the text. Notice that you cannot

display more of the text than is shown in the Clipboard Viewer window. The Picture format would be used if you pasted the text to a graphic program such as Paint.

3. Close the **Clipboard Viewer**.

4. Close **WordPad** without saving the current document.

Clipboard supports the *Rich Text Format (RTF)*. RTF is available in most word processing application programs, so RTF can be used to exchange formatted text between most word processing application programs. If the software application can format text in RTF format, it uses RTF when pasting to the Clipboard. How do you know that you have data in RTF display format on the Clipboard? You will see the RTF option in black type on the Clipboard Viewer's Display menu. If the application into which you are pasting information can read RTF, you can transfer the information without losing the formatting; if the application does not support RTF, the text is pasted in one of the other text formats and you may lose the formatting.

Data Sharing in Spreadsheet Format

A common use of data sharing is to transfer part of a spreadsheet to a word processing document. As with other Copy and Paste operations, to transfer data from a spreadsheet to a word processing document you must highlight the cells to be copied, copy the highlighted data to the Clipboard, and then paste the data from the Clipboard to the word processing document. The data are copied to the Clipboard with as much of the formatting as possible. Generally, any font changes are included, and the columns and rows are converted to the word processing software's table format.

Data Sharing in Graphic Format

The many different graphic formats can be classified into three categories: Bitmap, DIB Bitmap, and Picture (see Table 31-1).

BITMAP FORMAT

As you learned in Unit 6, bitmapped graphics are made of a pattern of screen pixels. The pixels that make up a bitmapped image are stored in the computer's memory as a table called a *map*. Each pixel in the map is represented by one or more *bits*. Each of these bits represents one pixel's location and color. To display an image in *bitmap* format, the computer reads the table and turns pixels on or off accordingly. The result is a bitmapped image.

A major disadvantage of bitmapped images occurs when you enlarge or reduce the image: You may alter its quality. If you enlarge the image, the pixels are "mapped" to a larger area, and the image loses some of its resolution. If you reduce the image, the pixels are packed more tightly together, and this tighter "map" may affect the value of the colors in the graphic.

DIB BITMAP FORMAT

The *device-independent bitmap (DIB Bitmap)* format allows you to display a graphic file regardless of which video mode you are using. Clipboard files that contain bitmapped graphics are device dependent. To display these graphic files, you must have the proper monitor. Example: You copy a 256-color image to the Clipboard and then save the data in a Clipboard file. But if you change to a different system—say, with a monitor that supports only 16 colors—you will no longer see the image. The Clipboard Viewer window will be blank. *But the graphic is still on the Clipboard!* The problem is that the Clipboard Viewer cannot display the graphic because the graphic was saved in a more complex video mode. The solution? Use the DIB Bitmap option on the Display menu. The DIB Bitmap format allows you to display a graphic file regardless of which video mode you are using.

PICTURE FORMAT

Picture images, also called *metafile* images, are vector graphics; that is, they are created on screen by connecting points with lines and arcs. Picture images are also known as *object-oriented images* because they are stored in the Clipboard not as the object but as a series of commands that redraw the image of the object on the display. For the Clipboard Viewer to display a Picture image, the Clipboard Viewer must process those commands. The same is true when you paste a Picture image into another application. That application must be able to issue the commands in order to display the image. If the application does not have that capability, and the image in the Clipboard is stored only in Picture format, then the application cannot display the image.

One advantage of Picture images is that they can be scaled to any size without losing clarity. Reason: A scaled image is redrawn with the same set of commands. Lines, circles, rectangles—all always have the same resolution regardless of size. The only limitations are the monitor's resolution and display.

EXERCISE ☐▷ 31.3

1. Start the **Paint** program.

2. Open the **Cornucopia** file on your Windows Template disk. Notice that this is a color graphic.

3. Use the **Select** tool to select the graphic. Copy the file to the Clipboard.

4. Open the **Clipboard Viewer**.

5. Click the Clipboard Viewer's **Display** menu and verify that the **Auto** option is selected.

6. Open **WordPad** and create a new document. Key the information below:

    ```
    Your Name[Enter]

    [Enter]
    ```

Your Class`[Enter]`

`[Enter]`

```
This document contains text that
was keyed and a color graphic
that was pasted from the
Clipboard. [Enter]
```

`[Enter]`

7. Paste the graphic into the document by choosing **Paste** from the **Edit** menu. The graphic will be pasted into the document, as shown in Figure 31-3.

8. Print the WordPad file.

9. Close **WordPad**, **Paint**, and the **Clipboard Viewer**. Do not save changes in WordPad or in Paint.

FIGURE 31-3
Pasting a Paint image

Saving Clipboard Files

At times, you may want to save the information stored on the Clipboard as a Clipboard file. With Clipboard, you save files "as usual" for Windows, using the Save As command from the File menu. Clipboard gives the files a **.clp** extension.

But when you save a Clipboard file, saving the file and all the available format options is not automatic. An Excel file, for example, has 10 different formats. Note the difference in the following two procedures:

- If you copy data from Excel into the Clipboard and then close Excel, you immediately lose all but three of these formats in your copied data.

- If you save the Clipboard contents to a Clipboard file before you close Excel, you save all 10 formats. You can then close Excel.

With Excel, and with many other applications, Clipboard is software independent. When the application is open, Clipboard saves a file and all its format options. Later, when this Clipboard file is opened, all the format options are available.

Creating Other Linking Shortcuts

There will be times when you will want to use an object in several documents or in a document that has not yet been created. You can do this by creating either a scrap of the object or a temporary link to that object and placing it on the desktop.

A *scrap* is a copy of an object that has been cut or copied from a source document and placed on the desktop. You can then copy or cut this object and paste it into your document or several documents. Scraps can be created in programs that support the drag-and-drop Windows feature.

FIGURE 31-4
Scrap icon on the desktop

To create a scrap, highlight the text or graphic object, select the Copy option on the Edit menu, right-click on the desktop, and select Paste. A Scrap icon similar to the one shown in Figure 31-4 displays. The name of the file is created by using the word *scrap* followed by the starting information of the material you selected.

You can create a document shortcut, or temporary link, to information in a document by:

1. Copying the information.

2. Right-clicking on the desktop.

3. Selecting the Paste Shortcut option. A shortcut icon appears on your desktop with an appropriate caption.

The advantage to using scraps and document shortcuts is that you do not have to have the destination document immediately available after you delete the information. This is useful when, for whatever reason, you cannot open the destination document or the destination document is located on a different computer. You can also copy scraps and document shortcuts onto a disk and move them between different computers.

Summary

This lesson covered how to share data using the Cut and Paste commands and Clipboard. You learned that:

▪ Data sharing allows you to create documents that consist of different types of data from different sources. Such documents are called compound documents. The document from which the data is copied is the source document. The document to which the data is pasted is the destination document.

▪ There are three primary ways in which you can share information or data in more than one location: using the Clipboard, embedding, and linking.

▪ The Clipboard Viewer is an accessory that shows you data stored on the Clipboard. The Clipboard Viewer's Display menu indicates the present format of the text, spreadsheet, or graphic on the Clipboard and permits you to select other formats for viewing the data. Which "other" formats depends on the source application displaying the data in the Clipboard Viewer.

▪ You may save Clipboard data in a Clipboard file, which will be given the extension **.clp**. The Clipboard is software independent; that is, Clipboard saves a file with its special formatting and makes the file available even after its application is closed. Clipboard files that contain graphics are device dependent; that is, to view these files you must have an appropriate monitor.

▪ An object is any data or block of information that is shared between two documents (or among three or more documents). An object always travels from a source document to a destination document.

LESSON 31 REVIEW QUESTIONS

MULTIPLE CHOICE

Complete the following questions by circling the correct multiple choice letter.

1. A procedure for sharing data between Windows applications is
   A. Copy and Paste
   B. linking
   C. embedding
   D. all of the above

2. The key to the Clipboard Viewer's data sharing is its
   A. File menu
   B. Display menu
   C. zoom feature
   D. none of the above

3. Rich Text Format
   A. is only available in the most advanced word processing application programs
   B. can be used for exchanging graphics files between most word processing application programs
   C. maintains character-formatting attributes
   D. all of the above

4. Clipboard files that contain graphics
   A. are device independent
   B. are software dependent
   C. always display using the OEM format
   D. none of the above

5. An example of an object is
   A. a block of text
   B. a dialog box
   C. a application program
   D. all of the above

MATCHING

Write the letter of the term in the right column that matches the definition in the left column.

_____ 1. Using data from one application in another application.

_____ 2. Any data or block of information shared between two documents.

_____ 3. A document that consists of different types of data from different sources.

_____ 4. A document from which data is copied.

_____ 5. A document to which data is pasted.

A. Destination document

B. Compound document

C. Source document

D. Object

E. Data sharing

LESSON 31 PROJECT

This project gives you the opportunity to review the concepts in this lesson and practice the techniques in the exercises. You will need your Windows Template disk and Windows Practice disk in order to complete this project.

1. Open **Paint**.

2. Open the **Picture** file on your Windows Template disk.

3. Modify the image:
   a. Click the **Text** tool.
   b. Click the **Draw Opaque** option (the top option in the selection area).
   c. Drag a text box at the top center of the drawing from the yellow chess piece to the blue one. The Text toolbar appears on your screen.

NOTE:

If the Text toolbar does not appear, select the Text Toolbar option on the View menu.

   d. Select the font: **Arial**, **Bold**, size **12**.
   e. Click in the text box and key your name and class.
   f. Click anywhere in the drawing area outside the text box to close the Text toolbar.

4. Select part of the graphic and copy it:
   a. Using the **Select** tool, select an area that encloses the yellow, pink, and blue chess pieces in the top half of the graphic.
   b. Choose **Copy** on the **Edit** menu.

5. Save the picture as a Clipboard file on your Windows Practice disk:
   a. Open the **Clipboard Viewer.**
   b. Verify that the image appears in the Clipboard Viewer with your name in the top center of the image.
   c. Click **Save As** on the **File** menu.
   d. Access the drive containing your Windows Practice disk.
   e. Double-click in the **File name** box and key the file name **Myfile.**

6. Close the **Clipboard Viewer** and **Paint**. Do not save changes to the drawing. If instructed, shut down Windows and your computer.

EMBEDDING OBJECTS

OBJECTIVES

Upon completion of this lesson, you will be able to:

■ Embed a new object.

■ Edit an embedded object.

■ Embed an object as an icon.

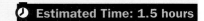 **Estimated Time: 1.5 hours**

The Copy and Paste process using the Clipboard is static; in other words, the pasted object is divorced both from its original document and from its original application program. *Object linking and embedding (OLE)* is dynamic; in other words, the embedded object remembers its origins. As its name implies, OLE uses two methods of data sharing: linking and embedding. In this lesson, you will learn how to embed objects.

Understanding OLE

An obvious advantage of OLE over the Cut, Copy, and Paste process is that it does not duplicate data and waste memory space. (The Copy and Paste process stores and re-stores the same object every time you paste it, forcing data to reside in two or more places). Another advantage is that OLE lets you place into documents an object that you cannot create directly in that document's application software. For example, OLE lets you embed a sound file or a video clip into a word processing or spreadsheet document. When the document's application program cannot render the data directly, it displays an icon to indicate where the object has been embedded. When you want to hear the sound or view the video, double-click the icon. Windows plays the object in the sound or video application in which the object was created. This process will be explained later in this text.

Windows applications that support OLE are called *OLE-aware*. But not all applications support the latest OLE features available with Windows 98.

OLE-aware documents permit linking and embedding as well as one or more of the following features:

- **In-place editing.** When a program supports in-place editing, the destination document's menus and toolbars are temporarily replaced by those of the object's source program. For example, if you wish to edit an Excel spreadsheet that has been embedded in a Word document, double-click the spreadsheet while you are in the Word document. The Excel menus and toolbars replace the Word menus and toolbars. When you finish editing the spreadsheet data, the Word menus and toolbars reappear.

- **Cross-application drag and drop.** Applications that support this OLE feature permit you to copy data between applications or between an application and a folder by dragging the data with the mouse from the source document or file to the destination document.

- **OLE automation.** Some OLE-aware applications permit you to use Microsoft Visual Basic and Visual Basic for Applications programs to create "scripts" or "macros" that copy and move data between and among OLE-aware applications.

Embedded Objects

Embedding an object means placing an object from a source document in a destination document. When you *embed* data, the data is duplicated in the destination document along with information about the application from which it came. If you wish to edit the data, double-click the embedded data. Windows remembers where the data came from and opens the source application with the data loaded into it.

For example, assume that you embed a portion of an Excel spreadsheet into a word processing document. Now you want to edit the data, so you double-click it. Even though you are in Word, Windows returns you to Excel and lets you work there, in the source application's environment. When you are finished editing, you save your changes and are returned to the word processing document.

OLE allows you to move in either of two directions: from source document to destination document, or from destination document to source document. In either case, the process is essentially the same, and your object will always be embedded in the destination document.

The process of embedding an object will be familiar to you from your study of WordPad in Lesson 18—it's the same as inserting an object:

- Position the cursor where you want the object to appear.

- Choose Object from the Insert menu.

- Choose either the Create New or Create from File button, and then choose an application to create the object, or Browse to locate an existing file.

In the next two exercises, you will embed a Paint graphic in a WordPad document. While the exercises use similar procedures, each exercise has a different starting point. In Exercise 32.1, you start in the destination document (a WordPad document). In Exercise 32.2, your starting point will be the source document (a Paint graphic). As you try both methods, you will see how OLE allows you flexibility in embedding objects and gives you control in editing embedded objects.

1. Open the WordPad document named **New Location Flier** on your Windows Template disk. Maximize the **WordPad** window.

2. Position the insertion point at the end of the last line of text and press **Enter**.

3. Embed an object into the document:
   a. Click **Object** on the **Insert** menu. The Insert Object dialog box appears (Figure 32-1).
   b. Click the **Create from File** button. The list box changes to allow you to key a file name.
   c. Click the **Browse** button and select the **New Location Map** file on your Windows Template disk.

   d. Click the **Insert** button. The **New Location Map.bmp** file name will be displayed in the File list box.
   e. Click the **OK** button. The bitmapped graphic will be embedded in the WordPad document, as shown in Figure 32-2.

4. Save the document on your Windows Practice disk as **Flier with Graphic**.

5. Print a copy of your completed document.

6. Close the document and exit **WordPad**.

FIGURE 32-1
Insert Object dialog box

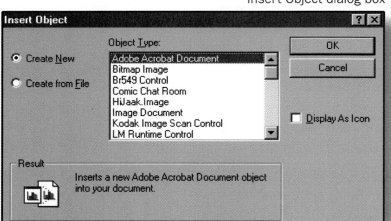

FIGURE 32-2

Graphic object embedded in WordPad file

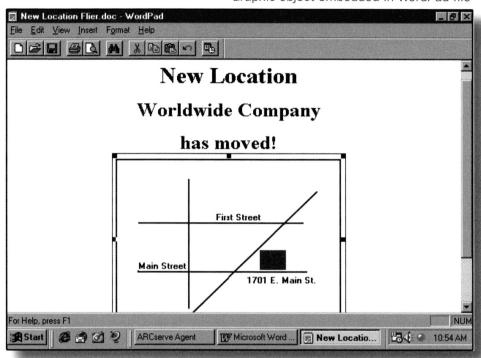

Now you'll practice embedding an object starting from the source document. Because both applications are OLE-aware, you can use Copy and Paste to embed the object.

E X E R C I S E ⟹ 32.2

1. Start **Paint** and open the **Sample Logo** file from your Windows Template disk. This graphic will be the source document.

2. Select the graphic using the **Select** tool. Drag a box around the graphic as closely as possible to the outside of the black rule around the logo.

3. Choose **Copy** from the **Edit** menu to copy the cutout to the Clipboard.

4. Close **Paint**. Do not save changes.

5. Start **WordPad** and open the **Graphic Memorandum** document on your Windows Template disk. Verify that the toolbar and format bar are visible.

6. Embed the **Sample Logo** graphic in the **Graphic Memorandum** document:
   a. Click an insertion point a double-space below the last line of text in the memorandum.
   b. Click the **Center** button on the format bar.
   c. Select **Paste** from the **Edit** menu. The graphic is embedded in the document.
   d. Click any white area in the document window to deselect the graphic.

7. Save the document on your Windows Practice disk as **Memo with Graphic**.

(continued on next page)

8. Print a copy of your completed document.

9. Select **Exit** on the **File** menu to close the document and exit **WordPad**.

Embedding a New Object

In the previous exercises you embedded objects that were already created. In addition, there may be times when you want to embed an object that doesn't already exist. For example, suppose you are creating a WordPad document and wish to include a graphic that doesn't exist yet. In this case, you would use the Create New button in the Insert Object dialog box (Figure 32-1). The Object Type list that then appears in the dialog box contains all the embeddable data types. Choose one of the types and click the OK button. Windows will either display the appropriate application's menus and toolbars or run the appropriate application. When you have finished creating the object, you can embed it by clicking outside the active window, as shown in Figure 32-3.

FIGURE 32-3
Embedding a newly created object

Click Outside Object to Return to WordPad

EXERCISE 32.3

1. Start **WordPad** and open the **Enrollment Fee** document on your Windows Template disk.

2. Embed a new graphic in the center of the document:
   a. Click an insertion point between the lines *No Enrollment Fee* and *Center for Sports & Wellness*.
   b. Select **Object** from the **Insert** menu.
   c. Verify that the **Create New** button and the **Bitmap Image** type are selected on the Insert Object dialog box, and then click the **OK** button. Paint's drawing window, toolbar, and menu bar will display (Figure 32-3).
   d. Use the Paint tools to draw a yellow and black happy face in the drawing window.
   e. Click outside the drawing window to embed the graphic and return to the WordPad document.
   f. Adjust the space around the graphic if desired.

3. Save the document on your Windows Practice disk as **Happy Face**.

4. Print a copy of your completed document.

5. Close the document and exit **WordPad**.

Editing an Embedded Object

To revise an embedded object, double-click the image in the destination document; the source application will open, allowing you to edit your object. For example, Figure 32-4 shows an object embedded in WordPad; the object has been opened so that it can be edited in Paint.

FIGURE 32-4
Editing an embedded object

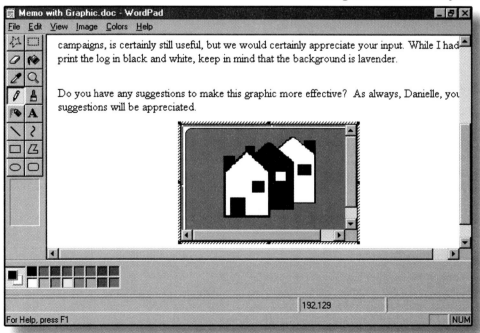

Do you understand why the source application must open? WordPad cannot edit graphics; Paint can. Embedding provides you with a way to edit in one application an object that was created in another application! Essentially, embedding simplifies the process of opening the source application and then returning to the destination document. In the meantime, of course, it allows you to edit the object—all without "leaving" your current application! When your editing is completed, click outside the editing window to return to WordPad and the document you are working on.

NOTE:

An embedded object retains its connection to its source application (Paint in our example) and is not connected to the document in which it was embedded.

EXERCISE ⟹ 32.4

1. Start **WordPad** and open the **Memo with Graphic** document on your Windows Practice disk.

2. Edit the text:
   a. Click an insertion point immediately after the period at the end of the first paragraph.
   b. Space once, then key the following:

   ```
   While I had to print the logo in
   black and white, keep in mind
   that the background is lavender.
   ```

3. Edit the graphic:
   a. Double-click the graphic at the bottom of the memorandum. The graphic displays in Paint's drawing window (Figure 32-4).

   b. Click the **Fill With Color** tool, click the color white on the color palette, and then click the graphic's background area. The background changes to white.
   c. Click outside the drawing window to return to the WordPad document.

4. Save the document on your Windows Practice disk as **Revised Graphic Memo**.

5. Print a copy of your completed document.

6. Close the document and exit **WordPad**.

Embedding an Object as an Icon

So far you have seen how OLE permits you to embed objects directly. A directly embedded object appears in the destination document in its "normal" state. In Exercise 32.3, for instance, you embedded a graphic directly in a WordPad document.

You can embed directly only objects created with OLE-aware applications. Non-OLE objects can be embedded only as icons. For example, if you wish to embed a sound recording (say, a reading of a text passage) or a full-motion video (say, a video of a complex manufacturing procedure) in your word processing document, you must embed the object as an icon. You can then play the recording or video by double-clicking its embedded icon.

You use the same process to embed an object as an icon as to embed it at its full size, except that after you have located the object and return to the Insert Object dialog box, you must click the Display As Icon check box before clicking the OK button.

When an icon represents embedded text, an embedded voice recording, or an embedded video or graphic, you must play the object in order to see the text, hear the voice, or see the video or graphic. To play an embedded icon, double-click the icon, which then opens the source application and loads the data, graphic, sound, or video.

E X E R C I S E ⟶ 32.5

1. Start **WordPad** and open the **New Location Flier** document on your Windows Template disk.

2. Embed an object into the document as an icon:
   a. Select **Object** on the **Insert** menu. The Insert Object dialog box appears.
   b. Click the **Create from File** button.
   c. Click the **Browse** button and select the **New Location Map** file on your Windows Template disk.
   d. Click the **Insert** button.
   e. Click the **Display As Icon** check box (Figure 32-5).

3. Click the **OK** button. The bitmapped graphic is embedded in the WordPad document as an icon (Figure 32-6).

4. Double-click the embedded icon to display the graphic. Notice that it displays in Paint, the source application.

5. Close **Paint** and **WordPad** without saving changes.

6. If instructed, shut down Windows and your computer.

FIGURE 32-5
Displaying an object as an icon

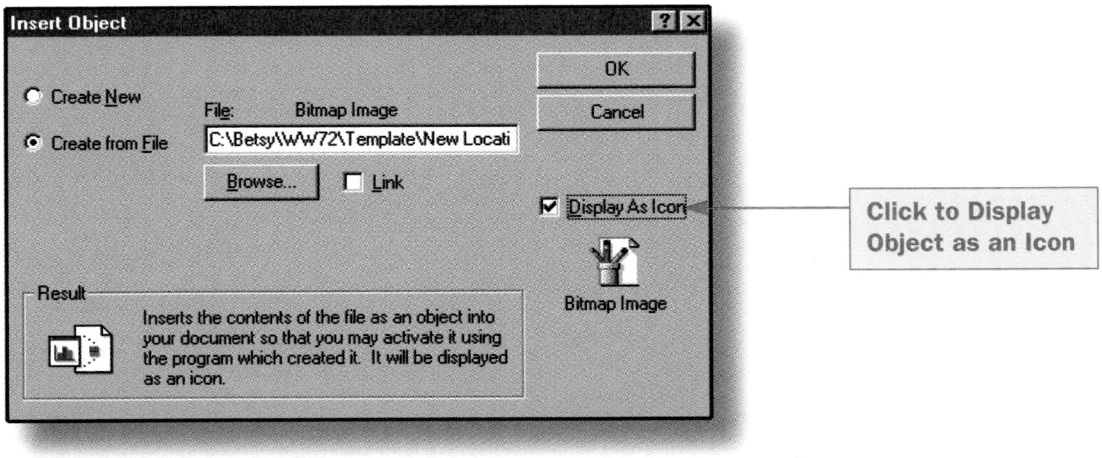

Insert Object

○ Create New
● Create from File

File: Bitmap Image
C:\Betsy\WW72\Template\New Locati

Browse... ☐ Link

☑ Display As Icon

OK
Cancel

Bitmap Image

Result
Inserts the contents of the file as an object into your document so that you may activate it using the program which created it. It will be displayed as an icon.

Click to Display Object as an Icon

FIGURE 32-6
Bitmap object embedded as an icon

Summary

This lesson covered how to embed objects and edit embedded objects. You learned that:

■ An obvious advantage of OLE over the Cut, Copy, and Paste process is that it does not duplicate data and waste memory space. (The Copy and Paste process stores and re-stores the same object every time you paste it, forcing data to reside in two or more places). Another advantage is that OLE lets you place into documents an object that you cannot create directly in that document's application software.

■ Windows applications that support OLE are called OLE-aware. But not all applications support the latest OLE features available with Windows 98.

■ Embedding an object means copying the object from a source document to a destination document. The source and destination may be created in two different applications.

■ When you embed data, the data is duplicated in the destination document along with information about the application from which it came. If you wish to edit the data, double-click the embedded data. Windows remembers where the data came from and opens the source application with the data loaded into it.

LESSON 32 REVIEW QUESTIONS

TRUE/FALSE

Each of the following statements is either true or false. Indicate your answer on the left by circling T if the statement is true and F if the statement is false.

T   F   1.   After an object is embedded, you can update it automatically from the source document.

T   F   2.   You can revise an embedded object by double-clicking its image in the destination document.

T   F   3.   An embedded icon can be part of a file, or it can be an entire file.

T   F   4.   All Windows applications support the OLE features that are available with Windows 98.

T   F   5.   When you edit an embedded object, you always use the destination program's menus and toolbar.

FILL IN THE BLANKS

Complete the following sentences by writing the correct word or words in the blanks provided.

1.   Windows applications that support object linking and embedding features are said to be _____.

2.   When the destination document's menus and toolbars are temporarily replaced by those of the object's source program, it means that an OLE-aware program has the _____ feature.

3.   If you want to create an object in a certain application and then insert that object in a file that was created in a different application, you would choose the _____ option in the Insert Object dialog box.

4.   To edit an embedded object, you _____-click it.

5.   Non-OLE objects can be embedded only as _____.

This project gives you the opportunity to review the concepts in this lesson and practice the techniques in the exercises. You will need your Windows Template disk and Windows Practice disk in order to complete this project.

1. Start **Paint**. Use the **Paste From** command to open the **Map** file on your Windows Template disk.

2. Edit the graphic: Using the **Fill With Color** tool, color the following states as indicated:
   a. Make California and all states that touch California (Oregon, Nevada, and Arizona) light gray (second color from the left on the bottom row).
   b. Make Texas red (third color from the left on the bottom row).
   c. Make Florida and the two states that touch Florida (Georgia and Alabama): green (fifth color from the left on the bottom row).

3. Save the graphic on your Windows Practice disk using the file name **Color Map**, and the **256-color bitmap** file type. Close Paint.

4. Open **WordPad** and create a new document. Use the following document settings:
   a. Font: **Arial**, **Regular**, size **10**.
   b. Ruler On.
   c. Page Setup: Left and Right margins, 1.5 inches; Top and Bottom margins, 1 inch.

5. Set a tab stop at 0.75 inch. Key the following text in the document. Center the district assignments (the last four lines of text).

   ```
   Date:[Tab] [Current Date][Enter][Enter]
   To:[Tab] Sales Representatives[Enter][Enter]
   From:[Tab] [Your Name], National Sales Manager[Enter][Enter]
   Subject:[Tab] NEW DISTRICT ASSIGNMENTS[Enter][Enter]

   After months of study and much consideration, new district assignments
   have been made. As illustrated on the map below, many of these changes
   have been made in the states assigned to the districts. The new
   districts and district managers are:[Enter][Enter]

   Western States - Joyce Lu[Enter]

   Southern States - Marshal Miller[Enter]

   Texas - James McDonald[Enter]

   Pacific Northwest - Stella White[Enter]
   ```

6. Save the document on your Windows Practice disk using the file name **New District Letter**.

7. Embed the Color Map graphic into your **New District Letter** document a double-space below the last line of text.

8. Save the document.

9. Edit the embedded object:
   a. Double-click the image to open it in the Paint window.
   b. Click the **Fill With Color** tool and click the yellow color in the color palette (fourth color from the left on the bottom) and color in **Oregon** and **Washington**.
   c. Click outside the Paint window to return to the WordPad document.

10. Save the changes, print a copy of your revised document, then close the document.

11. If instructed, shut down Windows and your computer.

LINKING OBJECTS

OBJECTIVES

Upon completion of this lesson, you will be able to:

- Create a link.

- Edit a linked document.

- Break or delete a link.

⏱ **Estimated Time: 1.5 hours**

Y‌ou learned in the last lesson that when you embed an object, it becomes part of its new destination document; a linked object does not. In this lesson, you will learn to distinguish between linking and embedding an object. You will also learn how to create, edit, and break a link.

Linked Objects

W‌hen you *link* data between two documents, the data you link is not actually stored in the destination document. Instead, the destination document stores only information about the data's origin. The destination document then uses this information to display the linked data so that it looks as if it is part of the document.

For example, when you link a graphic created in CorelDRAW to a Word document, the graphic appears as if it is in the Word document. But when you save the Word document, your saved file does not include the graphic, only the information Windows needs to locate the graphic the next time you open the file. In the meantime, if you edit the graphic in CorelDRAW, the edited graphic displays in your word processing document the next time the file is opened.

When you link an object, you are creating a reference to the original document that contains the information. Therefore, when you edit a linked object, you are actually editing the information in the source document.

Linking has one significant advantage over embedding: A linked object is always the latest version of that object. Linking allows you to share one object (your source file in the source application) with several destination documents (in the destination application). Further, linking allows you to edit and update that one file only. The revised object then automatically appears in all the destination documents to which it is linked. You do not need to revise the object in each of the destination files; linking makes that extra work unnecessary.

Another benefit: Linking uses less disk space because the linked object is saved on disk in only one place (its source document)—not in each destination document. One graphic, sound, or video file can occupy lots of disk space; imagine, then, the effect of duplicating such files! If you work with graphic, source, and video files, linking is an important space-saving feature.

To appreciate the power of linking, imagine coordinating an annual fundraiser for your company. You develop a monthly newsletter reporting on progress and encouraging your coworkers to contribute. You send a monthly report to your management. You send a monthly report to your regional office. You post notices on hallway bulletin boards to catch coworkers' attention. In each case, you use a graphic to visualize progress to date: a thermometer (see Figure 33-1) with marked numbers representing progress toward the goal of 100. You update the graphic weekly and save it in a file (of course!) that is linked to all your newsletters, reports, and notices.

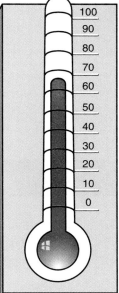

FIGURE 33-1
Frequently edited objects such as this one are ideal for linking

Creating a Link

You can create a link to a document by using the Paste Special option on the Edit menu or the Object option on the Insert menu.

■ Application programs that are OLE-aware (such as WordPad) have two Paste commands on their Edit menus: Paste and Paste Special. As you might expect, you use the Paste Special option when the Clipboard contains an object that you want to embed or link. The Paste Special dialog box controls whether Clipboard data are embedded or linked (Figure 33-2). If the Clipboard data are from an OLE source application, you use the Paste Link button to link the object to the destination document.

FIGURE 33-2
Paste Special dialog box

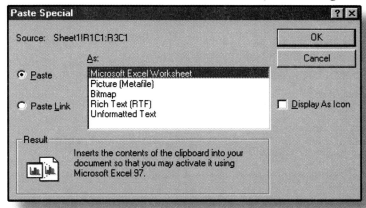

■ When the Clipboard data are not from an OLE-aware application, you must use the Object command on the Insert menu to link an object to the destination document. To link an object, click in the Link check box on the Insert Object dialog box.

In the following exercise, you will be linking a graphic created in Paint to a WordPad document using the Insert Object linking method. As you complete the exercise, note the similarities between embedding and linking:

- First, the steps involved in both procedures are the same.

- Further, whether you are embedding or linking, your starting point can be either the source or the destination application.

- Finally, the types of objects are the same (you can embed any object that you can link).

Remember, too, this basic difference between embedding and linking: Any change you make to a linked object appears in all objects associated with that object through links, including the source document. But a change you make to an embedded object is not reflected in its original source document.

EXERCISE 33.1

1. Start **WordPad** and open the **Special Sale** document on your Windows Template disk. Click an insertion point at the very top of the document.

2. Link an object to the document:
   a. Select **Object** on the **Insert** menu. The Insert Object dialog box appears.
   b. Click the **Create from File** button. The list box changes to a text box.
   c. Click the **Browse** button, locate and highlight the **Company Logo** file on your Windows Template disk, and then click the **Insert** button.

   d. In the Insert Object dialog box, click the **Link** check box (Figure 33-3).
   e. Click the **OK** button. The link between the source document and the destination document is now complete.

3. Save the document on your Windows Practice disk as **Linked Document.**

4. Print a copy of your completed document.

5. Close the document and exit **WordPad.**

FIGURE 33-3
Linking in the Insert Object dialog box

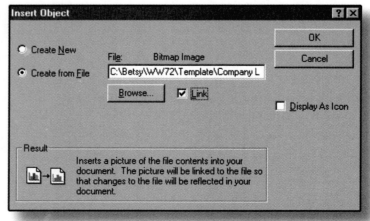

Editing a Linked Document

One of the advantages of linking data is the ease with which you can edit the data—you just edit the source data. The changes to the source data are reflected in the destination document. Two types of links are possible—automatic links and manual links. An *automatic link* is one that updates the linked data automatically every time you open the destination document, without any other action from you. Automatic links are sometimes called *hot links*. A *manual link* (also called a *warm link*) is updated only when you request it. How you instruct the source application to update the data varies from one application to another.

In most programs there is an Update Now button that allows you to instruct the source document to update the link. You can also lock a link so that it is not updated as the data are changed in the source document. When working with linked data, *the source document must be available in order for the update to occur*. For example, if the linked data's source document is stored on a floppy disk, that disk must be in one of the floppy drives whenever the destination document containing the linked data is opened, or the links cannot be updated.

EXERCISE ▷ 33.2

1. Start **WordPad** and open the **Linked Document** file you created in Exercise 33.1.

2. Verify that the Update: Automatic option button is selected:
   a. Click on the **Company Logo** graphic to select it.
   b. Select **Links** on the **Edit** menu. The Links dialog box (Figure 33-4) displays.
   c. Verify that the **Update: Automatic** button is selected. If not, click it to select it.
   d. Click the **Cancel** button to close the dialog box.

3. Edit the graphic by changing the fill color:
   a. Remove your Windows Practice disk and insert the Windows Template disk.
   b. Double-click the linked graphic. Its original version opens in Paint.
   c. Tile the windows as illustrated in Figure 33-5.
   d. Use the **Fill With Color** tool to fill the skyline area of the graphic with white.

   e. Watch the image in the WordPad document change as the Paint image is being edited. *Remember:* The original graphic has been changed, so any graphic linked to this original will also change.

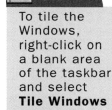

TIP

To tile the Windows, right-click on a blank area of the taskbar and select **Tile Windows Vertically** from the shortcut menu.

4. Save the changes to the graphic file and close Paint.

5. Save the updated WordPad document on your Windows Practice disk as **Edited Linked Document**.

6. Print a copy of your completed document.

7. Leave the document on screen for the next exercise.

FIGURE 33-4
Links dialog box

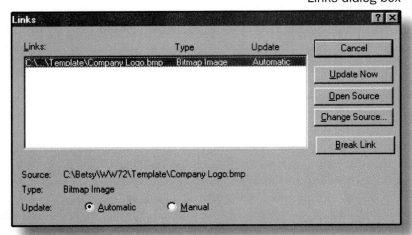

FIGURE 33-5
Tiling windows to review edits to linked object

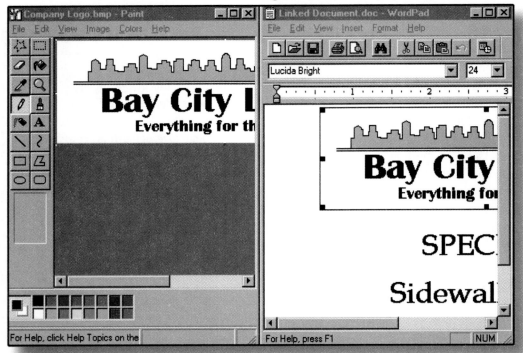

Changing the Update Option

There will be times when you will want to change the type of link used in a document. For example, you might manually link a graphic in a word processing document. You use a manual link because the graphic is still being refined, yet you need the graphic in the document for placement purposes. Because you used a manual link to the graphic, you do not have to wait for the graphic to update each time you access the word processing document. Of course, when the final graphic is created, you change the manual link to an automatic link.

As you have already seen, you use the Links command on the Edit menu to change links within a document. The dialog box that displays depends on the program that you are using, but it will list all the links currently active within your document (see Figure 33-4). There will be information summarizing the link and a choice for changing the type of link that exists. To change the link, select the link from the list and then click either the Automatic or the Manual Update button.

In Exercise 33.2 you used the Update: Automatic button to update a linked object. In Exercise 33.3 you will use the Update: Manual button to update a linked object.

EXERCISE 33.3

1. Change the Links Update to Manual:
   a. Select **Links** from the **Edit** menu. The Links dialog box appears.
   b. Verify that the **Company Logo.bmp** link is highlighted.
   c. Click the **Update: Manual** option button; then click the **Close** button to close the dialog box.

2. Edit the graphic by changing the background color:
   a. Insert the Windows Template disk, and then double-click the linked graphic.
   b. Tile the windows.
   c. Use the **Fill With Color** tool to fill the skyline area of the graphic with the light blue color (sixth color from the left on the bottom row) on the color palette.
   d. The background color of the graphic will change in the Paint window but not in the WordPad window because the manual update button is selected.

3. Save the changes to the graphic file, close the file, and exit **Paint**.

4. Update the graphic manually in the WordPad file:
   a. Select **Links** on the **Edit** menu.
   b. Position the **Links** dialog box so that you can see the graphic in the WordPad document.
   c. Click the **Update Now** button. Notice the graphic is immediately updated.

5. Reset the links update method to Automatic. Click the **Update: Automatic** option button; then click the **Close** button.

6. Save the changes and exit **WordPad**.

Breaking or Deleting a Link

At times you will want to break or delete a link. When you break a link, the object still exists in the destination document. When you delete a link, the object is deleted at the same time in the destination document.

To break a link, you must break the connection between the object in the source document and the object in the destination document. The original source document will still exist after you break the link. Once the link is broken, if you should want to change the object in the destination document, you will need to cut and paste it back into the source application, make your change(s), and then insert it back in the destination document using either Paste Special or the Insert Object dialog box.

EXERCISE 33.4

1. Start **WordPad** and open the **Edited Linked Document** file on your Windows Practice disk. If prompted, click the **Yes** button to update the links.

2. Break the link with the **Company Logo** graphic:
   a. Select the graphic.
   b. Select **Links** on the **Edit** menu. The Links dialog box appears.
   c. Verify that the **Company Logo.bmp** link is highlighted.
   d. Click the **Break Link** button at the right side of the dialog box. The Links message window (Figure 33-6) will display, asking if you want to break the link.
   e. Click the **Yes** button. The link will be removed from the Links dialog box.
   f. Click the **Close** button to close the dialog box.
   g. Save the document as **Unlinked Document**.

3. While the graphic still resides in the WordPad document, it is no longer linked to the Paint application. If it can, Windows converts the object to an embedded object. When the graphic is converted to an embedded object, it will not change as changes are made to the original graphic. However, you should not double-click on the graphic or you will replace the copy with the edited original, since the copy no longer exists.

4. Verify that the link has been broken. Choose **Links** from the **Edit** menu. Notice that the Links option on the menu is unavailable.

5. Close and exit **WordPad**. If instructed, shut down Windows and your computer.

FIGURE 33-6
Links message box

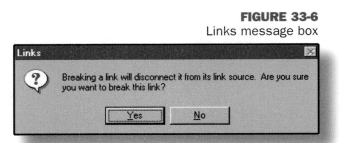

Summary

This lesson covered how to create, edit, and delete links. You learned that:

- Like an embedded object, a linked object is visible in the destination document. But unlike an embedded object, the linked data remain stored in the source document. When you link an object, you are creating a reference to the original document that contains the information. A linked object is always the latest version of that object.

- Because the link is a reference to the original document that contains the information; when you edit a linked object, you are actually editing the information in the source document.

- Linking has several advantages over embedding: A linked object is always the latest version of that object. Linking allows you to share one object (your source file in the source application) with several destination documents (in the destination application). Further, linking allows you to edit and update that one file only. The revised object then automatically appears in all the destination documents to which it is linked. And last, linking uses less disk space because the linked object is saved on disk in only one place (its source document)—not in each destination document.

- An automatic link is an active link; it automatically updates the data in all applications that are currently active. With a manual link, the source sends a message to the destination whenever the source data change.

LESSON 33 REVIEW QUESTIONS

TRUE/FALSE

Each of the following statements is either true or false. Indicate your answer on the left by circling T if the statement is true and F if the statement is false.

T F 1. The destination document cannot display a linked object.

T F 2. After an object is linked, it can only be updated manually.

T F 3. A linked object connects the source application to the destination document.

T F 4. When working with linked data, the source document must be available in order for an update to occur.

T F 5. When you break a link, the object is deleted in the destination document.

MULTIPLE CHOICE

Complete the following questions by circling the correct multiple choice letter.

1. When you break a link, the
    A. connection between the source document and the destination document is broken
    B. object is deleted from the destination document
    C. linked source file is deleted from the disk
    D. object can no longer be edited

2. A major difference between embedding an object and linking an object is that
    A. An embedded object is visible in the destination document; a linked object is not visible
    B. A linked object becomes part of the destination document; an embedded object does not
    C. An embedded object becomes part of a destination document; a linked object does not become a physical part of the destination document
    D. An embedded object cannot be edited within the destination document; a linked object can be edited within the destination document

3. A significant advantage that linking has over embedding is
    A. A linked object is always the latest version of that object
    B. Linking allows you to share one object with several destination documents, therefore requiring you to edit and update that one file only
    C. Linking uses less disk space because the linked object is saved on disk in only one place—not in each destination document
    D. All of the above

4. To update linked data automatically every time you open the destination document, you would use
    A. Manual links
    B. Automatic links
    C. OLE links
    D. None of the above

5. When you delete a link, the
    A. Object still exists in the destination document, but not the source document
    B. Object still exists in the source document, but not the destination document
    C. Object is deleted from both the source and the destination document
    D. Object still exists in both the source and the destination document but it cannot be edited

LESSON 33 PROJECT

This project gives you the opportunity to review the concepts in this lesson and practice the techniques in the exercises. You will need your Windows Practice disk in order to complete this project.

1. Open the **New District Letter** document you saved on your Windows Practice disk.

2. Click once on the graphic in the document and press the **Delete** key to delete the graphic.

3. Insert the **Color Map** graphic and link it to the document:
   a. Position the cursor two lines below the last line of text.
   b. Access the **Insert Object** dialog box, locate the **Color Map** file on your Windows Practice disk, and double-click to select it.
   c. Check the **Link** check box in the **Insert Object** dialog box, and then click the **OK** button.

4. Verify the link:
   a. Select **Links** on the **Edit** menu.
   b. Verify that the Bitmap Image **Color Map** is highlighted in the listing box.
   c. Verify that the **Update: Manual** button is checked.

5. Save the document as **Linked District Letter** on your Windows Practice disk. (You may need to use a new disk to store the document.) Close the document.

6. Edit the graphic image:
   a. Open and maximize **Paint**.
   b. Open the **Color Map** file on your Windows Practice disk.
   c. Draw an unfilled box around the map using the rectangle tool.
   d. Color the inside area around the map light blue.
   e. Save and close the graphic file.

7. Open and update the **Linked District Letter** document.

8. Update the link:
   a. Click the graphic to select.
   b. Choose **Links** on the **Edit** menu.
   c. Click the **Update Now** button. Do not close the dialog box.

9. Click the **Update: Automatic** button to select it, and then click the **Close** button.

10. Edit the graphic once again:
    a. Double-click the map graphic to open a copy of the **Color Map** file.
    b. Position the windows so you can see a portion of the contents of each window.
    c. Paint any five of the white states with the color of your choice.
    d. Select **Save** on Paint's **File** menu to save the change you made to the graphic.
    e. Click Paint's **Close** button to close the graphic file.

11. Save, print, and close the **Linked District Letter** document.

12. Close any open programs. If instructed, shut down Windows and your computer.

USING MY BRIEFCASE

OBJECTIVES

Upon completion of this lesson, you will be able to:

- Create a Briefcase.

- Use a Briefcase.

- Update duplicate files with a Briefcase.

⏱ Estimated Time: 1.5 hours

Business people who work in different locations, travel on business, or take work home often use a briefcase to transport their papers and files. Similarly, Windows 98 provides you with an electronic briefcase to transport folders and files from one computer to another. In this lesson, you will learn how to use the My Briefcase feature.

Introducing My Briefcase

When the Briefcase feature is set up on your computer, you will see the My Briefcase icon on your desktop (see Figure 34-1).

A Briefcase is a special type of system folder that helps you track multiple copies of a file and determine which one is the most up to date. Thus, a Briefcase does more than just transport files: It also permits you to synchronize duplicate files from two different computers. For example, you have a document on your office computer that you plan to finish while you are away on a business trip. You copy the document from your office computer to the Briefcase folder on your notebook computer (the specific procedure will be explained shortly). While you're on your trip, you complete the document in your Briefcase folder. Then when you return to your office, you use the Briefcase to update the copy of the document on your office computer.

FIGURE 34-1
My Briefcase icon

If your office computer is on a network and you share your files with others, it is possible that someone else has changed the document while you were away. If so, Briefcase informs you of changes and helps you reconcile the changes between the two documents. As you can see, a Briefcase is useful whenever you need to manage a file that resides on more than one computer.

Creating a Briefcase

You must have a Briefcase somewhere on your computer to use this feature. If you do not have My Briefcase displayed on your desktop, you can create it. Actually, you can create a Briefcase on any disk or in any folder. The advantage of placing the Briefcase on the desktop is that it is quickly accessible. When using the Briefcase, it is important to keep in mind that the Briefcase must be located on the computer to which you are moving the files. If you need to move a file from your office computer to your notebook computer, for instance, you must use the Briefcase on your notebook computer.

To create a Briefcase on the desktop, right-click on the desktop, select New from the shortcut menu, and then select Briefcase from the submenu. The Briefcase will be placed where you have clicked and it will have the name "New Briefcase." If you choose, you can rename the New Briefcase by using Rename from the shortcut menu. To create a Briefcase on a disk, select the drive or folder where you want to locate it, select New from the File menu, and then choose Briefcase from the submenu. To rename the Briefcase, choose Rename from the File menu.

Using a Briefcase

To use the Briefcase, copy the files you want to work on elsewhere to the Briefcase. You can use either My Computer or Explorer for this process: Locate the files you want to copy to the Briefcase, and then drag them to the Briefcase. The Briefcase is now ready to be transported to your other computer. If this other computer is not connected on a network or by a cable, you must move the Briefcase to a floppy disk and then use the floppy disk to transport the Briefcase to the second computer. To move the Briefcase to the floppy disk, drag the Briefcase folder icon to the floppy disk icon displayed in Explorer or My Computer.

When you are ready to use a file in your Briefcase, double-click the Briefcase to open it, and then double-click the file. You may want to move the Briefcase from the floppy disk to the hard disk of the other computer and work on the files there. When you have finished working with the files in your Briefcase, move the Briefcase back to the floppy disk.

In the following exercise, you will create a personal Briefcase on your computer.

NOTE:

You can rename a Briefcase by selecting it on the desktop, clicking on its name, and then keying the new name.

EXERCISE 34.1

This exercise assumes that the Briefcase feature has been installed on your computer (identified by the My Briefcase icon on the desktop). If your computer does not have this feature installed, ask your instructor for alternate instructions.

1. Right-click on the desktop, select **New** from the shortcut menu, and then select **Briefcase**. An icon labeled *New Briefcase* appears on the desktop (see Figure 34-2).

2. Right-click the **New Briefcase** icon; then select **Rename** from the shortcut menu.

3. Rename the Briefcase by keying your name before the word Briefcase, for example, *Mary Miller's Briefcase*.

4. Insert your Windows Template disk into the floppy disk drive.

5. Using **Explorer**, hold down the **Ctrl** key and drag the **Exercise 34.1 Report Form** document from your Windows Template disk to your desktop. A copy of the file appears on the desktop.

NOTE:

You are placing a copy of the template file on the desktop to avoid altering the file on your Template disk when you update the file in the next exercise. Usually, however, you can drag files directly to the Briefcase.

6. Remove your Windows Template disk from the floppy disk drive and insert your Windows Practice disk. Now let's pretend that you have created the **Exercise 34.1 Report Form** file on your work computer and that you want to take the file home to finish the report on your home computer. In order to take the file home, you will need to copy the file to your Briefcase and then move your Briefcase to a floppy disk.

7. Drag the **Exercise 34.1 Report Form** file from the desktop to your Briefcase. If the Welcome to the Windows Briefcase window displays, read it; then click the **Finish** button. Notice that the copy of the **Exercise 34.1 Report Form** file remains on your desktop.

8. Using **Explorer**, move your Briefcase from the desktop to your Windows Practice disk:
   a. Select the **Desktop** in the **Tree** pane. Your Briefcase folder should display in the Contents pane.
   b. Drag your **Briefcase** folder from the **Contents** pane to the floppy disk drive icon in the **Tree** pane that contains your Windows Practice disk. Your Briefcase and its contents are moved to the floppy disk, and your Briefcase icon disappears from your desktop.

9. In the **Tree** pane, click the floppy drive that contains your Windows Practice disk. Your Briefcase icon appears in the Contents pane along with the other items stored on your Windows Practice disk (see Figure 34-3).

10. Close all open windows and remove the Windows Practice disk from the drive.

11. You can now take the disk containing your Briefcase to any computer running Windows 98. Since you may not have access to another computer at this time, let's assume you are now at home and wish to complete the **Exercise 34.1 Report Form** document in your Briefcase.

12. Insert the disk containing your Briefcase (your Windows Practice disk) into the floppy disk drive.

13. Using **Explorer**, open the **Exercise 34.1 Report Form** file in your Briefcase:
  a. Navigate the **Tree** pane and display your Briefcase in the **Contents** pane.
  b. Double-click your **Briefcase** icon to open it.
  c. Double-click the **Exercise 34.1 Report Form** file to open it in **Notepad** (see Figure 34-4).

14. At the blinking insertion point, key the following text. Press **Enter** at the end of each line.

Your Name

Your Class

Current Date

15. Select **Save** from the **File** menu; then close the document window.

16. Close all open windows and remove the Windows Practice disk from the floppy drive.

FIGURE 34-2
New Briefcase icon

FIGURE 34-3
Transferring a Briefcase file

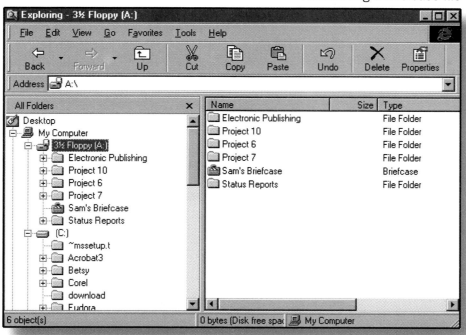

FIGURE 34-4
Exercise 34.1 Report Form in Notepad

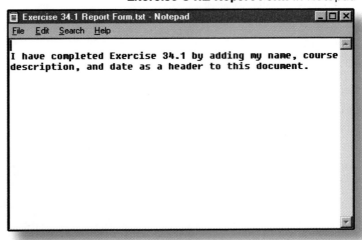

Updating Duplicate Files with a Briefcase

Now let's assume you are back at work and want to update the *Exercise 34.1 Report Form* file on your work computer to match the files stored in your Briefcase. Move your Briefcase back to the desktop, and then double-click to open it. From the Briefcase menu, select the Update All command to update all files in the Briefcase. Or select a file or files in the Briefcase window and then choose Update Selection from the Briefcase menu to update only the selected files. You can also use the Update All button or the Update Selection button on the Briefcase window's toolbar. Windows compares the files in your Briefcase to the corresponding files on your computer. The Update Briefcase window appears (Figure 34-5), telling you which files have been modified and asking if you wish to update them.

Update
All

Update
Selection

FIGURE 34-5
Update Briefcase window

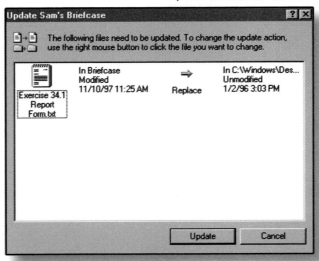

EXERCISE ⟹ 34.2

1. Insert the disk containing your Briefcase (your Windows Practice disk) into the floppy disk drive of your work computer.

2. Move your Briefcase to your computer's desktop using **Windows Explorer**.

3. Close **Explorer**.

4. Update the files:
   a. Double-click your **Briefcase** icon on the desktop to open it.
   b. Select **Update All** from the **Briefcase** menu (Figure 34-6).
   c. The Update Briefcase window appears, indicating that the **Exercise 34.1 Report Form** file has been modified and that this file should replace the unmodified file on the desktop.

5. Click the **Update** button to update the file. The older version of the file on your desktop is replaced with the newer version in your Briefcase.

6. Close all open windows.

7. Print a copy of the **Exercise 34.1 Report Form** file:
   a. Verify that your printer is on and that you have access to it.
   b. Right-click the **Exercise 34.1 Report Form** icon on the desktop; then select **Print** from the shortcut menu.

8. Delete your **Briefcase** and the **Exercise 34.1 Report Form** icon from your desktop.

9. If instructed, shut down Windows and your computer.

 TIP

You can delete objects on the desktop by dragging them to the Recycle Bin, or by right-clicking them and selecting Delete from the shortcut menu.

FIGURE 34-6
Briefcase menu

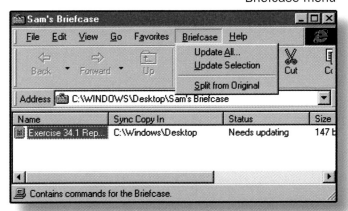

Summary

This lesson covered how to create, use, and update a Briefcase. You learned that:

- My Briefcase is a special type of system folder that helps you transport files from one computer to another and synchronize files from different computers. The Briefcase feature must be installed on both the computer from which you are moving files and the computer on which the files are to be used.

- The My Briefcase icon appears on your desktop if the Briefcase feature is installed on your computer.

- You can use the My Briefcase icon on the desktop or create your own. If you are using more than one Briefcase, each one must have a unique name.

- A Briefcase and its contents can be moved from one computer to another over a network or by using floppy disks.

LESSON 34 REVIEW QUESTIONS

TRUE/FALSE

Each of the following statements is either true or false. Indicate your answer on the left by circling T if the statement is true and F if the statement is false.

T F 1. The primary function of My Briefcase is to transport files from one computer to another.

T F 2. The Briefcase must be located on the computer to which you are moving files.

T F 3. You cannot change the "New Briefcase" name assigned to a briefcase when it is created.

T F 4. When updating files in a Briefcase, you only have the option to update all of them at once.

T F 5. You cannot delete a Briefcase from the desktop.

MULTIPLE CHOICE

Complete the following questions by circling the correct multiple choice letter.

1. A Briefcase is a special type of system folder that helps you
    A. track multiple copies of a file
    B. determine which copy of a file is the most up to date
    C. synchronize duplicate files from two different computers
    D. all of the above

2. When using a Briefcase, it is important to remember that the
   A. Briefcase need only be on the computer from which you are copying files
   B. Briefcase must be on the computer to which you are moving files
   C. Briefcase icon must appear on the desktop
   D. Briefcase can only be used if you are working on a network

3. To rename a Briefcase, you
   A. right-click on the Briefcase and select Rename on the shortcut menu
   B. select the New Briefcase icon on the desktop, click on its name, and then key a new name
   C. either A or B will work
   D. you cannot rename a Briefcase

4. To create a new Briefcase, you
   A. double-click on the desktop and select New Briefcase from the shortcut menu
   B. double-click the My Briefcase icon on the desktop
   C. right-click on the desktop, select New from the shortcut menu, and then select Briefcase
   D. none of the above will work

5. When you want to reconcile changes made to a particular file in a Briefcase, you
   A. select the file and then click the Update Selection button on the toolbar
   B. select the file and then click the Update All button on the toolbar
   C. right-click the Briefcase icon on the desktop and select Update from the shortcut menu
   D. can only update all the files in a Briefcase, not selected files

LESSON 34 PROJECT

This project gives you the opportunity to review the concepts in this lesson and practice the techniques in the exercises. You will need your Windows Template disk and Windows Practice disk in order to complete this project.

1. Using **Explorer**, copy the **Briefcase Practice** document from your Windows Template disk to your desktop.

2. Create a Briefcase on your computer's desktop and name the Briefcase **Project 34**.

3. Drag the **Briefcase Practice** document from your computer's desktop into the **Project 34 Briefcase**.

4. Move the **Project 34** Briefcase from the desktop to your Windows Practice disk.

5. Close all open windows, and remove your Windows Practice disk from the drive.

6. After a few seconds, insert your Windows Practice disk into the floppy drive, and open the **Briefcase Practice** file in your **Project 34** Briefcase.

403

7. Edit the document by doing the following:
   a. Move the cursor to the top left corner of the document, if necessary.
   b. Key your name, class, and the current date each on a separate line. Press **Enter** at the end of each line.

8. Save the changes to the document; then close all open windows and remove your Windows Practice disk from the floppy drive.

9. Insert your Windows Practice disk into the floppy drive, and move your **Project 34** Briefcase back onto your computer's desktop.

10. Update the files:
    a. Double-click the **Project 34** Briefcase icon to open it.
    b. Select the **Update All** option from the **Briefcase** menu.

11. Print a copy of the updated **Briefcase Practice** document on your desktop; then delete your Briefcase and the document from your desktop.

12. If instructed, shut down Windows and your computer.

USING NETWORK
NEIGHBORHOOD

OBJECTIVES

Upon completion of this lesson, you will be able to:

- Understand network basics.

- Log on to the network.

- Share files and printers.

- Disconnect from the network.

⏱ Estimated Time: 1.5 hours

The days of "unconnected" desktop computing—that is, of stand-alone computers with no connection to the outside world—will soon be history. Today's desktop computers connect people to others across the room, across buildings, across cities, across the continent, and across the globe. And the number of "connected" computers is growing. In this lesson, you will learn how computer networks operate and how to utilize a network.

Understanding Networks

Not surprisingly, Windows 98 facilitates your ability to network with others, to interact with "online communities," to collect information, to exchange files, and more. Windows 98 provides you with The *Microsoft Network (MSN)*, Microsoft's online service that offers an easy and consistent interface for networks and the Internet, as well as easy access to other online service providers.

The world of networks is exciting indeed, so let's begin. First let's become familiar with what networks are, then which kinds of networks you might use, and finally how to use networks.

What Is a "Network"?

A *network* is a combination of hardware and software connecting two or more computers. The connection allows the computers to communicate with each other and to share resources. *Shared resources* means not only files but also software, printers, folders, or CD-ROM drives can be shared. A key advantage of networks is that they promote sharing, rather than re-creating, information.

Networks can be categorized in a variety of ways. One way is to measure the network's scope—in other words, how many computers it "reaches" and where those computers are located:

- A *local area network* or *LAN* is a group of connected computers and computer devices located in a limited physical area.

- A *wide area network* or *WAN* is a group of many connected networks located over a larger geographical area that's served by local area networks.

- In a class by itself is the *Internet*, a global network of many computer networks.

Networks may also be categorized according to the source of their files or programs. Depending how a network shares, it may be labeled client/server or peer-to-peer. Both are discussed below.

Client/server networks, the most common type, rely on a dedicated file server. Dedicated means that one computer, called a *server*, is set apart on the network and designed for one purpose only: to store files and programs and share them with connected workstations. The *file server* is usually the most powerful computer on the network and is often called the host; it can be a personal computer, a minicomputer, or even a large mainframe computer. The connected workstations or the computers receiving the files and/or programs from the host are called the *clients*—thus the name client/server network. Figure 35-1 illustrates the relationship between the client computers and the host server.

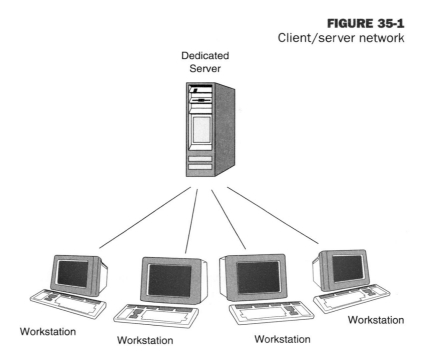

FIGURE 35-1
Client/server network

Dedicated
Server

Workstation
Workstation
Workstation
Workstation

Peer-to-peer networks do not rely on a dedicated server to store and deliver the software. Instead of the client/server relationship, each computer is a "peer," an equal, storing its own software; when necessary, however, a computer can share the files, folders, printers, or CD-ROM drives of the other computer or computers it is connected to. Figure 35-2 illustrates the relationship among computers in a peer-to-peer network.

FIGURE 35-2
Peer-to-peer network

Workstation

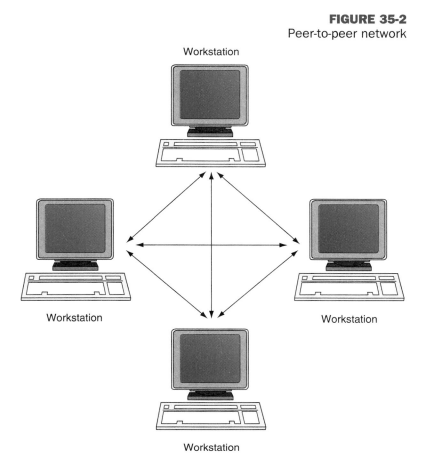

Workstation

Workstation

Workstation

There are, of course, advantages and disadvantages to each type of network. Client/server networks run faster than peer-to-peer networks and share application software more effectively, thanks to their dedicated servers and network operating system software. Furthermore, client/servers can handle more computers on the network and greater distance between computers and the network. As a result, client/server networks usually require a systems administrator to manage the network.

Peer-to-peer networks are generally inexpensive because they require no powerful computer "server," no expensive network operating software, and no special administration chores. Peer-to-peer networks are smaller; they can connect a maximum of 10 to 30 computers, depending on the power and the use of each computer, and are very easy to set up. If you need to network only a few computers at home or at work, a peer-to-peer network may be the quickest and best solution.

Establishing a Network Using the Direct Cable Connection

Windows 98 provides a special tool, the *Direct Cable Connection*, to connect two or more computers—and to facilitate the connection process, it provides the Direct Cable Connection Wizard. You need a cable, and you need to know the type of port connection on each computer. Of course, the computers must have Windows 98 installed with the Direct Cable Connection Wizard.

To access the Direct Cable Connection Wizard, choose Direct Cable Connection from the Accessories menu. Then follow the wizard's step-by-step instructions to complete the connection process. Once connected, both computers can share resources, although the sharing may be slow. The direct cable connection can be extremely useful if you have a portable computer and wish to connect to the network or to use shared resources on a desktop computer.

NOTE:

If Direct Cable Connection is not installed, you will not be able to complete some of the exercises in this lesson.

To Connect Host and Guest Computers

To use Direct Cable Connection, you must specify one computer as the host and the other (or others) as a guest. The Direct Cable Connection Wizard defines these terms for you in its opening screen, shown in Figure 35-3.

FIGURE 35-3
Direct Cable Connection Wizard opening screen

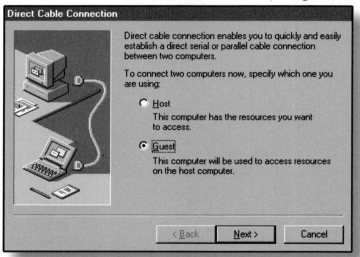

To set up the host computer, follow these steps:

1. Choose Communications from the Accessories menu and then click Direct Cabel Connection.

2. In the first wizard dialog box, click the Host option button, and then click the Next button.

3. Now the wizard asks you to select the port you want to use by highlighting the type of cable you are using (Figure 35-4). Plug in your cable and click the Next button.

FIGURE 35-4

Direct Cable Connection Wizard, step 2

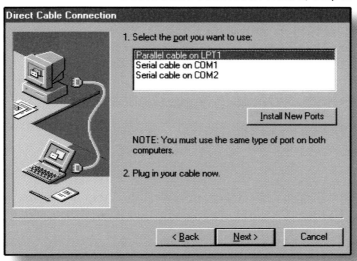

4. The wizard next gives you the chance to turn on File and Print Sharing. (You'll learn more about this feature later in this lesson.) Click the Next button.

5. The wizard informs you that the host computer has been successfully set up. Click the Finish button.

To set up the guest computer, follow the steps above, choosing the Guest option button in the first wizard dialog box.

To start using the cable connection, on the host computer choose Communications and then Direct Cable Connection from the Accessories menu. The screen shown in Figure 35-5 should appear. Click the Listen button to direct the host computer to wait for a connection. Next perform the same operation on the guest computer. Click the Connect button to connect the guest to the host.

FIGURE 35-5

Direct Cable Connection dialog box

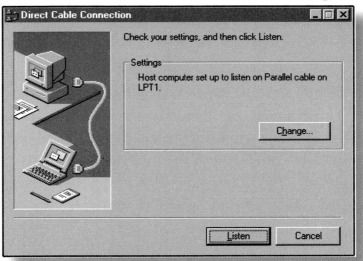

TO CONNECT MULTIPLE COMPUTERS

In most peer-to-peer networks, you will want to connect several computers with direct cable connections, rather than just two computers. Although no special networking software is necessary, network cards and regular cable (such as coaxial cable) are used to connect the computers.

The administration of multiple-computer peer-to-peer networks is more difficult than just connecting two computers as was described for a direct cable connection. You may need a network administrator to provide setup names to distinguish among all the computers and other available shared resources in the network.

Using Dial-Up Networking

Windows 98 provides another tool for connecting computers—*Dial-Up Networking*. If your computer is equipped with a *modem*, you can connect to another computer through a phone line. The other computer must also have a modem.

To use Dial-Up Networking, select Accessories on the Programs menu, select Communications, and click Dial-Up Networking. Then follow the instructions in the series of dialog boxes to establish a connection with another computer.

Network Neighborhood

Now, if you are connected to a network, let's see how you use Network Neighborhood to share resources in a workgroup.

The people you work with on a network comprise your *workgroup*, the users who have a common need to share files or programs. A workgroup can consist of two people in the same room or 200 people in different buildings in different cities throughout the country. They may be temporarily assigned to a special project, or they may be permanently teamed to work on seasonal, departmental, corporate, or other projects. A workgroup, then, is a team that shares responsibility for a project—and shares resources on a computer network.

What kind of *resources* does the team share? The folders, printers, and servers you have access to in your network. How do you know what they are? Double-click Network Neighborhood. If Windows 98's network components have been installed, you will see the Network Neighborhood icon on your desktop (Figure 35-6).

Network Neighborhood lets you "browse the network" and see icons (Figure 35-7) of all the folders, servers, printers, and other network resources that are available. Moreover, it lets you connect to any resource with the click of a mouse. Because Network Neighborhood uses a graphical user interface (GUI), it simplifies locating and connecting to computers in your workgroup or to servers on other networks—that is, if you have permission to attach. (Open Entire Network to see all the resources. If the resource you want does not appear, perhaps you do not have permission to access it.)

FIGURE 35-6
Network Neighborhood icon

Logging On to the Network

Connecting to the network is popularly called *logging on* or *signing in*. The usual log on process is to enter your user name and then your password. When you are connected, you can then use the network resources and interact with other users.

Depending on how your network is set up, you may log on before Windows opens or after Windows is running. In the following exercise, you will explore one way to log on to a network.

FIGURE 35-7
Network Neighborhood window

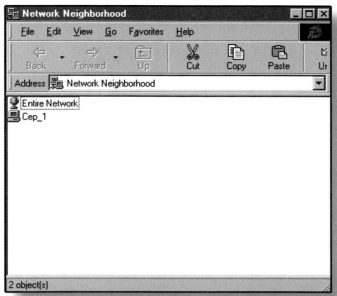

EXERCISE ⟹ 35.1

To complete this exercise, your computer must be connected to a network.

1. Start Windows 98, if it is not running. If any windows are open, close them.

2. Double-click the **Network Neighborhood** icon to open the Neighborhood. While your computer scans the network for other computers, the flashlight icon will display.

3. Select the icon that represents the server to which you wish to attach.

4. Choose **Attach As** from the **File** menu. The Enter Network Password box will appear.

5. Enter your password and click the **OK** button. If you have access privileges to that network, your password will complete the log on process. If it does not, ask your network administrator whether your network requires any special log on steps.

6. If you have access to only one network, your computer may display the Enter Network Password dialog box with your name in the User name box and with the server's name already listed.

Sharing Files and Printers

Clearly, you own the files and folders that you create; other users cannot access that information unless you allow them to do so. Similarly, without your approval others cannot access a printer attached to your computer. However, Windows makes it easy for you to allow others to share your files and your printer. You can turn on File and Print Sharing in the Control Panel.

EXERCISE ⇨ 35.2

1. Open the **Control Panel**.

2. Double-click the **Network** icon. The Network dialog box displays, as shown in Figure 35-8.

3. If necessary, click the **Configuration** tab, and select **Client for NetWare Networks**.

4. Click the **File and Print Sharing** button. A dialog box displays, as shown in Figure 35-9.

5. Select the **I want to be able to give others access to my files** check box to allow others in your workgroup to access your files.

6. Select the **I want to be able to allow others to print to my printer(s)** check box to allow others in your workgroup to access your printers; then click the **OK** button.

7. Choose the **OK** button in the **Network** dialog box.

FIGURE 35-8
Network dialog box

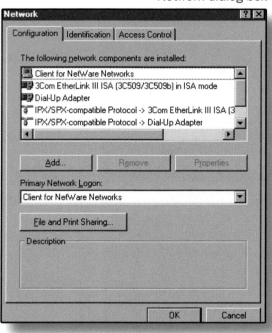

FIGURE 35-9
File and Print Sharing dialog box

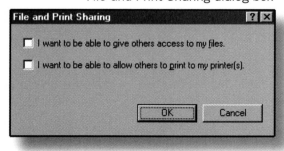

Opening Shared Folders

You can open a shared folder either from My Computer or from Windows Explorer. To open a shared folder on another computer from Network Neighborhood, follow these steps:

1. Double-click Network Neighborhood.

2. Double-click the computer or server where the folder is stored.

3. Double-click the folder you want to use.

Follow the same steps to open a folder from Windows Explorer. *Remember*: You must have access rights to open shared folders.

Providing Appropriate Access to Your Resources

You do not, of course, want to share your personal files and files that apply only to your work. But you do want to share certain appropriate files that other members of your workgroup may need. To distinguish between resources that you do and do not want to share, label your resources by selecting appropriate *access options*. You assign access options by selecting a file or folder, choosing Properties from the File menu, and clicking the Sharing tab in the Properties dialog box.

Here are the access options you can choose from:

- The Read Only option allows network users to only read files or only run programs that are in the folder—not change those files or programs in any way.

- The Full Access option allows users complete access to files and folders that are so designated. Users can read, create, change, delete, move, and so on.

- The Custom option lets you specify exactly what type of access a user has to your files.

E X E R C I S E ⟹ 35.3

1. In **My Computer** or in **Windows Explorer**, select a folder you want to share.

2. Choose **Properties** from the **File** menu. The Properties box displays.

3. In the Properties dialog box, click the **Sharing** tab, as shown in Figure 35-10.

4. Click the **Shared As** option button. Accept the default name or give it a new name in the Share Name box.

5. Add comments in the **Comment** text box, if you wish.

6. Click the **Add** button. The Add Users dialog box opens, as shown in Figure 35-11. Select the users you want to have access to the folder from the list box on the left. Determine the type of access for each user by clicking the **Read Only**, **Full Access**, or **Custom** buttons.

7. Click the **OK** button to close the **Add Users** dialog box. Then click **OK** again to close the Properties dialog box.

FIGURE 35-10
Sharing tab in the Properties dialog box

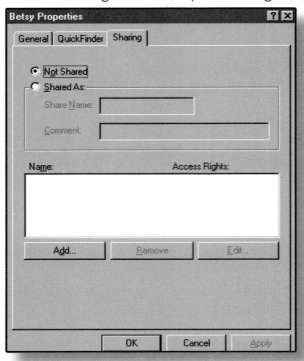

FIGURE 35-11
Add Users dialog box

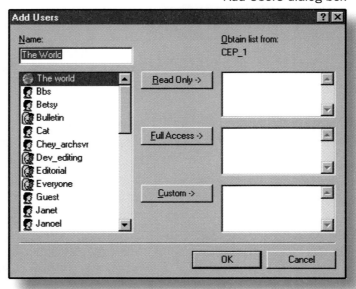

As you see in Figure 35-12, a shared folder is designated by a hand beneath the folder icon.

Logging Off or Disconnecting from the Network

When you are connected to a network, it is important that you exit or *log off* of the network properly. If you do not, you may leave files open or damage files. To log off or *sign off* a network, you follow essentially the same steps as to log on.

FIGURE 35-12
Shared folder

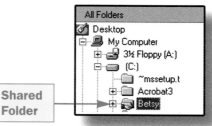

Shared Folder

E X E R C I S E ⟹ 35.4

1. Double-click **Network Neighborhood**.

2. Click the server icon that represents the server to which you are attached.

3. Choose **Log Out** from the **File** menu, and then choose **Yes** when asked to confirm.

4. Click the **OK** button when the Logging Out message box appears.

Using Net Watcher to Manage Resources

Windows includes a feature called *Net Watcher* that you can use to monitor and manage shared resources. To check whether Net Watcher is installed on your system, select System Tools from the Accessories menu. Net Watcher appears on the submenu.

Net Watcher shows you:

■ Who is connected to your computer.

■ How many users are connected to your computer.

■ What files and folders they are using.

■ How long they have been connected to your computer.

In addition, you can use Net Watcher to:

■ Disconnect a user.

■ Close a file being used.

■ Add folders to be shared.

■ Stop folders from being shared.

Summary

This lesson covered the basics of networks and introduced you to Windows' Network Neighborhood. You learned that:

- A network is a combination of hardware and software connecting two or more computers for the purpose of communicating and sharing resources.

- Networks can be categorized by their scope; for example, a local area network (LAN) is more limited than a wide area network (WAN). The Internet, a global network, is in a class by itself.

- A client/server network relies on a dedicated file server to store and "deliver" files and programs to all connected client workstations.

- A peer-to-peer network does not rely on a single dedicated computer to act as a file server.

- Direct Cable Connection is a Windows software tool that simplifies connecting two or more computers.

- Two computers can be linked by cable in a simple peer-to-peer network.

- Network Neighborhood displays all of a network's shared resources (that is, those to which you have access).

- Connecting to and disconnecting from a network is called logging on and logging off.

- To designate which network users can, and which cannot, access your resources, use the access options in the Add Users dialog box.

LESSON 35 REVIEW QUESTIONS

TRUE/FALSE

Each of the following statements is either true or false. Indicate your answer on the left by circling T if the statement is true and F if the statement is false.

T F 1. Access rights can be provided for others to share your resources.

T F 2. Net Watcher is the name that identifies the person administering the network.

T F 3. In a peer-to-peer network, each computer has its own software, but shares files and folders with others.

T F 4. Attaching to a network is called logging on or signing in.

T F 5. On a network, each user can access another's files or folders without permission.

MATCHING

Write the letter of the term in the right column that matches the definition in the left column.

_____ 1. A network that has a dedicated file server.

_____ 2. The global "network of networks."

_____ 3. A network that has no dedicated file server.

_____ 4. A computer that stores programs and files and provides them to workstations as needed.

_____ 5. Computer users who share files or programs.

A. Internet

B. Workgroup

C. Client/server network

D. Peer-to-peer network

E. File server

LESSON 35 PROJECT

This project gives you the opportunity to review the concepts in this lesson and practice the techniques in the exercises.

1. In **My Computer** or in **Windows Explorer**, select a folder you want to share.

2. Choose **Properties** from the **File** menu. Click the **Sharing** tab.

3. Click the **Shared As** option button. Accept the default name or give it a new name in the **Share Name** box.

4. Add comments in the **Comment** text box, if you wish.

5. Click the **Add** button. In the **Add Users** dialog box, select the users you want to have access to the folder from the list box on the left. Give each user **Read Only** access to the folder's contents.

6. "Unshare" the folder:
   a. Select the folder in either **My Computer** or **Windows Explorer**.
   b. Select **Properties** from the **File** menu, and click the **Sharing** tab.
   c. Click the **Not Shared** option and then click **Apply**.

7. In the **Control Panel**, open **Network**, click the **File and Print Sharing** button, and then deselect the sharing options. Click **OK** twice.

8. Close any open windows. Then shut down Windows and your computer.

UNIT 9 REVIEW QUESTIONS ▽

WRITTEN QUESTIONS

Answer the questions below on a separate piece of paper.

1. Describe the use of the Clipboard in sharing data among applications.

2. Briefly discuss why the Clipboard permits you to display data in different formats.

3. Define the term OLE, and give an example of how you might use OLE to produce business documents.

4. Distinguish between *embedding* an object and *linking* an object, and discuss the merits of each.

5. Briefly explain why an object might be embedded as an icon.

6. Explain the difference between an automatic link and a manual link.

7. Distinguish between the Paste and the Paste Special commands on the Edit menu, and give an example of when each might be used.

8. Explain the purpose of a scrap and give an example of how this feature might be used.

9. Briefly explain how My Briefcase uses floppy disks to transfer and synchronize folders and files.

10. In Network Neighborhood, how do you attach to a network? Explain the steps.

UNIT 9 APPLICATION ▽

SCANS

The project team for Corporate Communique client Townsend & Co. needs to get approval on the new masthead it has created for the company's corporate newsletter. Prepare a memo to send to the client.

Start WordPad and open the **Masthead Memo** document from the Windows Template disk. Click an insertion point at the end of the paragraph and press **Enter** three times. Embed the **TC Masthead** file on your Windows Practice disk that you created in the Unit 6 Application, and choose to display it as an icon.

Save the **Masthead Memo** document to your Windows Practice disk. Print a copy of the document. Double-click the icon to view the new masthead.

Close all open applications. If instructed, shut down Windows and your computer.

During your morning break, Bernice Larwin, from the Human Resources Department, asks you for advice. She has researched local labor market trends and wants to place her information on the company's computer network. She feels that most employees who access the data will need summary information only, and few employees will need more detailed "facts and figures" for a specific labor group. Of course, Bernice wants an easy way to update the data without having to rekey the document. A perfect project for you to practice your Windows OLE skills!

You offer to prepare a draft document for Bernice. She gives you her disk file (**Labor Market Projections** on your Windows Template disk) and a hard copy of the chart of the raw data used in the **Labor Market Projections** document (Figure U9-1).

FIGURE U9-1

LABOR MARKET TRENDS				
Industry Title	*1990*	*1995*	*Change*	*% Change*
Mining	2,300	2,800	500	21.7%
Construction	45,200	47,000	1,800	4.0%
Manufacturing	220,100	262,100	42,000	19.1%
Transportation & Public Utility	26,900	35,900	9,000	33.5%
Wholesale & Retail Trade	201,600	260,000	58,400	29.0%
Finance & Real Estate	57,200	76,600	19,400	33.9%
Services	233,800	295,800	62,000	26.5%
Public Administration	43,100	53,900	10,800	25.1%

You hurry back to your office to take on the challenge. Within a very short time, you develop your strategy. First, you will create a WordPad document containing the necessary data for each labor group, a document similar to the one you've sketched for the Mining Group (Figure U9-2).

FIGURE U9-2

Labor Market Projections -- Mining			
1990	1995	Change	% Change
2,300	2,800	500	21.7%

Next you will embed each of the WordPad documents as an icon in the **Labor Market Projections** document in the appropriate location (Figure U9-3).

MINING

Mining employment in the community is primarily concentrated in oil and gas extraction, with a small number in sand and gravel mining. Several large firms with international operations are located in the area and employment in the industry is subject to considerable fluctuation. Employment in mining dropped from an annual average of 3,900 in 1990 to 3,600 the following year.

Microsoft Word
Document

CONSTRUCTION

Construction employment in the area grew at an annual rate of 22 percent between 1990 and 1995. High interest rates and land cost, along with the weakening national economy, caused construction payrolls to decline by a total of

Use the WordPad program to create the two charts and embed them in the **Labor Market Projections** document according to the above plan. Print a copy of the completed **Labor Market Projections** document. Your instructor may wish to see how your embedded files work.

MULTIMEDIA ACCESSORIES

LESSON 36

PLAYING AND RECORDING SOUNDS

OBJECTIVES

Upon completion of this lesson, you will be able to:

- Understand Windows 98 sound tools.
- Play an audio CD.
- Create a play list.
- Record a sound.
- Use Volume Control.

⏱ **Estimated Time: 1.5 hours**

For many users, the most dramatic features of Windows 98 involve multimedia. Once you've had the opportunity to use (or just play with) multimedia for a short time, you may agree—and even if you don't, you will surely find Windows 98's multimedia features fascinating! Multimedia makes using computers easier, more fun, educational and entertaining, and extremely gratifying! In this lesson and the next, you will learn about Windows' multimedia tools and features.

What Is Multimedia?

Multimedia is the combining of text, sound, video, animation, and images. Windows lets you use multimedia to liven up your presentations, play interactive games, play audio CDs on your computer, see and hear famous speeches via an interactive multimedia encyclopedia (for example, Martin Luther King giving his famous "I have a dream" speech), add sounds to documents, and much, much more.

Plug and Play

Ordinarily, multimedia hardware requires a lot of time and effort to make and adjust settings to ensure that there are no hardware conflicts. Windows 98 makes installing all hardware a simple task. The Windows feature Plug and Play (introduced in Lesson 27) is designed to make installing hardware, such as peripherals and device drivers, quick and easy. *Peripherals* are system hardware devices such as monitors, modems, network cards, sound cards, graphics cards, and CD-ROM drives. A *device driver* is the program that controls a printer, a sound card, a CD-ROM drive, or some other piece of hardware.

When hardware manufacturers develop computer systems to run the newest software, they naturally provide the drivers needed to ensure hardware compatibility with Windows. As a result, you will be able to take full advantage of the sound and video that are an integral part of the latest multimedia software because Windows 98 provides increased support and greatly increased speed for digital audio and video compression, full-motion video, and games.

With Plug and Play, Windows does all the work for you. When you start your computer, Windows looks to see if any new hardware (for example, a modem or a CD-ROM drive) has been added. If it finds an added device that is Plug-and-Play compliant (that is, a device which is ready to use), Windows determines what the new hardware needs, makes the settings, and loads any necessary drivers. (Since Windows has a library of over 2,000 drivers, it's ready for most hardware!) As long as the hardware is Plug-and-Play compliant, Windows handles the installation.

Multimedia Hardware Requirements

Multimedia, as you just read, allows you to combine text, sound, video, animation, and images. True! But only if your computer is equipped with the appropriate hardware. Now let's look at some of the hardware you need to run multimedia programs: sound cards, DSP chips, CD-ROM drives, CD-R drives, video compact disks, digital video drives (DVDs), color monitors, video cards, RAM memory, and hard drives.

SOUND CARDS

Computers are equipped with small speakers, but for high-quality stereo sound, multimedia requires a *sound card* (also called a *sound board*). A sound card enables the computer to play and store sounds in disk files. Sound cards also make it possible to connect microphones, speakers, joysticks, electronic musical instruments, and other equipment to your computer.

DSP CHIPS

A *DSP (Digital Signal Processor) chip* located on newer, advanced sound cards enables enhanced audio capabilities with voice and *telephony* (the integration of Windows and telephone communications). Advanced sound cards also offer 3-D sound, which produces more realistic sounds by separating the audio tracks.

CD-ROM DRIVES

Because sound, graphics, and video files take up so much storage space, *CD-ROM* (compact disk–read-only memory) drives are preferred for such large files. For this reason, many multimedia programs are available only in CD form. Files on a CD read-only memory (ROM) disk can only be read; they cannot be changed (that is, you cannot write to or revise such files, nor can you save a new file on a read-only disk).

An advantage of using CD-ROM for storage is that CD-ROM disks can store up to 650MB on one disk; a high-density 3½-inch floppy disk can store only 1.4MB. A disadvantage is that CD-ROM drives are slower in retrieving information than hard disk drives (though CD-ROM drives are faster than floppy disks). Hard disk drives can retrieve data at a rate of up to 3MB per second—five times as fast as a quad-speed CD-ROM, which retrieves information at only 600KB per second.

Like hard drives, CD-ROM drives need a controller card in order to communicate with the rest of the computer. Many sound cards include the CD-ROM controller right on the sound card, which saves space for other devices. The most common type of controller card used with CD-ROM drives is called a SCSI (small computer standard interface) controller.

CD-ROM drives are of two types: internal and external. If your CPU has enough space for an additional drive, you can install an internal CD-ROM drive. If not, you can install an external CD-ROM drive that plugs into the parallel port or the SCSI card.

CD-R DRIVES

CD-R (compact disk–recordable) drives are compact disks that you can write to or record on, but only once: CD-Rs are forever! CD-Rs can be read by CD-ROM drives, but they are expensive. Despite their cost, CD-R drives are very popular (for example, with companies that want to save data that cannot be changed). Soon, CD-E (compact disk–erasable) drives will be available, drives on which you can read, write, and erase, just as with floppy disks.

VIDEO COMPACT DISKS AND DIGITAL VIDEO DRIVES

As future technology perfects the compression of sound and video, you will use small video compact disks and digital video drives (DVDs) to play a full-length movie on your computer. Compression techniques are quite remarkable if you consider that a single frame of full-color video (640 × 480 resolution) contains close to 1MB of data! Besides a full-length movie, the new video compact disks will hold an additional 10 gigabytes of data, thus allowing you to access other information from the same disk simultaneously.

Another technological advance: *Video cards* will let you display film from television, videodisc players, or VCRs in a small window in the corner of your computer screen. In that small corner window you can then display a football game or a news program as you work on your computer application.

COLOR MONITORS AND VIDEO CARDS

Color is an essential ingredient of multimedia, so you will want your computer to have a good color monitor (preferably an SVGA monitor) and a video card. The video card should support at least 1024 × 768 resolution in 256 colors. The better the monitor and video card, the clearer and more authentic the colors and images will be. Make sure your monitor is noninterlaced and has at least a .28 resolution.

RAM MEMORY

With technological advances come greater memory requirements—and thus the need for more *RAM (random access memory)*. Your computer will run with a minimum of 8MB of RAM—but possibly slowly because graphics and sound take up lots of storage space. To increase the computer's speed of operation and to handle large files, you will want to increase your system's RAM. Almost all computers have slots open on their motherboards where additional memory chips (or an additional board or card) can easily be added.

HARD DRIVES

For several reasons, a hard drive with ample storage capacity is an absolute necessity when you are using multimedia. First, multimedia packages store startup files on the hard drive. Second, if you want to create your own multimedia, you will need a hard drive to store your large files. And third, you may want to store images (logos, pictures, or other graphics), sounds, or music to use with presentation software packages, and presentations usually require considerable storage space. For these reasons and more, it will be to your advantage to have a very large hard drive.

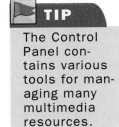

TIP

The Control Panel contains various tools for managing many multimedia resources.

Multimedia Accessories

Windows 98 includes several multimedia tools needed to run multimedia hardware. These tools include ActiveMovie Control, CD Player, Media Player, Sound Recorder, and Volume Control. You access ActiveMoview Control by selecting the Multimedia folder on the Accessories menu. The other tools are stored in the Entertainment folder on the Accessories menu (see Figure 36-1).

■ **ActiveMovie Control** lets you play movies, sounds, and other multimedia files from your computer, or from a local area network, an intranet, or the World Wide Web. ActiveMovie will be discussed in more detail in Lesson 37.

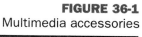

FIGURE 36-1
Multimedia accessories

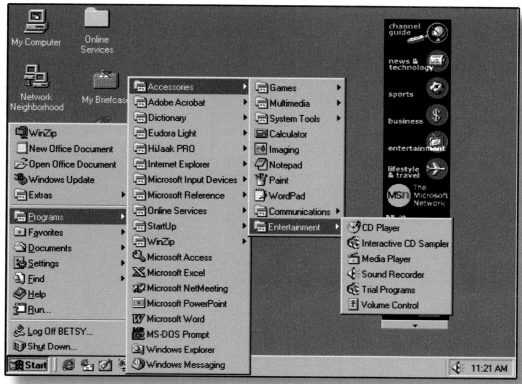

- **CD Player** can play regular audio CDs or specially created computer CDs.

- **Media Player** can play many sound and video files such as MIDI (.mid), waveform (.wav), and Video for Windows (.avi) files. Video for Windows will be covered more completely in Lesson 37.

- **Sound Recorder** records, edits, and plays waveform files. Windows includes some waveform files; you can also record your own waveform files, or you can buy software that contains waveform files.

- **Volume Control** lets you adjust the sound volume on any multimedia that you play using CD Player, Media Player, and Sound Recorder.

Managing Sound

Good audio or sound quality is an important ingredient of the multimedia you create or play. Before you use some of Windows' multimedia tools, let's take a closer look at how sound and audio are produced on the computer.

Sound can be of two types:

- **Analog** sound is the kind of sound your radio or tape player plays. *Analog* sound is a continuous wavelike transmission of sound.

- **Digital** sound is the kind of sound your computer uses. In Windows, a sample of sound appears on screen as a jagged line called a waveform or wave file. Analog sound is changed to *digital* sound when samples of analog waveforms of sound are captured, compressed, and then stored in digital form. If saved, this file will have the extension **.wav**.

Audio quality depends on several factors:

- **Sampling rate**. The higher the *sampling rate* (measured in kilohertz, kHz, or thousands of cycles per second) of a sound board, the better the audio quality. Sampling rates of 44.1 kHz are recommended.

- **Resolution**. Sound *resolution* is measured by the number of bits used to record the sample. The higher the resolution, the better the sound. A 16-bit sound board offers good resolution, but a 32-bit sound board is better. A sound board is a hardware component that enables the computer to reproduce and amplify recorded sounds. A sound board fits into an expansion slot in the back of your computer or on your motherboard.

- **Speaker quality**. As with stereo equipment, the better the speaker, the better the quality of your multimedia sound. Even the best sound board with a built-in amplifier will not compensate for the poor speakers that are packaged with most computer systems.

Audio Files

The two main types of digitized audio or sound played on computers are MIDI and waveform (waveform files are often referred to as "wave" files).

- *MIDI (musical instrument digital interface)* is a device that allows you to connect a sound mixer or an electronic musical instrument such as an electronic keyboard or an electric guitar to the computer. Instead of recording the sound itself (as a waveform file does), MIDI files store instructions or digitized electronic signals in the computer that tell the electronic musical instruments how to reproduce or play the sound. The MIDI sends the signals through a *synthesizer*, an electronic device that creates sounds, which is usually built right into sound cards. Your sound card must have a special MIDI port in order to connect the electronic instrument to the computer. MIDI files are always music files and have the extension **.mid**. Interestingly, a MIDI file lets you record a track with one instrument and play back the track using a different instrument! It is like looking at musical notes on sheet music for the piano—you may initially record and save the music on your home electronic keyboard, but you are now going to take the cassette or disk and play it back on a baby grand piano!

- *Waveform* files are digitized audio files that can store any type of sound (for example, your recorded voice), not just music, again using the extension **.wav**. Unlike MIDI files, waveform files can be played without a synthesizer. In addition, waveform files are usually larger than MIDI files.

Using CD Player

A CD-ROM drive in your computer lets you play both regular audio CDs and specially designed computer CDs. Popular titles include interactive multimedia packages such as Encarta or Compton's Interactive Encyclopedia, games such as MYST or Doom, reference materials such as atlases and literary works, and many educational titles (in math, science, reading, writing, etc.). Encarta, for example, has more than 26,000 articles, nine hours of sound files, more than 8,000 images, and 100 animations and video clips—quite an improvement over printed encyclopedias!

In Windows 98, installing or playing a CD is automated. Multimedia game and program CDs written for Windows are called AutoPlay CD-ROMs. All you do is load your CD in the drive; CD Player will automatically launch and start playing your CD. If the CD requires installation, Windows 98 will automatically start the installation wizard.

Windows' CD Player simulates the front of a real CD player (Figure 36-2). Like a stand-alone compact disk player, CD Player has the normal buttons to skip forward or backward through the tracks, to move to the next track, or to skip tracks. Menu options instruct CD Player to play the tracks in random order, to play continuously by starting over with the first track when the last track is finished, or to play only the beginning of a track.

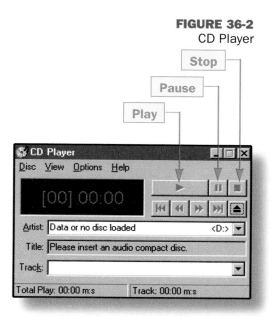

FIGURE 36-2
CD Player

CD Player offers you several options. For example, it lets you create a Play List of your audio CDs. Once you have entered the name of the disk and the artist, CD Player will recognize it and display the disk, artist, and track number whenever that disk is loaded. You can even name the tracks if you wish. Another option lets you select which tracks you want to play and the order in which you want to play them.

To minimize CD Player, click the Minimize button; the screen will clear, allowing you to use other programs while you listen. CD Player will be listed on the taskbar at the bottom of the screen so that you can easily recall it if needed. The taskbar will also display the track that is playing and the elapsed time.

E X E R C I S E 36.1

In order to complete this exercise, you will need an audio CD.

1. Insert the CD in the drive.

2. Click the **Start** button, choose **Programs**, **Accessories**, **Entertainment**, and then **CD Player** from the submenu (see Figure 36-1).

(continued on next page)

4 2 7

3. Click the **Play** button to start the play.

4. Adjust the volume:
   a. Select **Volume Control** from the **View** menu.
   b. Adjust the **Volume** sliders up or down to increase or decrease the volume to the desired level.
   c. Adjust the balance between your two speakers by moving the **Volume Control**

Balance slider left or right to get the desired balance.

5. Click the **Close** button.

6. Stop the play by clicking the **Stop** button.

7. Close **CD Player** by clicking the **Close** button.

CREATING A PLAY LIST

You can create a Play List in CD Player to specify which tracks to play and in what order.

With your CD in the drive, select Edit Play List from the Disc menu. The Disc Settings dialog box opens, as shown in Figure 36-3. You can enter the artist's name and the name of the CD in the text boxes at the top of the dialog box. The Available Tracks list shows the tracks on the current CD. The Play List box shows the order in which the tracks will be played. To change the order, click the Clear All button. Then, select a track from the Available Tracks list and click Add to place it in the Play List.

You can enter the name for a track in the Track text box at the bottom of the dialog box. After you type the name, click the Set Name button. The new name appears in both the Available Tracks list and the Play List.

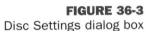

FIGURE 36-3
Disc Settings dialog box

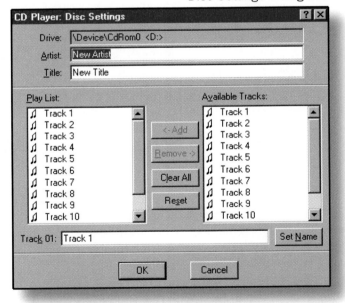

Using Sound Recorder to Record Sounds

Sound Recorder is a Windows utility that lets you record, edit, and play waveform (**.wav**) *sound files*. Waveform files store digitized *sound clips* such as a "ding" sound, spoken words, or music. Several waveform files come with Windows 98 and can be assigned to events, such as entering or exiting Windows. Also, by connecting a microphone to your sound card, you can record your own voice and link the waveform file to a document. You can even buy software that includes sound files which can be used with Windows.

EXERCISE ➡ 36.2

To complete this exercise, you will need a sound card and a microphone.

1. On the **Accessories** menu, select **Entertainment**, and then choose **Sound Recorder** from the submenu. As with the other players, Sound Recorder also closely resembles a real recorder (see Figure 36-4).

2. Make sure your microphone is plugged into the sound card and is turned on. Select **New** from the **File** menu.

3. Adjust the Playback and Recording properties if you wish:
   a. Select **Audio Properties** from the **Edit** menu.
   b. Make any changes needed in the dialog box; then click the **OK** button.

4. Start the recording by clicking the **Record** button. As you are recording, the green line will oscillate to indicate the sound levels. You can record for 60 seconds.

5. State your name, address, occupation, and phone number.

6. Stop the recording by clicking the **Stop** button.

7. Save the file as **Personal** on your Windows Practice disk.

8. Close the **Personal** file by clicking the **Close** button.

FIGURE 36-4
Sound Recorder

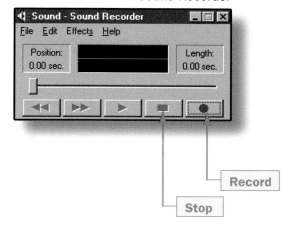

Using Volume Control

You can easily adjust the volume on any multimedia you play. Like other Windows multimedia components, Volume Control resembles real equipment, in this case a stereo control panel (Figure 36-5). In an earlier exercise you accessed Volume Control as a menu item. In Exercise 36.3 you will access Volume Control in another way.

FIGURE 36-5
Volume Control

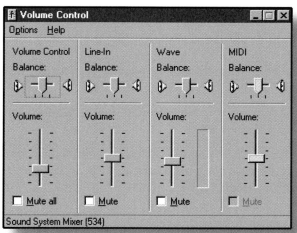

1. On the **Accessories** menu, select **Entertainment**, and then choose **Volume Control** from the submenu. The Volume Control panel appears (see Figure 36-5).

2. Display the devices you want to display and/or adjust the volume for playback, recording, or other types of devices, such as a microphone:
   a. Select **Properties** from the **Options** menu.
   b. Make the changes you want in the **Mixer** device, indicate at which point in the recording process the volume should be adjusted, and check the devices you want to display. When you have finished making changes, click the **OK** button.

3. Adjust the sliders up or down to the desired level to change the volume.

4. Change one of the settings and note the difference in the audio.

5. Close **Volume Control**.

6. If instructed, shut down Windows and your computer.

Summary

This lesson introduced you to some of Windows multimedia tools and features. You learned that:

- Multimedia combines many types of media, such as text, sound, video, animation, and graphics.

- Depending on the multimedia presentations you are using or developing, you will need hardware such as a sound card, DSP chips, a CD-ROM drive, CD-R drives, video compact disks, a digital video drive, a color monitor, additional RAM memory, and a hard drive.

- The Plug and Play feature of Windows recognizes new pieces of hardware, makes the settings necessary to incorporate the new hardware, and loads any drivers that are needed by the new hardware. Thus Plug and Play prevents any conflicts from occurring when adding peripherals. Products that are Plug-and-Play compliant bear the Plug and Play logo.

- Multimedia sound quality depends on your sound card and speakers. The higher the sound card's sampling rate and resolution, the better the sound.

- MIDI (musical instrument digital interface) is a device used to connect musical equipment such as a sound mixer or synthesizer, an electronic keyboard, or an electric guitar to a computer. MIDI files store instructions on how to reproduce the sounds; they do not store the sounds themselves. MIDI files have the extension **.mid**.

- Waveform is digitized audio. Waveform files can store any type of sound. Waveform files have the extension **.wav**.

- Windows 98 comes with these multimedia accessories: ActiveMovie lets you play movies, sounds, and other multimedia files. CD Player can play regular audio CDs or specially created computer CDs. Media Player can play many sound and video files such as MIDI, waveform, and Video for

Windows files. Sound Recorder records, edits, and plays waveform files. Windows includes some waveform files; you can also record you own waveform files, or you can buy software that contains waveform files.

■ Volume Control lets you adjust the sound volume on any multimedia that you play using CD Player, Media Player, and Sound Recorder. Volume Control gives you the opportunity to adjust the volume for playback, recording, or any type of sound device.

LESSON 36 REVIEW QUESTIONS

MATCHING

Write the letter of the term in the right column that matches the definition in the left column.

_____ 1. A continuous wavelike transmission of sound.

_____ 2. A software program that controls a piece of hardware, such as a CD-ROM drive.

_____ 3. Sound converted from analog waveforms for computer use.

_____ 4. A type of digitized audio that can store any type of sound.

_____ 5. A device that is necessary to play sounds and store them in disk files.

A. Device driver

B. Sound card

C. Digital

D. Waveform

E. Analog

MULTIPLE CHOICE

Complete the following questions by circling the correct multiple choice letter.

1. You can easily connect devices such as speakers, CD-ROM drives, and modems to a computer by using
   A. Plug and Play
   B. Plug and Run
   C. Multimedia
   D. Device Driver

2. A radio or a tape player produces
   A. digital sound
   B. analog sound
   C. MIDI sound
   D. none of the above

3. When you record a sound with an electronic keyboard, you get a
   A. digital file
   B. analog file
   C. MIDI file
   D. none of the above

4. The Windows utility you use to record, edit, and play waveform files is
   A. Media Player
   B. CD Player
   C. Sound Recorder
   D. Tape Recorder

5. You can find multimedia tools in the Accessories section and in
   A. Control Panel
   B. My Computer
   C. Tools
   D. Inbox

LESSON 36 PROJECT

This project gives you the opportunity to review the concepts in this lesson and practice the techniques in the exercises. In order to complete this project, you must have a CD-ROM drive and an audio CD.

1. Start Windows if it is not already running.

2. Open **CD Player**.

3. Place a CD in the drive.

4. Choose **Edit Play List** from the **Disc** menu. The CD Player: Disc Settings window opens.

5. In the **Artist** box, key the name of the artist of the inserted CD.

6. Tab to the **Title** section. In the **Title** box, key the title of the CD.

7. Create the Play List of tracks you want to play and the order in which you wish them to play:
   a. Click the **Clear All** button to start a new Play List.
   b. In the **Available Tracks** box, click the track that you want to play first, and then click the **Add** button.
   c. In the **Track number** box, key the name of the track, and then click **Set Name**. Then, whenever you edit the Play List, you will see the name of the track instead of just the track number.

8. Continue adding tracks until your Play List is complete. If you leave a track off the list, it will not play.

9. When you have finished adding the tracks to your Play List, click the **OK** button. You will return to the CD Player window.

10. The CD Player window now reflects the name of the artist, the title of the CD, and the first track that will play. Click the **Play** button. The first track from your Play List will begin to play.

11. Change to a different track:
    a. Click the down arrow at the end of the **Track** box. A drop-down window displays the Play List.
    b. Click a different track. The play will switch to that track.

12. Stop the play and close **CD Player**.

13. If instructed, shut down Windows and your computer.

USING MEDIA PLAYER AND ACTIVEMOVIE CONTROL

OBJECTIVES

Upon completion of this lesson, you will be able to:

- Play a sound file.

- Play a video file.

- Embed or link a sound file into a document.

- Link a media file to a document.

- Play a movie with ActiveMovie Control.

Estimated Time: 1.5 hours

You learned in the last lesson that good audio or sound is an important ingredient of multimedia. Good-quality video is equally important. In this lesson, you will learn how to use the Media Player and ActiveMovie Control accessories to play sound and video files.

Understanding Computers and Video

The ability to run video clips and animation on desktop computers is relatively new and very exciting. Television uses analog video, and the quality of analog video is far superior to that of digital video—that is, as of today. Today, analog videos that have been digitized for computers run at a slower number of frames per second (fps) because of the *compression* techniques used. Even the best digital videos run at only about 15 fps, compared to 24 fps for movies. As a result, digital video may appear jerky, as the early movies were.

Digital video files can be very large, depending on the length of the sequence. Generally, digital video requires a lot of disk space, a fast processor, and lots of memory. In most current applications, digital video runs in a small window on the monitor (running full-screen requires special software, boards, or chips). Windows 98 features *DCI (display control interface)* technology from Microsoft and Intel. DCI accelerates the speed of capturing video frames, allowing videos to run full screen.

To produce digital video for computers, you need to learn to create video sequences using a software utility program and a special hardware component, a *video capture card*. With this software and hardware, you can capture a single still image or a full video sequence using a video camera, a VCR (video cassette recorder), a videodisc player, or other device. Then you can convert the captured video or still image to a disk file, and you are on your way to producing multimedia!

Using Still Graphics and Images

Using a video capture card is not the only way to add still images and graphics to your multimedia presentations. You can use scanning equipment to convert photos and other images into digitized files, or you can use software programs such as Paint to create your own pictures. Another option: You can purchase clip art files on floppy disks or CD-ROM. Then you can simply copy ("clip") any of the predesigned graphics and import the "art" into your presentation. In addition, you can use a special camera that takes photos, digitizes them, and stores them on small disks, or you can send the digitized photos directly to your hard drive via a cable!

Using Media Player to Play Sound and Video Files

You can use Media Player to play sound and video files of many types. Because of Windows 98's enhanced support for sound, you will get a high-quality, realistic sound.

Although you can play an audio CD with Media Player, you have more control if you use CD Player for audio disks. As with CD Player, Media Player's controls look like the real thing on your screen, as shown in Figure 37-1.

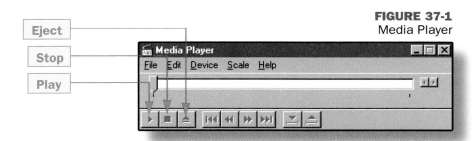

FIGURE 37-1
Media Player

Not only can Media Player play wave files (**.wav**) and MIDI (**.mid**) audio files, but Media Player also runs Video for Windows (**.avi**) files. A window opens that displays the clip as it plays. As mentioned earlier, Windows 98 can also display clips full screen.

To run a video full screen, the settings in Multimedia Properties must be changed as follows:

- Open the Control Panel.

- In Control Panel, double-click Multimedia.

- Click the Video tab.

- In the Show video in box, click the Full screen button to enable video clips to be played full screen.

 **NOTE:**

If you do not want the video to play full screen, the Show video in Window selection also allows you to change the size of the window in which a clip can be played.

Remember: Because CD-ROMs play video files more slowly, the videos may appear jerky, especially when compared to a VCR. To get a smoother play, you will have to either copy the file to the hard disk or get a faster CD-ROM drive. Video files require about 7MB of storage space for 1 minute of play, so it is difficult to store video files. A 1-minute, full-screen play requires about 1.5 gigabytes of space on your hard drive!

E X E R C I S E ▷ 37.1

1. Click the Start button, choose Programs, **Accessories**, **Entertainment**, and then choose **Media Player**.

2. Select **MIDI Sequencer** from the **Device** menu. The Open dialog box appears, displaying a list of files that can be played on Media Player (Figure 37-2).

3. Click **Beethoven's Fur Elise** (one of the standard Windows choices). If **Fur Elise** is not listed, click one of the other **.mid** or **.rmi** files.

4. Click the **Open** button. You will be returned to the Media Player.

5. Click the **Start** button to play the selection.

6. Adjust the volume:
   a. Select **Volume Control** from the **Device** menu. The Volume Control window appears.
   b. Adjust the volume and balance as necessary.

7. After the selection has played, leave Media Player open for the next exercise.

 **NOTE:**

If there are no MIDI files on your computer, follow steps 1–3 above, but in step 2, select the Sound option instead of MIDI Sequencer. Then choose one of the Wave (**.wav**) files, and play one of the files listed.

FIGURE 37-2
Open dialog box

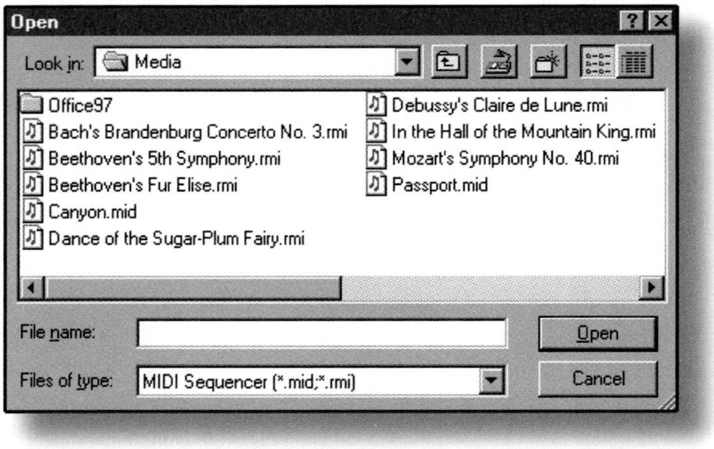

EXERCISE 37.2

You must have the Windows 98 installation CD to complete this exercise.

1. Insert the Windows 98 installation CD in the CD-ROM drive. Minimize the Microsoft Windows 98 window, if necessary.

2. In Media Player, choose **Video for Windows** from the **Device** menu.

3. In the Open dialog box, select the drive containing the Windows 98 CD.

4. Open the **CDSample** folder, and then the **Videos** folder.

5. Click the video **Gamepad**. (If **Gamepad** is not listed, choose one of the other files.)

6. Click the **Open** button. A window opens on screen.

7. On the **Media Player**, click the **Play** button. The video clip plays.

8. After the video clip has played, click the **Close** button to close the Gamepad window.

9. Close **Media Player**.

Using Multimedia Accessories to Insert Media Files into Documents

One exciting Windows feature you discovered earlier is its ability to link and embed files into the documents you create in different applications. Now you can embed media files in your text files as well! For example, you can annotate a spreadsheet by using Sound Recorder to create a file and then insert that sound into the spreadsheet; or you can record the sound from within the spreadsheet. Another example: You can create a multimedia resumé with your picture and the sound of your voice!

There are several methods to link and embed media files into documents:

■ In Exercise 37.3 you will start by choosing the media file from within Media Player and then open the document.

■ In Exercise 37.4 you will start by opening the document and then choosing the media file. The advantage of starting with Media Player is that you have the opportunity to change certain options.

An embedded media file appears as an icon in the document. A label describes the embedded object. To play the object, double-click its icon.

EXERCISE 37.3

1. Open **Media Player**.

2. Select **Sound** from the **Device** menu.

3. Locate and double-click the **Personal** file created in Exercise 36.2. (If you do not have that file, double-click one of the files from Windows.) You will be returned to the Media Player panel.

4. Select **Options** from the **Edit** menu.

(continued on next page)

5. In the **Options** window, make sure that the following are checked:
- **a.** Control Bar On Playback
- **b.** Border around object
- **c.** Play in client document

6. Click the **OK** button.

7. Select **Copy Object** from the **Edit** menu.

8. Open a new **WordPad** document in which you will embed the sound.

9. Embed the sound by selecting **Paste** from the **Edit** menu.

10. The embedded sound appears in the document as an icon, as shown in Figure 37-3.

11. Key a line of text that describes the embedded sound, as shown in Figure 37-3.

12. Play the embedded sound by double-clicking its icon.

13. Leave the document on screen.

FIGURE 37-3
Embedding a sound recording as an icon

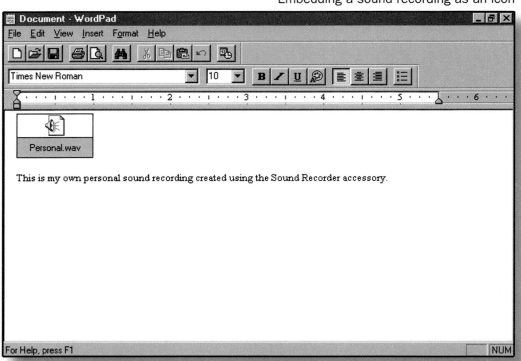

Linking Media Files from Within a Document

As mentioned earlier, another way to link a media file is from within the document itself. This method is a little faster and just as easy.

EXERCISE 37.4

1. Open a new **WordPad** document by selecting **New** from the **File** menu. Do not save the current document.

2. Key: **Linking a media file to a document**.

3. Choose **Object** from the **Insert** menu.

4. Click **Create from File**.

5. In the **File** box, key the following path: **C:\windows\media\ding.wav**.

NOTE:

If your wave files are located in a different directory, you will need to key the correct path (Figure 37-4).

6. Click a check mark in the **Link** box.

7. Click **Display As Icon**; then click the **OK** button. The sound icon now appears in the document.

8. Click to the right of the selected icon to deselect it. Figure 37-5 shows the results.

9. Double-click the icon. Windows will start Media Player, which will then play the file.

10. Close the **WordPad** document without saving.

FIGURE 37-4
Linking a sound object

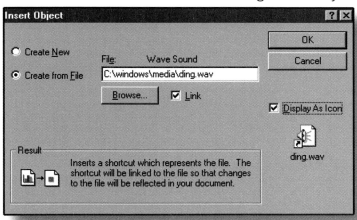

FIGURE 37-5
Sound file displayed as an icon

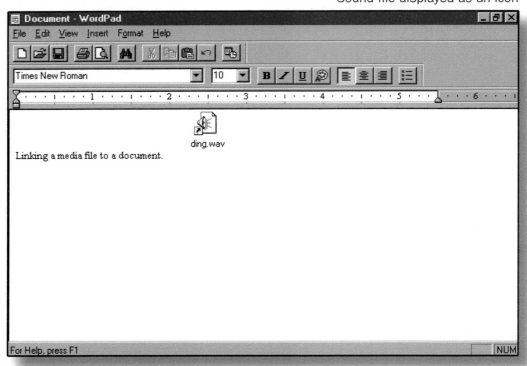

Using ActiveMovie Control

Windows' ActiveMovie multimedia accessory lets you play movies, sounds, and other multimedia files from your computer, a local area network, an intranet, or the Web.

To start ActiveMovie, select ActiveMovie Control from the Multimedia submenu. The Open dialog box appears. Select an ActiveMovie file (it might have an **.mpg** extension) to play. The ActiveMovie Control screen displays as shown in Figure 37-6. Click the Play button to play the movie.

FIGURE 37-6
ActiveMovie Control screen

EXERCISE ▷ 37.5

You will need the Windows 98 CD to complete this exercise.

1. Insert the Windows 98 CD in your CD-ROM drive. If necessary, minimize the Windows 98 opening window.

2. Start **ActiveMovie** by selecting **ActiveMovie Control** on the **Multimedia** submenu.

3. In the Open dialog box, select the drive containing the Windows 98 CD. Open the **CD-Sample** folder and then the **Videos** folder.

Double-click the **Greeting.mpg** file. (Double-click another **.mpg** file if the **Greeting** file is not available.)

4. In the ActiveMovie Control window, click the **Run** button and watch the movie.

5. When the movie is done, click the window's **Close** button to close **ActiveMovie Control**.

6. If instructed, shut down Windows and your computer.

Summary

This lesson covered the Windows Media Player and ActiveMovie Control accessories. You learned that:

■ Digital video files are generally very large and therefore require a large amount of disk space, a fast processor, and a great deal of RAM. With Windows 98, no special hardware or software is required to run digital video files full screen; without Windows 98, or special hardware or software, the video runs in a small window in the corner of your display.

■ Windows gives you the ability to link and embed sound or video files to create multimedia documents.

■ An embedded or linked media file appears as an icon in the document. A label describes the object. To play the object, double-click its icon.

■ Windows' ActiveMovie multimedia accessory lets you play movies, sounds, and other multimedia files from your computer, a local area network, an intranet, or the Web.

LESSON 37 REVIEW QUESTIONS

TRUE/FALSE

Each of the following statements is either true or false. Indicate your answer on the left by circling T if the statement is true and F if the statement is false.

T   F   1.   Media Player can play both sound and video files.

T   F   2.   Windows 98 features DCI technology which allows videos to run full screen.

T F 3. Media Player is the best Windows accessory for playing an audio CD.

T F 4. You cannot embed video clips, only sounds.

T F 5. You can choose to display a linked video clip or sound as an icon in the destination document.

MULTIPLE CHOICE

Complete the following questions by circling the correct multiple choice letter.

1. Media Player is used to play
   A. sound files
   B. video files
   C. CD audio
   D. all of the above

2. To start Media Player, click Start and then
   A. Programs, Accessories, Entertainment, and Media Player
   B. Programs, Multimedia, and Media Player
   C. Programs, Accessories, Media, and Media Player
   D. Control Panel, Accessories, Multimedia, and Media Player

3. You can insert media files into documents by
   A. linking
   B. embedding
   C. both a and b
   D. neither a nor b

4. The Windows technology that enables you to display videos full screen is
   A. Display Control Interface
   B. Digital Control Interface
   C. Video Capture Card
   D. Video for Windows

5. You can add still images and graphics to a multimedia presentation by
   A. scanning the image and converting it to a digitized format
   B. inserting a picture you create in a graphics or drawing program
   C. importing predesigned graphics or clip art
   D. all of the above will work

LESSON 37 PROJECT

This project gives you the opportunity to review the concepts in this lesson and practice the techniques in the exercises.

1. Start Windows if it is not already running. Start **Media Player**.

2. Select **Open** from the **File** menu.

3. In the **Files of type** box, click the down arrow and choose **Sound [*.wav]**.

4. Double-click **Chimes**. You will be returned to the Media Player window.

5. Choose **Options** from the **Edit** menu.

6. Click the **Auto Repeat** box to put a check mark in it.

7. Click the **OK** button.

8. Click the **Play** button on the **Media Player**. The chimes will play and repeat until you click the **Stop** button.

9. Choose **Options** from the **Edit** menu again.

10. Click **Auto Repeat** to remove the check mark.

11. Click the **OK** button. If you now click **Play**, the **Chime** file will play only one time.

12. Close **Media Player.**

13. If instructed, shut down Windows and your computer.

UNIT 10 REVIEW QUESTIONS

WRITTEN QUESTIONS

Answer the questions below on a separate piece of paper.

1. Define multimedia.

2. What pieces of hardware are needed to run multimedia?

3. What is the major advantage of CD-ROMs over disk drives?

4. What are two criteria that measure sound quality?

5. How do MIDI files differ from waveform files?

6. What equipment is needed to create video files?

7. How do you embed a media file in a document?

8. What are the five multimedia accessories that come with Windows 98?

9. What is the advantage of Plug and Play?

10. How would you change settings to display video in a full screen?

UNIT 10 APPLICATION

SCANS

Aleta Lopez, the president of Corporate Communique, wants to develop an "interactive" newsletter service that she can offer to the company's clients. As more and more businesses market themselves on the World Wide Web, it's important that a strong communications tool, like a newsletter, be available to Internet users. Before she can offer such a service, though, Aleta needs to determine Corporate Communique's capabilities in preparing newsletters that can engage and involve online users using Windows' multimedia tools.

Start WordPad and prepare a report for Aleta that explains Windows 98's sound and video capabilities. Then, describe how you could incorporate audio and video segments in a newsletter for Townsend & Co. As you know, Townsend is a residential real estate company. The market it wants to reach consists of homebuyers and sellers. An online newsletter should include information on properties for sale, the names and phone numbers of agents, and perhaps some general information on the residential real estate market.

Save the report as **TC Multimedia Newsletter** to your Windows Practice disk. Print a copy, and then close all open applications. If instructed, shut down Windows and your computer.

CRITICAL THINKING

Windows 98 is new to your department. Your manager, Mr. Frost, would like to use some of the multimedia features to enliven a presentation that he plans to make for some customers.

Since he is very busy preparing the text of his presentation, he asks you to write him a memo suggesting which Windows multimedia tools he should use, and include some specific sound or video file examples.

You decide to use WordPad to write the memo. Further, you will link some media files to each suggestion. Then, when Mr. Frost loads the memo, he can click the icons to hear or see your suggestions.

In your memo, be sure to:

- State appropriate times to use a media file (for example, he might play music from a MIDI file before the presentation, while attendees are arriving).

- Give examples of multimedia types that are available.

- Give examples of specific files that would be appropriate for each type of multimedia you suggest.

- Link the files to the examples so that Mr. Frost can try out your suggestions.

- Suggest volume levels for each example. (Would you use the same volume level for a file playing prior to the beginning of the presentation that you would use during the presentation itself?)

INTERNET EXPLORER

UNIT 11

Estimated Time for Unit 11: 10.75 hours

447

LESSON 38

BROWSING THE WORLD WIDE WEB

OBJECTIVES

Upon completion of this lesson, you will be able to:

■ Start Internet Explorer and load a home page.

■ Navigate a Web page using the keyboard navigation keys.

■ Access and display Web pages using a variety of techniques.

■ Add and delete quick links buttons.

Estimated Time: 2 hours

In previous lessons you learned how Windows 98 receives and processes information in a variety of media, such as text, graphics, sound, video clips, and animation. This multimedia capability also permits Windows 98 to utilize hypertext documents. A *hypertext document* contains any number of *links*, which are pointers to other hypertext documents and to the computer on which the hypertext document is stored. The capability to utilize hypertext documents is the basis for the Internet; a network of computers that provides an electronic link to information on almost every topic that you can imagine. In the next five lessons, you will learn how to use Windows 98 tools to access and use the expansive base of information that's available on the Internet.

While the Internet has many components, when people say "the Internet," they are generally referring to just one of its components—the *World Wide Web* (or more simply, the *Web*). The hypertext documents that make up the Web are called *Web pages*. The Web gets its name from the fact that its structure resembles a spider web; that is, links connect you from one location to another and most pages are linked to other pages. You must use an application program called a *Web browser* in order to access and display the contents of a Web page. Windows 98 built-in browser, Internet Explorer, permits you to view the text and graphics on Web pages and to play the audio and video contents on these pages.

Starting Internet Explorer

You start Internet Explorer by double-clicking on the Internet Explorer icon (see Figure 38-1) on your desktop, or by selecting Internet Explorer in the Internet Explorer folder on the Programs submenu on the Start menu. Before launching Windows 98, Internet Explorer will first check for an active connection to the Internet. An *active connection* means that your computer is communicating to the Internet through a network connection or a modem. If Windows 98 does not find an active connection, a Connect To dialog box displays, as shown in Figure 38-2.

TIP

You can also start Internet Explorer by clicking its icon on the Quick Launch toolbar.

FIGURE 38-1
Internet
Explorer icon

FIGURE 38-2
Connect To dialog box

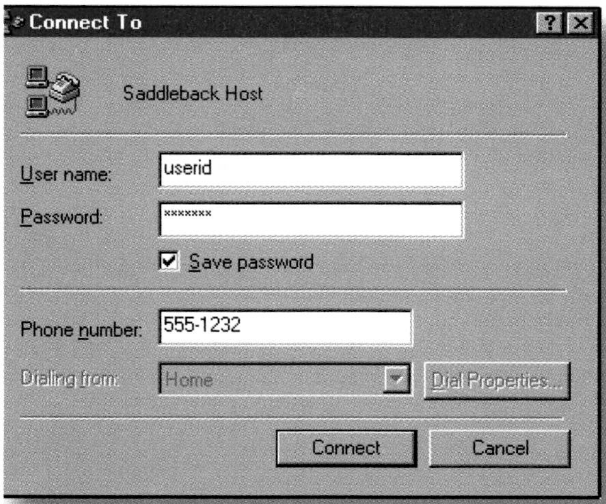

Connect To

Saddleback Host

User name: userid

Password: xxxxxxx

☑ Save password

Phone number: 555-1232

Dialing from: Home   Dial Properties...

Connect   Cancel

After entering your user name and password, click the OK button. Your modem will dial your post office server and attempt to make an active connection to the Internet. Once connected, Internet Explorer's start page displays. The *start page* is the first page you see each time you launch Internet Explorer. It is also called the *home page*.

NOTE:

The start page you see when you start Internet Explorer may differ from the one shown in this text.

E X E R C I S E ⟩ **38.1**

Before your begin this exercise, ask your instructor or lab assistant if a user name and password are required to connect your computer to the Internet.

1. Double-click the **Internet Explorer** icon on the desktop.

2. If a Connect To dialog box displays, enter the user name and password provided by your instructor or laboratory assistant, and then click the **Connect** button.

If you are unsuccessful in connecting to the Internet or you cancel the connection, Internet Explorer displays a window like the one shown in Figure 38-3, indicating the Internet site specified cannot be opened. When you establish an active connection, the Internet Explorer window displays as shown in Figure 38-4.

FIGURE 38-3

FIGURE 38-3
Message window that displays when you are unsuccessful in connecting to the Internet

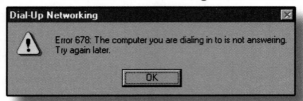

FIGURE 38-4
Internet Explorer window

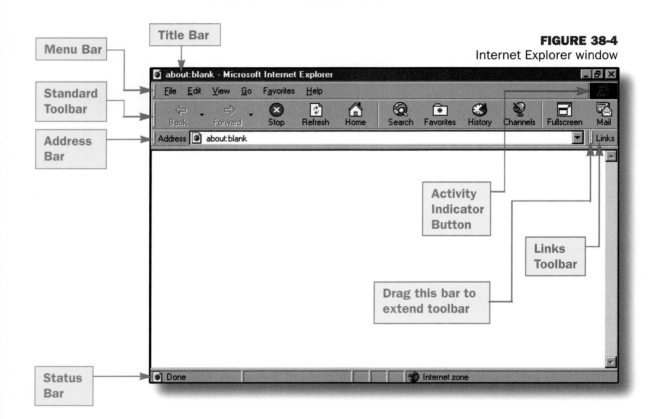

Examining the Internet Explorer Screen

As you can see in Figure 38-4, the Internet Explorer window contains features common to most Windows 98 windows—a title bar, menu bar, toolbar, Address bar, display area, and a status bar. You might notice that some of these features look differently in the Internet Explorer window than in other windows. You might also notice that the window is characterized by some new elements as well. To fully understand how to use Internet Explorer, you need a working knowledge of the following five features:

■ **Activity indicator**. The Internet Explorer button to the right of the menu bar is animated when Internet Explorer is sending and receiving data from the Internet.

■ **Standard toolbar**. The Standard toolbar contains tools for navigating, displaying, editing, and printing Web pages.

■ **Address bar**. The Address bar contains a text box where you key and display the location (address) for a Web page.

■ **Links toolbar**. The Links toolbar contains five buttons that link (jump) to specific Web pages. These buttons are called *quick links* because they represent a fast way to get to a specific Web page. Often, the Links toolbar looks more like a button than a toolbar. You can drag the white vertical bar to extend the toolbar and display its buttons.

■ **Status bar**. The status bar at the bottom of the Internet Explorer window supplies information about the Web page displayed or being received in the main window. When you position the pointer over a link in the displayed page, the status bar shows the destination of that link. If a Web page is being received, the status bar will display information about the progress of the transfer of the page.

Modifying Internet Explorer's Toolbars

As was mentioned above, the Links toolbar looks like a button at the end of the Address bar. Combining toolbars on the same line minimizes the space they take up and shows more of the display window.

When more than one toolbar occupies the same line, you can view the hidden toolbar by double-clicking the bar or by dragging the white vertical bar left or right. You can remove a toolbar from the display by deselecting it on the View menu's Toolbars submenu.

E X E R C I S E 38.2

1. Select the **Toolbars** option on the **View** menu and verify that **Standard Buttons**, **Address Bar**, and **Links** are selected (checked). Select any toolbar that is not checked.

2. If necessary, arrange the toolbars as they appear in Figure 38-5:
   a. Double-click on the word **Links** to display the full Links toolbar.
   b. Point to the word **Links** and then press and hold down the mouse button. The pointer

should turn into a four-headed arrow. Drag the toolbar so that it is below the Address Bar.
   c. Point on the word **Address** on the Address Bar and drag the Address bar below the Links toolbar. Notice that each toolbar now occupies its own line. Your Internet Explorer window should have all three toolbars displayed on separate lines as shown in Figure 38-5.

FIGURE 38-5
Modifying the toolbar display

Browsing the Web

The act of using Internet Explorer to jump from Web page to Web page and to view and interact with items on a page is referred to as *browsing*. You browse the Web in several different ways:

- Key the address of a new Web page in the Address bar text box.

- Use the keyboard's arrow keys.

- Click the Internet Explorer navigation buttons on the Standard toolbar.

- Click a link on the currently displayed page.

- Click one of the buttons on the Links toolbar.

- Choose a page from a list of previously viewed pages.

- Choose a page from a list of favorite pages.

Keying an Address

Every Web page has a unique Web address known as a *Uniform Resource Locator*, or *URL*. A typical URL looks like that shown in Figure 38-6. The first part of this URL, **http://**, specifies the Internet method of access or *protocol*, and is an acronym for *Hypertext Transfer Protocol*. The protocol is always keyed in lowercase letters. The colon and two forward slashes separate the method of access from the second part of the URL, the domain name.

The *domain name* is the Internet address of the computer where the Web page is located (**www.budgettravel.com** in our example). The domain always contains at least one period. Occasionally, a third part of the URL is used that indicates a file name or folder (**country.htm** in Figure 38-6). When this is done, a forward slash (/) separates the file specifications from the domain.

FIGURE 38-6
A typical Uniform Resource Locator (URL)

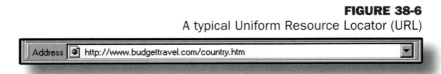

Web site addresses are becoming very common. You see them in advertisements, hear them mentioned on the radio, see them displayed on television, and learn of them through conversations with others. You can access these sites or any Web site by keying its URL in the Address bar text box and pressing Enter.

The Address bar has an AutoComplete feature that will automatically complete an address if it recognizes the address you are keying as one that has been entered before. As soon as you see the Auto-Complete text appear in the text box, you can press Enter and the page will be loaded.

E X E R C I S E ⟹ 38.3

You need to have Internet Explorer open and an active connection to the Internet in order to complete this exercise.

1. Double-click in the Address bar text box to set an insertion point or highlight any currently displayed text.

2. Key the following URL exactly as shown. Do not use any spaces and be sure to use two forward slashes: **http://fic.info.gov**.

3. Press **Enter**. Monitor the Internet Explorer's activity by watching the status bar at the bottom left of the main window. Also, notice the activity indicator.

The Federal Information Center home page will display as shown in Figure 38-7. The links on this page are frequently updated, so the page may not look exactly like the example in the figure when you access it.

4. Click in the Address bar text box to highlight the Federal Information Center home page address.

5. Key the following URL exactly as shown. Do not use any spaces, and be sure to use two forward slashes as shown: **http://www.microsoft.com**.

6. Press **Enter**. The Microsoft Corporation home page will display as shown in Figure 38-8. (The contents of this page change constantly. Don't be alarmed if your screen looks differently than Figure 38-8)

(continued on next page)

FIGURE 38-7
The Federal Information Center home page

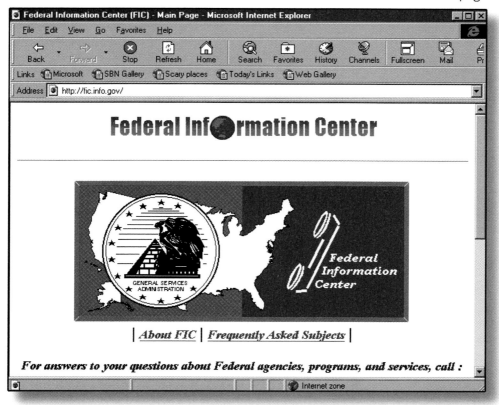

FIGURE 38-8
The Microsoft Corporation home page

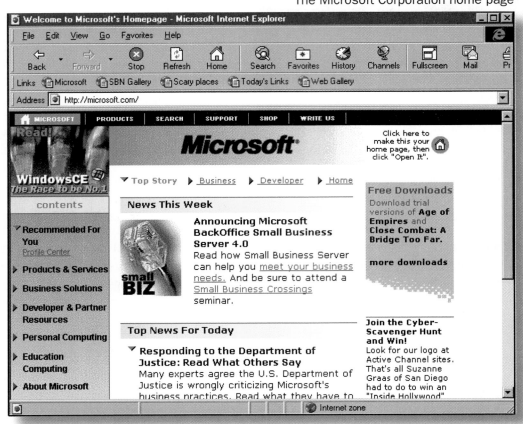

EXERCISE 38.3 CONTINUED

7. Start keying the Federal Information Center home page URL again: **http://fic.info.gov**. As soon as you see the complete URL appear in the Address bar text box, press **Enter** to load the page.

8. Start keying the Microsoft Corporation home page URL again: **http://www.microsoft.com**.

As soon as you see the complete URL appear in the Address text box, press **Enter**.

9. Leave the Microsoft home page displayed on screen for the next exercise.

Using the Keyboard

Web pages are often so large that they cannot fit on one screen, so Internet Explorer permits you to use the keys on your keyboard to display different portions of a page. The navigation keys, Home, End, Page Up, and Page Down, and the arrow keys can be used to move within any page.

EXERCISE ▭⟩ 38.4

You must have the Microsoft home page displayed and an active Internet connection in order to complete this exercise.

1. Press the **End** key to move to the end of the Microsoft Web page.

2. Press the **Home** key to move back to the top of the page.

3. Press the **Page Down** key. The Web page moves one screen down.

4. Press the **Page Up** key. The display returns to the top of the Web page.

5. Press the **down arrow** key three times slowly. Notice the page moves up to display a small portion each time the key is pressed.

6. Press the **End** key to move to the end of the Web page.

7. Press the **Page Up** key to return to the top of the Web page.

8. Leave the Microsoft home page on screen for the next exercise.

Using Navigation Buttons

As you learned early in this course, the Standard toolbar contains navigation buttons to help you move from page to page (or document to document). These buttons are identified in Figure 38-9. As you navigate the Web, Internet Explorer keeps track of the sites you've visited and saves images from these pages on your hard disk so they'll load faster should you return. The pages are saved on your hard disk in an area called the *disk cache*. The disk cache is cleared each time you shut down your computer, and a new disk cache is created each time you start Internet Explorer.

Clicking the Back button will move you back or up the list of previously visited sites. If you have not jumped from the start page, the Back button will be grayed out. Clicking the Forward button will move you forward or down the list of previously visited sites. When the Forward button is grayed out, you're already on the last page visited during the session.

Clicking the Stop button permits you to abort the present action. Clicking the Refresh button reloads the current page. You may want to reload a page because the page is displaying incorrectly or was displayed incompletely.

Each time you launch Internet Explorer, the same page will display. This page is called the start (or home) page because it is the first page you see each time you start Internet Explorer. You can return to the start page at any time during a session by clicking the Home button.

FIGURE 38-9
Navigation keys on the Standard toolbar

EXERCISE 38.5

You must have completed Exercise 38.4 and maintained the connection to the Microsoft Corporation Web page in order to complete this exercise.

1. Click the **Back** button on the toolbar to return to the previously displayed Web page (the Federal Information Center).

   The page displays more quickly than it did previously because it is stored in your computer's disk cache, so your computer did not have to download it a second time.

2. Click the **Forward** button on the toolbar to move forward to the Microsoft Corporation Web page.

   This page will also display more quickly than the first time it was accessed. The next step must be done quickly, so read the entire instruction before you do anything.

3. Click the **Refresh** button. While the page is reloading, click the **Stop** button.

4. Click the **Back** button to return to the Federal Information Center Web page.

Clicking a Link

Most Web pages contain links to other Web pages, files, and online services. A link may be a word, phrase, or sentence or a graphic such as an icon or a map. Text links are easy to spot because they are usually a different color and underlined. Graphic links don't have any special visual clues, so they are more difficult to identify. You can identify any link on a page by moving the mouse pointer around the page. When the mouse pointer is placed over a link, it changes to an icon of a pointing finger, and the URL of the link will display in the status bar.

When you click a link, the browser sends a signal to that Web site to access and load the Web page you have chosen. The rate at which a page loads is dependent on the speed of your connection and the complexity of the page. If you don't want to wait for a page to display, you can click another link on the displayed page. When you click a second link, Internet Explorer stops downloading the first page and begins downloading the new page.

EXERCISE 38.6

You must have the Federal Information Center Web page displayed in order to complete this exercise.

1. Move the pointer over the first link, **About FIC**, on the Federal Information Center page. Notice the URL is displayed in the status bar at the bottom of the window.

2. Click the link. The new page may take a minute or two to appear. Watch the status bar to monitor the jump.

3. Click the link, **FIC FAQs**, near the top of the page.

4. Scroll to the bottom of the page,

 INTERNET If you try to access a link and a long time passes without anything happening, click the Stop button to cancel the jump to the link.

and then point (*don't* click) on each of the graphics. Notice that the pointer changes to a hand with a finger indicating these are links.

5. Click a graphic link of your choice in the bottom portion of the page.

6. After the page finishes loading, click the **Back** button.

7. Continue clicking the **Back** button until the Federal Information Center home page is displayed.

Using the Quick Links Buttons

The buttons on the Links toolbar provide a one-click connection to specific Web pages. These buttons are called quick links because the buttons are always available when the Links toolbar is displayed and they are a direct link to a specific Web site. When Internet Explorer is first installed, the quick links buttons are set to Microsoft Web sites, but they can be deleted and new quick links sites can be added.

To add a quick link, drag the icon for the page from the Address bar text box to a desired location on the Links toolbar. You can rearrange your quick links buttons by dragging them to a different location on the Links toolbar. You can also delete a quick link by right-clicking the button, then selecting Delete from the shortcut menu.

E X E R C I S E ⟼ 38.7

1. Point to the far left quick link button on the **Links** toolbar. After a few seconds of pointing to the button, a window displays showing the URL of the link.

2. Click the quick link button to which you were pointing. The Web site identified in step one above is accessed and the page is loaded and displayed in the Internet Explorer window.

3. Double-click in the Address text box, and then key the URL for the Disney Web page exactly as shown: **http://www.disney.com**. Then press **Enter**.

4. Monitor the loading of the page. When the page is fully loaded, drag the icon at the far left of the Address text box over the word *Links* on the **Links** toolbar. A quick link button is created for the site and placed on the Links toolbar.

5. Right-click on the **Disney** quick link button, then click the **Delete** option from the shortcut menu.

6. Click the **Yes** button if a Confirm File Delete window displays.

Printing a Web Page

Internet Explorer permits you to print the text and the graphic portion of a Web page. To print a page, click the Print button on the toolbar, or choose Print from the File menu.

1. The Disney Web page should still be on your screen. Verify that your printer is on and you have access to it.

2. Select **Print** on the **File** menu. In the Print dialog box, click **OK**. Leave the Disney Web page on the screen for the next exercise.

Using the History Tools

Internet Explorer keeps track of the Web pages you've visited by placing them on a history list. When you click the down arrow in the Address bar text box, a list of the pages you've recently visited will display as shown in Figure 38-10. It is faster to use this feature to return to a previous page than using the Back button, because you don't have to pause at every intermediate page.

FIGURE 38-10
History list on Address Bar

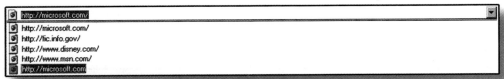

Because a history list is limited in the number of sites it can hold, you can use the History button on the Standard toolbar if you wish to return to a site you've visited in a previous online session. When you click the History button, a list like that shown in Figure 38-11 appears in the left pane of the Internet

FIGURE 38-11
History list displayed when you click the History button

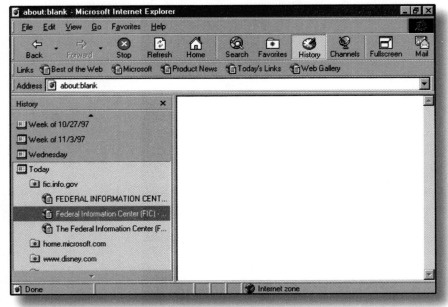

Explorer window. Sites you've visited are placed in folders and sorted by week; the current week is shown by day. When you click on the day or week, the display expands to show folder icons. Each folder is a different site (such as **home.microsoft.com**) that you've visited. When you click on the site folder, each page you visited on that site is displayed.

EXERCISE ➡ 38.9

1. Click on the down arrow on the Address bar text box to display the History list of pages you've visited.

2. Click on the **Disney** Web page URL, **http://www.disney.com/**.

3. Click on the first link on the Disney Web page.

4. Wait for the page to load, and then click on the down arrow on the Address text box to display the History list.

5. Click on the Federal Information Center Web page URL, **http://fic.info.gov/**.

6. Click the **Home** button.

7. Click on the **History** button on the Standard toolbar. The History pane opens on the left side of the screen. The history of sites visited during the current week is shown by day.

8. If necessary, click on the **Today** folder icon to display the sites you've visited today. Click on the first site folder to display the pages at that site that you've visited. Click the first page listed in the site folder.

9. Wait for the page to load, and then click the **Home** button. Click the **History** button to hide the history pane.

10. Close **Internet Explorer** by clicking its **Close** button.

11. If instructed, shut down Windows and your computer.

Summary

This lesson introduced you to Windows' Internet Explorer program. You learned that:

■ The World Wide Web utilizes hypertext documents called Web pages. A hypertext document contains links that are pointers to other hypertext documents and to the computer on which the document is stored.

■ The Web gets its name from the fact that its structure resembles a spider web.

- You must use a Web browser such as Windows 98 Internet Explorer to access and display the contents of a Web page.

- The Internet Explorer window has many of the same elements that are common to all windows. When Internet Explorer is first opened, the Address bar and Links toolbar appear side by side beneath the Standard toolbar. You can expand the Links toolbar by double-clicking the Links "button." Each of the toolbars can be displayed on its own line, one beneath the other. The window also has an activity indicator that is animated when Internet data is being sent and received.

- Every Web page has a unique Web address called an URL. The URL consists of a protocol and a domain name. A colon and two forward slashes follow the protocol; the domain name always contains at least one period. Occasionally a URL also includes a file name or folder name.

- Web pages visited are saved in the disk cache once they are displayed. The disk cache is cleared each time you shut down your computer and a new disk cache is created each time you start Internet Explorer. The Forward and Back buttons on the Standard toolbar permit you to move forward and backward through the disk cache. The Stop button aborts the loading of the current page, and the Home button loads the start or home page.

- Both the text and graphic elements of a Web page can be printed by clicking the Print button on the toolbar or by selecting Print on the File menu.

- Most Web pages contain a word, phrase, sentence, or graphic link to other Web pages. Text links are generally a different color and underlined. The pointer will change to an icon of a pointing finger when placed over a graphic or text link. Quick links buttons are a direct link to a specific Web site. Quick links can be added, deleted, and rearranged on the Links toolbar.

- Internet Explorer maintains a record of the most recently viewed Web pages on a history list. Clicking the History button on the Standard toolbar displays a list of all viewed pages for multiple online sessions.

LESSON 38 REVIEW QUESTIONS

TRUE/FALSE

Each of the following statements is either true or false. Indicate your answer on the left by circling T if the statement is true and F if the statement is false.

T F 1. The World Wide Web is just another name for the Internet.

T F 2. An active connection to the Internet means that your computer is communicating with the Internet through a network connection or a modem.

T F 3. The only way to jump from one Web page to another Web page is to click on a link on the currently displayed page.

T F   4. The start page is the first page you see each time you start Internet Explorer.

T F   5. The Internet Explorer maintains the addresses of only the last three sites you visited on its history list.

FILL IN THE BLANKS

Complete the following sentences by writing the correct word or words in the blanks provided.

1. Each Web page has a unique Web address known as a(n) _____.

2. The _____ is a network of computers that provide electronic links to information on almost every topic that you can imagine.

3. A(n) _____ is a program that lets you access and display the contents of a Web page.

4. The _____ is the first page you see each time you launch Internet Explorer.

5. Internet Explorer keeps track of the pages you've visited on a(n) _____.

LESSON 38 PROJECT

This project gives you the opportunity to review the concepts in this lesson and practice the techniques in the exercises.

1. Start **Internet Explorer**.

2. If necessary, display the **Links** toolbar.

3. Click the **Product News** quick link.

4. Click the first link on the Web page. Print the page.

5. Click the **Web Gallery** quick link on the Links toolbar.

6. Click the first link on the Web page. Print the page.

7. Click the **Back** button.

8. Click the **Forward** button.

9. Click the **Home** button.

10. Close **Internet Explorer**. If instructed, shut down Windows and your computer.

WORKING WITH FAVORITE WEB PAGES

OBJECTIVES

Upon completion of this lesson, you will be able to:

■ Change Internet Explorer's start page.

■ Create and maintain a Favorites menu list.

■ Create and maintain a Favorites folder.

⏱ Estimated Time: 1 hour

Now that you understand how to browse the Web, you can search for specific Web pages and save them for future use. In this lesson, you learn how to save and manage Web pages on your computer.

Changing the Start Page

Each time you launch Internet Explorer, the same page is loaded in the display window. As you know, Internet Explorer refers to this page as the start, or home, page. You can change the home page to any Web page or a blank page to suit your tastes or needs. The page you choose can be located on your computer's hard drive or at a site somewhere on the Web.

To change the start page, start Internet Explorer and display the page you want to use as your new start page. Then, select Internet Options from the View menu. The Internet Options dialog box appears, as shown in Figure 39-1. Select the General tab and then click the Use Current button in the Home page section.

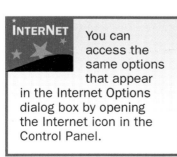

INTERNET You can access the same options that appear in the Internet Options dialog box by opening the Internet icon in the Control Panel.

FIGURE 39-1
Internet Options dialog box

1. Start **Internet Explorer** and access the **Federal Information Center** Web page by keying its URL (**http://fic.info.gov/**) in the Address text box. Press **Enter**.

2. Once the page is displayed, select **Internet Options** from the **View** menu.

3. Click the **General** tab, if necessary. Notice that the URL for Internet Explorer's current home page is shown in the Address text box in the Home page section of the dialog box.

4. Click the **Use Current** button in the Home page section to set the start page to the Federal Information Center Web page.

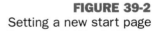

TIP

You can also key a URL in the Address text box in the Home page section to set the start page.

5. Click the **OK** button.

6. Close **Internet Explorer** by clicking its **Close** button. Restart Internet Explorer by double-clicking its icon on the desktop. The Federal Information Center Web page should display as your new start page.

7. You can also set a blank page as your home page. Select **Internet Options** from the **View** menu.

8. Click the **Use Blank** button in the **Home page** section to set the start page to a blank page. The address **about.blank** will display in the Address text box.

9. Click the **OK** button.

10. Click the **Home** button to display the start page. Your display area should be blank, as shown in Figure 39-2.

FIGURE 39-2
Setting a new start page

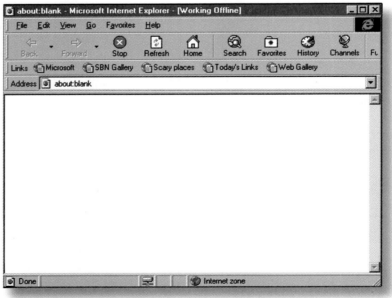

Creating a Favorites List

As you navigate the Web, you will locate some interesting sites that you will want to visit again and again. Internet Explorer calls these sites *favorites* and allows you to save the sites to a favorites list. Other browsers might call these lists "bookmarks." As you can see in Figure 39-3, the Favorites list is like an electronic address book with Web page names.

Adding a Web Page to the Favorites List

Internet Explorer allows you to add any Web page to the Favorites list. To add a page to the Favorites list, go to the Web page and then select the Add to Favorites option from the Favorites menu (see Figure 39-4). The next time you display the Favorites menu, the new item will be listed on the bottom portion of the menu.

As shown in Figure 39-4, the Favorites list may contain folders as well as favorite sites. Later in this lesson you will learn how you can organize your favorites by creating folders and placing your favorites into the folders.

FIGURE 39-3
Favorites list

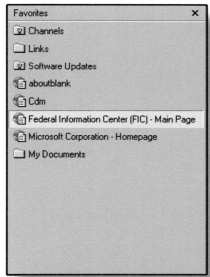

FIGURE 39-4
Favorites menu

EXERCISE 39.2

1. Click once in Internet Explorer's **Address** text box to highlight the current entry.

2. Key the URL, **http://www.cocacola.com/museum/**, and press **Enter**.

3. Wait until the page has completed loading.

4. Select the **Add to Favorites** option from the **Favorites** menu. The Add Favorite dialog box displays as shown in Figure 39-5. The Name text

(continued on next page)

box at the bottom of the dialog box contains a title for the page rather than the URL you keyed. Since items on the Favorites list are listed by title, you can accept this title or key something different if you would like to give the item a more descriptive title.

Before you add the Web page to your Favorites list, you're offered the opportunity to subscribe to the site. *Subscribing* means Internet Explorer will surf the Web checking for any recent changes to the page and will either download the actual content from the site or just tell you that something has changed. You either accept the default to indicate you do not wish to subscribe to the page or select one of the other choices. The Create in button allows you to select a particular folder in which to store the favorite. You will learn more about the folders option later in this lesson.

TIP

You can also add a favorite to the Favorites list by right-clicking on the Web page and choosing Add to Favorites from the shortcut menu that displays.

5. Make sure the option to add the page to your favorites is selected. Then highlight the text in the **Name** text box, key **Exercise 39.2 Favorite**, and click **OK**.

6. Click once in Internet Explorer's Address text box to highlight the current entry.

7. Key the URL **http://www.jellybelly.com/**, and then press **Enter**.

8. Wait until the page has completed loading. Right-click on the page, and then select the **Add to Favorites** option from the shortcut menu.

9. In the **Add Favorite** dialog box, click an insertion point at the far right of the name in the **Name** text box. Use the **Backspace** key to edit the name so that it reads **Jelly Belly Online**, and then click **OK**. Remain in this screen for the next exercise.

FIGURE 39-5
Add Favorite dialog box

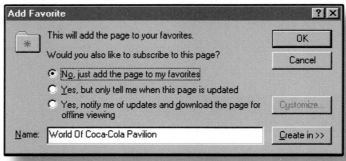

Displaying a Web Page

To display a page on the Favorites list, open the Favorites menu and select the page from the list at the bottom of the menu. Or click the Favorites button on the Standard toolbar. The Favorites list displays in the left panel of the Explorer window, as shown in Figure 39-6.

FIGURE 39-6
Clicking the Favorites button to display the Favorites list

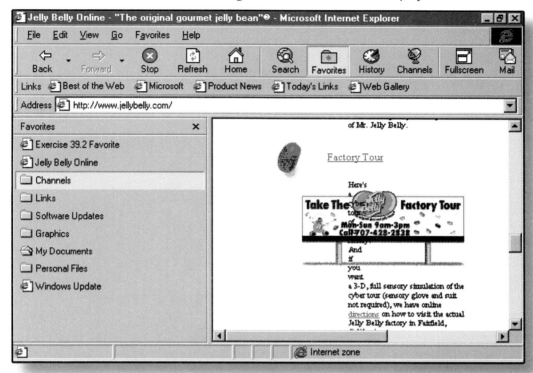

EXERCISE 39.3

1. Click the **Favorites** button on the **Standard** toolbar.

2. Click the **Exercise 39.2 Favorite** item on the **Favorites** list.

3. After the page loads, click the **Jelly Belly Online** item on the list. Remain in this screen for the next exercise.

Editing the Favorites List

Because the Web is constantly changing, your favorites may also change. For instance, you may find an item is no longer of value and you would like to delete it from your Favorites list. Or perhaps you've accepted a default page name and it's difficult to remember, so you want to rename it. The Organize Favorites option on the Favorites menu permits you to make these changes and edit your favorites list.

Deleting a Favorite from the Favorites List

To remove a favorite from the Favorites list, select the Organize Favorites option from the Favorites menu. An Organize Favorites dialog box displays, as shown in Figure 39-7. Once you select the favorite you wish to delete, the buttons for moving, renaming, and deleting favorites will become active. When you click the Delete button, the Confirm File Delete dialog box displays asking you to confirm the deletion.

FIGURE 39-7
Organize Favorites dialog box

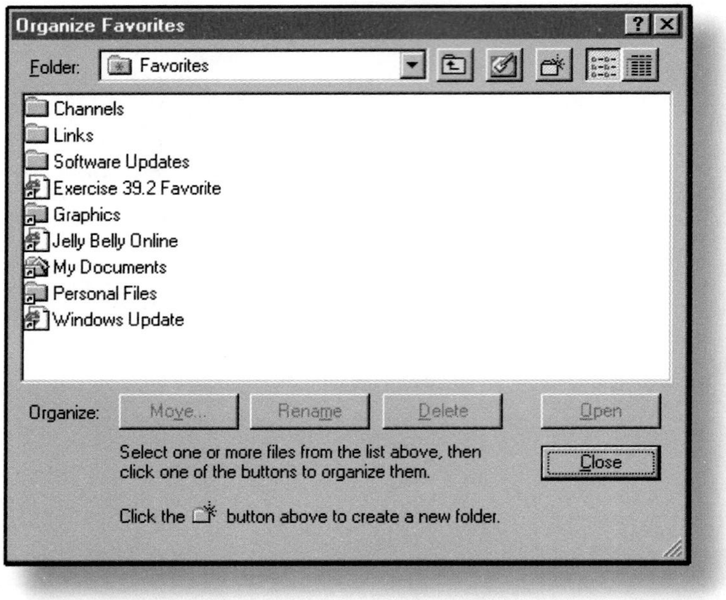

EXERCISE 39.4

1. Select the **Organize Favorites** option from the **Favorites** menu.

2. Click the **Exercise 39.2 Favorite** on the list, and then click the **Delete** button.

3. Click the **Yes** button on the **Confirm File Delete** dialog box.

4. Verify that **Exercise 39.2 Favorite** has been deleted from the Favorites list. You may have to move the Organize Favorites dialog box to see the list.

5. In the **Organize Favorites** dialog box, click the **Jelly Belly Online** page. Click the **Rename** button. Notice the item's title is highlighted

and ready for you to key a new name or modify the existing name.

6. Key the new name, **Jelly Belly Co. Home Page**, and then click **Close**.

7. Verify that the name has been changed on the Favorites list.

8. Click the **Close** button on the Favorites window to close it.

Working with Favorites Folders

After saving a number of favorites, you will probably want to group them or organize them into a logical sequence. You can organize your favorites by placing them in folders. For example, you might create folders and sort your favorites by topic or in alphabetical order such as A-E, F-K, and so on.

You create a new folder by opening the Organize Favorites dialog box (see Figure 39-7). Click the Create New Folder button at the top of the dialog box. The new folder will be placed at the bottom of the favorites listing, as shown in Figure 39-8. Key a name for the folder and press Enter. Then you can drag Web pages listed in the dialog box into the new folder. The next time you open the Favorites list, the new folder appears in the list.

FIGURE 39-8
Creating a new folder for favorite Web pages

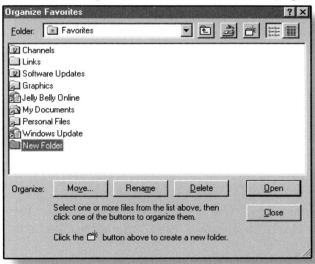

EXERCISE 39.5

1. Select the **Organize Favorites** option from the **Favorites** menu.

2. Click the **Create New Folder** button on the toolbar. A new folder appears at the bottom of the list with the name, **New Folder**, highlighted.

3. Key the folder name, **Lesson 39 Favorites**, and then press **Enter**.

4. Select the **Jelly Belly Co. Home Page** and drag it into the **Lesson 39 Favorites** folder.

(continued on next page)

5. Click **Close**.

6. Click the **Favorites** menu to display the Favorites list. Notice the new folder is now displayed on the list. The right-pointing arrow next to the folder indicates that a submenu will

open to display the Web pages contained in the folder, as shown in Figure 39-9.

7. Press **Esc** twice to close the menu. Remain in this screen for the next exercise.

FIGURE 39-9
Folder on the Favorites list

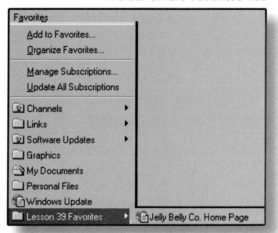

NOTE:

You can nest folders. For example, you might have a folder named **Vendors** that contains subfolders named **Monitors**, **Printers**, and **Computers**. You could then save Web pages to the appropriate folder.

Changing the View

You probably noticed that the Organize Favorites dialog box contains buttons on its toolbar that let you change the view of the display window from List to Detail. The Large Icons and Small Icons view options are also available. To select one of those views, right-click on an empty space in the dialog box. Select View on the shortcut menu to display a submenu listing the four view options.

EXERCISE 39.6

1. Select **Organize Favorites** from the **Favorites** menu.

2. Right-click on an empty space in the display area of the dialog box.

3. Click **View**, and then select **Large Icons** from the submenu. The Favorites list will display in a large icon format similar to the one shown in Figure 39-10.

4. Double-click on the **Lesson 39 Favorites** folder icon to display the favorites in this folder.

5. Click the **Up One Level** button on the toolbar to display the Favorites folder listing.

6. Right-click on the **Lesson 39 Favorites** folder, and then select the **Delete** option from the shortcut menu.

7. Click **Yes** in the Confirm Folder Delete dialog box.

8. Click **Close** to close the Organize Favorites dialog box.

9. Close **Internet Explorer**. If instructed, shut down Windows and your computer.

FIGURE 39-10
Changing the view in the Organize Favorites dialog box

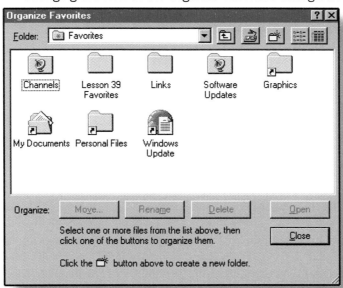

Summary

This lesson covered how to organize your favorite Web pages so that you have quick and easy access to them. You learned that:

- Each time you launch Internet Explorer, the start or home page appears. You can change the start page to any Web page or to a blank page. You use the Internet Options dialog box which is accessed from the View menu to do this.

- Web pages and sites you wish to visit frequently are called favorites. Your favorites can be saved on a Favorites list. There are two ways to view the Favorites list; by displaying the Favorites menu or by clicking the Favorites button on the Standard toolbar to display the list in the left panel of the Explorer window. The Favorites panel remains displayed until you close it.

- You use the Add Favorites option on the Favorites menu to add items to your Favorites list.

- Your Favorites list can be modified in several ways. You can rename or delete items from the list. You can also organize your favorites into folders and subfolders. To do this you use the options in the Organize Favorites dialog box, which is accessed from the Favorites menu.

- You can change the view of the Organize Favorites display window by clicking one of the two display buttons on the toolbar or by right-clicking on an empty space in the dialog box and selecting the View option from the shortcut menu.

LESSON 39 REVIEW QUESTIONS

TRUE/FALSE

Each of the following statements is either true or false. Indicate your answer on the left by circling T if the statement is true and F if the statement is false.

T F 1. Any page but a blank page may be used as Internet Explorer's start page.

T F 2. Internet Explorer favorites are Web pages that have widespread popular appeal.

T F 3. You can organize your favorites in folders.

T F 4. A favorites folder cannot contain subfolders, only your favorite Web pages.

T F 5. The Favorites menu displays only the names of favorite Web pages, not favorite folders you create.

MULTIPLE CHOICE

Complete the following questions by circling the correct multiple choice letter.

1. The start page is
   A. loaded each time you launch Internet Explorer
   B. changed in the Organize Favorites dialog box
   C. also called the favorite page
   D. all of the above

2. Internet Explorer's Favorites list
   A. is similar to an electronic address book
   B. is the same as bookmarks in other browsers
   C. can contain folders that store your favorite Web pages
   D. all of the above

3. Internet Explorer's Favorites folders
   A. do not appear on the Favorites menu
   B. cannot contain subfolders
   C. may be displayed in different views in the Organize Favorites dialog box
   D. cannot be renamed

4. To change the home page that displays when you start Internet Explorer, you
   A. select Internet Options on the View menu and make changes on the General tab of the Internet Options dialog box
   B. select New on the File menu and key the URL of the Web page you want to display as the home page
   C. click the Home button on the toolbar and key the URL of the new home page in the Address text box
   D. you cannot change the home page

5. If you subscribe to a Web page, it means that
   A. you must visit the Web site on a regular basis to read about updates
   B. updates to the page's content are automatically sent to your computer
   C. you receive a hard copy of updates to the page in the mail on a regular basis
   D. you cannot delete the page from your Favorites list

LESSON 39 PROJECT

This project gives you the opportunity to review the concepts in this lesson and practice the techniques in the exercises.

1. Start **Internet Explorer**.

2. Make sure the Links toolbar is displayed. Click the **Web Gallery** quick link.

3. Make this page the new Internet Explorer home page.

4. Click the **What's New** link on the new home page.

5. Save the page that displays to the Favorites list. In the **Add Favorite** dialog box, verify that you do *not* want to subscribe to the page. Change the name of the page to **Project 39 Favorite**.

6. Open the **Organize Favorites** dialog box and create a new folder. Name the folder **[your name] Favorites**.

7. Move the **Project 39 Favorite** into your new folder. Then close the **Organize Favorites** dialog box.

8. Click the **Home** button on the toolbar.

9. On the **Favorites** menu, click your new folder and then select the **Project 39 Favorite** page.

10. Open the **Organize Favorites** dialog box and delete your new folder.

11. Change the home page back to the blank page.

12. Close **Internet Explorer**. If instructed, shut down Windows and your computer.

SENDING AND RECEIVING ELECTRONIC MAIL

LESSON

40

OBJECTIVES

Upon completion of this lesson, you will be able to:

- Create, send, and reply to e-mail messages.

- Attach a file to an e-mail message.

- Read and print e-mail messages.

- Manage and use an Address Book.

⏱ **Estimated Time: 1.75 hours**

*E*lectronic mail, or *e-mail* as it is more commonly called, is the exchange of messages between computers. E-mail differs from other Internet applications in that the sending and receiving computers do not have to be connected directly with each other to make it work. In this lesson, you will learn how to use Windows' Outlook Express to send and receive e-mail.

Understanding E-Mail

E-mail is a client/server system. That is, you need an e-mail program (the client) on your computer and you need an e-mail post office program running on a host computer (the server). The client program communicates with the server program over the Internet to send and receive mail.

E-mail client programs differ in their use and in the way they handle messages, but they all include a mechanism that gives them the following capabilities:

- Creating and sending messages to a post office server.

- Receiving messages from a post office server.

- Displaying messages.

- Storing copies of messages that have been sent and received.

E-mail is no longer a technology of the future; it is in fact, the single most common Internet application. Internet Explorer comes with its own mail client program called Outlook Express.

Starting Outlook Express

Y ou can start Outlook Express from Internet Explorer: Click the Mail button on the toolbar and select the Read Mail option (see Figure 40-1).

FIGURE 40-1
Starting Outlook Express

The Outlook Express window is shown in Figure 40-2. You will notice that it is similar to the Explorer window. It contains a menu bar, a toolbar, and a status bar. Unlike Explorer, it has a three-paned display window. The two panes on the right side work together. The upper pane is where a list of messages in a selected folder is contained. The lower pane is where the message selected in the message list is displayed. On the left side are the folders into which you can file your mail. Five mail folders are automatically created when Outlook Express is installed:

- The Inbox contains e-mail messages you have received.

- The Outbox acts as a temporary storage area for messages waiting to be sent.

- The Sent Items folder keeps a copy of the messages that have already been sent.

- The Deleted Items folder keeps a copy of the items you have deleted.

- The Drafts folder is where messages in the process of being completed are kept.

FIGURE 40-2
Outlook Express opening window

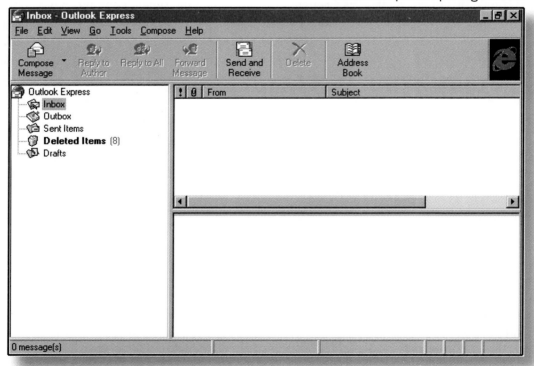

E X E R C I S E 40.1

1. Start **Internet Explorer.**

2. Click the **Mail** button on the Standard toolbar.

3. Select the **Read Mail** option on the **Mail** menu.

4. If a message box similar to the one shown in Figure 40-3 displays, choose **Don't dial a connection** from the drop-down list box, and then click the **OK** button.

FIGURE 40-3
Connection message box

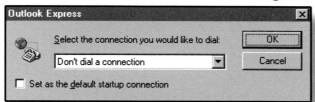

Creating a Mail Account Profile

Outlook Express must be customized in order for you to connect properly with your e-mail server and to access your e-mail mailbox. Choosing Accounts on the Tools menu opens the Internet Accounts dialog box (Figure 40-4), which lets you provide your personal e-mail account profile to Outlook Express. Click the Add button and then choose the Mail option. The Internet Connection Wizard starts, as shown in Figure 40-5. This wizard guides you through the creation of your mail account profile.

■ In the first dialog box, key your name (or the name you want to appear in the From field in your outgoing messages), and then click Next.

■ The next dialog box instructs you to key your e-mail address (this address is assigned by your e-mail administrator); then click Next.

■ Enter the name of your Incoming and Outgoing post office mail server (these are domain names that are assigned by your e-mail administrator), and then click Next.

■ Enter your logon e-mail account name and password (these are assigned by your e-mail administrator), and then click Next.

■ Enter a name of your choice (this will become the Account name in the Internet Accounts Dialog box); then click Next.

■ Choose one of the three connection types to indicate whether you want to connect using a phone line, a local area network (LAN), or a manual connection. Then click Next.

■ If you choose to connect using a phone line, you must create a new dial-up connection or select one of the existing dial-up connections. Then click Next.

■ In the final dialog box, the wizard congratulates you for successfully entering all of the required information. To save the setting, click Finish.

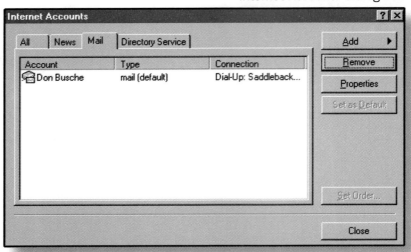

FIGURE 40-4
Internet Accounts dialog box

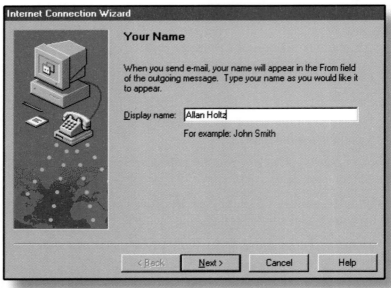

FIGURE 40-5
Internet Connection Wizard dialog box

EXERCISE 40.2

You will need to complete this exercise only if you have your own e-mail account or if your instructor has assigned you an e-mail account. You will need the following information before you begin: your complete e-mail address (for example, *myname@myserver.com*);

the name of your incoming mail server (for example, *mail.school.edu*); the name of your outgoing mail server (may be the same as your incoming mail server); your e-mail log on name and password (for example, *dsmith*; your password will be assigned by your e-mail administrator); and the type of connection (for example, dial-up or direct connection).

1. Choose the **Accounts** option on the **Tools** menu.

2. Click the **Add** button, and then choose **Mail**.

3. Key your first and last name, and then click **Next**.

4. Key your Internet e-mail address; then click **Next**.

5. Complete the E-mail Server window:
   a. Key the incoming mail server address, and then press **Tab**.
   b. Key the outgoing mail server address, and then click **Next**.

6. Complete the Internet Mail Logon window:
   a. Key your e-mail account name; then press **Tab**.
   b. Key your e-mail password; then click Next.

7. Key your Internet mail account name, and then click **Next**.

8. Choose the appropriate connection type from the list; then click **Next**.

9. If the Dial-up Connection window displays, choose an existing connection type from the list; then click **Next**.

10. Click **Finish**. Remain in this screen for the next exercise.

Creating and Sending Mail

Messages may be created and sent to any Internet mail user, but you must know the recipient's e-mail address. An individual's e-mail address, like your e-mail address, consists of an account name followed by the @ symbol, followed by the Internet address (domain name) of the computer where the account is located.

Creating an electronic mail message is very easy with Outlook Express. First, click the Compose Message button on the toolbar (or select the New Message option from the Compose menu) to display the New Message window, as shown in Figure 40-6. The window contains a fill-in form that provides space for a header and a message.

When filling in the header:

■ Use the *To:* field to identify the individual or individuals for whom the message is intended. Key the e-mail address or use the Address Book feature (explained later in this lesson) to insert the name in this field. If you are keying more than one e-mail address, separate the addresses with a comma.

■ Use the *Cc:* field to send a copy of the message to another individual. Key the individual's e-mail address or choose the address from the Address Book.

■ Use the *Bcc:* field to send a blind carbon copy to another individual. Sending a blind carbon copy means that the recipient does not know a copy is being sent to another individual. Key the individual's name or choose the name from the Address Book.

■ Use the *Subject:* line to describe the content of the message. Keep your subject line short. What you key here is displayed in the message list window; therefore, it is important for the text to be short and descriptive.

FIGURE 40-6
New Message window

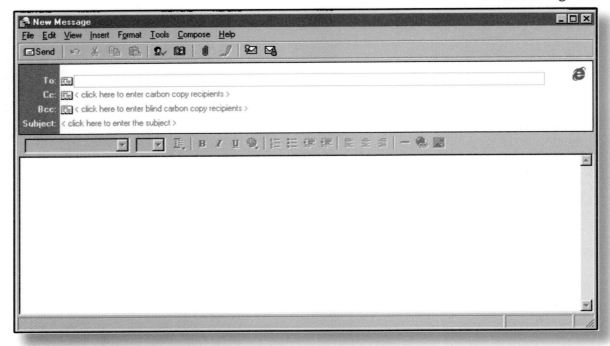

The message area at the bottom of the window is where you key your message. You are free to use the Format menu options to change the text's font and paragraph attributes. The Format menu options are similar to the ones used in many Windows applications. You can also display (if necessary) and use an optional Format toolbar (accessed from the View menu) to format your message.

EXERCISE ▭▷ 40.3

In this exercise, you will create and send an e-mail message to yourself; therefore, before you begin this lesson you must have an e-mail account and know your e-mail address.

1. Click the **Compose Message** button on the toolbar.

2. Complete the message header:
   a. Key your e-mail address in the **To:** field. It should look something like this: *my-name@myhost.com*

   b. Press **Tab** to move to the Cc: field.
   c. Press **Tab** again to leave the Cc: field blank.
   d. Press **Tab** to leave the Bcc: field blank.
   e. Key **E-mail from [Your Name]** on the Subject line, and then press **Tab**.

3. Key the following message in the message area:

   This is my attempt at sending an e-mail message using Windows 98 Outlook Express.

4. Click the **Send** button on the toolbar (or choose **Send Message** from the **File** menu) to send the message. If you have a direct connection to the Internet, the message will be sent. If you have a dial-up connection to the Internet, your post office server will be dialed, you will be logged on to the host computer, and your message will be sent.

5. Leave the Outlook Express window open for the next exercise.

Reading and Deleting Mail

When the Inbox folder is selected in the left pane, its contents are displayed in the message list pane in the upper right of the window. New messages that you *have not* yet read are shown in bold and are preceded by a closed envelope icon, while messages that you have read are shown in regular type and are preceded with an open envelope icon. The author, subject, and date and time received are displayed for each message.

Several icons may appear to the left of the author's name. Three of these are described below.

- A red exclamation mark icon indicates a high-priority message, while a down arrow indicates a low-priority message. If the priority is normal, no icon will appear in this space.

- A paper clip indicates that a file is attached to the message.

- An open envelope signifies the message has been read, while a closed envelope signifies the message has not been read.

You can read or delete any message in the listing. To read a message, click the message. The message displays in the preview pane, as shown in Figure 40-7. Notice the preview pane has a scroll bar so you can view a long document.

FIGURE 40-7
A typical message displayed in the preview pane

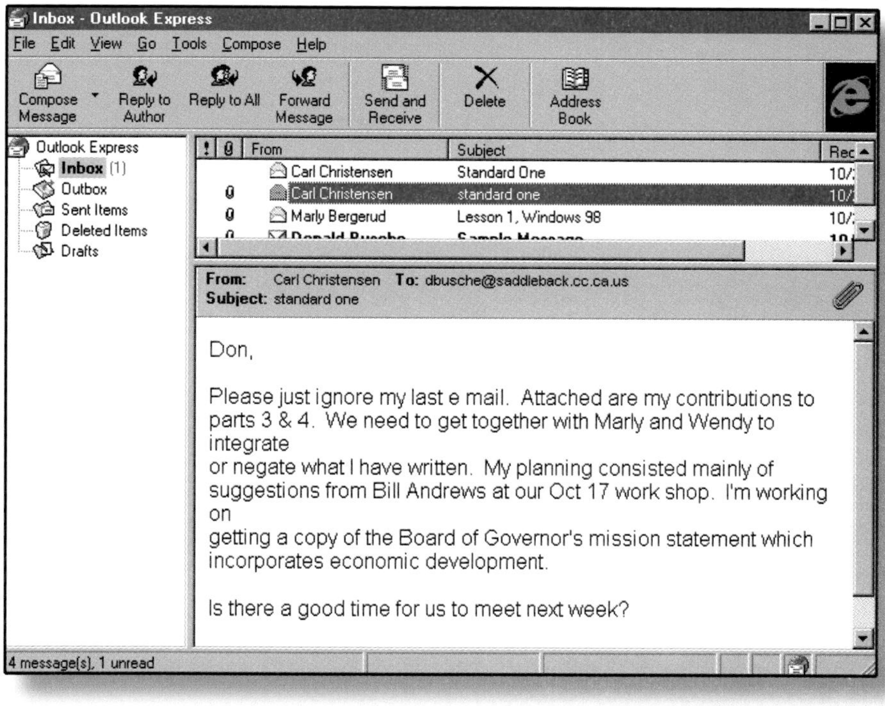

481

Outlook Express gives you a choice of actions after you have read a message. You can reply to the author of the message, forward the message to someone else, save the message to a different folder, or delete the message. We'll discuss the first three options later in this lesson. To delete a message, select it and then click the Delete button on the toolbar; or right-click the message, and then choose the Delete option.

EXERCISE ⇨ 40.4

1. Click the **Send and Receive** button on the Outlook Express toolbar. If you have a direct connection to the Internet, any messages for you will be placed in your Inbox. If you have a dial-up connection to the Internet, your post office server will be dialed, you will be logged on to the host computer, and your messages will be placed in your Inbox.

2. Click the **Inbox** in the Folders window, if it is not already selected.

3. Click the e-mail message you sent yourself in Exercise 40.3. The message should have the subject *E-mail from [Your Name]*.

4. Read the message, and then click the **Delete** button on the toolbar.

5. Leave the Outlook Express window open for the next exercise.

Using Address Book

The *Address Book* feature of Outlook Express helps simplify addressing e-mail messages. The Address Book is a database of e-mail addresses. When you want to send a message to a person in your Address Book, you simply select the address to fill in the header section of the message.

To display an address book, choose Address Book on the Tools menu, or click the Address Book button on the toolbar. The Address Book window displays, as shown in Figure 40-8.

Adding a New Address Book Entry

To add an entry to the Address Book, click the New Contact button on the toolbar or choose New Contact from the File menu. Outlook Express displays the Properties dialog box, as shown in Figure 40-9. On the Personal tab, you enter the name and e-mail address, as well as

FIGURE 40-8
Address Book window

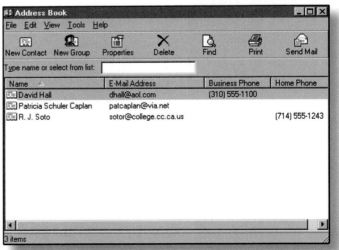

other pertinent information, for the new Address Book entry. You can enter additional information on the individuals or businesses in your Address Book on the other tabs in the Properties dialog box. Once you've entered the appropriate information, click the OK button to close the dialog box.

FIGURE 40-9
Adding an entry to the Address Book

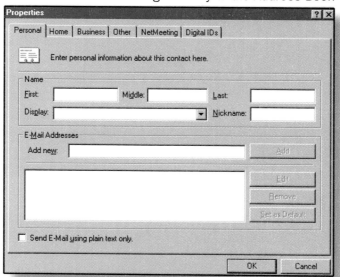

EXERCISE 40.5

1. Click the **Address Book** button on the toolbar.

2. Click the **New Contact** button on the Address Book toolbar.

3. Select the **Personal** tab, if necessary, and enter the following information:
   a. Key your first name in the First text box; then press **Tab**.
   b. Key your middle name in the Middle text box; then press **Tab** (or if you wish, just press **Tab** to skip this field).
   c. Key your last name in the Last text box; then press **Tab**.
   d. Press **Tab** again to skip the Nickname field and move to the Add new text box in the E-Mail Addresses section of the

dialog box. Key your complete e-mail address.
   e. Click the **Add** button to the right of the Add new text box.
   f. Click the **OK** button to close the Properties dialog box.

4. Close the **Address Book**.

5. Click the **Compose Message** button on the toolbar.

6. With the New Message window open, click the file card icon in the **To:** field. The Select Recipients dialog box opens, as shown in Figure 40-10.

(continued on next page)

7. Select your name from the list box and click the **To: ->** button to move the name to the To box.

8. Click the **OK** button to close the dialog box. When the dialog box closes, the selected name (your name in this exercise) appears in the To: field of the New Message dialog box.

9. Click in the **Subject** field and key **Sample Message Using Address Book**; then press **Tab**.

10. Key the following message in the message area:

```
The address in the To: field was
inserted using Address Book.
Please let me know if this
message is received.
```

11. Click the **Send** button to send the message.

12. If the message is placed in your Outbox to be sent later, click the **Send and Receive** button on the toolbar to log on to your Internet host computer and send the message.

13. Remain in this screen for the next exercise.

FIGURE 40-10
Select Recipients dialog box

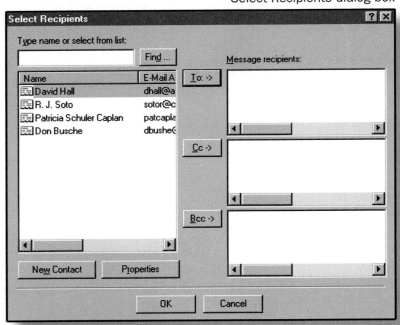

Printing Mail

To print a message, select the message and then choose Print from the File menu, or right-click on the selected message and choose Print.

EXERCISE ▷ 40.6

1. Click the **Send and Receive** button to check your mail and download any messages that you may have on the host computer.

2. Click the message that you sent to yourself in Exercise 40.5.

3. Print the message:
   a. Verify that you have access to your printer and your printer is turned on.

   b. Choose **Print** from the **File** menu.
   c. Verify the printer settings, and then click the **OK** button.

4. Notice that the printed message contains both the message header and the message. Leave the Outlook Express window open for the next exercise.

Replying to Mail

Often you will find that you need to respond to an e-mail message that you receive. You could create an entirely new message. However, the simplest and quickest way to respond to an e-mail message is to use Outlook Express's Reply to options.

You have the choice of replying just to the sender of the message, or replying to everyone listed in the header. You also have the option to include the original message in your reply or to delete it. The advantage of including the original message is that the originator of the message knows exactly what you are referring to in your reply. The disadvantage of including the original message is that the message is longer, so it takes up more computer resources.

To reply to a message, click the Reply to Author or the Reply to All button on the toolbar. These options also are available on the Compose menu. By default, the text of the original message is included at the end of your reply. The reply is separated from your message with a line and is indented. If you prefer not to include the original message, you can change the default in the Options dialog box.

EXERCISE ▷ 40.7

1. Click the **Send and Receive** button to check your mail and download any messages that you may have on the host computer.

2. Click the message that you sent to yourself in Exercise 40.5. Read the message, and then click the **Reply to Author** button on the toolbar.

3. Key the following reply:

   A short note to let you know
   that your message was received.

4. Click the **Send** button or choose the **Send Message** option on the **File** menu.

5. Click the **Send and Receive** button on the toolbar.

6. Notice that the subject line for the message is preceded by *Re:*, indicating that it is a reply. Select the message to read. Leave the Outlook Express window open for the next exercise.

Attaching a File to a Message

Sending a copy of a file along with your e-mail message is a way to transfer data from your computer to a recipient's computer. The file is called an *attachment*. In order to send and read attachments, your mail server must support a protocol called MIME (Multipurpose Internet Mail Extensions).

MIME is an Internet mail standard that allows e-mail messages to have Rich text (bold, italics, other fonts, colors, and so on), character sets other than English, images, and sounds.

Outlook Express makes it easy to attach a file to a new message. Files can be inserted in mail messages in two ways:

- **Text only**. The contents of the file display as unformatted ASCII text. Only text files can be inserted as text.

- **An attachment**. The file is maintained as a computer file. An icon that represents the type of file (text, sound and video clip, graphic, or program) is displayed in the document. Click the icon to access the file.

The processes used to insert and attach files are similar. First complete the header for the message in the New Message dialog box. Then choose File Attachment from the Insert menu, or click the Insert File icon on the New Message toolbar (see Figure 40-11). The Insert Attachment dialog box appears, as shown in Figure 40-12.

If you know the exact file name, key the name in the File name textbox, or browse the directory window and locate the file. Click OK, and Outlook Express will open a new window at the bottom of the message window for attached files. You can repeat the process to attach multiple files to your e-mail message. Figure 40-13 shows a New Message window with an attached file.

In the following exercise, you will compose an e-mail message, attach a file, send the message to one of your classmates, and send yourself a copy of the message.

FIGURE 40-11
Insert File icon on the toolbar

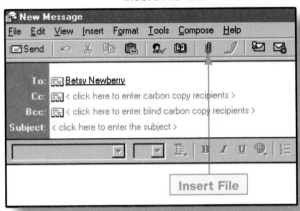

FIGURE 40-12
Insert Attachment dialog box

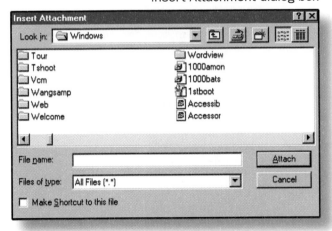

FIGURE 40-13
New Message window with an attached file

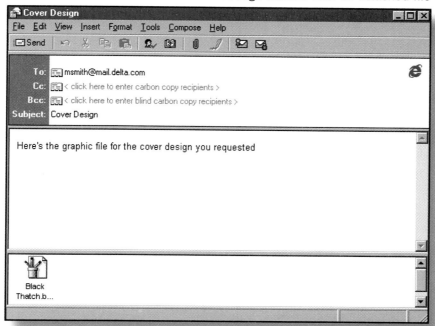

EXERCISE 40.8

You need your Windows Template disk and the e-mail address of a classmate to complete this exercise.

1. Place your Windows Template disk in the appropriate floppy drive.

2. In **Outlook Express**, click the **Compose Message** button on the toolbar.

3. Complete the message header:
   a. Key the e-mail address of the classmate to whom you wish to send the message and press **Tab**.
   b. Key your e-mail address in the Cc: field and press **Tab**.
   c. Key **Inserting a File** on the Subject line; then press **Tab**.

4. Attach the **Mail Document** file from your Windows Template disk as an attached file:
   a. Click the **Insert File** icon on the toolbar.
   b. Locate the **Mail Document** file on your Windows Template disk.
   c. Select the file.
   d. Click the **Attach** button. The file icon appears in the window beneath the message window.

5. Click the **Send** button.

Working with Attachments

When you receive a mail message with an attachment, you can view the attachment and save it to disk.

- **To view an attachment**: Display the message. Double-click the file attachment icon. If you have a program that is associated with the file, the file will open. If no program on your hard disk is associated with the attachment's file type, the file will not open. In this case, you will have to save the file to disk, and then obtain the necessary program and use it to open the attachment.

- **To save an attachment**: Select the message with the attachment in the message list. Choose Save Attachments on the File menu, and then select the attachment from the submenu. The Save Attachment As dialog box appears, as shown in Figure 40-14. Select a location for the file, and click Save.

FIGURE 40-14
Save Attachment As dialog box

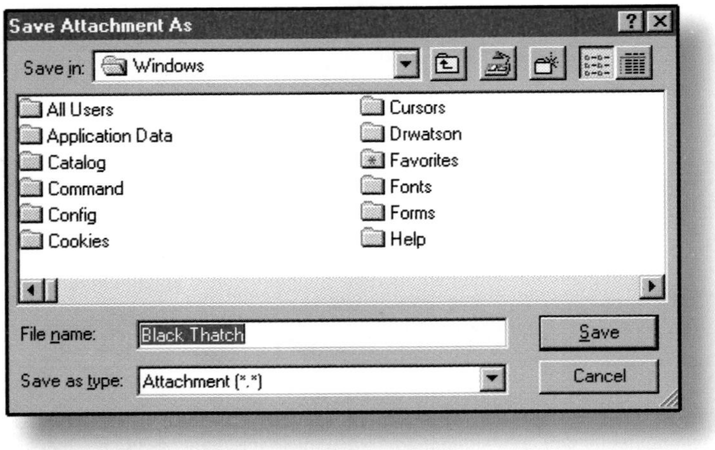

EXERCISE 40.9

You need your Windows Practice disk to complete this exercise.

1. Place your Windows Practice disk in the appropriate floppy drive.

2. In Outlook Express, click the **Send and Receive** button on the toolbar to review any mail in your mailbox.

3. Click the **Inbox** in the Folders window if it is not already selected.

4. Click the copy of the e-mail message you sent yourself in Exercise 40.8. The message should have an attachment.

5. Save the attachment as a file on your Windows Practice disk:
   a. Choose **Save Attachments** from the **File** menu.
   b. Click **Mail Document** on the submenu.
   c. Select the floppy drive in which you placed your Windows Practice disk from the Save in drop-down list box.
   d. Click the **Save** button.

6. In the Outlook Express window, delete all the messages addressed to you from the message list: Select each one and then press the **Delete** button on the toolbar.

7. Close **Outlook Express** and **Internet Explorer**. If instructed, shut down Windows and your computer.

Summary

This lesson covered Microsoft Outlook Express. You learned that:

■ The Internet Connection Wizard simplifies creating mail account profiles.

■ Outlook Express provides a client/server mail program to send, receive, and manage your electronic mail messages.

■ The Outlook Express window consists of three panes: a folder list in the left pane, a message list in the upper-right pane, and a preview window in the lower-right pane.

■ E-mail messages are placed in the Inbox folder. Unread messages are shown in bold. An exclamation mark indicates a high-priority message and a down arrow indicates a low priority message. A paper clip denotes an attached file.

■ The Outlook Express Address Book feature permits you to save and insert e-mail addresses in the header section of your e-mail messages.

■ E-mail messages contain a header with To, Cc, and Subject fields and a message area that contains the message. Application files, images, video clips, and sound clips can be attached to a mail message.

■ To view an attached file, display the message and double-click the attached file icon. You choose Save Attachments on the File menu to save the attached file on your system.

LESSON 40 REVIEW QUESTIONS

TRUE/FALSE

Each of the following statements is either true or false. Indicate your answer on the left by circling T if the statement is true and F if the statement is false.

T F 1. E-mail is considered the most common Internet application.

T F 2. E-mail messages may be created and sent to any Internet mail user.

T F 3. An attachment is the original message that is included in a replay to an e-mail message.

T F 4. A high-priority message is indicated in the message list window by a closed envelope icon.

T F 5. The easiest way to reply to an e-mail message is to compose a new message.

FILL IN THE BLANKS

Complete the following sentences by writing the correct word or words in the blanks provided.

1. In the Outlook Express message list, new messages that you have not read are shown in _____ type.

2. In the Outlook Express message list, messages that you have read are shown in _____ type.

3. Outlook Express simplifies addressing messages with a database feature called _____.

4. A reply is indented and separated from the original message with a(n) _____.

5. A(n) _____ is a copy of a file that's transmitted along with your e-mail message to a recipient's computer.

LESSON 40 PROJECT

This project gives you the opportunity to review the concepts in this lesson and practice the techniques in the exercises. Before you start this exercise you will need one of your classmate's e-mail address.

1. Start **Internet Explorer** and then start **Outlook Express**.

2. Add a classmate's e-mail address to the Address Book.

3. Compose and send an e-mail message to one of your classmates:
   a. Click the **Compose Message** button on the toolbar.
   b. Enter the classmate's name in the **To:** field by using the Address Book.
   c. Skip the Cc: field.
   d. Key **Mail Message** as the Subject.

4. Key the following text in the message area:

   ```
   This is an attempt at sending a mail message in Outlook Express. Please
   reply to this message.
   ```

5. Send the message.

6. Give your classmate a few minutes to respond to your e-mail message. Click the **Send and Receive** button and select the **Inbox** folder, if necessary.

7. Print the e-mail message containing the reply. Then delete the message from the message list.

8. Close **Outlook Express** and **Internet Explorer**. If instructed, shut down Windows and your computer.

USING INTERNET SEARCH TOOLS

OBJECTIVES

Upon completion of this lesson, you will be able to:

■ Search the Web using AutoSearch.

■ Search the Web using different search engines.

■ Search the Web using Boolean logic.

■ Search the Web using a subject guide.

⏱ **Estimated Time: 2 hours**

Picture the Web—a library with more than 40 million pages of information on topics ranging from sports and travel to science and technology. These pages are stored randomly—they are not listed alphabetically by topic, nor are they numbered according to any type of classification system. Now put yourself in that picture, trying to locate the information and files in which you are interested. An impossible task? No, because Web users have several search tools to help them locate information. In this lesson, you will learn how to use various tools to search the Web and locate specified information.

Searching the Web

You can search the Web for information by using a *search engine*. A search engine is a server that processes requests for information and helps you locate Web pages that contain information related to your request. To find information on the Web, you can use Internet Explorer's AutoSearch tool. Or you can use one of several search engines that are available on the Web.

Using AutoSearch

Internet Explorer's AutoSearch makes an information search simple. If you are searching for a term, simply enter the term or terms (referred to as *keywords*) in the Address text box in the Internet Explorer window. If you are searching for a single keyword (for example, *clown*), type a question mark (or the word *Go* or *Find*), space once, type the keyword (in this case, *clown*), and then press Enter. (See Figure 41-1.)

FIGURE 41-1
Using AutoSearch to search for a single keyword

If you are searching for a phrase (for example, *U.S. Constitution*), key the words with a space after each, and then press Enter. Do *not* key the question mark or the words *Go* or *Find*. (See Figure 41-2.)

After Internet Explorer executes the search, it displays a Web results page like the page shown in Figure 41-3. The page lists links that contain the key word or phrase. These links are called *hits*. A hit may also include a few lines of text from the Web page. Click on any of the links to display the corresponding page.

FIGURE 41-2
Using AutoSearch to search for a phrase

FIGURE 41-3
AutoSearch results page for the phrase *U.S. Constitution*

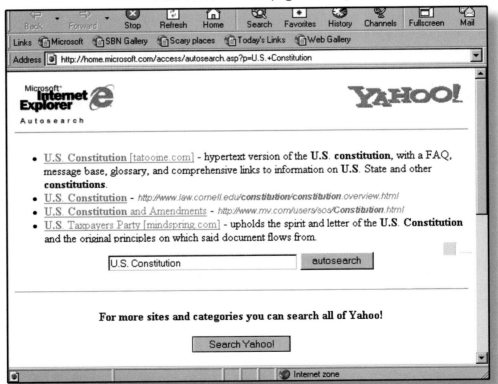

EXERCISE ▭▷ 41.1

1. Start **Internet Explorer**.

2. Click the Address text box and type the following phrase: **discount air travel**. Then press **Enter**.

3. Verify that you have access to your printer and that it is turned on. Select **Print** on the

File menu and click **OK** to print the results page.

4. Click the **Home** button. Leave the Internet Explorer window open for the next exercise.

Understanding Search Engines

In the previous exercise, you might have noticed that the word *Yahoo!* appeared on the results page. That's because Internet Explorer used a search engine called Yahoo! to search a database of Web resources, locate the information, and display a list of URLs that match your request with links to each one. The database that Yahoo! used was created by a program called a *spider* or *robot*. This spider program travels the Web on a frequent basis, following links and adding Web page entries to its index.

There are about a half dozen major general-purpose Internet search engines, and about ten times as many specialized ones. Each search engine follows a slightly different set of rules to conduct its search; as a result, each engine will produce a different list of URLs in response to the same request.

If you're looking for a popular Web site, you can probably find it with almost any search engine. But if you want *everything* related to a specific subject, repeat the same search using several different search engines.

Accessing the Search the Web Page

Clicking the Search button on the Explorer toolbar opens a Search pane on the left side of the Explorer window, similar to the one shown in Figure 41-4. The Search pane displays the search engine that's currently being used. You can change the engine by selecting a different one from the Choose provider drop-down list. Choose the List of all providers option on the drop-down list and the Search the Web page displays in the right pane of the Explorer window. As you see in Figure 41-5, this page contains links to various search engines and other search tools.

The same five search tools that are listed in the Choose Provider drop-down list are also displayed in the top left corner of the Search the Web window. A number of other search tools are listed by category at the bottom of the window:

■ **General Search**. Searches the entire Web.

■ **Guides**. Searches Web sites organized by category and/or location.

■ **White Pages**. Searches for phone numbers, addresses, and e-mail names of individuals.

■ **Newsgroups**. Searches postings of users to electronic discussion groups.

■ **Chat Guides**. Searches daily schedules and links to live (real-time) communications between two or more individuals.

FIGURE 41-4
Search pane in Internet Explorer window

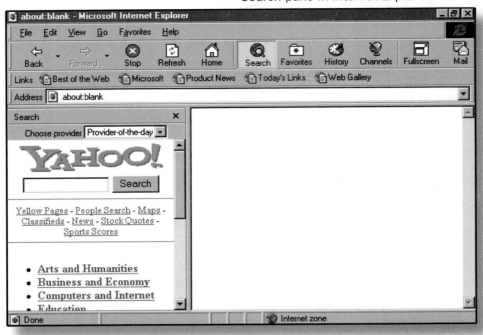

FIGURE 41-5
Search the Web page

Links to
Search
Engines

- **Specialty**. Searches special-interest and content-specific sites.

- **International**. Searches Web sites in different countries and in different languages.

E X E R C I S E ⟶ 41.2

1. In the Internet Explorer window, click the **Search** button on the toolbar.

2. Choose **List of all providers** on the Choose provider drop-down list. The Search the Web page displays.

3. Use the scroll arrows to bring the seven categories of search tools into view.

4. Click the **Excite** search engine button. Wait for the Excite search page to display. Leave the Internet Explorer window open for the next exercise.

Performing a Search with a Search Engine

Using a search engine is like using AutoSearch. You might have noticed an empty text box and accompanying "search" button in both the Infoseek and Excite Web search pages. You enter a keyword or words in this text box and then click the Search button.

For example, say you want to gather information on studying in a foreign country. You might type the keywords *study abroad programs* in the text box. Then you click the Search button to start the search. After a short time, a Search Results page, similar to Figure 41-6, displays. The page contains the word or phrase used in the search and shows the number of hits. Each hit is preceded by a percentage figure called a *relevance rating*. The relevance rating represents how "confident" the search engine is that the hit contains information relevant to your request. The closer the rating is to 100%, the more relevant the information.

FIGURE 41-6
Typical search results page

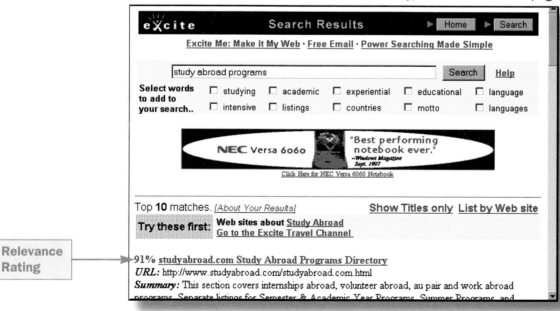

If the search finds more hits than can be displayed on the results page, a Next Results button appears at the bottom of the page. The Next Results button appears at the bottom of the page only when there are more hits than will fit on the display page.

EXERCISE ▭▷ 41.3

1. The Excite Search the Web page should be displayed on your screen. Key the following phrase in the search text box: **dog obedience training**. Click **Search**.

2. Click the first hit on the page.

3. When the page displays, close the **Search** pane by clicking its **Close** button.

4. Print the Web page:
   a. Verify that your printer is on and that you have access to it.
   b. Select **Print** on the **File** menu.

5. Leave the Internet Explorer window open for the next exercise.

Refining Your Search

So far, you have performed basic searches, where you only had to enter a keyword or phrase. Most search engines also offer the ability to conduct advanced searches—that is, they allow you to refine your searches by including search options. The types of options vary from one search engine to another.

The options common to most search engines let you:

■ Give more weight to one keyword than you give to another.

■ Exclude words that might produce unwanted results.

■ Search for proper names.

By using advanced search options, you can limit your search results. That can be a big benefit when you are searching millions of files!

SEARCHING USING BOOLEAN LOGIC

Most of the popular search engines allow you to use *Boolean logic* to refine your search. The term Boolean logic describes certain logical operations that are used to combine search options or exclude search terms.

The four basic Boolean operators are *AND*, *OR*, *NOT*, and *AND NOT*. Table 41-1 explains these operators and gives examples of their uses.

TABLE 41-1
Refining a search using Boolean logic

Boolean Operators

Operator	Symbol	Meaning	Example	Use when the search results . . .
AND	&	Include all words	campaign AND reform AND Congress	*Must* contain the words, phrase, or name
OR	|	Include any word	alien OR ufo	*Can* contain the words, phrase, or name
NOT	!	Do not include a word	Simpson NOT Homer	*Must not* contain the words, phrase, or name
AND NOT		Include some words and exclude others	immigrant AND NOT Mexico	*Must* contain a certain word, phrase, or name *and not others*

Here are some important things to remember when using Boolean operators:

1. Use the words rather than the symbols. The words are easier to remember and are common to nearly all search engines. Enter the words in uppercase letters (lowercase is acceptable but uppercase makes your keywords stand out).

2. To query on a phrase, enclose the phrase in quotation marks. For example, if you were researching the effect of automobile emissions on global warming, you would enter "global warming" AND "automobile emission." The ability to query on phrases is a very important feature of search engines.

3. Double-check capitalization when searching on proper names of people, companies, or products.

EXERCISE ▷ 41.4

1. Access the InfoSeek search engine Web page:
   a. Click the **Search** button on the toolbar.
   b. In the **Search pane**, select **List of all providers** from the Choose provider drop-down list.
   c. In the Search the Web page, click the **Infoseek** button.
   d. Click the **Search** button on the toolbar to close the Search pane.

(continued on next page)

2. Conduct a search to answer this question: *What is California doing about welfare reform?*
   a. Key the search terms exactly as shown below in the text box and then click **Seek**: **"welfare reform" AND California**
   b. Print a copy of the first results page.

3. Access the Excite search engine Web page:
   a. Click the **Search** button on the toolbar.
   b. In the Search pane, select **List of all providers** from the Choose provider drop-down list. In the Search the Web page, click the **Excite** button.
   c. Click the **Search** button on the toolbar to close the Search pane.

4. Conduct a search to answer this question: *What summer job opportunities are available other than working at a summer camp?*
   a. Key the search terms exactly as shown below and then press **Enter**: **"summer jobs" AND NOT "summer camp"**
   b. Print a copy of the first results page.

5. Write your name in the upper right corner of the printouts. Leave the Internet Explorer window open for the next exercise.

SEARCHING THE WEB USING A SUBJECT GUIDE

To simplify searches, some engines provide a *subject guide* on the Search the Web page (Figure 41-7). Subject guides allow you to "follow a path" from a broad category of information to more specific categories. Clicking a link in a subject guide jumps you to a page with more specific categories that help you narrow your search. You continue to make selections from the subject guides until a results page displays with links.

FIGURE 41-7
Yahoo! subject guide

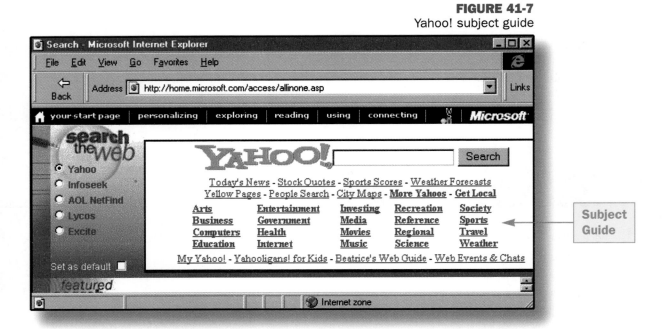

UNIT 11: INTERNET EXPLORER

For example, suppose you use the Yahoo! subject guide to find information on courses you can take from your home. You would proceed as follows:

1. Access the Yahoo! search page.

2. Click the Education link (refer to Figure 41-7). A guide similar to that shown in Figure 41-8 displays.

3. Click the Distance Learning link. A guide similar to that shown in Figure 41-9 opens.

4. Click the Courses link. A page like that shown in Figure 41-10 appears.

FIGURE 41-8
Clicking the Education link narrows the search

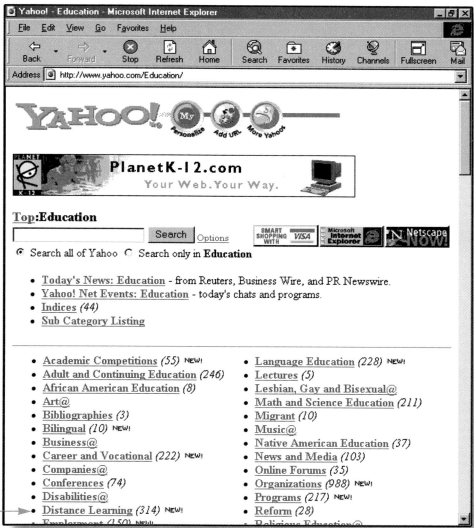

Click this Link

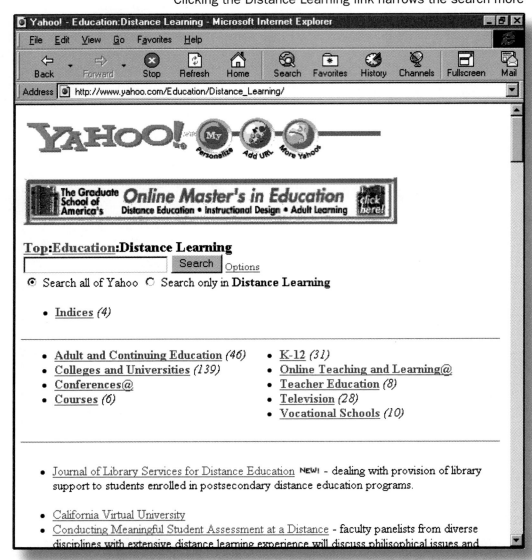

FIGURE 41-10
Clicking the Courses link further narrows the search

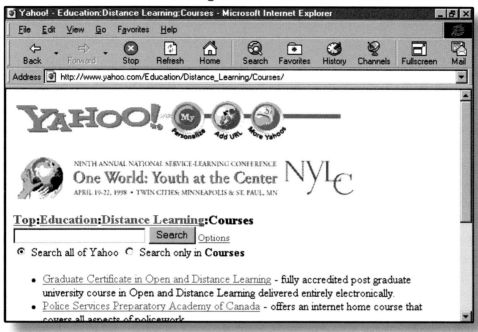

Notice in Figure 41-10 that the search path to the current Web page is displayed above the Search text box: Education, Distance Learning, and Courses.

EXERCISE 41.5

1. Access the Yahoo! search page:
   a. Click the **Search** button on the toolbar.
   b. In the Search pane, select **List of all providers** from the Choose provider drop-down list. Click the **Yahoo!** button on the search page.
   c. Click the **Search** button on the toolbar to close the Search pane.

2. Conduct a search to fill in the blank in this piece of movie trivia: *Beauty and the Beast was Disney's ___th animated feature to be made from a classic fairy tale:*
   a. Click the **Entertainment** link on the Yahoo! search page.

   b. Scroll down the page until you locate the **Trivia** link and then click on it.
   c. Click the **Movies** link.
   d. Scroll down the page until you locate the link **Index - Movie Trivia Links** and then click on it.
   e. Click on **Beauty and the Beast Trivia**.
   f. Scroll the page until you find the answer to the question. Print only the page containing the answer.

3. Close the **Internet Explorer** window. If instructed, shut down Windows and your computer.

Summary

This lesson covered methods for searching the Web using various search engines. You learned that:

■ Search engines are tools that help you locate information on the Web. Internet Explorer's AutoSearch tool allows you to search the Web quickly and simply. To search for a phrase, key the phrase in the Address text box and press Enter. To search for a single keyword, type a question mark or the words *Go* or *Find*, press the spacebar, and then enter the keyword.

■ Each search engine has different search rules, and will yield different results. Therefore, when you want detailed information about a topic, you should use several search engines.

■ Internet Explorer's Search button and Search pane make locating a search engine easy. Choose the List of all providers option from the Choose provider drop-down list to display a Web page with links to the popular search tools.

■ Besides basic searches (like those that AutoSearch provides), search engines are capable of more advanced searches in which you can specify options that include or exclude words and terms (for example, proper names). Most of the popular search engines allow you to use the Boolean operators AND, OR, NOT and AND NOT (either in word or in symbol form) to narrow your searches.

■ Subject guides allow you to "follow a path" from a broad category of information to more specific categories. Clicking a link in a subject guide jumps you to a page with more specific categories to choose from. You continue to make selections from the subject guides until a results page displays with links.

LESSON 41 REVIEW QUESTIONS

TRUE/FALSE

Each of the following statements is either true or false. Indicate your answer on the left by circling T if the statement is true and F if the statement is false.

T   F   1.   To perform an AutoSearch of the Internet, you key search terms in the text box on the Search the Web page.

T   F   2.   An AutoSearch for a keyword must be preceded by a question mark or the words *Go* or *Find*.

T   F   3.   The links that display on a Web search results page are called subject guides.

T   F   4.   Most result pages typically display the first 10 hits and include a button at the bottom of the page that you can click to view additional hits.

T   F   5.   Subject guides allow you to "follow a path" from a specific category of information to broader categories.

MULTIPLE CHOICE

Complete the following questions by circling the correct multiple choice letter.

1. Which of the following is not a Boolean operator?
   A. AND
   B. AND NOT
   C. OR
   D. EXCLUDE

2. When searching for a phrase with AutoSearch, which procedure should you follow?
   A. Key a question mark, space once, key the phrase, and then press Enter
   B. Key the word *Go*, space once, key the phrase, and then press Enter
   C. Key the word *Find*, space once, key the phrase, and then press Enter
   D. Key the phrase and then press Enter

3. Which of the following searches is most likely to give you a result with a reference to F. Scott Fitzgerald *without* a reference to his book *The Great Gatsby*?
   A. "F. Scott Fitzgerald" NOT Gatsby
   B. F. Scott Fitzgerald NOT Gatsby
   C. "F. Scott Fitzgerald" AND NOT Gatsby
   D. Any of the above

4. The links on a search results page are called
   A. Boolean operators
   B. Hits
   C. Search engines
   D. Relevance ratings

5. Which of the following hits is likely to have the information that's most relevant to a search on studying abroad?
   A. 81% Study Abroad Programs Directory
   B. 10% Study Abroad Directory
   C. 50% Studying and Working Abroad
   D. 75% Study Out of Residence

LESSON 41 PROJECT

This project gives you the opportunity to review the concepts in this lesson and practice the techniques in the exercises. You will need your Windows Practice disk in order to complete this project.

1. Start **Internet Explorer**. Place your Windows Practice disk in the appropriate disk drive.

2. Access the Yahoo! search engine Web page:
   a. Click the **Search** button on the toolbar.
   b. Choose **List of all providers** from the Choose provider drop-down list.

    c. Close the **Search** pane.

    d. Click the **Yahoo!** button.

3. Use the subject guide to locate movie reviews of two current movies of your choice:

    a. Click **Entertainment**.

    b. Click **Movies and Films**.

    c. Click **Reviews**.

    d. Select **Capsule Reviews**.

    e. Select one of the links to see the movies reviewed.

    f. Locate a review for two movies of your choice.

4. Save each review as a text file:

    a. Display the review in Internet Explorer's display window.

    b. Choose **Save As** on the **File** menu to open the Save As dialog box.

    c. Select the drive that contains your Windows Practice disk from the Save in drop-down list.

    d. Highlight the name in the File name text box. Key the file name: **Movie Review 1**.

    e. Click the Save as type drop-down list arrow to display the file type options.

    f. Choose **Text File (*.txt)**.

    g. Click the **Save** button.

    h. Find a review for a second movie of your choice, and following steps 4a–g above, save the review as **Movie Review 2**.

5. Open your movie reviews in **WordPad**. Print a copy of each review.

6. Close **Internet Explorer** and **WordPad**. If instructed, shut down Windows and your computer.

DOWNLOADING FILES

OBJECTIVES

Upon completion of this lesson, you will be able to:

- Save Web Pages and display them offline.

- Download files from FTP archives.

- Download files from Gopher servers.

- Determine what safety precautions you need to take when downloading files.

⏱ **Estimated Time: 2 hours**

As you have already learned, you can save information you find on the Web to a disk and then access it later. In this lesson, you learn more about saving Web pages and downloading files.

Saving Web Pages

You can save a Web page in one of two ways: as a text file or as an HTML document.

When you save a Web page as a text file, features such as graphic images, links, colors, and type styles are lost. This method should be used only if the information you want to save will still be valuable without its text and graphic formats. Once you save the file, you can open it in a word processing program, edit it, and print it.

Saving a Web page as an HTML document retains its text formatting, but not its graphic images. Instead, a small icon that represents the image appears on the document. You can reopen the document in Internet Explorer and use links, but you will not see the graphic images that originally appeared on the page. You can also open an HTML format file in a word processing program such as Microsoft Word.

Saving a Web Page as an HTML File

Saving a Web page in HTML format is similar to saving any document: Choose Save As on the File menu. Enter a name in the File name text box. Then, click the Save button. You do not need to choose a file type since the default file type for Web pages is the HTML format.

1. Start **Internet Explorer.**

2. Make sure the Links toolbar is displayed. If it is not, select **Toolbars** on the **View** menu, and then click **Links**.

3. Click the first quick links button on the toolbar. Wait for the page to load.

4. Place your Windows Practice disk in the appropriate drive.

5. Save the page as an HTML file:
   a. Choose **Save As** on the **File** menu to open the Save As dialog box.
   b. Select the drive that contains your Windows Practice disk from the Save in drop-down list.
   c. Highlight the name in the File name text box. Key the new file name: **Web HTML File**.
   d. Click the **Save** button.

6. Click the **Home** button to display the home page. Leave Internet Explorer open for the next exercise.

Opening an HTML File in Internet Explorer

You can open an HTML file in Internet Explorer. Choose Open on the File menu, locate the file you want to open, and double-click it. Text formats are retained, but since graphic images could not be saved with the file, Internet Explorer displays a small icon where each image appeared in the original Web page (see Figure 42-1).

FIGURE 42-1
Icons represent graphic images

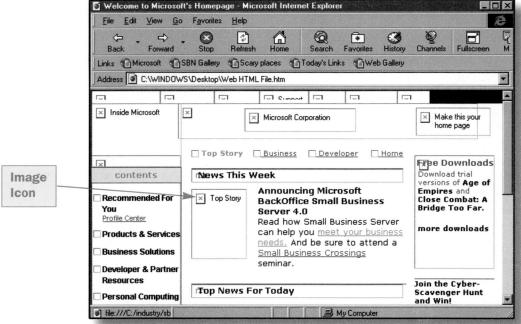

EXERCISE 42.2

1. Choose **Open** from the **File** menu.

2. In the Open dialog box, click the **Browse** button. In the second Open dialog box, select the drive containing your Windows Practice disk from the Look in drop-down list.

3. Double-click **Web HTML File**. In the dialog box, verify that the correct file is in the Open text box, and click **OK**. Notice that the page is displayed with its original formatting, but the graphics are missing. Leave Internet Explorer open for the next exercise.

Saving a Web Page as a Text File

To save a Web page as a text file, choose Save As on the File menu. Enter a name in the File name text box. Click the Save as type drop-down list arrow and select Text File (*.**txt**). Then click the Save button.

EXERCISE 42.3

1. Verify that your Windows Practice disk is in the appropriate drive.

2. Click the first quick links button on the toolbar. Wait for the page to load.

3. Save the page as a text file:
   a. Choose **Save As** on the **File** menu to open the Save As dialog box.
   b. Select the drive that contains your Windows Practice disk from the Save in drop-down list.
   c. Highlight the name in the File name text box. Key the new file name: **Web Text File**.
   d. Click the **Save as type** drop-down list arrow to display the file type options.
   e. Choose **Text File (*.txt)** from the Save as type list.
   f. Click the **Save** button.

4. Click the **Home** button. Leave Internet Explorer open for the next exercise.

Opening a Text File in Internet Explorer

To open a text file in Internet Explorer, follow these steps:

1. Choose Open on the File menu.

2. Click Browse in the first Open dialog box.

3. In the second Open dialog box, select Text Files from the Files of type list box.

4. Double-click on the file you want to open. In the dialog box, verify that you've selected the correct file to open and click OK. The file will open and only the text will display in the Internet Explorer window (see Figure 42-2).

FIGURE 42-2
Web page saved as a text file and opened in Internet Explorer

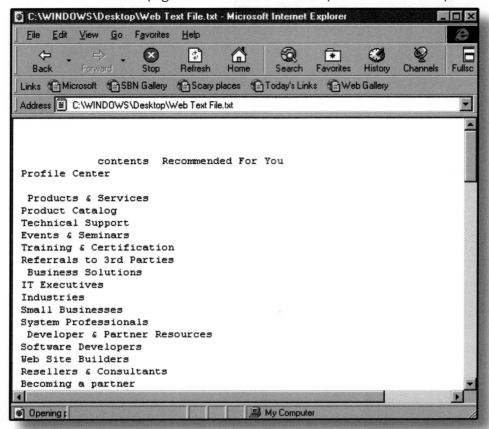

EXERCISE ⟐ 42.4

1. Select **Open** from the **File** menu.

2. In the Open dialog box, click the **Browse** button. In the second Open dialog box, select the drive containing your Windows Practice disk from the Look in drop-down list.

3. Select **Text Files** from the Files of type drop-down list box.

4. Double-click **Web Text File** to open the file in the Internet Explorer window. Notice that only the unformatted text appears. Remain in this screen for the next exercise.

File Transfer

Internet Explorer can be used to send and receive electronic files from one computer to another, a process known as *file transfer*. File transfer includes sending (*uploading*) and receiving (*downloading*) files. The transfer process is nearly the same as copying a file from one disk to another. In both instances, you make a copy of the original file and then place the copy in a different location.

Transferring files between computers involves the use of *file transfer protocol* (*FTP*). FTP allows for the transfer of files between machines with different character sets and different ways of formatting files.

To use FTP, you must connect to an FTP host computer. An FTP host computer is distinguishable by its URL, which begins with **ftp://**. A complete URL for an FTP site would look something like **ftp://domain/directory/filename**. The *domain* is the name of the FTP host computer you want to access; the *directory* (or folder) is where the file is stored; and *filename* is the name of the file you want to download. Table 42-1 lists some popular FTP sites.

TABLE 42-1
Popular sites where files can be uploaded or downloaded

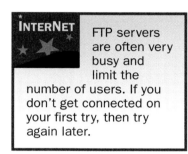

INTERNET FTP servers are often very busy and limit the number of users. If you don't get connected on your first try, then try again later.

FTP Sites

FTP Site	URL
America Online	ftp://ftp.aol.com
Microsoft Corporation	ftp://ftp.microsoft.com
Oakland Archives	ftp://oak.oakland.edu
SimTel Archives	ftp://ftp.coast.net
Smithsonian Institute	ftp://photo1.si.edu
U.S. Supreme Court	ftp://ftp.cwru.edu

Once you log on to an FTP host computer, you'll see its public directories (or folders), similar to the ones shown in Figure 42-3. Public directories are those directories to which everyone has access. When you find a directory you want to access, just click it. A file list and/or other folders will display. Many FTP host computers display an icon preceding each link that indicates if the link is a file or a directory. All FTP host computers list information about the items in a folder, including each item's name, date and time of creation, and file size. When you locate the file you want, simply click it.

Downloading a Text or Graphic File

If you've selected a text file (**.txt**) or a graphic file (**.gif** or **.jpg**), the file will load and display on your screen. After viewing the file, you can click the Back button to close it, or choose Save As on the File menu to save it to disk.

FIGURE 42-3
FTP host

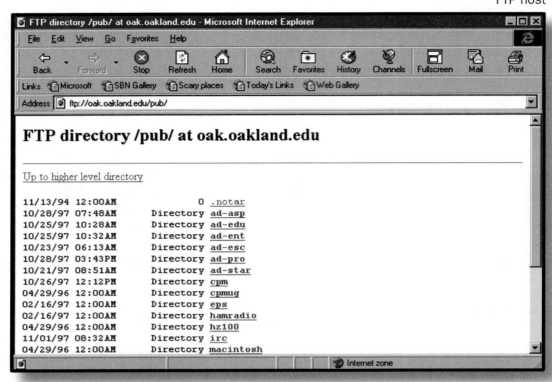

EXERCISE 42.5

1. Open **Internet Explorer** if it is not already open.

2. Click in the **Address** text box, key the ftp address **ftp://wuarchive.wustl.edu** and then press **Enter**. The FTP root folder displays as shown in Figure 42-4.

3. Scroll to the bottom of the page to display the directory listing (see Figure 42-5), then click the **multimedia** directory link.

4. Click the **images** directory link.

5. Click the **jpeg** directory link.

6. Click the **f** directory link.

7. Click on the file **f16.jpg**.

8. After the graphic displays, click the **Home** button on the toolbar to log off the ftp server and return to your home page.

FIGURE 42-4

Smithsonian FTP root directory

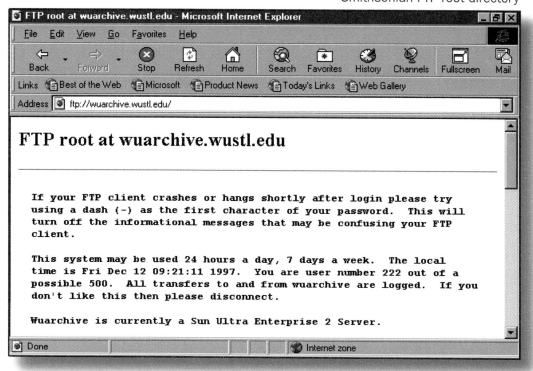

FIGURE 45-5

Public directory listing on the Smithsonian FTP server

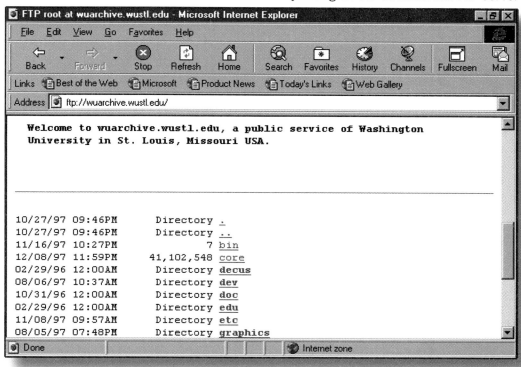

Downloading Program Files

When you select a program file, such as files with the extensions **.zip**, **.exe**, **.com**, and so on, the File Download dialog box opens, as shown in Figure 42-6. You are prompted to indicate whether you want to run the program from the host computer, or save the program to disk. Few FTP host computers allow you to run a program. You must, therefore, select the default option to save the program to a disk. Once you click the OK button, the familiar Save As dialog box is displayed, as shown in Figure 42-7. Indicate where you want the program file saved and enter a name for it.

FIGURE 42-6
File Download dialog box

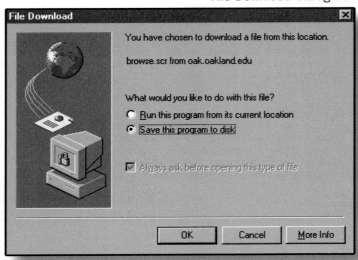

FIGURE 42-7
Save As dialog box

Compressed Files

Files are frequently stored on the Internet in a compressed format. *Compressed files* are files that have been made smaller so that they take up less disk space. Since they are smaller than the original file, compressed files transfer much more quickly. As you would expect, a compressed file must be decompressed (expanded) before it can be used. If you are browsing an FTP directory and see a file name with the extension **.zip**, that is a clue that the file is a compressed file.

The file name also gives you a clue as to which decompression program to use. A decompression program is a general-purpose program that restores a compressed file to its original size. You can download decompression programs from many FTP sites.

Downloading Files with a Gopher

A gopher is a menu-driven Internet service that helps you locate information and services from Internet host computers. Host computers that offer gopher services are called gopher servers. Some of the more popular gopher servers are listed in Table 42-2.

TABLE 42-2
Popular sites for menu-driven gopher Internet service

Gopher Servers

Gopher Site	URL
Library of Congress	gopher://marvel.loc.gov
National Public Radio	gopher://gopher.npr.org
University of Minnesota	gopher://gopher.tc.umn.edu
U.S. Senate	gopher://gopher.senate.gov
U.S. House of Representatives	gopher://gopher.house.gov
United National	gopher://gopher.undp.org

When using a gopher, you are presented with a list of links similar to those used by an FTP sever. Clicking one of the links may display another list of links or retrieve and display a file.

You access a gopher server the same way you access an FTP host computer—by keying a URL. A gopher URL is constructed like this: ***gopher://domain/directory/filename.*** When you access a gopher server, its root Web page looks similar to the one shown in Figure 42-8.

FIGURE 42-8
Typical gopher root Web page

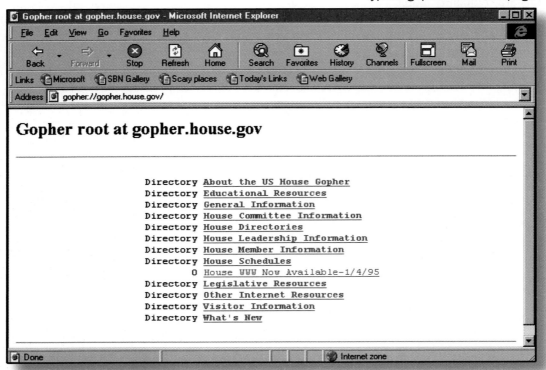

You navigate the gopher Web page just as you did the FTP page.

EXERCISE ▷ 42.6

1. Click in the Address text box, key **gopher://gopher.house.gov**, and then press **Enter**. The root folder displays as shown in Figure 42-8.

2. Click the **House Schedules** directory link.

3. Click the current year **House Calendar** link. Wait for the text file to display.

4. Save the file to your Windows Practice disk:
   a. Choose **Save As** on the **File** menu.
   b. Enter **Exercise 42.6** in the **File name** text box.

   c. From the Save as type list, choose **Text File (*.txt)**.
   d. From the Save in list, choose the drive in which you have placed your Windows Practice disk.
   e. Click the **Save** button.

5. Close **Internet Explorer**.

6. Open the **Exercise 42.6** file in **WordPad** and print a copy of it.

7. Close **WordPad**. If instructed, shut down Windows and your computer.

Protecting Against Computer Viruses

While FTP and Gopher sites appear to be an inexpensive and convenient way to obtain software programs, downloading must be done with caution. Careless downloading of files can infect your system with a computer virus. A computer *virus* is a computer program that's designed as a prank or as sabotage. It replicates itself by attaching to other programs and carrying out unwanted and sometimes damaging operations. A computer virus has three distinct stages of life:

1. It enters a computer system and locates a receptive home.

2. It reproduces itself within the system.

3. It is activated to perform the task for which it was designed.

Some viruses are nuisances and others cause serious damage to your computer system and its programs. The more hostile viruses often alter data files. The best defense against a computer virus is to avoid it in the first place. The next best thing is to kill it at an early stage, before it has had a chance to spread, and certainly before it has been activated. Programs that launch "search-and-destroy" missions in a computer system are called *vaccine programs*. They seek out viruses and try to disable those they find.

To protect your system from computer viruses, observe the following rules:

- Always download files to a floppy disk so that the files cannot get near your hard disk until you have checked them with a vaccine program.

- Purchase and use a vaccine program.

Summary

This lesson covered how to save and download Web pages and content. You learned that:

- Web pages can be saved as HTML documents or plain text documents. When a page is saved as an HTML document, all of its formatting except for the graphic images are saved. When a Web page is saved as a text file, only the text is saved; all of the formatting is lost.

- Both HTML files and text files can be opened in Internet Explorer and in a word processing program.

- The file transfer process makes an electronic duplicate, or copy, of an original file and places that copy in a new specified location. Sending a file is known as uploading; receiving a file is called downloading. The Internet program that supports file transfer is called FTP, or file transfer protocol.

- FTP can only be used on FTP host computers. FTP host computers have a distinguishable URL that follows the format: **ftp://domain/directory/filename**. When you log on to an FTP host computer, you are placed in a public directory (folder). When you select a text or graphic file on the FTP host computer, the file will load and display in the browser window. You can then save or print the file. File types other than text or graphics cannot be displayed; they must be saved to disk.

- Files are often stored in a compressed format for easy transfer. These files must be decompressed with a utility program before they can be used.

- A gopher is a menu-driven service that supports file transfer. Host computers that offer gopher services are called gopher servers.

- A computer virus is a computer program that replicates itself by attaching to other programs and carrying out unwanted and sometimes damaging operations. The best defense against a computer virus is to avoid it; the next best defense is to use a vaccine program to kill it in an early stage.

LESSON 42 REVIEW QUESTIONS

TRUE/FALSE

Each of the following statements is either true or false. Indicate your answer on the left by circling T if the statement is true and F if the statement is false.

T   F   1.   The HTML format cannot be retained when a Web page is saved to disk.

T   F   2.   A Web page saved to disk can be opened and edited in a word processing program.

T   F   3.   A compressed file must be decompressed before it can be downloaded.

T   F   4.   Saving a Web page as an HTML document retains all formats except for links.

T   F   5.   A file with an **.exe** extension can be run from an FTP host computer.

FILL IN THE BLANKS

Complete the following sentences by writing the correct word or words in the blanks provided.

1.   The FTP URL format is _____,

2.   The _____ file format is the default format when saving a Web page.

3.   A(n) _____ is a computer program designed as a prank or as sabotage.

4.   A(n) _____ is a menu-driven Internet service that helps you locate information and services from Internet host computers.

5.   Receiving a file on your computer is also called _____.

LESSON 42 PROJECT

This project gives you the opportunity to review the concepts in this lesson and practice the techniques in the exercises. You will need your Windows Practice disk in order to complete this project.

1. Open **Internet Explorer**.

2. Use **AutoSearch** to locate a copy of the Declaration of Independence:
   a. In the **Address** text box, key **United States Declaration of Independence** and press **Enter**.
   b. Scroll the listing on the results page until you locate **Government Documents: Declaration of Independence**.
   c. Click **Declaration of Independence [csuchico.edu]**.

3. Save the document to your Windows Practice disk as a text file with the file name **Independence**.

4. Open the file in **WordPad**, and print only the first page.

5. Close **WordPad** and **Internet Explorer**. If instructed, shut down Windows and your computer.

UNIT 11 REVIEW QUESTIONS ▽

WRITTEN QUESTIONS

Answer the questions below on a separate piece of paper.

1. What are the basic elements of a URL?

2. Distinguish between a text link and a graphic link on a Web page.

3. Define Internet Explorer's AutoComplete feature and explain how it works.

4. What is the difference between the History pane in the Explorer window and the History list?

5. How does the Favorites list simplify returning to previously visited Web pages?

6. When would you use the Outlook Express Reply to Author button? When would you use the Reply to All button?

7. How does the Address Book feature of Outlook Express simplify addressing e-mail messages?

8. Distinguish between the two ways a file may be attached to an e-mail message.

9. Distinguish between searching the Web using a keyword search engine and a subject guide.

10. What does uploading a file mean? What does downloading mean?

UNIT 11 APPLICATION ▽

SCANS

Earthwares Nursery, a large landscaping and nursery business, has approached Corporate Communique to develop a quarterly newsletter that it can distribute to existing and potential customers. Earthwares would like Corporate Communique to create a sample newsletter.

To do so, Corporate Communique must first educate itself on the landscaping and nursery business. Use your Internet search tools to find information on related topics. Topics that you might want to research include seasonal planting guides, lawn care, and landscape design. You'll also want to find resources from which you can download artwork, such as photos of landscape designs or plant specimens, to include in the newsletter.

Once you have gathered information, send an e-mail (to one of your classmates or your instructor) that outlines the articles that could be included in the sample newsletter. Make sure you include details on where you found your information.

Print a copy of your e-mail message. Then, close all open applications. If instructed, shut down Windows and your computer.

CRITICAL THINKING

You plan to attend a five-day Internet World Conference in Paris, France. Since you have earned vacation time, you decide to extend your stay for an additional week. You want to visit two other cities in France during your vacation. The conference is scheduled from March 2 through March 9 of next year. To make the most of your trip, you decide to use the World Wide Web to plan your itinerary and estimate your expenses. From your experience with search engines, you decide the travel directory on the Excite search page will locate all the information you need.

Because you are a methodical person, you make the following list of things you need to do.

NEED TO FIND:

- A flight that departs from your home city and arrives in Paris on March 1 and returns 14 days later.

- Hotels in each of the cities you visit.

- Sights to see.

- Train connections between the cities you plan to visit.

- A selection of restaurants.

NEED TO DETERMINE:

- The best price for the round-trip flight to Paris.

- The cost of all other items. Convert all prices from French francs to American dollars (use the currency converter at *http://www.xe.net/currency/*).

After you obtain the necessary information, use WordPad to create an itinerary for your trip. Include the following information on your itinerary: Date, City, Comments, and Price. Use the comments section to include your arrival and departure dates and time, as well as the name and address of each hotel.

APPENDIX

COMPUTER BASICS: SOFTWARE AND HARDWARE

Software: Systems, Applications, and Utilities Software

To begin, note that all microcomputer systems have two major components: hardware and software. As you will see later, *hardware* refers to any or all of the pieces of equipment that make up a computer system (monitor, mouse, keyboard, etc.). *Software* is a broad term used to mean system instructions or applications of all kinds. Both are essential components. Without software, a computer system would be like a television that receives no broadcast signal, or a VCR that has no videotapes. A microcomputer must be given instructions, and computer instructions are often simply called software.

Even if you know little about computers, you won't be surprised to hear that there are many, many, many software programs developed for different purposes. Learning about software programs is easier if you envision them in three distinct groups or families:

1. *Systems software.* Systems software is the software used to operate computer systems. Without systems software, your computer would not have the instructions necessary to run. Windows 98 is systems software and because it manages the software programs and the hardware it is called an *operating system.*

2. *Applications software.* The second broad category of software includes all the other specific applications software used for word processing, database management, spreadsheets, graphics, and so on. There are thousands of applications software programs that belong in this category.

3. *Utilities software.* Perhaps you are not yet familiar with utilities software, programs developed specifically to help you manage your files and your computer system. Utilities are tools, such as those found in Windows' *System Tools*, that help you get the most out of your computer. For instance, a utilities software package can check your disks for bad areas, manage your files if more than one person is using your computer, create more free space on hard and floppy disks, and back up your files.

The discussion that follows will introduce you to these three families of software—systems software, applications software, and utilities software—and will explain their uses. Let's take a closer look at each group.

Systems Software

Systems software describes the special programs or instructions needed to operate the computer system. Systems software is also called OS for "operating system." An earlier OS is *DOS (disk operating system).* Without systems software or an operating system, you would not be able to use or even start your computer. They *boot*, or start, the activity in a computer when you first turn it on. An OS is the supervisor; it controls all aspects of file management, including storing, retrieving, and printing files. An OS also supervises and coordinates the loading of applications software programs.

An earlier version of Windows, Windows 3.1, simplified the use of "DOS power." With Windows 3.1, users didn't need to memorize many different DOS commands. DOS worked in the background, performing tasks that users were often unaware of. For Windows 3.1 users, knowing DOS was helpful but not essential. The next version of Windows, Windows 95, helped decrease that dependency on knowing much about DOS.

Now all that has changed. Windows 98 does not rely on DOS to run Windows applications; however, it will use DOS to run any older DOS-based applications and to support certain older hardware devices. There are a few characteristics of operating systems that are important to recognize:

- Most operating systems for microcomputers allow one user to do one job at a time.

- Advanced operating systems such as Windows 98 allow *one or more users* to run programs at the same time, thus it is a *multiuser* operating system.

- Running *two or more tasks* at the same time is referred to as a *multitasking* operating system.

- These are not to be confused with one other term, *multiprocessing,* which is two or more CPUs sharing the processing workload, thus allowing several programs to be completed at the same time.

- *Plug and Play* support is a recognizable symbol of today's enhanced technology being built into newer versions of operating systems. With *Plug and Play* you can add hardware to a system and the system handles the configuration and driver loading automatically.

Applications Software

With the appropriate software, you can use your computer system to perform a variety of functions. You can write letters, create a financial report, develop a long list of names and addresses, create illustrations and charts, even send data from your computer to another computer. Each function or use represents a specific application.

- When you write letters and other documents, you use word processing software.

- When you create financial reports, you use a spreadsheet application.

- When you develop lists of customer names and addresses, you use database management software.

- When you create illustrations or charts, you use graphics software.

- When you send information or data from your computer to another, you use communications software.

- When you use multiple applications developed by the same vendor or manufacturer, the group of applications software is referred to as a software suite.

These represent only a few of the thousands of applications software packages available today. Key applications are discussed below.

WORD PROCESSING SOFTWARE

The purpose of a word processing application is to create, store, and revise text documents of all kinds and all lengths. Word processing makes it easy to change or correct text copy; to format text; to boldface, italicize, or otherwise "enhance" text; and much, much more.

One feature common to word processors is a spell checker. The software includes a computerized word list of perhaps hundreds of thousands of words. When you command the program to check the spelling in a document, it compares each word in the document against its word list and identifies those words not found in its list. By highlighting these possible misspellings, the spell checker helps you avoid many common errors.

WordPerfect, AmiPro, and Word are just a few of the many word processing applications software available today.

SPREADSHEET SOFTWARE

If you have never seen spreadsheet software, just imagine an accountant's multicolumn paper worksheet—only this spreadsheet is electronic, on-screen instead of on paper.

On paper, you enter figures in pencil in the various columns and then make your computations. On an electronic spreadsheet, you use the keyboard or the keypad to enter figures in cells (boxes formed by the intersections of columns and rows). You can place not only numbers (that is, values) but also words and formulas in the cells. For example, in a cell at the bottom of a Total column you might enter a formula to add all the numbers in the column above. Whenever you enter the command to do so, the applications software performs all the math for you. Perhaps best of all, whenever you change any of the values, the software recalculates everything for you! Spreadsheets provide a fast, accurate, easy way to do analyses, projections, forecasts, etc. Three of the most popular spreadsheet applications programs are Excel, Lotus 1-2-3, and Quattro Pro.

DATABASE MANAGEMENT SOFTWARE

A database is an organized collection of data or information; for example, customers' names, addresses, phone numbers, account numbers, etc. Database software allows you to maintain the data by:

■ Adding new entries to the database.

■ Deleting old entries.

■ Editing entries to correct existing data.

You can also organize information from the database in a variety of ways. For example, you can manipulate the data to show only those customers in selected states, only those entries in selected ZIP codes, all or part of the list in ascending or descending order by dollar purchases in the last year, all or part of the database entries in alphabetic order, or all or part of the database by account number. Some popular database programs are Access, Oracle, and FoxPro.

Imagine the added power and convenience when you are able to use database software with other applications software, such as word processing. With your word processing software, you create one "shell" letter to send to all your customers. With your database software, you specify a list of, say, 2,500 customers' names and addresses stored in the database file. Then you instruct your applications program to combine the text of that letter with the name-and-address list. The result? 2,500 personalized letters!

GRAPHICS SOFTWARE

Drawing illustrations by hand is not easy for most people. But creating them with a graphics program is easy, even for those of us who claim no artistic skills.

Graphics software enables you to create attractive, professional visuals for written reports, newsletters, news releases, oral presentations, and so on. Examples of graphics software programs are CorelDraw, QuarkXPress, PowerPoint, and Adobe Photoshop. These are only a few examples which represent different categories of graphics software. The categories and the capabilities within them vary tremendously based upon the type of graphics the software was designed for—and they include such specialty areas as presentation graphics, desktop publishers, business graphics, photo editors, and illustration software.

Two ways to differentiate many graphics packages are as paint programs and draw programs.

■ A paint program creates dot after dot after dot on the screen until a line is complete. Each dot is called a pixel, derived from the sounds in *picture element*. Because of the way a paint program takes each dot, or bit, and maps the dots into a line, a paint program is a bitmapped program.

■ A draw program places two points on the screen, one at the beginning and the other at the end of the object to be drawn, and then instructs the software to connect those two points and draw the object. Thus, a draw program is an object-oriented program.

When you're not feeling particularly artistic, you may not want to create your own graphics. Instead, you'd prefer ready-made sketches, drawings, and photographs. Enter clip art, already prepared graphics stored on disk. You can use clip art with paint, draw, and word processing programs. Imagine being able to choose from a virtually endless variety of sketches, drawings, and photographs that you can incorporate into your documents!

COMMUNICATIONS SOFTWARE

You can send and receive data electronically with communications software such as ProComm, WinFax Pro, or you can use Windows 98's Internet Explorer Outlook Express, and Hyperterminal communications tools. With communications software, you can access the Internet, the "information superhighway."

Electronic mail or e-mail is a communications application that allows you to create, edit, and then send messages electronically from your computer to others. On the other end, each receiver gets an e-mail message that he or she can display on screen, save, or print. The receiver, of course, can also send you a response.

APPLICATIONS SOFTWARE SUITES

A few software manufacturers have packaged several of their compatible applications together in what is now called a suite or integrated software. A few examples of software suites are Lotus Smart-Suite, Microsoft Office, and Corel PerfectOffice. Some reasons users buy software as a suite are that the applications may be easier to use because they have all been developed by the same vendor, the applications work smoothly together, and it is usually less expensive to buy software packaged in this way.

Utilities Software

A utility program has one purpose: to help manage your computer files and your computer system. Your systems software may include its own utility program (System Tools, for example), or you may purchase a program such as Symantec Norton Utilities or PC Tools.

Utilities software provides simple ways to copy, rename, delete, and print files; format disks; create directories; and change the date or time currently on the system. A *defragmenting* utility, such as Windows 98's Disk Defragmenter, helps gather all the pieces of a file and collect them into one place on the hard disk. Other utilities include screen savers, virus protection programs, and utilities very specific to one type of hardware, such as printer utilities. The value of utility software increases as you accumulate many files, as you will see.

Hardware: Computer Systems and Peripherals

So much for software. Now, how about hardware? In microcomputer jargon, hardware means "equipment," and hardware is what most of us think of when we think of "computers." A computer system generally includes input devices, output devices, a central processing unit (CPU), and storage devices. Each is discussed in detail below.

Input Devices

Several input devices are used today for general purpose computer applications.

THE KEYBOARD

Clearly the most commonly used input device, the keyboard allows you to communicate with the microcomputer and to enter ("input") words, numbers, or commands. Today, when you use a keyboard, what you are doing is called *keyboarding*, or *keying in*, rather than typing. While keyboards differ slightly in design from one manufacturer to another, all offer alphanumeric keys, function keys, and a numeric keypad. The split keyboard model manufactured by Microsoft Corporation is a recent ergonomic design to relieve wrist pressure and improve posture while keyboarding (typing).

- The alphanumeric keys are all the standard letter and number keys, plus a few special keys that help you issue commands (such as the Alt and Ctrl keys, discussed later).

- The function keys are the keys labeled F1 through F10 or F12. They may be grouped in two vertical columns to the left of the alphanumeric keys, or they may be grouped in a single horizontal row above the alphanumeric keys. The layout varies depending on the keyboard's manufacturer. Each function key directs the software to perform a specific task. Correspondence between key and function varies from one software program to another. For example, in one program F1 may issue the Print command, but in another program F5 may issue the Print command.

- The numeric keypad at the right can be used to input numbers or to move the cursor. For instance, if the Num Lock ("Number Lock," located immediately above the keypad) is "on," pressing 2, 4, 6, or 8 on the keypad will display those numbers on the screen. But if you turn Num Lock off, those same keys become cursor or directional keys and control cursor movement on the screen.

- To increase keyboard efficiency, keys can be used in combination to perform additional functions. For instance, you can press and hold down the Alt or Ctrl key and then press a second key to issue a command called a "keyboard shortcut."

- Some keys serve as toggle switches. A *toggle* switch is an on/off switch, similar to an electric light switch. The Num Lock key is a toggle key. Press it once and it's on; press it again and it's off. As you become familiar with software programs, you will notice how other toggle keys are used.

- Under Windows software, all keyboards are remappable, which means you can change the value or function of any key on the keyboard. You may wish, for example, to substitute foreign language characters for some of the standard keyboard characters.

- Most keyboards have a directional arrow keypad—a separate set of four directional arrow keys located between the alphanumeric keys and the numeric keypad. Above this set of directional keys, your keyboard will have a set of six keys labeled Insert, Home, Page Up, Delete, End, and Page Down. These keys perform the functions indicated.

THE MOUSE

The mouse's unique name comes from its general shape and the wire that simulates its "tail." Some mouse devices, however, are not connected by wire; they operate through infrared light, similar to a TV remote control or a garage door opener. While its name may be cute, the mouse is a hard-working laborer and an exceptionally useful input device. The mouse operates by detecting motion on a surface and sending tracking information to the mouse port or serial port. Indeed, for many users, the mouse is the easiest and most natural way to use Windows and similar programs that require you to point to and select icons, menus, and menu options. To actually select an item such as an icon, you click once or twice on one of the mouse buttons, which then sends a signal to the computer directing it to select the object. Using a mouse is virtually a necessity to be productive in Windows.

As you cup the mouse in the palm of your hand, you roll the mouse on your desktop (it rolls freely because it sits on a ball). Because the mouse controls the on-screen pointer, each movement moves the pointer, allowing you to reach (and then select) Windows icons, menus, and options without using the keyboard. With the mouse you can open or close windows, open or close menus, select menu commands, and much more. The mouse buttons have different functions, which you will discover when using Windows 98.

THE TRACKBALL

Like a mouse, a trackball is a pointing device, but it works differently. The mouse rests on and rolls on a ball. Actually, a trackball is a roller-bearing mouse, upside down. You rotate the ball itself in the desired direction, and as you do so you move the cursor on the screen.

A trackball may be freestanding. That is, it may be a separate mouse-like device on your desktop. This type of trackball requires less desk space than a mouse (remember, the base is stationary; only the ball rotates). A second type of trackball is built in as part of the keyboard. Depending on the manufacturer, this small protuberance may be positioned between the *G* and *H* keys, in front of the spacebar, or on the right or left edge of the keyboard. The types of trackball devices are changing rapidly.

TOUCH SCREENS

The name *touch screen* defines this input device: You can touch the screen in a certain location, and your touch produces an electronic signal that the software can then interpret. For example, imagine two on-screen boxes, one labeled "yes" and the other "no." Depending on which box you touch, a unique electronic impulse will signal the software to perform a certain task.

GRAPHIC INPUT DEVICES

Graphic data, such as photos or drawings, can be input and then processed on a computer through a variety of devices: a light pen, a digitizer, and a graphics tablet.

- A light pen is usually attached to the computer and can create or change existing graphics. When the pen touches the display screen, a sensing device within the pen activates an area on the screen and the software begins to perform its functions.

- A digitizer changes points, lines, and curves from a drawing, photograph, or a sketch to digital impulses and transmits them to a computer where the data can be used to reproduce the drawing on a screen or printer.

- A graphics tablet allows you to select specific options on the computer using a hand-held device that passes over the options.

PEN INPUT DEVICES

One input method lets you "write" on a flat screen using a special "pen"; that is, a device that looks like a pen and is hooked up to the computer system. Using the pen, you enter data or select processing options. Another input pen device is a light pen, a pen-shaped object with a light-sensitive cell at its end used in conjunction with the screen. Pen input devices provide a very comfortable, familiar, and easy method of input, especially for people who have worked primarily with pencil and paper and are unfamiliar with a keyboard.

VOICE INPUT

As its name indicates, voice input employs speech recognition. It allows you to enter data and issue computer commands by speaking. Previously, most voice input systems were not very sophisticated but they are becoming a popular method for entering data without a keyboard and they have also become affordable. Voice input systems are especially useful to people who must use both hands while recording information (for example, surgeons and mechanics). More simply, though, voice input is great for people who have poor keyboarding skills.

SCANNERS

Another remarkable input device, the optical scanner, "reads" or takes a picture of text or graphics and electronically converts the picture or image to a digitized format that your software can use. The result is a bitmap, which can be stored or displayed on a screen. The denser the bitmap, the higher or greater the resolution. Because a scanned image is already bitmapped, you can edit pictures or images with graphics software.

Optical character reader (OCR) software can be used to transform the "picture" of text into alphanumeric characters that you can then use and/or edit in any document with word processing software, just as if you keyed them yourself.

Scanners vary in size from hand-held devices that scan only a strip at a time, to half-page or larger full-page devices that can scan many pages per minute. With a sheet-fed scanners, the sheet slides through the scanner and the information is translated into computer-usable data. A flatbed scanner is a device that moves across the page being scanned and gives you added capabilities for scanning materials from books and periodicals.

DIGITAL CAMERAS

Digital cameras allow you to take pictures (still shots) and send the results in a digitized format into your computer via a cable connection to your computer. Then, using graphics software, you can edit the pictures and prepare them for desktop publishing or multimedia presentations or place them on a Web page. The quality of pictures taken with ordinary cameras and film still produce a greater quality picture than that of digital cameras.

With the addition of a video-capture board on your computer, sometimes called a motion-capture board, you can take action shots or moving pictures for use in multimedia presentations or programs. Motion video input requires a great deal of memory and speed, as well as a considerable amount of space on a hard drive. Once the video is stored, film-editing software exists for editing the moving pictures you wish to use.

Output Devices

Now let's address the most popular output devices.

MONITORS

A monitor (or screen) displays stored data or text and is therefore an output device. A monitor resembles a television and handles communication between you and the computer. You issue commands on screen, instructing the computer to perform a certain function. And when the computer gives you a message, a prompt, or other information, it also displays the data on screen. The monitor is attached to the computer through a short cable connected to the computer's display "adapter" port. The display or graphics adapter (also known as the video adapter, graphics card, or video card) is the internal component inside your computer which is attached internally to one part of the processing portion of the computer, the motherboard. The graphics adapter generates the output you see on your monitor.

Most monitors can display a minimum of 80 characters of text per line and 25 lines of text or graphics per screen. Larger screens are available that display a greater area—very useful for applications that require you to see a full page at a time.

Resolution is one of the most important qualities to look for when acquiring a monitor because it measures the sharpness and the clarity of the on-screen image. Resolution is expressed in the number of pixels displayed horizontally and vertically. A high-resolution monitor uses more dots or pixels to display an image or letter, and the greater the number of pixels, the higher the resolution and the sharper the image.

Monitors are either monochrome or color. The monochrome monitor uses one color to display text—usually green, white, or amber on a black background. Graphics are produced by showing various shades of that one color.

Color monitors, on the other hand, display many colors, depending on the quality of the monitor and the type of display adapter card. The most common types of color monitors and adapter cards used today include VGA, Super VGA, PGA, XGA, and AVGA. The computer industry has developed standards for display devices that vary in support of color and resolution.

- VGA (video graphics display) provides support for up to 256 colors (resolution 640×480).

- Super VGA provides 256 colors and a resolution ranging from 800×600 to 1280×1024.

- PGA (professional graphics array) and XGA (extended graphics array) are the names given to the video graphics adapters that were developed by Intel Corporation and IBM for a faster, higher resolution (1024×768) in window environments.

- AVGA (accelerated video graphics array) is the name given to display adapters that now best support the graphics image creations of Windows software. AVGA, referred to as today's standard for video adapters, supports a resolution of 1200×1600.

Manufacturers often offer upgrades for display adapters, which is an inexpensive way to improve a system's graphics performance when using Windows software.

In addition to the type of adapter card used with Windows software, another critical component that determines the screen resolution, color depth, and overall performance of Windows software is the size of its display memory. It is common to need and to purchase video adapters with memory ranging in size from 1MB to 2MB; some even come with up to 8MB of video memory. Not only does the size of video memory affect performance but the *type* of video memory or RAM is critical and the types available are:

- DRAM (Dynamic RAM): This is the least costly video RAM and is used on low-end graphics adapters.

- EDO (Extended Data Out) DRAM: This type of RAM is slightly faster than DRAM and is becoming the standard on low-end adapters.

- VRAM (Video RAM): This type of RAM is best for graphics operations and is much faster than DRAM.

- WRAM (Window RAM): This uses special graphics features that allow the adapter to process graphics faster. It uses fewer components and will be cheaper than VRAM.

PRINTERS

A printer is an output device and a basic part of most computer systems because in the past the purpose of creating a document is most often to print it or create what is called a hard copy of the document. When the majority of the people you interact with are able to use electronic communications, then the method of output will change drastically from hard copy to electronically delivered copy.

Let's look at two basic types of printers: impact and nonimpact printers.

Impact printers available today vary in speed, quality, and price. The most common printers used on microcomputers are dot matrix and small-page printers. The least expensive impact device is the dot-matrix printer, which uses a hammerlike device to form dots, which in turn form printed characters. These inexpensive printers are fairly slow and produce, at best, near-letter-quality (NLQ) documents similar to an output resembling the appearance of a typewritten document. Their cost makes them good choices for rough drafts.

Laser printers and ink-jet printers are relatively fast nonimpact printers that produce superior-quality documents in a wide range of typefaces. Laser printers produce exceptionally sharp, crisp, professional-looking text copy and graphics. Using a process similar to photocopying, they produce images by an intense, narrow beam of light capable of carrying millions of images simultaneously. This beam of light is merged with a process that uses light to shape characters on a surface (usually paper) as a toner is applied. Because nonimpact printing is a "once through the printer" process, you cannot print carbon copies, nor use glossy paper. The cost of laser printers runs from a few hundred dollars to many thousands of dollars, depending on speed, quality of output, types of paper that can be used, and whether they print black only or color.

Ink-jet printers are a viable, cost-effective type of nonimpact dot-matrix printer used for producing high-quality black and white or color print. Using a process similar to photocopying, they produce images or letters by electrostatically spraying a very fine hairlike stream of ink dots into paper. Ink-jet printers are used a great deal in the home market, as well as in the segment of the business market needing low-cost color print.

The quality of a printer's output is measured in *dots per inch (dpi),* ranging from a low of 300 dpi to 1200 dpi resolution or higher. Although this quality has improved in the last couple of years for the average desktop printers, their output quality cannot match the high-resolution of imagesetters used in professional print shops with dpi of 1270 and 2540, etc.

MODEMS

A modem may be used as either an input or output device. A modem is a device that connects your computer to your telephone line—a hookup that allows your computer to communicate with other computers worldwide (that is, other computers that have modems). Here, *communicate* means that you can send data or receive data from others through your modem hookup.

A modem can be internal (inside your computer where you cannot see it) or it can be external (a device that sits on your desktop). In either case, your modem can have built-in fax capabilities, allowing you to send or receive faxes right from your desktop computer. An internal modem is located on an expansion board or a PCMCIA card that plugs into a slot inside the computer. If you have used up all of the slots in your motherboard and do not have room for a modem, you may want to use an external modem.

Modems are identified by their speed, measured in *bits per second (bps)*. The most common speeds are 2400 bps, 9600 bps, 14,400 bps, 28,800 bps, and 33,600 bps, with the higher numbers being faster. You will want to use a fast modem if you plan to do a lot of communicating or interaction with the Internet.

The Computer Motherboard

The motherboard is the heart of all microcomputers. It is called a motherboard because all other features and peripherals—such as the CPU, memory chips, the keyboard, and the mouse controllers and ports—must plug into it to operate.

CENTRAL PROCESSING UNIT (CPU)

The central processing unit is the motor or brain of any computer system and is located on the motherboard. The CPU is usually powered by one tiny computer chip, known as a microprocessor. Some computers use multiple chips for augmenting the performance of different tasks, and together perform all the CPU's work. Internal memory and even your clock may be found on chips inside the computer on the motherboard. Yet most microcomputers today use just one microprocessor, on one chip that may be smaller than your little fingernail. Becoming more popular for high-end computer users are some computers that use two microprocessors, better known as dual-processing systems.

Every chip has thousands of miniature electronic circuits placed on a very thin, tiny piece of silicon covered with a protective plastic coating. These electronic circuits hold instructions and data that they communicate to the other CPU components through tiny metal prongs. These prongs connect the chips to boards inside the computer.

The instructions stored on the microprocessor allow it to perform calculations and/or process information. One or more microprocessor chips direct the hardware and software and control how information enters and leaves the system. The CPU is responsible for much of the computer's main work, including, for example, changing or manipulating data to produce information.

A word about "chip power": The power of a processor chip is measured by capacity (that is, the amount of data a chip can "grab" or hold at one time) and speed (the time it takes to process data). (You might similarly "measure" a moving truck by its capacity and its speed: How many cubic feet of space does the truck have? How fast can it travel?) For a computer chip, capacity is measured in bits and speed is measured in megahertz (MHz).

Chips are referred to by name, such as 486DX, Pentium, MMX Pentium, or Pentium Pro (with varying speeds of 100MHz to 300MHz and higher).

MEMORY CHIPS

Besides using chips for processing, the computer system also uses chips for other tasks, such as storing data or instructions. These chips are called *memory* chips and are considered the computer's main memory. Memory chips are physically packaged on small circuit boards called SIMMs (single inline memory modules) and are installed on the motherboard along with the CPU chip. There are primarily two types of memory chips: RAM (random access memory) and ROM (read-only memory).

RAM (Random Access Memory). RAM chips allow the computer to store data electronically. RAM chips create a temporary storage center for the applications software you are currently using and the data you are entering into the computer's memory as you type or key information. But note the word temporary! When you turn off your microcomputer, everything stored in RAM disappears. For this reason, RAM is sometimes called volatile memory.

The capacity of RAM storage depends on the memory chips in each computer. RAM is usually measured in thousands, millions, billions, or trillions of bytes. Think of a byte as one character—a letter, a number, or a symbol—that the computer stores in memory.

- KB or K stands for *kilobyte*, or thousands of bytes.

- MB or M stands for *megabyte*, or millions of bytes.

- GB or G stands for *gigabyte*, or billions of bytes.

- TB or T stands for *terabyte*, or trillions of bytes.

A typical older computer system may have as RAM memory 640K, 1 MB, 2 MB, or 4 MB. Newer PCs come standard with a minimum of 8 MB, 16 MB, or 32 MB of RAM which can be upgraded. Thus, a computer with 8 MB of RAM memory can store approximately 8 million bytes. Another type of RAM memory, called *DRAM (dynamic random access memory)*, can vary in size from 4 MB to 128 MB or even larger and is known for its ability to refresh itself thousands of times per second.

Increasing your RAM memory is one of the easiest ways to add to the capabilities of your computer. When you wish to increase the amount of RAM memory on your computer, you must determine what kind of RAM memory you have and which of these types of RAM your computer's motherboard can accept: DIPs (dual inline packages), SIPs (single inline packages), or SIMMs.

Cache Memory. Since the amount of main memory or RAM on your computer is one of the most important features in determining how your computer performs, adding on to that memory would seem to be a reasonable way to increase performance. As a result, another type of memory called cache memory, a second smaller area in RAM memory, may be added or enhanced to improve your computer's performance in retrieving data. Cache memory sizes typically range from 128KB to 1MB (typically Pentium systems come with 256KB of cache memory standard).

ROM (Read-Only Memory). Your microcomputer needs operating instructions the moment you start your computer system. It cannot get instructions from RAM because, as you now know, RAM stores data only temporarily. The computer gets operating instructions from a special chip, the ROM, or read-only memory chip, which is installed in the computer by the manufacturer. This ROM is usually referred to as the ROM–BIOS (read-only memory–basic input/output system). ROM–BIOS is simply a set of programs built into this type of computer memory chip that provides the most basic, low-level control and supervision of the computer's operations. Actually, BIOS is like a translator between the computer hardware and the software programs that you run, controlling the hardware and responding to any demands that the hardware makes. For instance, when you are working on a computer with multitasking software, such as Windows, the BIOS helps the computer memory separate the instructions it has been given so that you can work on several tasks at the same time, such as printing one spreadsheet while you are working on another.

Because information stored on a ROM chip cannot be changed or altered and the data is retained when the system is turned off, ROM is considered nonvolatile. "Read only" usually means you cannot write to a ROM chip as you can to other chips. Newer ROM chips, however, do allow you to write to ROM memory. Some may be written over only once (EPROMs, erasable programmable read-only memory) and then the data is stored permanently and cannot be changed or altered. Others (EEPROMs) allow you to write over and over again.

A recent development in ROM chip technology is the flash-memory chip. Commonly used in the form of flash-memory cards, these chips are especially useful in answering machines, cellular phones, and digital cameras, as well as PCs. In fact, flash memory is ideally suited for portable PCs because flash memory is dense and lightweight, requires no power to retain data, and costs little. The standard flash-memory card for laptop PCs is the PCMCIA card (Personal Computer Memory Card International Association). Note that high-capacity flash-memory cards require a special disk drive called a flash disk drive.

Storage Devices

The need for permanent storage should now be obvious. The most common permanent storage devices are disks—or more specifically, floppy disks and hard disks. However, optical storage device and magnetic tape storage devices are also available.

FLOPPY DISKS

The most common permanent storage devices are 3½- and 5¼-inch floppy disks. The larger disks are flexible; the smaller ones are rigid, tougher, and usually contained in a cartridge. In both cases, the outer housing protects a thin inner layer of Mylar. Data is stored magnetically on this special material.

How much data can be stored on a disk? That depends on the density of the disk and the capacity of the disk drive. Here, density loosely measures the storage capacity of a disk. Three common density measurements are:

1. Low density, also called double density (labeled DD or 2D)

2. High density (labeled HD)

3. High capacity

As technology progresses, the trend is toward high-capacity disks and disk drives, such as the floptical disk (which stores approximately 21MB of data) and the flash disk. The flash disk seems especially promising for future use. It offers almost instant access to data, has low power requirements, is resistant to shock, and is very portable.

Table A-1 lists the approximate storage capacity in bytes of a variety of disks (the actual storage capacity depends on the disk drive, which is discussed next).

TABLE A-1
The approximate storage capacity of disks.

DISK	DOUBLE DENSITY	HIGH DENSITY	HIGH CAPACITY
3½ inch	720KB	1.44MB	
5¼ inch	360KB	1.2MB	
Flash-memory card			40–500MB
Floptical			21MB

DISK DRIVES

In order for disks to store or save data, the data must be written to the disk. In order to retrieve data, the data must be read from the disk. Question: "What tool does this reading and writing?" Answer: "The disk drive transfers data to and from the disk."

The number and types of drives vary on computer systems. Most have both a hard disk drive and at least one floppy drive. Systems that have two floppy drives may have one 3½- and one 5¼-inch drive, so that they can handle disks of either size. Like floppy disks, drives too are of three types: low density, high density, and high capacity. Low-density floppy disks can be used both in low-density and high-density drives, but high-density disks can be used only in high-density drives, and high-capacity disks can be used only in high-capacity drives.

Openings for floppy disks are usually on the front of the CPU. A small light on many floppy drives signals when the drive is activated.

Zip drives may replace the now-standard 3½-inch, 1.44MB floppy disk drives. Zip drives use cartridges that can hold 100MB or more of data—great for backup, for primary storage, for large graphic or multimedia storage, and for transporting data easily between systems.

HARD DISKS

Because hard disks are usually permanently installed within the computer and are not visible, they are also known as fixed disks. Some of the newer hard disks are removable cartridge hard disks.

Hard disks are much faster and can store more data than most floppy disks. Most computer users store their programs and much of their needed data on the hard disk and use their floppy disks for copying and backing up information.

Hard disk capacity is measured in megabytes, gigabytes, or terabytes. Hard disks on most PCs sold today have storage capacities that range from approximately 500MB to 4GB. Because a flash-memory card (PCMCIA) about the size of a credit card can store up to 500MB, flash memory is being used to replace hard disk drives in subnotebook and some pen-computer systems—wherever weight is a serious consideration.

DISK DRIVE DESIGNATIONS

Traditionally, disk drives are named or designated by letters, with A and B reserved for floppy drives, and C, D, and so on reserved for hard drives. The hard drive is always labeled drive C, regardless of whether the system has one or more floppy drives.

Why are these letters important? Because you must use them often to tell the computer where stored data is located and to issue specific commands. For example, when you start Windows and click on My Computer, you will see a screen that displays the drives (floppy, hard, CD-ROM, tape, etc.) your computer has. Each drive is designated by a letter, called a disk drive designator.

As "smart" as your computer may be, you must tell it where you stored files, where you saved documents, and so on. These letters, the disk drive designators, identify where items are stored for your system.

MAGNETIC TAPE

For added safety, many computer users create duplicate or backup copies of files, "just in case." The more valuable the data and the harder it is to replace, the more important it is to create backup files. Another way to inexpensively back up data, other than from hard disk to floppy disk, is to use magnetic tape drives or tape cartridges as a permanent storage device. But magnetic tape has a drawback: Some tape drives retrieve data very slowly.

OPTICAL STORAGE DEVICES

Optical storage devices use laser technology to record data; that is, they use lasers (controlled beams of light) to record and store data on special optical media. Laser technology can also record magnetic data on magneto-optical material and can read data that has been prerecorded. One key advantage of using optical storage technology is that it permits you to store vast amounts of data. Another is that it provides superior data integrity. Therefore, it is particularly useful for data backup or for archiving. The two best known kinds of optical storage are CD-ROM and MO, both of which are discussed below.

CD-ROM (Compact Disk–Read-Only Memory) Disks. Here the "disk" is an optical disk that records and stores vast amounts of data. Software manufacturers now commonly offer CD-ROM versions of their software at a lower cost than traditional floppy disk versions. In any case, CD-ROM technology is commonly used for multimedia applications (graphics, photographs, sound, and motion video). A CD-ROM disk holds a minimum of 680MB of data, with common storage capacities from 2GB to 9GB.

CD-ROM drives obviously can store much more data than can some hard disks. The basic drawback of a CD-ROM drive compared to a hard disk drive is that CD-ROM drives can be slow at accessing data. How slow is slow? Hard disks take as little as a hundredth of a second to do a task that might take a CD-ROM a full second to do. Does this matter to you? As is true with all applications for computer users, it depends on the individual needs of each person or for each task. As a result, CD-ROMs are now available in varying speeds referenced by how fast the disk spins (2X, 8X, 12X, 24X, and higher). When using CD-ROM for capturing video and sound, as well as data, a minimum of 32MB of main memory is desirable.

MO (Magneto-Optical) Drives. MO disk drives use 5¼- or 3½-inch cartridges filled with magnetic read/write media to store about 600MB of data under laser control. MO drives offer more permanent data storage than conventional hard disks and floppy disk drives.

Optical technology is considered durable and reliable under normal use. Since the surface of the disk is sealed in a plastic coating and is touched only by the laser light beam, information written to an optical disk lasts a very long time.

A disadvantage of CD-ROM is the slow data access time compared to most high-capacity hard drives. Also, you cannot change or update data that has already been written. (Note that for some, this is an advantage because it helps protect data.) Another disadvantage is that storing so much data on one disk adds to the difficulty of accessing information. The disadvantages of MO technology are the cost for replacement (about $200 for a 5¼-inch cartridge) and a question of compatibility between cartridges manufactured by different vendors.

What's next? Future optical storage devices will have even greater density than current CD-ROM and MO technology. Look for holographic devices capable of storing 120 GB of data in one cubic centimeter.

Ports and Expansion Slots

Many enhancements are available to increase the capabilities of your microcomputer. Most of these enhancements are devices that must be connected to the computer through a port or an additional expansion slot.

Most computers have two types of ports: parallel and serial. Parallel ports are most often used to connect your computer to a printer. Data transmitted through a parallel port moves quickly because it is sent eight bits at a time over eight separate lines. Serial ports are most often used for modems and the mouse. A serial port transmits data more slowly, because the information is sent one bit at a time over a single line.

Another kind of port, the SCSI (small computer system interface) port, can transport data or electronic signals to the disk drives at very high speeds. This type of port is especially useful for multimedia and multitasking applications. Other types of ports can help manage multiple drives: IDE (intelligent drive electronics) ports and EIDE ("enhanced IDE") ports.

Expansion slots are areas inside the computer where additional circuit boards can be plugged in to expand the computer's capabilities. When buying a PC, pay attention to the number and types of ports it has and how many slots it has for future expansion.

Plug and Play

You have become aware of different pieces of hardware that either are needed to make your computer work or which you may want to add to your computer to enhance its capabilities. In either case, changing the hardware of a machine, such as adding a CD-ROM to your system or a modem, is a task that few end users attempt and many trained technicians can find difficult and time consuming.

Plug and Play is Microsoft's design to make the personal computer add-on hardware devices, drivers, and operating system work together automatically without user intervention. Therefore, when adding on components to a Plug-and-Play compatible computer you must make certain the new components are Plug and Play, which provides substantial benefits to you, the user, and to the computer vendors. The computer is easier to use because you do not have to be worried about setting switches, about hardware conflicts, or loading drivers manually. Vendors like making Plug and Play hardware because they know you will have an easy time installing it and making it work and they can pass the savings from their reduced support costs on to you, the consumer.

GLOSSARY

A

Accessibility Options Windows 98 features designed especially to assist users with movement, sight, or hearing disabilities.

Access Options Selections that permit a network user to specify (1) who can share that user's resources and (2) which specific resources each user can share.

Accessories (1) Windows programs that assist with everyday computer tasks (for example, Notepad, Calculator, Phone Dialer, WordPad, and Paint); (2) Windows utilities (called System Tools) that help manage your computer resources; (3) Windows programs for telecommunications, fax, and multimedia; and (4) games.

Active Connection A computer connection that allows you to communicate with the Internet through a network or modem.

Active Desktop Windows 98 desktop that allows quick access to specified Web sites.

Active Window The window or icon currently in use. The title bar of the active window is always highlighted (or displayed in a different color) to distinguish it from other open windows that may be visible in a tiled or cascaded screen.

Address Bar The space in a window that displays the name of the open folder or object.

Address Book An electronic database of the individuals to whom and the businesses to which you often send e-mail or fax messages.

All Folders The left pane of the Explorer window.

Analog Describes signals transmitted over telephone lines (as opposed to digital signals, which are computer signals).

Applets A diminutive of the word *applications*; used to describe Windows utility programs such as the Clipboard Viewer.

Application File Icon In Explorer or My Computer, an icon that represents a software application and that, when chosen, opens the software program.

Applications Software Software designed to handle a wide range of tasks, such as word processing or database management (for example, Microsoft Excel, WordPerfect, and Lotus 1-2-3).

Attachment A file that is attached to an e-mail message.

Attribute A flag assigned to a file to indicate the file type (Archive, Read-only, Hidden, or System) and whether the file has been changed since it was last backed up.

Automatic Link In object linking and embedding (OLE), a feature that updates an object whenever the original file "linked" to that object is edited or changed.

B

Bitmap Method of storing computer graphic images on a grid (or *map*) of the screen in which (1) each square (pixel) equals one bit and (2) each bit represents *on* or *off*, that is, *color* or *no color*.

Bitmapped Fonts Screen and printer fonts that create characters dot by dot. Bitmapped fonts are displayed on screen, pixel by pixel.

Bits The basic or smallest units of computer information (derived from **b**inary dig**it**). 8 bits = 1 byte.

Bits Per Second (bps) Measurement used to indicate the speed of a *modem*.

Block *See Highlight.*

.bmp The original format for **Bit**m**ap** (thus the extension **.bmp**). *See Bitmap*.

Boolean Logic Term used to describe certain operations that combine or limit search options.

Boot To start (or restart) the computer system by loading its operating system (DOS or Windows) into memory.

Borders The four edges that make up a window outline.

Briefcase *See My Briefcase*.

Browse To look for a file, a folder, a workgroup, a drive, or a network using the Browse button.

Browsing Jumping from Web page to Web page, viewing and interacting with items on the pages.

Built-In Fonts Resident fonts.

Bullets Symbols such as dots or diamonds that appear at the beginning of a line of text.

Byte Unit of measure equal to 8 bits; a byte defines a single character. Memory-storage capacity is typically measured in bytes. Byte quantities are usually listed in thousands (*kilobytes*, or *KB*), millions (*megabytes*, or *MB*), billions (*gigabytes*, or *GB*), and trillions (*terabytes*, or *TB*).

C

Calculator The Windows accessory that allows you to perform numeric, scientific, or statistical calculations.

Call Log A detailed record of phone calls kept by Phone Dialer, a Windows 98 accessory.

Capacity The amount of information a disk can hold. *See Double-Density and High-Density*.

Cartridge Fonts Typefaces or fonts available on a cartridge (also called font cartridge) that plugs into the printer (HP LaserJet laser printers, for example).

Cascade Arrangement of open windows in an overlapping, staggered format so that (except for the topmost window) only the title bars are legible.

CD-ROM (Compact Disk–Read-Only Memory) A high-capacity, disk-storage system that reads files using a laser.

CD-R (Compact Disk–Recordable) Compact disk that you can write to or record on one time.

Channels Web sites that can be accessed through the *Active Desktop* Internet Explorer Channel bar.

Character Map A Windows accessory that lists standard symbols, as well as nonstandard characters such as special symbols and foreign-language letters, that users can then paste into text.

Check Boxes Boxes that serve as toggle switches to select or deselect features.

Clicking Pressing once—and then quickly releasing—a mouse button.

Clients On a network, computers or other devices that rely on services or resources provided by another computer—the server.

Client/Server Networks A form of distributed network computing in which two computers (often called *nodes* in networking) execute an application by assuming the roles of client and server, thereby increasing efficiency, performance, flexibility, and (for some applications) reliability and data integrity.

Clipboard Both (1) the Windows' accessory and (2) the temporary storage area that holds data being transferred between documents or between applications using the Cut, Copy, and Paste commands.

Clipboard Viewer A window that displays the contents of the Clipboard (that is, displays what has been cut or copied to the Clipboard).

Close Button Clicking the Close button issues the Close command, which then shuts down a window (or a dialog box) or exits the program.

Color Box In Paint, the palette of colors you can use to apply foreground and background colors.

Color Scheme The combination of colors in Windows' screen elements.

Combo Box A combination text box and list box.

Command An instruction to perform an operation or execute a program.

Command Buttons In dialog boxes, buttons that, when clicked, carry out actions such as Cancel or Open. An ellipsis (...) following a command button name (Browse...) indicates that another dialog box will appear if this command is chosen.

Command Processor The program that permits you to issue DOS commands.

Command Prompt The character or characters that appear at the begining of the DOS command line (for example, C:> or B:>). This prompt (also known as the DOS Prompt or simply the C prompt) indicates that the computer is ready to receive input.

COM Port (COMmunications Port) *See Serial Port*.

Compound Documents Documents that contain information created by using more than one application (thus *compound*).

Compressed Files Files that have been made smaller so they take up less disk space or take less time to download or upload.

Compression The process of condensing data, thereby allowing a disk drive to fit nearly twice as much data on a disk.

Configure Install and supply settings for a device such as a printer.

Contents Pane The Contents pane in the Explorer window gives a more detailed view of the structure by displaying all the folders and files contained in the drive or folder currently selected in the Tree pane.

Control Menu A list of commands for minimizing, maximizing, moving, and closing (and thus *controlling*) a window, as well as certain application icons and dialog boxes. The Control menu displays at the upper left corner of a window, to the left of the title bar.

Control Panel Windows' central location for configuring or changing system hardware, software, and settings.

Copy A command that duplicates selected data or a file or folder, and places that data, file, or folder on the Clipboard, where it can then be transferred elsewhere.

Cursor On screen, the blinking box, blinking vertical line, hand with a pointing finger, or arrowhead that indicates your current position.

Cut A command that removes ("cuts") highlighted text, a selected graphic, or a file or folder and places the removed data in a temporary storage area, the Clipboard. From the Clipboard you can place the item elsewhere, in effect moving the item.

Cutout In Paint, an area defined by a selection tool.

D

DCI (Display Control Interface) A technology used in Windows 98 that accelerates the speed of capturing video frames, allowing videos to run full screen.

Default In any given set of choices, the choice that is preselected; the selection that is in effect when you open a program; the settings established during the installation process.

Default Printer The currently-selected printer, the one that the system will go to automatically at the next print command.

Default Settings *See Default.*

Defragmenting Refers to a utility that gathers pieces of a file dispersed in computer storage and collects them in one place on the hard drive.

Demodulate Convert signals from analog to digital.

Desktop (1) In the opening Windows' screen, the entire background area where windows, icons, and dialog boxes represent your work area. (2) The Desktop utility program (in Control Panel) that allows you to customize the background pattern of the desktop and other items to suit your needs and/or working environment.

Destination (1) In file copying, the target location where files, objects, or other information is being copied. (2) A document or program into which an object is embedded or linked.

Destination Document *See Destination*, definition (2).

Device Driver System software that controls a device or component, such as a printer driver or a mouse driver.

Device-Independent Bitmap (DIB) A format that allows you to display a graphic file regardless of which video mode you are using.

Dialog Box An information-exchange window in which the user selects options, sets defaults, chooses items from lists, and otherwise provides information Windows needs before it can execute a command.

Dial-Up Networking The accessory used to connect two computers that each have a modem to share information between them, even if the computers are not on a network.

Digital Type of sound or video in which analog waveforms are captured and compressed.

Direct Cable Connection A special tool provided in Windows 98 to connect two or more computers.

Disk The magnetic element that stores data electronically, allowing the data to be retrieved for future use.

Disk Cache An area on your hard disk used to temporarily store information, such as Web pages you have visited, until you turn off your computer.

Disk Defragmenter A Windows accessory that is capable of repositioning the files on your disk so that it performs optimally.

Disk Drive Device that reads data from and writes data to a disk. Personal computers usually have at least two drives, one hard drive and one floppy drive.

Disk Drive Icons Graphic representations of floppy disk drives, hard disk drives, network drives, RAM drives, or CD-ROM drives.

Disk Label A name applied to a disk.

Document File Icon In Explorer or My Computer, an icon that represents an associated file and that, when chosen, opens both the document file and its associated application.

Document Window A window within an application (such as WordPad) that displays data created in that application. More than one document window can be open at a time.

Domain Name The Internet address of the computer where a Web page is located.

DOS (Disk Operating System) *Systems software*; the instructions loaded into the system when the computer is booted.

DOS Prompt *See* **Comand Prompt.**

Dots Per Inch (dpi) Measurement used to indicate the quality of a printer's output.

Double-Click To press and release a mouse button twice in rapid succession.

Double-Density Describes disk capacity of 360KB or 720KB.

Download To *receive* a file *from* a remote computer via a modem.

Downloadable Fonts Fonts (also called *soft fonts*) stored on the hard disk and sent to the printer as needed.

Drag *See* **Dragging.**

Dragging A special method of using a mouse to move a window or a graphic object across the screen—specifically, by (1) selecting the object to be moved and (2) pressing and holding down the mouse button while moving the mouse (and at the same time moving the object).

Dragging and Dropping Dragging a window or an object across the screen and then releasing the mouse button to position the object.

DRAM (Dynamic Random Access Memory) A type of random access memory that has the ability to refresh itself thousands of times per second.

Drawing Tools Line tools and shape tools provided in the Windows accessory Paint.

Drive Icon *See* **Disk Drive Icons.**

Driver *See* **Device Driver.**

Drop-Down List Boxes Menus of options listed in boxes, which can be accessed by clicking the down-arrow icon to the right of the displayed options.

Drop-Down Menu *See* **Submenu.**

DSP (Digital Signal Processor) Chip A computer chip that enables advanced audio capabilities such as voice and telephone.

E

Edit Revise or change the words in text.

8.3 Alias The name Windows 98 assigns a long file name when placing it in a DOS environment.

Electronic Mail (E-Mail) Notes, messages, and files sent among different computers that share telecommunications or network services or through an Internet service provider.

Embed To insert information (an *object*) that was created in one document (the *source*) into another document (the *destination*).

Embedding *See* **Embed.**

Extension The optional suffix (three characters maximum, preceded by a period) following a file name, often for the purpose of indicating the type of file [for example, **.bat** to indicate a batch file (as in **setup.bat**) and **.txt** to indicate a text file (as in the file name **readme.txt**)].

F

Fast Alt+Tab A keystroke feature that allows you to quickly switch to the last application window you used, or switch to the next application window.

Fat-Bit Editor Paint's Zoom mode, which enlarges each bit (makes it "fat") so you can edit it.

Favorites Web sites you can store to return to quickly again and again.

File Loosely, instructions or information grouped into one division, separated from all other divisions or files, and labeled distinctly from all the others.

File Attribute *See Attribute*.

File Format The structure, which differs from one application program to another, for storing a file in memory. One application may not be able to read the file format of another application.

File Name The label or name given to any specific file or folder. In Windows 98, a file name may be up to 255 characters long and may include spaces, punctuation marks, and special characters.

File Name Extension *See Extension*.

File Server *See Server*.

File Transfer A process to send electronic files from one computer to another.

File Transfer Protocol (FTP) An agreed-on set of rules that control data flow between computers and screen data for errors introduced during the transmission process.

File Type A designation given to a file object, such as bitmapped, text, or spreadsheet, and usually indicated in the file name extension.

Fixed Disk *See Hard Disk*.

Floppy Disk A portable disk, either 5¼ or 3½ inches square, that can be inserted into a floppy disk drive.

Folder A place or container in which documents, program files, and other folders are stored on your disks. Formerly referred to as a *directory*.

Font A complete set of all the letters (characters), all the numbers, and all the symbols (including punctuation marks) of the same size and the same weight within any given typeface family.

Font Size *See Type Size*.

Format (1) File format: The way information is structured in a file, often specific to one application. (2) Text format: The arrangement of text on a page.

Formatting (1) Process of initializing and preparing a disk for information storage and retrieval. During the formatting process, the computer arranges the magnetic disk surface in a series of tracks and sectors for storing information. (2) Process of changing the appearance of documents.

Fragmented Files Files that are not stored in contiguous clusters on a disk, which makes accessing the files slower.

FTP *See File Transfer Protocol*.

G

Gigabyte (GB) A unit of measurement approximately equal to 1,024MB or one billion bytes.

Gopher On the Internet, a menu-based server that can point you to information and can help you find files to download.

Graphical User Interface (GUI) Describes computer-user interaction in which the user relies on an easy-to-use visual setting—that is, familiar graphical images or icons (as in Windows)—rather than a difficult, word-based setting that requires memorization of complicated commands.

H

Handles The small boxes surrounding a high-lighted object to indicate it is selected.

Hard Disk A permanent or *fixed* disk, usually mounted inside the computer and therefore unseen.

Hardware Any piece (or all) of the equipment that makes up a computer system (for example, keyboard, mouse, disk drives, and monitor).

Hidden Attribute Used to hide a file so its name does not display when you use conventional commands to show or list files, thereby protecting the file from being deleted.

Hidden Files In a folder listing, files that are unlisted and unseen because they have the *Hidden attribute*, usually to protect the files from accidental erasure.

High-Density Describes a disk capacity of 1.2MB or 1.44MB.

Highlight To "select" an object, a block of text, or an icon—and therefore identify it before issuing a command or an action that will affect the selected item.

Hits Hyperlinks on a Web-search result page that will connect you directly to relevant Web sites.

Home Page The first screen that appears when you start your Internet browser; or the first page you see at a Web site.

Hot Links Active connections between two programs that allow them to share data so that any update in one file will automatically update the other file.

Hue The position of a color along the color spectrum (green, for example, is between yellow and blue).

HyperTerminal A Windows program that facilitates electronic communication; requires a modem.

Hypertext Document A multimedia document that contains *links,* or pointers, to other hypertext documents.

Hypertext Transfer Protocol The protocol, or set of rules, used to access many sites on the World Wide Web, **http://**.

I

I-Beam Pointer Shape the mouse pointer assumes (that is, the letter *I*) when the mouse moves into a text-editing area.

Icons Graphic images or symbols that represent applications (programs), files, disk drives, documents, embedded objects, or linked objects.

Import Retrieving an existing file and inserting it into another file.

In-Place Editing The temporary replacement of a document's menus and toolbars by those of the object's source program, thus allowing the document to be edited without actually opening the source program.

Insertion Point The location where the next keystrokes will be inserted, clearly marked by the cursor.

Interface The way a user communicates with the computer.

Internet A global communications network that connects many different, smaller networks and online services throughout the world.

Internet Explorer The Web browser included in Windows 98.

K

Keyboard Commands Commands issued in a Windows 98 software application by pressing a letter in combination with the Alt key. The letters available for keyboard commands are indicated with underlining on menus.

Keyboarding Also refered to as *keying in*, entering, or inputting data—words, numbers, or commands, using a computer keyboard.

Keying In *See Keyboarding.*

Keywords The terms you use to search the Web with a *search engine*.

Kilobyte (KB) A unit of measurment equal to 1,024 bytes (frequently rounded to 1,000 bytes) of information or storage.

L

LAN *See Local Area Network*.

Landscape The term that identifies the position of standard 8½-by-11-inch paper when the 11-inch dimension is left to right.

Launch Internet Explorer Browser Button A special button on an application toolbar, that, when clicked, starts the Internet Explorer browser.

Linking Making a connection or bond between an object in a destination document and the object created by the source application. As a result of the linking, any changes to the source document are automatically updated in the destination document simultaneously.

Links Pointers in a *hypertext document* that connect with other hypertext documents.

List Boxes Boxes (within an application window or another dialog box) that list choices available. If all choices cannot fit on screen at once, a scroll bar will display.

Local Area Network (LAN) A communications system that uses cables or telephone lines to join two or more computer workstations, thereby permitting them to share hardware and software.

Logging On/Off The processes of connecting to and then disconnecting from a remote computer.

Long File Name A standard Windows 98 filename can be up to 255 characters long, as compared to the older 8-character filenames in Windows 3.1, thus *long* file names.

Luminosity The brightness of the color.

M

Manual Link A link that does not automatically update changes in the destination document, but instead requires the user to open the Links dialog box and click the Update Now button.

Map A grid used in a bitmapped figure in which each square or *pixel* equals one *bit*.

Marking In a non-Windows application, selecting text so that it can be copied onto the Clipboard.

Maximize/Restore Button Small box on the right side of the title bar that, when clicked on, enlarges a window to its largest possible size.

Megabyte (MB) A unit of measurement approximately one million bytes, or 1,024 kilobytes.

Memory Any of several temporary storage areas computers use to hold information and applications during working sessions.

Menu List of commands or options grouped under specific headings or titles (*File*, *Edit*, etc.) on a window's menu bar.

Menu Bar In every application window, a listing of menus between two horizontal lines directly under the title bar.

Metafile Images Vector graphics.

MIDI (Musical Instrument Digital Interface) The standard protocol between musical instruments and computers.

Minimize Button Small box on the title bar that, when clicked, reduces a window to an icon.

Modem A device that converts computer (digital) signals to telephone (analog) signals and vice versa, thereby allowing computers to communicate by, and to send and receive data over, ordinary phone lines.

Modifying Tools In the Windows accessory Paint, the tools used to select objects, erase, change colors, and magnify.

Mouse A pointing device that serves as a faster, more effective alternative to the keyboard in communicating instructions.

Mouse Buttons The buttons on the mouse that let you choose options or perform mouse operations.

Mouse Pad A pad that sits under a mouse and facilitates its movement.

Mouse Pointer *See Pointer*.

Move To remove a file from its original location and place it in a new location, in a different folder, or on a different disk.

MS-DOS Microsoft's disk operating system, popularly known as DOS, a standard operating system for 16-bit personal computers.

.msp The format for Microsoft Paint files.

Multimedia The combined use of various media (sound, images, animation, and video, for example) on a computer system; a Windows accessory that lets you control multimedia devices.

Multiprocessing Refers to two or more CPUs sharing the processing workload and thus allowing several programs to run at the same time.

Multitasking Running two or more distinct computer operations simultaneously—one in the foreground, the other(s) in the background.

Multiuser Refers to a computer operating system, such as Windows 98, that allows one or more users to run programs at the same time.

My Briefcase A Windows 98 program that updates duplicate sets of files and folders between two different computers.

My Computer A desktop icon that provides a quick route to folders, files, and other objects on your computer.

N

Net Watcher A feature in Windows 98 that allows you to monitor and manage shared resources.

Network A combination of hardware and software connecting two or more computers. *See Local Area Network and Wide Area Network.*

Network Neighborhood A quick way to see what devices are on your network and a way to browse through your network.

Network Printer A printer that all network users share.

Notepad An accessory program in Windows in which you can create short, simple, unformatted documents.

O

Object Any data (pasted graphic image, text, chart, sound file, animation, etc.) created in a Windows client application using *OLE* and linked to the server application where it was created.

Object Icons Icons representing objects in a display window.

Object Linking and Embedding (OLE) A Windows feature that permits sharing data between applications by embedding and linking data in a document of one application that was created in another application.

Object-Oriented Images Picture images stored in the Clipboard not as the object, but as a series of commands that redraw the image of the object on the display.

OLE *See Object Linking and Embedding.*

OLE-Aware Windows applications that support OLE.

Opaquely Option for moving or copying a *cutout* in Paint in which all parts of the cutout retain their original colors at the new location.

Operating System *Systems software,* such as Windows 98, that manages the hardware and the software programs in a computer system.

Optical Character Reader (OCR) Refers to software that can transform a scanned "picture" of text into alphanumeric characters that you can then edit in a word processing program.

Option Buttons Small, round buttons that appear in a dialog box.

Outline Fonts Fonts created by drawing lines between points; also called vector fonts.

Outlook Express Windows 98's mail client program.

P

Paint A Windows accessory that you can use to create, edit, and view drawings.

Painting Tools In the Windows accessory Paint, the two tools used to "paint" or color objects.

Panes Distinct portions of a window.

Panose Information File A computer file for particular fonts that stores information about the font's size, attributes, and design.

Parallel Port Computer connection (named LPT1, LPT2, or LPT3) through which information is sent in segments, not bit by bit. Generally, printers are connected to parallel ports.

Parent Folder A folder that contains other folders.

Paste A Windows Edit menu command that places the contents of the Clipboard in a specified location.

Path The written out "track" or location that describes a file's location in reverse order, by naming first the disk drive designation letter, then the folder (and subfolder, if any), and then finally the file name itself (its extension is optional), each major part separated by a reverse slash (\ ).

.pcx The bitmapped graphics format used by Paint.

Peer-to-Peer Networks Network in which all connected computers are viewed as equals (thus "peer"), managing their own local resources and responsible for making them available to other nodes on the network.

Pel A unit of measure (pixel element or picture element); the individual dot that makes up an image.

Peripherals System hardware devices such as monitors, modems, network cards, sound cards, graphics cards, and CD-ROM drives.

Personal Information Managers (PIMs) Desktop accessories (Notepad, Calculator, and Phone Dialer) that help you manage and coordinate your work.

Phone Dialer The Windows accessory that dials voice telephone calls, logs phone calls, and provides speed-dial memory.

Picas Units of measurement for type. There are 6 picas in an inch.

Picture Images Vector graphics that are created by connecting points with lines and arcs.

PIF See Program Information File.

Pixel A single dot in a graphic; the smallest unit displayed on screen. Derived from picture elements, pixels are sometimes called *pels*.

Plug and Play A Windows 98 feature that automatically detects and configures a new hardware device when it is added to or removed from your computer system.

Pointer The mouse-controlled, on-screen graphic that may take the shape of an I-beam, an arrow, or some other form, depending on its particular function.

Points Units of measurement for type. There are 12 points in a pica and 72 points in an inch.

Pop-Up An item in a Help screen displayed with an underscore. Clicking the pop-up displays a box that defines the term.

Port The specific position (usually on the back of the CPU) where cables are connected from the computer to devices such as printers, modems, and monitors.

Portrait The term that identifies the position of standard 8½-by-11-inch paper when the 8½-inch dimension is left to right.

Primary Button The left mouse button.

Printer Peripheral device that produces hard copy.

Printer Driver File that provides an application program (Windows, for example) with the information it needs to communicate with a specific printer.

Printer Fonts Fonts designed to produce printed copy.

Print Preview Before printing, an on-screen representation of what your printed document will look like.

Program Information File (PIF) Here, program refers to a non-Windows application. A PIF provides Windows with the information it needs to load and run a specific non-Windows application—information about memory requirements, its screen display, and so on.

Protocol A set of rules that define how, for example, peripheral devices communicate with the computer and with one another, or a specific Internet method of access.

Q

Quick Links Buttons on the Links toolbar in Internet Explorer that are direct *links* to specific Web sites.

R

RAM (Random Access Memory) The memory area that stores, temporarily, applications currently being used, as well as any application files currently being created or edited. (The contents of RAM are erased when the computer is turned off.)

Read-Only Attribute An attribute assigned to a file that allows users to *only* read the file and not change or delete the file.

Read-Only File A file that has been assigned the Read-only attribute.

Recycle Bin A Windows feature that holds temporarily any file you delete from the hard disk, allowing you to recover a deleted file "just in case."

Relevance Rating Number that indicates how confident a *search engine* is that particular *hits* contain information relevant to your request. The closer the rating is to 100%, the more relevant the information.

Resident Fonts Fonts stored in the printer. *See Built-In Fonts.*

Resize Tab A large spot that you can "grab" with your mouse to resize a window.

Resolution Measures the number of dots in a screen image or a printer image, or the number of bits used to record a sound sample.

Resource A feature or component of a computer that can be used by a program or by another computer through a network; for example, a disk drive, a file, a printer, a modem, or another server.

Rich Text Format (RTF) A file format that enables different applications to exchange and use formatted documents.

Right-Clicking Clicking the right mouse button.

Right-Drag To *drag* an object while holding down the right mouse button.

Root The primary source of a disk; the top-level position of a disk; the folder from which all other folders branch. Each disk has only one root.

Robot *See Spider.*

S

Sampling Rate How fast a sound board processes sound samples.

Sans Serif A typeface that has no serifs.

Saturation The purity of color.

Scaleable Typeface One complete font (letters, numbers, punctuation marks, and symbols) in a given design (its *typeface)* that can be adjusted (scaled) to any size.

ScanDisk A Windows accessory that checks a disk or disk drive for faults or errors.

Scanner A computer device that can convert a paper drawing or photograph to an electronic computer file.

Scientific Calculator A Windows calculator that supports trigonometric, scientific, and number-conversion operations.

Scrap A portion of a document that you send to the desktop.

Screen Fonts Fonts designed to display type on screen.

Screen Saver A moving on-screen image that automatically appears when the mouse or keyboard is not used for a specific time (say, 60 or 90 seconds) in order to protect the screen (thus *screen saver)* from potential damage (called burn-in) that might result from overexposure of the screen to a stationary image.

Scroll Bars Rectangular boxes (on-screen position varies) that contain scroll arrows and scroll bars, which facilitate "moving" through a list, the contents of a window or screen, or any other data that do not fit in the display area. The scroll arrows and scroll boxes may move left and right, or they may move up and down.

Scroll To move (by way of scroll arrows) through a list, a block of text, or any other materials larger than the current window or screen.

Search Engine A server that processes requests for information and locates Web pages about a particular subject.

Select *See Highlight.*

Serial Port Computer connection (named COM1, COM2, COM3, or COM4) through which information is sent bit by bit (that is, *serially*). Generally, modems are connected to serial ports.

Serif A small stem at the ends of letters in a serif font.

Server A computer that is dedicated to one or more workstations, with which the computer shares its disk space and for which it provides various resources. The server usually stores the control programs that coordinate data sent across the network and allows access to other resources on the network.

Shared Resources Hardware, software, or information made available to (thus shared with) network users. Examples are public folders, a file server, a network printer, or a CD-ROM drive.

Shareware Free software programs (utilities, graphics, games, etc.). Although the programs are made available for free, if you use them, you are expected to pay a small registration fee.

Shortcut An icon that contains a direct route to a specific object; the icon can be identified by an arrow located in the lower left corner of the icon.

Shortcut Button A button in a Help entry that provides a shortcut for performing an action associated with the Help topic.

Shortcut Key On a menu, an underlined letter that can be combined with the Alt key to issue a menu command. For example, pressing the shortcut key Alt+E opens the Edit menu. Shortcut key combinations are listed to the right of the command name on the menu.

Shortcut Menu A menu that contains commonly selected options, accessed by right-clicking an object.

Shortcut Menu Button The secondary mouse button, usually the button on the right.

Sign In/Sign Off *See Logging On/Off.*

Sliders Scroll bars in a dialog box.

Soft Fonts *See Downloadable Fonts.*

Software Computer instructions; the directions or commands that make *hardware* work, including application programs, disk operating systems, and device drivers.

Sound Board A hardware component that enables a computer to reproduce and amplify recorded sounds, and play them through speakers attached to the computer system.

Sound Card *See Sound Board.*

Sound Clips Sounds that are stored on your computer as files. A sound clip may be created, played, edited, and inserted into documents.

Sound Files Audio files that can be played if a *sound board* is installed (a sound board converts digital information to analog waveforms, which can be heard through a speaker).

Source In file copying, the name of the file to be copied to a new destination; that is, to a target.

Source Document In an OLE application, the document in which the linked object was created—and therefore, the document that is edited when the link is updated.

Spider A program created to travel the World Wide Web, following links and adding items to an index of subjects.

Standard Calculator A Windows Calculator that performs common mathematical operations.

Standard Desktop *See Desktop, definition (1).*

Standard Toolbar The bar usually near the top of a window that contains buttons that instantly execute commands.

Start Button The command button on the taskbar that, when clicked, opens the Start menu.

Start Menu The menu that displays when you click the Start button; the starting point for all the Windows 98 menus and programs.

Start Page The first screen that appears at a Web site.

Startup File An executable file that runs a program.

Statistics Box A box that holds your entered series of statistical values (needed because Calculator's display can hold only a single value at a time).

Status Bar A message or information area, usually located at the bottom of a window, that displays specific details about disk capacity.

Style (Font) The appearance of a typeface, such as bold, italic, or underlined.

Subfolder A folder within a parent folder.

Subject Guide A listing of broad categories you can use in some search engines, following a path to more specific categories.

Submenu A secondary menu that opens when you click a menu option with a right-pointing arrow after it.

Subscribing Asking Internet Explorer to surf a specific Web site to check for recent changes.

Synchronize In My Briefcase, the ability to compare and then update files and folders that are duplicated.

Synthesizer An electronic piano-like keyboard or device used with Windows' *MIDI* files to generate sounds not from "recordings" but from digital instructions.

Systems Software The software used to operate or give instructions to computer systems.

System Tools A Windows accessory that supplies utilities to maintain your computer system.

T

Tab Stop The place where the cursor will stop when you press the Tab key.

Taskbar A bar usually located at the bottom of the screen, that lets you quickly switch between tasks of open programs, files, or folders. The taskbar includes the Start button, as well as buttons for any open program(s) and document(s).

Telephony The integration of Windows and telephone communications.

Terabyte (TB) A unit of measurement approximately 1 trillion bytes, or 1,024 gigabytes.

Text Boxes Boxes (within a dialog box) in which you enter information. When the dialog box opens, a text box may be blank or may contain text.

Text Editor An application that can be used to create, view, and modify text files to a limited extent.

Text Files Files (also known as data files) containing only letters, digits, and symbols from the ASCII character set.

Text String The text copy that you key in the Find what text box.

Text Tool In the Windows accessory Paint, the tool that allows you to add text to a graphic.

Thumbnail In Paint, a small box that shows normal view while you are zoomed in.

Tile Arrangement of open windows side by side (like tiles on a floor) so the contents of each are visible.

Title Bar Horizontal band in an application window, a document window, or a dialog box that displays the name of the application running in the window, the name of the data file in the window, or the name of the dialog box.

Toggle A key or menu option that can be turned off and on like a switch.

Toolbar *See Standard Toolbar.*

Tool Box Paint's collection of drawing, coloring, and painting tools (located on the left side of the Paint screen).

Tools In Paint, the individual icons in the tool box that represent drawing, painting, modifying, and coloring capabilities.

Touch Screen An input device that allows you to touch a computer screen in a particular location to produce an electronic signal that the software can interpret.

Trackball An upside-down mouse.

Transfer Protocol *See File Transfer Protocol.*

Transparently Option for moving or copying a *cutout* in Paint in which the background color assumes the underlying color of the location to which it is moved or copied.

Tree Pane The left pane of the Explorer window.

TrueType Fonts Fonts that print exactly as they appear on the screen and that are scaleable; that is, can be sized to any height.

Typeface The design of one "family" of letters, numbers, symbols, and punctuation marks, such as Times Roman, Helvetica, and Courier.

Type Size Printers measure type in *points* and *picas*: 12 points = 1 pica; 6 picas = 1 inch.

U

Undo Edit menu command that lets you reverse a recent change.

Upload To send a file from one computer to another via modem.

URL (Universal Resource Locator) On the Internet, the **http://** addresses that identify Web pages.

Utilities Software A program that helps computer performance.

V

Vaccine Program A program that seeks out viruses and tries to disable the viruses it finds.

Vectors Lines drawn between points. Vectors are used to create *outline fonts* and vector graphics.

Video Capture Card Digital video hardware component that, used in combination with a software utility program, allows you to capture a single still image or a full video sequence using a video camera, a VCR, or a videodisc player.

Video Cards Hardware components that allow you to display film in a small window on your computer screen.

Virtual Machines Blocks of memory configured to perform DOS operations just as if the blocks were an older DOS-based computer.

Virus Deliberate computer software; a virus replicates itself by attaching to other programs and carrying out unwanted and sometimes damaging operations.

W

Wallpaper Decorative graphic image that serves as background on the desktop, behind all open windows.

WAN *See Wide Area Network.*

Warm Links *Manual links* between two files that update the linked information only when you request it.

Waveform Digitized audio files that store any type of sound, not just music; waveform files can be played by a sound card.

Web *See World Wide Web.*

Web Browser A tool that lets you point to and view Web pages while it converts the information sent from a Web site and displays it as a Web page with text and graphics.

Web Pages Single screens of text and graphics and links to other pages all over the world.

What's This? A dialog box Help feature that offers information about dialog box options.

Wide Area Network (WAN) As opposed to a *local area network (LAN)*, a WAN serves a larger area, likewise providing data communication capability.

Wildcard Character A symbol (*) that can be used to replace a character or a sequence of characters in certain DOS commands or in file names.

Window The screen display of a program, document, listing, or work area—or a portion of the screen display. The actual "window" may be delimited by borders.

Windows A visual or picture-oriented environment.

Windows Explorer A program that lets you browse through, open, and manage your computer's disk drives, folders, and files (that is, move, copy, rename, and delete files).

Wizard A utility program that uses step-by-step instructions to lead you through the execution of a Windows task.

Word Pad An easy-to-use Windows 98 word processing program with many editing and formatting capabilities.

Word Wrap Automatic text advance from the end of one line to the next while keying, precluding the need to press Enter (except at the end of a paragraph).

Workgroup In a networked environment, a group of computers used by people sharing the same resources.

Workspace The section in an active window in which you can enter text, edit data, create graphics, etc.

World Wide Web (WWW) A graphical system of linking or pointing to documents and sites on the Internet.

Z

Zoom The option used to magnify a drawing, thus making it useful for editing.

INDEX

L

labels, disk, 62, 64

landscape orientation, 198, 541

LANs (local area networks), 406, 541

laptop computers. *See* notebook computers

laser printers, 528

Launch Internet Explorer Browser button, 17, 541

launching. *See* starting

lines, drawing, 228, 230

linked objects, 386–387, 541

 breaking links, 392

 changing update option, 391

 creating links, 387–388

 deleting, 392

 editing, 389

 media files, 439

 updating, 389

links

 automatic, 389, 391

 document shortcuts, 370

 in Help entries, 30, 35

 hot, 389, 391

 hypertext, 448, 456, 541

 manual, 389, 391

 quick, 451, 457

 warm, 389, 391

 on Web, 30, 456

Links toolbar, 451, 457

list boxes, 23, 541

local area networks (LANs), 406, 541

Log Off command, 8

logging off, 415, 541

logging on, 410, 541

logic, Boolean, 496–497

long file names, 71, 541

LPT ports, 312

luminosity, of colors, 294–295, 541

M

magnetic tape, 532

magneto-optical (MO) drives, 532–533

mail. *See* e-mail

manual links, 389, 391, 541

maps, 541

margins

 in Notepad documents, 149

 in WordPad documents, 197–198

marking, 357, 541

Maximize/Restore button, 17, 18, 541

maximizing windows, 18

MBs. *See* megabytes

Media Player, 425, 435–436, 437

megabytes (MBs), 529, 541

memory, 542

 cache, 530

 in Calculator, 166

 chips, 529–530

 requirements for multimedia, 424

 ROM (read-only), 530

 use by DOS-based applications, 340

 video display, 527

 See also RAM

menu bar, 16, 17, 19, 542

menus, 19, 542

 arrows on, 21

 colors in, 20

 displaying, 19

 ellipses on, 20

 highlighted options, 20

 selecting options, 21

 selection letters, 20

 shortcut keys, 20, 21

 sub-, 21

 underlined letters, 186–187

messages, e-mail. *See* e-mail

metafile images, 368, 542

microprocessors, 529

Microsoft Network (MSN), 405

MIDI files, 426, 435, 542

MIME (Multipurpose Internet Mail Extensions), 486

Minimize button, 17, 18, 542

minimizing windows, 18

MO (magneto-optical) drives, 532–533

modems, 528, 542

 Dial-Up Networking, 410

 settings in Phone Dialer, 176

 speeds, 528

portrait orientation, 198, 544

ports, 312, 533, 544

previewing
 Notepad documents, 150
 printing, 544
 WordPad documents, 192

primary button, 11, 544

Print dialog box, 34, 192–194

Print Help dialog box, 33

Print Preview window, 192, 193

printer drivers, 310, 319, 544

printer fonts, 319–320, 544

printers, 527–528, 544
 configuring, 310–312
 default, 312
 dot-matrix, 528
 impact, 528
 ink-jet, 528
 laser, 528
 ports, 312
 removing, 313
 sharing, 412

printing
 drawings, 233
 e-mail messages, 484
 Help topics, 33–34
 Notepad documents, 149–151
 orientation, 150
 previewing, 192, 544
 Web pages, 457
 WordPad documents, 192–194

program files, downloading, 512

Program Information Files (PIFs), 338–344, 544

Program Speed Dial dialog box, 174

Programs menu, 7

Properties button, 50

protocols, 452, 544

Q

question mark (?) icon (What's This?), 39

Quick Launch Toolbar, 4, 6

quick links, 451, 544
 adding, 457
 deleting, 457

QuickFinder, 135

quitting. *See* exiting

R

radio buttons. *See* option buttons

RAM (random access memory), 424, 529, 545
 amounts, 529
 increasing, 530
 types, 527

read-only attribute, 123, 124, 545

read-only files, 124, 545

read-only memory (ROM), 530

Recycle Bin, 6, 74, 545
 opening window, 75
 restoring deleted files or folders, 75

Refresh option, 52

Regional Settings, 300

relevance ratings, 495, 545

removing
 background patterns, 280
 file attributes, 124
 fonts, 326
 printers, 313
 See also deleting

renaming
 Briefcases, 397
 files, 120
 folders, 72–73, 120
 shortcut icons, 93

Replace dialog box, 206

replacing text, 155, 206

replying, to e-mail, 485

resident fonts, 320, 545

resize tab, 17, 545

resizing
 objects in drawings, 238
 objects in WordPad, 216
 windows, 18

resolution, 545
 of monitors, 527
 sound, 426

resources, 545
 shared, 405, 410, 415

Restore button, 17, 18

S

tools (Paint), 548
  drawing, 227, 229–230
  modifying, 228, 237–239
  painting, 227, 231
  selection, 237
  text, 228, 247–248
touch screens, 525, 548
trackballs, 10, 525, 548
transfer protocol. *See* FTP (file transfer protocol)
transparent cutouts, 238, 548
Tree pane, 106–107, 548
TrueType fonts, 319, 320, 548
type sizes, 318, 548
typefaces, 317, 548
  distinguishing, 322
  sans serif, 322
  scaleable, 319
  serif, 322
  See also fonts
typing. *See* keying

U

undeleting files and folders, 75
Undo button, 49
Undo command, 155, 200, 548
Unicode text
  in Clipboard, 365
  documents, 189
Universal Resource Locators. *See* URLs
Update Briefcase window, 400
uploading files, 508, 548
URLs (Universal Resource Locators), 452, 548
utilities software, 520, 523, 548

V

vaccine programs, 515, 548
vector fonts, 319
vectors, 549
video, 434
  ActiveMovie Control, 424, 440
  digital, 434, 537
  DVDs (digital video drives), 424
  embedding files in documents, 437

files, 435–436
  linking files, 439
  playing, 435–436
  producing, 434
  See also multimedia
video adapters, 527
video capture cards, 434, 526, 549
video cards, 424, 549
video compact disks, 424
Views button, 50
virtual machines (VMs), 335, 549
viruses, 515, 549
VMs. *See* virtual machines
voice input systems, 526
Volume Control, 425, 429

W

wallpaper, 277, 281–282, 549
WANs. *See* wide area networks
warm links, 389, 391, 549
waveform (.wav) files, 426, 428, 435, 549
Web, 448, 551
  browsing, 452, 455–457
  links, 30
  searching, 134–135, 491–501
  subject guides, 498–501
  Windows 98 page, 33
Web browsers, 50, 448, 549
  starting, 50
  See also Internet Explorer
Web pages, 448, 549
  addresses, 452
  displaying My Computer as, 51
  Favorites list, 7–8, 465–470
  finding, 50–51, 134–135, 491–501
  history list, 458–459
  links on, 456
  moving through, 454–455
  printing, 457
  quick links, 451, 457
  saving as HTML files, 505
  saving as text files, 505, 507
  start page, 449, 455, 463
What's This?, 39, 549
wide area networks (WANs), 406, 549